CRIMINAL LITIGATION AND SENTENCING

Fifth Edition

Cavendish
Publishing
Limited

London • Sydney

CRIMINAL LITIGATION AND SENTENCING

Fifth Edition

Peter Hungerford-Welch, LLB, Barrister
Principal Lecturer
Inns of Court School of Law

Cavendish
Publishing
Limited

London • Sydney

Fifth edition first published in Great Britain 2000 by Cavendish Publishing Limited, The Glass House, Wharton Street, London WC1X 9PX

Telephone: +44 (0)20 7278 8000   Facsimile: +44 (0)20 7278 8080

Email: info@cavendishpublishing.com

Visit our Home Page on http://www.cavendishpublishing.com

Hungerford-Welch, Peter

Criminal litigation and sentencing – 5th edn

1 Criminal justice, Administration of – England   2 Criminal justice – Administration of – Wales   3 Criminal procedure – England   4 Criminal procedure – Wales   5 Sentences (Criminal procedure) – England   6 Sentences (Criminal procedure) – Wales

I. Title

345.4'2'05

ISBN 1 85941 559 8

Printed and bound in Great Britain

Dedicated to Jane Hungerford-Welch

PREFACE

This book started life as *Lecture Notes on Criminal Litigation and Sentencing*. It was – and is – an expanded version of lectures which I deliver to the students doing the Bar Vocational Course at the Inns of Court School of Law.

After three editions under the Lecture Notes banner, it was felt that the book should be expanded to make it useful for practitioners (both solicitors and barristers) as well as for students, pupil barristers and trainee solicitors. I hope that the book will also be of interest, and use, to anyone else who wants to know a little more about how our system of criminal justice operates.

To cater for this wide audience, the text (which has been revised) is supplemented with statutory materials relevant to each chapter. I hope that the book still provides a comprehensive treatment of criminal procedure and sentencing, but without becoming so technical that the reader is left with mental indigestion.

My thanks go to Cavendish for their hard work in putting this book together. Special thanks go to my wife, Jane, without whose help and encouragement this book would never have seen the light of day. Any errors are, of course, my fault!

There have been numerous statutory changes, not to mention a tide of case law, since the last edition.

I have endeavoured to state the law as at July 2000.

Peter Hungerford-Welch
Barrister (Inner Temple)
Principal Lecturer at the Inns of Court School of Law

CONTENTS

Contents

Contents

Contents

Contents

Contents

Contents

TABLE OF CASES

J

K

L

M

R

S

TABLE OF STATUTES

TABLE OF STATUTORY INSTRUMENTS

CHAPTER 1

PRELIMINARIES

1.1 INTRODUCTION

In this first chapter, we examine how a defendant is brought before the criminal courts. We consider what happens when a suspect is taken to a police station for questioning. We see how the decision to prosecute a suspect is taken. We also look at the structure and personnel of the criminal courts, and at the advocates who appear before them.

1.1.1 Some basic terminology

A defendant in a criminal case always makes his first appearance in a magistrates' court. Some cases are tried in the magistrates' court (comprising lay justices or a stipendiary magistrate); others are tried by a judge and jury in the Crown Court. An offence is a summary offence if it must be tried in a magistrates' court. An offence is an indictable offence if it may or must be tried in the Crown Court; where an indictable offence may be tried by a magistrates' court instead of the Crown Court, it is known as an 'either way' offence.

1.2 COMMENCING PROCEEDINGS

There are three ways of bringing someone before the criminal courts:
- summons;
- arrest without warrant, followed by charge;
- arrest with warrant, followed by charge.

1.3 SUMMONS

Suppose that my poor driving nearly causes an accident; I am stopped by the police and warned that I am to be reported for driving without due care and attention.

1.3.1 The initial decision to prosecute

The police officer who stopped me files a written report on the incident which will be considered by a senior police officer in the process department of that division of the police force. Thus, the initial decision whether or not to prosecute me is taken by a senior police officer. In some cases, however, the police may consult with the Crown Prosecution Service before commencing proceedings.

1.3.2 Laying the information

Before a summons can be issued, an 'information' has to be laid at a magistrates' court. Where proceedings are commenced by the police, this will be done by a police officer. The information must state:

- the name and address of the person laying the information, who is known as the 'informant' (in the case of a police prosecution this will be the police officer who reported the offence or a senior officer, depending on the policy of that police force);
- the name and address of the accused;
- the brief facts of the case as alleged by the informant;
- the statutory provision (if any) allegedly contravened by the accused.

In *Rubin v Director of Public Prosecutions* [1990] 2 QB 80, it was held that an information must be laid in the name of an individual, not a body. Thus, an information must state the name of an individual officer, not, for example, 'Thames Valley Police'. However, this point is of limited practical significance; a police prosecution can continue even if the officer who signs the information dies before the case has been disposed of (*Hawkins v Bepey* [1980] 1 WLR 419; [1980] 1 All ER 797).

The information may be laid before a magistrate or a magistrates' clerk, and this may be done orally (in which case, the informant attends the magistrates' court) or in writing. Usually, an information is laid in writing; a standard form, prescribed by the Magistrates' Courts (Forms) Rules 1981, is sent to the nearest magistrates' court.

The volume of prosecutions means that a bundle of informations in respect of all the cases where a decision to prosecute has been taken will be prepared by the police process department and sent to the magistrates' court.

As we shall see in Chapter 4, an information may allege only one offence (r 12 of the Magistrates' Courts Rules 1981). This means that, if a suspect is alleged to have committed more than one offence, a separate information has to be laid in respect of each offence.

We shall also see in Chapter 4 that an information alleging a summary offence must be laid within six months of the alleged commission of the offence (s 127 of the Magistrates' Courts Act 1980). Thus, the date when the information is laid can be important.

A written information is laid as soon as it is received in the clerk's office, even if it is not considered by a clerk or a magistrate until later (*R v Manchester Justices ex p Hill* [1983] 1 AC 328; [1982] 2 All ER 963).

Some courts have computer links with local police stations. In those cases, the information is laid when it is fed by the police into the computer link, even if a print out is not produced at the court until later (*R v Pontypridd Juvenile Court ex p B* [1988] Crim LR 842).

In *R v Kennet Justices ex p Humphrey and Wyatt* [1993] Crim LR 787, it was held that the prosecutor can lay an information by means of sending a letter to the magistrates' court: no standard form needs to be used, provided that the document contains the essential elements of an information. In that case, the defendants were charged with either way offences. The Crown Prosecution Service sent a letter to the magistrates' court informing the court that it had been decided to proceed with purely summary offences instead. It was held by the Divisional Court that the letter was sufficient to amount to the informations which had to be laid in order to proceed with the new offences.

1.3.3   Issuing a summons

Once an information has been laid, a summons may then be issued by a magistrate or clerk (usually the latter), provided that:

- In the case of a summary offence:
  - (a) the alleged offence was committed or is suspected to have been committed in the county served by that court; or
  - (b) the defendant named on the summons is to be tried jointly with someone else who will be tried by a court in the same county as the court issuing the summons in the present case and who is in custody; or
  - (c) the defendant is already accused of an offence (summary or indictable) at a court in that county.
- In the case of an indictable offence:
  - (a) the offence was committed or is suspected to have been committed in that county; or
  - (b) the accused resides or is believed to reside in that county; or
  - (c) the defendant named on the summons is to be tried jointly with someone else who will be tried by a court in the same county as the court issuing the summons in the present case and who is in custody (see ss 1(2) and 2(6) of the Magistrates' Courts Act 1980).

Furthermore, in deciding whether or not to issue a summons, the magistrate or clerk should ensure that the facts stated in the information disclose an offence known to law, that any time limits relating to the commencement of the prosecution have been complied with, and that the particular court has jurisdiction under s 1(2) of the Magistrates' Courts Act 1980 (see above) (*R v Gateshead Justices ex p Tesco Stores Ltd* [1981] QB 470; [1981] 1 All ER 1027).

In *R v Liverpool Justices ex p Knibb* [1991] COD 53, it was held that, before issuing a summons, a clerk or magistrate must ascertain that the essential ingredients of the offence are *prima facie* present (that is, that the facts alleged in the information contain all the ingredients of the offence); that the offence alleged is not out of time; that the court has jurisdiction; that the informant has the necessary authority to prosecute, and that the application for the summons is not vexatious. In *R v Bradford Justice ex p Sykes* (1999) 163 JP 224, it was argued that a clerk or magistrate, before issuing a summons, must make inquiries into the background of the information which has been laid. The Divisional Court held that, where an information has been laid, a clerk or a magistrate is entitled to make inquiries beyond the material before him before issuing a summons, but there is no duty to do so.

1.3.4   Contents of summons

The summons must give the substance of the allegation against the accused. It will set out the statutory provision contravened (if appropriate, as it usually will be since most offences are statutory), together with a short summary of the facts of the case: r 98 of the Magistrates' Courts Rules 1981.

In the case of an allegation of careless driving, for example, the particulars would be set out as follows:

> On 26 August 2001, driving a mechanically propelled vehicle, namely, a Ford Cortina motor car registration number D123 ABC, on a road, namely, Warmington High Street, without due care and attention, contrary to s 3 of the Road Traffic Act 1988.

Although an information may allege only one offence, there is no objection to a summons referring to more than one information. So, if the accused is alleged to have committed a number of offences, the allegations will be detailed in a schedule on the summons.

The summons will also show the address of the court which the defendant is to attend, and the date and time of the first court appearance which the accused has to make in respect of this offence.

The standard form for a summons is shown at the end of this chapter.

1.3.5 Serving the summons

The summons is then served, usually by the court posting it to the defendant's last known address (that is, the address he gave to the police). If this is ineffective (for example, it is returned undelivered by the Post Office), the summons may be served by personal delivery (a police officer will hand the summons to the defendant) or even by leaving it with someone at the defendant's last known address (r 99(1) of the Magistrates' Courts Rules 1981).

1.4 ARREST WITHOUT WARRANT

Under s 24 of the Police and Criminal Evidence Act 1984, a police officer may arrest someone without a warrant if:

- the person is committing (or the officer has reasonable grounds to believe that he is committing) an arrestable offence; or
- the officer has reasonable grounds to believe that an arrestable offence has been committed and also has reasonable grounds to believe that the person arrested has committed that offence; or
- the person is about to commit (or the officer has reasonable grounds to believe that the person is about to commit) an arrestable offence.

1.4.1 Meaning of 'arrestable offence'

An arrestable offence is defined by s 24 of the Police and Criminal Evidence Act 1984 as one which is:

- punishable by a fixed term of imprisonment (for example, murder); or
- punishable by a maximum sentence of imprisonment of five years or more; or
- another specified offence referred to in s 24(2), for example, certain offences under the Customs and Excise Management Act 1979, the Official Secrets Acts 1920 and 1989, and (more commonly) offences under the Football (Offences) Act 1991, taking a conveyance without the owner's consent (s 12 of the Theft Act 1968), going equipped for stealing (s 25 of the Theft Act 1968); attempts to commit any of these offences (except taking a conveyance) are also arrestable offences.

Schedule 2 of the Police and Criminal Evidence Act 1984 preserves other statutory powers of arrest, such as arrest for breach of a condition of bail (s 7 of the Bail Act 1976) and arrest for failure to provide a road-side breath specimen (s 6(5) of the Road Traffic Act 1988).

1.4.2   Meaning of 'reasonable grounds'

In *O'Hara v Chief Constable, Royal Ulster Constabulary* [1997] 2 WLR 1; [1997] 1 All ER 129, the House of Lords considered the meaning of 'reasonable grounds' in the context of s 12(1)(b) of the Prevention of Terrorism (Temporary Provisions) Act 1984 (now s 14(1) of the Prevention of Terrorism (Temporary Provisions) Act 1989), which applies the same test as s 24 of the Police and Criminal Evidence Act 1984. It was held that, for a police officer to have reasonable grounds to effect an arrest, the question is whether a reasonable person would be of that opinion, having regard to the information which was in the mind of the arresting officer. In other words, the test is partly subjective (the officer must have formed a genuine suspicion in his own mind that the suspect has committed the offence in question) and partly objective (there must be reasonable grounds for that suspicion). The House of Lords went on to hold that the information acted on by the officer need not be based on his own observations: he is entitled to form a suspicion on the basis of what he has been told. It is not necessary to prove what was known to the person who gave the information to the police officer or to prove that any facts on which the officer based his suspicion were actually true.

This test is compatible with the requirements of Art 5 of the European Convention on Human Rights (the right to liberty). This has been held to require an arrest to be based on reasonable suspicion, in the sense of the existence of facts or information which would satisfy an objective observer that the suspect may have committed the offence (*Fox, Campbell and Hartley v UK* 13 EHRR 157).

1.4.3   Information on arrest

When someone is arrested, they should, at the time of the arrest, be informed (by the person making the arrest) in non-technical language, of the reason for the arrest even if the reason is obvious (s 28(3), (4) of the Police and Criminal Evidence Act and *Abbassy v Metropolitan Police Commissioner* [1990] 1 WLR 385; [1990] 1 All ER 193). Article 5(2) of the European Convention on Human Rights requires that everyone who is arrested shall be informed promptly, in a language which he understands, of the reasons for his arrest and of any charge against him. This means that the suspect must be told 'in simple, non-technical language that he can understand, the essential legal and factual grounds for his arrest so as to be able, if he sees fit, to apply to a court to challenge its lawfulness' (*Fox, Campbell and Hartley v UK* 13 EHRR 157).

Section 28 of the Police and Criminal Evidence Act is satisfied if an officer other than the arresting officer informs the person arrested of the reason for the arrest (*Dhesi v Chief Constable of West Midlands Police* (2000) *The Times*, 9 May.

The suspect should also be cautioned that if he does not mention, when questioned, something he later relies on in court, it may harm his defence, and that anything he does say may be given in evidence (see 1.7.1 below).

1.4.4   Citizen's arrest

Under s 24 of the Police and Criminal Evidence Act 1984, a member of the public may arrest someone who is in the act of committing (or whom he has reasonable grounds to suspect is committing) an arrestable offence.

Where an arrestable offence has already been committed, a member of the public can arrest someone who is (or whom he has reasonable grounds for suspecting is) guilty of that offence.

The police powers of arrest are wider, in that a police officer only has to have reasonable grounds for suspecting that an arrestable offence has been committed before he can arrest anyone whom he reasonably suspects of committing it.

Thus, if a member of the public (for example, a store detective) arrests someone who he reasonably suspects of committing an arrestable offence, the arrest will not be valid if an arrestable offence has not in fact been committed (*R v Self* [1992] 1 WLR 657; [1992] 3 All ER 476). In *Self* the defendant was arrested by a store detective, with the help of a member of the public, on suspicion of shoplifting. There was a struggle in which the member of the public was kicked and punched by the defendant. The defendant was charged with theft and assault. He was acquitted of the theft but convicted of assault. The Court of Appeal held that the conviction for the assault could not be sustained. The store detective and the person assisting him had no right to detain the defendant: no arrestable offence had in fact been committed by the defendant and therefore there was no right to effect a 'citizen's arrest'.

Furthermore, a member of the public cannot arrest someone who is apparently about to commit an arrestable offence, whereas a police officer can.

A citizen who makes an arrest should deliver the person arrested into the hands of the police as soon as practicable: s 30(1)(b) of the Police and Criminal Evidence Act. The police will then be responsible for charging the suspect if they decide to proceed with the case.

1.4.5   Non-arrestable offences

In the case of non-arrestable offences (that is, those not within s 24) the police may only arrest a suspect if one or more of the so-called 'general arrest conditions' set out in s 25 of the Police and Criminal Evidence Act 1984 is satisfied. These include instances where:

- the suspect refuses to give his name and his identity cannot readily be ascertained (for example, from a document such as a driving licence in his possession); or
- the police officer has reasonable grounds for doubting whether the name given by the suspect is his real name; or
- the suspect has failed to supply his address; or
- the police officer has reasonable grounds for doubting whether the address given by the suspect is one at which it will be possible to effect service of a summons on the suspect; or
- the police officer has reasonable grounds for believing that it is necessary to arrest the suspect in order to prevent him from causing physical injury to another person or to himself; or
- the police officer has reasonable grounds for believing that it is necessary to arrest the suspect in order to prevent him from causing damage to property; or
- the police officer reasonably thinks that it is necessary to arrest the suspect in order to prevent him from committing an offence against public decency or from obstructing the highway; or
- the police officer reasonably thinks that it is necessary to arrest the suspect in order to protect a child or other vulnerable (for example, mentally ill) person.

Grounds 1–4 are cases where arrest is appropriate because it is doubtful that a summons could be served and therefore arrest is the only way of commencing proceedings. The remaining grounds enable the police to deal with emergency situations.

In *Edwards v DPP* (1993) 97 Cr App R 301, it was held that for an arrest under s 25 of the Police and Criminal Evidence Act 1984 to be valid, the relevant ground should be in mind of the police officer at the time the arrest is made. Furthermore, there must be evidence (especially what is said by the police officer to the suspect when the arrest is made) that this is the case.

Only a police officer may make an arrest for a non-arrestable offence.

Thus, a suspect can only be arrested if it is alleged that he has committed an arrestable offence (unless the general arrest conditions set out above apply). On the other hand, an information may be laid and a summons issued in respect of any offence.

1.5 VOLUNTARY ATTENDANCE AT POLICE STATION

Sometimes, a person will agree to go to a police station to be interviewed by the police without first being arrested. Someone who has not been arrested but who is 'helping the police with their inquiries' is free to leave at any time unless and until he is arrested (s 29 of the Police and Criminal Evidence Act 1984).

1.6 AFTER ARREST: DETENTION AT POLICE STATION

After the suspect has been arrested, he will be detained at the police station.

- The suspect is taken to a 'designated police station' (that is, under s 35, one with facilities for the detention of suspects) as soon as practicable after arrest:
  s 30(1) of the Police and Criminal Evidence Act 1984. The only exception is where the presence of the suspect elsewhere 'is necessary in order to carry out such investigations as it is reasonable to carry out immediately' (s 30(10)); it may be necessary, for example, to search the suspect's home.
- The time of suspect's arrival at police station is called the 'relevant time'. This is the moment from which the length of the suspect's detention starts to be measured.
- On arrival at the police station the suspect is taken to the custody officer, defined by s 36 as an officer of the rank of a Sergeant or above who is unconnected with the investigation of the case.

1.6.1 Duties of the custody officer

The duties of the custody officer are:
- to inform the suspect of his rights (for example, the right under s 56 to have someone informed of his arrest and the right under s 58 to consult in private with a solicitor);
- to decide whether there is sufficient evidence for the suspect to be charged or whether to authorise detention without charge;
- to keep a custody record documenting all that occurs during the suspect's detention, for example, meal breaks and interviews;
- to seize and retain anything in the possession of the prisoner, except for clothes and personal effects (which may only be seized if the custody officer thinks the prisoner will use them to cause injury to himself or others, or damage to property, or to escape).

1.6.2 Charging the suspect

If there is sufficient evidence the suspect must be charged (s 37(7)). To charge a suspect, the custody officer tells the suspect what offence(s) he is accused of. The suspect is cautioned that he does not have to say anything, that it may harm his defence if he does not mention something he later relies on in court, and that anything he does say will be written down and may be given in evidence. The suspect is then asked if he has anything to say. Any reply must be noted down.

1.6.3 Police bail

After a suspect has been charged, he must be released on police bail (with the condition that he attend a specified magistrates' court on a specified date and at a specified time) unless any of the exceptions contained in s 38 of the Police and Criminal Evidence Act 1984 apply. Under s 38, bail may only be withheld from a person who has been charged if:

(a) the suspect refuses to give his name or address (or there are doubts as to the correctness of the name or address given);

or

(b) if the custody officer has reasonable grounds to believe that:

    (i)   the suspect will fail to appear in court;

    or

    (ii) continued detention of the suspect is necessary to prevent the suspect from committing an offence (provided that the person has been arrested for an imprisonable offence);

    or

    (iii) continued detention of the suspect is necessary to prevent him from causing physical injury to any other person or from causing damage to property (this ground applies only where the person has been arrested for a non-imprisonable offence; there is no need for this specific ground where the suspect has been arrested for an imprisonable offence because such conduct would be covered by the other ground – risk of a subsequent offence – for withholding bail in the case of imprisonable offences);

    or

    (iv) continued detention of the suspect is necessary to prevent the suspect from interfering with the administration of justice or with police investigations;

    or

    (v) continued detention of the suspect is necessary for his own protection.

In deciding whether there is a risk that the defendant will abscond, or commit a further offence, or interfere with witnesses, the custody officer will have to apply the same criteria as a magistrates' court (s 38(2A) of the Police and Criminal Evidence Act 1984). These criteria are considered in section 2.4.1 below.

1.6.4   Imposition of conditions on police bail

Where a person is released on police bail (under s 38 of the Police and Criminal Evidence Act 1984) having been charged with an offence, the custody officer has power under s 3A of the Bail Act 1976 to impose any condition on the grant of bail which a court could impose (with certain exceptions such as a requirement of residence in a bail hostel).

The custody officer may only impose conditions on the police bail if those conditions are necessary to prevent the defendant from absconding, or committing an offence while on bail, or interfering with witnesses, or obstructing the course of justice (s 3A(5) of the Bail Act 1976).

Section 3A(4) of the Bail Act 1976 allows a custody officer, at the request of the accused, to vary the conditions of bail which were imposed when the defendant was charged.

Where conditions are attached to police bail, reasons have to be given and recorded (s 5A of the Bail Act 1976). Furthermore, where conditions have been attached to police bail, the defendant may apply to a magistrates' court to vary those conditions, although it should be borne in mind that the court also has the power to withhold bail altogether or to make the conditions more onerous (s 43B of the Magistrates' Courts Act).

Section 46 of the Crime and Disorder Act 1998 inserts a s 47(3A) into the Police and Criminal Evidence 1984. This provides that where a custody officer grants bail to someone who has been charged with an offence, he must specify the date of the person's appearance in the magistrates' court; that date should normally 'be not later than the first sitting of the court after the person is charged with the offence'. This has the effect that the first court appearance of the accused should take place at the next available sitting of the magistrates whether the suspect is released on police bail or not.

1.6.5   Release without charge on police bail

Sometimes police release a suspect without charge but require him to return to the police station at a later date (for example, for further questioning or to give the police further time in which to decide whether or not to charge him). In such a case, the suspect is released on police bail. Where a suspect has been released on police bail with the condition that he should return to the police station on a specified date, he may be arrested without a warrant if he fails to attend the police station at the appointed time (s 46A of the Police and Criminal Evidence Act 1984).

Section 34 of the Police and Criminal Evidence Act 1984 provides that where a person returns to the police station to answer police bail (or is arrested for failing to do so) he is to be regarded as having been arrested for the original offence at that moment. It follows that the suspect is in the same position as a person who is being detained without charge and so the custody timetable set out in the subsequent paragraphs applies.

1.6.6   Detention without charge

If there is insufficient evidence for the suspect to be charged, he must be released (either unconditionally or with the proviso that he return to the police station on a specified date) unless it is necessary for the police to detain him without charge in order to:

- secure or preserve evidence relating to the offence for which the suspect has been arrested (for example, the police fear that the suspect would hide relevant evidence or warn accomplices); or
- obtain such evidence by questioning the suspect (see s 37(2) of the Police and Criminal Evidence Act 1984).

1.6.7   Detention without charge: reviews

If the suspect is detained without charge, the detention is subject to periodic reviews according to the timetable set out in ss 40–44 of the Police and Criminal Evidence Act 1984.

Under s 40 reviews take place as follows:

- six hours from the 'relevant time', by an officer of the rank of Inspector or above who is not directly involved in the investigation of the case;
- 15 hours from the 'relevant time', again by an Inspector unconnected with the case;

At each of these reviews, the review officer has to be satisfied that the conditions of continued detention set out at 1.6.6 above continue to be satisfied.

Before deciding whether to authorise the continued detention of the suspect, the review officer must give the suspect (unless he is asleep or otherwise unfit by reason of his condition or behaviour), or any solicitor who is representing him and who is available at the time of the review, the opportunity to make representations about the continued detention (s 40(12)–(14)).

A review may be postponed if, having regard to the circumstances prevailing at the latest time when that review should take place, it is not practicable to carry out the review then (for example, because the suspect is then being interviewed and it would wreck the interview if it were to be suspended for a review to take place, or because no review officer is readily available at that time). Where a review is postponed, it must take place as soon as practicable after the time it should have taken place and a reason for the delay must be noted on the custody record (s 40(4), (5), (7)). A postponement of one review does not affect the time when subsequent reviews have to take place (s 40(6)).

An officer conducting a review of the detention of a person who has been arrested but not charged, cannot do so by means of a live video link. The Act requires the reviewing officer and the detainee to be physically present together in the same place at the same time: *R v Chief Constable of Kent ex p Kent Police Federation* (1999) *The Times*, 1 December. In that case, Lord Bingham CJ also expressed doubts as to the legality of the guidance note 15C in Code C of the PACE Codes of Practice, which provides for a review to be conducted by telephone.

After 24 hours from the 'relevant time' have elapsed the suspect can only be detained without charge if the provisions of ss 42ff (set out below) apply (s 41). Otherwise he must be released (with or without bail): s 41(7).

If the suspect is released because 24 hours have elapsed, he cannot be re-arrested without a warrant for the offence for which he was previously arrested unless new evidence comes to light after his release (s 41(9)).

1.6.8   Detention beyond 24 hours

If, and only if, the offence is a 'serious arrestable offence', once the suspect has been detained for 24 hours, an officer of the rank of superintendent or above can authorise detention for up to a further 12 hours (s 42).

Thus, the maximum period of detention in a case which does not involve a serious arrestable offence is 24 hours.

In addition to the requirement that this power to detain without charge for more than 24 hours can only be exercised in the case of a serious arrestable offence, the officer giving permission for continued detention must be satisfied that:

- the investigation is being carried out diligently and expeditiously; and
- the suspect's continued detention is necessary to secure or preserve evidence relating to the offence for which the suspect has been arrested or to obtain such evidence by questioning the suspect (in other words the same requirements as s 37(2), set out at 1.6.6 above).

1.6.9   Serious arrestable offence

The term 'serious arrestable offence' is defined in s 116 of the Police and Criminal Evidence Act 1984 as:

- an offence from the list in Sched 5 of the Act, namely:
  - (a)   treason;

(b)   murder;

(c)   manslaughter;

(d)   rape;

(e)   kidnapping;

(f)   incest with a girl under 13;

(g)   buggery with a boy under 16 or a person who has not consented;

(h)   indecent assault which constitutes an act of gross indecency;

(i)   causing explosions likely to endanger life or property contrary to the Explosive Substances Act 1883, s 2;

(j)   intercourse with a girl under 13 contrary to the Sexual Offences Act 1956, s 5;

(k)   possession of firearms with intent to injure contrary to the Firearms Act 1968, s 16;

(l)   use of firearms and imitation firearms to resist arrest contrary to the Firearms Act 1968, s 17;

(m)   carrying firearms with criminal intent contrary to the Firearms Act 1968, s 18;

(n)   hostage taking contrary to Taking of Hostages Act 1982, s 1;

(o)   hijacking contrary to Aviation Security Act 1982, s 1;

(p)   torture contrary to Criminal Justice Act 1988, s 134;

(q)   causing death by dangerous driving contrary to Road Traffic Act 1988, s 1;

(r)   causing death by careless driving when under the influence of drink or drugs contrary to Road Traffic Act 1988, s 3A;

(s)   endangering safety at aerodromes contrary to Aviation and Maritime Security Act 1990, s 1;

(t)   hijacking of ships contrary to Aviation and Maritime Security Act 1990, s 9;

(u)   seizing or exercising control of fixed platforms contrary to Aviation and Maritime Security Act 1990, s 10;

(v)   indecent photographs and pseudo-photographs of children contrary to Protection of Children Act 1978, s 1;

(w)   publication of obscene matter contrary to Obscene Publications Act 1959, s 2;

- under s 116(2)(c), any of the offences mentioned in paragraphs (a) to (f) of s 1(3) of the Drug Trafficking Act 1994;

- an offence under Prevention of Terrorism (Temporary Provisions) Act 1989, s 2, 8, 9, 10, or 11;

- under s 116(3)–(6);
- any other arrestable offence is a serious arrestable offence if its commission has led to, is intended or is likely to lead to, or consists of making a threat which if carried out would lead to:
  - (i) serious harm to the security of the state or to public order;
  - (ii) serious interference with the administration of justice or with the investigation of offences or of a particular offence;
  - (iii) the death of any person;
  - (iv) serious injury to any person;
  - (v) substantial financial gain to any person;
  - (vi) serious financial loss to any person.

The latter two provisions generally mean that a substantial amount of money is involved. However, as regards the last item on this list, s 116(7) provides that 'loss is serious for the purposes of this section if, having regard to all the circumstances, it is serious for the person who suffers it'. In *R v McIvor* [1987] Crim LR 409, for example, it was held that the loss of £800 was not a 'serious financial loss' to a relatively prosperous loser.

1.6.10   Detention beyond 36 hours

After 36 hours have elapsed since the 'relevant time', the suspect can only be detained further without being charged if this is permitted by a magistrates' court (s 43).

The application for a warrant for continued detention is made 'in camera' (that is, with the public excluded) before two or more lay justices (s 45). The application has to be made on oath. The suspect has a right to be present and to be legally represented at this hearing.

Section 43(14) stipulates that any information submitted in support of an application for a warrant of continued detention must state:

(a) the nature of the offence for which the suspect has been arrested;

(b) the general nature of the evidence in which he was arrested;

(c) what inquiries have been made by the police and what inquiries they propose to make; and

(d) the reasons for believing that the continued detention of the suspect is necessary for the purpose of making such further inquiries.

Before they can issue a warrant for continued detention, the magistrates have to be satisfied that:

- the detention without charge of the suspect is necessary to secure or preserve evidence relating to the offence for which he was arrested or to obtain such evidence by questioning him;

- the offence is a serious arrestable offence; and
- the police are conducting the investigation diligently and expeditiously.

The police should apply for permission to detain the suspect before the initial 36 hour period has expired; if this is not practicable then the application must be made to the magistrates not later than 42 hours after the initial detention (s 43(5)).

The magistrates can only issue a warrant allowing a maximum period of no more than a further 36 hours' detention: s 43(12). If the police need even more time, they can make a further application under s 44 to the magistrates for continued permission to detain the suspect without charge. However, the magistrates cannot authorise a period of detention which would mean that the suspect has been in custody for a total of more than 96 hours from the relevant time (s 44(3)).

Once 96 hours have elapsed from the relevant time, the suspect must be released, either unconditionally or on bail to return to the police station. Following his release the suspect cannot be re-arrested without a warrant for the same offence unless new evidence has come to light (s 43(19)).

The standard form for the warrant of continued detention (and the endorsement allowing further detention) appears at the end of this chapter.

1.7 INTERVIEWING SUSPECTS

Code of Practice C, issued to the police under the Police and Criminal Evidence Act 1984, sets out detailed rules for the detention and interviewing of suspects. It requires, for example, that suspects be given two light meals and a main meal each day and that they are given at least eight hours rest per day: Code C 8 and Code C 12.2. In *R v Weerdesteyn* [1995] 1 Cr App R 405, the Court of Appeal confirmed that where customs officers interview a suspect the provisions of the Police and Criminal Evidence Act 1984 and the Codes of Practice apply just as they do in the case of a police interview.

1.7.1 The caution

Code C 10.1 says that a person whom there are grounds to suspect of an offence must be cautioned before any questions about it are put to him regarding his involvement or suspected involvement in that offence. This definition of when a caution must be administered excludes preliminary questions, for example, to establish the suspect's identity.

Code C 10.4 sets out the terms of the caution:

You do not have to say anything. But it may harm your defence if you do not mention when questioned something which you later rely on in court. Anything you do say may be given in evidence.

Minor deviations from this form of words do not constitute a breach of the Code C provided the sense of the caution is preserved.

This caution must be given both upon arrest (Code C 10.3) and before the suspect is questioned. When there is a break in questioning, the interviewing officer must ensure that the suspect is aware that he remains under caution (Code C 10.5).

When the suspect is charged, the caution is repeated in the same terms except that the word 'now' replaces the words 'when questioned' (Code C 16.2).

1.7.2 The interview

Code C 11.1 provides that, except in emergencies, an interview may only take place at a police station. If the interview is not tape-recorded, a record must be made showing what is said; this should be done during or as soon as practicable after the interview; the record should be signed by the maker and the person interviewed should be given the opportunity to read and correct the record: Code C 11.5–13.

1.7.3 Role of solicitor during police interviews

Guidance from the Law Society says that a solicitor who is present when a suspect is being interviewed by the police should intervene if the police officers:

- ask unfair questions;
- ask questions which do not relate to the alleged offence(s);
- misrepresent the law;
- claim to know things but without having any factual basis for that knowledge;
- produce or refer to evidence which has not been shown to the suspect or the solicitor;
- misrepresent information;
- put pressure on the suspect by questioning him in a burdensome manner, by behaving abusively, or by attempting to influence the suspect's decision making.

1.7.4 Special rules for juveniles and persons at risk

Special rules apply to protect juveniles and other vulnerable groups.

- A juvenile should not be placed in a cell unless no other secure accommodation is available and the custody officer takes the view that secure accommodation is necessary.

- A juvenile, or someone who is mentally ill or mentally handicapped, should not be interviewed unless an 'appropriate adult' (parent, guardian, or social worker) is present.

The appropriate adult should be told that they are not there simply to observe but that they have an important role to play in advising the person being interviewed, in ensuring that the interview is conducted fairly, and in facilitating communication between the police and the juvenile (Code C 11.16). See, also, *DPP v Blake* [1989] 1 WLR 432; 88 Cr App R 179, where it was held that a parent is not an appropriate adult if the juvenile and parent are estranged; a social worker should be the appropriate adult in such a case.

In *DPP v Cornish* (1997) *The Times*, 27 January, the Divisional Court held that where a juvenile is interviewed by the police in the absence of an appropriate adult and there is an application for the interview to be excluded under s 76 of the Police and Criminal Evidence Act 1984, the court should hear evidence as to who was at the interview and how the interview went in order to determine the effect of the absence of an appropriate adult.

In *R v Aspinall* [1999] 2 Cr App R 115, the defendant suffered from schizophrenia, and so was a person at risk; he was interviewed by the police in the absence of an appropriate adult. The Court of Appeal held that even though the defendant appeared able to understand procedures and answer questions, this did not obviate the need for the presence of an appropriate adult. The interview should therefore have been ruled inadmissible under s 78 of the Police and Criminal Evidence Act 1984.

1.8 DETENTION AFTER CHARGE

As soon as the investigating officer thinks there is sufficient evidence to prosecute the suspect, the suspect must be taken to the custody officer. If the custody officer agrees that there is sufficient evidence against the suspect, the suspect will be charged. The custody officer tells the suspect what offence(s) he is accused of and, after cautioning the suspect, asks if he has anything to say. Anything said by the suspect in answer to the charge must be noted down.

If the suspect is not granted bail under s 38 of the Police and Criminal Evidence Act 1984, he must be taken before the magistrates' court not later than the day after the day he is charged (ignoring Sundays) (s 46). The magistrates will then decide whether or not to grant bail, using the criteria laid down in the Bail Act 1976 (set out in Chapter 2).

1.8.1 Further questioning

Code C 16.5 provides that, once the suspect has been charged, the suspect cannot be asked further questions about the offence(s) with which he has been charged unless further questions are necessary:

- to prevent or minimise harm or loss to some other person or to the public; or
- for clearing up an ambiguity in a previous answer or statement; or
- in the interests of justice to enable the suspect to have put to him information concerning the offence which has come to light since he was charged.

1.9 ACCESS TO LEGAL ADVICE: S 58 OF THE POLICE AND CRIMINAL EVIDENCE ACT 1984

Under s 58 of the Police and Criminal Evidence Act 1984, the suspect has a right, upon request, to consult with a solicitor in private at any time. The solicitor can be the defendant's own solicitor or a duty solicitor (see Chapter 11, 11.2 for details of the duty solicitor scheme).

1.9.1 Denial of access to legal advice

This right can be denied by the police for up to 36 hours from the relevant time, but only if the following conditions are satisfied:

- denial is on the authority of a superintendent or more senior officer; and
- the offence is a 'serious arrestable offence' (defined at 1.6.9 above); and
- there are reasonable grounds for believing that allowing immediate access to a solicitor would lead to:
  - (a) interference with evidence connected with a serious arrestable offence; or
  - (b) interference with or injury to other persons; or
  - (c) alerting of other persons suspected of committing a serious arrestable offence (that is, other miscreants would be tipped off); or
  - (d) hindrance to the recovery of the proceeds of a serious arrestable offence.

In *R v Samuel* [1988] QB 615; [1988] 2 All ER 135, it was held that the suspicion must relate to the particular solicitor whom the suspect wishes to see. The police must therefore have grounds to suspect the honesty of that solicitor or else think him particularly naive.

1.9.2   The Code of Practice – access to legal advice

Code C 6.1 says that (unless the provisions of s 58 of the Police and Criminal Evidence Act 1984 apply) all people in police detention must be informed that they may at any time consult privately with a solicitor and that independent legal advice is available free of charge from the duty solicitor. Code C 6.4 says that the police must not try to dissuade the suspect from obtaining legal advice. Under Code C 6.5, if a suspect declines legal advice, the custody officer should ask the suspect his reasons for doing so and any reasons given should be entered on the custody record.

If a suspect asks for legal advice, he may not be interviewed before he has received that legal advice (or if he initially refused legal advice but changes his mind during the course of an interview, the interview must be suspended until he has received that advice).

However, Code C 6.6 provides that, where the suspect nominates a particular solicitor but that solicitor cannot be contacted or refuses to attend, an inspector may authorise an interview to take place without a solicitor being present if the suspect has been told about the duty solicitor scheme but has declined to ask for the duty solicitor (or no duty solicitor is available).

The notes for guidance in Code C. 6D make it clear that the role of the solicitor is to protect and advance the legal rights of his client and that on occasions this may require the solicitor to give advice which has the effect of preventing the suspect from giving evidence which strengthens the case against him. The solicitor is entitled to intervene to challenge questions which are improper or which are put in an improper manner. Under Code C 6.9, the solicitor may only be required to leave the interview if his conduct is such that the investigating officer is unable properly to put questions to the suspect (and, under Code C 6.10, such removal should be approved by an officer of at least the rank of superintendent, or inspector if a superintendent is not available, who is not connected with the investigation of the case).

1.9.3   Wrongful denial of access to legal advice

Should there be wrongful exclusion of a solicitor, any confession obtained by the police may well be held inadmissible at trial under s 78 of the Police and Criminal Evidence Act 1984 which allows the court to exclude any prosecution evidence which would have an adverse effect on the fairness of the proceedings. See, for example, *R v Mason* [1988] 1 WLR 139; [1987] 3 All ER 481, where the police deceived a solicitor into thinking that the case against his client was stronger than it was and, because the legal advice was based on this fact, the police had effectively denied legal advice to the defendant. The Court of Appeal said that his subsequent confession should have been excluded.

1.9.4 European Convention on Human Rights

Article 6 of the European Convention on Human Rights guarantees the right to legal representation. Denial of access to a solicitor during a police interview may violate this provision, especially if adverse inferences can be drawn from the defendant's failure to answer questions (*Murray v UK* 22 EHRR 29). It is for this reason that s 58 of the Youth Justice and Criminal Evidence Act 1999 prevents adverse inferences being drawn (under s 34 of the Criminal Justice and Public Order Act 1994) from a suspect's silence where the suspect was not allowed the opportunity to consult a solicitor.

In *Averill v UK* (2000) *The Times*, 20 June, the defendant was denied access to a solicitor for the first 24 hours of his detention for questioning. He failed to mention when questioned matters he later relied on at his trial, and adverse inferences were drawn at trial from his silence. The European Court of Human Rights held that the defendant had been fully apprised of the implications of remaining silent. It was clear from the reasoning of the judge (this was a Northern Ireland trial by judge alone) that there was substantial evidence against the defendant irrespective of the adverse inferences, and so the defendant had not been convicted on the basis of adverse inferences alone. There was, therefore, no violation of Art 6.1 (the right to a fair hearing) in the drawing of the adverse inferences. However, there was a violation of Art 6.3(c) (right to access to legal assistance): as a matter of fairness, access to a lawyer should have been guaranteed to the applicant before his interrogation began; the denial of access to a solicitor during the first 24 hours of detention failed to comply with the requirements of Art 6.3(c). This seems to go further than *Murray*.

In *Magee v UK* (2000) *The Times*, 20 June, the defendant had been held by the police for over 48 hours without access to legal advice under the Prevention of Terrorism Act. The European Court of Human Rights held that to deny access to a lawyer for such a long period was incompatible with the rights of the accused under Art 6 of the Convention. However, the Court took particular account of the austerity of the conditions of the Holding Centre where the defendant had been detained and the fact that he had been held incommunicado during the breaks between bouts of questioning by teams of police officers. The intimidating atmosphere was specifically devised to sap his will; as a matter of procedural fairness, said the Court, this should have been counterbalanced by access to a solicitor.

1.10   ARREST WITH A WARRANT

Under ss 1(1)(b), (3) and (4) of the Magistrates' Courts Act 1980, a warrant for the suspect's arrest may only be issued if:

(a) the information is in writing and substantiated on oath; and

(b) either:

    (i)   the offence to which the warrant relates is an indictable offence or is punishable with imprisonment; or

    (ii)   the person's address is not sufficiently established for a summons to be served on him.

Whereas a magistrate or a justices' clerk may issue a summons, only a magistrate is empowered to issue an arrest warrant.

The warrant requires the police to arrest the suspect and take him before the magistrates' court named on the warrant (usually the issuing court).

Where the offence charged is an indictable offence, a warrant may be issued even if a summons has previously been issued; this would be appropriate if, for example, the summons was returned by the Post Office undelivered.

In practice, it is quite rare for an arrest warrant to be sought.

The more serious offences carry a power of arrest without warrant (so a warrant is unnecessary) and in other cases it is preferable to issue a summons. If the summons cannot be served, however, the police can go back to the magistrate to apply for an arrest warrant.

An arrest warrant issued to commence criminal proceedings can be endorsed with a requirement that the accused be released on bail after his arrest. It is unlikely that such a warrant would be so endorsed, however, as a warrant will normally be sought only where the defendant is clearly evading service of the summons.

In *R v Enfield Magistrates' Court ex p Caldwell* (1997) 161 JP 336, the Divisional Court held that an information laid to secure an arrest warrant has the effect of commencing a prosecution in that case (and so has the same effect as laying an information without also asking for an arrest warrant).

The form of the arrest warrant prescribed in the Magistrates' Courts (Forms) Rules 1981 is shown at the end of the chapter.

1.11   THE CODES OF PRACTICE

The five Codes of Practice issued under the Police and Criminal Evidence Act 1984 are known as Codes A, B, C , D and E.

1.11.1　Code A

Code of Practice for the exercise by police officers of statutory powers of stop and search (this Code deals with the exercise of the power vested in the police to stop people and search them for stolen or prohibited articles under s 1 of the Police and Criminal Evidence Act 1984, dealt with below).

1.11.2　Code B

Code of Practice for the searching of premises by police officers and the seizure of property found by police officers on person or premises (this Code deals with the exercise of the powers of search conferred on the police by s 17 of the Police and Criminal Evidence Act 1984, also dealt with below).

1.11.3　Code C

Code of Practice for the detention, treatment and questioning of persons by police officers (see above).

1.11.4　Code D

Code of Practice for the identification of persons by police officers. This Code governs matters such as the conduct of identification parades and the taking of finger prints. It provides, for example, that an identification parade (which should only take place with the consent of the suspect) should be conducted by an officer of the rank of inspector or above; the parade should consist of at least eight people (in addition to the suspect) who so far as possible resemble the suspect in age, height, general appearance and position in life. The participants stand in line and each one must be clearly numbered. Witnesses are brought in one at a time; they are told that the person they saw may or may not be on the parade and that, if they can make a positive identification, they should do so by indicating the number of the person concerned. In *R v Quinn* [1995] 1 Cr App R 480, the Court of Appeal said that if the Code of Practice on identification parades is not complied with, a conviction based on evidence of identification from the parade will be quashed.

1.11.5　Code E

Code of Practice on tape-recording. This Code deals with the procedure to be adopted in tape-recorded interviews; all interviews in respect of indictable (including triable either way) offences must be tape-recorded unless it is not reasonably practicable to do so as a result of equipment failure and the custody officer considers that the interview should not be delayed.

1.11.6   Breaches of the Codes

Breaches of the provisions of the Codes do not mean that any evidence obtained in breach of the Code in question (for example, a confession) is automatically inadmissible, but if there have been breaches of the Code, any evidence so obtained may well be ruled inadmissible as a result. See, for example, *R v Delaney* (1988) 88 Cr App R 338, *R v Bryce* [1992] 4 All ER 567 and *R v Joseph* [1993] Crim LR 206.

1.12   POLICE POWERS OF SEARCH

The Police and Criminal Evidence Act 1984 also contains powers regarding police searches of people, vehicles and premises.

1.12.1   Power to stop and search

Section 1 of the Police and Criminal Evidence Act 1984 empowers a police officer to search any person or vehicle for stolen or prohibited articles provided that the officer has reasonable grounds for suspecting that such articles will be found. The term 'stolen' article is self-explanatory.

The term 'prohibited' article means:

- an offensive weapon (that is, made or adapted for use for causing injury to person or intended by the person having it for such use); or
- an article made or adapted for use in burglary, theft, taking a conveyance without authority, or obtaining property by deception.

1.12.2   Searching premises

It may also be necessary for the police to enter and search premises. Usually, a search warrant is required, but there are circumstances where the police can proceed without a warrant.

- Entry with a warrant

  Section 8 of the Police and Criminal Evidence Act 1984 allows a Justice of the Peace to issue the police with a warrant to enter and search premises provided that there are reasonable grounds for believing that:

  (a) a serious arrestable offence has been committed; and

(b) there is material on the premises specified in the warrant which is likely to be of substantial value to the investigation of the offence; and

(c) the material sought is likely to be relevant evidence; and

(d) it is not practicable to communicate with any person entitled to grant entry to the premises, or entry will not be granted unless a warrant is produced, or the purpose of the search may be frustrated if police are unable to effect immediate entry.

Under s 15 of the Police and Criminal Evidence Act 1984, an application for a search warrant must specify the premises which the police wish to enter and search and must identify the material to be sought. Where a constable knows that premises include or consist of a number of dwellings in separate occupation, the application must specify the particular dwelling(s) which the police wish to enter and search: *R v South Western Magistrates' Court ex p Cofie* [1997] 1 WLR 885.

A police officer may seize and retain anything for which a search has been authorised under the warrant (s 8(2)).

In *R v Chesterfield Justices ex p Bramley* [2000] 1 All ER 411, the Divisional Court held as follows: (a) when executing a search warrant under s 8(1) of the 1984 Act, a police officer is not entitled to remove items from the premises in order to sift through them for the purpose of deciding whether or not they fall within the scope of the warrant; (b) there is no absolute prohibition on seizing an item which is in fact subject to legal professional privilege (see 1.12.3 below), provided that the police officer who seizes it does not have reasonable grounds for believing that it is privileged; (c) if there is no lawful authority for seizing some of the items that are seized during a search, those items must be returned, but the search remains valid for the items that were properly seized.

A specimen warrant is shown at the end of the chapter.

- Entry without warrant

  Two statutory provisions enable the police to enter and search premises without a warrant.

  o Section 17 of the Police and Criminal Evidence Act 1984 empowers the police to enter and search premises to execute an arrest warrant, to arrest someone for an arrestable offence, or to save life or limb or prevent serious damage to property.

  o Section 18(1) of the Police and Criminal Evidence Act 1984 allows a police officer to enter and search any premises occupied or controlled by a person who is under arrest for an arrestable offence if the officer has reasonable grounds to suspect that there is on the premises evidence relating to the offence for which the suspect has been arrested or to some other arrestable offence which is connected with or similar to that offence.

The officer may seize and retain anything for which he may search but the scope of the search must be restricted to whatever is reasonably required to search for the evidence referred to in s 18(1) (s 18(2), (3)).

Normally, such a search should be authorised in writing by an officer of at least the rank of inspector (s 18(4)). A search may take place without such authorisation and without taking the suspect to the police station first if his presence is necessary at some other place for the effective investigation of the offence (s 18(5)).

A police officer who is exercising a statutory power to enter someone's home by the use of the reasonable force should explain the reason for exercising that power of entry to any occupant unless it is impracticable to do so (*O'Loughlin v Chief Constable of Essex* [1998] 1 WLR 374).

1.12.3 Legal privilege

The police cannot gain access to material which is subject to legal privilege. This material is defined by s 10(1) of the Police and Criminal Evidence Act 1984 as meaning communications between a lawyer and his client (or any person representing his client) made in connection with the giving of legal advice to the client; and communications between a lawyer and his client (or any person representing his client) or between such an adviser or his client or any such representative and any other person made in connection with or in contemplation of legal proceedings and for the purpose of such proceedings.

1.12.4 Excluded and special procedure material

The police can only gain access to 'excluded material' or 'special procedure material' by obtaining a warrant from a circuit judge under s 9 of the Police and Criminal Evidence Act 1984.

Excluded material is defined by s 11(1) of the Police and Criminal Evidence Act 1984:

(a) personal records[1] which a person has acquired or created in the course of any trade, business, profession or other occupation or for the purposes of any paid or unpaid office and which he holds in confidence;

---

1 Documentary and other records concerning an individual (whether living or dead) who can be identified from them and relating:
   (a) to his physical or mental health;
   (b) to spiritual counselling or assistance given or to be given to him; or
   (c) to counselling or assistance given or to be given to him, for the purposes of his personal welfare, by any voluntary organisation or by any individual who:
         (i) by reason of his office or occupation has responsibilities for personal welfare; or
         (ii) be reason of an order of a court has responsibilities for his supervision.

(b) human tissue or tissue fluid which has been taken for the purposes of diagnosis or medical treatment and which a person holds in confidence;

(c) journalistic material[2] which a person holds in confidence and which consists:

    (i) of documents; or

    (ii) of records other than documents.

Special procedure material is defined by s 14:

(a) material other than items subject to legal privilege and excluded material, in the possession of a person who:

    (i) acquired or created it in the course of any trade, business, profession or other occupation or for the purpose of any paid or unpaid office (s 14(1), (2)); and

    (ii) holds it in confidence;

(b) journalistic material, other than excluded material.

The procedure for applying to a circuit judge for access to excluded material or special procedure material under s 9 is set out in Sched 1.

The judge may only make an access order if satisfied on the balance of probabilities that one of the sets of access conditions is fulfilled.

The first set of access conditions (Sched 1, para 2) requires that:

(a) there are reasonable grounds for believing that a serious arrestable offence has been committed and that on the premises to be searched there is special procedure material which is likely to be of substantial value to the investigation and is likely to be relevant evidence;

(b) other methods of obtaining the special procedure material have failed or have not been tried because it appeared they would be bound to fail;

(c) it is in the public interest to produce or allow access to the material, having regard to the benefit to the investigation and the circumstances under which the person holds the material.

The second set of access conditions (Sched 1, para 3) requires that there be reasonable grounds for believing that there is excluded material on the premises, in respect of which a magistrate would have had power to grant a search warrant but for the removal of that power by s 9(2).

A judge also has the power to issue a warrant authorising a constable to enter and search premises (Sched 1, para 12). Where the material is excluded material, the judge must be satisfied that the second set of access conditions (see previous paragraph) is fulfilled and that there has been a failure to comply with an access order.

---

2   Material acquired or created for the purposes of journalism and which is in the possession of a person who acquired or created it for the purposes of journalism (s 13).

A judge may also issue a warrant to enter and search premises if satisfied that either set of access conditions is fulfilled and that any of the following conditions are also fulfilled:

(a) that it is not practicable to communicate with a person entitled to grant entry to the premises; or

(b) that it is practicable to communicate with a person entitled to grant entry to the premises but it is not practicable to communicate with a person entitled to grant access to the material; or

(c) there is a statutory restriction of disclosure or obligation of secrecy and that disclosure would be a breach of that statutory restriction or obligation unless a warrant were granted; or

(d) that service of notice of an application for an order would seriously prejudice the investigation.

1.13   ALTERNATIVES TO PROSECUTION

1.13.1   Adults

Not every arrest results in the person arrested being charged and having to go to court. The police have the alternative of administering a caution instead. This is not to be confused with the warning given before questioning (see 1.7.1 above). Rather it is a warning that committing a further offence will result in court action.

The present arrangements for cautions of adults are set out in Home Office Circular 18/1994.

The purpose of a formal caution is:

• to deal quickly and simply with less serious offenders;

• to divert such offenders from unnecessary court appearances;

• to reduce the chances of their re-offending.

A caution does not count as a previous conviction but if the person re-offends, the caution will be cited in court. Records of a caution are usually kept for three years (or until the offender attains the age of 18) whichever is the longer.

Before administering a caution, the police should consider two questions:

• are the circumstances such that a caution is likely to be effective in preventing the offender from re-offending?;

• is a caution appropriate to the offence?

As regards the latter question, the guidelines make it clear that a caution is never appropriate for really serious indictable only offences, such as rape. A caution may, in exceptional circumstances, be appropriate for an indictable only offence (for example, one child taking another's pocket-money by force, which is robbery).

Offences that are triable either way may not be appropriate for cautioning if they are serious in the present case (for example, an offence which is racially motivated; theft in breach of trust; an offence carried out in a systematic and organised way).

A caution may only be administered if:

- there is sufficient evidence of the offender's guilt for there to be a realistic prospect of conviction;
- the offender admits the offence; and
- the offender consents to the caution (in the case of a juvenile, consent is given by a parent or guardian).

There is a presumption against prosecuting certain categories of offender (for example, the elderly, those who suffer from mental illness or impairment and those who are severely disabled). The guidance from the Home Office makes it clear, however, that members of these groups should be prosecuted if the seriousness of the offence requires this. That guidance also says that the presumption in favour of diverting juveniles from the courts does not mean that they should automatically be cautioned merely because they are juveniles.

The guidelines go on to say that a practical demonstration of regret (for example, apologising to the victim or offering to put matters right) may support the use of a caution. However, it should be noted that conditions cannot be attached to a caution (so the police cannot say that the offender will only be cautioned if she pays compensation to the victim).

The police are encouraged to seek the views of the victim as to the seriousness of the offence, the extent of any harm or loss, and any reparation by the offender.

A caution should normally be administered at a police station by a uniform officer of the rank of inspector or above. A juvenile should only be cautioned in the presence of a parent or guardian.

If the offender is elderly, infirm or otherwise vulnerable, a caution may be administered at the offender's home in the presence of a friend or relative.

It is the intention of the Home Office that offenders should not usually receive more than one caution; subsequent offences should lead to prosecution. Cautioning for a subsequent offence should only take place if:

- the later offence is trivial; or
- there has been a sufficient lapse of time since the first caution to suggest that the caution had some effect in preventing re-offending.

The Home Office circular adds that there is no intention to inhibit the practice of taking action short of a formal caution by giving an oral warning. Such a warning, or informal caution, is not recorded and cannot be cited in subsequent court proceedings.

If a formal caution is administered in breach of the Home Office guidelines, then judicial review may be sought to quash the caution and have it deleted from police records. See *R v Metropolitan Police Commissioner ex p P* (1996) 8 Admin LR 6, where a caution was quashed because the recipient of the caution had not admitted the offence and also because the police had made no attempt to establish whether the person, a child under 14, knew that his behaviour had been seriously wrong.

Where the suspect makes a clear and unequivocal admission, it is acceptable to administer a formal caution (as an alternative to commencing a prosecution) even if the admission was not obtained in an interview complying with Code C of the Codes of Practice; however, as a matter of good practice, the police should ensure that a formal interview (complying with Code C) takes place (*R v Chief Constable of Lancashire Constabulary ex p Atkinson* (1998) 192 JP 275).

Normally, where someone has been cautioned for an offence, they will not subsequently be prosecuted for that same offence. However, in *Hayter v L* [1998] 1 WLR 854, the prosecutor's son was assaulted by the respondents. The respondents admitted the offence and were cautioned by the police. The prosecutor then commenced a private prosecution. The magistrates stayed the prosecution as an abuse of process. The Divisional Court held that the administration of a caution did not mean that a subsequent private prosecution would be an abuse of process and so the justices were wrong to stay the prosecution. It should be borne in mind, however, that the DPP has power under the Prosecution of Offences Act 1985 to take over and terminate a private prosecution if it is in the public interest to do so: see 1.14.1 below.

1.13.2   Juveniles

A slightly system applies to young offenders. Section 65 of the Crime and Disorder Act 1998 applies (by virtue of s 65(1)) to cases where:

(a) the police have evidence that a child or young person has committed an offence;

(b) there is sufficient evidence against the youngster that, if he were prosecuted, there would be a realistic prospect that he would be convicted of the offence;

(c) the youngster admits to the police that he committed the offence;

(d) the youngster has not previously been convicted of any offence; and

(e) the police are satisfied that it would not be in the public interest for the youngster to be prosecuted.

In such a case, s 65(2) provides that the police may *reprimand* the youngster if he has not previously been reprimanded or warned.

Under s 65(3), the police may warn a youngster who comes within s 65(1) if:

(a) he has not previously been warned; or

(b) where he has previously been warned, the present offence was committed more than two years after the date of the previous warning and the police consider that the present offence is not sufficiently serious to require a charge to be brought.

Section 65(3) goes on to state that no person may be warned more than twice.

Under s 65, the usual sequence of events would be:

- first offence: reprimand;
- second offence: warning;
- third offence: prosecution (or a second warning if the present offence is more than two years after the first warning and the present offence is not so serious as to require prosecution).

However, s 65(4) states that where the youngster has not previously been reprimanded, a warning may be administered, rather than a reprimand, if the police consider that the offence is so serious as to require a warning.

Similarly, there is nothing to stop the police from prosecuting a youngster for a first or second offence where the seriousness of the offence makes that an appropriate course of action.

Under s 65(5), reprimands and warnings must be administered at a police station and in the presence of an appropriate adult. The effect of re-offending must be explained to the youngster and to the adult.

Under s 66(2), where a warning has been administered, a youth offending team must, unless they consider it inappropriate to do so, arrange for the youngster to participate in a rehabilitation programme, with the aim of preventing him from re-offending.

Where a person has been warned under s 65 and is subsequently convicted of an offence committed within two years of the warning, the court dealing with him for the later offence cannot impose a conditional discharge unless it takes the view that there are exceptional circumstances relating to the offence or to the offender which justify its doing so (s 66(4)).

Reprimands, warnings, and failure to participate in a rehabilitation programme, may be cited in criminal proceedings in the same way as previous convictions may be cited (s 66(5)).

The current requirement that a reprimand or warning may only be given in a police station will be removed under the Criminal Justice and Court Services Bill 2000. This will give the police flexibility to arrange for 'restorative conferences' in more suitable locations, such as the offices of the youth offending team responsible for assessing the young offender and providing the intervention programme. The Bill gives the police an explicit power to grant bail pending delivery of reprimands and final warnings.

1.14   THE DECISION TO PROSECUTE

Assuming the case is not one where the police consider that a caution is appropriate, the decision to charge someone following their arrest, or to lay an information, is taken by the police. The Crown Prosecution Service (CPS) then take over the conduct of the prosecution (s 3(2)(a) of the Prosecution of Offences Act 1985). The case will be reviewed by a Crown Prosecutor, who may decide to continue with the original charge(s), substitute different ones, or even discontinue proceedings altogether.

1.14.1   Discontinuing proceedings

The Director of Public Prosecutions (DPP), the head of the CPS, can at any 'preliminary stage' of the proceedings discontinue any criminal proceedings by serving a notice of discontinuance under s 23 of the Prosecution of Offences Act 1985. The case will be reviewed by a Crown Prosecutor, who may decide to continue with the original charge(s), substitute different ones, or even discontinue proceedings altogether.

This will be done where it becomes apparent that the case against the defendant is not as strong as it first seemed (for example, new evidence comes to light or a prosecution witness changes his story). In the year ending March 1996, 12% of cases in the magistrates' court were discontinued. Section 23(2) defines the term 'preliminary stage'. In the case of a summary offence, it is too late to serve a notice under s 23 once the trial has begun. In the case of an indictable offence, it is too late to serve a notice if committal proceedings have taken place or summary trial has begun.

To discontinue proceedings, the DPP simply serves a notice on the clerk to the justices. The DPP must inform the defendant and must give reasons for the decision to discontinue the proceedings. As discontinuance does not prevent the institution of further proceedings in respect of the offence (s 23(9)), the defendant may serve a counter-notice requiring that the proceedings continue; this would be the case where the defendant wishes to have his name cleared by an acquittal.

If the decision to discontinue the prosecution is taken after the preliminary stages have been completed, the prosecution can discontinue proceedings at trial by offering no evidence at trial.

In *Cooke v DPP* (1992) 95 Cr App R 233, it was held that s 23 only provides an additional method of discontinuing proceedings. The other ways of discontinuing proceedings (such as withdrawing a summons or charge or offering no evidence) remain available.

In *R v Grafton* [1992] QB 101; [1992] 4 All ER 609, it was held that the decision to discontinue proceedings is entirely a matter for the prosecution; the agreement of the court is not required. This applies both in the magistrates' court and the Crown Court.

The powers of the Director of Public Prosecutions to discontinue a prosecution under s 23 of the Prosecution of Offences Act may be contrasted with the power of the Attorney General (who is a member of the government but who is also responsible to parliament) to enter a *nolle prosequi*. This power enables the Attorney General to terminate a prosecution at any time after the bill of indictment (see Chapter 8, 8.2 below) has been signed. This power is exercised only rarely but its exercise cannot be challenged in the courts (*Gouriet v Union of Post Office Workers* [1978] AC 435).

1.14.2   Deciding to prosecute

The Code of Conduct for Crown Prosecutors states that a prosecution should only be started or continued if there is a 'realistic prospect of conviction'. This means that a court is more likely than not to convict the defendant of the charge alleged. In deciding whether or not this 51% test is satisfied, the Crown Prosecutor should consider both the admissibility and the likely reliability of the evidence against the defendant. Thus, the Crown Prosecutor must take account of any challenges which the defence may make to the admissibility of evidence and must also see if there are discrepancies between what the various prosecutions witnesses have said to the police and whether a prosecution witness might have a motive for lying.

The Crown Prosecution Service should also consider whether a prosecution is in the public interest. For example, if the offence is a trivial one, and so in the event of conviction the court would be likely to impose only a very small or nominal penalty, the CPS might take the view that it is not in the public interest to continue proceedings. Similarly, a prosecution may not be in the public interest if it is likely to have an adverse effect on the physical or mental health of the victim or the offender. However, the Code makes it clear that 'the more serious the offence, the more likely it is that a prosecution will be needed in the public interest'.

In *R v DPP ex p C* [1995] 1 Cr App R 136, it was held that the decision by the Crown Prosecution Service not to prosecute a person was susceptible to judicial review if the Crown Prosecutor who took the decision failed to act in accordance with the policy set out in the Code of Conduct for Crown Prosecutors. In the present case, which involved an allegation that a man had committed buggery on his wife, a Crown Prosecutor decided that there was sufficient evidence against the man but that it was not in the public interest to prosecute him. The Code of Conduct states that in the case of a serious sexual assault, where the evidential sufficiency criterion is satisfied (so that there is a realistic prospect of conviction), it will normally be in the public interest to prosecute the alleged offender. The Divisional Court emphasised that the power to review the decisions of the CPS will be exercised sparingly: it would only be used if the decision not to prosecute was arrived at because of an unlawful policy, or because of a failure to act in accordance with the Code of Practice or where a decision was perverse.

In *R v DPP ex p Manning* (2000) *The Times*, 19 May, the Divisional Court repeated that, although a decision by the DPP not to prosecute is susceptible to judicial review, the review power is to be exercised sparingly. The court went on to hold that there is no general obligation on the DPP to give reasons for a decision not to prosecute. However, in a case where one might reasonably expect there to be a prosecution (in this case, there had been a death in custody and a properly directed coroner's jury had returned a verdict of unlawful killing implicating a person who, although not named, was clearly identified and whose whereabouts were known), reasons for a decision not to prosecute should be given.

In *R v DPP ex p Treadaway* (1997) *The Times*, 31 October, the Divisional Court held that when deciding whether or not to prosecute a person for conduct which a civil court has found proven, the prosecutor must analyse the civil court's findings very carefully.

In the absence of dishonesty or bad faith or other exceptional circumstances, the decision of the DPP to consent to a prosecution where such consent is required is not amenable to judicial review; challenges to such proceedings should be made in the context of the criminal trial or by way of appeal against conviction following such trial (*R v DPP ex p Kebilene* [1999] 3 WLR 972; [1999] 4 All ER 801).

1.14.3   Private prosecutions

Where a member of the public commences a 'private prosecution', they do so by laying an information. A member of the public can bring a private prosecution for any offence unless the offence is one for which the consent of the Attorney General or the Director of Public Prosecutions is required before a prosecution can take place. This is because s 6(1) of the Prosecution of Offences Act 1985 preserves the right of any person to institute criminal proceedings in any case unless the consent of the Director of Public Prosecutions or the Attorney General is necessary in order to commence a prosecution. Such consent is only needed for a very small number of offences. The Attorney General's consent is required (*inter alia*) for offences of bribery under the Public Bodies Corrupt Practices Act 1889 (see s 4) and the Prevention of Corruption Act 1906 (see s 2); offences under the Official Secrets Act 1911 (see s 8); for offences of inciting racial hatred and similar offences under the Public Order Act 1986 (see s 27); for offences under the Explosive Substances Act 1883 (see s 7); and for most offences under the Prevention of Terrorism (Temporary Provisions) Act 1989 (see s 19). The consent of the Director of Public Prosecutions is required (*inter alia*) for offences of theft or criminal damage where the property belongs to the spouse of the accused (see s 30(4) of the Theft Act 1968); for offences of assisting offenders and wasting police time (see ss 4(4) and 5(3) of the Criminal Law Act 1967); for homosexual offences where either partner is under the age of consent (s 8 of the Sexual Offences Act 1967); incest (see Schedule 2 of the Sexual Offences Act 1956); aiding and abetting a suicide (see s 2 of the Suicide Act 1961); and riot (see s 7 of the Public Order Act 1986).

A member of the public can only commence criminal proceedings by laying an information as he will not be granted an arrest warrant by a magistrate; someone who effects a 'citizen's arrest' (an arrest without a warrant) will have to hand the suspect over to the police.

Section 6(2) of the Prosecution of Offences Act 1985 enables the Director of Public prosecution to take over the conduct of any criminal proceedings. Once the DPP has taken over the conduct of the proceedings, he is free to discontinue them if he thinks it appropriate to do so.

Where the Crown Prosecution Service have already commenced proceedings against a defendant and a member of the public seeks to lay an information against that defendant alleging another offence arising out of the same incident, the court should be reluctant to issue a summons. In *R v Tower Bridge Magistrates ex p Chaudhry* [1993] 3 WLR 1154; [1994] 1 All ER 44, for example, the applicant's son was killed in a road accident. The Crown Prosecution Service brought proceedings against the other driver alleging driving without due care and attention. The applicant laid an information which alleged causing death by reckless driving (it would now be causing death by dangerous driving). The stipendiary magistrate refused to issue a summons and that refusal was upheld by the Divisional Court.

1.14.4 Prosecutions by public bodies other than the police

Where a public body, such as the Inland Revenue, HM Customs and Excise, or a local authority, commences a prosecution, this is normally done by an employee of the public body laying an information at a magistrates' court. Indeed, this is the only way for the proceedings to be commenced if the offence is not an arrestable offence. Even in the case of arrestable offences, the usual method for a public body to commence a prosecution is by laying down an information. However, in some cases (provided that the offence is an arrestable offence, as defined in s 24 of the Police and Criminal Evidence Act 1984, see 1.4.1 above) the suspect may be arrested by a representative of the public body.

Representatives of such bodies are not police officers and so are, in effect, making a 'citizen's arrest'. The person arrested will be taken to a police station to be charged by the custody officer.

In *R v Stafford Justices ex p Customs and Excise Commissioners* [1990] 3 WLR 656, followed in *R v Croydon Justices ex p Holmberg* [1992] Crim LR 892, it was held that proceedings commenced in this way are not taken over by the police (and thence by the Crown Prosecution Service) but are conducted by the relevant public body.

1.14.5   What happens next?

As we shall see in Chapter 3, some offences have to be tried in the magistrates' court ('summary trial', dealt with in Chapter 4) while others may be tried in that court if the defendant and the magistrates agree; the remaining offences have to be tried before a judge and jury in the Crown Court ('trial on indictment', dealt with in Chapter 9).

Even if a case is ultimately tried in the Crown Court, the case will nevertheless start in the magistrates' court:

• In the case of proceedings which are commenced by the laying of an information and the issue of a summons, it is the magistrates' court which issues the summons and the summons will require the defendant to attend the magistrates' court which issued it.

• If the suspect is arrested and charged by the police, he may be granted police bail under s 38 of the Police and Criminal Evidence Act 1984. In that case, he will be handed a charge sheet which tells him the date, time and place of his first court appearance, which will be in the magistrates' court.

• If, after charge, the suspect is not granted police bail, then he will be held in custody by the police until the next sitting of the magistrates' court. At that hearing, the magistrates will decide whether to grant him bail or not. On bail, see Chapter 2.

1.15   THE MAGISTRATES' COURT

The magistrates' court usually comprises three lay justices and a legally qualified clerk.

The lay justices are ordinary members of the public who have put themselves forward to sit as Justices of the Peace (JPs). They are appointed by the Lord Chancellor under s 6 of the Justices of the Peace Act 1979. They are unpaid, although they can claim reimbursement for travel expenses and loss of earnings. Each magistrate has to sit at least 26 times a year (although many sit more often than this). They receive basic training in the law, the evidence and the procedure which they are likely to encounter.

Because they have only very elementary training, the lay justices need the help of their clerk. The clerk must be a barrister or solicitor of at least five years' standing (or else have been an assistant clerk for at least five years). The assistant clerks do not have to be legally qualified, but if they are not so qualified they can only do work 'behind the scenes' and cannot act as clerks in court.

In the cities, there may well be a stipendiary magistrate (to be re-named District Judge under the Access to Justice Act 1999). As the name suggests, these magistrates receive a salary. Stipendiary magistrates are appointed by the Queen, on the recommendation of the Lord Chancellor, from amongst barristers and solicitors of at least seven years' standing. A stipendiary magistrate can try a case sitting alone (except in the youth court) whereas at least two lay justices must be sitting for a summary trial to take place. Because a stipendiary magistrate is legally qualified and sits alone, cases in front of such magistrates tend to be disposed of more quickly than those that are heard by lay justices.

Both solicitors and barristers have complete rights of audience in the magistrates' court.

1.16 THE CROWN COURT

The Crown Court is always presided over by a professional judge. Where the Crown Court is trying a case, the judge always sits with a jury. Very serious offences are usually tried by a High Court judge; most cases however will be tried by a circuit judge or a part time judge called a recorder. Thus, murder must be tried by a High Court judge; manslaughter and rape will usually be tried by a High Court judge but may be tried by a circuit judge; other offences can be tried by a High Court judge, a circuit judge or a recorder. See ss 8 and 75 of the Supreme Court Act 1981 and s 24 of the Courts Act 1971. The post of assistant recorder (effectively, a probationary recorder) is being phased out.

A circuit judge or recorder is addressed as 'your Honour'; a High Court judge (or any judge sitting at the Central Criminal Court) is addressed as 'my Lord'.

High Court judges are appointed by the Queen, on the recommendation of the Lord Chancellor, from amongst the ranks of barristers of at least 10 years' standing. Most will have acted as deputy (that is, part time) High Court judges beforehand. A circuit judge may also be made a High Court judge.

Circuit judges and recorders are appointed by the Queen on the recommendation of the Lord Chancellor. Barristers and solicitors of at least 10 years' standing may be appointed recorders. Only barristers of 10 years' standing or solicitors or barristers who have been recorders for at least three years are eligible for appointment as circuit judges.

The allocation of work in the Crown Court is governed by a Practice Note (1995).

Offences triable in the Crown Court are classified as follows:

Class 1: Murder, treason; to be tried by a High Court judge;

Class 2: Manslaughter, infanticide, child destruction, abortion, rape, sexual intercourse with a girl under 13, incest with a girl under 13; usually tried by a High Court judge;

Class 3: All offences triable only on indictment other than those in classes 1, 2 and 4; triable by a High Court judge, circuit judge or recorder;

Class 4: Wounding or causing grievous bodily harm with intent, robbery, all triable either way offences; to be tried by a circuit judge, recorder or assistant recorder.

Crown Courts are classified as first, second, or third tier. The first tier courts can try all indictable offences; the third tier can try only less serious indictable offences. This is because third tier Crown Court do not have the services of a High Court judge; first tier courts always do and second tier courts sometimes do.

When the Crown Court is sitting as an appellate court from the magistrates' court, it comprises a circuit judge or recorder and two lay justices (though up to four lay justices may sit).

Barristers, and solicitors with at least three years' post-qualification experience, have rights of audience for trials on indictment. However, where the Crown Court is hearing an appeal from the magistrates' court, or a committal for sentence from the magistrates' court (see Chapter 4), all barristers and solicitors have rights of audience.

1.17   CROWN PROSECUTORS

All Crown Prosecutors have to be either barrister or solicitors (s 1(3) of the Prosecution of Offences Act 1985).

Crown Prosecutors have 'all the powers of the Director [of Public Prosecutions] as to the institution and conduct of proceedings' (s 1(6)). Thus a Crown Prosecutor can authorise the commencement of proceedings where the consent of the Director of Prosecutions is required (s 1(7)). Similarly, a Crown Prosecutor can discontinue proceedings under s 23 of the Prosecution of Offences Act 1985.

Crown Prosecutors, whether barrister or solicitors, may conduct trials in the magistrates' court and in the Crown Court but, in most cases, the Crown Prosecution Service will brief counsel to prosecute in trials on indictment.

1.18   OPEN COURT

Both the magistrates' court and the Crown Court normally sit in open court and there is a strong presumption that they should do. However, any court does have a discretion to sit 'in camera' (that is, to exclude the public) if this is necessary for the administration of justice. Decisions to sit 'in camera' are therefore very rare (see, generally *Attorney General v Leveller Magazine Ltd* [1979] AC 440; [1979] 1 All ER 745).

1.19   DISCLOSURE UNDER THE CRIMINAL PROCEDURE AND INVESTIGATIONS ACT 1996

The Criminal Procedure and Investigations Act (CPIA) 1996 puts on a statutory footing requirements for pre-trial disclosure by the prosecution to the defence and by the defence to the prosecution.

Under s 1 of the CPIA 1996, the statutory disclosure provisions apply to all trials in the magistrates' court or Youth Court where the defendant pleads not guilty and to all cases being tried in the Crown Court.

1.19.1   Disclosure by prosecution

Section 3(1) of the CPIA 1996 requires the prosecutor to:
  (a) disclose to the accused any prosecution material which has not previously been disclosed to the accused and which in the prosecutor's opinion might undermine the case for the prosecution against the accused; or
  (b) give to the accused a written statement that there is no material of a description mentioned in para (a).

Section 3(6) enables the prosecutor to withhold material if 'the court, on an application by the prosecutor, concludes it is not in the public interest to disclose it and orders accordingly'. The relevant court is the one in which the defendant will be tried (so, following committal for trial, the magistrates will have no jurisdiction in respect of disclosure; cf *R v CPS ex p Warby* (1994) 158 JP 190; [1994] Crim LR 281). See 1.19.10 below.

'Prosecution material' is defined by s 3(2) as material 'which is in the prosecutor's possession, and came into his possession in connection with the case for the prosecution against the accused'. This would seem to represent a narrowing of the common law duty of disclosure, which applied to material of which the prosecuting lawyers were unaware (for example, forensic evidence which had not been passed on to the lawyers).

The duty to disclose is defined very broadly (anything which might undermine the Crown's case). It follows that it would extend to information which casts doubt on the reliability of a prosecution witness by undermining their credibility. This would include revealing the fact that the witness has sought a reward payable on the defendant's conviction (as in *R v Rasheed* (1994) 158 JP 914).

In *R v Guney* [1998] 2 Cr App R 242, the Court of Appeal held that the defence are entitled to be informed of any convictions or disciplinary findings recorded against a police officer involved in the present case, and of any decisions by trial judges where a trial was stopped, or Court of Appeal judgements where a conviction was quashed, because of misconduct or lack of veracity of identified police officers who are also involved in the present case.

1.19.2 Compulsory disclosure by defence

Section 5 of the CPIA 1996 makes provision for compulsory disclosure by the defendant where the case is to be tried in the Crown Court. Under s 5(1) of the CPIA 1996, the requirement for disclosure by the defence applies once the prosecution have made disclosure of their material under s 3. Section 5(5) requires the defendant to give a 'defence statement to the court and the prosecutor'. This 'defence statement' is defined by s 5(6) as 'a written statement':

- (a) setting out in general terms the nature of the accused's defence;
- (b) indicating the matters on which he takes issue with the prosecution; and
- (c) setting out, in the case of each such matter, the reason why he takes issue with the prosecution.

The General Council of the Bar has given guidance on the involvement of counsel in the drafting of defence statements. The guidance notes that it will normally be more appropriate for instructing solicitors to draft the defence statement, since counsel will generally have had little involvement in the case at this stage. However, there is no reason why a barrister should not draft a defence statement. Before doing so, counsel must ensure that the defendant:

- (a) understands the importance of the accuracy and adequacy of the defence statement; and
- (b) has had the opportunity of carefully considering the statement drafted by counsel and has approved it.

1.19.3 Alibi evidence

Special provisions apply where the defendant relies on an alibi. Evidence in support of an alibi is defined by s 5(8) as 'evidence tending to show that by reason of the presence of the accused at a particular place or in a particular area at a particular time he was not, or was unlikely to have been, at the place where the offence is alleged to have been committed at the time of its alleged commission'.

The defence of alibi applies only to offences which are linked to a particular time and place. If, for example, the defendant is charged with living off immoral earnings and claims in his defence that he was out of the country at the time he is alleged to have been so doing, this defence does not amount to an alibi because the allegation is not specific to a particular place (*R v Hassan* [1970] 1 QB 423; [1970] 1 All ER 745).

An alibi is concerned with the defendant's whereabouts at the time of the offence itself, not at times which are related to circumstantial evidence relied on by the prosecution. In *R v Lewis* [1969] 2 QB 1; [1969] 1 All ER 79, the defendant was charged with dishonestly receiving two stolen postal orders on 14 February. The prosecution adduced evidence that he cashed the two postal orders on 16 February as part of the evidence showing that he had dishonestly received them on 14 February. It was held that his whereabouts on 16 February were so removed from the offence itself as not to amount to an alibi.

This case should be contrasted with *R v Fields* [1991] Crim LR 38. The defendant was allegedly seen twice by a prosecution witness, once during the robbery with which he was charged and once three hours before the robbery. The defendant had no alibi for the time of the robbery itself but said that three hours before the robbery he was 25 miles away and so could not have been the person seen by the witness. This was held to amount to an alibi even though it did not relate to the time of the offence itself. This decision of the Court of Appeal is a rather surprising one; however, it may be justified on the basis that the two sightings were very close together in time and that they were inextricably linked given the evidence of the witness; also, that the person seen three hours before the robbery was at the scene in order to prepare for the robbery and so his presence there could be said to be part of the robbery itself. It is likely that this decision will be confined to its facts.

In *R v Johnson* [1994] Crim LR 949; [1994] 15 Crim App R(S) 827, it was held that evidence only amounts to alibi evidence if it is evidence that the defendant was somewhere other than the place where the offence was committed at the relevant time; evidence which simply shows that the defendant was not present at the commission of the offence is not alibi evidence.

Where the defence statement discloses an alibi, s 5(7) requires the defence statement to give particulars of the alibi. Those particulars must include:

(a) the name and address of any witness the accused believes is able to give evidence in support of the alibi, if the name and address are known to the accused when the statement is given;

(b) any information in the accused's possession which might be of material assistance in finding any such witness, if his name or address is not known to the accused when the statement is given.

Presumably the particulars of alibi should set out where the defendant claims to have been at the relevant time even if the only evidence in support of that alibi is to come from the defendant himself (cf *R v Jackson* [1973] Crim LR 356, a case decided under the legislation which dealt with alibis prior to the enactment of the CPIA 1996).

1.19.4   Voluntary disclosure by defence

Where the defendant is to be tried in the magistrates' court (or, if a juvenile, the Youth Court), s 6 of the CPIA 1996 makes provision for voluntary disclosure by the defence. Section 6(2) provides that in those cases the defendant *may* give a defence statement to the prosecutor and, if he does so, must also give such a statement to the court.

The incentive for the defence to make disclosure even though it is not compulsory is that if they do so a further duty of disclosure is then imposed upon the prosecution.

1.19.5   Secondary disclosure by the prosecution

Section 7 of the CPIA 1996 imposes a further duty of disclosure on the prosecution whenever the defence have made compulsory disclosure (under s 5, in the case of Crown Court trials) or voluntary disclosure (under s 6, in the case of magistrates' court or Youth Court trials). Section 7(2) requires the prosecutor, once a defence statement has been given, to:

(a) disclose to the accused any prosecution material which has not previously been disclosed to the accused and which might be reasonably expected to assist the accused's defence as disclosed by the defence statement given under s 5 or 6; or

(b) give to the accused a written statement that there is no material of a description mentioned in para (a).

'Prosecution material' has the same definition as under s 3.

As with the initial duty of disclosure, it is open to the prosecution to seek an order from the court that material should be withheld on the ground that it is not in the public interest to disclose it (s 7(5)). Again, the relevant court is the one in which the trial is to take place.

1.19.6   Defence application for disclosure

Section 8(2) of the CPIA 1996 provides that where the accused has given a defence statement under s 5 or s 6 and has reasonable cause to believe that the prosecutor has failed to disclose prosecution material which might reasonably be expected to assist the accused's defence (as disclosed by the defence statement), the defendant may apply to the court for an order requiring the prosecutor to disclose such material to the defence. Again, it is open to the prosecutor to argue that disclosure is not in the public interest (s 8(4)).

1.19.7 Continuing disclosure duty of prosecution

Section 9(2) of the CPIA 1996 applies to all times between disclosure by the prosecution under s 3 and the end of the case (that is, the acquittal or conviction of the defendant or the prosecution deciding not to proceed with the case). This continuing duty of the prosecutor is defined by s 9(2) as a duty to:

> ... keep under review the question whether at any given time there is prosecution material which:
>
> (a) in his opinion might undermine the case for the prosecution against the accused; and
>
> (b) has not been disclosed to the accused.

Section 9(2) then provides that 'if there is such material at any time the prosecutor must disclose it to the accused as soon as is reasonably practicable'.

Section 9(5) places a slightly different duty on the prosecutor once secondary disclosure has been made by the prosecution under s 7. This duty is to:

> ... keep under review the question whether at any given time there is prosecution material which:
>
> (a) might reasonably be expected to assist the accused's defence as disclosed by the defence statement given under s 5 or 6; and
>
> (b) has not been disclosed to the accused.

Again, any such material must be disclosed as soon as is reasonably practicable.

'Prosecution material' has the same definition as under s 3.

Section 9(8) enables the prosecution to apply for an order that it is not in the public interest to disclose material which would otherwise have to be disclosed under s 9.

1.19.8 Time limits

Regulation 2 of the CPIA 1996 (Defence Disclosure Time Limits) Regulations 1997 (SI 1997/684) defines the 'relevant period' for ss 5 and 6 as beginning with the day when the prosecutor complies (or purports to comply) with s 3 of the CPIA 1996 and expiring 14 days later.

Regulation 3 provides for the extension of that period by the court, on application by the accused, if the court is satisfied that the accused could not reasonably have acted within that period. No limit is prescribed for the length of such extension. Regulation 4 enables the accused to apply for further extensions of time.

Regulation 5 provides that where the 14 day period would otherwise expire on a Saturday or Sunday, or on Christmas Day or Good Friday or any other bank holiday, it will be deemed to expire on the next working day.

No 'relevant periods' have been prescribed for s 3 or 7 of the Act and so these remain governed by the transitional provisions in s 13. For s 3, the prosecutor must act 'as soon as is reasonably practicable' after the accused has pleaded not guilty (in the case of summary trials) or has been committed or transferred for trial, etc (in the case of Crown Court trials). For s 7, the prosecutor must act 'as soon as is reasonably practicable after the accused gives a defence statement under s 5 or 6'.

Rule 8(4) of the Crown Court (Criminal Procedure and Investigations Act 1996) (Disclosure) Rules 1997 (SI 1997/698) and r 8(4) of the Magistrates' Courts (Criminal Procedure and Investigations Act 1996) (Disclosure) Rules 1997 (SI 1997/703) provide that, where the accused applies for an extension of time, the prosecutor may make written representations to the court within 14 days of being given notice of the application by the accused. On receipt of these representations (or at the expiry of the 14 day period, where no representations have been made), the court considers the application and may, if it wishes, do so at a hearing (r 8(5)). If there is a hearing, it is *inter partes* and the prosecutor and applicant are entitled to make representations to the court (r 8(6)). The hearing is held in open court (r 9(2)).

Section 10 of the CPIA 1996 provides that a failure by the prosecution to observe those time limits does not constitute grounds for staying the proceedings for abuse of process (s 10(2)) unless the delay is such that the accused is denied a fair trial (s 10(3)).

1.19.9   Faults in disclosure by defence

If the defendant:

(a) fails to give a defence statement under s 5 (compulsory disclosure prior to Crown Court trial) or does so but fails to comply with the time limit (see above); or

(b) gives voluntary disclosure under s 6 (prior to summary trial) but does so after the expiry of the time limit; or

(c) sets out inconsistent defences in the defence statement; or

(d) at his trial puts forward a defence which is different from any defence set out in the defence statement; or

(e) at his trial adduces evidence in support of an alibi without having given particulars of the alibi in the defence statement (this applies to all Crown

Court trials but it only applies to summary trials if the defendant has made voluntary disclosure under s 6); or

(f) at his trial calls a witness to give evidence in support of an alibi without having given particulars of that witness in the alibi notice (again, this applies to all Crown Court trials but it only applies to summary trials if the defendant has made voluntary disclosure under s 6),

then s 11(3) of the CPIA 1996 enables the court or, with the leave of the court, the prosecution (or a co-defendant where two defendants are running different defences) to 'make such comment as appears appropriate' (s 11(3)(a)). Section 11(3) also enables the magistrates or the jury, as the case may be, to 'draw such inferences as appear proper in deciding whether the accused is guilty of the offence concerned' (s 11(3)(b)).

Section 11(5) provides that 'a person shall not be convicted on an offence solely on an inference drawn under sub-s (3)'.

Section 11(4) provides that where the accused puts forward at trial a defence which is different from any defence set out in a defence statement given under s 5 (trial on indictment) or s 6 (summary trial) the court, in deciding whether comments should be made or adverse inferences drawn, should have regard:

(a) to the extent of the difference in the defences; and

(b) to whether there is any justification for it.

Section 11 does not require leave for cross-examination of a defendant on differences between his defence at trial and the defence statement served in accordance with s 5 of the Act; s 11 merely precludes comment on, or invitation to the jury to draw an inference from, such differences unless the court gives leave (*R v Tibbs* (2000) *The Times*, 28 February).

1.19.10 Public interest immunity

It is open to the prosecution to seek permission from the court to withhold material that would otherwise have to be disclosed, on the basis of public interest immunity (see 1.19.13 for details of the procedure to be followed in such a case). A common example of this is where the prosecution wish to protect the identity of an informant (as in *R v Turner* [1995] 1 WLR 264; [1995] 3 All ER 432). In *R v Davis, Rowe and Johnson* (2000) *The Times*, 24 April, the Court of Appeal noted that the judgement of the European Court of Human Rights in the case of *Rowe and Davis v United Kingdom* (2000) *The Times*, 1 March, was highly critical of the procedure adopted prior to the coming into force of the Criminal Procedure and Investigations Act 1996 but did not criticise the procedure used under that Act to deal with public interest immunity applications.

Where a magistrates' court has ruled that it is not in the public interest to disclose prosecution material, the defendant may apply to the magistrates for a review of the question whether it is still not in the public interest to disclose that material (s 14(2)).

Where a Crown Court has ruled that it is not in the public interest to disclose prosecution material, the court itself must keep under review the question whether it is still not in the public interest to disclose that material (s 15(3)). Although the Crown Court has to keep the matter under review without the need for any application by the defence, it is open to the defendant to apply to the court for a review of the question (s 15(4)).

Where magistrates rule on disclosure, it may be that they hear matters which are prejudicial to the defendant. In these circumstances, it is a matter for their discretion whether they disqualify themselves from conducting the trial itself (*R v South Worcestershire Justices ex p Lilley* [1995] 1 WLR 1595; [1995] 4 All ER 186).

1.19.11 Confidentiality

Where prosecution material has been disclosed to the defendant, the defendant may only use that material in connection with the forthcoming trial or an appeal following that trial unless the material is in the public domain because it has been displayed or communicated to the public in open court (s 17).

Contravention of s 17 is a contempt of court (s 18(1)). Where the prosecution disclosure was in the context of a summary trial, the contempt will be dealt with by the magistrates' court and the penalty is a custodial sentence of up to six months and/or a fine of up to £5,000; where the prosecution disclosure was in the context of trial on indictment, the contempt will be dealt with by the Crown Court and the penalty is up to two years 'custody and/or a fine.

1.19.12 Common law disclosure

Prior to the CPIA 1996, disclosure was governed almost exclusively by case law. Section 21 of the CPIA 1996 provides that the Act replaces the common law regarding the circumstances in which disclosure has to be made (s 21(1)). However, the Act does not 'affect the rules of common law as to whether disclosure is in the public interest' (s 21(2)).

Many of the public interest cases are ones where the prosecution did not want to reveal to the defence the identity of a person because the prosecution feared that the person would be intimidated or otherwise put at risk (for example, a regular police informant). However, as was said in *R v Keane* [1994] 1 WLR 746; [1994] 2 All ER 478, if the evidence proves the defendant's innocence, or would assist in avoiding a miscarriage of justice, the balance must come down resoundingly in favour of disclosing that evidence.

In *R v Reilly* [1994] Crim LR 279, the prosecution refused to disclose the identity of an informant who was not going to be called as a prosecution witness. It was held by the Court of Appeal that the need to protect an informant had to give way to the need to allow the defence to present a tenable case in its best light (which may involve impugning the informant). The Crown had to choose between disclosing the identity of the informant or discontinuing the case against the defendant (and in fact chose the latter course).

In *R v Turner* [1995] 1 WLR 264; [1995] 3 All ER 432, however, the Court of Appeal took a slightly tougher line and said that the court should only accede to an application by the defence for disclosure of the identity of an informant if it was satisfied that the information was essential to the running of the defence. In the instant case, it appeared that the informant had participated in the events surrounding the crime and the defence case was that the defendant had been set up. Accordingly, the judge should have decided that the balance came down firmly in favour of disclosure.

The prosecution generally cannot claim immunity from disclosure in respect of documents which the trial judge has not viewed personally (*R v K* (1993) 97 Cr App R 342). However, in *R v W* (1996) *The Times*, 12 July, it was said to be sufficient for the judge to rely on the judgment of an independent barrister appointed to·read the documents where the volume of papers is such that the judge does not have time to read them personally.

In *R v Brown* [1997] 3 All ER 769; [1997] 3 WLR 447, the Crown had failed to disclose to the defence information which reflected on the credibility of two defence witnesses. It was held by the House of Lords that the Crown is not under a duty to disclose to the defence material which is relevant only to the credibility of defence witnesses. Although this case was not one to which the CPIA 1996 applied (since the relevant provisions of the Act were not in force at the relevant time), the House of Lords held that such material is not material which might assist the defence case. It follows that it would not be disclosable under s 7 of the CPIA 1996.

In *R v Mills* [1997] 3 All ER 780, the House of Lords held that the prosecution should provide the defence with a copy of the statement made by a witness whom the prosecution does not propose to call at the trial (not just supply the defence with the name and address of that witness) even if the prosecution take the view that the witness is not a credible witness. Failure to do so may render a conviction unsafe. Such statements would now have to be disclosed under s 7 of the CPIA 1996 if they might assist the defence case.

In *R v DPP ex p Lee* [1999] 2 Cr App R 304, the Divisional Court noted that the 1996 Act does not specifically address disclosure during the period between arrest and committal to the Crown Court. The court said that, in most cases, prosecution disclosure can wait until after committal without jeopardising the defendant's right to a fair trial. However, the prosecutor must always be alive to the need to make advance disclosure of material that should be disclosed at an earlier stage. Examples given by the court include: (a) previous convictions of a complainant if that information could reasonably be expected to assist the defence when applying for bail; (b) material which might enable a defendant to make a pre-committal application to stay the proceedings as an abuse of process; (c) material which might enable a defendant to submit that he should only be committed for trial on a lesser charge, or perhaps that he should not be committed for trial at all; (d) depending on what the defendant chooses to reveal about his case at this early stage, material which would enable the defendant and his legal advisers to make preparations for trial which would be significantly less effective if disclosure were delayed, for example, names of any witnesses whom the prosecution do not intend to use. Any disclosure by the prosecution prior to committal would not normally exceed the primary disclosure which, after committal, would be required by s 3 of the 1996 Act (that is, material which in the prosecutor's opinion might undermine the case for the prosecution).

1.19.13   Procedure for making applications under the CPIA 1996

The procedure for the making of applications by the prosecution for permission to withhold material, and by the defence for an order requiring the prosecution to disclose material, is set out in the Crown Court (Criminal Procedure and Investigations Act 1996) (Disclosure) Rules 1997 (SI 1997/698) and the Magistrates' Courts (Criminal Procedure and Investigations Act 1996) (Disclosure) Rules 1997 (SI 1997/703).

Applications by the prosecution

Where the prosecutor wishes to make an application under s 3(6), 7(5), 8(5) or 9(8) of the CPIA 1996, a notice of application must be served on:

(a) the appropriate officer of the Crown Court or the clerk to the justices, as the case may be; and

(b) (subject to the proviso in r 2(4) of the Crown Court Rules and r 2(5) of the Magistrates' Courts Rules) on the accused.

This notice must (subject to the proviso in r 2(3) of the Crown Court Rules and r 2(4) of the Magistrates' Courts Rules) 'specify the nature of the material to which the application relates' (r 2(2) of both sets of Rules).

Where the prosecutor 'has reason to believe that to reveal to the accused the nature of the material to which the application relates would have the effect of disclosing that which the prosecutor contends should not in the public interest be disclosed', the prosecutor does not have to specify the nature of the material to which the application refers (r 2(3) of the Crown Court Rules and r 2(4) of the Magistrates' Courts Rules). This would be the case, for example, where the material in question is from an informant whom the prosecutor does not intend to call as a witness at the trial and the prosecutor believes that, once the accused finds out that there was an informant, he would be able to work out who that informant was.

Where the prosecutor 'has reason to believe that to reveal to the accused the fact that an application is being made would have the effect of disclosing that which the prosecutor contends should not in the public interest be disclosed', the prosecutor does not have to inform the accused that an application is being made (r 2(4) of the Crown Court Rules and r 2(5) of the Magistrates' Courts Rules).

In a case where the prosecutor serves notice on the accused that an application is being made, the hearing is *inter partes* and both the prosecutor and the accused are entitled to make representations to the court (r 3(3) of the Crown Court Rules and r 3(2) of the Magistrates' Courts Rules).

Rule 3(4) of the Crown Court Rules (r 3(3) of the Magistrates' Courts Rules) provides that, where the prosecutor applies to the court for leave to make representations in the absence of the accused, the court may for that purpose sit in the absence of the accused and any legal representative of his. Thus, the accused (and his legal representatives) can be excluded from part of the hearing.

In a case where the prosecutor did not serve notice of the application on the accused, the hearing is *ex parte* and only the prosecutor is entitled to make representations to the court (r 3(5) of the Crown Court Rules and r 3(4) of the Magistrates' Courts Rules).

A hearing under r 3 may be held in private (r 9(2) of both sets of Rules).

Where the court rules that it is in the public interest that material should not be disclosed, the court must state, and record, its reasons for doing so (r 4(2) of both sets of Rules).

The accused must be notified of the making of the order unless the case was one where the accused was not informed that an application was being made (r 4(3) of both sets of Rules).

Applications by the accused under s 15(4) for review of non-disclosure order

Where the accused wishes to make an application under s 15(4) of the CPIA 1996, the application must be in writing and must 'specify the reason why the accused believes the court should review the question' whether it is still in the public interest for the material to be withheld (r 5(2) of both sets of Rules).

The court is empowered to determine the application without a hearing (r 5(5) of the Crown Court Rules and r 5(6) of the Magistrates' Courts Rules). However, under r 5(6) of both sets of rules, an application may only be determined without a hearing if the court is satisfied that there are no grounds on which the court might conclude that it is in the public interest to disclose material to any extent. Thus, it is only hopeless applications that can be determined without a hearing.

The hearing is *inter partes*, and the accused and the prosecutor are entitled to make representations to the court (r 5(7) of the Crown Court Rules and r 5(5) of the Magistrates' Courts Rules). However, after hearing the accused's representations, the prosecutor can apply to the court for leave to make representations in the absence of the accused (r 5(8) of the Crown Court Rules and r 5(7) of the Magistrates' Courts Rules). Furthermore, where the order to which the application relates was one made after an application where the accused was not informed that the application was being made, the review hearing is *ex parte* and only the prosecutor is entitled to make representations to the court (r 5(9) of the Crown Court Rules and r 5(8) of the Magistrates' Courts Rules).

A hearing under r 5 may be held in private (r 9(2) of both sets of Rules).

Application by the accused under s 8(2)

Where the accused wishes to make an application under s 8(2) of the 1996 Act, the application must be made in writing and must specify the material to which the application relates, that the material has not been disclosed to the accused, and the reason why the material might be expected to assist the applicant's defence as disclosed by the defence statement (r 7(2) of both sets of Rules).

The prosecutor has to give written notice to the court within 14 days of being informed of the accused's application that either he wishes to make representations to the court concerning the material to which the application relates or, if he does not wish to make representations, that he is willing to disclose that material (r 7(6) of the Crown Court Rules and r 7(4) of the Magistrates' Courts Rules).

Rule 7(5) of the Crown Court Rules (r 7(6) of the Magistrates' Courts Rules) enables the court to determine the application without a hearing but r 7(7) of the Crown Court Rules (r 7(6) of the Magistrates' Courts Rules) stipulates that the application must not be determined without a hearing if:

- the prosecutor has given notice that he wishes to make representations and the court considers that those representations should be made at a hearing; or
- the court considers a hearing to be necessary in the interests of justice.

The hearing is *inter partes* and the prosecutor and the applicant are entitled to make representations to the court (r 7(8) of the Crown Court Rules and r 7(5) of the Magistrates' Courts Rules). Rule 7(9) of the Crown Court Rules (r 7(7) of the Magistrates' Courts Rules) enables the prosecutor to apply for leave to make representations in the absence of the accused and any legal representative of the accused.

A hearing under r 7 may be held in private (r 9(2) of both sets of rules).

1.19.14 Disclosure and the European Convention on Human Rights

The 'equality of arms' principle implicit in Art 6 of the European Convention on Human Rights requires the prosecution or police to disclose to the defence material in their possession, including material which might assist the defendant to exonerate himself and material that might undermine the credibility of a prosecution witness (*Jespers v Belgium* (1981) – a decision of the Commission)

In *Edwards v UK* (1992) 15 EHRR 417, the European Court of Human Rights said that 'it is a requirement of fairness that the prosecuting authorities disclose to the defence all material evidence for or against the accused'.

In *Rowe and Davis v UK* (2000) *The Times*, 1 March, the European Court of Human Rights held that the procedure which existed prior to the implementation of the Criminal Procedure and Investigations Act 1996 was unfair, and so inconsistent with the right to a fair trial, because, at that time, the prosecution were able to withhold material without the permission of the judge. However, in *Jasper v UK*, it was held by the Court (by a slim 9:8 majority) that the procedure under 1996 Act is fair, on the basis that the judge is able to look after the interests of the defence.

1.20   INFORMATION

INFORMATION

(MC Act 1980, s 1; MC Rules 1981, r 41)

.... Magistrates' Court (Code:)

Date:

Accused:

Address:

Alleged offence:

The information of: [Name of Informant]

Address:

Telephone No:

who [upon oath] states that the accused committed the offence of which particulars are given above. Taken [upon oath] before me

Justice of the Peace
[Justices' Clerk]

Note: the prosecutor only has to swear an oath when laying the information if an arrest warrant is being sought.

1.21   SUMMONS

SUMMONS

(MC Act 1980, s 1; MC Rules 1981, r 98)

.... Magistrates' Court (Code:)

Date:

To the accused: [name]

of: [address]

You are hereby summoned to appear on [date] at [time] am/pm before the Magistrates' Court at [place] to answer to the following information

Alleged offence:

Prosecutor:

Address:

Date of information:

Justice of the Peace

[Justices' Clerk]

1.22 SUMMONS FORM USED WHERE THE SUSPECT FACES MORE THAN ONE INFORMATION

Where the accused faces more than one information, the following form of summons is used:

SUMMONS

(MC Act 1980, s 1; MC Rules 1981, r 98)

.... Magistrates' Court (Code:)

Date:

To the accused: [name]

of: [address]

You are hereby summoned to appear on [date] at [time] am/pm before the Magistrates' Court at [place] to answer to the informations of which particulars are given in the Schedule hereto.

Prosecutor:
Address:

Justice of the Peace

[Justices' Clerk]

SCHEDULE

Date of Information

Alleged Offence
[particulars and statute]

1.23   WARRANT FOR ARREST AT FIRST INSTANCE

When proceedings are commenced by the issue of a warrant for the arrest of the suspect, the warrant takes the following form:

WARRANT OF ARREST AT FIRST INSTANCE

*(Bail Act 1976, s 3; MC Act 1980, ss 1, 13, 14, 117;
MC Rules 1981, rr 95, 96)*

.... Magistrates' Court (Code:)

Date:

Accused:

Address:

Alleged offence: [short particulars and statute]

	Information having been laid before me on [oath] [affirmation] by [name of informant] on [date of information] that the accused committed the above offence
Direction:	You, the constables of [County] Police Force, are hereby required to arrest the accused and bring the accused before the Magistrates' Court at [place] immediately [unless the accused is released on bail as directed below]
*Bail:	On arrest, after complying with the condition(s) specified in Schedule I hereto, the accused shall be released on bail, subject to the condition(s) specified in Schedule II hereto, and with a duty to surrender to the custody of the above Magistrates' Court on [date] at [time] am/pm.

Justice of the Peace

*Delete if bail not granted

SCHEDULE I

Conditions to be complied with before release on bail

To provide suret[y][ies] in the sum of £   [each] to secure the accused's surrender to custody at the time and place appointed.

SCHEDULE II

Conditions to be complied with after release on bail

1.24 WARRANT TO ENTER AND SEARCH PREMISES

WARRANT TO ENTER AND SEARCH PREMISES

(PCE Act 1984, s 15)

.... Magistrates' Court (Code:)

Date

On this day an application supported by an information was made by: [specify name of applicant]
for the issue of a warrant under: [state enactment under which warrant is to be issued]
to enter and search the premises at: [specify premises]
and search for: [identify, so far as is practicable, the articles or persons to be sought].

Authority is hereby given for any constable [accompanied by ....]
to enter the said premises on one occasion only within one month from the date of issue of this warrant and to search for the articles or persons in respect of which the above application is made.

Justice of the Peace

ENDORSEMENT
(to be made by constable executing the warrant)

1 [The following articles or persons sought were found: (list)] or [no article or person sought was found]
2 [The following articles other than articles which were sought were seized: (list)] or [no other article was seized]

Signature of constable...................................

Date...

1.25   WARRANT OF FURTHER DETENTION

WARRANT OF FURTHER DETENTION

(PCE Act 1984, s 43)

.... Magistrates' Court (Code:)

Date and time:
Person to whom warrant applies: Age: Years
Address:
Offence for which under arrest:

Starting time of detention (relevant time as defined in s 41 of PCE Act 1984):

Decision: The above court, to which an application on oath sup-
                   ported by an information has been made by a constable
                   of the [County] Police Force, is satisfied that there are
                   reasonable grounds for believing that the further deten-
                   tion of the person named above and brought before the
                   court today is justified in accordance with s 43(4) of the
                   Police and Criminal Evidence Act 1984.
                   You, the constables of the above named Police Force, are
                   hereby authorised to keep the person named above in
                   police detention for [   ] hours from the time of issue of
                   this warrant.

Justice of the Peace

ENDORSEMENT OF EXTENSION OR FURTHER EXTENSION
(s 44 PCE Act 1984)

The court, being satisfied that there are reasonable grounds for believing that the further detention of the person named above is justified, in exercise of its powers under s 44 of the Police and Criminal Evidence Act 1984, hereby extends/[further extends] the warrant for [   ] hours from the expiry of the period authorised above.

Justice of the Peace

Date and time of endorsement:

TABLE OF STATUTORY AND OTHER MATERIALS

STATUTORY MATERIALS

MAGISTRATES' COURTS ACT 1980

Section 1: Issue of summons to accused or warrant for his arrest

(1) Upon an information being laid before a justice of the peace for an area to which this section applies that any person has, or is suspected of having, committed an offence, the justice may, in any of the events mentioned in sub-section (2) below, but subject to sub-sections (3) to (5) below:

    (a) issue a summons directed to that person requiring him to appear before a magistrates' court for the area to answer to the information; or

    (b) issue a warrant to arrest that person and bring him before a magistrates' court for the area or such magistrates' court as is provided in sub-section (5) below.

(2) A justice of the peace for an area to which this section applies may issue a summons or warrant under this section:

    (a) if the offence was committed or is suspected to have been committed within the area; or

    (b) if it appears to the justice necessary or expedient, with a view to the better administration of justice, that the person charged should be tried jointly with, or in the same place as, some other person who is charged with an offence, and who is in custody, or is being or is to be proceeded against, within the area; or

    (c) if the person charged resides or is, or is believed to reside or be, within the area; or

    (d) if under any enactment a magistrates' court for the area has jurisdiction to try the offence; or

    (e) …

(3) No warrant shall be issued under this section unless the information is in writing and substantiated on oath.

(4) No warrant shall be issued under this section for the arrest of any person who has attained the age of 18 unless:

    (a) the offence to which the warrant relates is an indictable offence or is punishable with imprisonment; or

    (b) the person's address is not sufficiently established for a summons to be served on him.

(5) Where the offence charged is not an indictable offence:

    (a) no summons shall be issued by virtue only of paragraph (c) of sub-section (2) above; and

    (b) any warrant issued by virtue only of that paragraph shall require the person charged to be brought before a magistrates' court having jurisdiction to try the offence.

(6) Where the offence charged is an indictable offence, a warrant under this section may be issued at any time notwithstanding that a summons has previously been issued.

(7) A justice of the peace may issue a summons or warrant under this section upon an information being laid before him notwithstanding any enactment requiring the information to be laid before two or more justices.

(8) The areas to which this section applies are commission areas [defined in the Justices of the Peace Act 1979, section 1, as any county, any London commission area and the City of London.

Section 47: Service of summons out of time after failure to prove service by post

Where any enactment requires, expressly or by implication, that a summons in respect of an offence shall be issued or served within a specified period after the commission of the offence, and service of the summons may under the rules be effected by post, then, if under the rules service of the summons is not treated as proved, but it is shown that a letter containing the summons was posted at such time as to enable it to be delivered in the ordinary course of post within that period, a second summons may be issued on the same information; and the enactment shall have effect, in relation to that summons, as if the specified period were a period running from the return day of the original summons.

MAGISTRATES' COURTS RULES 1981 (SI 1981/552 AS AMENDED)

Rule 4: Information and complaint

(1) An information may be laid or complaint made by the prosecutor or complainant in person or by his counsel or solicitor or other person authorised in that behalf.

(2) Subject to any provision of the Magistrates' Courts Act 1980 and any other enactment an information or complaint need not be in writing or on oath.

(3) It shall not be necessary in an information or complaint to specify or negative an exception, exemption, proviso, excuse or qualification, whether or not it accompanies the description of the offence or matter of complaint contained in the enactment creating the offence or on which the complaint is founded.

Rule 67: Proof of service

(1) The service on any person of a summons, process, notice or document required or authorised to be served in any proceedings before a magistrates' court, and the handwriting or seal of a justice of the peace or

other person on any warrant, summons, notice, process or documents issued or made in any such proceedings, may be proved in any legal proceedings by a document purporting to be a solemn declaration in the prescribed form made before a justice of the peace, commissioner for oaths, clerk of a magistrates' court or registrar of a county court ...

(2) The service of any process or other document required or authorised to be served, the proper addressing, pre-paying and posting or registration for the purposes of service of a letter containing such a document, and the place, date and time of posting or registration of any such letter, may be proved in any proceedings before a magistrates' court by a document purporting to be a certificate signed by the person by whom the service was effected or the letter posted or registered.

...

Rule 98: Form of summons

(1) A summons shall be signed by the justice issuing it or state his name and be authenticated by the signature of the clerk of a magistrates' court.[3]

(2) A summons requiring a person to appear before a magistrates' court to answer an information or complaint shall state shortly the matter of the information or complaint and shall state the time and place at which the defendant is required by the summons to appear.

(3) A single summons may be issued against a person in respect of several informations or complaints; but the summons shall state the matter of each information or complaint separately and shall have effect as several summonses, each issued in respect of one information or complaint.

Rule 99: Service of summons

(1) Service of a summons issued by a justice of the peace on a person other than a corporation may be effected:

(a) by delivering it to the person to whom it is directed; or

(b) by leaving it for him with some person at his last known or usual place of abode; or

(c) by sending it by post in a letter addressed to him at his last known or usual place of abode.

(2) [Revoked.]

(3) Service for the purposes of the Magistrates' Courts Act 1980 of a summons issued by a justice of the peace on a corporation may be effected by delivering it at, or sending it by post to, the registered office of the

---

3   (1) The signature of the justice may be affixed by means of a rubber stamp facsimile not only by the justice himself but by a clerk or clerk's assistant with the specific or general authority of the justice (*R v Brentford Justices ex p Catlin* [1975] QB 455). (2) Under the Justices' Clerks Rules 1970 (SI 1970/231), a clerk may issue a summons.

corporation, if that office is in the United Kingdom, or, if there is no registered office in the United Kingdom, any place in the United Kingdom where the corporation trades or conducts its business.

(4) Paragraph (3) shall have effect in relation to a document (other than a summons) issued by a justice of the peace as it has effect in relation to a summons so issued, but with the substitution of references to England and Wales for the references to the United Kingdom.

(5) Any summons or other document served in a manner authorised by the preceding provisions of this rule shall, for the purposes of any enactment other than the Act of 1980 or these Rules requiring a summons or other document to be served in any particular manner, be deemed to have been as effectively served as if it had been served in that manner; and nothing in this rule shall render invalid the service of a summons or other document in that manner.

(6) Sub-paragraph (c) of paragraph (1) shall not authorise the service by post of:

    (a) a summons requiring the attendance of any person to give evidence or produce a document or thing; or

    (b) ...

(8) Where this rule or any other of these Rules provides that a summons or other document may be sent by post to a person's last known or usual place of abode that rule shall have effect as if it provided also for the summons or other document to be sent in the manner specified in the rule to an address given by that person for that purpose.

    ...

Rule 100: Statement of offence

(1) Every information, summons, warrant or other document laid, issued or made for the purposes of, or in connection with, any proceedings before a magistrates' court for an offence shall be sufficient if it describes the specific offence with which the accused is charged, or of which he is convicted, in ordinary language avoiding as far as possible the use of technical terms and without necessarily stating all the elements of the offence, and gives such particulars as may be necessary for giving reasonable information of the nature of the charge.

(2) If the offence charged is one created by or under any Act, the description of the offence shall contain a reference to the section of the Act, or, as the case may be, the rule, order, regulation, byelaw or other instrument creating the offence.

THE JUSTICES' CLERKS RULES 1970

Rule 3

The things specified in the Schedule to these Rules, being things authorised to be done by, to or before a single justice of the peace for a petty sessions area may be done by, to or before the justices' clerk for that area.

Rule 4

(1) The things specified in the Schedule to these Rules (except in paragraphs 13 to 15D), being things authorised to be done by, to or before a justices' clerk, may be done instead by, to or before:

    (a) a person appointed by a magistrates' courts committee to assist him;

    (b) where he is a part time justices' clerk, any member of his staff who has been appointed by the magistrates' courts committee to assist him as such; or

    (c) any officer appointed by the committee of magistrates to be his deputy or to assist him, provided that that person, member or officer has been specifically authorised by the justices' clerk for that purpose; and any reference in the Schedule to a justices' clerk shall be taken to include such a person, member or officer.

    ...

SCHEDULE

1   The laying of an information or the making of a complaint, other than an information or complaint substantiated on oath.

2   The issue of any summons, including a witness summons.

2A (1) The issue of a warrant of arrest, whether or not endorsed for bail, for failure to surrender to the court, where there is no objection on behalf of the accused.

    (2) The issue of a warrant of distress.

3   The adjournment of the hearing of a complaint if the parties to the complaint consent to the complaint being adjourned.

4   (1) The further adjournment of criminal proceedings with the consent of the prosecutor and the accused if, but only if:

    (a) the accused, not having been remanded on the previous adjournment, is not remanded on the further adjournment; or

    (b) the accused, having been remanded on bail on the previous adjournment, is remanded on bail on the like terms and conditions.

    (2) The remand of the accused on bail at the time of further adjourning the proceedings in pursuance of sub-paragraph (1)(b) above.

(3) The further adjournment of criminal proceedings, where there is no objection by the prosecutor, where the accused, having been remanded on bail on the previous adjournment, is remanded on bail on the like terms and conditions in his absence.

(4) The remand of the accused on bail in his absence at the time of further adjourning the proceedings in pursuance of sub-paragraph (3) above.

(5) The appointment of a later time as the time at which a person, who has been granted bail under the Police and Criminal Evidence Act 1984 subject to a duty to appear before a magistrates' court, is to appear, and the enlargement of any sureties for that person at that time, in accordance with section 43(1) of the Magistrates' Courts Act 1980, provided there is no objection by the prosecutor.

4A (1) The committal of a person for trial on bail in accordance with section 6(2) and (3)(b) of the Magistrates' Courts Act 1980 where, having been remanded on bail on the previous adjournment, he is released on bail on the like terms and conditions.

...

4B (1) The asking of an accused whether he pleads guilty or not guilty to a charge, after having stated to him the substance of the information laid against him.

(2) The fixing or setting aside of a date, time and place for the trial of an information.

...

6 The allowing of further time for payment of a sum enforceable by a magistrates' court.

...

STOP AND SEARCH POWERS

POLICE AND CRIMINAL EVIDENCE ACT 1984

Section 1: Power of constable to stop and search persons, vehicles, etc

(1) A constable may exercise any power conferred by this section:

(a) in any place to which at the time when he proposes to exercise the power the public or any section of the public has access, on payment or otherwise, as of right or by virtue of express or implied permission; or

(b) in any other place to which people have ready access at the time when he proposes to exercise the power but which is not a dwelling.

(2) Subject to sub-section (3) to (5) below, a constable:

  (a) may search

    (i) any person or vehicle;

    (ii) anything which is in or on a vehicle,

    for stolen or prohibited articles or any article to which sub-section (8A) below applies; and

  (b) may detain a person or vehicle for the purpose of such a search.

(3) This section does not give a constable power to search a person or vehicle or anything in or on a vehicle unless he has reasonable grounds for suspecting that he will find stolen or prohibited articles or any article to which sub-section (8A) below applies.

(4) If a person is in a garden or yard occupied with and used for the purposes of a dwelling or on other land so occupied and used, a constable may not search him in the exercise of the power conferred by this section unless the constable has reasonable grounds for believing:

  (a) that he does not reside in the dwelling; and

  (b) that he is not in the place in question with the express or implied permission of a person who resides in the dwelling.

(5) If a vehicle is in a garden or yard occupied with and used for the purposes of a dwelling or on other land so occupied and used, a constable may not search the vehicle or anything in or on it in the exercise of the power conferred by this section unless he has reasonable grounds for believing:

  (a) that the person in charge of the vehicle does not reside in the dwelling; and

  (b) that the vehicle is not in the place in question with the express or implied permission of a person who resides in the dwelling.

(6) If in the course of such a search a constable discovers an article which he has reasonable grounds for suspecting to be a stolen or prohibited article or an article to which sub-section (8A) below applies, he may seize it.

(7) An article is prohibited for the purposes of this Part of this Act if it is:

  (a) an offensive weapon; or

  (b) an article:

    (i) made or adapted for use in the course of or in connection with an offence to which this sub-paragraph applies; or

    (ii) intended by the person having it with him for such use by him or by some other person.

(8) The offences to which sub-section (7)(b)(i) above applies are:

  (a) burglary;

  (b) theft;

  (c) offences under section 12 of the Theft Act 1968 (taking motor vehicle or other conveyance without authority); and

  (d) offences under section 15 of that Act (obtaining property by deception).

(8A) This sub-section applies to any article in relation to which a person has committed, or is committing or is going to commit an offence under section 139 of the Criminal Justice Act 1988.

(9) In this Part of this Act 'offensive weapon' means any article:

    (a) made or adapted for use for causing injury to persons; or

    (b) intended by the person having it with him for such use by him or by some other person.

Section 2: Provisions relating to search under s 1 and other powers

(1) A constable who detains a person or vehicle in the exercise:

    (a) of the power conferred by section 1 above; or

    (b) of any other power:

        (i) to search a person without first arresting him; or

        (ii) to search a vehicle without making an arrest,

    need not conduct a search if it appears to him subsequently:

        (i) that no search is required; or

        (ii) that a search is impracticable.

(2) If a constable contemplates a search, other than a search of an unattended vehicle, in the exercise:

    (a) of the power conferred by section 1 above; or

    (b) of any other power, except the power conferred by section 6 below and the power conferred by section 27(2) of the Aviation Security Act 1982:

        (i) to search a person without first arresting him; or

        (ii) to search a vehicle without making an arrest,

    it shall be his duty, subject to sub-section (4) below, to take reasonable steps before he commences the search to bring to the attention of the appropriate person:

        (i) if the constable is not in uniform, documentary evidence that he is a constable; and

        (ii) whether he is in uniform or not, the matters specified in sub-section (3) below,

    and the constable shall not commence the search until he has performed that duty.

(3) The matters referred to in sub-section (2)(ii) above are:

    (a) the constable's name and the name of the police station to which he is attached;

    (b) the object of the proposed search;

    (c) the constable's grounds for proposing to make it; and

    (d) the effect of section 3(7) or (8) below, as may be appropriate.

(4) A constable need not bring the effect of section 3(7) or (8) below to the attention of the appropriate person if it appears to the constable that it will not be practicable to make the record in section 3(1) below.

(5) In this section 'the appropriate person' means:

(a) if the constable proposes to search a person, that person; and

(b) if he proposes to search a vehicle, or anything in or on a vehicle, the person in charge of the vehicle.

(6) On completing a search of an unattended vehicle or anything in or on such a vehicle in the exercise of any such power as is mentioned in sub-section (2) above a constable shall leave a notice:

(a) stating that he has searched it;

(b) giving the name of the police station to which he is attached;

(c) stating that an application for compensation for any damage caused by the search may be made to that police station; and

(d) stating the effect of sub-section 3(8) below.

(7) The constable shall leave the notice inside the vehicle unless it is not reasonably practicable to do so without damaging the vehicle.

(8) The time for which a person or vehicle may be detained for the purposes of such a search is such time as is reasonably required to permit a search to be carried out either at the place where the person or vehicle was first detained or nearby.

(9) Neither the power conferred by section 1 above nor any other power to detain and search a person without first arresting him or to detain and search a vehicle without making an arrest is to be construed:

(a) as authorising a constable to require a person to remove any of his clothing in public other than an outer coat, jacket or gloves; or

(b) as authorising a constable not in uniform to stop a vehicle.

(10) This section and section 1 apply to vessels, aircraft and hovercraft as they apply to vehicles.

Section 3: Duty to make records concerning searches

(1) Where a constable has carried out a search in the exercise of any such power as is mentioned in section 2(1) above, other than a search:

(a) under section 6 below; or

(b) under section 27(2) of the Aviation Security Act 1982,

he shall make a record of it in writing unless it is not practicable to do so.

(2) If:

(a) a constable is required by sub-section (1) above to make a record of a search; but

(b) it is not practicable to make the record on the spot,

he shall make it as soon as practicable after the completion of the search.

(3) The record of a search of a person shall include a note of his name, if the constable knows it, but a constable may not detain a person to find out his name.

(4) If a constable does not know the name of a person whom he has searched, the record of the search shall include a note otherwise describing that person.

(5) The record of a search of a vehicle shall include a note describing the vehicle.

(6) The record of a search of a person or a vehicle:

    (a) shall state:

        (i) the object of the search;

        (ii) the grounds for making it;

        (iii) the date and time when it was made;

        (iv) the place where it was made;

        (v) whether anything, and if so what, was found;

        (vi) whether any, and if so what, injury to a person or damage to property appears to the constable to have resulted from the search; and

    (b) shall identify the constable making it.

(7) If a constable who conducted a search of a person made a record of it, the person who was searched shall be entitled to a copy of the record if he asks for one before the end of the period specified in sub-section (9) below.

(8) If:

    (a) the owner of a vehicle which has been searched or the person who was in charge of the vehicle at the time when it was searched asks for a copy of the record of the search before the end of the period specified in sub-section (9) below; and

    (b) the constable who conducted the search made a record of it,

    the person who made the request shall be entitled to a copy.

(9) The period mentioned in sub-sections (7) and (8) above is the period of 12 months beginning with the date on which the search was made.

(10) The requirements imposed by this section with regard to records of searches of vehicles shall apply also to records of searches of vessels, aircraft and hovercraft.

    ...

Section 8: Power of justice of the peace to authorise entry and search of premises

(1) If on an application made by a constable a justice of the peace is satisfied that there are reasonable grounds for believing:

    (a) that a serious arrestable offence has been committed; and

(b) that there is material on premises specified in the application which is likely to be of substantial value (whether by itself or together with other material) to the investigation of the offence; and

(c) that the material is likely to be relevant evidence; and

(d) that it does not consist of or include items subject to legal privilege, excluded material or special procedure material;[4] and

(e) that any of the conditions specified in sub-section (3) below applies,

he may issue a warrant authorising a constable to enter and search the premises.

(2) A constable may seize and retain anything for which a search has been authorised under sub-section (1) above.

(3) The conditions mentioned in sub-section 1(e) above are:

(a) that it is not practicable to communicate with any person entitled to grant entry to the premises;

(b) that it is practicable to communicate with a person entitled to grant entry to the premises but it is not practicable to communicate with any person entitled to grant access to the evidence;

(c) that entry to the premises will not be granted unless a warrant is produced;

(d) that the purpose of a search may be frustrated or seriously prejudiced unless a constable arriving at the premises can secure immediate entry to them.

(4) In this Act 'relevant evidence', in relation to an offence, means anything that would be admissible in evidence at a trial for that offence.

(5) The power to issue a warrant conferred by this section is in addition to any such power otherwise conferred.

...

Section 15: Search warrants – safeguards

(1) This section and section 16 below have effect in relation to the issue to constables under any enactment, including an enactment contained in an Act passed after this Act, of warrants to enter and search premises; and an entry on or search of premises under a warrant is unlawful unless it complies with this section and section 16 below.

(2) Where a constable applies for any such warrant, it shall be his duty:

(a) to state:

(i) the ground on which he makes the application; and

(ii) the enactment under which the warrant would be issued;

---

4   See ss 9 to 14, and Sched 1.

    (b) to specify the premises which it is desired to enter and search; and

    (c) to identify, so far as practicable, the articles or persons to be sought.

(3) An application for such a warrant shall be made *ex parte* and supported by an information in writing.

(4) The constable shall answer on oath any question that the justice of the peace or judge hearing the application asks him.

(5) A warrant shall authorise an entry on one occasion only.

(6) A warrant:

    (a) shall specify:

        (i) the name of the person who applies for it;

        (ii) the date on which it is issued;

        (iii) the enactment under which it is issued; and

        (iv) the premises to be searched; and

    (b) shall identify, so far as is practicable, the articles or persons to be sought.

(7) Two copies shall be made of a warrant.

(8) The copies shall be clearly certified as copies.

Section 16: Execution of warrants

(1) A warrant to enter and search premises may be executed by any constable.

(2) Such a warrant may authorise persons to accompany any constable who is executing it.

(3) Entry and search under a warrant must be within one month from the date of its issue.

(4) Entry and search under a warrant must be at a reasonable hour unless it appears to the constable executing it that the purpose of a search may be frustrated on an entry at a reasonable hour.

(5) Where the occupier of premises which are to be entered and searched is present at the time when a constable seeks to execute a warrant to enter and search them, the constable:

    (a) shall identify himself to the occupier and, if not in uniform, shall produce to him documentary evidence that he is a constable;

    (b) shall produce the warrant to him; and

    (c) shall supply him with a copy of it.

(6) Where:

    (a) the occupier of such premises is not present at the time when a constable seeks to execute such a warrant; but

    (b) some other person who appears to the constable to be in charge of the premises is present,

sub-section (5) above shall have effect as if any reference to the occupier were a reference to that other person.

(7) If there is no person present who appears to the constable to be in charge of the premises, he shall leave a copy of the warrant in a prominent place on the premises.

(8) A search under a warrant may only be a search to the extent required for the purpose for which the warrant was issued.

(9) A constable executing a warrant shall make an endorsement on it stating:

(a) whether the articles or persons sought were found; and

(b) whether any articles were seized, other than articles which were sought.

...

Section 17: Entry for purpose of arrest, etc

(1) Subject to the following provisions of this section, and without prejudice to any other enactment, a constable may enter and search any premises for the purpose:

(a) of executing:

(i) a warrant of arrest issued in connection with or arising out of criminal proceedings; or

(ii) a warrant of commitment issued under section 76 of the Magistrates' Courts Act 1980;

(b) of arresting a person for an arrestable offence;

(c) of arresting a person for an offence under:

(i) section 1 (prohibition of uniforms in connection with political objects) of the Public Order Act 1936;

(ii) any enactment contained in sections 6 to 8 or 10 of the Criminal Law Act 1977 (offences relating to entering and remaining on property);

(iii) section 4 of the Public Order Act 1986 (fear or provocation of violence);

(iv) section 76 of the Criminal Justice and Public Order Act 1994 (failure to comply with interim possession order);

(ca) of arresting, in pursuance of section 32(1A) of the Children and Young Persons Act 1969, any child or young person who has been remanded or committed to local authority accommodation under section 23(1) of that Act;

(cb) of recapturing any person who is, or is deemed for any purpose to be, unlawfully at large while liable to be detained:

(i) in a prison, remand centre, young offender institution or secure training centre training centre; or

(ii) in pursuance of section 53 of the Children and Young Persons Act 1933 (dealing with children and young persons guilty of grave crimes), in any other place;

(d) of recapturing any person whatever who is unlawfully at large and whom he is pursing; or

(e) of saving life or limb or preventing serious damage to property.

(2) Except for the purpose specified in paragraph (e) of sub-section (1) above, the powers of entry and search conferred by this section:

    (a) are only exercisable if the constable has reasonable grounds for believing that the person whom he is seeking is on the premises; and

    (b) are limited, in relation to premises consisting of two or more separate dwellings, to powers to enter and search:

        (i) any parts of the premises which the occupiers of any dwelling comprised in the premises used in common with the occupiers of any other such dwelling; and

        (ii) any such dwelling in which the constable has reasonable grounds for believing that the person whom he is seeking may be.

(3) The powers of entry and search conferred by this section are only exercisable for the purposes specified in sub-section (1)(c)(ii) or (iv) above by a constable in uniform.

(4) The power of search conferred by this section is only a power to search to the extent that is reasonably required for the purpose for which the power of entry is exercised.

...

Section 18: Entry and search after arrest

(1) Subject to the following provisions of this section, a constable may enter and search any premises occupied or controlled by a person who is under arrest for an arrestable offence, if he has reasonable grounds for suspecting that there is on the premises evidence, other than items subject to legal privilege, that relates:

    (a) to that offence; or

    (b) to some other arrestable offence which is connected with or similar to that offence.

(2) A constable may seize and retain anything for which he may search under sub-section (1) above.

(3) The power to search conferred by sub-section (1) above is only a power to search to the extent that is reasonably required for the purpose of discovering such evidence.

(4) Subject to sub-section (5) below, the powers conferred by this section may not be exercised unless an officer of the rank of inspector or above has authorised them in writing.

(5) A constable may conduct a search under sub-section (1) above:

    (a) before taking the person to a police station; and

    (b) without obtaining an authorisation under sub-section (4) above, if the presence of that person at a place other than a police station is necessary for the effective investigation of the offence.

(6) If a constable conducts a search by virtue of sub-section (5) above, he shall inform an officer of the rank of inspector or above that he has made the search as soon as practicable after he has made it.

(7) An officer who:

(a) authorises a search; or

(b) is informed of a search under sub-section (6) above,

shall make a record in writing:

(i) of the grounds for the search; and

(ii) of the nature of the evidence that was sought.

(8) If the person who was in occupation or control of the premises at the time of the search is in police detention at the time the record is made, the officer shall make the record as part of his custody record.

...

Section 23: Meaning of 'premises', etc

In this Act:

'premises' includes any place and, in particular, includes:

(a) any vehicle, vessel, aircraft or hovercraft;

(b) any offshore installation; and

(c) any tent or movable structure.

...

POWERS OF ARREST

POLICE AND CRIMINAL EVIDENCE ACT 1984

Section 24: Arrest without warrant for arrestable offences

(1) The powers of summary arrest conferred by the following sub-sections shall apply:

(a) to offences for which the sentence is fixed by law;

(b) to offences for which a person of 21 years of age or over (not previously convicted) may be sentenced to imprisonment for a term of five years (or might be so sentenced but for the restrictions imposed by section 33 of the Magistrates' Courts Act 1980); and

(c) to the offences to which sub-section (2) below applies,

and in this Act 'arrestable offence' means any such offence.

(2) The offences to which this sub-section applies are:

(a) offences for which a person may be arrested under the customs and excise Acts, as defined in section 1(1) of the Customs and Excise Management Act 1979;

(b) offences under the Official Secrets Act 1920 that are not arrestable offences by virtue of the term of imprisonment for which a person may be sentenced in respect of them;

(bb) offences under any provision of the Official Secrets Act 1989 except section 8(1), (4) or (5);

(c) offences under section 22 (causing prostitution of women) or 23 (procuration of a girl under 21) of the Sexual Offences Act 1956;

(d) offences under section 12(1) (taking motor vehicle or other conveyance without authority etc) or 25(1) (going equipped for stealing etc) of the Theft Act 1968; and

(e) any offence under the Football (Offences) Act 1991;

(f) an offence under section 2 of the Obscene Publications Act 1959 (publication of obscene matter);

(g) an offence under section 1 of the Protection of Children Act 1978 (indecent photographs and pseudo-photographs of children);

(h) an offence under section 166 of the Criminal Justice and Public Order Act 1994 (sale of tickets for designated football matches by unauthorised persons);

(i) an offence under section 19 of the Public Order Act 1986 (publishing, etc material intended or likely to stir up racial hatred);

(j) an offence under section 167 of the Criminal Justice and Public Order Act 1994 (touting for hire car services);

(k) an offence under section 1(1) of the Prevention of Crime Act 1953 (prohibition of the carrying of offensive weapons without lawful authority or reasonable excuse);

(l) an offence under section 139(1) of the Criminal Justice Act 1988 (offence of having article with blade or point in public place);

(m) an offence under section 139A(1) or (2) of the Criminal Justice Act 1988 (offence of having article with blade or point (or offensive weapon) on school premises).

(3) Without prejudice to section 2 of the Criminal Attempts Act 1981, the powers of summary arrest conferred by the following sub-sections shall also apply to the offences of:

(a) conspiring to commit any of the offences mentioned in sub-section (2) above;

(b) attempting to commit any such offence other than an offence under section 12(1) of the Theft Act 1968;

(c) inciting, aiding, abetting, counselling or procuring the commission of any such offence;

and such offences are also arrestable offences for the purposes of this Act.

(4) Any person may arrest without a warrant:

(a) anyone who is in the act of committing an arrestable offence;

(b) anyone whom he has reasonable grounds for suspecting to be committing such an offence.

(5) Where an arrestable offence has been committed, any person may arrest without a warrant:

(a) anyone who is guilty of the offence;

(b) anyone whom he has reasonable grounds for suspecting to be guilty of it.

(6) Where a constable has reasonable grounds for suspecting that an arrestable offence has been committed, he may arrest without a warrant anyone whom he has reasonable grounds for suspecting to be guilty of the offence.

(7) A constable may arrest without a warrant:

(a) anyone who is about to commit an arrestable offence;

(b) anyone whom he has reasonable grounds for suspecting to be about to commit an arrestable offence.

Section 25: General arrest conditions

(1) Where a constable has reasonable grounds for suspecting that any offence which is not an arrestable offence has been committed or attempted, or is being committed or attempted, he may arrest the relevant person if it appears to him that service of a summons is impracticable or inappropriate because any of the general arrest conditions are satisfied.

(2) In this section 'the relevant person' means any person whom the constable has reasonable grounds to suspect of having committed or having attempted to commit the offence or of being in the course of committing or attempting to commit it.

(3) The general arrest conditions are:

(a) that the name of the relevant person is unknown to, and cannot be readily ascertained by, the constable;

(b) that the constable has reasonable grounds for doubting whether a name furnished by the relevant person as his name is his real name;

(c) that:

(i) the relevant person has failed to furnish a satisfactory address for service; or

(ii) the constable has reasonable grounds for doubting whether an address furnished by the relevant person is a satisfactory address for service;

(d) that the constable has reasonable grounds for believing that arrest is necessary to prevent the relevant person:

(i) causing physical injury to himself or any other person;

(ii) suffering physical injury;

(iii) causing loss of or damage to property;

(iv) committing an offence against public decency; or

(v) causing an unlawful obstruction of the highway;

(e) that the constable has reasonable grounds for believing that arrest is necessary to protect a child or other vulnerable person from the relevant person.

(4) For the purposes of sub-section (3) above an address is a satisfactory address for service if it appears to the constable:

(a) that the relevant person will be at it for a sufficiently long period for it to be possible to serve him with a summons; or

(b) that some other person specified by the relevant person will accept service of a summons for the relevant person at it.

(5) Nothing in sub-section 3(d) above authorises the arrest of a person under sub-paragraph (iv) of that paragraph except where members of the public going about their normal business cannot reasonably be expected to avoid the person to be arrested.

(6) This section shall not prejudice any power of arrest conferred apart from this section.

...

Section 28: Information to be given on arrest

(1) Subject to sub-section (5) below, where a person is arrested, otherwise than by being informed that he is under arrest, the arrest is not lawful unless the person arrested is informed that he is under arrest as soon as is practicable after his arrest.

(2) Where a person is arrested by a constable, sub-section (1) applies regardless of whether the fact of the arrest is obvious.

(3) Subject to sub-section (5) below, no arrest is lawful unless the person arrested is informed of the ground for the arrest at the time of, or as soon as is practicable after, the arrest.

(4) Where a person is arrested by a constable, sub-section (3) above applies regardless of whether the ground for the arrest is obvious.

(5) Nothing in this section is to be taken to require a person to be informed:

(a) that he is under arrest; or

(b) of the ground for the arrest,

if it was not reasonably practicable for him to be so informed by reason of his having escaped from arrest before the information could be given.

Section 29: Voluntary attendance at police station, etc

Where for the purpose of assisting with an investigation a person attends voluntarily at a police station or at any other place where a constable is present or accompanies a constable to a police station or any such other place without having been arrested:

    (a) he shall be entitled to leave at will unless he is placed under arrest;

    (b) he shall be informed at once that he is under arrest if a decision is taken by a constable to prevent him from leaving at will.

Section 30: Arrest elsewhere than at a police station

(1) Subject to the following provisions of this section, where a person:

    (a) is arrested by a constable for an offence; or

    (b) is taken into custody by a constable after being arrested for an offence by a person other than a constable,

at any place other than a police station, he shall be taken to a police station by a constable as soon as practicable after the arrest.

(2) Subject to sub-sections (3) and (5) below, the police station to which an arrested person is taken under sub-section (1) above shall be a designated police station.

(3) A constable to whom this sub-section applies may take an arrested person to any police station unless it appears to the constable that it may be necessary to keep the arrested person in police detention for more than six hours.

(4) Sub-section (3) above applies:

    (a) to a constable who is working in a locality covered by a police station which is not a designated police station; and

    (b) to a constable belonging to a body of constables maintained by an authority other than a police authority.

(5) Any constable may take an arrested person to any police station if:

    (a) either of the following conditions is satisfied:

        (i) the constable has arrested him without the assistance of any other constable and no other constable is available to assist him;

        (ii) the constable has taken him into custody from a person other than a constable without the assistance of any other constable and no other constable is available to assist him; and

    (b) it appears to the constable that he will be unable to take the arrested person to a designated police station without the arrested person injuring himself, the constable or some other person.

(6) If the first police station to which an arrested person is taken after his arrest is not a designated police station, he shall be taken to a designated police station not more than six hours after his arrival at the first police station unless he is released previously.

(7) A person arrested by a constable at a place other than a police station shall be released if a constable is satisfied, before the person arrested reaches a police station, that there are no grounds for keeping him under arrest.

(8) A constable who releases a person under sub-section (7) above shall record the fact that he has done so.

(9) The constable shall make the record as soon as is practicable after the release.

(10) Nothing in sub-section (1) above shall prevent a constable delaying taking a person who has been arrested to a police station if the presence of that person elsewhere is necessary in order to carry out such investigations as it is reasonable to carry out immediately.

(11) Where there is delay in taking a person who has been arrested to a police station after his arrest, the reasons for the delay shall be recorded when he first arrives at a police station.

(12) Nothing in sub-section (1) above shall be taken to affect:

(a) paragraphs 16(3) or 18(1) of Schedule 2 to the Immigration Act 1971;

(b) section 34(1) of the Criminal Justice Act 1972; or

(c) section 15(6) and (9) of the Prevention of Terrorism (Temporary Provisions) Act 1989 and paragraphs 7(4) and 8(4) and (5) of Schedule 2 and paragraphs 6(6) and 7(4) and (5) of Schedule 5 to that Act.

(13) Nothing in sub-section (10) above shall be taken to affect paragraph 18(3) of Schedule 2 to the Immigration Act 1971.

Section 31: Arrest for further offence

Where:

(a) a person:

(i) has been arrested for an offence; and

(ii) is at a police station in consequence of that arrest; and

(b) it appears to a constable that, if he were released from that arrest, he would be liable to arrest for some other offence,

he shall be arrested for that other offence.

Section 32: Search upon arrest

(1) A constable may search an arrested person, in any case where the person to be searched has been arrested at a place other than a police station, if the constable has reasonable grounds for believing that the arrested person may present a danger to himself or others.

(2) Subject to sub-sections (3) to (5) below, a constable shall also have power in any such case:

    (a) to search the arrested person for anything;

        (i) which he might use to assist him to escape from lawful custody; or

        (ii) which might be evidence relating to an offence; and

    (b) to enter and search any premises in which he was when arrested or immediately before he was arrested for evidence relating to the offence for which he has been arrested.

(3) The power to search conferred by sub-section (2) above is only a power to search to the extent that is reasonably required for the purpose of discovering any such thing or any such evidence.

(4) The powers conferred by this section to search a person are not to be construed as authorising a constable to require a person to remove any of his clothing in public other than an outer coat, jacket or gloves but they do authorise a search of a person's mouth.

(5) A constable may not search a person in the exercise of the power conferred by sub-section (2)(a) above unless he has reasonable grounds for believing that the person to be searched may have concealed on him anything for which a search is permitted under that paragraph.

(6) A constable may not search premises in the exercise of the power conferred by sub-section (2)(b) above unless he has reasonable grounds for believing that there is evidence for which a search is permitted under that paragraph on the premises.

(7) In so far as the power of search conferred by sub-section (2)(b) above relates to premises consisting of two or more separate dwellings, it is limited to a power to search:

    (a) any dwelling in which the arrest took place or in which the person arrested was immediately before his arrest; and

    (b) any parts of the premises which the occupier of any such dwelling uses in common with the occupiers of any other dwellings comprised in the premises.

(8) A constable searching a person in the exercise of the power conferred by sub-section (1) above may seize and retain anything he finds, if he has reasonable grounds for believing that the person searched might use it to cause physical injury to himself or to any other person.

(9) A constable searching a person in the exercise of the power conferred by sub-section (2)(a) above may seize and retain anything he finds, other than an item subject to legal privilege, if he has reasonable grounds for believing:

    (a) that he might use it to assist him to escape from lawful custody; or

    (b) that it is evidence of an offence or has been obtained in consequence of the commission of an offence.

(10) Nothing in this section shall be taken to affect the power conferred by section 15(3), (4) and (5) of the Prevention of Terrorism (Temporary Provisions) Act 1989.

DETENTION AND QUESTIONING OF SUSPECTS BY POLICE

POLICE AND CRIMINAL EVIDENCE ACT 1984

Section 34: Limitations on police detention

(1) A person arrested for an offence shall not be kept in police detention except in accordance with the provisions of this Part of this Act.

(2) Subject to sub-section (3) below, if at any time a custody officer:

    (a) becomes aware, in relation to any person in police detention, that the grounds for the detention of that person have ceased to apply; and

    (b) is not aware of any other grounds on which the continued detention of that person could be justified under the provisions of this Part of this Act,

it shall be the duty of the custody officer, subject to sub-section (4) below, to order his immediate release from custody.

(3) No person in police detention shall be released except on the authority of a custody officer at the police station where his detention was authorised or, if it was authorised at more than one station, a custody officer at the station where it was last authorised.

(4) A person who appears to the custody officer to have been unlawfully at large when he was arrested is not to be released under sub-section (2) above.

(5) A person whose release is ordered under sub-section (2) above shall be released without bail unless it appears to the custody officer:

    (a) that there is need for further investigation of any matter in connection with which he was detained at any time during the period of his detention; or

    (b) that proceedings may be taken against him in respect of any such matter,

and, if it so appears, he shall be released on bail.

(6) For the purposes of this Part of this Act a person arrested under section 6(5) of the Road Traffic Act 1988 is arrested for an offence.

(7) For the purposes of this Part of this Act a person who returns to a police station to answer bail or is arrested under section 46A below shall be treated as arrested for an offence and the offence in connection with which he was granted bail shall be deemed to be that offence.

Section 35: Designated police stations

(1) The chief officer of police for each police area shall designate the police stations in his area which, subject to section 30(3) and (5) above, are to be

the stations in that area to be used for the purpose of detaining arrested persons.

(2) A chief officer's duty under sub-section (1) above is to designate police stations appearing to him to provide enough accommodation for that purpose.

(3) Without prejudice to section 12 of the Interpretation Act 1978 (continuity of duties) a chief officer:

(a) may designate a station which was not previously designated; and

(b) may direct that a designation of a station previously made shall cease to operate.

(4) In this Act 'designated police station' means a police station for the time being designated under this section.

Section 36: Custody officers at police stations

(1) One or more custody officers shall be appointed for each designated police station.

(2) A custody officer for a designated police station shall be appointed:

(a) by the chief officer of police for the area in which the designated police station is situated; or

(b) by such other police officer as the chief of police for that area may direct.

(3) No officer may be appointed a custody officer unless he is of at least the rank of sergeant.

(4) An officer of any rank may perform the functions of a custody officer at a designated police station if a custody officer is not readily available to perform them.

(5) Subject to the following provisions of this section and to section 39(2) below, none of the functions of a custody officer in relation to a person shall be performed by an officer who at the time when the function falls to be performed is involved in the investigation of an offence for which that person is in police detention at that time.

(6) Nothing in sub-section (5) above is to be taken to prevent a custody officer:

(a) performing any function assigned to custody officers:

(i) by this Act; or

(ii) by a code of practice issued under this Act;

(b) carrying out the duty imposed on custody officers by section 39 below;

(c) doing anything in connection with the identification of a suspect; or

(d) doing anything under sections 7 and 8 of the Road Traffic Act 1988.

(7) Where an arrested person is taken to a police station which is not a designated police station, the functions in relation to him which at a designated police station would be the functions of a custody officer shall be performed:

(a) by an officer who is not involved in the investigation of an offence for which he is in police detention, if such an officer is readily available; and

(b) if no such officer is readily available, by the officer who took him to the station or any other officer.

(8) References to a custody officer in the following provisions of this Act include references to an officer other than a custody officer who is performing the functions of a custody officer by virtue of sub-section (4) or (7) above.

(9) Where by virtue of sub-section (7) above an officer of a force maintained by a police authority who took an arrested person to a police station is to perform the functions of a custody officer in relation to him, the officer shall inform an officer who:

(a) is attached to a designated police station; and

(b) is of at least the rank of inspector,

that he is to do so.

(10)The duty imposed by sub-section (9) above shall be performed as soon as it is practicable to perform it.

Section 37: Duties of custody officer before charge

(1) Where:

(a) a person is arrested for an offence:

(i) without a warrant; or

(ii) under a warrant not endorsed for bail,

(b) [repealed],

the custody officer at each police station where he is detained after his arrest shall determine whether he has before him sufficient evidence to charge that person with the office for which he was arrested and may detain him at the police station for such period as is necessary to enable him to do so.

(2) If the custody officer determines that he does not have such evidence before him, the person arrested shall be released either on bail or without bail, unless the custody officer has reasonable grounds for believing that his detention without being charged is necessary to secure or preserve evidence relating to an offence for which he is under arrest or to obtain such evidence by questioning him.

(3) If the custody officer has reasonable grounds for so believing, he may authorise the person arrested to be kept in police detention.

(4) Where a custody officer authorises a person who has not been charged to be kept in police detention, he shall, as soon as is practicable, make a written record of the grounds for the detention.

(5) Subject to sub-section (6) below, the written record shall be made in the presence of the person arrested who shall at that time be informed by the custody officer of the grounds for his detention.

(6) Sub-section (5) above shall not apply where the person arrested is, at the time when the written record is made:

    (a) incapable of understanding what is said to him;

    (b) violent or likely to become violent; or

    (c) in urgent need of medical attention.

(7) Subject of section 41(7) below, if the custody officer determines that he has before him sufficient evidence to charge the person arrested with the offence for which he was arrested, the person arrested:

    (a) shall be charged; or

    (b) shall be released without charge, either on bail or without bail.

(8) Where:

    (a) a person is released under sub-section (7)(b) above; and

    (b) at the time of his release a decision whether he should be prosecuted for the offence for which he was arrested has not been taken,

it shall be the duty of custody officer so to inform him.

(9) If the person arrested is not in a fit state to be dealt with under sub-section (7) above, he may be kept in police detention until he is.

(10) The duty imposed on the custody officer under sub-section (1) above shall be carried out by him as soon as practicable after the person arrested arrives at the police station or, in the case of a person arrested at the police station, as soon as practicable after the arrest.

(11)–(14)   [Repealed]

(15) In this Part of this Act:

'arrested juvenile' means a person arrested with or without a warrant who appears to be under the age of 17;

'endorsed for bail' means endorsed with a direction for bail in accordance with section 117(2) of the Magistrates' Courts Act 1980.

Section 38: Duties of custody officer after charge

(1) Where a person arrested for an offence otherwise than under a warrant endorsed for bail is charged with an offence, the custody officer shall, subject to section 25 of the Criminal Justice and Public Order Act 1994, order his release from police detention, either on bail or without bail, unless:

    (a)   if the person arrested is not an arrested juvenile;

        (i) his name or address cannot be ascertained or the custody officer has reasonable grounds for doubting whether a name or address furnished by him as his name or address is his real name or address;

(ii) the custody officer has reasonable grounds for believing that the person arrested will fail to appear in court to answer to bail;

(iii) in the case of a person arrested for an imprisonable offence, the custody officer has reasonable grounds for believing that the detention of the person arrested is necessary to prevent him from committing an offence;

(iv) in the case of a person arrested for an offence which is not an imprisonable offence, the custody officer has reasonable grounds for believing that the detention of the person arrested is necessary to prevent him from causing physical injury to any other person or from causing loss of or damage to property;

(v) the custody officer has reasonable grounds for believing that the detention of the person arrested is necessary to prevent him from interfering with the administration of justice or with the investigation of offences or of a particular offence; or

(vi) the custody officer has reasonable grounds for believing that the detention of the person arrested is necessary for his own protection;

(b) if he is an arrested juvenile:

(i) any of the requirements of paragraph (a) above is satisfied; or

(ii) the custody officer has reasonable grounds for believing that he ought to be detained in his own interests.

(2) If the release of a person arrested is not required by sub-section (1) above, the custody officer may authorise him to be kept in police detention.

(2A) The custody officer, in taking the decisions required by sub-section (1)(a) and (b) above (except (a)(i) and (vi) and (b)(ii)), shall have regard to the same considerations as those which a court is required to have regard to in taking the corresponding decisions under paragraph 2 of Part I of Schedule 1 to the Bail Act 1976.

(3) Where a custody officer authorises a person who has been charged to be kept in police detention, he shall, as soon as practicable, make a written record of the grounds for the detention.

(4) Subject to sub-section (5) below, the written record shall be made in the presence of the person charged who shall at that time be informed by the custody officer of the grounds for his detention.

(5) Sub-section (4) above shall not apply where the person charged is, at the time when the written record is made:

(a) incapable of understanding what is said to him;

(b) violent or likely to become violent; or

(c) in urgent need of medical attention.

(6) Where a custody officer authorises an arrested juvenile to be kept in police detention under sub-section (1) above, the custody officer shall, unless he certifies:

(a) that, by reason of such circumstances as are specified in the certificate, it is impracticable for him to do so; or

(b) in the case of an arrested juvenile who has attained the age of 12 years, that no secure accommodation is available and that keeping him in other local authority accommodation would not be adequate to protect the public from serious harm from him,

secure that the arrested juvenile is moved to local authority accommodation.

(6A) In this section:

'local authority accommodation' means accommodation provided by or on behalf of a local authority (within the meaning of the Children Act 1989);

'secure accommodation' means accommodation provided for the purpose of restricting liberty;

'sexual offence' and 'violent offence' have the same meanings as in Part I of the Criminal Justice Act 1991

and any reference, in relation to an arrested juvenile charged with a violent or sexual offence, to protecting the public from serious harm from him shall be construed as a reference to protecting members of the public from death or serious personal injury, whether physical or psychological, occasioned by further such offences committed by him.

(6B) Where an arrested juvenile is moved to local authority accommodation under sub-section (6) above, it shall be lawful for any person acting on behalf of the authority to detain him.

(7) A certificate made under sub-section (6) above in respect of an arrested juvenile shall be produced to the court before which he is first brought thereafter.

(7A) In this section 'imprisonable offence' has the same meaning as in Schedule 1 to the Bail Act 1976.

(8) In this Part of this Act 'local authority' has the same meaning as in the Children Act 1989.

Section 39: Responsibilities in relation to persons detained

(1) Subject to sub-sections (2) and (4) below, it shall be the duty of the custody officer at a police station to ensure:

(a) that all persons in police detention at that station are treated in accordance with this Act and any code of practice issued under it and relating to the treatment of persons in police detention; and

(b) that all matters relating to such persons which are required by this Act or by such codes of practice to be recorded are recorded in the custody records relating to such persons.

(2) If the custody officer, in accordance with any code of practice issued under this Act transfers or permits the transfer of a person in police detention:

(a) to the custody of a police officer investigating an offence for which that person is in police detention; or

(b) to the custody of an officer who has charge of that person outside the police station,

the custody officer shall cease in relation to that person to be subject to the duty imposed on him by sub-section (1)(a) above; and it shall be the duty of the officer to whom the transfer is made to ensure that he is treated in accordance with the provisions of this Act and of any such codes of practice as are mentioned in sub-section (1) above.

(3) If the person detained is subsequently returned to the custody of the custody officer, it shall be the duty of the officer investigating the offence to report to the custody officer as to the manner in which this section and the codes of practice have been complied with while that person was in custody.

(4) If an arrested juvenile is moved to local authority accommodation under section 38(6) above, the custody officer shall cease in relation to the person to be subject to the duty imposed on him by sub-section (1) above.

(5) [Repealed.]

(6) Where:

(a) an officer of higher rank than the custody officer gives directions relating to a person in police detention; and

(b) the directions are at variance:

(i) with any decision made or action taken by the custody officer in the performance of a duty imposed on him under this Part of this Act; or

(ii) with any decision or action which would but for the directions have been made or taken by him in the performance of such a duty,

the custody officer shall refer the matter at once to an officer of the rank of superintendent or above who is responsible for the police station for which the custody officer is acting as custody officer.

Section 40: Review of police detention

(1) Reviews of the detention of each person in police detention in connection with the investigation of an offence shall be carried out periodically in accordance with the following provisions of this section:

(a) in the case of a person who has been arrested and charged, by the custody officer; and

(b) in the case of a person who has been arrested but not charged, by an officer of at least the rank of inspector who has not been directly involved in the investigation.

(2) The officer to whom it falls to carry out a review is referred to in this section as a 'review officer'.

(3) Subject to sub-section (4) below:

(a) the first review shall be not later than six hours after the detention was first authorised;

(b) the second review shall be not later than nine hours after the first;

(c) subsequent reviews shall be at intervals of not more than nine hours.

(4) A review may be postponed:

(a) if, having regard to all the circumstances prevailing at the latest time for it specified in sub-section (3) above, it is not practicable to carry out the review at that time;

(b) without prejudice to the generality of paragraph (a) above:

(i) if at that time the person in detention is being questioned by a police officer and the review officer is satisfied that an interruption of the questioning for the purpose of carrying out the review would prejudice the investigation in connection with which he is being questioned; or

(ii) if at that time no review officer is readily available.

(5) If a review is postponed under sub-section (4) above it shall be carried out as soon as practicable after the latest time specified for it in sub-section (3) above.

(6) If a review is carried out after postponement under sub-section (4) above, the fact that it was so carried out shall not affect any requirement of this section as to the time at which any subsequent review is to be carried out.

(7) The review officer shall record the reasons for any postponement of a review in the custody record.

(8) Subject to sub-section (9) below, where the person whose detention is under review has not been charged before the time of the review, section 37(1) to (6) above shall effect in relation to him, but with the substitution:

(a) of references to the person whose detention is under review for references to the person arrested; and

(b) of references to the review officer for references to the custody officer.

(9) Where a person has been kept in police detention by virtue of section 37(9) above, section 37(1) to (6) shall not have effect in relation to him but it shall be the duty of the review officer to determine whether he is yet in a fit state.

(10) Where the person whose detention is under review has been charged before the time of the review, section 38(1) to (6) above shall have effect in relation to him, but with the substitution of references to the person whose detention is under review for references to the person arrested.

(11) Where:

(a) an officer of higher rank than the review officer gives directions relating to a person in police detention; and

(b) the directions are at variance:

(i) with any decision made or action taken by the review officer in the performance of a duty imposed on him under this Part of this Act; or

(ii) with any decision or action which would but for the directions have been made or taken by him in the performance of such a duty, the review officer shall refer the matter at once to an officer of the rank of superintendent or above who is responsible for the police station for which the review officer is acting as review officer in connection with the detention.

(12) Before determining whether to authorise a person's continued detention the review officer shall give:

(a) that person (unless he is asleep); or

(b) any solicitor representing him who is available at the time of the review, an opportunity to make representations to him about the detention.

(13) Subject to sub-section (14) below, the person whose detention is under review or his solicitor may make representations under sub-section (12) above either orally or in writing.

(14) The review officer may refuse to hear oral representations from the person whose detention is under review if he considers that he is unfit to make such representations by reason of his condition or behaviour.

Section 41: Limits on period of detention without charge

(1) Subject to the following provisions of this section and to sections 42 and 43 below, a person shall not be kept in police detention for more than 24 hours without being charged.

(2) The time from which the period of detention of a person is to be calculated (in this Act referred to as 'the relevant time'):

(a) in the case of a person to whom this paragraph applies, shall be:

(i) the time at which that person arrives at the relevant police station; or

(ii) the time 24 hours after the time of that person's arrest,

whichever is the earlier;

(b) in the case of a person arrested outside England and Wales, shall be:

(i) the time at which that person arrives at the first police station to which he is taken in the police area in England or Wales in which the offence for which he was arrested is being investigated; or

(ii) the time 24 hours after the time of that person's entry into England and Wales, whichever is the earlier;

(c) in the case of a person who:

(i) attends voluntarily at a police station; or

(ii) accompanies a constable to a police station without having been arrested,

and is arrested at the police station, the time of his arrest;

(d) in any other case, except where sub-section (5) below applies, shall be the time at which the person arrested arrives at the first police station to which he is taken after his arrest.

(3) Sub-section (2)(a) above applies to a person if:

    (a) his arrest is sought in one police area in England and Wales;

    (b) he is arrested in another police area; and

    (c) he is not questioned in the area in which he is arrested in order to obtain evidence in relation to an offence for which he is arrested,

and in sub-paragraph (i) of that paragraph 'the relevant police station' means the first police station to which he is taken in the police area in which his arrest was sought.

(4) Sub-section (2) above shall have effect in relation to a person arrested under section 31 above as if every reference in it to his arrest or his being arrested were a reference to his arrest or of his being arrested for the offence for which he was originally arrested.

(5) If:

    (a) a person is in police detention in a police are in England and Wales ('the first area'); and

    (b) his arrest for an offence is sought in some other police area in England and Wales ('the second area'); and

    (c) he is taken to the second area for the purposes of investigating that offence, without being questioned in the first area in order to obtain evidence in relation to it,

the relevant time shall be:

    (i) the time 24 hours after he leaves the place where he is detained in the first area; or

    (ii) the time at which he arrives at the first police station to which he is taken in the second area,

whichever is the earlier.

(6) When a person who is in police detention is removed to hospital because he is in need of medical treatment, any time during which he is being questioned in hospital or on the way there or back by a police officer for the purpose of obtaining evidence relating to an offence shall be included in any period which falls to be calculated for the purposes of this Part of this Act, but any other time while he is in hospital or on his way there or back shall not be so included.

(7) Subject to sub-section (8) below, a person who at the expiry of 24 hours after the relevant time is in police detention and has not been charged shall be released at that time either on bail or without bail.

(8) Sub-section (7) above does not apply to a person whose detention for more than 24 hours after the relevant time has been authorised or is otherwise permitted in accordance with section 42 or 43 below.

(9) A person released under sub-section (7) above shall not be re-arrested without a warrant for the offence for which he was previously arrested unless new evidence justifying a further arrest has come to light since his release; but this sub-section does not prevent an arrest under section 46A below.

Section 42: Authorisation of continued detention

(1) Where a police officer of the rank of superintendent or above who is responsible for the police station at which a person is detained has reasonable grounds for believing that:

    (a) the detention of that person without charge is necessary to secure or preserve evidence relating to an offence for which he is under arrest or to obtain such evidence by questioning him;

    (b) an offence for which he is under arrest is a serious arrestable offence; and

    (c) the investigation is being conducted diligently and expeditiously,

he may authorise the keeping of that person in police detention for a period expiring at or before 36 hours after the relevant time.

(2) Where an officer such as is mentioned in sub-section (1) above has authorised the keeping of a person in police detention for a period expiring less than 36 hours after the relevant time, such an officer may authorise the keeping of that person in police detention for a further period expiring not more than 36 hours after that time if the conditions specified in sub-section (1) above are still satisfied when he gives the authorisation.

(3) If it is proposed to transfer a person in police detention to another police area, the officer determining whether or not to authorise keeping him in detention under sub-section (1) above shall have regard to the distance and the time the journey would take.

(4) No authorisation under sub-section (1) above shall be given in respect of any person:

    (a) more than 24 hours after the relevant time; or

    (b) before the second review of his detention under section 40 above has been carried out.

(5) Where an officer authorises the keeping of a person in police detention under sub-section (1) above, it shall be his duty:

    (a) to inform that person of the grounds for his continued detention; and

    (b) to record the grounds in that person's custody record.

(6) Before determining whether to authorise the keeping of a person in detention under sub-section (1) or (2) above, and officer shall give:

    (a) that person; or

    (b) any solicitor representing him who is available at the time when it falls to the officer to determine whether to give the authorisation,

an opportunity to make representations to him about the detention.

(7) Subject to sub-section (8) below, the person in detention or his solicitor may make representations under sub-section (6) above either orally or in writing.

(8) The officer to whom it falls to determine whether to give the authorisation may refuse to hear oral representations from the person in detention if he

considers that he is unfit to make such representations by reason of his condition or behaviour.

(9) Where:

    (a) an officer authorises the keeping of a person in detention under sub-section (1) above; and

    (b) at the time of the authorisation he has not yet exercised a right conferred on him by section 56 or 58 below,

the officer:

    (i)   shall inform him of that right;

    (ii) shall decide whether he should be permitted to exercise it;

    (iii) shall record the decision in his custody record; and

    (iv) if the decision is to refuse to permit the exercise of the right, shall also record the grounds for the decision in that record.

(10) Where an officer has authorised the keeping of a person who has not been charged in detention under sub-section (1) or (2) above, he shall be released from detention, either on bail or without bail, not later than 36 hours after the relevant time, unless:

    (a) he has been charged with an offence; or

    (b) his continued detention is authorised or otherwise permitted in accordance with section 43 below.

(11) A person released under sub-section (10) above shall not be re-arrested without a warrant for the offence for which he was previously arrested unless new evidence justifying a further arrest has come to light since his release, but this sub-section does not prevent an arrest under section 46A below.

Section 43: Warrants of further detention

(1) Where, on an application on oath made by a constable and supported by an information, a magistrates' court is satisfied that there are reasonable grounds for believing that the further detention of the person to whom the application relates is justified, it may issue a warrant of further detention authorising the keeping of that person in police detention.

(2) A court may not hear an application for a warrant of further detention unless the person to whom the application relates:

    (a) has been furnished with a copy of the information; and

    (b) has been brought before the court for the hearing.

(3) The person to whom the application relates shall be entitled to be legally represented at the hearing and, if he is not so represented but wishes to be so represented:

    (a) the court shall adjourn the hearing to enable him to obtain representation; and

    (b) he may be kept in police detention during the adjournment.

(4) A person's further detention is only justified for the purposes of this section or section 44 below if:

    (a) his detention without charge is necessary to secure or preserve evidence relating to an offence for which he is under arrest or to obtain such evidence by questioning him;

    (b) an offence for which he is under arrest is a serious arrestable offence; and

    (c) the investigation is being conducted diligently and expeditiously.

(5) Subject to sub-section (7) below, an application for a warrant of further detention may be made:

    (a) at any time before the expiry of 36 hours after the relevant time; or

    (b) in a case where:

        (i) it is not practicable for the magistrates' court to which the application will be made to sit at the expiry of 36 hours after the relevant time; but

        (ii) the court will sit during the 6 hours following the end of that period,

    at any time before the expiry of the said 6 hours.

(6) In a case to which sub-section (5)(b) above applies:

    (a) the person to whom the application relates may be kept in police detention until the application is heard; and

    (b) the custody officer shall make a note in that person's custody record:

        (i) of the fact that he was kept in police detention for more than 36 hours after the relevant time; and

        (ii) of the reason why he was so kept.

(7) If:

    (a) an application for a warrant of further detention is made after the expiry of 36 hours after the relevant time; and

    (b) it appears to the magistrates' court that it would have been reasonable for the police to make it before the expiry of that period,

    the court will dismiss the application.

(8) Where on an application such as is mentioned in sub-section (1) above a magistrates' court is not satisfied that there are reasonable grounds for believing that the further detention of the person to whom the application relates is justified, it shall be its duty:

    (a) to refuse the application; or

    (b) to adjourn the hearing of it until a time not later than 36 hours after the relevant time.

(9) The person to whom the application relates may be kept in police detention during the adjournment.

(10) A warrant of further detention shall:

    (a) state the time at which it is issued;

(b) authorise the keeping in police detention of the person to whom it relates for the period stated in it.

(11) Subject to sub-section (12) below, the period stated in a warrant of further detention shall be such period as the magistrates' court thinks fit, having regard to the evidence before it.

(12) The period shall not be longer than 36 hours.

(13) If it is proposed to transfer a person in police detention to a police area other than that in which he is detained when the application for a warrant of further detention is made, the court hearing the application shall have regard to the distance and the time the journey would take.

(14) Any information submitted in support of an application under this section shall state:

(a) the nature of the offence for which the person to whom the application relates has been arrested;

(b) the general nature of the evidence on which that person was arrested;

(c) what inquiries relating to the offence have been made by the police and what further inquiries are proposed by them;

(d) the reasons for believing the continued detention of that person to be necessary for the purposes of such further inquiries.

(15) Where an application under this section is refused, the person to whom the application relates shall forthwith be charged or, subject to sub-section (16) below, released, either on bail or without bail.

(16) A person need not be released under sub-section (15) above:

(a) before the expiry of 24 hours after the relevant time; or

(b) before the expiry of any longer period for which his continued detention is or has been authorised under section 42 above.

(17) Where an application under this section is refused, no further application shall be made under this section in respect of the person to whom the refusal relates, unless supported by evidence which has come to light since the refusal.

(18) Where a warrant of further detention is issued, the person to whom it relates shall be released from police detention, either on bail or without bail, upon or before the expiry of the warrant unless he is charged.

(19) A person released under sub-section (18) above shall not be re-arrested without a warrant for the offence for which he was previously arrested unless new evidence justifying a further arrest has come to light since his release; but this sub-section does not prevent an arrest under section 46A below.

Section 44: Extension of warrants of further detention

(1) On an application made by a constable and supported by an information a magistrates' court may extend a warrant of further detention issued under section 43 above if it is satisfied that there are reasonable grounds for

believing that the further detention of the person to whom the application relates is justified.

(2) Subject to sub-section (3) below, the period for which a warrant of further detention may be extended shall be such period as the court thinks fit, having regard to the evidence before it.

(3) The period shall not:

(a) be longer than 36 hours; or

(b) end later than 96 hours after the relevant time.

(4) Where a warrant of further detention has been extended under sub-section (1) above, or further extended under this sub-section, for a period ending before 96 hours after the relevant time, on an application such as is mentioned in that sub-section a magistrates' court may further extend the warrant if it is satisfied as there mentioned; and sub-sections (2) and (3) above apply to such extensions as they apply to extensions under sub-section (1) above.

(5) A warrant of further detention shall, if extended or further extended under this section be endorsed with a note of the period of the extension.

(6) Sub-sections (2), (3) and (14) of section 43 above shall apply to an application made under this section as they apply to an application made under that section.

(7) Where an application under this section is refused, the person to whom the application relates shall forthwith be charged or, subject to sub-section (8) below, released, either on bail or without bail.

(8) A person need not be released under sub-section (7) above before the expiry of any period for which a warrant of further detention issued in relation to him has been extended or further extended on an earlier application made under this section.

Section 45: Detention before charge – supplementary

(1) In sections 43 and 44 of this Act 'magistrates' court' means a court consisting of two or more justices of the peace sitting otherwise than in open court.

(2) Any reference in this Part of this Act to a period of time or a time of day is to be treated as approximate only.

Section 46: Detention after charge

(1) Where a person:

(a) is charged with an offence; and

(b) after being charged:

(i) is kept in police detention; or

(ii) is detained by a local authority in pursuance of arrangements made under section 38(6) above, he shall be brought before a magistrates' court in accordance with the provisions of this section.

(2) If he is to be brought before a magistrates' court for the petty sessions area in which the police station at which he was charged is situated, he shall be brought before such a court as soon as is practicable and in any event not later than the first sitting after he is charged with the offence.

(3) If no magistrates' court for that area is due to sit either on the day on which he is charged or on the next day, the custody officer for the police station at which he was charged shall inform the clerk to the justices for the area that there is a person in the area to whom sub-section (2) above applies.

(4) If the person charged is to be brought before a magistrates' court for a petty sessions area other than that in which the police station at which he was charged is situated, he shall be removed to that area as soon as is practicable and brought before such a court as soon as is practicable after his arrival in the area and in any event not later than the first sitting of a magistrates' court for that area after his arrival in the area.

(5) If no magistrates' court for that area is due to sit either on the day on which he arrives in the area or on the next day:

   (a) he shall be taken to a police station in the area; and

   (b) the custody officer at that station shall inform the clerk to the justices for the area that there is a person in the area to whom sub-section (4) applies.

(6) Subject to sub-section (8) below, where a clerk to the justices for a petty sessions area has been informed:

   (a) under sub-section (3) above that there is a person in the area to whom sub-section (2) above applies; or

   (b) under sub-section (5) above that there is a person in the area to whom, sub-section (4) above applies,

the clerk shall arrange for a magistrates' court to sit not later than the day next following the relevant day.

(7) In this section 'the relevant day':

   (a) in relation to a person who is to be brought before a magistrates' court for the petty sessions area in which the police station at which he was charged is situated, means the day on which he was charged; and

   (b) in relation to a person who is to be brought before a magistrates' court for any other petty sessions area, means the day on which he arrives in the area.

(8) Where the day next following the relevant day is Christmas Day, Good Friday or a Sunday, the duty of the clerk under sub-section (6) above is a duty to arrange for a magistrates' court to sit not later than the first day after the relevant day which is not one of those days.

(9) Nothing in this section requires a person who is in hospital to be brought before a court if he is not well enough.

Section 46A: Power of arrest for failure to answer police bail

(1) A constable may arrest without a warrant any person who, having been released on bail under this Part of this Act subject to a duty to attend at a police station, fails to attend at that police station at the time appointed for him to do so.

(2) A person who is arrested under this section shall be taken to the police station appointed as the place at which he is to surrender to custody as soon as practicable after the arrest.

(3) For the purposes of:

(a) section 30 above (subject to the obligation in sub-section (2) above); and

(b) section 31 above,

an arrest under this section shall be treated as an arrest for an offence.

Section 47: Bail after arrest

(1) Subject to sub-section (2) below, a release on bail of a person under this Part of this Act shall be a release on bail granted in accordance with sections 3, 3A, 5 and 5A of the Bail Act 1976 as they apply to bail granted by a constable.

(1A) The normal powers to impose conditions of bail shall be available to him where a custody officer releases a person on bail under section 38(1) above (including that sub-section as applied by section 40(10) above) but not in any other cases.

In this sub-section, 'the normal powers to impose conditions of bail' has the meaning given in section 3(6) of the Bail Act 1976.

(2) Nothing in the Bail Act 1976 shall prevent the re-arrest without warrant of a person released on bail subject to a duty to attend at a police station if new evidence justifying a further arrest has come to light since his release.

(3) Subject to sub-sections (3A) and (4) below, in this Part of this Act references to 'bail' are references to bail subject to a duty:

(a) to appear before a magistrates' court at such time and such place; or

(b) to attend at such police station at such time,

as the custody officer may appoint.

(3A) Where a custody officer grants bail to a person subject to a duty to appear before a magistrates' court, he shall appoint for the appearance:

(a) a date which is not later than the first sitting of the court after the person is charged with the offence; or

(b) where he is informed by the clerk to the justices [justices' chief executive] for the relevant petty sessions area that the appearance cannot be accommodated until a later date, that later date.

(4) Where a custody officer has granted bail to a person subject to a duty to appear at a police station, the custody officer may give notice in writing to that person that his attendance at the police station is not required.

(5) [Repealed]

(6) Where a person who has been granted bail and either has attended at the police station in accordance with the grant of bail or has been arrested under section 46A above is detained at a police station, any time during which he was in police detention prior to being granted bail shall be included as part of any period which falls to be calculated under this Part of this Act.

(7) Where a person who was released on bail subject to a duty to attend at a police station is re-arrested, the provisions of this Part of this Act shall apply to him as they apply to a person arrested for the first time; but this sub-section does not apply to a person who is arrested under section 46A above or has attended a police station in accordance with the grant of bail (and who accordingly is deemed by section 34(7) above to have been arrested for an offence).

...

Section 54: Searches of detained persons

(1) The custody officer at a police station shall ascertain and record or cause to be recorded everything which a person has with him when he is:

(a) brought to the station after being arrested elsewhere or after being committed to custody by an order or sentence of a court; or

(b) arrested at the station or detained there, as a person falling within section 34(7), under section 37 above.

(2) In the case of an arrested person the record shall be made as part of his custody record.

(3) Subject to sub-section (4) below, a custody officer may seize and retain any such thing or cause any such thing to be seized and retained.

(4) Clothes and personal effects may only be seized if the custody officer:

(a) believes that the person from whom they are seized may use them:

(i) to cause physical injury to himself or any other person;

(ii) to damage property;

(iii) to interfere with evidence; or

(iv) to assist him to escape; or

(b) has reasonable grounds for believing that they may be evidence relating to an offence.

(5) Where anything is seized, the person from whom it is seized shall be told the reason for the seizure unless he is:

(a) violent or likely to become violent; or

(b) incapable of understanding what is said to him.

(6) Subject to sub-section (7) below, a person may be searched if the custody officer considers it necessary to enable him to carry out his duty under sub-section (1) above and to the extent that the custody officer considers necessary for that purpose.

(6A) A person who is in custody at a police station or is in police detention otherwise than at a police station may at any time be searched in order to ascertain whether he has with him anything which he could use for any of the purposes specified in sub-section (4)(a) above.

(6B) Subject to sub-section (6C) below, a constable may seize and retain, or cause to be seized and retained, anything found on such a search.

(6C) A constable may only seize clothes and personal effects in the circumstances specified in sub-section (4) above.

(7) An intimate search may not be conducted under this section.

(8) A search under this section shall be carried out by a constable.

(9) The constable carrying out a search shall be of the same sex as the person searched.

Section 56: Right to have someone informed when arrested

(1) When a person has been arrested and is being held in custody in a police station or other premises, he shall be entitled, if he so requests, to have one friend or relative or other person who is known to him or who is likely to take an interest in his welfare told, as soon as practicable except to the extent that delay is permitted by this section, that he has been arrested and is being detained there.

(2) Delay is only permitted:

   (a) in the case of a person who is in police detention for a serious arrestable offence; and

   (b) if an officer of at least the rank of superintendent authorises it.

(3) In any case the person in custody must be permitted to exercise the right conferred by sub-section (1) above within 36 hours from the relevant time, as defined in section 41(2) above.

(4) An officer may give an authorisation under sub-section (2) above orally or in writing but, if he gives it orally, he shall confirm it in writing as soon as is practicable.

(5) Subject to sub-section (5A) below an officer may only authorise delay where he has reasonable grounds for believing that telling the named person of the arrest:

   (a) will lead to interference with or harm to evidence connected with a serious arrestable offence or interference with or physical injury to other persons; or

   (b) will lead to the alerting of other persons suspected of having committed such an offence but not yet arrested for it; or

   (c) will hinder the recovery of any property obtained as a result of such an offence.

(5A) An officer may also authorise delay where the serious arrestable offence is a drug trafficking offence or an offence to which Part VI of the Criminal Justice Act 1988 applies (offences in respect of which confiscation orders under that Part may be made) and the officer has reasonable grounds for believing:

  (a) where the offence is a drug trafficking offence, that the detained person has benefited from drug trafficking and that the recovery of the value of that person's proceeds of drug trafficking will be hindered by telling the named person of the arrest; and

  (b) where the offence is one to which Part VI of the Criminal Justice Act 1988 applies, that the detained person has benefited from the offence and that the recovery of the value of the property obtained by that person from or in connection with the offence or of the pecuniary advantage derived by him from or in connection with it will be hindered by telling the named person of the arrest.

(6) If a delay is authorised:

  (a) the detained person shall be told the reason for it; and

  (b) the reason shall be noted on his custody record.

(7) The duties imposed by sub-section (6) above shall be performed as soon as is practicable.

(8) The rights conferred by this section on a person detained at a police station or other premises are exercisable whenever he is transferred from one place to another; and this section applied to each subsequent occasion on which they are exercisable as it applies to the first such occasion.

(9) There may be no further delay in permitting the exercise of the right conferred by sub-section (1) above once the reason for authorising delay ceases to subsist.

(10) In the foregoing provisions of this section references to a person who has been arrested include references to a person who has been detained under the terrorism provisions and 'arrest' includes detention under those provisions.

(11) In its application to a person who has been arrested or detained under the terrorism provisions:

  (a) sub-section (2)(a) above shall have effect as if for the words 'for a serious arrestable offence' there were substituted the words 'under the terrorism provisions';

  (b) sub-section (3) above shall have effect as if for the words from 'within' onwards there were substituted the words 'before the end of the period beyond which he may no longer be detained without the authority of the Secretary of State'; and

  (c) sub-section (5) above shall have effect as if at the end there were added 'or

  (d) will lead to interference with the gathering of information about the commission, preparation or instigation of acts of terrorism; or

  (e) by alerting any person, will make it more difficult:

    (i) to prevent an act of terrorism; or

(ii) to secure the apprehension, prosecution or conviction of any person in connection with the commission, preparation or instigation of an act of terrorism.'

Section 58: Access to legal advice

(1) A person arrested and held in custody in a police station or other premises shall be entitled, if he so requests, to consult a solicitor privately at any time.

(2) Subject to sub-section (3) below, a request under sub-section (1) above and the time at which it was made shall be recorded in the custody record.

(3) Such a request need not be recorded in the custody record of a person who makes it at a time while he is at a court after being charged with an offence.

(4) If a person makes such a request, he must be permitted to consult a solicitor as soon as is practicable except to the extent that delay is permitted by this section.

(5) In any case he must be permitted to consult a solicitor within 36 hours from the relevant time, as defined in section 41(2) above.

(6) Delay in compliance with a request is only permitted:

(a) in the case of a person who is in police detention for a serious arrestable offence; and

(b) if an officer of at least the rank of superintendent authorises it.

(7) An officer may give an authorisation under sub-section (6) above orally or in writing but, if he gives it orally, he shall confirm it in writing as soon as is practicable.

(8) Subject to sub-section (8A) below an officer may only authorise delay where he has reasonable grounds for believing that the exercise of the right conferred by sub-section (1) above at the time when the person detained desires to exercise it:

(a) will lead to interference with or harm to evidence connected with a serious arrestable offence or interference with or physical injury to other persons; or

(b) will lead to the alerting of other persons suspected of having committed such an offence but not yet arrested for it; or

(c) will hinder the recovery of any property obtained as a result of such an offence.

(8A) An officer may also authorise delay where the serious arrestable offence is a drug trafficking offence or an offence to which Part VI of the Criminal Justice Act 1988 applies and the officer has reasonable grounds for believing:

(a) where the offence is a drug trafficking offence, that the detained person has benefited from drug trafficking and that the recovery of the value of that person's proceeds of drug trafficking will be hindered by the exercise of the right conferred by sub-section (1) above; and

(b) where the offence is one to which Part VI of the Criminal Justice Act 1988 applies, that the detained person has benefited from the offence and that the recovery of the value of the property obtained by that person from or in connection with the offence or of the pecuniary advantage derived by him from or in connection with it will be hindered by the exercise of the right conferred by sub-section (1) above.

(9) If delay is authorised:

(a) the detained person shall be told the reason for it; and

(b) the reason shall be noted on his custody record.

(10) The duties imposed by sub-section (9) above shall be performed as soon as is practicable.

(11) There may be no further delay in permitting the exercise of the right conferred by sub-section (1) above once the reason for authorising delay ceases to subsist.

(12) The reference in sub-section (1) above to a person arrested includes a reference to a person who has been detained under the terrorism provisions.

(13) In the application of this section to a person who has been arrested or detained under the terrorism provisions:

(a) sub-section (5) above shall have effect as if for the words from 'within' onwards there were substituted the words 'before the end of the period beyond which he may no longer be detained without the authority of the Secretary of State';

(b) sub-section (6)(a) above shall have effect as if for the words 'for a serious arrestable offence' there were substituted the words 'under the terrorism provisions'; and

(c) sub-section (8) above shall have effect as if at the end there were added 'or

(d) will lead to interference with the gathering of information about the commission, preparation or instigation of acts of terrorism; or

(e) by alerting any person, will make it more difficult:

(i) to prevent an act of terrorism; or

(ii) to secure the apprehension, prosecution or conviction of any person in connection with the commission, preparation or instigation of an act of terrorism.

(14) If an officer of appropriate rank has reasonable grounds for believing that, unless he gives a direction under sub-section (15) below, the exercise by a person arrested or detained under the terrorism provisions of the right conferred by sub-section (1) above will have any of the consequences specified in sub-section (8) above (as it has effect by virtue of sub-section (13) above), he may give a direction under that sub-section.

(15) A direction under this sub-section is a direction that a person desiring to exercise the right conferred by sub-section (1) above may only consult a solicitor in the sight and hearing of a qualified officer of the uniformed branch of the force of which the officer giving the direction is a member.

(16) An officer is qualified for the purpose of sub-section (15) above if:

  (a) he is of at least the rank of inspector; and

  (b) in the opinion of the officer giving the direction he has no connection with the case.

(17) An officer is of appropriate rank to give a direction under sub-section (15) above if he is of at least the rank of Commander or Assistant Chief Constable.

(18) A direction under sub-section (15) above shall cease to have effect once the reason for giving it ceases to subsist.

CRIME AND DISORDER ACT 1998

Section 65: Reprimands and warnings

(1) Sub-sections (2) to (5) below apply where:

  (a) a constable has evidence that a child or young person ('the offender') has committed an offence;

  (b) the constable considers that the evidence is such that, if the offender were prosecuted for the offence, there would be a realistic prospect of his being convicted;

  (c) the offender admits to the constable that he committed the offence;

  (d) the offender has not previously been convicted of an offence; and

  (e) the constable is satisfied that it would not be in the public interest for the offender to be prosecuted.

(2) Subject to sub-section (4) below, the constable may reprimand the offender if the offender has not previously been reprimanded or warned.

(3) The constable may warn the offender if:

  (a) the offender has not previously been warned; or

  (b) where the offender has previously been warned, the offence was committed more than two years after the date of the previous warning and the constable considers the offence to be not so serious as to require a charge to be brought,

  but no person may be warned under paragraph (b) above more than once.

(4) Where the offender has not been previously reprimanded, the constable shall warn rather than reprimand the offender if he considers the offence to be so serious as to require a warning.

(5) The constable shall:

  (a) give any reprimand or warning at a police station and, where the offender is under the age of 17, in the presence of an appropriate adult; and

  (c) explain to the offender and, where he is under that age, the appropriate adult in ordinary language:

(i) in the case of a reprimand, the effect of sub-section (5)(a) of section 66 below;

(ii) in the case of a warning, the effect of sub-sections (1),(2),(4) and (5)(b) and (c) of that section, and any guidance issued under sub-section (3) of that section.

(6) The Secretary of State shall publish, in such manner as he considers appropriate, guidance as to:

(a) the circumstances in which it is appropriate to give reprimands or warnings, including criteria for determining:

(i) for the purposes of sub-section (3)(b) above, whether an offence is not so serious as to require a charge to be brought; and

(ii) for the purposes of sub-section (4) above, whether an offence is so serious as to require a warning;

(b) the category of constable by whom reprimands and warnings may be given; and

(c) the form which reprimands and warnings are to take and the manner in which they are to be given and recorded.

(7) In this section 'appropriate adult', in relation to a child or young person, means:

(a) his parent or guardian or, if he is in the care of a local authority or voluntary organisation, a person representing that authority or organisation;

(b) a social worker of a local authority social services department;

(c) if no person falling within paragraph (a) or (b) above is available, any responsible person aged 18 or over who is not a police officer or a person employed by the police.

(8) No caution shall be given to a child or young person after the commencement of this section.

(9) Any reference (however expressed) in any enactment passed before or in the same Session as this Act to a person being cautioned shall be construed, in relation to any time after that commencement, as including a reference to a child or young person being reprimanded or warned.

CRIMINAL PROCEDURE AND INVESTIGATIONS ACT 1996

Section 1: Application of this Part

(1) This Part applies where:

(a) a person is charged with a summary offence in respect of which a court proceeds to summary trial and in respect of which he pleads not guilty;

(b) a person who has attained the age of 18 is charged with an offence which is triable either way, in respect of which a court proceeds to summary trial and in respect of which he pleads not guilty; or

(c) a person under the age of 18 is charged with an indictable offence in respect of which a court proceeds to summary trial and in respect of which he pleads not guilty.

(2) This Part also applies where:

(a) a person is charged with an indictable offence and he is committed for trial for the offence concerned;

(b) a person is charged with an indictable offence and proceedings for the trial of the person on the charge concerned are transferred to the Crown Court by virtue of a notice of transfer given under section 4 of the Criminal Justice Act 1987 (serious or complex fraud);

(c) a person is charged with an indictable offence and proceedings for the trial of the person on the charge concerned are transferred to the Crown Court by virtue of a notice of transfer served on a magistrates' court under section 53 of the Criminal Justice Act 1991 (certain cases involving children);

(d) a count charging a person with a summary offence is included in an indictment under the authority of section 40 of the Criminal Justice Act 1988 (common assault, etc); or

(e) a bill of indictment charging a person with an indictable offence is preferred under the authority of section 2(2)(b) of the Administration of Justice (Miscellaneous Provisions) Act 1933 (bill preferred by direction of Court of Appeal, or by direction or with consent of a judge).

...

Section 2: General interpretation

(1) References to the accused are to the person mentioned in section 1(1) or (2).

(2) Where there is more than one accused in any proceedings this Part applies separately in relation to each of the accused.

(3) References to the prosecutor are to any person acting as prosecutor, whether an individual or a body.

(4) References to material are to material of all kinds, and in particular include references to:

(a) information; and

(b) objects of all descriptions.

(5) References to recording information are to putting it in a durable or retrievable form (such as writing or tape).

(6) This section applies for the purposes of this Part.

Section 3: Primary disclosure by prosecutor

(1) The prosecutor must:

(a) disclose to the accused any prosecution material which has not previously been disclosed to the accused and which in the prosecutor's opinion might undermine the case for the prosecution against the accused; or

(b) give to the accused a written statement that there is no material of a description mentioned in paragraph (a).

(2) For the purposes of this section prosecution material is material:

(a) which is in the prosecutor's possession, and came into his possession in connection with the case for the prosecution against the accused; or

(b) which, in pursuance of a code operative under Part II, he has inspected in connection with the case for the prosecution against the accused.

(3) Where material consists of information which has been recorded in any form the prosecutor discloses it for the purposes of this section:

(a) by securing that a copy is made of it and that the copy is given to the accused; or

(b) if in the prosecutor's opinion that is not practicable or desirable, by allowing the accused to inspect it at a reasonable time and a reasonable place or by taking steps to secure that he is allowed to do so,

and a copy may be in such form as the prosecutor thinks fit and need not be in the same form as that in which the information has already been recorded.

(4) Where material consists of information which has not been recorded the prosecutor discloses it for the purposes of this section by securing that it is recorded in such form as he thinks fit and:

(a) by securing that a copy is made of it and that the copy is given to the accused; or

(b) if in the prosecutor's opinion that is not practicable or not desirable, by allowing the accused to inspect it at a reasonable time and a reasonable place or by taking steps to secure that he is allowed to do so.

(5) Where material does not consist of information the prosecutor discloses it for the purposes of this section by allowing the accused to inspect it at a reasonable time and a reasonable place or by taking steps to secure that he is allowed to do so.

(6) Material must not be disclosed under this section to the extent that the court, on an application by the prosecutor,[5] concludes that it is not in the public interest to disclose it and orders accordingly.

(7) Material must not be disclosed under this section to the extent that:

(a) it has been intercepted in obedience to a warrant issued under section 2 of the Interception of Communications Act 1985; or

(b) it indicates that such a warrant has been issued or that material has been intercepted in obedience to such a warrant.

---

5   See the Crown Court (Criminal Procedure and Investigations Act 1996) (Disclosure) Rules 1997 SI 1997/698 and the Magistrates' Courts (Criminal Procedure and Investigations Act 1996) (Disclosure) Rules 1997 SI 1997/703.

(8) The prosecutor must act under this section during the period which, by virtue of section 12, is the relevant period for this section.

...

Section 5: Compulsory disclosure by accused

(1) Subject to sub-section (2) to (4), this section applies where:

(a) this Part applies by virtue of section 1(2); and

(b) the prosecutor complies with section 3 or purports to comply with it.

(2) Where this Part applies by virtue of section 1(2)(b), this section does not apply unless:

(a) a copy of the notice of transfer; and

(b) copies of the documents containing the evidence,

have been given to the accused under regulations made under section 5(9) of the Criminal Justice Act 1987.

(3) Where this Part applies by virtue of section 1(2)(c), this section does not apply unless:

(a) a copy of the notice of transfer; and

(b) copies of the documents containing the evidence,

have been given to the accused under regulations made under paragraph 4 of Schedule 6 to the Criminal Justice Act 1991.

(4) Where this Part applies by virtue of section 1(2)(e), this section does not apply unless the prosecutor has served on the accused a copy of the indictment and a copy of the set of documents containing the evidence which is the basis of the charge.

(5) Where this section applies, the accused must give a defence statement to the court and the prosecutor.

(6) For the purposes of this section a defence statement is a written statement:

(a) setting out in general terms the nature of the accused's defence;

(b) indicating the matters on which he takes issue with the prosecution; and

(c) setting out, in the case of each such matter, the reason why he takes issue with the prosecution.

(7) If the defence statement discloses an alibi the accused must give particulars of the alibi in the statement, including:

(a) the name and address of any witness the accused believes is able to give evidence in support of the alibi, if the name and address are known to the accused when the statement is given;

(b) any information in the accused's possession which might be of material assistance in finding any such witness, if his name or address is not known to the accused when the statement is given.

(8) For the purposes of this section evidence in support of an alibi is evidence tending to show that by reason of the presence of the accused at a particular place or in a particular area at a particular time he was not, or was unlikely to have been, at the place where the offence is alleged to have been committed at the time of its alleged commission.

(9) The accused must give a defence statement under this section during the period which, by virtue of section 12, is the relevant period for this section.[6]

Section 6: Voluntary disclosure by accused

(1) This section applies where:

    (a) this Part applies by virtue of section 1(1); and

    (b) the prosecutor complies with section 3 or purports to comply with it.

(2) The accused:

    (a) may give a defence statement to the prosecutor; and

    (b) if he does so, must also give such a statement to the court.

(3) Sub-sections (6) to (8) of section 5 apply for the purposes of this section as they apply for the purposes of that.

(4) If the accused gives a defence statement under this section he must give it during the period which, by virtue of section 12, is the relevant period for this section.[7]

Section 7: Secondary disclosure by prosecutor

(1) This section applies where the accused gives a defence statement under section 5 or 6.

(2) The prosecutor must:

    (a) disclose to the accused any prosecution material which has not previously been disclosed to the accused and which might be reasonably expected to assist the accused's defence as disclosed by the defence statement given under section 5 or 6; or

    (b) give to the accused a written statement that there is no material of a description mentioned in paragraph (a).

(3) For the purposes of this section prosecution material is material:

    (a) which is in the prosecutor's possession, and came into his possession in connection with the case for the prosecution against the accused; or

    (b) which, in pursuance of a code operative under Part II, he has inspected in connection with the case for the prosecution against the accused.

---

6   See the Criminal Procedure and Investigations Act 1996 (Defence Disclosure Time Limits) Regulations 1997 (SI 1997/684).

7   *Ibid.*

(4) Sub-sections (3) to (5) of section 3 (method by which prosecutor discloses) apply for the purposes of this section as they apply for the purposes of that.

(5) Material must not be disclosed under this section to the extent that the court, on an application by the prosecutor,[8] concludes that it is not in the public interest to disclose it and orders accordingly.

(6) Material must not be disclosed under this section to the extent that:

(a) it has been intercepted in obedience to a warrant issued under section 2 of the Interception of Communications Act 1985; or

(b) it indicates that such a warrant has been issued or that material has been intercepted in obedience to such a warrant.

(7) The prosecutor must act under this section during the period which, by virtue of section 12, is the relevant period for this section.

Section 8: Application by accused for disclosure

(1) This section applies where the accused gives a defence statement under section 5 or 6 and the prosecutor complies with section 7 or purports to comply with it or fails to comply with it.

(2) If the accused has at any time reasonable cause to believe that:

(a) there is prosecution material which might be reasonably expected to assist the accused's defence as disclosed by the defence statement given under section 5 or 6; and

(b) the material has not been disclosed to the accused,

the accused may apply to the court for an order requiring the prosecutor to disclose such material to the accused.

(3) For the purposes of this section prosecution material is material:

(a) which is in the prosecutor's possession, and came into his possession in connection with the case for the prosecution against the accused;

(b) which, in pursuance of a code operative under Part II, he has inspected in connection with the case for the prosecution against the accused; or

(c) which falls within sub-section (4).

(4) Material falls within this sub-section if in pursuance of a code operative under Part II the prosecutor must, if he asks for the material, be given a copy of it or be allowed to inspect it in connection with the case for the prosecution against the accused.

(5) Material must not be disclosed under this section to the extent that the court, on an application by the prosecutor,[9] concludes that it is not in the public interest to disclose it and orders accordingly.

---

8   See the Crown Court (Criminal Procedure and Investigations Act 1996) (Disclosure) Rules 1997 SI 1997/698 and the Magistrates' Courts (Criminal Procedure and Investigations Act 1996) (Disclosure) Rules 1997 SI 1997/703.

9   *Ibid.*

(6) Material must not be disclosed under this section to the extent that:

    (a) it has been intercepted in obedience to a warrant issued under section 2 of the Interception of Communications Act 1985; or

    (b) it indicates that such a warrant has been issued or that material has been intercepted in obedience to such a warrant.

Section 9: Continuing duty of prosecutor to disclose

(1) Sub-section (2) applies at all times:

    (a) after the prosecutor complies with section 3 or purports to comply with it; and

    (b) before the accused is acquitted or convicted or the prosecutor decides not to proceed with the case concerned.

(2) The prosecutor must keep under review the question whether at any given time there is prosecution material which:

    (a) in his opinion might undermine the case for the prosecution against the accused; and

    (b) has not been disclosed to the accused,

and if there is such material at any time the prosecutor must disclose it to the accused as soon as is reasonably practicable.

(3) In applying sub-section (2) by reference to any given time the state of affairs at that time (including the case for the prosecution as it stands at that time) must be taken into account.

(4) Sub-section (5) applies at all times:

    (a) after the prosecutor complies with section 7 or purports to comply with it; and

    (b) before the accused is acquitted or convicted or the prosecutor decides not to proceed with the case concerned.

(5) The prosecutor must keep under review the question whether at any given time there is prosecution material which:

    (a) might be reasonably expected to assist the accused's defence as disclosed by the defence statement given under section 5 or 6; and

    (b) has not been disclosed to the accused,

and if there is such material at any time the prosecutor must disclose it to the accused as soon as is reasonably practicable.

(6) For the purposes of this section prosecution material is material:

    (a) which is in the prosecutor's possession, and came into his possession in connection with the case for the prosecution against the accused; or

    (b) which, in pursuance of a code operative under Part II, he has inspected in connection with the case for the prosecution against the accused.

(7) Sub-sections (3) to (5) of section 3 (method by which prosecutor discloses) apply for the purposes of this section as they apply for the purposes of that.

(8) Material must not be disclosed under this section to the extent that the court, on an application by the prosecutor,[10] concludes that it is not in the public interest to disclose it and orders accordingly.

(9) Material must not be disclosed under this section to the extent that:

(a) it has been intercepted in obedience to a warrant issued under section 2 of the Interception of Communications Act 1985; or

(b) it indicates that such a warrant has been issued or that material has been intercepted in obedience to such a warrant.

Section 10: Prosecutor's failure to observe time limits

(1) This section applies if the prosecutor:

(a) purports to act under section 3 after the end of the period which, by virtue of section 12, is the relevant period for section 3; or

(b) purports to act under section 7 after the end of the period which, by virtue of section 12, is the relevant period for section 7.

(2) Subject to sub-section (3), the failure to act during the period concerned does not on its own constitute grounds for staying proceedings for abuse of process.

(3) Sub-section (2) does not prevent the failure constituting such grounds if it involves such delay by the prosecutor that the accused is denied a fair trial.

Section 11: Faults in disclosure by accused

(1) This section applies where section 5 applies and the accused:

(a) fails to give a defence statement under that section;

(b) gives a defence statement under that section but does so after the end of the period which, by virtue of section 12, is the relevant period for section 5;

(c) sets out inconsistent defences in a defence statement given under section 5;

(d) at his trial puts forward a defence which is different from any defence set out in a defence statement under section 5;

(e) at his trial adduces evidence in support of an alibi without having given particulars of the alibi in a defence statement given under section 5; or

(f) at his trial calls a witness to give evidence in support of an alibi without having complied with sub-section (7)(a) or (b) of section 5 as regards the witness in giving a defence statement under that section.

---

10 See the Crown Court (Criminal Procedure and Investigations Act 1996) (Disclosure) Rules 1997 SI 1997/698 and the Magistrates' Courts (Criminal Procedure and Investigations Act 1996) (Disclosure) Rules 1997 SI 1997/703.

(2) This section also applies where section 6 applies, the accused gives a defence statement under that section, and the accused:

    (a) gives the statement after the end of the period which, by virtue of section 12, is the relevant period for section 6;

    (b) sets out inconsistent defences in the statement;

    (c) at his trial puts forward a defence which is different from any defence set out in the statement;

    (d) at his trial adduces evidence in support of an alibi without having given particulars of the alibi in the statement; or

    (e) at his trial calls a witness to give evidence in support of an alibi without having complied with sub-section (7)(a) or (b) of section 5 (as applied by section 6) as regards the witness in giving the statement.

(3) Where this section applies:

    (a) the court or, with the leave of the court, any other party may make such comment as appears appropriate;

    (b) the court or jury may draw such inferences as appear proper in deciding whether the accused is guilty of the offence concerned.

(4) Where the accused puts forward a defence which is different from any defence set out in a defence statement given under section 5 or 6, in doing anything under sub-section (3) or in deciding whether to do anything under it the court shall have regard:

    (a) to the extent of the difference in the defences; and

    (b) to whether there is any justification for it.

(5) A person shall not be convicted of an offence solely on an inference drawn under sub-section (3).

(6) Any reference in this section to evidence in support of an alibi shall be construed in accordance with section 5.

Section 14: Public interest – review for summary trials

(1) This section applies where this Part applies by virtue of section 1(1).

(2) At any time:

    (a) after a court makes an order under section 3(6), 7(5), 8(5) or 9(8); and

    (b) before the accused is acquitted or convicted or the prosecutor decides not to proceed with the case concerned,

the accused may apply to the court for a review of the question whether it is still not in the public interest to disclose the material affected by its order.

(3) In such a case the court must review that question, and if it concludes that it is in the public interest to disclose material to any extent:

    (a) it shall so order; and

    (b) it shall take such steps as are reasonable to inform the prosecutor of its order.

(4) Where the prosecutor is informed of an order made under sub-section (3) he must act accordingly having regard to the provisions of this Part (unless he decides not to proceed with the case concerned).

Section 15: Public interest – review in other cases

(1) This section applies where this Part applies by virtue of section 1(2) [Crown Court trials].

(2) This section applies at all times:

(a) after a court makes an order under sections 3(6), 7(5), 8(5) or 9(8); and

(b) before the accused is acquitted or convicted or the prosecutor decides not to proceed with the case concerned.

(3) The court must keep under review the question whether at any given time it is still not in the public interest to disclose material affected by its order.

(4) The court must keep the question mentioned in sub-section (3) under review without the need for an application; but the accused may apply to the court for a review of that question.

(5) If the court at any time concludes that it is in the public interest to disclose material to any extent:

(a) it shall so order; and

(b) it shall take such steps as are reasonable to inform the prosecutor of its order.

(6) Where the prosecutor is informed of an order made under sub-section (5) he must act accordingly having regard to the provisions of this Part (unless he decides not to proceed with the case concerned).

...

OTHER MATERIALS

CODE FOR CROWN PROSECUTORS

3 Review

3.1 Proceedings are usually started by the police. Sometimes, they may consult the Crown Prosecution Service before charging a defendant. Each case that the police send to the Crown Prosecution Service is reviewed by a Crown Prosecutor to make sure that it meets the tests set out in this Code. Crown Prosecutors may decide to continue with the original charges, to change the charges or sometimes to stop the proceedings.

3.2 Review, however, is a continuing process so that Crown Prosecutors can take into account any change in circumstances. Wherever possible, they talk to the police first if they are thinking about changing the charges or stopping the proceedings. This gives the police the chance to provide more information that may affect the decision. The Crown Prosecution Service and the police work closely together to reach the right decision, but the final responsibility for the decision rests with the Crown Prosecution Service.

4   The Code tests

4.1 There are two stages in the decision to prosecute. The first stage is the evidential test. If the case does not pass the evidential test, it must not go ahead, no matter how important or serious it may be. If the case does pass the evidential test, Crown Prosecutors must decide if a prosecution is needed in the public interest.

4.2 This second stage is the public interest test. The Crown Prosecution Service will only start or continue a prosecution when the case has passed both tests. The evidential test is explained in section 5 and the public interest test is explained in section 6.

5   The evidential test

5.1 Crown Prosecutors must be satisfied that there is enough evidence to provide a 'realistic prospect of conviction' against each defendant on each charge. They must consider what the defence case may be and how that is likely to affect the prosecution case.

5.2 A realistic prospect of conviction is an objective test. It means that a jury or bench of magistrates, properly directed in accordance with the law, is more likely than not to convict the defendant of the charge alleged.

5.3 When deciding whether there is enough evidence to prosecute, Crown Prosecutors must consider whether the evidence can be used and is reliable. There will be many cases in which the evidence does not give any cause for concern. But there will also be cases in which the evidence may not be as strong as it first appears. Crown Prosecutors must ask themselves the following questions:

Can the evidence be used in court?

(a)   Is it likely that the evidence will be excluded by the court? There are certain legal rules which might mean that evidence which seems relevant cannot be given at a trial. For example, is it likely that the evidence will be excluded because of the way in which it was gathered or because of the rule against using hearsay as evidence? If so, is there enough other evidence for a realistic prospect of conviction?

Is the evidence reliable?

(b) Is it likely that a confession is unreliable, for example, because of the defendant's age, intelligence or lack of understanding?

(c) Is the witness's background likely to weaken the prosecution case? For example, does the witness have any dubious motive that may affect his or her attitude to the case or a relevant previous conviction?

(d) If the identity of the defendant is likely to be questioned, is the evidence about this strong enough?

5.4 Crown Prosecutors should not ignore evidence because they are not sure that it can be used or is reliable. But they should look closely at it when deciding if there is a realistic prospect of conviction.

6 The public interest test

6.1 In 1951, Lord Shawcross, who was Attorney General made the classic statement on public interest, which has been supported by Attorneys General ever since: 'It has never been the rule in this country – I hope it never will be – that suspected criminal offences must automatically be the subject of prosecution' (House of Commons Debates, volume 483, column 681, 29 January 1951).

6.2 The public interest must be considered in each case where there is enough evidence to provide a realistic prospect of conviction. In cases of any seriousness, a prosecution will usually take place unless there are public interest factors tending against prosecution which clearly outweigh those tending in favour. Although there may be public interest factors against prosecution in a particular case, often the prosecution should go ahead and those factors should be put to the court for consideration when sentence is being passed.

6.3 Crown Prosecutors must balance factors for and against prosecution carefully and fairly. Public interest factors that can affect the decision to prosecute usually depend on the seriousness of the offence or the circumstances of the offender. Some factors may increase the need to prosecute but others may suggest that another course of action would be better.

The following list of some common public interest factors, both for and against prosecution, are not exhaustive. The factors that apply will depend on the facts in each case.

Some common public interest factors in favour of prosecution

6.4 The more serious the offence, the more likely it is that a prosecution will be needed in the public interest. A prosecution is likely to be needed if:

    (a)   a conviction is likely to result in a significant sentence;

    (b)   a weapon was used or violence was threatened during the commission of the offence;

    (c)   the offence was committed against a person serving the public (for example, a police or prison officer, or a nurse);

    (d)   the defendant was in a position of authority or trust;

    (e)   the evidence shows that the defendant was a ringleader or an organiser of the offence;

    (f)   there is evidence that the offence was premeditated;

    (g)   there is evidence that the offence was carried out by a group;

    (h)   the victim of the offence was vulnerable, has been put in considerable fear, or suffered personal attack, damage or disturbance;

    (i)   the offence was motivated by any form of discrimination against the victim's ethnic or national origin, sex, religious beliefs, political views or sexual preference;

    (j)   there is a marked difference between the actual or mental ages of the defendant and the victim, or if there is any element of corruption;

    (k)   the defendant's previous convictions or cautions are relevant to the present offence;

    (l)   the defendant is alleged to have committed the offence whilst under an order of the court;

    (m) there are grounds for believing that the offence is likely to be continued or repeated, for example, by a history of recurring conduct; or

    (n)   the offence, although not serious is itself, is widespread in the area where it was committed.

Some common interest public interest factors against prosecution

6.5 A prosecution is less likely to be needed if:

    (a)   the court is likely to impose a very small or nominal penalty;

    (b)   the offence was committed as a result of a genuine mistake or misunderstanding (these factors must be balanced against the seriousness of the offence);

    (c)   the loss or harm can be described as minor and was the result of a single incident, particularly if it was caused by a misjudgment;

(d)   there has been a long delay between the offence taking place and the date of the trial, unless:

- the offence is serious;

- the delay has been caused in part by the defendant;

- the offence has only recently come to light; or

- the complexity of the offence has meant that there has been a long investigation;

(e)   a prosecution is likely to have a very bad effect on the victim's physical or mental health, always bearing in mind the seriousness of the offence;

(f)   the defendant is elderly or is, or was at the time of the offence, suffering from significant mental or physical ill health, unless the offence is serious or there is a real possibility that it may be repeated. The Crown Prosecution Service, where necessary applies Home Office guidelines about how to deal with mentally disordered offenders. Crown Prosecutors must balance the desirability of diverting a defendant who is suffering from significant mental or physical ill health with the need to safeguard the general public;

(g)   the defendant has put right the loss or harm that was caused (but defendants must not avoid prosecution simply because they can pay compensation); or

(h)   details may be made public that could harm sources of information, international relations or national security.

6.6. Deciding on the public interest is not simply a matter of adding up the number of factors on each side. Crown Prosecutors must decide how important each factor is in the circumstances of each case and go on to make an overall assessment.

The relationship between the victim and the public interest

6.7 The Crown Prosecution Service acts in the public interest, not just in the interests of any one individual. But Crown Prosecutors must always think very carefully about the interests of the victim, which are an important factor, when deciding where the public interest lies.

Youth offenders

6.8 Crown Prosecutors must consider the interests of a youth when deciding whether it is in the public interest to prosecute. The stigma of a conviction can cause very serious harm to the prospects of a youth offender or a young adult. Young offenders can sometimes be dealt with without going to court. But Crown Prosecutors should not avoid prosecuting simply because of the defendant's age. The seriousness of the offence or the offender's past behaviour may make prosecution necessary.

Police cautions

6.9 The police make the decision to caution an offender in accordance with Home Office guidelines. If the defendant admits the offence, cautioning is the most common alternative to a court appearance. Crown Prosecutors, where necessary, apply the same guidelines and should look at the alternatives to prosecution when they consider the public interest. Crown Prosecutors should tell the police if they think that a caution would be more suitable than a prosecution.

7 Charges

7.1 Crown Prosecutors should select charges which:

    (a)   reflect the seriousness of the offending;

    (b)   give the court adequate sentencing powers; and

    (c)   enable the case to be presented in a clear and simple way.

This means that Crown Prosecutors may not always continue with the most serious charge where there is a choice. Further, Crown Prosecutors should not continue with more charges than are necessary.

7.2 Crown Prosecutors should never go ahead with more charges than are necessary just to encourage a defendant to plead guilty to a few. In the same way, they should never go ahead with a more serious charge just to encourage a defendant to plead guilty to a less serious one.

7.3 Crown Prosecutors should not change the charge simply because of the decision made by the court or the defendant about where the case will be heard.

8 Mode of trial

8.1 The Crown Prosecution Service applies the current guidelines for magistrates who have to decide whether cases should be tried in the Crown Court when the offence gives the option. (See the 'National Mode of Trial Guidelines' issued by the Lord Chief Justice.) Crown Prosecutors should recommend Crown Court trial when they are satisfied that the guidelines require them to do so.

8.2 Speed must never be the only reason for asking for a case to stay in the magistrates' courts. But Crown Prosecutors should consider the effect of any likely delay if they send a case to the Crown Court, and any possible stress on victims and witnesses if the case is delayed.

9 Accepting guilty pleas

9.1 Defendants may want to plead guilty to some, but not all, of the charges. Or they may want to plead guilty to a different, possibly less serious, charge because they are admitting only part of the crime. Crown Prosecutors should only accept the defendant's plea if they think the court is able to pass a sentence that matches the seriousness of the offending. Crown Prosecutors must never accept a guilty plea just because it is convenient.

10 Restarting a prosecution

10.1 People should be able to rely on decisions taken by the Crown Prosecution Service. Normally, if the Crown Prosecution Service tells a suspect or defendant that there will not be a prosecution, or that the prosecution has been stopped, that is the end of the matter and the case will not start again. But occasionally there are special reasons why the Crown Prosecution Service will restart the prosecution, particularly if the case is serious.

10.2 These reasons include:

  (a) rare cases where a new look at the original decision shows that it was clearly wrong and should not be allowed to stand;

  (b) cases which are stopped so that more evidence which is likely to become available in the fairly near future can be collected and prepared. In these cases, the Crown Prosecutor will tell the defendant that the prosecution may well start again;

  (c) cases which are stopped because of a lack of evidence but where more significant evidence is discovered later.

      ...

HUMAN RIGHTS ACT 1998

[The provisions of the European Convention on Human Rights that have effect under the Act are set out in Sched 1. Those that are relevant to criminal litigation and sentencing are set out below.]

Schedule 1

THE ARTICLES

THE CONVENTION

RIGHTS AND FREEDOMS

Article 2: Right to life

1   Everyone's right to life shall be protected by law. No one shall be deprived of his life intentionally save in the execution of a sentence of a court following his conviction of a crime for which this penalty is provided by law.

2   Deprivation of life shall not be regarded as inflicted in contravention of this Article when it results from the use of force which is no more than absolutely necessary:

(a) in defence of any person from unlawful violence;

(b) in order to effect a lawful arrest or to prevent the escape of a person lawfully detained;

(c) in action lawfully taken for the purpose of quelling a riot or insurrection.

Article 3: Prohibition of torture

No one shall be subjected to torture or to inhuman or degrading treatment or punishment.

Article 4: Prohibition of slavery and forced labour

1   No one shall be held in slavery or servitude.

2   No one shall be required to perform forced or compulsory labour.

3   For the purpose of this Article the term 'forced or compulsory labour' shall not include:

(a) any work required to be done in the ordinary course of detention imposed according to the provisions of Article 5 of this Convention or during conditional release from such detention;

(b) any service of a military character or, in case of conscientious objectors in countries where they are recognised, service exacted instead of compulsory military service;

(c) any service exacted in case of an emergency or calamity threatening the life or well-being of the community;

(d) any work or service which forms part of normal civic obligations.

Article 5: Right to liberty and security

1   Everyone has the right to liberty and security of person. No one shall be deprived of his liberty save in the following cases and in accordance with a procedure prescribed by law:

(a) the lawful detention of a person after conviction by a competent court;

(b) the lawful arrest or detention of a person for non-compliance with the lawful order of a court or in order to secure the fulfilment of any obligation prescribed by law;

(c) the lawful arrest or detention of a person effected for the purpose of bringing him before the competent legal authority on reasonable suspicion of having committed an offence or when it is reasonably considered necessary to prevent his committing an offence or fleeing after having done so;

(d) the detention of a minor by lawful order for the purpose of educational supervision or his lawful detention for the purpose of bringing him before the competent legal authority;

(e) the lawful detention of persons for the prevention of the spreading of infectious diseases, of persons of unsound mind, alcoholics or drug addicts or vagrants;

(f) the lawful arrest or detention of a person to prevent his effecting an unauthorised entry into the country or of a person against whom action is being taken with a view to deportation or extradition.

2   Everyone who is arrested shall be informed promptly, in a language which he understands, of the reasons for his arrest and of any charge against him.

3   Everyone arrested or detained in accordance with the provisions of paragraph 1(c) of this Article shall be brought promptly before a judge or other officer authorised by law to exercise judicial power and shall be entitled to trial within a reasonable time or to release pending trial. Release may be conditioned by guarantees to appear for trial.

4   Everyone who is deprived of his liberty by arrest or detention shall be entitled to take proceedings by which the lawfulness of his detention shall be decided speedily by a court and his release ordered if the detention is not lawful.

5   Everyone who has been the victim of arrest or detention in contravention of the provisions of this Article shall have an enforceable right to compensation.

Article 6: Right to a fair trial

1   In the determination of his civil rights and obligations or of any criminal charge against him, everyone is entitled to a fair and public hearing within a reasonable time by an independent and impartial tribunal established by law. Judgment shall be pronounced publicly but the press and public may be excluded from all or part of the trial in the interest of morals, public order or national security in a democratic society, where the interests of juveniles or the protection of the private life of the parties so require, or to the extent strictly necessary in the opinion of the court in special circumstances where publicity would prejudice the interests of justice.

2   Everyone charged with a criminal offence shall be presumed innocent until proved guilty according to law.

3   Everyone charged with a criminal offence has the following minimum rights:

(a) to be informed promptly, in a language which he understands and in detail, of the nature and cause of the accusation against him;

(b) to have adequate time and facilities for the preparation of his defence;

(c) to defend himself in person or through legal assistance of his own choosing or, if he has not sufficient means to pay for legal assistance, to be given it free when the interests of justice so require;

(d) to examine or have examined witnesses against him and to obtain the attendance and examination of witnesses on his behalf under the same conditions as witnesses against him;

(e) to have the free assistance of an interpreter if he cannot understand or speak the language used in court.

Article 7: No punishment without law

1   No one shall be held guilty of any criminal offence on account of any act or omission which did not constitute a criminal offence under national or international law at the time when it was committed. Nor shall a heavier penalty be imposed than the one that was applicable at the time the criminal offence was committed.

2   This Article shall not prejudice the trial and punishment of any person for any act or omission which, at the time when it was committed, was criminal according to the general principles of law recognised by civilised nations.

Article 8: Right to respect for private and family life

1   Everyone has the right to respect for his private and family life, his home and his correspondence.

2   There shall be no interference by a public authority with the exercise of this right except such as is in accordance with the law and is necessary in a

democratic society in the interests of national security, public safety or the economic well being of the country, for the prevention of disorder or crime, for the protection of health or morals, or for the protection of the rights and freedoms of others.

Article 9: Freedom of thought, conscience and religion

1   Everyone has the right to freedom of thought, conscience and religion; this right includes freedom to change his religion or belief and freedom, either alone or in community with others and in public or private, to manifest his religion or belief, in worship, teaching, practice and observance.

2   Freedom to manifest one's religion or beliefs shall be subject only to such limitations as are prescribed by law and are necessary in a democratic society in the interests of public safety, for the protection of public order, health or morals, or for the protection of the rights and freedoms of others.

Article 10: Freedom of expression

1   Everyone has the right to freedom of expression. This right shall include freedom to hold opinions and to receive and impart information and ideas without interference by public authority and regardless of frontiers. This Article shall not prevent States from requiring the licensing of broadcasting, television or cinema enterprises.

2   The exercise of these freedoms, since it carries with it duties and responsibilities, may be subject to such formalities, conditions, restrictions or penalties as are prescribed by law and are necessary in a democratic society, in the interests of national security, territorial integrity or public safety, for the prevention of disorder or crime, for the protection of health or morals, for the protection of the reputation or rights of others, for preventing the disclosure of information received in confidence, or for maintaining the authority and impartiality of the judiciary.

Article 11: Freedom of assembly and association

1   Everyone has the right to freedom of peaceful assembly and to freedom of association with others, including the right to form and to join trade unions for the protection of his interests.

2   No restrictions shall be placed on the exercise of these rights other than such as are prescribed by law and are necessary in a democratic society in the interests of national security or public safety, for the prevention of disorder or crime, for the protection of health or morals or for the protection of the rights and freedoms of others. This Article shall not prevent the imposition of lawful restrictions on the exercise of these rights by members of the armed forces, of the police or of the administration of the State.

Article 14: Prohibition of discrimination

The enjoyment of the rights and freedoms set forth in this Convention shall be secured without discrimination on any ground such as sex, race, colour, language, religion, political or other opinion, national or social origin, association with a national minority, property, birth or other status.

Article 18: Limitation on use of restrictions on rights

The restrictions permitted under this Convention to the said rights and freedoms shall not be applied for any purpose other than those for which they have been prescribed.

CHAPTER 2

BAIL

2.1   INTRODUCTION

In this chapter, we see what happens at the defendant's first court appearance and the subsequent adjournments before the case is ready to proceed to its next stage. In particular, we examine the principles which govern whether the defendant should be held in custody or granted bail prior to the trial.

2.2   ADJOURNMENTS

Adjournments are often necessary to enable the defendant to instruct solicitors or to give the prosecution a chance to prepare advance information or committal statements (see below). At each adjournment, the defendant is told the next date upon which he must attend court.

The granting of an adjournment is a matter for the court's discretion, but the rules of natural justice require that both sides should be allowed to prepare and present their cases properly (*R v Thames Magistrates' Court ex p Polemis* [1974] 1 WLR 1371; [1974] 2 All ER 1219).

In *R v Kingston-upon-Thames Justices ex p Martin* [1994] Imm AR 172, it was said that the following factors should be taken into account in deciding whether or not to grant an adjournment: the importance of the proceedings, the likely adverse consequences for the person seeking the adjournment, the risk of prejudice if the application is not granted, the convenience of the court and the interests of justice in ensuring that cases are dealt with efficiently, and the extent to which the applicant has been responsible for the circumstances which have led to the application for an adjournment.

In *R v Sunderland Justices ex p Dryden* (1994) *The Times*, 18 May, it was held that, where a defendant applied for an adjournment in order to obtain expert evidence, the magistrates could not refuse that application on the ground that the expert called by the prosecution was independent.

In *R v Highbury Juvenile Court ex p DPP* [1993] COD 390, the case had been adjourned three times. On the next occasion the case was listed, a prosecution witness failed to attend. The defendant argued that his recollection of the events leading up to the charge was becoming dim and that the case should be dismissed. The magistrates refused a prosecution application for an adjournment and, as the prosecution were unable to call any evidence, dismissed the case. It was held by the Divisional Court (rather surprisingly) that the magistrates had acted perversely in refusing a fourth adjournment. However, in view of the delay, the Divisional Court took no action and so the acquittal stood.

It is common for there to be several adjournments before the prosecution and the defence are ready to proceed with the case. An adjournment is only refused if the court takes the view that the party requesting the adjournment *should* be in a position to proceed now.

2.3   REMANDS: PROCEDURE IN COURT

Where a defendant is before the court because he has been arrested and charged, an adjournment is called a remand.

The remand may be in custody or on bail. This is governed by the Bail Act 1976 (see 2.4 below).

It is usually the Crown Prosecution Service who make the formal application for the adjournment (although there is no reason why it could not be the defence, if the prosecution are ready to proceed but the defence are not).

The Crown Prosecution Service representative is asked by the court if there are any objections to bail and, if so, to summarise them. The objections are based on a form in the Crown Prosecution Service file which has been filled in by the police. A list of the defendant's previous convictions (if any) will also be handed to the court.

There is no requirement for formal evidence of the matters which give rise to the objections to bail to be given (*R v Mansfield Justices ex p Sharkey* [1985] QB 613; [1985] 1 All ER 19). The Crown Prosecution Service objections to bail are simply given by the Crown Prosecution Service representative in court; a police officer will not give evidence.

The defendant may then make an application for bail. The defence will try to show that the prosecution objections are ill founded or that the objections can be met by the imposition of conditions.

In *R v Isleworth Crown Court ex p Commissioner of Customs and Excise* [1990] Crim LR 859, it was said that the prosecution have a right to reply to the defence submissions if this is necessary to correct alleged mis-statements of fact in what the defence have said.

The court then comes to a decision. If bail is refused, the court must say why. The reason(s) must be based on the grounds for withholding bail set out in the Bail Act (see 2.4 below) and must be recorded in a certificate which is handed to the defendant.

Rule 4(1), (2) of the Justices' Clerks Rules 1970 provides that a clerk has the power to further adjourn proceedings with the consent of the prosecutor and of the accused if:

(a) the accused is not on already bail (because the proceedings were commenced by the laying of an information and the issue of a summons); or

(b) the accused is on bail and is remanded (by the clerk) on bail on the same terms and conditions as before.

Rule 4(3), (4) of the Justices' Clerks Rules 1970 enables the clerk to further adjourn proceedings where there is no objection from the prosecutor and the accused, having been remanded on bail on a previous occasion, is remanded (by the clerk) on the same terms and conditions in his absence.

2.4 BAIL ACT 1976

Section 4 of the Bail Act 1976 creates a presumption in favour of bail prior to conviction. This presumption also applies after conviction, but only where the case is adjourned for pre-sentence reports.

Where s 4 does not apply (for example, when the defendant appeals against conviction or sentence or where the defendant is committed for sentence following summary conviction of an either way offence, see Chapter 3), the court nevertheless has a discretion to grant bail.

2.4.1 Imprisonable offences

If the defendant is charged with (or has been convicted of) an offence which is punishable with imprisonment, the presumption in favour of bail may be rebutted if the court finds that one or more of the grounds for withholding bail set out in the paragraphs which comprise Sched 1, Pt I of the Bail Act applies. Those grounds are:

- under para 2, that the court is satisfied that there are substantial grounds for believing that the defendant will:
  (i) fail to surrender to custody; or
  (ii) commit offence(s) while on bail; or
  (iii) interfere with witnesses or otherwise obstruct the course of justice in relation to himself or someone else; or
- under para 3, that the court is satisfied that the defendant should be kept in custody for his own protection (or welfare if a juvenile); or
- under para 4, that the defendant is already serving a custodial sentence; or
- under para 5, that the court is satisfied that lack of time since the commencements of proceedings means that it has been impracticable to obtain the information needed to decide the question of bail properly; or
- under para 6, that in the course of the present proceedings the defendant has been arrested for absconding under s 7 of the Bail Act.

- under para 2A, that the defendant is accused of an indictable (including triable either way) offence and it appears to the court that the defendant was on bail in respect of proceedings for another offence at the time he is alleged to have committed the present offence.

Where the defendant has been convicted and the case is adjourned for a pre-sentence report to be prepared, there is an additional ground (under para 7) for withholding bail, namely, that it would be impracticable to make the report without keeping the defendant in custody.

The factors which have to be taken into account in deciding whether or not the grounds set out in Sched 1 are made out are listed in para 9. They are:

- The nature of the offence and the probable method of dealing with the defendant for that offence, that is, the gravity of the offence. The point is that if a custodial sentence is likely, that is an incentive to abscond.

- The defendant's character and antecedents. This refers to any previous convictions. These may make a custodial sentence more likely (especially if the defendant, if convicted of the present offence, will be in breach of a suspended sentence of imprisonment).

  Note that, if a magistrate hears about a defendant's previous convictions in the course of a bail application, that magistrate is disqualified from trying the defendant if a summary trial takes place subsequently (s 42 of the Magistrates' Courts Act 1980).

- Associations and community ties: 'associations' is generally taken to refer to undesirable friends with criminal records. Examining the defendant's 'community ties' involves looking at how easy it would be for the defendant to abscond and how much he has to lose by absconding. How long has the defendant lived at his present address? Is he single or married? Does he have dependant children? Is he in employment? How long has he had his present job? Does he have a mortgage or a protected tenancy?

- Bail record: has the defendant absconded or committed offences while on bail in the past. Note that, if the defendant has absconded in the proceedings in respect of the present offence, that is a *ground* for withholding bail. Absconding in earlier proceedings is merely evidence that he may do so again.

- Strength of prosecution evidence: if the defendant has a good chance of acquittal (for example, the prosecution case rests on uncorroborated identification evidence) it can be argued that there is no point in the defendant absconding.

- The Criminal Justice and Court Services Bill 2000 adds a s 4(9) to the Bail Act 1976: this says that, in taking any decisions on bail, the court must have regard to any misuse of controlled drugs by the defendant.

2.4.2 Murder, manslaughter and rape

Under para 9A of Sched 1, Pt I, of the Bail Act 1976, a court granting bail to someone accused of murder, manslaughter, rape, attempted murder, or attempted rape must state and record its reasons for granting bail. This applies only if the application for bail was opposed by the prosecution on the grounds that the defendant might abscond, or commit further offences, or interfere with witnesses. Nevertheless, the presumption in favour of bail (s 4) continues to apply.

Furthermore, s 25 of the Criminal Justice and Public Order Act (as amended by s 56 of the Crime and Disorder Act 1998) applies where the defendant is charged with murder, attempted murder, manslaughter, rape, or attempted rape and has previously been convicted of one of these offences in the past. In a case to which s 25 applies, bail may only be granted if there are exceptional circumstances which justify the grant of bail.

2.4.3 Non-imprisonable offences

A defendant who is charged with (or convicted of) a non-imprisonable need not be granted bail if:

- the court is satisfied that he should be kept in custody for his own protection; or
- he is already serving a custodial sentence; or
- he has already been bailed in the course of the present proceedings and has been arrested for absconding, under s 7 of the Act.

These provisions are contained in Sched 1, Pt II, of the Act.

It is very rare for bail to be refused in the case of non-imprisonable offences. Note that bail cannot be refused on the grounds that the defendant is likely to abscond or to commit offences while on bail.

2.4.4 Bail and the European Convention on Human Rights

Under Art 5 of the Convention, which safeguards the right to liberty, a person charged with an offence must be released pending trial unless there are 'relevant and sufficient' reasons to justify continued detention (*Wemhoff v Germany* 1 EHRR 55). The case law of the European Court shows that this is interpreted in a way that is very similar to the UK's Bail Act 1976. The grounds accepted by the European Court of Human Rights for withholding bail include:

- the risk that the defendant will fail to appear at the trial. This has been defined as requiring 'a whole set of circumstances which give reason to suppose that the consequences and hazards of flight will seem to him to be a lesser evil than continued imprisonment' (*Stogmuller v Austria* 1 EHRR 155). The court can take account of 'the character of the person involved, his morals, his home, his occupation, his assets, his family ties, and all kinds of links with the country in which he is being prosecuted' (*Neumeister v Austria* 1 EHRR 91). The likely sentence is relevant but cannot of itself justify the refusal of bail (*Letellier v France* 14 EHRR 83);

- the risk that the defendant will interfere with the course of justice (for example, interfering with witnesses, warning other suspects, destroying relevant evidence). There must be an identifiable risk and there must be evidence in support (*Clooth v Belgium* 14 EHRR 717);

- preventing the commission of further offences; there must be good reason to believe that the defendant will commit offences while on bail (*Toth v Austria* 14 EHRR 717);

- the preservation of public order: bail may be withheld where the nature of the alleged crime and the likely public reaction to it are such that the release of the accused may give rise to public disorder (*Letellier v France* 14 EHRR 83).

Article 5 of the Convention also allows the imposition of conditions on the grant of bail.

It should be noted that the 'equality of arms' principle applies to bail applications (*Woukam Moudefo v France* 13 EHRR 549). This includes:

- the right to disclosure of prosecution evidence for purposes of making a bail application: *Lamy v Belgium* 11 EHRR 529 (the decision of the Divisional Court, *R v DPP ex p Lee* [1999] 2 Cr App R 304, largely accords with this);

- the requirement that the court should give reasons for the refusal of bail (*Tomasi v France* 15 EHRR 1) and should permit renewed applications for bail at reasonable intervals (*Bezicheri v Italy* 12 EHRR 210). Both these requirements are satisfied by the Bail Act.

2.5   CONDITIONS

If the magistrates grant unconditional bail, the defendant's only duty is to attend court on the date of the next hearing (s 3(1)).

If the court thinks it is necessary to impose conditions in order to prevent the defendant from absconding or committing offences or interfering with witnesses or otherwise obstructing the course of justice whether in relation to himself or any other person, then the court may attach one or more conditions to the defendant's bail (para 8(1), Sched 1, Pt I).

2.5.1   Examples of commonly imposed conditions

Sureties and security are the only conditions specifically mentioned in the Bail Act 1976. However, the court can impose any condition it thinks appropriate, provided that the condition is necessary on the grounds set out in the previous paragraph.

Commonly imposed conditions include:

- surety (where one or more persons, other than the defendant, promise to pay a specified sum to the court if the defendant absconds; see 2.6 below for further details);
- security (where the defendant deposits money or one or more valuable items with the court). If the defendant absconds the court can order the forfeiture of some or all of the security;
- residence (that is, living and sleeping at a specified address);
- residence in a bail hostel (in which case it is also a condition that the defendant must comply with the hostel rules (s 3(6ZA));
- reporting to a specified police station (on specified days and at specified times);
- curfew (requiring the defendant to stay indoors during specified hours at night time);
- not to enter a particular building or to go to a specified place or to go within a specified distance of a certain address;
- not to contact, directly or indirectly, the victim or any named prosecution witnesses;
- surrender of defendant's passport to the police;
- the court can require the defendant, before the time appointed for him to surrender to custody, to attend an interview with his solicitor (s 3(6)(e)).

2.5.2   When may conditions be imposed?

In *R v Mansfield Justices ex p Sharkey* [1985] QB 613; [1985] 1 All ER 193, Lord Lane CJ said that whereas there have to be substantial grounds for believing that the defendant will abscond, commit further offences etc for bail to be withheld altogether, the test for the imposition of conditions is a lower one. To impose conditions on the grant of bail, it is enough if the justices 'perceive a real and not a fanciful risk' of the defendant absconding, committing further offences etc.

2.5.3   Non-imprisonable offence

In *R v Bournemouth Magistrates ex p Cross* (1989) 89 Cr App R 90, it was held that conditions may be imposed when bail is granted to someone who is charged with a non-imprisonable offence.

2.5.4   Breaking conditions of bail

If the defendant is granted conditional bail but then breaches a condition of that bail, he is liable to be arrested under s 7 of the Bail Act 1976. No warrant is required by the police to arrest the defendant if he is in breach of a condition of his bail. After his arrest, he must be brought before a justice of the peace within 24 hours (s 7(4)). It is likely that his bail will be withdrawn, so that he will be held in custody pending trial, or else bail will be granted again but subject to even more stringent conditions.

Where a defendant is granted conditional bail by the Crown Court following an appeal to that court against the refusal of bail by a magistrates' court, if the defendant is arrested under s 7 of the Bail Act 1976 for breach of a condition of his bail, he must be taken before a magistrate, not a judge of the Crown Court (*Re Marshall* (1994) 159 JP 688).

2.5.5   Application for variation of conditions

Where bail is granted subject to conditions the defendant or the prosecution may apply to vary those conditions. Similarly, if unconditional bail was granted, the prosecution may apply to the court which granted bail for conditions to be added (see s 3(8) of the Bail Act 1976)).

The power to vary conditions of bail under s 3(8) of the Bail Act 1976 is conferred on the court which imposed those conditions and, where that court has committed a defendant on bail to the Crown Court for trial, on the Crown Court. During the period between committal to the Crown Court by the magistrates and the defendant's surrender to custody at the Crown Court, the magistrates' court and the Crown Court have concurrent jurisdiction (so either could vary the conditions). Once the arraignment has taken place (that is, the defendant has surrendered to the custody of the Crown Court) the magistrates no longer have any jurisdiction in relation to the grant of bail. So, in *R v Lincoln Justices ex p Mawer* (1995) 160 JP 21, the defendant was granted conditional bail by the Crown Court following her arraignment, the conditions being the same as those which the magistrates had originally imposed; the Divisional Court held that the magistrates' court could not entertain an application to vary the conditions imposed by the Crown Court.

2.6 SURETIES

In this section, we examine in greater detail one of the commonly imposed conditions of bail, namely sureties.

Under s 8(1) of the Bail Act 1976, the court may grant bail on condition that the defendant provides one or more surety for the purpose of ensuring that he surrenders to custody.

2.6.1 Granting of bail subject to surety

In deciding whether to grant bail subject to a surety, the court has to consider the suitability of the proposed surety. Section 8(2) provides that regard must be had to:

- the financial resources of the proposed surety: could the surety pay the sum which he is promising to pay?;
- the character of the proposed surety and whether he has previous convictions: is the surety a trustworthy person?;
- the 'proximity' of the proposed surety to the accused. (Is the proposed surety a friend, relative or employer? How far away does he live from the defendant?) The most important consideration under this heading is the relationship of proposed surety to the defendant: will the surety have the ability to control the defendant so as to ensure that he attends court when he should?

If the proposed surety is in court, he gives evidence of these matters and confirms that he understands the obligations he will be undertaking.

If the defence are aware that someone has offered to act as a surety but that person is not in court, and the magistrates are satisfied that she is a satisfactory surety, the court may grant bail subject to the named surety entering into the recognisance (that is, signing the formal document which sets out the agreement to act as surety) in front of a magistrate, a magistrates' clerk, or at a police station in front of an officer of the rank of inspector or above (s 8(4)). The defendant remains in custody until this has been done.

If there is no one whom the defence can offer as a surety at the time of the hearing, the magistrates may grant bail subject to a surety who is acceptable to the police entering into a recognisance at a police station. Again, the defendant stays in custody until a satisfactory surety has entered into a recognisance.

In fixing the amount of the surety, the court has regard to the seriousness of the offence, the degree of risk that the defendant will abscond, and to the means of the proposed surety.

It is quite common to have two or more sureties. If the court will only grant bail subject to a recognisance of a certain amount and that amount is beyond the means of the proposed surety, then another person will have to be found. It should be noted that the defendant cannot stand as a surety for himself (s 3(2) of the Bail Act 1976).

In *R v Birmingham Crown Court ex p Ali* (1999) 163 JP 145, the Divisional Court said that 'it is irresponsible (and possibly a matter for consideration by a professional disciplinary body) for a qualified lawyer or legal executive to tender anyone as a surety unless he or she has reasonable grounds for believing that the surety will, if necessary, be able to meet his or her financial undertaking' (at p 147, *per* Kennedy LJ). The same goes for a court official; unless the surety has the benefit of separate legal advice, the court official should make some inquiries to satisfy himself or herself that the surety will, if necessary, be able to pay.

2.6.2   Forfeiture of recognizance

If the defendant fails to surrender to custody when he should, there is a presumption that the full sum promised by the surety will be forfeited, unless it appears fair and just that a lesser sum should be forfeited or none at all. See s 120 of the Magistrates' Courts Act 1980.

The burden of showing that the amount promised by the surety should not be forfeited (or that only part of that sum should be forfeited) lies on the surety (*R v Uxbridge Justices ex p Heward-Mills* [1983] 1 WLR 56; [1983] 1 All ER 53).

The relevant factors were considered in *R v Southampton Justices ex p Green* [1976] QB 11; [1975] 2 All ER 1073, *R v Horseferry Road Justices ex p Pearson* [1976] 1 WLR 511; [1976] 2 All ER 264, *R v Reading Crown Court ex p Bello* [1992] 3 All ER 353 and *R v Wood Green Crown Court ex p Howe* [1992] 1 WLR 702; [1992] 3 All ER 366:

* *The surety's means*

  Has there been a change in financial circumstances since he agreed to act as surety which would make it unfair to order him to forfeit the sum promised?

* *Culpability*

  Did the surety take all reasonable steps to secure the defendant's attendance at court, again making it unfair to penalise the surety?

If a surety has a change of mind (for example, decides that the defendant is unlikely to attend court after all) and wishes to withdraw from the surety, he should give written notice to this effect to the police (see *Bello* above). The police can then arrest the defendant without a warrant. Even though the surety can only formally withdraw from the recognisance with the agreement of the court, a surety who has given written notice to the police would not normally forfeit the money promised if the defendant did indeed abscond (see *Howe* (above)).

However, in *R v Maidstone Crown Court ex p Lever and Connell* [1995] 2 All ER 35; [1995] 1 WLR 928, the Court of Appeal took a rather tougher line. In that case, one of two sureties discovered that the defendant had not been home for two nights. That surety telephoned the other surety and the police. Attempts by the police to reapprehend the defendant were unsuccessful. The judge ordered the first surety to forfeit £35,000 (out of a recognizance of £40,000) and the other £16,000 (out of a recognizance of £19,000). The two sureties sought judicial review of this decision. The Court of Appeal upheld the judge's decision. It was said that a lack of culpability on the part of the surety (or even commendable diligence by the surety), although a relevant factor, was not in itself a reason for reducing or setting aside the obligation into which the surety had freely entered. It was added that the court had a broad discretion as to whether and to what extent it would be fair and just to remit some or all of a recognizance and that the exercise of that discretion will only be set aside if it is perverse. In the instant case, a remission of about 15% could not be said to be perverse.

In *Lever and Connell* (above), the court endeavoured to give general guidance. Butler-Sloss LJ said that 'the presence or absence of culpability is a factor but the absence of culpability ... is not in itself a reason to reduce or set aside the obligation entered into by the surety to pay in the event of a failure to bring the defendant to court' but there may be circumstances where the amount forfeited might be reduced because the surety had made considerable efforts to carry out his undertakings. Rose LJ said that the amount to be forfeited may be reduced because the surety 'has made very considerable efforts to carry out his or her undertaking'.

It should be noted that s 120 of the Magistrates' Courts Act 1980 (as amended by s 55 of the Crime and Disorder Act 1998) provides that, where a person stands as a surety but the accused fails to attend court, the magistrates' court must:

(a) declare the recognizance to be forfeited; and

(b) issue a summons to the surety requiring him to appear before the court to show cause why he should not be ordered to pay the sum promised.

If the surety fails to attend that hearing, the court may proceed in his absence if satisfied that he was served with the summons.

In *Kaur v DPP* (2000) 164 JP 127, the Divisional Court noted that justices have a wide discretion under s 120 of the Magistrates' Courts Act 1980 to remit the recognizance of a surety where the defendant fails to surrender. The court went on to hold that the justices can only have regard to the assets of the surety; assets of third parties are irrelevant. Regard must be had to the surety's share in the equity of the matrimonial home; however, the impact on the surety and others, if the matrimonial home has to be sold to satisfy the recognizance, is a relevant factor in deciding whether to remit all or part of the recognizance. The court went on to say that lack of culpability on the part of the surety is not in itself a reason for not remitting the recognizance (as was held in *R v Maidstone Crown Court ex p Lever*, above)

In *R v Birmingham Crown Court ex p Ali* (1999) 163 JP 145, it was held that, where there has been no proper means inquiry and the surety then applies for a reduction in the amount of the recognizance to be forfeited (under s 120 of the Magistrates' Courts Act 1980), the sum should be reduced (if necessary) to a sum that the surety could be expected to pay in full within two, or at the most three, years.

2.7   REPEATED BAIL APPLICATIONS

Schedule 1, Pt IIA, of the Bail Act 1976 (inserted by s 154 of the Criminal Justice Act 1988) provides that, at the first hearing after that at which bail was refused, the defendant can make a bail application whether or not it is based on arguments which were advanced on the first occasion.

Thus, the defendant may make bail applications on his first and second appearances before the court and may advance precisely the same arguments in each application if he so wishes. Or, if no application is made on the first appearance, the defendant may make an application on his second appearance.

Thereafter, a material change of circumstances (that is, something relevant to bail) is required if a further bail application is to be made. So, in subsequent remands, the court should only consider whether the circumstances have changed since last fully argued bail application was heard (for example, a possible surety comes forward or the defendant is offered employment).

This provision is based on *R v Nottingham Justices ex p Davies* [1981] QB 38; [1980] 2 All ER 77, in which the Divisional Court said the defendant should be allowed two fully argued applications. This was because the first application is usually under-prepared due to lack of time, and so fairness demands that a second application be heard. Thereafter, however, the court would simply be hearing arguments that had been heard before; hence, the requirement of a change in circumstances so that a third application for bail can only be made if there is some fresh material for the court to consider.

In *R v Dover and East Kent Justices ex p Dean* [1992] Crim LR 33, the defendant did not make a bail application on his first appearance at court and he consented to being remanded in his absence (under s 128 of the Magistrates' Courts Act 1980) for the next three weeks. On the occasion of his next appearance before the court (a month after his first appearance), the defendant sought to make a bail application. The magistrates would not let him do so, but the Divisional Court held that remands in the defendant's absence do not count as hearings for the purpose of determining whether a bail application can be made. The defendant's second appearance was to be regarded as the second hearing (even though the case had been listed in the intervening weeks) and so he had a right to make a bail application.

In *R v Calder Justices ex p Kennedy* [1992] Crim LR 496, it was similarly held that, if the magistrates remand the defendant in custody on the basis that there is insufficient information before the court to make a decision on bail (a permitted ground for refusing bail under Sched 1, Pt I, para 5 of the Bail Act 1976), this hearing does not count for the purposes of s 154. So, a full bail application may be made on the occasion of the defendant's next appearance and if that application is unsuccessful a second fully argued bail application can be made on his subsequent appearance before the court.

2.8   CHALLENGING THE REFUSAL OF BAIL

In this section, we consider the various ways of challenging a refusal of bail. The starting point is the right of the defendant to know why bail was refused in the first place.

2.8.1   Record of reasons

Section 5(3) of the Bail Act 1976 says that whenever the defendant is refused bail, the court must give its reasons for withholding bail and (under s 5(1)) the defendant must be given a copy of the record of the decision. The same applies where bail is granted subject to conditions.

Thus, the defendant receives a document setting out which ground or grounds for withholding bail (from those specified in Sched 1 of the Act) and what factors were taken into account (that is, from the list in Sched 1 para 9) in deciding that the grounds were made out.

For example, the record of the decision might say that bail is being withheld because the court is satisfied that there are substantial grounds believing that the accused will:

* *Fail to surrender to custody*

  Reasons: accused has two previous convictions for absconding;

  accused is unemployed and of no fixed abode.

* *Commit an offence while on bail*

  Reasons: accused has three previous convictions for offences similar to that presently charged;

  accused has no apparent income;

  two of accused's previous convictions are for offences committed while on bail.

2.8.2   Certificate that full argument heard

Furthermore, s 5(6A) says that, if a magistrates' court refuses bail after hearing a fully argued bail application, it must provide the defendant with a certificate that this is the case. If the magistrates allow a defendant to make a third application because there has been a material change of circumstances but do not grant bail, they must state in the certificate what change of circumstances persuaded them to hear the application.

Once the defendant has a certificate that full argument has been heard, he may apply for bail to the Crown Court if the magistrates refuse bail (see 2.9.1 below).

The standard forms for the recording of the various decisions regarding bail are shown at the end of a chapter, as is the form for the certificate that the court has heard a fully-argued bail application.

2.9   OPTIONS OPEN TO DEFENDANT WHEN BAIL REFUSED

In order to challenge the refusal of bail (or to challenge the imposition of conditions):

- The defendant may make a further application in the magistrates' court if this is permissible under Sched 1, Pt IIA, of the Bail Act 1976 (above), that is, this is only the defendant's second bail application or the defendant can show that there has been a material change of circumstances.

- The defendant may apply for bail to the Crown Court under s 81(1) of the Supreme Court Act 1981 or to the High Court under s 22 of the Criminal Justice Act 1967. Note that, if the defendant is legally aided, the legal aid certificate automatically covers a bail application to the Crown Court. It is quite rare for defendants to apply to the High Court since criminal legal aid is not available; an application would have to be made for emergency civil legal aid. Alternatively, the defendant can ask the Official Solicitor (an official appointed by the Lord Chancellor) to act for him in the High Court.

2.9.1   Crown Court bail application: procedure

An application may be made to the Crown Court if the defendant has a certificate (under s 5(6A) of the Bail Act 1976) from the magistrates' court that a fully argued bail application was made there.

The defendant must give at least 24 hours' notice to the Crown Prosecution Service. The defendant has no right to be present at the Crown Court hearing (and usually is not present) (r 19(5) of the Crown Court Rules 1982). The hearing is usually (though not invariably) in chambers (that is, the public are excluded and robes are not worn): r 27(2)(a). Otherwise, the procedure is the same as the magistrates' court, with the prosecution summarising the objections to bail and the defence replying.

2.9.2 High Court bail application: procedure

An application for bail to the High Court is made by summons, served on the prosecution at least 24 hours before the hearing date, supported by an affidavit saying why bail should have been granted. The hearing, in front of a High Court judge, is in chambers (that is, the public are excluded). See Ord 79, r 9 of the Rules of the Supreme Court.

If a defendant wishes to challenge the refusal of bail (or the imposition of conditions on the grant of bail) in the High Court, he must use the procedure set out in RSC Ord 79, r 9. Judicial review is not available in such a case (*R v Croydon Crown Court ex p Cox* [1997] 1 Cr App R 20).

2.9.3 Relationship between Crown Court and High Court regarding bail

If the defendant applies unsuccessfully to the Crown Court, he could then apply to the High Court; if the defendant applies unsuccessfully to the High Court he could then apply to the Crown Court. However, the second court must be told that an unsuccessful application has already been made to the other court (*R v Reading Crown Court ex p Malik* [1981] QB 451; [1981] 1 All ER 249). In practice, applications are rarely made to both courts, not least because the prospects of ultimately being granted bail are remote. The fact that a legal aid certificate automatically covers a Crown Court bail application means that Crown Court bail applications are much more common than High Court applications.

2.10 PROSECUTION CHALLENGES TO THE GRANT OF BAIL

Two mechanisms exist to enable the prosecution to challenge the grant of bail to a defendant.

2.10.1 Prosecution appeals against grant of bail

The Bail (Amendment) Act 1993 allows the prosecution to appeal, in certain circumstances, against decisions by magistrates to grant bail.

Section 1 of the Bail (Amendment) Act 1993 provides that where a magistrates' court grants bail to someone who is charged with (or convicted of):

- an offence punishable by a term of imprisonment of five years or more; or

- taking a conveyance without authority or aggravated vehicle taking (s 12 and 12A of the Theft Act 1968),

    the prosecution may appeal to the Crown Court against the granting of bail.

Private prosecutions (that is, prosecutions other than those brought by the Crown Prosecution Service or other public bodies) are excluded from the scope of the Bail (Amendment) Act 1993. Furthermore, for the Act to apply, the prosecution must have opposed bail in the magistrates' court. If the prosecution wish to exercise the right of appeal, oral notice of appeal is given to the magistrates at the conclusion of the bail hearing and written notice of appeal must be served on the magistrates' court and on the defendant within two hours of the conclusion of the bail hearing. The defendant is held in custody pending the Crown Court hearing, which must take place within 48 hours (excluding weekends).

In *R v Isleworth Crown Court ex p Clarke* [1998] 1 Cr App R 257, the Divisional Court held that the requirement that the prosecutor must give oral notice of appeal against the decision to grant bail 'at the conclusion of the proceedings' was satisfied in a case where such notice had been given to the magistrates' court clerk about five minutes after the court rose.

The appeal is by way of re-hearing, and the judge hearing the appeal may remand the defendant in custody or may grant bail subject to such conditions (if any) as he thinks fit.

The need to have a written notice following the oral notice of appeal is to enable the question of whether or not to appeal to be considered by a Senior Crown Prosecutor.

Guidance issued to Crown Prosecutors by the CPS says that the power to appeal against a grant of bail must be used judiciously and responsibly; it should not be used merely because the prosecutor disagrees with the decision of the magistrates. Rather, the power should only be used in cases of 'grave concern'. The test to be applied is whether there is a serious risk of harm to any member of the public or other significant public interest grounds. Is there a risk to the victim of the alleged offence (for example, the defendant has previous convictions for similar offences against that victim or victims of a similar type)? Is there a strong indication that the defendant will abscond (for example, he has no right to remain in Britain or has substantial assets abroad)? Is the case one involving national security or large-scale drug trafficking and, if so, is there real doubt about the true identity of the defendant and a lack of community ties?

Where a Crown Court judge allows a prosecution appeal against the grant of bail by a magistrates' court under the Bail (Amendment) Act 1993, the judge must state the period for which the defendant is to be remanded in custody (in other words, the judge must specify the date on which the defendant is to appear in the magistrates' court), and that period must be in accordance with the periods specified in s 128 or 128A of the Magistrates' Courts Act 1980 (see 2.12 below). This is because the defendant is still under the jurisdiction of the magistrates' court: *R v Szakal* [2000] 1 Cr App R 248.

In *R v Middlesex Guildhall Crown Court ex p Okoli* (2000) *The Times*, 2 August, the Divisional Court had to consider the effect of the 48 hour time limit (contained in s 1(8)). On 7 June 2000, the defendant was granted bail by a magistrates' court. The prosecution sought to appeal under the Bail (Amendment) Act 1993. The appeal was listed for 3.00 pm on 9 June. The defendant argued that this was more than 48 hours after the notice of appeal had been given, and so the Crown Court had no jurisdiction to hear the appeal. It was held that where an oral notice of appeal against a decision to grant bail has been given, the appeal hearing must commence within 48 hours of the date – not the time – on which notice of appeal was given. The Crown Court therefore had jurisdiction in the present case.

2.10.2 Prosecution application for reconsideration of grant of bail

Section 5B of the Bail Act 1976 provides that, where a magistrates' court has granted bail, or the defendant has been granted police bail, the prosecution may apply to the magistrates' court for that decision to be reconsidered. The court has power to impose conditions if the original grant of bail was without condition, to vary any conditions that were imposed originally, or to withhold bail. This provision only applies where the defendant is accused of an indictable (including triable either way) offence. Section 5B clearly envisages the possibility of such an application being made in the absence of the defendant; however, s 5B(9) requires notice of the application to be given to the defendant and for the defendant to be given an opportunity to make written or oral representations to the court.

An application is only possible under s 5B if it is based on information which was not available when the original decision regarding bail was taken.

2.10.3 The two procedures compared

It follows that the two main differences between the prosecution appeal against the grant of bail and the prosecution application for re-consideration of the grant of bail are:

(i) an application for re-consideration depends on new information coming to light;

(ii) an appeal is made to the Crown Court whereas an application for re-consideration is made to the magistrates' court.

2.11 WHAT HAPPENS IF THE DEFENDANT FAILS TO ATTEND COURT?

The defendant 'surrenders' to custody by attending the correct court on the correct date and at the correct time and by complying with that court's procedure for surrender, for example, reporting to a particular office or a particular person (*DPP v Richards* [1988] QB 701; [1988] 3 All ER 406). As it was put in *R v Central Criminal Court ex p Guney* [1996] AC 616; [1996] 2 All ER 705, a defendant surrenders to custody when he puts himself at the direction of the court or an officer of the court. Having surrendered, the defendant must remain within the precincts of the court.

2.11.1 The offence of absconding

Failure without reasonable cause to surrender to custody is itself an offence (s 6(1) of the Bail Act 1976).

According to a Practice Direction (1987), if the defendant has absconded but is now before the court, it should be left to the prosecution to invite the court to take action if the prosecutor thinks it appropriate to do so. There is then a hearing to determine whether or not the defendant is guilty of absconding.

The prosecution are generally quite keen for action to be taken where a defendant has absconded. This is because, if the defendant is convicted of failing to answer his bail, this conviction can be used in any later proceedings against the defendant to show a risk that he will abscond again (Sched 1, Pt I, para 9(c) of the Bail Act 1976).

Failure to answer bail which was granted by a court (that is, rather than the police) will be dealt with by the court at which the proceedings in respect of which bail was granted are to be to be heard. In other words, if the defendant is to be tried for the original offence in the magistrates' court, the Bail Act offence will be dealt with at the end of the summary trial. If the defendant is to be tried in the Crown Court, the Bail Act offence will be dealt with after the trial on indictment (although the Bail Act offence will be heard by a judge sitting alone, not by a jury).

Failure to answer police bail is dealt with by the police laying an information; the allegation is then tried at the magistrates' court. The information must be laid within six months of the failure to surrender (*Murphy v DPP* [1990] 1 WLR 601; [1990] 2 All ER 390).

Under s 6(5) of the Bail Act, failure to surrender is punishable either on summary conviction or as if it were a criminal contempt of court. In *R v Lubega* (1999) 163 JP 221, the appellant arrived at the Crown Court 20 minutes late. The judge dealt with the matter as a contempt of court. The question for the Court of Appeal was whether the judge was entitled to treat the late arrival as a contempt of court. The court held that if the appellant had committed any offence it was contrary to s 6(1) of the Bail Act 1976. The effect of s 6(5) is not to convert an offence under the Act into a contempt of court, but rather to provide a speedy method of disposing of the matter. The judge was therefore not entitled to deal with the matter as a contempt of court.

Section 6(7) of the Bail Act 1976 provides that a person convicted of absconding is liable to up to three months' imprisonment or a fine of up to £5,000 in the magistrates' court or to 12 months' imprisonment and an unlimited fine in the Crown Court; the latter applies whether the defendant has been committed to the Crown Court for sentence (under s 6(6) of the Bail Act 1976) or, if the offence is being dealt with by the Crown Court, because the defendant had been sent for trial in the Crown Court before he absconded (see *Schiavo v Anderton* [1987] QB 20; [1986] 3 All ER 10).

2.11.2 Reasonable cause

An offence is only committed under s 6 if the defendant has no reasonable cause for the failure to surrender.

Section 6(3) states that it is for the accused to prove that he had reasonable cause for his failure to surrender to custody. As is always the case when a defendant bears a burden of proof, it is the civil standard, that is the balance of probabilities.

In *R v Liverpool City Justices ex p Santos* (1997) *The Times*, 23 January, QBD, it was held that a mistake by a solicitor may, depending on the circumstances, be a reasonable excuse for a defendant's failure to surrender to bail.

If reasonable cause exists at the time the defendant should have surrendered, then he should surrender as soon as reasonably practicable thereafter.

In *R v How* [1993] Crim LR 201, following the earlier decision in *R v Watson* (1990) 12 Cr App R(S) 227, the Court of Appeal emphasised that when the court is dealing with an allegation of absconding, the defendant must be given an opportunity to explain the failure to surrender to custody, or (if the defendant admits the offence) to put forward any mitigation. Furthermore, where the defendant denies the offence, he should be given the chance to adduce evidence that he had good cause for the failure to surrender (*R v Boyle* [1993] Crim LR 40).

2.11.3 Bench warrant

If the defendant was originally arrested and charged, failing to attend court is not only an offence itself (s 6 of the Bail Act 1976) but also enables the court to grant a warrant for the defendant's arrest (s 7(1) of the Bail Act 1976). Such a warrant is known as a 'bench warrant'.

Under s 7(2), if the defendant surrenders to custody by attending court on the appropriate day, but then absents himself from the court, this is a breach of bail and a bench warrant may be issued.

If there is a suggestion that the defendant has a good reason for not attending court (but there is not sufficient information to be sure of this), the court may issue a bench warrant but 'back it for bail'. In other words, the warrant is endorsed with a direction to the police to release the defendant once he has been arrested and informed of the next date he must attend court. This serves to warn the defendant that failure to attend court may lead to his arrest.

If the defendant clearly has a good reason for not attending court, the court should simply adjourn the case in the absence of the defendant, with the defendant being remanded on bail as before (s 129(3) of the Magistrates' Courts Act 1980). This is sometimes known as 'enlarging bail'.

If no good reason is apparent, a warrant (not backed for bail) will be issued.

Under the Magistrates' Courts (Miscellaneous Amendments) Rules 1993, a clerk is empowered to issue an arrest warrant (whether or not endorsed for bail) if there is no objection on behalf of the accused.

The standard form for a bench warrant is shown at the end of this chapter.

2.11.4 Failure to attend to answer summons

If the defendant was supposed to attend court to answer a summons (that is, he was not originally arrested and charged), a bench warrant can only be granted if the information upon which the summons was based is substantiated on oath and the offence alleged is one which is imprisonable (s 1 of the Magistrates' Courts Act 1980).

2.11.5 After arrest under a bench warrant

After arrest pursuant to a bench warrant not backed for bail, the defendant will be taken before the court which granted bail and the question of whether or not he should be released on bail (perhaps with more stringent conditions) or kept in custody will be decided by the court. The defendant should be taken before the court within 24 hours of arrest (excluding Sundays).

As a result of absconding, the defendant no longer has a presumption in favour of bail operating in his favour in the present proceedings (Sched 1, Pt I, para 6, of the Bail Act 1980). In other words, absconding becomes a ground for withholding bail for the rest of the time that proceedings are active in respect of the offence for which bail was granted.

2.11.6   Police powers

The police may arrest a defendant (under s 7(3) of the Bail Act 1976, without a warrant) if they have reasonable grounds for believing:

- that the defendant is not likely to surrender to custody; or
- that the defendant has broken or is likely to break any condition which was imposed when bail was granted; or
- that a surety has given written notice that he no longer wishes to act as a surety and that, in his opinion, the defendant is unlikely to surrender.

2.11.7   After arrest without a bench warrant

When the defendant has been arrested under s 7(3), he should be taken before the court within 24 hours (s 7(4)). The court has to decide whether the accused is indeed likely to fail to surrender to custody or has broken (or is likely to breach) any condition of his bail. In *R v Governor of Glen Parva Young Offender Institution ex p G* [1998] 2 All ER 295, the defendant was arrested for breach of bail conditions; he was taken to the cells of a magistrates' court within 24 hours of arrest but was not brought before a magistrate until two hours after the expiry of the 24 hour time limit. The Divisional Court held that the detention after 24 hours was unlawful: s 7(4) of the Bail Act 1976 requires the defendant to be brought before a justice of the peace (not merely brought within the court precincts) within 24 hours of arrest.

In *R v Liverpool Justices ex p DPP* [1993] QB 233; [1992] 3 All ER 249, it was held that where the police arrest someone who is in breach of a bail condition or whom the police believe to be about to abscond (powers conferred by s 7 of the Bail Act 1976), a single lay justice has the power to remand the defendant in custody or to grant bail subject to further conditions.

2.11.8   Proceeding with the case in the defendant's absence

In some instances, it may be possible to continue with the case even though the defendant is not present in the courtroom. This is dealt with in connection with the various types of hearing: mode of trial hearings, summary trial, committal proceedings, and trial on indictment (see Chapters 3, 4, 7 and 9).

2.12 PERIOD OF REMAND IN CUSTODY PRIOR TO CONVICTION

The maximum period of a remand in custody prior to conviction is eight clear days unless s 128A of the Magistrates' Courts Act 1980 applies (s 128(6) of the Magistrates' Courts Act 1980).

The term 'eight *clear* days' means that if a hearing takes place on Monday, the next hearing must take place no later than the following Wednesday.

Section 128A allows a remand in custody for up to 28 days but does not apply to the first remand hearing, as the defendant must have previously been remanded in custody for the same offence. Furthermore, for s 128A to apply, the next hearing must be 'effective', in the sense that the mode of trial hearing or committal proceedings or summary trial will take place. Both prosecution and defendant must be allowed to make representations before a remand in excess of eight days is ordered but the defendant's consent is not required.

2.12.1 Remands in absence of defendant

The provisions of s 128A should be contrasted with remands in the absence of the defendant which are possible, under s 128(3A)–(3E), provided that the defendant has a solicitor acting for him in the case (though not necessarily present in court) and the defendant consents to not being present at future remand hearings. A maximum of three remands *in absentia* means that the defendant has to appear in court once a month.

Whether s 128 or s 128A applies, the defendant can still apply for bail during the 28 day period by giving notice to the court that he wishes to do so.

2.12.2 Remand after conviction

Following summary conviction, there may be a remand in custody of up to three weeks to enable the preparation of a pre-sentence report (dealing with the most suitable method of dealing with the defendant) (s 10(3) of the Magistrates' Courts Act 1980).

2.12.3 Place of remand

Remand in custody means that the defendant is held in prison or (if aged 17–20) in a remand centre. However, s 128(7) of the Magistrates' Courts Act 1980 allows a remand to police custody for a maximum of three clear days. Section 128(8) states that this is only possible if it is necessary for the purpose of making inquiries into offences other than those presently before court (see Chapter 1, 1.8.1 above). The defendant must be brought back to the magistrates' court as soon as the need to question him ceases.

Where a defendant has been remanded in custody, he will have to be brought to the court from the place he is detained on the next date when he is due to appear in court (this is sometimes known as being 'produced'). The defendant will be kept in cells adjacent to the court until his case is called on. At that point he will be escorted into the dock.

Section 57 of the Crime and Disorder Act 1998 allows preliminary hearings (that is, hearings before the start of the trial) to take place even though the defendant is not present in court provided that he is in custody in prison and, by means of a live television link or otherwise, he is able to see and hear the court and to be seen and heard by it.

It should be noted that a person who is in remand in the cells of the court (for example, waiting to be taken up to the courtroom) has a common law right to consult a solicitor as soon as reasonably practicable of he so wishes (*R v Chief Constable of South Wales ex p Merrick* [1994] 1 WLR 663; [1994] 2 All ER 560).

2.13   EARLY ADMINISTRATIVE HEARINGS

Section 50 of the Crime and Disorder Act 1998 provides for 'early administrative hearings' in the magistrates' court. It provides that, where the accused has been charged with an offence at a police station, the magistrates' court before whom he appears for the first time may (unless the offence or one of them is triable only on indictment) consist of a single magistrate (s 50(1)). At this hearing, the accused must be asked if he wishes to receive legal aid; if he does, his eligibility for it must be determined; and if it is determined that he is eligible for it, he should be granted legal aid (s 50(2)). The single justice may then remand the accused in custody or on bail (s 50(3)). Such a hearing may also be conducted by a justices' clerk, with the important proviso that the clerk is not empowered to remand the accused in custody and may only vary conditions of bail imposed by the police if the prosecution and accused both consent to the clerk doing so.

2.14   CUSTODY TIME LIMITS

Section 22 of the Prosecution of Offences Act 1985 provides for 'custody time limits'. For indictable offences, the custody time limit from first appearance to committal proceedings is 70 days. For offences which are triable either way and the case is to be tried summarily, the custody time limit from first appearance to the start of the trial is 70 days unless the mode of trial hearing takes place within 56 days in which case the time limit is 56 days. Following committal proceedings, the time limit from committal to arraignment at the Crown Court is 112 days.

These provisions apply to proceedings in the youth court even though the usual distinction between summary and indictable offences does not apply there (*R v Stratford Youth Court ex p S* [1998] 1 WLR 1758).

For the purposes of s 22, proceedings for an offence are taken to have begun when the accused is charged with the offence or an information is laid charging him with the offence (s 22(11ZA)).

The start of a trial on indictment is taken to occur when a jury is sworn to consider the issue of guilt or fitness to plead or, if the court accepts a plea of guilty before a jury is sworn, when that plea is accepted (s 22(11A)). The start of a summary trial is taken to occur when the court begins to hear evidence for the prosecution at the trial or, if the court accepts a plea of guilty, that plea is accepted (s 22(11B)).

In *R v Leeds Crown Court ex p Whitehead* (2000) 164 JP 102, the custody time limit applicable to the defendant was due to expire on 15 October 1998. The trial commenced on 14 October 1998. On 26 January 1999, the trial was stopped and the jury were discharged. A fresh trial date was set for 13 September 1999; the defendant was remanded in custody. The defendant argued that the custody time limit provisions were applicable to the period after the abandonment of the first trial. The Divisional Court held that, since the custody time limit provisions cease to apply at the start of the trial (that is, when a jury is sworn in), the time limit provisions do not apply to the period between when a trial is aborted in the Crown Court and the retrial. However, the court went on to say that, if a trial is aborted and a retrial ordered, the judge should be vigilant to protect the interests of the accused by taking steps to fix a speedy retrial, or by considering the grant of bail, or even staying the proceedings as an abuse of process.

2.14.1 Expiry of time limit

Under reg 8 of the Prosecution of Offences (Custody Time Limits) Regulations 1987 (SI 1987 No 299), where a custody time limit has expired:

- the defendant has an absolute right to bail; and
- the court cannot require sureties as a condition of granting bail (but it can impose other conditions, such as conditions of residence, reporting to a police station, etc). Any application for the imposition of conditions must be made by the prosecution to the Crown Court (with written notice being served on the defendant beforehand).

If the defendant is granted bail because the custody time limit has expired, his right to bail continues only until he is arraigned (that is, when he pleads guilty or not guilty). Thereafter, the court can withhold bail if any of the reasons for doing so under the Bail Act apply (*R v Croydon Crown Court ex p Lewis* (1994) 158 JP 886).

Also, under s 22(4) of the 1985 Act, where the time limit expires, the court must stay the proceedings against the accused. Section 22B enables the proceedings to be re-instituted in certain limited circumstances.

2.14.2 Extending the time limit

Section 22(3) of the 1985 Act empowers the appropriate court, at any time before the expiry of a time limit imposed by the regulations, to extend (or further extend) that limit. The appropriate court to do so is the Crown Court if the defendant has been committed or sent for trial to the Crown Court; otherwise the application should be made to the magistrates' court.

The court can only extend the custody time limit if it is satisfied:

(a) that the need for the extension is due to:

   (i)   the illness or absence of the accused, a necessary witness, a judge or a magistrate;

   (ii)   a postponement which is occasioned by the ordering by the court of separate trials in the case of two or more accused or two or more offences; or

   (iii) some other good and sufficient cause,

and

(b) that the prosecution has acted with all due diligence and expedition.

Guidance was given by the Court of Appeal in *R v Manchester Crown Court ex p McDonald* [1999] 1 All ER 805. The court held that, to grant an extension of the custody time limit, the court must first be satisfied on the balance of probabilities that both statutory conditions in s 22(3) are met. The prosecutor must show that there is a sufficient basis for the court to be satisfied that there is good reason to grant an extension (sub-s (3)(a)). The court still has to make this decision even if the parties agree to the extension or if there is no objection to it from the defence. This requirement will not be satisfied merely because of the seriousness of the offence or by the fact that only a short extension is required. To satisfy the second requirement (under sub-s 3(b)), it must be shown that the prosecutor has acted with the diligence and expedition to be shown by a competent prosecutor conscious of his duty to bring the case to trial as quickly as reasonably and fairly possible. This involves having regard to the nature and complexity of the case, the extent of preparation necessary, the conduct of the defence, and the extent to which the prosecutor depends on the co-operation of people outside his control. Staff shortages are not relevant. Difficulty in finding an appropriate judge will only be relevant if the case needs to be tried by a judge of particular seniority. Further, the Divisional Court will only interfere if the court below reaches a decision that no reasonable court could reach.

Delays caused by police under-staffing will not amount to a good reason for extending time (*R v Southampton Crown Court ex p Roddie* [1991] 1 WLR 303; [1991] 2 All ER 931).

In *R v Leeds Crown Court ex p Briggs (No. 1)* [1998] 2 Cr App R 413, the Divisional Court noted that the seriousness of the offence is not, of itself, enough to justify an extension of time but the complexity of the case might be. The Divisional Court in that case also held that the court should give reasons explaining its decision that there is good and sufficient cause to extend time and that the prosecution has acted with all due expedition.

In *R v Leeds Crown Court ex p Bagoutie* (1999) *The Times*, 31 May, the Divisional Court held that where there is an application for an extension of the custody time limits and the court is satisfied that that there is good and sufficient cause for the extension but is not satisfied that the prosecution have acted with all due expedition, the court is not obliged to refuse the application for an extension if it concludes that the failure to exercise due expedition has not caused or contributed to the need for the extension. It follows that the court is not obliged to refuse an extension in a case where there has been avoidable delay by the prosecution but that delay has had no effect on the ability of the prosecution and the defence to be ready for trial on a predetermined trial date.

In *R v Norwich Crown Court ex p Parker and Ward* (1992) 96 Cr App R 68, it was held that the court can decide whether or not to extend time on the basis of submissions from counsel; in other words, there is no need for evidence to be called if the court thinks that this would be unnecessary.

The application to extend the time limit must be made prior to the expiry of the limit: once the limit has expired, there is no power to extend it (*R v Sheffield Justices ex p Turner* [1991] 2 QB 472; [1991] 1 All ER 858).

In *R v Great Yarmouth Magistrates ex p Thomas* [1992] Crim LR 116, the defendant was charged with importing cannabis. The prosecution applied for an extension of the custody time limit, but the court refused to extend time. The defendant was released on bail but was immediately arrested by police for possessing cannabis with intent to supply. The Divisional Court held that there was nothing to stop the prosecution from bringing several charges against a defendant based on the same or similar facts, even if this resulted in there being several custody time limits in operation. However, the magistrates should ensure that the prosecution are not abusing the process of the court by doing so. In *R v Stafford Crown Court ex p Uppall* (1995) 159 JP 86, the defendant was charged with rape. At the expiry of the custody time limit (an application for an extension of time having been refused), the prosecution preferred an additional charge of false imprisonment arising out of the same facts as the rape. It was held that where an additional charge is brought against a defendant who is already charged with an offence, the second offence has its own custody time limit and this is the case whether or not the second charge is based on additional evidence. It was also said that when the CPS are considering bringing further charges against a defendant, they should review the evidence at the earliest opportunity and, wherever possible, comply with the initial custody time limit. However, the CPS would not be guilty of abuse of process unless it was established that they brought further charges simply for the purpose of extending the time limit.

In *R v Maidstone Crown Court ex p Hollstein* [1995] 3 All ER 503, the defendant had been arrested for arson on 19 January 1994. The custody time limit following committal for trial was extended to 22 July, the date the trial was expected to start. The trial did not start on 22 July but no application to extend the custody time limit was made. On 27 July the defendant was arraigned (although the trial did not in fact start on that date) and the defendant was remanded in custody. It was said by the Queen's Bench Division that it was not permissible to arraign a defendant simply to deprive the accused of the right to bail he would otherwise have enjoyed upon the expiry of the custody time limit. See, also, *R v Maidstone Crown Court ex p Clark* [1995] 1 WLR 831; [1995] 3 All ER 513, where the defendant was served with a large amount of evidential material on the date he was supposed to be entering a plea. As the custody time limit was about to expire, the prosecution wanted the defendant to be arraigned, even though he needed more time to consider the evidence just served on him. Again, the Divisional Court said that it was improper to arraign a defendant simply to defeat the custody time limit provisions.

In such cases, however, judicial review is not available to challenge the arraignment. This is because judicial review cannot be sought in respect of matters relating to Crown Court trials (s 29(3) of the Supreme Court Act 1981; see Chapter 10, 10.14 below). The only remedy available to a defendant in such a case is to seek a writ of *habeas corpus* (*R v Leeds Crown Court ex p Hussain* [1995] 3 All ER 527; [1995] 1 WLR 1329).

Under s 22(7) of the Prosecution of Offences Act 1985, where a magistrates' court decides to extend, or further extend, a time limit, the accused may appeal against the decision to the Crown Court. Under sub-s (8), where a magistrates' court refuses to extend, or further extend, a time limit, the prosecution may appeal against the refusal to the Crown Court. Sub-section (9) provides that an appeal under sub-s (8) may not be commenced after the expiry of the limit in question and also provides that where such an appeal is commenced before the expiry of the limit, the limit shall be deemed not to have expired before the determination or abandonment of the appeal.

2.15   DELAY BEFORE OR DURING PROCEEDINGS

We have already seen that, if a defendant is remanded in custody prior to trial, the custody time limits restrict the length of time that the defendant can be kept in custody unless the prosecution are able to justify extending the custody time limit. Once the custody limit has expired, then, unless the prosecution obtain an extension, the defendant has to be released on bail. However, the prosecution continues against him.

Nevertheless, there are instances when a case can be terminated as a result of delay.

In *R v Willesden Justices ex p Clemmings* (1987) 87 Cr App R 280, and in *R v Derby Crown Court ex p Brooks* (1984) 80 Cr App R 164, it was said that there are two types of delay which empower the court to stop the proceedings against the accused:

- the prosecution have deliberately manipulated or misused the process of the court so as to take unfair advantage of the accused (for example, delaying proceedings in the hope that a defence witness will no longer be available to give evidence); or

- the accused is able to show that he has been, or will be, prejudiced in the preparation or conduct of his defence by delay on the part of the prosecution which, although not deliberate, was nonetheless unjustifiable.

Delay may arise before or after proceedings are commenced.

2.16   THE TWO TYPES OF DELAY

The two types of delay which have been identified, abuse of process and prejudice to the defendant, have been considered in a number of cases.

2.16.1   Deliberate delay: abuse of process

In *R v Brentford Justices ex p Wong* (1981), the prosecution laid an information alleging careless driving. The information was laid just before the expiry of the six month time limit which applies to summary offences. The prosecution asked for the summons not to be served straightaway, however, as they had not yet decided whether or not to proceed with the case. The summons was served five months later. The Divisional Court said that the magistrates had a discretion to dismiss the case because of the delay, which had been a deliberate attempt to gain further time in which to reach a decision.

2.16.2   Inadvertent delay: prejudice to defendant

To succeed in having a case dismissed on the basis of delay which is not deliberate, the defence must show both inordinate delay as a result of inefficiency on the part of the prosecution and that the defence have been, or will be, prejudiced by that delay (*per* Lloyd LJ in *R v Gateshead Justices ex p Smith* (1985) 149 JP 681). In that case, there was a delay of more than two years between the issue and the service of the summons and the trial was eventually fixed for a date over three years after the alleged offences. This was said to be inordinate and prejudicial delay and it was therefore held that the case should therefore proceed no further.

In *R v Oxford City Justices ex p Smith* (1982) 75 Cr App R 200, the summons was inadvertently sent to the wrong address; the summons was eventually served nearly two years later. The prosecution had the correct address and the delay was a result of their inefficiency; further, it was found that the defence would be handicapped as a result of the delay and its effect on the memories of any relevant witnesses. It was held that the case should be dismissed.

On the other hand, in *R v Grays Justices ex p Graham* [1982] QB 1239; [1982] 3 All ER 653, committal proceedings held more than two years after the alleged offences were held not to cause undue prejudice to the accused. The Court of Appeal held that the delay was not sufficiently prolonged to amount to an abuse of process and apparently accepted the prosecution contention that the offences involved (cheque fraud) take a long time to investigate.

In *R v Central Criminal Court ex p Randle* [1991] 1 WLR 1087; [1992] 1 All ER 370, the defendants were charged with offences arising out of the escape from prison of the spy George Blake. The offences had occurred some 23 years ago but the defendants had published a book about what they had done in 1989. The prosecution case was based on the book and so the Divisional Court held that the defendants could not claim that they were prejudiced by the failing memory of witnesses.

In *R v Canterbury and St Augustine's Justices ex p Barrington* (1994) 158 JP 325, an information was laid against the defendant alleging a drink-driving offence. The defendant left the address he had given the police before the summons was served. The police had no other address from him. The summons was not served until nearly four years after the alleged offence. The court reiterated the familiar principle that a stay would only be ordered if the defendant could show, on the balance of probabilities, that no fair trial could take place because of the degree of prejudice caused by the delay. That involved looking at the case as a whole. Here, the defendant conceded that it was unlikely that he would have any defence to the summons; in the circumstances, the justices had not erred in concluding that a fair trial was possible despite the delay.

In *R v Telford Justices ex p Badhan* [1991] 2 QB 78; [1991] 2 All ER 854, the defendant was charged with a rape which was alleged to have occurred over 14 years ago. The Divisional Court held that the test to be applied was not whether the prosecution could be blamed for the delay but whether the accused could show, on the balance of probabilities, that a fair trial was no longer possible. In that case, it was not and the case stopped there. In *R v Dutton* [1994] Crim LR 910, it was re-emphasised that it is for the defendant to show, on the balance of probabilities, that the delay is such that a fair trial is not possible.

These decisions followed the Court of Appeal decision on the *Attorney General's Reference (No 1 of 1990)* in which it was said that a stay of proceedings on the ground of delay should rarely be ordered in the absence of fault on the part of the prosecution and should never be ordered where the delay was due merely to the complexity of the case or contributed to by the actions of the defendant himself.

In *R v Birchall* (1995) *The Times*, 23 March, the defendant faced charges of rape and indecent assault arising out of incidents which allegedly took place 15–20 years ago. The judge refused to stay the proceedings for abuse of process. The Court of Appeal (perhaps surprisingly) upheld this decision but allowed the defendant's appeal against conviction because the judge had failed to warn the jury about the difficulties which the defendant would have in defending himself against such old charges.

Similarly, in *R v B* [1996] Crim LR 406, the appellant was charged with rape and indecent assault, the offences allegedly having been committed 19 years earlier. The Court of Appeal, upholding the decision of the trial judge to allow the trial to take place said that, provided that there could still be a fair trial, a lapse of time was not a sufficient reason for granting a stay of the case. However, the judge in this case had failed to direct the jury on the difficulties which the defendant faced in defending the case in the light of the lapse of time. It was on that basis that the appeal was allowed.

Likewise, in *R v Wilkinson* [1996] 1 Cr App Rep 81, convictions for indecent assault, gross indecency and incest were upheld even though the acts were committed some 15–28 years ago. The judge had held that a fair trial was possible and the Court of Appeal would not impugn that decision. Also, the judge had given a warning to the jury that the defence had difficulties in adducing precise evidence because of the lapse of time.

A note of caution on the use of authorities in applications to stay proceedings on the ground of delay was sounded by the Divisional Court in *R v Newham Justices ex p C* [1993] Crim LR 130; comparing the facts of the instant case with the facts of earlier reported cases will rarely be of assistance. It is a question of fact whether the particular defendant is able to show that a fair trial is no longer possible.

The right to a fair trial under Art 6 of the European Convention on Human Rights includes the right to have a trial within a reasonable time. Time runs from the date of the charge. Account is taken of the complexity of the case, the conduct of the defendant, and the conduct of the prosecution. A more rigorous standard applies where the accused is in custody. The 'custody time limits' under the Prosecution of Offences Act 1985 would seem to accord with these principles.

2.16.3 Code of Conduct for Crown Prosecutors

According to the Code of Conduct for Crown Prosecutors, it may not be in the public interest to prosecute where there has been a long delay between the offence taking place and the date of the trial. However, this will not be so if the offence is serious, or the delay has been caused in part by the defendant, or the offence has only recently come to light, or the complexity of the offence has meant that there has been a long investigation.

2.17 RECORD OF DECISION TO GRANT UNCONDITIONAL BAIL

RECORD OF DECISION TO GRANT UNCONDITIONAL BAIL (CRIMINAL CASES)

(Bail Act 1976, s 5; MC Rules 1981, rr 66, 90)

.... Magistrates' Court (Code:)

Date:

Accused:

Date of birth:

Alleged offences[s]: [short particulars and statute]

Decision: The accused is granted bail with a duty to surrender to the custody of [place] Magistrates' Court on [date] at [time] am/pm {or [the Crown Court at the time and place for the time being appointed by that court]}.

Signature ....
Justice of the Peace
[Clerk of the Court present during these proceedings]

2.18 RECORD OF DECISION TO GRANT CONDITIONAL BAIL

RECORD OF DECISION TO GRANT CONDITIONAL BAIL (CRIMINAL CASES)

(Bail Act 1976, s 5; MC Rules 1981, rr 66, 90)

.... Magistrates' Court (Code:)

Date:

Accused:

Date of birth:

Alleged offence[s]:   [short particulars and statute]

Decision: The accused is granted bail, with a duty to surrender to the custody of [place] Magistrates' Court on [date] at [time] am/pm {or [the Crown Court at the time and place for the time being appointed by that court]}; the bail being subject to the following conditions:

Conditions: Conditions to be complied with before release on bail
To provide suret[y][ies] in the sum of £ [each] to secure the accused's surrender to custody at the time and place appointed.
†
Conditions to be complied with after release on bail
†

*Reasons: The above conditions were imposed on the grant of bail for the following reason(s):

Signature ....
Justice of the Peace
[Clerk of the Court present during these proceedings]

*   Delete if section 4 of the Bail Act 1976 does not apply.
†   Insert condition(s) as appropriate.

2.19   RECORD OF DECISION TO WITHHOLD BAIL

RECORD OF DECISION TO WITHHOLD BAIL (CRIMINAL CASES)

(Bail Act 1976, s 5; MC rules 1981, rr 66, 90)

.... Magistrates' Court (Code:)

Date:

Accused:

Date of birth:

Alleged offence[s]:   [short particulars and statute]

Decision: The court, having found that the exception(s) to the right to bail specified in the first column of the Schedule hereto applies [apply] for the reason(s) specified in the second column of the said Schedule, withholds bail.
The accused is [remanded in] [committed to] custody for appearance before [place] Magistrates' Court on [date] at [time] am/pm] {or [the Crown Court at the time and place for the time being appointed by that court]}.

Signature ....
Justice of the Peace
[Clerk of the Court present during these proceedings]

SCHEDULE

Exception(s) to right to bail (Include relevant Part and paragraph number(s) of Schedule I to Bail Act 1976)	Reason(s) for applying the Exception(s) specified in first column

2.20   CERTIFICATE AS TO HEARING A FULL ARGUMENT ON APPLICATION FOR BAIL

CERTIFICATE AS TO HEARING A FULL ARGUMENT ON APPLICATION FOR BAIL (CRIMINAL CASES)

(Bail Act 1976, s 5; MC Rules 1981, rr 66, 90)

.... Magistrates' Court (Code:)

Date:

Accused:

Date of birth:

Alleged offence[s]:   [short particulars and statute]

I hereby certify that, at a hearing this day, the court heard full argument on an application for bail made [by] [on behalf of] the accused, before refusing the application and remanding the accused in custody under section [ ] of the Magistrates' Courts Act 1980.

[The court has not previously heard full argument on an application for bail by or on behalf of the accused in these proceedings]

[The court has previously heard full argument from the accused on an application for bail, but is satisfied [that there has been the following change in his circumstances:] [that the following new considerations have been placed before it:]]

Signature ....
Justice of the Peace
[or By order of the Court
Clerk of the Court]

2.21 RECORD OF DECISION TO VARY CONDITIONS OF BAIL OR IMPOSE CONDITIONS ON BAIL GRANTED UNCONDITIONALLY

RECORD OF DECISION TO VARY CONDITIONS OF BAIL OR IMPOSE CONDITIONS ON BAIL GRANTED UNCONDITIONALLY (CRIMINAL CASES)

(Bail Act 1976, s 5; MC Rules 1981, rr 66, 90)

.... Magistrates' Court (Code:)

Date:

Accused:

Date of birth:

Alleged offence[s]:   [short particulars and statute]

The accused having been granted bail by the above Magistrates' Court on [date] with a duty to surrender to the custody of [place] Magistrates' Court on [date] at [time] am/pm appointed by that court [and the said bail being subject to conditions].

Application having been made by [the defendant] [the prosecutor] under section 3(8) of the Bail Act 1976 for [variation] [imposition] of bail conditions.

Decision: The condition(s) to be complied with by the accused in respect of the said bail shall now be as specified in Schedule I and II hereto

*Reasons: The conditions of bail were [varied] [imposed] for the following reason(s):

Signature ....
Justice of the Peace
[Clerk of the Court present during these proceedings]

*Delete if section 4 of the Bail Act 1976 does not apply.

(contd overleaf)

SCHEDULE I

Conditions to be complied with before on bail

To provide suret[y][ies] in the sum of £   [each] to secure the defendant's surrender to custody at the time and place appointed.
†

SCHEDULE II

Conditions to be complied with after release on bail

†

† Insert condition(s) as appropriate

2.22   RECORD OF DECISION TO GRANT BAIL

RECORD OF DECISION TO GRANT BAIL
(SERIOUS CRIMINAL CASES)

(Bail Act 1976, s 5; Schedule 1; MC Rules 1981, rr 66, 90)

.... Magistrates' Court (Code:)

Date:

Accused:

Address:

Alleged offence[s]:   [short particulars and statute]

Decision: The accused is granted bail, with a duty to surrender to the custody of [place] Magistrates' Court on
[date] at [time] am/pm {or [the Crown Court at
the time and place for the time being appointed by
that court]}. The Court heard representations as to
whether the exceptions to the right to bail in paragraph 2 of Schedule 1 (to the Bail Act) 1976 were
satisfied, but decided that it should grant bail for
the following reasons:

Reasons   The Court stated that the reasons for its decisions
were that:#

*Conditions: *Conditions to be complied with before release on bail*

(contd overleaf)

To provide suret[y][ies] in the sum of £   [each] to secure the accused's
surrender to custody at the time
and place appointed.

Conditions to be complied with after release on bail

†

‡   The above conditions were imposed on the grant
of bail for the following reason(s):

Signature ....
Justice of the Peace
[Clerk of the Court present during these proceedings]

Insert reason(s) as required by para 9A, Part 1, Schedule 1, to
           the Bail Act 1976 (s 145 of the Criminal Justice Act 1988).
*   Delete if unconditional.
†   Insert condition(s) as appropriate.
‡   Delete if s 4 of the Bail Act 1976 does not apply.

2.23   WARRANT OF ARREST ON FAILURE TO SURRENDER BAIL

WARRANT OF ARREST ON FAILURE TO SURRENDER TO BAIL

(Bail Act 1976, s 7; MC Act 1980, s 117; MC Rules 1981, rr 95, 96)

.... Magistrates' Court (Code:)

Date:

Accused:

Alleged offence:	[short particulars statute]
	The accused having been released on bail with a duty to surrender to the custody of the above Magistrates' Court on this day at [time] and having failed to surrender to custody as required
Direction:	You, the constables of [County] Police Force, are hereby required to arrest the accused and bring the accused before the above Magistrates' Court immediately [unless the accused is released on bail as directed below].
*Bail	On arrest, after complying with the condition(s) specified in Schedule I hereto, the accused shall be released on bail subject to the condition(s) specified in Schedule II hereto and with a duty to surrender to the custody of the above Magistrates' Court on [date] at [time] am/pm.

Justice of the Peace
[or By order of the Court
Clerk of the Court]

*Delete if bail is not granted.

SCHEDULE 1

Conditions to be complied with before release on bail

To provide sure[y][ies] in the sum of £   [each] to secure the accused's surrender to custody at the time and place appointed.

†

SCHEDULE II

Conditions to be complied with after release on bail

†

†   Insert condition(s) as appropriate (including in Schedule I directions under MC Rules 1981, r 85 in respect of any pre-release conditions).

TABLE OF STATUTORY MATERIALS

STATUTORY MATERIALS

BAIL ACT 1976

Preliminary

Section 1: Meaning of 'bail in criminal proceedings'

(1) In this Act 'bail in criminal proceedings' means:

    (a) bail grantable in or in connection with proceedings for an offence to a person who is accused or convicted of the offence; or

    (b) bail grantable in connection with an offence to a person who is under arrest for the offence or for whose arrest for the offence a warrant (endorsed for bail) is being issued.

(2) In this Act 'bail' means bail grantable under the law (including common law) for the time being in force.

(3) Except as provided by section 13(3) of this Act, this section does not apply to bail in or in connection with proceedings outside England and Wales.

(4) [Repealed.]

(5) This section applies:

    (a) whether the offence was committed in England or Wales or elsewhere; and

    (b) whether it is an offence under the law of England and Wales, or of any other country or territory.

(6) Bail in criminal proceedings shall be granted (and in particular shall be granted unconditionally or conditionally), in accordance with this Act.

Section 2: Other definitions

(1) In this Act, unless the context otherwise requires, 'conviction' includes:

    (a) a finding of guilt;

    (b) a finding that a person is not guilty by reason of insanity;

    (c) a finding under section 11(1) of the Powers of Criminal Courts (Sentencing) Act 2000 (remand for medical examination) that the person in question did the act or made the omission charged; and

    (d) a conviction of an offence for which an order is made placing the offender on probation or discharging him absolutely or conditionally.

(2) In this Act, unless the context otherwise requires: 'bail hostel' means premises for the accommodation of persons remanded on bail, 'child' means a person under the age of 14, 'court' includes a judge of a court or a justice of the peace and, in the case of a specified court, includes a judge or (as the case may be) justice having powers to act in connection with proceedings before that court;

...

'offence' includes an alleged offence;

...

'surrender to custody' means, in relation to a person released on bail, surrendering himself into the custody of the court or of the constable (according to the requirements of the grant of bail) at the time and place for the time being appointed for him to do so;

'vary', in relation to bail, means imposing further conditions after bail is granted, or varying or rescinding conditions;

'young person' means a person who has attained the age of 14 and is under the age of 17.

(3) Where an enactment (whenever passed) which relates to bail in criminal proceedings refers to the person bailed appearing before a court it is to be construed unless the context otherwise requires as referring to his surrendering himself into the custody of the court.

(4) Any reference in this Act to any other enactment is a reference thereto as amended, and includes a reference thereto as extended or applied, by or under any other enactment, including this Act.

Incidents of bail in criminal proceedings

Section 3: General provisions

(1) A person granted bail in criminal proceedings shall be under a duty to surrender to custody, and that duty is enforceable in accordance with section 6 of this Act.

(2) No recognisance for his surrender to custody shall be taken from him.

(3) Except as provided by this section:

(a) no security for his surrender to custody shall be taken from him;

(b) he shall not be required to provide a surety or sureties for his surrender to custody; and

(c) no other requirement shall be imposed on him as a condition of bail.

(4) He may be required, before release on bail, to provide a surety or sureties to secure his surrender to custody.

(5) He may be required, before release on bail, to give security for his surrender to custody.

The security may be given by him or on his behalf.

(6) He may be required to comply, before release on bail or later, with such requirements as appear to the court to be necessary to secure that:

(a) he surrenders to custody;

(b) he does not commit an offence while on bail;

(c) he does not interfere with witnesses or otherwise obstruct the course of justice whether in relation to himself or any other person;

(d) he makes himself available for the purpose of enabling inquiries or a report to be made to assist the court in dealing with him for the offence, and, in any Act, 'the normal powers to impose conditions of bail' means the powers to impose conditions under paragraph (a), (b) or (c) above.

(e) before the time appointed for him to surrender to custody, he attends an interview with an authorised advocate or authorised litigator, as defined by section 119(1) of the Courts and Legal Services Act 1990.

(6ZA) Where he is required under sub-section (6) above to reside in a bail hostel or probation hostel, he may also be required to comply with the rules of the hostel.

(6A) In the case of a person accused of murder the court granting bail shall, unless it considers that satisfactory reports on his mental condition have already been obtained, impose as conditions of bail:

(a) a requirement that the accused shall undergo examination by two medical practitioners for the purpose of enabling such reports to be prepared; and

(b) a requirement that he shall for that purpose attend such an institution or place as the court directs and comply with any other directions which may be given to him for that purpose by either of those practitioners.

(6B) Of the medical practitioners referred to in sub-section (6A) above at least one shall be a practitioner approved for the purposes of section 12 of the Mental Health Act 1983.

(7) If a parent or guardian of a child or young person consents to be surety for the child or young person for the purposes of this sub-section, the parent or guardian may be required to secure that the child or young person complies with any requirement imposed on him by virtue of sub-section (6) or (6A) above but:

(a) no requirement shall be imposed on the parent or the guardian of a young person by virtue of this sub-section where it appears that the young person will attain the age of 17 before the time to be appointed for him to surrender to custody; and

(b) the parent or guardian shall not be required to secure compliance with any requirement to which his consent does not extend and shall not, in respect of those requirements to which his consent does extend, be bound in a sum greater than £50.

(8) Where a court has granted bail in criminal proceedings that court or, where that court has committed a person on bail to the Crown Court for trial or to be sentenced or otherwise dealt with, that court or the Crown Court may on application:

(a) by or on behalf of the person to whom bail was granted; or

(b) by the prosecutor or a constable,

vary the conditions of bail or impose conditions in respect of bail which has been granted unconditionally.

(8A) Where a notice of transfer is given under a relevant transfer provision, sub-section (8) above shall have effect in relation to a person in relation to whose case the notice is given as if he had been committed on bail to the Crown Court for trial.

(9) This section is subject to sub-section (3) of section 11 of the Powers of Criminal Courts (Sentencing) Act 2000 (conditions of bail on remand for medical examination).

(10) This section is subject, in its application to bail granted by a constable, to section 3A of this Act.

In sub-section (8A) above 'relevant transfer provision' means:

(a) section 4 of the Criminal Justice Act 1987; or

(b) section 53 of the Criminal Justice Act 1991.

Section 3A: Conditions of bail in case of police bail

(1) Section 3 of this Act applies, in relation to bail granted by a custody officer under Part IV of the Police and Criminal Evidence Act 1984 in cases where the normal powers to impose conditions of bail are available to him, subject to the following modifications.

(2) Sub-section (6) does not authorise the imposition of a requirement to reside in a bail hostel or any requirement under paragraph (d).

(3) Sub-section (6ZA), (6A) and (6B) shall be omitted.

(4) For sub-section (8), substitute the following:

(8) where a custody officer has granted bail in criminal proceedings he or another custody officer serving at the same police station may, at the request of the person to whom it was granted, vary the conditions of bail; and in doing so he may impose conditions or more onerous conditions.

(5) Where a constable grants bail to a person no conditions shall be imposed under sub-sections (4), (5), (6) or (7) of section 3 of this Act unless it appears to the constable that it is necessary to do so for the purpose of preventing that person from:

(a) failing to surrender to custody; or

(b) committing an offence while on bail; or

(c) interfering with witnesses or otherwise obstructing the course of justice, whether in relation to himself or any other person.

(6) Sub-section (5) above also applies on any request to a custody officer under sub-section (8) of section 3 of this Act to vary the conditions of bail.

Bail for accused persons and others

Section 4: General right to bail of accused persons and others

(1) A person to whom this section applies shall be granted bail except as provided in Schedule 1 to this Act.

(2) This section applies to a person who is accused of an offence when:

    (a) he appears or is brought before a magistrates' court or the Crown Court in the course of or in connections with proceedings for the offence; or

    (b) he applies to a court for bail or for a variation of the condition of bail in connection with the proceedings.

This sub-section does not apply as respects proceedings on or after a person's conviction of the offence or proceedings against a fugitive offender for the offence.

(3) This section also applies to a person who, having been convicted of an offence, appears or is brought before a magistrates' court to be dealt with under Part II of Schedule 3 to the Powers of Criminal Courts (Sentencing) Act 2000 (breach of certain community orders).

(4) This section also applies to a person who has been convicted of an offence and whose case is adjourned by the court for the purpose of enabling inquiries or a report to be made to assist the court in dealing with him for the offence.

(5) Schedule 1 to this Act also has effect as respects conditions of bail for a person to whom this section applies.

(6) In Schedule 1 to this Act 'the defendant' means a person to whom this section applies and any reference to a defendant whose case is adjourned for inquiries or a report is a reference to a person to whom this section applies by virtue of sub-section (4) above.

(7) This section is subject to section 41 of the Magistrates' Courts Act 1980 (restriction of bail by magistrates' court in cases of treason).

(8) This section is subject to section 25 of the Criminal Justice and Public Order Act 1994 (exclusion of bail in cases of homicide and rape).[1]

---

1   Section 25 of the Criminal Justice and Public Order Act (no bail for defendants charged with or convicted of homicide or rape after previous conviction of such offences):

    (1) A person who in any proceedings has been charged with or convicted of an offence to which this section applies in circumstances to which it applies shall not be granted bail in those proceedings.

    (2) This section applies, subject to sub-section (3) below, to the following offences, that is to say: (a) murder; (b) attempted murder; (c) manslaughter; (d) rape; or (e) attempted rape.

    (3) This section applies to a person charged with or convicted of any such offence only if he has previously been convicted by or before a court in any part of the United Kingdom of any such offence or of culpable homicide and, in the case of a previous conviction of manslaughter or of culpable homicide, if he was then sentenced to imprisonment or, if he was then a child or young person, to long term detention under any of the relevant enactments.

    (4) This section applies whether or not an appeal is pending against conviction or sentence.

    (5) In this section, 'conviction' includes: (a) a finding that a person is not guilty by reason of insanity; (b) a finding under section 4A(3) of the Criminal Procedure (Insanity) Act 1964 (cases of unfitness to plead) that a person did the act or made the omission charged against him; and (c) a conviction of an offence for which an order is made placing the offender on probation or discharging him absolutely or conditionally; and 'convicted' shall be construed accordingly ...

Supplementary

Section 5: Supplementary provisions about decisions on bail

(1) Subject to sub-section (2) below, where:

    (a) a court or constable grants bail in criminal proceedings; or

    (b) a court withholds bail in criminal proceedings from a person to whom section 4 of this Act applies; or

    (c) a court, officer of a court or constable appoints a time or place or a court or officer of a court appoints a different time or place for a person granted bail in criminal proceedings to surrender to custody; or

    (d) a court or constable varies any conditions of bail or imposes conditions in respect of bail in criminal proceedings,

that court, officer or constable shall make a record of the decision in the prescribed manner and containing the prescribed particulars and, if requested to do so by the person in relation to whom the decision was taken, shall cause him to be given a copy of the record of the decision as soon as practicable after the record is made.

(2) Where bail in criminal proceedings is granted by endorsing a warrant of arrest for bail the constable who releases on bail the person arrested shall make the record required by sub-section (1) above instead of the judge or justice who issued the warrant.

(3) Where a magistrates' court or the Crown Court:

    (a) withholds bail in criminal proceedings; or

    (b) imposes conditions in granting bail in criminal proceedings; or

    (c) varies any conditions of bail or imposes conditions in respect of bail in criminal proceedings,

and does so in relation to a person to whom section 4 of this Act applies, then the court shall, with a view to enabling him to consider making an application in the matter to another court, give reasons for withholding bail or for imposing or varying the conditions.

(4) A court which is by virtue of sub-section (3) above required to give reasons for its decision shall include a note of those reasons in the record of its decision and shall (except in a case where, by virtue of sub-section (5) below, this need not be done) give a copy of that note to the person in relation to whom the decision was taken.

(5) The Crown Court need not give a copy of the note of the reasons for its decision to the person in relation to whom the decision was taken where that person is represented by counsel or a solicitor unless his counsel or solicitor requests the court to do so.

(6) Where a magistrates' court withholds bail in criminal proceedings from a person who is not represented by counsel or a solicitor, the court shall:

    (a) if it is committing him for trial to the Crown Court, or if it issues a certificate under sub-section (6A) below inform him that he may apply to the High Court or to the Crown Court to be granted bail;

     (b) in any other case, inform him that he may apply to the High Court for that purpose.

(6A) Where in criminal proceedings:

     (a) a magistrates' court remands a person in custody under section 11 of the Powers of Criminal Courts (Sentencing) Act 2000 (remand for medical examination) or any of the following provisions of the Magistrates' Courts Act 1980:

          (i) section 5 (adjournment of inquiry into offence);

          (ii) section 10 (adjournment of trial); or

          (iii) section 18 (initial procedure on information against adult for offence triable either way),

     after hearing full argument on an application for bail from him; and

     (b) either:

          (i) it has not previously heard such argument on an application for bail from him in those proceedings; or

          (ii) it has previously heard full argument from him on such an application but it is satisfied that there has been a change in his circumstances or that new considerations have been placed before it,

     it shall be the duty of the court to issue a certificate in the prescribed form that they heard full argument on his application for bail before they refused the application.

(6B) Where the court issues a certificate under sub-section (6A) above in a case to which paragraph (b)(ii) of that sub-section applies, it shall state in the certificate the nature of the change of circumstances or the new considerations which caused it to hear a further fully argued application.

(6C) Where a court issues a certificate under sub-section (6A) above it shall cause the person to whom it refuses bail to be given a copy of the certificate.

 (7) Where a person has given security in pursuance of section 3(5) above, and a court is satisfied that he failed to surrender to custody then, unless it appears that he had reasonable cause for his failure, the court may order the forfeiture of the security.

 (8) If the court orders the forfeiture of a security under sub-section (7) above, the court may declare that the forfeiture extends to such amount less than the full value of the security as it thinks fit to order.

[Sub-sections (8A) to (9A) detail procedure for taking and forfeiting a security.]

(10) In this section 'prescribed' means, in relation to the decision of a court or an officer of a court, prescribed by Supreme Court Rules, Courts-Martial Appeal Rules, Crown Court Rules or Magistrates' Courts Rules, as the case requires or, in relation to a decision of a constable, prescribed by direction of the Secretary of State,

(11) This section is subject, in its application to bail granted by a constable, to section 5(a) of this Act.

Section 5A: Supplementary provisions in case of police bail

(1) Section 5 of this Act applies, in relation to bail granted by a custody officer under Part IV of the Police and Criminal Evidence Act 1984 in cases where the normal powers to impose conditions of bail are available to him, subject to the following modifications.

(2) For sub-section (3) substitute the following:

(3) Where a custody officer, in relation to any person:

(a) imposes conditions in granting bail in criminal proceedings; or

(b) varies any conditions of bail or imposes conditions in respect of bail, in criminal proceedings,

the custody officer shall, with a view to enabling that person to consider requesting him or another custody officer, or making an application to a magistrates' court, to vary the conditions, give reasons for imposing or varying the conditions.

(3) For sub-section (4) substitute the following:

(4) A custody officer who is by virtue of sub-section (3) above required to give reasons for his decision shall include a note of those reasons in the custody record and shall give a copy of that note to the person in relation to whom the decision was taken.

(4) Sub-sections (5) and (6) shall be omitted.

Section 5B: Reconsideration of decisions granting bail

(1) Where a magistrates' court has granted bail in criminal proceedings in connection with an offence, or proceedings for an offence, to which this section applies or a constable has granted bail in criminal proceedings in connections with proceedings for an offence, that court or the appropriate court in relation to the constable may, on application by the prosecutor for the decision to be reconsidered:

(a) vary the conditions of bail;

(b) impose conditions in respect of bail which has been granted unconditionally; or

(c) withhold bail.

(2) The offences to which this section applies are offences triable on indictment and offences triable either way.

(3) No application for the reconsideration of a decision under this section shall be made unless it is based on information which was not available to the court or constable when the decision was taken.

(4) Whether or not the person to whom the application relates appears before it, the magistrates' court shall take the decision in accordance with section 4(1) and (Schedule 1) of this Act.

(5) Where the decision of the court on a reconsideration under this section is to withhold bail from the person to whom it was originally granted the court shall:

    (a) if that person is before the court, remand him in custody; and

    (b) if that person is not before the court, order him to surrender himself forthwith into the custody of the court.

(6) Where a person surrenders himself into the custody of the court in compliance with an order under sub-section (5) above, the court shall remand him in custody.

(7) A person who has been ordered to surrender to custody under sub-section (5) above may be arrested without warrant by a constable if he fails without reasonable cause to surrender to custody in accordance with the order.

(8) A person arrested in pursuance of sub-section (7) above shall be brought as soon as practicable, and in any event within 24 hours after his arrest, before a justice of the peace for petty sessions area in which he was arrested and the justice shall remand him in custody.

In reckoning for the purposes of this sub-section any period of 24 hours, no account shall be taken of Christmas Day, Good Friday or any Sunday.

(9) Magistrates' court rules shall include provision:

    (a) requiring notice of an application under this section and of the grounds for it to be given to the person affected, including notice of the powers available to the court under it;

    (b) for securing that any representations made by the person affected (whether in writing or orally) are considered by the court before making its decision; and

    (c) designating the court which is the appropriate court in relation to the decision of any constable to grant bail.

Section 6: Offence of absconding by person released on bail

(1) If a person who has been released on bail in criminal proceedings fails without reasonable cause to surrender to custody he shall be guilty of an offence.

(2) If a person who:

    (a) has been released on bail in criminal proceedings; and

    (b) having reasonable cause therefore, has failed to surrender to custody,

    fails to surrender to custody at the appointed place as soon after the appointed time as is reasonably practicable he shall be guilty of an offence.

(3) It shall be for the accused to prove that he had reasonable cause for his failure to surrender to custody.

(4) A failure to give to a person granted bail in criminal proceedings a copy of the record of the decision shall not constitute a reasonable cause for that person's failure to surrender to custody.

(5) An offence under sub-section (1) or (2) above shall be punishable either on summary conviction or as if it were a criminal contempt of court.

(6) Where a magistrates' court convicts a person of an offence under sub-section (1) or (2) above the court may, if it thinks:

(a) that the circumstances of the offence are such that greater punishment should be inflicted for that offence than the court has power to inflict; or

(b) in a case where it commits that person for trial to the Crown Court for another offence, that it would be appropriate for him to be dealt with for the offence under sub-section (1) or (2) above by the court before which he is tried for the other offence,

commit him in custody or on bail to the Crown Court for sentence.

(7) A person who is convicted summarily of an offence under sub-section (1) or (2) above and is not committed to the Crown Court for sentence shall be liable to imprisonment for a term not exceeding three months or to a fine not exceeding level 5 on the standard scale or to both and a person who is so committed for sentence or is dealt with as for such a contempt shall be liable to imprisonment for a term not exceeding 12 months or to a fine or to both.

(8) In any proceedings for an offence under sub-section (1) or (2) above a document purporting to be a copy of the part of the prescribed record which relates to the time and place appointed for the person specified in the record to surrender to custody and to be duly certified to be a true copy of that part of the record shall be evidence of the time and place appointed for that person to surrender to custody.

(9) For the purposes of sub-section (8) above:

(a) 'the prescribed record' means the record of the decision of the court, officer, or constable made in pursuance of section 5(1) of this Act;

(b) the copy of the prescribed record is duly certified if it is certified by the appropriate officer of the court or, as the case may be, by the constable who took the decision or a constable designated for the purpose by the officer in charge of the police station from which the person to whom the record relates was released;

(c) 'the appropriate officer' of the court is:

(i) in the case of a magistrates' court, the justices' clerk or such other officer as may be authorised by him to act for the purpose;

(ii) in the case of the Crown Court, such officer as may be designated for the purpose in accordance with arrangements made by the Lord Chancellor;

(iii) in the case of the High Court, such officer as may be designated for the purpose in accordance with arrangements made by the Lord Chancellor;

(iv) in the case of the Court of Appeal, the registrar of criminal appeals or such other officer as may be authorised by him to act for the purpose;

(v) in the case of the Courts-Martial Appeal Court, the registrar or such other officer as may be authorised by him to act for the purpose.

Section 7: Liability to arrest for absconding or breaking conditions of bail

(1) If a person who has been released on bail in criminal proceedings and is under a duty to surrender into the custody of a court fails to surrender to custody at the time appointed for him to do so the court may issue a warrant for his arrest.

(2) If a person who has been released on bail in criminal proceedings absents himself from the court at any time after he has surrendered into the custody of the court and before the court is ready to begin or to resume the hearing of the proceedings, the court may issue a warrant for his arrest; but no warrant shall be issued under this sub-section where that person is absent in accordance with leave given to him by or on behalf of the court.

(3) A person who has been released on bail in criminal proceedings and is under a duty to surrender into the custody of a court may be arrested without warrant by a constable:

(a) if a constable has reasonable grounds for believing that that person is not likely to surrender to custody;

(b) if the constable has reasonable grounds for believing that that person is likely to break any of the conditions of his bail or has reasonable grounds for suspecting that that person has broken any of those conditions; or

(c) in a case where that person was released on bail with one or more surety or sureties, if a surety notifies in writing that that person is unlikely to surrender to custody and that for that reason the surety wishes to be relieved of his obligations as a surety.

(4) A person arrested in pursuance of sub-section (3) above:

(a) shall, except where he was arrested within 24 hours of the time appointed for him to surrender to custody, be brought as soon as practicable and in any event within 24 hours after his arrest before a justice of the peace for the petty sessions area in which he was arrested; and

(b) in the said excepted case shall be brought before the court at which he was to have surrendered to custody.

In reckoning for the purposes of this sub-section any period of 24 hours, no account shall be taken of Christmas Day, Good Friday or any Sunday.

(5) A justice of the peace before whom a person is brought under sub-section (4) above may, subject to sub-section (6) below, if of the opinion that that person:

(a) is not likely to surrender to custody; or

(b) has broken or is likely to break any condition of his bail,

remand him in custody or commit him to custody, as the case may require, or alternatively, grant him bail subject to the same or to different conditions, but if not of that opinion shall grant him bail subject to the same conditions (if any) as were originally imposed.

(6) Where the person so brought before the justice is a child or young person and the justice does not grant him bail, sub-section (5) above shall have effect subject to the provisions of section 23 of the Children and Young Persons Act 1969 (remands to the care of local authorities).

Section 8: Bail with sureties

(1) This section applies where a person is granted bail in criminal proceedings on condition that he provides one or more surety or sureties for the purpose of securing that he surrenders to custody.

(2) In considering the suitability for that purpose of a proposed surety, regard may be had (amongst other things) to:

(a) the surety's financial resources;

(b) his character and any previous convictions of his; and

(c) his proximity (whether in point of kinship, place of residence or otherwise) to the person for whom he is to be surety.

(3) Where a court grants a person bail in criminal proceedings on such a condition but is unable to release him because no surety or no suitable surety is available, the court shall fix the amount in which the surety is to be bound and sub-sections (4) and (5) below, or in a case where the proposed surety resides in Scotland sub-section (6) below, shall apply for the purpose of enabling the recognizance of the surety to be entered into subsequently.

(4) Where this sub-section applies the recognizance of the surety may be entered into before such of the following persons or descriptions of persons as the court may by order specify or, if it makes no such order, before any of the following persons, that is to say:

(a) where the decision is taken by a magistrates' court, before a justice of the peace, a justices' clerk or a police officer who either is of the rank of inspector or above or is in charge of a police station or, if magistrates' courts rules so provide, by a person of such other description as is specified in the rules;

(b) where the decision is taken by the Crown Court, before any of the persons specified in paragraph (a) above or, if Crown Court rules so provide, by a person of such other descriptions as is specified in the rules;

(c) where the decision is taken by the High Court or the Court of Appeal, before any of the persons specified in paragraph (a) above or, if Supreme Court rules so provide, by a person of such other description as is specified in the rules;

(d) where the decision is taken by the Courts-Martial Appeal Court, before any of the persons specified in paragraph (a) above or, if Courts-Martial Appeal Rules so provide by a person of such other description as is specified in the rules,

and Supreme Court Rules, Crown Court rules, Courts-Martial Appeal Rules or Magistrates' Courts Rules may also prescribe the manner in which a recognizance which is to be entered into before such a person is to be entered into and the persons by whom and the manner in which the recognizance may be enforced.

(5) Where a surety seeks to enter into his recognizance before any person in accordance with sub-section (4) above but that person declines to take his recognizance because he is not satisfied of the surety's suitability, the surety may apply to:

(a) the court which fixed the amount of the recognizance in which the surety was to be bound; or

(b) a magistrates' court for the petty sessions area in which he resides;

for that court to take his recognizance and that court shall, if satisfied or his suitability, take his recognizance.

(6) Where this sub-section applies, the court, if satisfied of the suitability of the proposed surety, may direct that arrangements be made for the recognizance of the surety to be entered into in Scotland before any constable, within the meaning of the Police (Scotland) Act 1967, having charge at any police office or station in like manner as the recognizance would be entered into in England or Wales.

(7) Where, in pursuance of sub-section (4) or (6) above, a recognizance is entered into otherwise than before the court that fixed the amount of the recognizance, the same consequences shall follow as if it had been entered into before that court.

Miscellaneous

Section 9: Offence of agreeing to indemnify sureties in criminal proceedings

(1) If a person agrees with another to indemnify that other against any liability which that other may incur as a surety to secure the surrender to custody of a person accused or convicted of or under arrest for an offence, he had that other person shall be guilty of an offence.

(2) An offence under sub-section (1) above is committed whether the agreement is made before or after the person to be indemnified becomes a surety and whether or not he becomes a surety and whether the agreement contemplates compensation in money or in money's worth.

(3) Where a magistrates' court convicts a person of an offence under sub-section (1) above the court may, if it thinks:

(a) that the circumstances of the offence are such that greater punishment should be inflicted for that offence than the court has power to inflict; or

(b) in a case where it commits that person for trial to the Crown Court for another offence, that it would be appropriate for him to be dealt with for the offence under sub-section (1) above by the court before which he is tried for the other offence,

commit him in custody or on bail to the Crown Court for sentence.

(4) A person guilty of an offence under sub-section (1) above shall be liable:

(a) on summary conviction, to imprisonment for a term not exceeding 3 months or to a fine not exceeding the statutory maximum or to both; or

(b) on conviction on indictment or if sentenced by the Crown Court on committal for sentence under sub-section (3) above, to imprisonment for a term not exceeding 12 months or to a fine or to both.

(5) No proceedings for an offence under sub-section (1) above shall be instituted except by or with the consent of the Director of Public Prosecutions.

[Sections 10 and 11 repealed.]

SCHEDULE 1

PERSONS ENTITLED TO BAIL: SUPPLEMENTARY PROVISIONS

PART I DEFENDANTS ACCUSED OR CONVICTED OF IMPRISONABLE OFFENCES

Defendants to whom Part I applies

1 Where the offence or one of the offences of which the defendant is accused or convicted in the proceedings is punishable with imprisonment the following provisions of this Part of this Schedule apply.

Exceptions to right of bail

2 The defendant need not be granted bail if the court is satisfied that there are substantial grounds for believing that the defendant, if released on bail (whether subject to conditions or not) would:

(a) fail to surrender to custody; or

(b) commit an offence while on bail; or

(c) interfere with witnesses or otherwise obstruct the course of justice, whether in relation to himself or any other person.

2A The defendant need not be granted bail if:

(a) the offence is an indictable offence or an offence triable either way; and

(b) it appears to the court that he was on bail in criminal proceedings on the date of the offence.

3   The defendant need not be granted bail if the court is satisfied that the defendant should be kept in custody for his own protection or, if he is a child or young person, for his own welfare.

4   The defendant need not be granted bail if he is in custody in pursuance of the sentence of a court or of any authority acting under any of the Services Acts.

5   The defendant need not be granted bail where the court is satisfied that it has not been practicable to obtain sufficient information for the purpose of taking the decisions required by this Part of this Schedule for want of time since the institution of the proceedings against him.

6   The defendant need not be granted bail if, having been released on bail in or in connection with the proceedings for the offence, he has been arrested in pursuance of section 7 of this Act.

Exception applicable only to defendant whose case is adjourned for inquiries or a report

7   Where his case is adjourned for inquiries or a report, the defendant need not be granted bail if it appears to the court that it would be impracticable to complete the inquiries or make the report without keeping the defendant in custody.

Restriction of conditions of bail

8

(1) Subject to sub-paragraph (3) below, where the defendant is granted bail, no conditions shall be imposed under sub-sections (4) to (7) (except sub-section (6) (d)) of section 3 of this Act unless it appears to the court that it is necessary to do so for the purpose of preventing the occurrence of any of the events mentioned in paragraph 2 of this Part of this Schedule.

(1A) No condition shall be imposed under section 3(6)(d) of this Act unless it appears necessary to do so for the purpose of enabling inquiries or a report to be made.

(2) Sub-paragraph (1) and (1A) above also apply on any application to the court to vary the conditions of bail or to impose conditions in respect of bail which has been granted unconditionally.

(3) The restriction imposed by sub-paragraph (1A) above shall not apply to the conditions required to be imposed under section 3(6A) of this act or operate to override the direction in section 11(3) of the Powers of Criminal Courts (Sentencing) Act 2000 to a magistrates' court to impose conditions of bail under section 3(6)(d) of this Act of the description specified in the said section 30(2) in the circumstances so specified.

Decisions under paragraph 2

9   In taking the decisions required by paragraph 2 or 2A of this Part of this Schedule, the court shall have regard to such of the following considerations as appear to it to be relevant, that is to say:

(a) the nature and seriousness of the offence or default (and the probable method of dealing with the defendant for it);

(b) the character, antecedents, associations and community ties of the defendant;

(c) the defendant's record as respects the fulfilment of his obligations under previous grants of bail in criminal proceedings;

(d) except in the case of a defendant whose case is adjourned for the inquiries or a report, the strength of the evidence of his having committed the offence or having defaulted,

as well as to any other things which appear to be relevant.

9A

(1) If:

(a) the defendant is charged with an offence to which this paragraph applies; and

(b) representations are made as to any of the matters mentioned in paragraph 2 of this Part of this Schedule; and

(c) the court decides to grant him bail,

the court shall state the reasons for its decision and shall cause those reasons to be included in the record of the proceedings.

(2) The offences to which this paragraph applies are:

(a) murder;

(b) manslaughter;

(c) rape;

(d) attempted murder; and

(e) attempted rape.

Cases under section 128A of the Magistrates' Courts Act 1980

9B Where the court is considering exercising the power conferred by section 128A of the Magistrates' Courts Act 1980 (power to remand in custody for more than 8 clear days), it shall have regard to the total length of time which the accused would spend in custody if it were to exercise the power.

PART II DEFENDANTS ACCUSED OR CONVICTED OF NON-IMPRISONABLE OFFENCES

Defendants to whom Part II applies

1 Where the offence or every offence of which the defendant is accused or convicted in the proceedings is one which is not punishable with imprisonment the following provisions of this Part of this Schedule apply.

Exceptions to right to bail

2 The defendants need not be granted bail if:

(a) it appears to the court that, having been previously granted bail in criminal proceedings, he has failed to surrender to custody in accordance with his obligations under the grant of bail; and

(b) the court believes, in view of that failure, that the defendant, if released on bail (whether subject to conditions or not) would fail to surrender to custody.

3 The defendant need not be granted bail if the court is satisfied that the defendant should be kept in custody for his own protection or, if he is a child or young person, for his own welfare.

4 The defendant need not be granted bail if he is in custody in pursuance of the sentence of a court or of any authority acting under any of the Services Acts.

5 The defendant need not be granted bail if, having been released on bail in or in connection with the proceedings for the offence, he has been arrested in pursuance of section 7 of this Act.

PART IIA DECISIONS WHERE BAIL REFUSED ON PREVIOUS HEARING

1 If the court decides not to grant the defendant bail, it is the court's duty to consider, at each subsequent hearing while the defendant is a person to whom section 4 above applies and remains in custody, whether he ought to be granted bail.

2 At the first hearing after that at which the court decided not to grant the defendant bail he may support an application for bail with any argument as to fact or law that he desires (whether or not he has advanced that argument previously).

3 At subsequent hearings the court need not hear arguments as to fact or law which it has heard previously.

PART III INTERPRETATION

1 For the purposes of this Schedule the question whether an offence is one which is punishable with imprisonment shall be determined without regard to any enactment prohibiting or restricting the imprisonment of young offenders or first offenders.

...

3 References in this Schedule to a defendant's being kept in custody or being in custody include (where the defendant is a child or young person) references to his being kept or being in the care of a local authority in pursuance of a warrant of commitment under section 23(1) of the Children and Young Persons Act 1969.

4   In this Schedule:

...

'default', in relation to the defendant, means the default for which he is to be dealt with under Part II of Schedule 3 of the Powers of Criminal Courts (Sentencing) Act 2000.

...

MAGISTRATES' COURTS ACT 1980

Section 42: Restriction on justices sitting after dealing with bail

(1) A justice of the peace shall not take part in trying the issue of an accused's guilt on the summary trial of an information if in the course of the same proceedings the justice has been informed, for the purpose of determining whether the accused shall be granted bail, that he has one or more previous convictions.

(2) For the purposes of this section any committal proceedings from which the proceedings on the summary trial arose shall be treated as part of the trial.[2]

Section 43: Bail on arrest

(1) Where a person has been granted bail under Part IV of the Police and Criminal Evidence Act 1984 subject to a duty to appear before a magistrates' court, the court before which he is to appear may appoint a later time as the time at which he is to appear and may enlarge the recognizances of any sureties for him at that time.

(2) The recognizance of any surety for any person granted bail subject to a duty to attend at a police station may be enforced as if it were conditioned for his appearance before a magistrates' court for the petty sessions area in which the police station named in the recognizance is situated.

Section 43A: Functions of magistrates' court where a person in custody is brought before it with a view to his appearance before the Crown Court

(1) Where a person in custody in pursuance of a warrant issued by the Crown Court with a view to his appearance before the Crown Court is brought before a magistrates' court in pursuance of section 81(5) of the Supreme Court Act 1981:

---

2   This sub-section applies where committal proceedings are discontinued in favour of summary trial under s 25(3) of the Magistrates' Courts Act 1980.

(a) the magistrates' court shall commit him in custody or release him on bail until he can be brought or appear before the Crown Court at the time and place appointed by the Crown Court;

(b) if the warrant is endorsed for bail, but the person in custody is unable to satisfy the conditions endorsed, the magistrates' court may vary those conditions, if satisfied that it is proper to do so.

...

Section 43B: Power to grant bail where police bail has been granted

(1) Where a custody officer:

(a) grants bail to any person under Part IV of the Police and Criminal Evidence Act 1984 in criminal proceedings and imposes conditions; or

(b) varies, in relation to any person, conditions of bail in criminal proceedings under section 3(8) of the Bail Act 1976,

a magistrates' court may, on application by or on behalf of that person, grant bail or vary the conditions.

(2) On an application under sub-section (1) the court, if it grants bail and imposes conditions or if it varies the conditions, may impose more onerous conditions.

(3) On determining an application under sub-section (1) the court shall remand the applicant, in custody or on bail in accordance with the determination, and where the court withholds bail or grants bail the grant of bail made by the custody officer shall lapse.

(4) In this section 'bail in criminal proceedings' and 'vary' have the same meanings as they have in the Bail Act 1976.

BAIL (AMENDMENT) ACT 1993

Section 1: Prosecution right of appeal

(1) Where a magistrates' court grants bail to a person who is charged with or convicted of:

(a) an offence punishable with a term of imprisonment of 5 years or more; or

(b) an offence under section 12 (taking a conveyance without authority) or 12A (aggravated vehicle taking) of the Theft Act 1968,

the prosecution may appeal to a judge of the Crown Court against the granting of bail.

(2) Sub-section (1) above applies only where the prosecution is conducted:

(a) by or on behalf of the Director of Public Prosecutions; or

(b) [persons prescribed the Secretary of State – currently, the Serious Fraud Office, the Department of Trade and Industry, the Commissioners of Customs & Excise, the Department of Social Security, the Post Office, the Commissioners of Inland Revenue.]

(3) Such an appeal may be made only if:

(a) the prosecution made representations that bail should not be granted; and

(b) the representations were made before it was granted.

(4) In the event of the prosecution wishing to exercise the right of appeal set out in sub-section (1) above, oral notice of appeal should be given to the magistrates' court at the conclusion of the proceedings in which such bail has been granted and before the release from custody of the person concerned.

(5) Written notice of appeal shall thereafter be served on the magistrates' court and the person concerned within two hours of the conclusion of such proceedings.

(6) Upon receipt from the prosecution of oral notice of appeal from its decision to grant bail the magistrates' court shall remand in custody the person concerned, until the appeal is determined or otherwise disposed of.

(7) Where the prosecution fails, within the period of two hours mentioned in sub-section (5) above, to serve one or both of the notices required by that sub-section, the appeal shall be deemed to have been disposed of.

(8) The hearing of an appeal under sub-section (1) above against a decision of the magistrates' court to grant bail shall be commenced with forty-eight hours, excluding weekends and any public holiday (that is to say, Christmas Day, Good Friday or a bank holiday), from the date on which oral notice of appeal is given.

(9) At the hearing of any appeal by the prosecution under this section, such appeal shall be by way of re-hearing, and the judge hearing any such appeal may remand the person concerned in custody or may grant bail subject to such conditions (if any) as he thinks fit.

(10) In relation to a child or young person (within the meaning of the Children and Young Persons Act 1969):

(a) the reference in sub-section (1) above to an offence punishable by a term of imprisonment is to be read as a reference to an offence which would be so punishable in the case of an adult; and

(b) the reference in sub-section (6) above to remand in custody is to be read subject to the provisions of section 23 of the Act of 1969 (remands to local authority accommodation).

MAGISTRATES' COURTS RULES 1981 (SI 1981/552 AS AMENDED)

Rule 84A

(1) An application under section 43B(1) of the Magistrates' Courts Act 1980 shall:

    (a) be made in writing;

    (b) contain a statement of the grounds upon which it is made;

    (c) specify the offence with which the applicant was charged before his release on bail;

    (d) specify, or be accompanied by a copy of the note of, the reasons given by the custody officer for imposing or varying the conditions of bail; and

    (e) specify the name and address of any surety provided by the applicant before his release on bail to secure his surrender to custody.

(2) Any such application shall be sent to the clerk of:

    (a) the magistrates' court (if any) appointed by the custody officer as the court before which the applicant has a duty to appear; or

    (b) if no such court has been appointed, a magistrates' court acting for the petty sessions area in which the police station at which the applicant was granted bail or at which conditions of his bail were varied, as the case may be, is situated,

and, in either case, a copy shall be sent to a custody officer appointed for that police station.

(3) The clerk to whom an application is sent under paragraph (2) shall send a notice in writing of the date, time and place fixed for the hearing of the application to:

    (a) the applicant;

    (b) the prosecutor; and

    (c) any surety in connection with bail in criminal proceedings granted to, or the conditions of which were varied by a custody officer in relation to, the applicant.

(4) The time fixed for the hearing shall be not later than 72 hours after receipt of the application. In reckoning for the purposes of this paragraph any period of 72 hours, no account shall be taken of Christmas Day, Good Friday, and bank holiday, or any Saturday or Sunday.

    ...

Rule 86

(1) Where a magistrates' court has fixed the amount in which a person (including any surety) is to be bound by a recognisance, the recognisance may be entered into:

(a) in the case of a surety in connection with bail in criminal proceedings where the accused is in prison or other place of detention, before the governor or keeper of the prison or place as well as before the persons mentioned in section 8(4)(a) of the Bail Act 1976;

(b) ...

Rule 90A

Where the court hears full argument as to bail, the clerk of the court shall take a note of that argument.

Rule 93A

(1) Where the prosecution wishes to exercise the right of appeal under section 1 of the Bail (Amendment) Act 1993 (hereafter in this rule referred to as 'the 1993 Act'), to a judge of the Crown Court against a decision to grant bail, the oral notice of appeal must be given to the clerk of the magistrates' court and to the person concerned, at the conclusion of the proceedings in which such bail was granted and before the release of the person concerned.

(2) When oral notice of appeal is given, the clerk of the magistrates' court shall announce in open court the time at which such notice was given.

(3) A record of the prosecution's decision to appeal and the time the oral notice of appeal was given shall be made in the register and shall contain the particulars set out in the appropriate form prescribed for the purpose.

(4) Where an oral notice of appeal has been given the court shall remand the person concerned in custody by a warrant of commitment in the appropriate form prescribed for the purpose.

(5) On receipt of the written notice required by section 1(5) of the 1993 Act, the court shall remand the person concerned in custody by a warrant of commitment in the appropriate form prescribed for the purpose, until the appeal is determined or otherwise disposed of.

(6) A record of the receipt of the written notice of appeal shall be made in the same manner as that of the oral notice of appeal under paragraph (3) above.

(7) If, having given oral notice of appeal, the prosecution fails to serve a written notice of appeal within the two hour period referred to in section 1(5) of the 1993 Act the clerk of the magistrates' court shall, as soon as practicable, by way of written notice to the persons in whose custody the person concerned is, direct the release of the person concerned on bail as granted by the magistrates' court and subject to any conditions which it imposed.

...

(9) The clerk of the magistrates' court shall record the prosecution's failure to serve a written notice of appeal, or its service of a notice of abandonment, in the appropriate form prescribed for the purpose.

(10) Where a written notice of appeal has been served on the clerk of the magistrates' court, he shall provide as soon as practicable to the

appropriate officer of the Crown Court a copy of that written notice, together with:

(a) the notes of argument made by the clerk under rule 90A of these Rules; and

(b) a note of the date, or dates, when the person concerned is next due to appear in the magistrates' court, whether he is released on bail or remanded in custody by the Crown Court.

(11) References in this rule to 'the person concerned' are references to such a person within the meaning of section 1 of the 1993 Act.

Rule 93B

(1) The appropriate court for the purposes of section 5B of the Bail Act 1976 in relation to the decision of a constable to grant bail shall be:

(a) the magistrates' court (if any) appointed by the custody officer as the court before which the person to whom bail was granted has a duty to appear; or

(b) if no such court has been appointed, a magistrates' court acting for the petty sessions area in which the police station at which bail was granted is situated.

(2) An application under section 5B(1) of the Bail Act 1976 shall:

(a) be made in writing;

(b) contain a statement of the grounds on which it is made;

(c) specify the offence which the proceedings in which bail was granted were connected with, or for;

(d) specify the decision to be reconsidered (including any conditions of bail which have been imposed and why they have been imposed); and

(e) specify the name and address of any surety provided by the person to whom the application relates to secure his surrender to custody.

(3) The clerk of a magistrates' court to which an application has been made under section 5B of the Bail Act 1976 shall fix a date, time and place for the hearing of the application and shall give notice of the application and of the date, time and place so fixed in the prescribed form to the person affected and send a copy of the notice to the prosecutor who made the application and to any surety specified in the application.

(4) The time fixed for the hearing shall be not later than 72 hours after receipt of the application. In reckoning for the purpose of this paragraph any period of 72 hours, no account shall be taken of Christmas Day, Good Friday, any bank holiday or any Sunday.

(5) Service of a notice to be given under paragraph (3) to the person affected may be effected by delivering it to him.

(6) At the hearing of an application under section 5B of the Bail Act 1976 the court shall consider any representations made by the person affected (whether in writing or orally) before taking any decision under that section

with respect to him; and, where the person affected does not appear before the court, the court shall not take such a decision unless it is proved to the satisfaction of the court, on oath or in the manner prescribed by paragraph (1) of rule 67, that the notice required to be given under paragraph (3) was served on him before the hearing.

(7) Where the court proceeds in the absence of the person affected in accordance with paragraph (6):

(a) if the decision of the court is to vary the conditions of bail or impose conditions in respect of bail which has been granted unconditionally, the clerk of the court shall notify the person affected in the prescribed form;

(b) if the decision of the court is to withhold bail, the order of the court under section 5B(5)(b) of the Bail Act 1976 (surrender to custody) shall be signed by the justice issuing it or state his name and be authenticated by the signature of the clerk of the court and shall be in the prescribed form.

(8) Service of any of the documents referred to in paragraph (7) may be effected by delivering it to the person to whom it is directed or by leaving it for him with some person at his last known or usual place of abode.

HIGH COURT JURISDICTION TO GRANT BAIL

Criminal Justice Act 1967, section 22(1)

Where a magistrates' court withholds bail in criminal proceedings or imposes conditions in granting bail in criminal proceedings, the High Court may, subject to section 25 of the Criminal Justice and Public Order Act 1994, grant bail or vary the conditions.

CROWN COURT JURISDICTION TO GRANT BAIL

Supreme Court Act 1981, section 81

(1) The Crown Court may, subject to section 25 of the Criminal Justice and Public Order Act 1994, grant bail to any person:

(a) who has been committed in custody for appearance before the Crown Court or in relation to whose case a notice of transfer has been given under a relevant transfer provision; or

(b) who is in custody pursuant to a sentence imposed by a magistrates' court, and who has appealed to the Crown Court against his conviction or sentence; or

(c) who is in the custody of the Crown Court pending the disposal of his case by that court; or

(d) who, after the decision of his case by the Crown Court, has applied to that court for the statement of a case for the High Court on that decision; or

(e) who has applied to the High Court for an order of *certiorari* to remove proceedings in the Crown Court in his case into the High Court, or has applied to the High Court for leave to make such an application; or

(f) to whom the Crown Court has granted a certificate under section 1(2) or 11(1A) of the Criminal Appeal Act 1968 or under sub-section (1B) below; or

(g) who has been remanded in custody by a magistrates' court on adjourning a case under:

  (i) section 5 (adjournment of inquiry into offence);

  (ii) section 10 (adjournment of trial);

  (iii) section 18 (initial procedure on information against adult for offence triable either way); or

  (iv) section 30 (remand for medical examination),

  of the Magistrates' Courts Act 1980,

and the time during which a person is released on bail under any provision of this sub-section shall not count as part of any term of imprisonment or detention under his sentence.

...

(1J) The Crown Court may only grant bail to a person under sub-section (1)(g) if the magistrates' court which remanded him in custody has certified under section 5(6A) of the Bail Act 1976 that it heard full argument on his application for bail before it refused the application.

...

(4) The Crown Court, on issuing a warrant for the arrest of any person, may endorse the warrant for bail, and in any such case:

(a) the person arrested under the warrant shall, unless the Crown Court otherwise directs, be taken to a police station; and

(b) the officer in charge of the station shall release him from custody if he, and any sureties required by the endorsement and approved by the officer, enter into recognizances of such amount as may be fixed by the endorsement.

Provided that in the case of bail in criminal proceedings (within the meaning of the Bail Act 1976) the person arrested shall not be required to enter into a recognizance.

(5) A person in custody in pursuance of a warrant issued by the Crown Court with a view to his appearance before that court shall be brought forthwith before either the Crown Court or a magistrates' court.

...

REMANDS

MAGISTRATES' COURTS ACT 1980

Section 128: Remand in custody or on bail

(1) Where a magistrates' court has power to remand any person, then, subject to section 4 of the Bail Act 1976 and to any other enactment modifying that power, the court may:

    (a) remand him in custody, that is to say, commit him to custody to be brought before the court, subject to sub-section (3A) below, at the end of the period of remand or at such earlier time as the court may require; or

    (b) where it is inquiring into or trying an offence alleged to have been committed by that person or has convicted him of an offence, remand him on bail in accordance with the Bail Act 1976, that is to say, by directing him to appear as provided in sub-section (4) below; or

    (c) except in a case falling within paragraph (b) above, remand him on bail by taking from him a recognizance (with or without sureties) conditions as provided in that sub-section,

and may, in a case falling within paragraph (c) above, instead of taking recognizances in accordance with that paragraph, fix the amount of the recognizances with a view to their being taken subsequently in accordance with section 119 above.

(1A) Where:

    (a) on adjourning a case under section 5, 10(1) or 18(4) above the court proposes to remand or further remand a person in custody; and

    (b) he is before the court; and

    (c) [repealed];

    (d) he is legally represented in that court,

it shall be the duty of the court:

      (i) to explain the effect of sub-sections (3A) and (3B) below to him in ordinary language; and

      (ii) to inform him in ordinary language that, notwithstanding the procedure for a remand without his being brought before a court, he would be brought before a court for the hearing and determination of at least every fourth application for his remand, and of every application for his remand heard at a time when it appeared to the court that he had no legal representative acting for him in the case.

(1B) For the purposes of sub-section (1A) above a person is to be treated as legally represented in a court if, but only if, he has the assistance of a legal representative to represent him in the proceedings in that court.

(1C) After explaining to an accused as provided by sub-section (1A) above, the court shall ask him whether he consents to the hearing and determination of such applications in his absence.

(2) Where the court fixes the amount of a recognizance under sub-section (1) above or section 8(3) of the Bail Act 1976 with a view to its being taken subsequently the court shall in the meantime commit the person so remanded to custody in accordance with paragraph (a) of the said sub-section (1).

(3) Where a person is brought before the court after remand, the court may further remand him.

(3A) Subject to sub-section (3B) below, where a person has been remanded in custody and the remand was not a remand under section 128A below for a period exceeding 8 clear days, the court may further remand him (otherwise than in the exercise of the power conferred by that section) on an adjournment under section 5, 10(1) or 18(4) above without his being brought before it if it is satisfied:

(a) that he gave his consent, either in response to a question under sub-section (1C) above or otherwise, to the hearing and determination in his absence of any application for his remand on an adjournment of the case under any of those provisions; and

(b) that he has not by virtue of this sub-section been remanded without being brought before the court on more than two such applications immediately preceding the application which the court is hearing; and

(c) [repealed];

(d) that he has not withdrawn his consent to their being so heard and determined.

(3B) The court may not exercise the power conferred by sub-section (3A) above if it appears to the court, on an application for a further remand being made to it, that the person to whom the application relates has no legal representative acting for him in the case (whether present in court or not).

(3C) Where:

(a) a person has been remanded in custody on an adjournment of a case under section 5, 10(1) or 18(4) above; and

(b) an application is subsequently made for his further remand on such an adjournment; and

(c) he is not brought before the court which hears and determines the application; and

(d) that court is not satisfied as mentioned in sub-section (3A) above,

the court shall adjourn the case and remand him in custody for the period for which it stands adjourned.

(3D) An adjournment under sub-section (3C) above shall be for the shortest period that appears to the court to make it possible for the accused to be brought before it.

(3E) Where:

(a) on an adjournment of a case under section 5, 10(1) or 18(4) above a person has been remanded in custody without being brought before the court; and

(b) it subsequently appears:

(i) to the court which remanded him in custody; or

(ii) to an alternate magistrates' court to which he is remanded under section 130 below,

that he ought not to have been remanded in custody in his absence, the court shall require him to be brought before it at the earliest time that appears to the court to be possible.

(4) Where a person is remanded on bail under sub-section (1) above the court may, where it remands him on bail in accordance with the Bail Act 1976 direct him to appear or, in any other case, direct that his recognizance be conditioned for his appearance:

(a) before that court at the end of the period of remand; or

(b) at every time and place to which during the course of the proceedings the hearing may be from time to time adjourned,

and, where it remands him on bail conditionally on his providing a surety during an inquiry into an offence alleged to have been committed by him, may direct that the recognizance of the surety be conditioned to secure that the person so bailed appears:

(c) at every time and place to which during the course of the proceedings the hearing may be from time to time adjourned and also before the Crown Court in the event of the person so bailed being committed for trial there.

(5) Where a person is directed to appear or a recognizance is conditioned for a person's appearance in accordance with paragraph (b) or (c) of sub-section (4) above, the fixing at any time of the time for him next to appear shall be deemed to be a remand; but nothing in this sub-section or sub-section (4) above shall deprive the court of power at any subsequent hearing to remand him afresh.

(6) Subject to the provisions of sections 128A and 129 below, a magistrates' court shall not remand a person for a period exceeding 8 clear days, except that:

(a) if the court remands him on bail, it may remand him for a longer period if he and the other party consent;

(b) where the court adjourns a trial under section 10(3) above or section 11 of the Powers of Criminal Courts (Sentencing) Act 2000, the court may remand him for the period of the adjournment;

(c) where a person is charged with an offence triable either way, then, if it falls to the court to try the case summarily but the court at the time is not so constituted, and sitting in such a place, as will enable it to proceed with the trial, the court may remand him until the next occasion on which it will be practicable for the court to be so constituted, and to sit in such a place, as aforesaid, notwithstanding that the remand is for a period exceeding 8 clear days.

(7) A magistrates' court having power to remand a person in custody may, if the remand is for a period not exceeding 3 clear days, commit him to detention at a police station.

(8) Where a person is committed to detention at a police station under subsection (7) above:

(a) he shall not be kept in such detention unless there is a need for him to be so detained for the purposes of inquiries into other offences;

(b) if kept in such detention, he shall be brought back before the magistrates' court which committed him as soon as that need ceases;

(c) he shall be treated as a person in police detention to whom the duties under section 39 of the Police and Criminal Evidence Act 1984 (responsibilities in relation to persons detained) relate;

(d) his detention shall be subject to periodic review at the times set out in section 40 of that Act (review of police detention).

Section 128A: Remands in custody for more than eight days

...

(2) A magistrates' court may remand the accused in custody for a period exceeding 8 clear days if:

(a) it has previously remanded him in custody for the same offence; and

(b) he is before the court,

but only if, after affording the parties an opportunity to make representations, it has set a date on which it expects that it will be possible for the next stage in the proceedings, other than a hearing relating to a further remand in custody or on bail, to take place, and only:

(i) for a period ending not later than that date; or

(ii) for a period of 28 clear days,

whichever is the less.

(3) Nothing in this section affects the right of the accused to apply for bail during the period of the remand.

...

Section 129: Further remand

(1) If a magistrates' court is satisfied that any person who has been remanded is unable by reason of illness or accident to appear or be brought before the court at the expiration of the period for which he was remanded, the court may, in his absence, remand him for a further time; and section 128(6) above shall not apply.

(2) Notwithstanding anything in section 128(1) above, the power of a court under sub-section (1) above to remand a person on bail for a further time:

(a) where he was granted bail in criminal proceedings, includes power to enlarge the recognizance of any surety for him to a later time;

...

(3) Where a person remanded on bail is bound to appear before a magistrates' court at any time and the court has no power to remand him under sub-section (1) above, the court may in his absence:

(a) where he was granted bail in criminal proceedings, appoint a later time as the time at which he is to appear and enlarge the recognizances of any sureties for him to that time;

...

and the appointment of the time or the enlargement of his recognizance shall be deemed to be a further remand.

(4) Where a magistrates' court commits a person for trial on bail and the recognizance of any surety for him has been conditioned in accordance with paragraph (a) of sub-section (4) of section 128 above the court may, in the absence of the surety, enlarge his recognizance so that he is bound to secure that the person so committed for trial appears also before the Crown Court.

Section 130: Transfer of remand hearings

(1) A magistrates' court adjourning a case under sections 5, 10(1) or 18(4) above, and remanding the accused in custody, may, if he has attained the age of 17, order that he be brought up for any subsequent remands before an alternate magistrates' court nearer to the prison where he is to be confined while on remand

...

CHAPTER 3

CLASSIFICATION OF OFFENCES

3.1   INTRODUCTION

In this chapter, we examine how the decision is made as to which court (magistrates' court or Crown Court) the offence should be tried in, if that offence is one which can be tried in either court.

Mode of trial can be determined in any magistrates' court; it does not matter where in England and Wales the offence was allegedly committed (s 2 of the Magistrates' Courts Act 1980).

3.2   CLASSIFICATION OF OFFENCES

According to Sched 1 of the Interpretation Act 1978, there are three types of criminal offence:

- summary offences, that is, offences which are triable only in the magistrates' court;
- indictable offences, which are either:
  - (i)   triable only on indictment (that is, triable only in the Crown Court); or
  - (ii) triable either way (that is, triable either in the magistrates' court or the Crown Court).

To determine which category a particular offence falls into one should look at:

- Sched 1 of the Magistrates' Courts Act 1980,[1] which lists a number of offences that are triable either way; or

---

1   The offences listed in Sched 1 of the Magistrates' Courts Act 1980 include the following:
   - inflicting bodily injury (Offences Against the Person Act 1861, s 20);
   - assault with intent to resist apprehension (Offences Against the Person Act 1861, s 38);
   - assault occasioning bodily harm (Offences Against the Person Act 1861, s 47);
   - unlawful intercourse with a girl under 16 (Sexual Offences Act 1956, s 6);
   - indecency between men (Sexual Offences Act 1956, s 13);
   - assisting offenders (Criminal Law Act 1967, s 4(1)), where the offence to which it relates is triable either way;
   - concealing arrestable offences and giving false information (Criminal Law Act 1967, s 5(1)), where the offence to which it relates is triable either way;

Footnote continued overleaf

- at the statute which creates the offence: If the penalty refers both to summary conviction and to conviction on indictment, the offence is triable either way; if it refers only to conviction on indictment, the offence can be tried only in the Crown Court; if it refers only to summary conviction, the offence can be tried only in the magistrates' court.

Thus, if an offence is in the list in Sched 1 of the 1980 Act or its penalty is expressed in a way which refers to summary trial and trial on indictment, it is triable either way.

A list showing how some of the more common offences are classified appears at the end of this chapter.

The rest of this chapter examines how it is decided where an offence which is triable either way should be tried.

3.3 INDICATION AS TO A DEFENDANT'S INTENDED PLEA: THE PLEA BEFORE VENUE HEARING

Section 49 of the Criminal Procedure and Investigations Act 1996 inserts a s 17A and a s 17B into the Magistrates' Courts Act 1980.

Section 17A applies where a defendant who has attained the age of 18 is charged with an offence that is triable either way. The s 17A procedure has to be carried out in the presence of the defendant. It begins with the charge being written down (if this has not already been done) and being read to the defendant. The court then explains to the defendant that he may indicate whether he intends to plead guilty or not guilty. The defendant must also be warned that if he indicates an intention to plead guilty he will be regarded as having actually pleaded guilty and that the magistrates then have the power to commit him for sentence to the Crown Court (under s 3 of the Powers of

---

1   *Continued*

- all indictable offences under the Theft Act 1968 *except:*
    - (i)   robbery, aggravated burglary, blackmail and assault with intent to rob;
    - (ii) burglary comprising the commission of, or an intention to commit, an offence which is triable only on indictment; and
    - (iii) burglary in a dwelling if any person in the dwelling was subjected to violence or the threat of violence;
- destroying or damaging property (Criminal Damage Act 1971, s 1(1));
- arson (Criminal Damage Act 1971, s 1(1) and (3));
- threats to destroy or damage property (Criminal Damage Act 1971, s 2);
- possessing anything with intent to destroy or damage property (Criminal Damage Act 1971, s 3);
- committing an indecent assault upon a person whether male or female; and
- aiding, abetting counselling or procuring any of the above offences (except the two offences under the Criminal Law Act 1967).

Criminal Courts (Sentencing) Act 2000) if they take the view that their sentencing powers are inadequate.

The defendant is then asked whether he intends to plead guilty or not guilty.

If the defendant indicates that he intends to plead guilty, the magistrates must proceed as if the case were a summary trial and the defendant had pleaded guilty.

If the defendant indicates that he intends to plead not guilty, the court goes through the mode of trial procedure set out in ss 18–21 of the Magistrates' Courts Act 1980 (and described at 3.4 below). Where the defendant refuses to indicate how he intends to plead, the court must assume that he intends to plead not guilty and so must go through the mode of trial procedure.

The effect of these provisions is that where a defendant is charged with an either way offence and indicates to the magistrates that he intends to plead guilty, he will be regarded as having agreed to summary trial and as having actually pleaded guilty. If the case is a serious one, in the sense that it calls for a sentence beyond the powers of the magistrates, the defendant will be committed for sentence to the Crown Court. The object of this reform is to ensure that defendants who intend to plead guilty do not end up in the Crown Court unless the case is a serious one.

Where the defendant indicates an intention to plead guilty to one or more either way offences but is also committed to the Crown Court for trial in respect of an either way offence to which he intends to plead not guilty, or in respect of an offence which is triable only on indictment, the magistrates may commit him to the Crown Court for sentence (under s 4 of the Powers of Criminal Courts (Sentencing) Act 2000 – see Chapter 4, 4.13.4) in respect of the offence(s) to which he had indicated a guilty plea.

A Home Office Circular (45/1997) makes the point that some defendants, especially unrepresented defendants, may find the 'plea before venue' hearing difficult to understand. The Circular says:

> The court may wish to take account of the following points in framing its invitation:
>
> - the defendant will want to know whether his case will be dealt with that day in court. The court may wish to make this clear when explaining what will happen if the defendant indicates a plea of guilty or not guilty;
>
> - the defendant must understand that an indication of a guilty plea will lead to conviction and sentence. But some defendants may be confused if the court tries to distinguish between plea indication and plea taking. It may be clearer to inform the defendant that if he tells the court that he intends to plead guilty, the outcome will be that he will be convicted of the offence, that the prosecutor will tell the court about the facts of the case, that the defence will have the opportunity to respond, and that the court will then proceed to consider sentence either on the same day or at a later date if the

court requires more information about the case before deciding on the appropriate sentence;

- the defendant must also understand that the court has the discretion to commit him to Crown Court for sentence (under s 38 of the 1980 Act) if it considers the offence to be so serious that its own sentencing powers are not sufficient to impose a great enough punishment;

- the defendant should be given every opportunity to say that he understands what is likely to happen if he takes a particular course. It may be preferable, during the explanation of the procedure, to pause at the end of each stage and ask the defendant whether he understands what has just been said;

- the defendant should be asked at the end of the explanation whether he understands and whether there is anything on which he would like further explanation.

The Home Office Circular contains an Annex with a suggested form of wording for the use of the magistrates' court when inviting the defendant to indicate his plea. It is as follows:

This/these offence(s) may be tried either by this court or by the Crown Court before a Judge and jury.

Whether or not this court can deal with your case today will depend upon your answers to the questions which I am going to put to you. Do you understand?

You will shortly be asked to tell the court whether you intend to plead guilty or not guilty to (certain of) the offence(s) [that is, only the offences which are triable either way] with which you are charged. Do you understand?

If you tell us that you intend to plead guilty, you will be convicted of the offence(s). We may then be able to deal with (part of) your case at this hearing. The prosecutor will tell us about the facts of the case, you (your representative) will have the opportunity to respond (on your behalf), and we shall then go on to consider how to sentence you. Do you understand?

We may be able to sentence you today, or we may need to adjourn the proceedings until a later date for the preparation of a pre-sentence report by the Probation Service. If we believe that you deserve a greater sentence than we have the power to give you in this court, we may decide to send you to the Crown Court, either on bail or in custody, and you will be sentenced by that court, which has greater sentencing powers. Do you understand?

[In cases where s 4 of the Powers of Criminal Courts (Sentencing) Act 2000 applies:

If you indicate a guilty plea for this/these offence(s), even if we believe that our own sentencing powers are great enough to deal with you here, we may still send you to the Crown Court to be sentenced for this/these offence(s) because you have also been charged with [a] related offence(s) [for which you have already been committed for trial in that court [for which you will be committed for trial in that court.] Do you understand?]

> If, on the other hand, you tell us that you intend to plead not guilty, or if you do not tell us what you intend to do, we shall go on to consider whether you should be tried by this court or by the Crown Court on some future date. If we decide that it would be appropriate to deal with your case in this court, we shall ask you if you are content for us to do so or whether you wish to have your case tried in the Crown Court.
>
> Before I ask you how you intend to plead, do you understand everything I have said or is there any part of what I have said which you would like me to repeat or explain?

Section 17B of the Magistrates' Courts Act 1980 deals with the situation where a defendant who has attained the age of 18 is charged with an either way offence and:

(a) the defendant is represented by a lawyer; and

(b) the defendant's disorderly conduct means that it is not practicable for proceedings under s 17A to continue in his presence.

In such a case, the charge is written down (if not already done) and read to the lawyer. The lawyer is then asked whether the defendant intends to plead guilty or not guilty. If the lawyer indicates that the defendant intends to plead guilty the case is regarded as a summary trial in which the defendant has pleaded guilty. If the lawyer indicates that the client intends to plead not guilty, or if the lawyer fails to indicate the defendant's intention regarding the plea, the court proceeds to the mode of trial hearing.

Further guidance on the impact of the 'plea before venue' procedure was given by the Court of Appeal in *R v Rafferty* [1999] 1 Cr App R 235. The court held that (i) where the defendant is charged with an either way offence and indicates a guilty plea at the plea before venue hearing and is then committed for sentence to the Crown Court, he is entitled to a greater discount for his guilty plea than the defendant who delays pleading guilty until he appears in the Crown Court (see, also, Chapter 12, 12.8.1); (ii) when a person who is on bail enters a guilty plea at the plea before venue hearing, the usual practice should be to continue his bail, even if it is anticipated that a custodial sentence will be imposed by the Crown Court, unless there is good reason for remanding him in custody.

In *R v Horseferry Road Magistrates' Court ex p Rugless* (2000) 164 JP 311, the defendant indicated a guilty plea at the 'plea before venue' hearing; the court accepted jurisdiction and ordered a pre-sentence report, stating that all sentencing options were to remain open with the exception of committal to the Crown Court for sentence. At the next hearing, the magistrates committed the defendant to the Crown Court for sentence (see s 3 of the Powers of Criminal Courts (Sentencing) Act 2000). The Divisional Court held that the defendant had a legitimate expectation that he would be sentenced in the magistrates' court. The subsequent decision to commit him for sentence was in breach of this legitimate expectation; accordingly it was appropriate to quash the decision to commit for sentence.

3.4   MODE OF TRIAL HEARING: PROCEDURE

What follows will alter substantially with the coming into force of the Criminal Justice (Mode of Trial) Bill 2000. Until that time, the procedure at a mode of trial hearing is as follows.

Where the defendant indicates an intention to plead not guilty (or gives no indication of his intended plea) in respect of one or more offences which are triable either way, the court then goes through the mode of trial procedure contained in ss 18–21 of the Magistrates' Courts Act 1980.

- The charge is read to the defendant, but he is not asked to plead guilty or not guilty.

- The court asks if the accused is aware of his right to receive advance information of the prosecution case (see 3.12 below); if a request for disclosure has been made, the court will ask if the request has been complied with.

- The prosecution make representations as to the appropriate mode of trial. This involves a brief summary of the facts of the alleged offence so that the magistrates can assess the seriousness of the offence. The prosecution will base their submissions on the Practice Note (Mode of Trial Guidelines) referred to at 3.5.1 below.

- The defence then have the chance of making representations as to the appropriate mode of trial. If the defendant wishes to be tried at the Crown Court no representations will be made since even if the magistrates decide that the case is suitable for summary trial, the defendant can nevertheless choose trial on indictment. If, on the other hand, the prosecution ask for trial on indictment but the defendant wishes to be tried summarily, the defendant will first have to persuade the magistrates to accept jurisdiction (that is, to rule that the case is suitable for summary trial).

- Having heard the representations, the magistrates come to their decision whether or not to offer the defendant the option of summary trial.

- If the magistrates decide that the case is not suitable for summary trial, committal proceedings will take place either immediately or else on a later occasion (see Chapter 7).

- If the magistrates decide that the case is suitable for summary trial, the defendant will be asked whether he wishes to be tried in the magistrates' court or by a judge and jury in the Crown Court. Before the defendant announces his choice, the court must first warn him that if he consents to summary trial and is convicted he may be sent to the Crown Court to be sentenced (under s 3 of the Powers of Criminal Courts (Sentencing) Act 2000 (see Chapter 4, 4.13.1 below)). The defendant then announces his choice. In *R v Southampton Magistrates Court ex p Sansome* [1999] 1 Cr App R (S) 112, the court approved the form of wording in Stone's *Justices' Manual* (para 1-438) where the magistrates decide that the case is suitable for summary trial: 'It appears to this court more suitable for you to be tried here. You may now consent to be tried by this court, but if you wish, you may choose to be tried by a jury instead. If you are tried by this court and are found guilty, this court may still send you to the Crown Court for sentence if it is of the opinion that greater punishment should be inflicted for the offence than it has power to impose. Do you wish to be tried by this court or do you wish to be tried by a jury?'

Thus, summary trial of an either way offence is only possible if both the magistrates and the defendant agree to it.

3.5 MODE OF TRIAL: RELEVANT FACTORS

Section 19(3) of the Magistrates' Courts Act 1980 states that in deciding whether or not a case is suitable for summary trial, the magistrates should have regard to:

- the nature of the case;
- whether the circumstances make the offence one of serious character;
- whether the punishment which a magistrates' court would have power to inflict for that offence would be adequate;
- any other circumstances which appear relevant to the mode of trial decision.

Section 19(1) also requires the court to take account of any representations made by the prosecution and the defence.

The key question which the magistrates must ask themselves is whether six months' imprisonment (12 months if the accused is charged with two or more offences which are triable either way) would be adequate punishment.

3.5.1 Guidelines

To help the magistrates decide which is the appropriate mode of trial in any case, the Lord Chief Justice issued the guidelines mentioned above. Those guidelines set out the following principles:

- the court should never make its decision on the ground of convenience;
- the court should assume for the purpose of deciding mode of trial that the prosecution version of the facts is correct;

- the fact that the defendant will, in the event of conviction, be asking for other offences to be taken into consideration (see Chapter 12, 12.9.1 below) is not a relevant consideration;

- if the case involves complex questions of fact or difficult questions of law, the court should consider committing the defendant to the Crown Court for trial;

- where two or more defendants are jointly charged, the magistrates must consider each defendant separately; it would be wrong to refuse to try a defendant summarily in a case which is suitable for summary trial merely because another defendant is to be tried in the Crown Court. This provision is based on the decision of the House of Lords in *R v Brentwood Justices ex p Nicholls* [1992] 1 AC 1; [1991] 3 All ER 359, followed in *R v Ipswich Justices ex p Callaghan* (1995) 159 JP 748. The same approach was taken in *R v Wigan Justices ex p Layland* (1995) 160 JP 223, where it was held that s 19 of the Magistrates' Courts Act 1980 requires the justices to make a decision about mode of trial before the defendant or defendants are put to their election. Once a decision has been made, it should not be changed on the basis that one or more of the defendants elects Crown Court trial.

- The original version of the guidelines (issued in 1990) said that the magistrates, in determining mode of trial, should assume that the defendant has no previous convictions (indeed it was held in *R v Colchester Justices ex p NE Essex Building Co* [1977] 1 WLR 1109; [1977] 3 All ER 567 that any previous convictions must not be revealed to the magistrates at this stage) and should not take account of any personal mitigating circumstances. However, the revised version of the mode of trial guidelines omits the principle that the defendant's antecedents are irrelevant. Similarly, the revised guidelines omit the principle stated in the original version that the magistrates should ignore any personal mitigating circumstances. The present position thus appears to be that in determining mode of trial the magistrates may take account of all the factors to which they would have regard if they were passing sentence (see Chapter 12).

- There is a presumption in favour of summary trial unless the case has aggravating features which render the magistrates' sentencing powers inadequate. The guidelines go on to give examples of aggravating features for particular offences. For example:
  (i)   burglary of a dwelling house is more serious if committed when the building is likely to be occupied, or if there is also vandalism;
  (ii) theft is more serious if committed in breach of trust or over a prolonged period;
  (iii) offences of violence are more serious if a weapon is used or if the victim is vulnerable (for example, elderly or infirm) or if the victim is someone whose job brings him into contact with the public (for example, a bus driver, a publican or a police officer);

(iv) dangerous driving is more serious if there is grossly excessive speed or a prolonged course of dangerous driving or other related offences are committed as well.

Amount involved: where property has been stolen and not recovered, regard should be had to its value. The guidelines say that the magistrates should decline jurisdiction if the value involved exceeds twice the amount they can order to be paid by way of compensation. Since the magistrates can order compensation of £5,000 per offence, this means that they should decline jurisdiction if the value of unrecovered property exceeds £10,000.

3.5.2 Summary

The question which the magistrates should ask themselves at a mode of trial hearing is: 'Assuming that what the prosecution say about the offence is correct and assuming the defendant has no previous convictions, is six months' imprisonment (or 12 months for two or more offences) likely to be sufficient punishment?'

3.6 PRESENCE OF DEFENDANT

The defendant must be present at the mode of trial hearing unless either:
- his disorderly conduct makes it impracticable for the hearing to continue with him present (s 18(3) of the Magistrates' Courts Act); or
- there is a good reason for the defendant's absence (for example, he is too ill to attend court) and his legal representative is in court and states that the defendant has consented to the proceedings going on in the defendant's absence (s 23(1) of the Magistrates' Courts Act).

3.7 WHERE SHOULD THE DEFENDANT CHOOSE TO BE TRIED?

If the magistrates do not offer the defendant the chance of summary trial, the defendant has no choice in the matter: the trial can only take place in the Crown Court. If the magistrates do accept jurisdiction, should the defendant agree to summary trial?

3.7.1 The advantages of summary trial

The advantages of summary trial are as follows:

- The main advantage of summary trial is that the trial procedure is less formal. This means that the trial is less daunting, a fact which may be particularly relevant if the defendant is going to be unrepresented at trial, as will be the case if the defendant is not granted legal aid and yet cannot afford legal representation (see Chapter 11 for the criteria which determine whether legal aid should be granted).

- Summary trial takes a shorter time than does a trial in the Crown Court. A case which would take half a day in the magistrates' court would take probably a whole day in the Crown Court. This means that summary trial is cheaper. This too is relevant if the defendant is not legally aided but has chosen to pay for representation (but see, also, Chapter 11 for details of the circumstances where a successful defendant can recover his legal costs).

- It is sometimes said that an advantage of summary trial is that there is a limit on the sentence which the magistrates' court can pass (six months' imprisonment for one 'either way' offence, 12 months for two or more). However, this advantage is largely nullified by the power of the magistrates to commit the defendant to be sentenced in the Crown Court under s 3 of the Powers of Criminal Courts (Sentencing) Act 2000 (see Chapter 4, 4.13.1).

3.7.2 The advantages of trial on indictment

The advantages of trial on indictment are as follows:

- Jurors tend to be less 'case hardened' than magistrates. Magistrates, who sit regularly, may well have heard the same story before and therefore find it less convincing. Also, magistrates tend to be more trusting of police evidence than do jurors.

  The figures do show that there is a greater chance of acquittal in the Crown Court. It must be borne in mind that these are national figures and there are considerable local variations.

- In the magistrates' court the justices are triers of law and fact whereas in the Crown Court the judge is the trier of law and the jurors are the triers of fact. Two advantages of Crown Court trial flow from this fact:

  (a) Where the admissibility of a piece of evidence is challenged, in the Crown Court, the challenge is made in the absence of the jury and, if the judge rules the evidence inadmissible, the jury hear nothing of this evidence. In the magistrates' court, however, the justices themselves have to rule on any question concerning the admissibility of evidence. If they decide that a particular piece of evidence is inadmissible, they must then put it from their minds. It is difficult to be sure that the justices are able to ignore, for example, evidence that the defendant made a confession even where they have ruled that the confession is inadmissible. In *R v Ormskirk Justices ex p Davies* [1994] Crim LR 850, it was held that one bench cannot delegate to another bench the duty of hearing and determining questions of admissibility; such decisions must be taken by the bench actually trying the case.

(b) (i) If there is a point of law to be decided, it is easier to deal with that point in the Crown Court, presided over by a professional judge, than in the magistrates' court, where the justices (who have only elementary legal training) depend on their clerk for advice on questions of law.

(ii) Legal errors are also easier to detect in the Crown Court, as the judge has to set out the relevant law in the summing up to the jury (see Chapter 9).

• Another advantage of trial on indictment is said to be that the prosecution have to disclose copies of the statements made by the witnesses they will be calling at the Crown Court. This is because committal proceedings (Chapter 7) cannot take place unless the prosecution have served their witness statements on the defence. This advantage is less marked as a result of the advance information rules (see 3.12 below) which have to be complied with before mode of trial is decided.

Another factor which might be relevant is the length of time the defendant will have to wait for a summary trial or a trial on indictment to take place. This depends very much on local conditions, as waiting lists vary considerably.

3.8   FAILURE TO FOLLOW THE CORRECT PROCEDURE IN DETERMINING MODE OF TRIAL

If the magistrates fail to follow the correct procedure in the mode of trial hearing (for example, the defendant is not warned of the possibility of being committed for sentence to the Crown Court) and a summary trial then takes place, the summary trial will be invalid and the Divisional Court (see Chapter 6) will order the magistrates to go through the mode of trial procedure again. See *R v Kent Justices ex p Machin* [1952] 2 QB 355; [1952] 1 All ER 1123, where a conviction by the magistrates was quashed by the Divisional Court because the magistrates' court failed to warn the defendant of the possibility of being committed for sentence following summary conviction; and *R v Cardiff Justices ex p Cardiff City Council* (1987) *The Times*, 24 February, where an acquittal following summary trial which took place after a defective mode of trial hearing was quashed by the Divisional Court.

In *R v Northampton Justices ex p Commissioners of Customs and Excise* [1994] Crim LR 598, the defendant was charged with fraudulent evasion of VAT (triable either way) involving £193,000. The magistrates, having heard representations, held that the case was suitable for summary trial. The prosecution appealed against this decision. The Divisional Court held that, in view of the seriousness of the alleged offence, the decision reached by the magistrates was so unreasonable that it should be quashed.

3.9 CHANGING THE DECISION AS TO MODE OF TRIAL

Once the decision as to mode of trial has been taken, it is nonetheless possible for that decision to be altered.

3.9.1 From summary trial to trial on indictment

Section 25(2) of the Magistrates' Courts Act 1980 says that, during a summary trial, the magistrates may terminate the trial at any time before the close of the prosecution case and hold committal proceedings instead (so that, if there is a case to answer, the defendant will be committed for trial to the Crown Court). This may happen if either the defendant or the magistrates have a change of mind or if the defendant is allowed to change his plea from guilty to not guilty.

In *R v Horseferry Road Magistrates' Court ex p K* [1996] 3 All ER 719, the Divisional Court held that the power to change from summary trial applies only once the trial has begun. The fact that the defendant has entered a plea of not guilty does not mean that the trial has begun. That only happens once the court has started to hear evidence or, for example, submissions on a preliminary point of law which has a direct bearing on the guilt or innocence of the accused.

3.9.2 The magistrates have a change of mind

The magistrates may have a change of mind regarding mode of trial if, during a summary trial, they decide as they hear the prosecution evidence that the case is in fact more serious than they thought when they agreed to summary trial. However, in such a case, it should be noted that they could simply continue with the summary trial and, if they convict the defendant, commit him to the Crown Court to be sentenced (s 38 of the Magistrates' Courts Act 1980; see Chapter 4, 4.13.1).

If the defendant consents to summary trial and pleads guilty, it is then too late to change to committal proceedings unless the defendant asks to change his plea first (*R v Dudley Justices ex p Gillard* [1986] AC 442; [1985] 3 All ER 634).

In the case of a plea of guilty, the only course of action if the magistrates, on hearing the facts of the case set out more fully by the prosecution, decide that the case is too serious for them to deal with is to commit the defendant to the Crown Court for sentence under s 3 of the Powers of Criminal Courts (Sentencing) Act 2000.

3.9.3 The defendant has a change of mind

The magistrates have a discretion to allow the defendant to withdraw his consent to summary trial.

The test to be applied in deciding whether to exercise this discretion in the defendant's favour was set out in *R v Birmingham Justices ex p Hodgson* [1985] QB 1131; [1985] 2 All ER 193, where the defendant did not realise that he had a defence to the charge, and *R v Highbury Corner Magistrates ex p Weekes* [1985] QB 1147, where a 17 year old defendant did not understand what a Crown Court was. The test to be applied in deciding whether to allow a defendant to withdraw his consent to summary trial is: did the defendant understand the 'nature and significance' of the choice which was put before him at the mode of trial hearing? In deciding this question, the magistrates should have regard to factors such as:

- whether the defendant knew that he had a possible defence to the charge;
- whether the defendant had access to legal advice before making his decision as to mode of trial;
- the defendant's age and apparent intelligence;
- possibly, whether the defendant has previous convictions (and so is likely to know something about criminal procedure); it should be remembered, however, that if the magistrates are made aware of the defendant's previous convictions, those magistrates will not be able to continue with the trial anyway, and so if the defendant's application is not allowed the trial with have to begin again in front of a bench which is unaware of the defendant's criminal record.

It should be noted that the burden of proof lies on the defendant to show that he did not understand the nature and significance of the choice (*R v Forest Magistrates ex p Spicer* [1988] Crim LR 619).

3.9.4 The defendant successfully applies to change his plea

In *R v Bow Street Magistrates ex p Welcombe* (1992) 156 JP 609, it was held that if, during a summary trial, the defendant is allowed to change his plea from guilty to not guilty, the defendant must also be given the opportunity to elect trial on indictment if he so wishes.

3.10 FROM TRIAL ON INDICTMENT TO SUMMARY TRIAL

Section 25(3) of the Magistrates' Courts Act 1980 provides that, at any time during committal proceedings, the justices may offer the defendant the chance of summary trial. This is the case whether it is the defendant or the justices who have a change of mind. It must be emphasised, however, that summary trial can only take place if both the defendant and the magistrates agree to it. It follows that if the magistrates decide that the case is not as serious as they thought when they declined jurisdiction, a summary trial cannot take place without the defendant's consent. The defendant should be warned (or reminded if he was informed earlier) that he may be committed for sentence to the Crown Court if he is convicted by the magistrates.

Where the magistrates decide that the case is, in fact, suitable for summary trial, there will have to be an adjournment before the summary trial can start. This is because all the evidence at committal proceedings is in the form of written statements. Witnesses will have to attend court to give oral evidence at the summary trial.

3.11 CRIMINAL DAMAGE: THE SPECIAL PROVISIONS

Section 22 of the Magistrates' Courts Act 1980 sets out a special procedure to be applied in cases of criminal damage (excluding arson) where the value involved is less than £5,000.

The first step is therefore to ascertain the 'value involved'. This is defined as the cost of repair or, if the article is damaged beyond repair, replacement. The value may be ascertained on the basis of representations by the prosecution and defence. There is no obligation on the magistrates to hear evidence as to the value (though they have a discretion to do so) (*R v Canterbury Justices ex p Klisiak* [1982] QB 398; [1981] 2 All ER 129).

Where there is more than one charge of criminal damage but the charges constitute a series of offences, the value involved in each offence is added up and it is the aggregate sum which is the value involved for the purpose of determining whether the special procedure applies (s 22(11)).

Where the value involved is £5,000 or less, the case *must* be tried summarily. The maximum sentence in such a case is three months' imprisonment or a fine up to £2,500 (that is, half the usual penalty); furthermore there can be no committal for sentence to the Crown Court under s 3 of the Powers of Criminal Courts (Sentencing) Act 2000.

Where the value is more than £5,000, the usual mode of trial procedure applies. If the defendant consents to summary trial and is convicted the usual penalties apply and a s 3 committal is possible.

If there is doubt as to whether the value involved is more or less than £5,000, the magistrates must offer the defendant the chance of summary trial. If the defendant accepts summary trial the lower penalties (three months' imprisonment or a fine of up to £2,500 and no s 3 committal) apply.

There is no appeal against the decision of the magistrates as to the value involved.

It must be emphasised that these special provisions apply only to criminal damage (and to offences under s 12A of the Theft Act 1968, aggravated vehicle taking, but only where the only aggravating feature alleged is criminal damage). In the case of theft, for example, the defendant has an unfettered right to Crown Court trial no matter how small the value of the property stolen.

In *R v Ward and others* (1996) *The Times*, 12 November, the Court of Appeal held that where a defendant is convicted of conspiracy to cause criminal damage, and the value of the damage is less than £5,000, the Crown Court can impose a sentence in excess of the maximum for the substantive offence.

The 'plea before venue' procedure established by s 17A of the Magistrates' Courts Act 1980 (see 3.3 above) applies to all offences which are triable either way, including cases of criminal damage where the value involved is less than £5,000. The defendant should therefore be given an opportunity to indicate his plea at a 'plea before venue' hearing. On a guilty indication, the court will deal with the case summarily and proceed to consider sentence. Home Office Circular 45/1997 says that the limitation on the court's sentencing powers under s 33 of the Act (three months' imprisonment and/or a £2,500 fine in cases where the value involved in the criminal damage is less than £5,000) does not apply in such cases, since the procedure set out in s 17A is not subject to s 22. This means, says the Circular, that the court has the power to impose the maximum penalties or to commit the defendant for sentence to the Crown Court under s 3 or 4 of the Powers of Criminal Courts (Sentencing) Act 2000. If the defendant indicates that he will plead not guilty (or gives no indication), the court should then go through the s 22 procedure, hearing representations as to the value involved and trying the case summarily if the value is £5,000 or less, or going through the standard mode of trial procedure if the value is more than £5,000.

3.12 CRIMINAL JUSTICE (MODE OF TRIAL) BILL 2000

The government intends to remove the defendant's right to elect trial for either way offences. In the Criminal Justice (Mode of Trial) (No 2) Bill of 2000, it is proposed that ss 19 to 22 of the Magistrates' Courts Act 1980 should be amended.

Under the amended version of s 19, the magistrates' court will be empowered to decide whether the offence ought to be tried summarily or on indictment.

In coming to its decision, the court would consider (under s 19(2)):

(a) the nature of the case;

(b) any circumstances of the offence (but not of the accused) which appear to the court to be relevant;

(c) whether, having regard to the circumstances of the offence (but still ignoring the circumstances of the offender), the court's sentencing powers would be adequate to deal with this offence.

The first version of the Bill required the court to have regard to the likely effect of conviction on the defendant's reputation. However, this was felt to discriminate unfairly against those with previous convictions. The (No 2) Bill went to the other extreme, and excluded all consideration of the circumstances of the offender.

The prosecution and defence would still be able to make representations as to the appropriate forum for the trial (s 19(3)).

Under the Bill, s 20(2) of the Magistrates' Court Act 1980 will provide that, if the magistrates decide that the offence ought to be tried summarily, the accused can only be tried summarily.

As is currently the case, where the magistrates decide that the offence ought to be tried in the Crown Court, summary trial is not possible (s 20(3)).

The magistrates will have to give reasons for the decision as to mode of trial (s 20(1)(b)).

Under s 20(4), the accused will have a right of appeal to the Crown Court (the appeal will be to a judge sitting alone, without lay justices) against a decision that he ought to be tried summarily. This right of appeal will only apply where the defendant made representations at the mode of trial hearing, under s 19(3), that he ought to be tried on indictment.

The special procedure for dealing with criminal damage (s 22 of the Magistrates' Courts Act 1980) is also amended by the Mode of Trial Bill. It remains the case that, where the value involved (as defined by Sched 2 of the 1980 Act) is £5,000 or less, the offence must be treated as if it is triable only summarily. If the court is satisfied that the value involved exceeds £5,000, then the court will go through the normal mode of trial procedure set out in the amended version of ss 19–21 of the 1980 Act.

3.13 THE ADVANCE INFORMATION RULES

The Magistrates' Courts (Advance Information) Rules 1985 provide that, in the case of offences which are triable either way, the prosecution must, if the defence so request, supply the defence with either a summary of the prosecution case or copies of the statements of the prosecution witnesses. The choice of whether to supply a summary or the witness statements lies with the prosecution (r 4(1)).

The prosecution may only refuse to comply with a request under the Rules if they think that compliance would lead to the intimidation of witnesses or other interference with the course of justice (r 5).

At the mode of trial hearing, the court must ensure that the defendant is aware of the right to advance information and that, if advance information has been requested, the prosecution have complied with that request (r 6(1)).

If the prosecution fail to comply with the request for advance disclosure, the magistrates' court has no power to order the prosecution to comply (*R v Dunmow Justices ex p Nash* (1993) 157 JP 1153). All the court can do is to adjourn the mode of trial hearing (if necessary more than once) or, if satisfied that the defence have not been prejudiced by the prosecution's failure to comply with the Rules, proceed to determine mode of trial anyway (r 7(1)).

Furthermore, the court cannot dismiss the charges brought by the prosecution because of non-compliance with the Rules (*King v Kucharz* (1989) 153 JP 336).

The purpose of the Advance Information Rules is to make it unnecessary for the defendant to elect Crown Court trial simply so that committal proceedings (in which the prosecution case has to be revealed) then have to take place.

If the prosecution offer only a summary of their case, they can sometimes be encouraged to supply copies of the witness statements if the defence indicate that they may well consent to summary trial if they do not have to elect Crown Court trial merely in order to obtain witness statements.

In the case of summary offences, the Advance Information Rules do not apply. However, the prosecution may make voluntary disclosure and so it is worthwhile for the defence to ask.

Home Office Circular 45/1997 points out that early service of advance information will help the defendant and his legal representatives to prepare for the 'plea before venue' hearing. The Circular notes that CPS aim to serve advance information on the first of the following occasions:

- a request by the defendant or his representative;
- notification by the court that legal aid has been granted;
- the defendant's first appearance in court (where he is remanded on bail).

In *R v Stratford Justices ex p Imbert* [1999] 2 Cr App R 276, the Divisional Court held that Art 6 of the European Convention on Human Rights (which guarantees the right to a fair trial) does not require that prosecution witness statements should be disclosed to the defence before summary trial in the magistrates' court. The court held that disclosure of the witness statements is not necessary to achieve the 'equality of arms' required by the European Court of Human Rights in cases such as *Foucher v France* (1997) 25 EHRR 234. The decision in *ex p Imbert* seems to accord with the view taken by the European Court of Human Rights, that the accused must be informed of the nature of the charge against him and the material facts on which it is based, but not necessarily the evidence in support (*Brozicek v Italy* 12 EHRR 371).

3.14   SECTION 40 OF THE CRIMINAL JUSTICE ACT 1988

Section 40 of the Criminal Justice Act 1988 applies if the defendant is committed for trial in respect of an indictable (that is, indictable only or triable either way) offence and the witness statements also disclose any one or more of the following summary offences:

- common assault;
- taking a conveyance without the owner's consent (s 12 of the Theft Act 1968);
- driving a motor vehicle while disqualified;
- criminal damage where the value involved is £5,000 or less;
- assaulting a prison officer or a secure training centre officer.

The summary offence(s) may then be included on the indictment if they are founded on the same facts as the indictable offence or if they form part of a series of offences (along with the indictable offence) of the same or a similar character. This is the same test as that which applies to the joinder of counts on an indictment (see Chapter 8, 8.9).

The effect of this is that the get away driver at a robbery who has taken the car without the owner's consent can be indicted for robbery and for taking the conveyance (even though the latter is a summary offence) and the burglar who commits criminal damage in order to effect entry to the premises can be charged with burglary and criminal damage (even if the value of the criminal damage is less than £5,000).

It is the prosecution who decide whether or not the linked summary offence(s) should appear on the indictment so that the Crown Court can try the summary offence(s) as well as the indictable offence.

Where s 40 applies the summary offence(s) appear on the indictment and are tried as if indictable. Note, however, that if the defendant is convicted of a s 40 summary offence the Crown Court cannot impose more than six months imprisonment and/or a £5,000 fine (that is, the maximum which the magistrates' court could have imposed).

In *R v Wrench* [1996] Crim LR 265, the appellant was accused of offences involving children. The DPP decided to bypass committal proceedings and use the transfer procedure in s 53 of the Criminal Justice Act 1988 (see Chapter 7, 7.12.3 below). A summary offence (common assault) was added to the indictment, purportedly under s 40 of the Criminal Justice Act 1988. The Court of Appeal doubted whether the addition of the summary offence was lawful, since the wording of s 40 requires evidence of the summary offence to come to light in committal proceedings; in the present case, there had been no committal proceedings.

3.15   SECTION 41 OF THE CRIMINAL JUSTICE ACT 1988

Section 41 of the Criminal Justice Act 1988 provides that, if the magistrates commit the defendant for trial on indictment in respect of one or more offences which are triable either way, they may also commit the defendant for a plea to be taken in respect of any summary offence, provided that the summary offence:

- is punishable with imprisonment or with disqualification from driving; and
- arises out of circumstances which are the same as or connected with the either way offence(s).

If, and only if, the defendant is convicted of the either way offence (either pleading guilty or being found guilty by the jury) the summary offence(s) will be put to the defendant for plea. The summary offence(s) will thus not appear on the indictment and will not be tried by the jury. Thereafter:

- if, having been convicted of the either way offence(s), the defendant pleads guilty to the summary offence(s), the Crown Court can pass any sentence which the magistrates could have imposed in respect of the summary offence(s) to which the defendant has pleaded guilty;
- if the defendant is acquitted of the either way offence(s) or, having been convicted of the either way offence(s), pleads not guilty to the summary offence(s), the prosecution can either indicate that they do not wish to proceed with the summary offence(s) or proceedings in respect of the summary offence(s) must be continued in the magistrates' court.

It is the magistrates rather than the prosecution who decide whether or not to commit a summary offence to the Crown Court for the plea to be taken.

In *R v Miall* [1992] QB 836; [1992] 3 All ER 153, the defendant was committed for trial for perverting the course of justice. The magistrates tried to commit him, under s 41, for the plea to be taken in respect of a summary offence, driving with excess alcohol. It was held that s 41 could not be invoked as the offence on the indictment (perverting the course of justice, a common law offence) was triable only on indictment, not triable either way.

In *R v Foote* (1992) 94 Cr App R 82, the defendant was committed for trial to the Crown Court in respect of a charge of reckless (now called dangerous) driving. The magistrates also tried to commit him under s 41 of the Criminal Justice Act 1988 for a plea to be taken in respect of a charge of careless driving arising out of the same incident. The defendant pleaded not guilty to the reckless driving and the prosecution decided to accept that plea; the court then tried to invoke s 41 to take a plea in respect of the charge of careless driving. This was held to be wrong, because s 41 could not apply where the defendant had not been convicted of the either way offence.

In *R v Bird* [1995] Crim LR 745, the defendant was sent for trial in the Crown Court on charges of possession of an offensive weapon (an either way offence) and driving while disqualified (a summary offence to which s 40 applies). By virtue of s 41, he was committed for plea in respect of a charge of driving without insurance. He was acquitted of the charge of possession of an offensive weapon but convicted of driving while disqualified. The Court of Appeal held that, since the defendant had been convicted on indictment of driving while disqualified, that offence was to be treated as an indictable offence. It followed that the Crown Court was entitled to deal with the summary offence of no insurance under s 41.

3.16   ADJUSTING THE CHARGES TO DICTATE MODE OF TRIAL

It is possible for the prosecution to drop the existing charge and replace it with a new charge. This will usually be done in open court. The prosecution will indicate that they do not wish to proceed on the existing charge (by offering no evidence if the defendant has already pleaded not guilty; by giving notice of discontinuance or by withdrawing the summons if he has not entered a plea). The new charge is brought either by the police further charging the defendant outside court or by the prosecution laying an information orally in open court. Under r 4(1) of the Magistrates' Courts Rules 1981, an information may be laid by the prosecutor or by counsel or solicitor (or someone else) authorised on behalf of the prosecutor.

Sometimes, the effect of replacing one charge with another will be to replace an offence which is triable either way with one which is triable only summarily, thus depriving the accused of the possibility of Crown Court trial. In *R v Canterbury Justices ex p Klisiak* [1982] QB 398; [1981] 2 All ER 129, it was held that the prosecution could only be prevented from doing this in 'the most obvious circumstances which disclose blatant injustice' (*per* Lord Lane CJ).

In *R v Sheffield Justices ex p DPP* [1993] Crim LR 136, the magistrates stayed proceedings against a defendant where the prosecution declined to proceed with a charge of assault occasioning actual bodily harm (triable either way) and substituted a charge of common assault (a summary offence). The Divisional Court granted a prosecution application for judicial review, holding that it is a matter for the prosecution which charge to proceed with. The court would only intervene where there was evidence of bad faith (that is, manipulating the system). In the present case, the charge of common assault was appropriate on the facts and there was no prejudice to the defendant.

It is also possible for a charge which is triable either way to be replaced by an offence which is triable only on indictment. However, in *R v Brooks* (1985) Crim LR 385, the Court of Appeal warned that it would be unjust and wrong for the prosecution to do this if the magistrates have already accepted jurisdiction in respect of the either way offence; the prosecution would be frustrating that decision by changing the charge.

The Code of Conduct for Crown Prosecutors says that charges should be chosen which reflect the seriousness of the offending, give the court adequate sentencing powers, and enable the case to be presented in a clear and simple way. The Code goes on to say that Crown Prosecutors should not continue with more charges than necessary and should never go ahead with a more serious charge just to encourage a defendant to plead guilty to a less serious one. Finally, the Code states that the charge should not be changed simply because of the decision made by the court or the defendant about where the case will be heard.

3.17 SOME COMMON OFFENCES TRIABLE ONLY ON INDICTMENT

The following is a list of some of the more common offences which are triable only on indictment:

- murder;
- manslaughter;
- wounding/causing grievous bodily harm with intent (Offences Against the Person Act 1861, s 18);
- rape (Sexual Offences Act 1956, s 1);
- intercourse with a girl under 13 (Sexual Offences Act 1956, s 5);
- buggery (Sexual Offences Act 1956, s 12);
- incest (Sexual Offences Act 1956, ss 10 and 11);

- robbery (Theft Act 1968, s 8);
- aggravated burglary (that is, burglary while possessing a weapon (Theft Act 1968, s 10);
- blackmail (Theft Act 1968, s 21);
- burglary comprising commission of or intent to commit an offence triable only on indictment (Theft Act 1968, s 9);
- burglary of a dwelling house where someone is subjected to violence or the threat of violence;
- criminal damage or arson committed with intent to endanger life or recklessness as to the endangerment of life (Criminal Damage Act 1971, s 1(2));
- causing death by dangerous driving (Road Traffic Act 1988, s 1);
- possession of a firearm with intent to endanger life (Firearms Act 1968, s 16);
- use of a firearm to resist arrest (Firearms Act 1968, s 17);
- possession of a firearm with intent to resist arrest or to commit an indictable offence (Firearms Act 1968, s 18);
- riot (Public Order Act 1986, s 1);
- perjury (Perjury Act 1911, s 1);
- perverting the course of justice;
- conspiracy.

3.18   COMMON OFFENCES TRIABLE EITHER WAY

The following is a list of some of the more common offences which are triable either way:

- inflicting grievous bodily harm (Offences Against the Person Act 1861, s 20);
- unlawful wounding (Offences Against the Person Act 1861, s 20);
- assault with intent to resist arrest (Offences Against the Person Act 1861, s 38);
- unlawful sexual intercourse with a girl under 16 (Sexual Offences Act 1956, s 6);
- gross indecency between men (Sexual Offences Act 1956, s 13);
- indecent assault (Sexual Offences Act 1956, s 14 (on a woman), s 15 (on a man));
- living on the earnings of prostitution (Sexual Offences Act 1956, s 30)
- theft (Theft Act 1968, s 1);

- handling stolen goods (Theft Act 1968, s 22);
- obtaining property by deception (Theft Act 1968, s 15);
- burglary (except in cases set out in previous list) (Theft Act 1968, s 9);
- going equipped for burglary/theft (Theft Act 1968, s 25);
- obtaining services by deception (Theft Act 1978, s 1);
- evading liability by deception (Theft Act 1978, s 2);
- making off without payment (Theft Act 1978, s 3);
- criminal damage (unless intent to endanger life etc) (Criminal Damage Act 1971, s 1);
- dangerous driving (Road Traffic Act 1988, s 2);
- carrying a loaded firearm in a public place (Firearms Act 1968, s 19);
- shortening a shot gun (Firearms Act 1968, s 4);
- having an offensive weapon in a public place (Prevention of Crime Act 1953, s 1);
- violent disorder (Public Order Act 1986, s 2);
- affray (Public Order Act 1986, s 3);
- stirring up racial hatred (Public Order Act 1986, s 18);
- all offences under the Forgery and Counterfeiting Act 1981;
- possessing/supplying/producing controlled drugs (Misuse of Drugs Act 1971, ss 4 and 5).

3.19   COMMON OFFENCES TRIABLE SUMMARILY

The following is a list of the most common offences which are triable only summarily:
- road traffic offences (except causing death by dangerous driving and dangerous driving);
- threatening behaviour (Public Order Act 1986, s 4);
- assaulting a police officer in the execution of his duty (Police Act 1996, s 89(1));
- resisting or wilfully obstructing a police officer in the execution of his duty (Police Act 1996, s 89(2));
- wasting police time (Criminal Law Act 1967, s 5);
- soliciting (Street Offences Act 1959, s 1);
- interfering with a motor vehicle (Criminal Attempts Act 1981, s 9);
- offences made summary by s 40 of the Criminal Justice Act 1988:

(i) common assault;

(ii) criminal damage where the value involved is less than £5,000 (Criminal Damage Act 1971, s 1);

(iii) driving whilst disqualified (Road Traffic Act 1988, s 103);

(iv) taking a conveyance without authority (Theft Act 1968, s 12).

TABLE OF STATUTORY AND OTHER MATERIALS

STATUTORY MATERIALS

MAGISTRATES' COURTS ACT 1980

Section 17: Certain offences triable either way

(1) The offences listed in Schedule 1 to this Act shall be triable either way.

(2) Sub-section (1) above is without prejudice to any other enactment by virtue of which any offence is triable either way.

Section 17A: Initial procedure – accused to indicate intention as to plea

(1) This section shall have effect where a person who has attained the age of 18 years appears or is brought before a magistrates' court on an information charging him with an offence triable either way.

(2) Everything that the court is required to do under the following provisions of this section must be done with the accused present in court.

(3) The court shall cause the charge to be written down, if this has not already been done, and to be read to the accused.

(4) The court shall then explain to the accused in ordinary language that he may indicate whether (if the offence were to proceed to trial) he would plead guilty or not guilty, and that if he indicates that he would plead guilty:

    (a) the court must proceed as mentioned in sub-section (6) below; and

    (b) he may be committed for sentence to the Crown Court under section 3 of the Powers of Criminal Courts (Sentencing) Act 2000 if the court is of such opinion as is mentioned in sub-section (2) of that section.

(5) The court shall then ask the accused whether (if the offence were to proceed to trial) he would plead guilty or not guilty.

(6) If the accused indicates that he would plead guilty the court shall proceed as if:

    (a) the proceedings constituted from the beginning the summary trial of the information; and

    (b) section 9(1) above [start of summary trial] was complied with and he pleaded guilty under it.

(7) If the accused indicates that he would plead not guilty section 18(1) below shall apply.

(8) If the accused in fact fails to indicate how he would plead, for the purposes of this section and section 18(1) below he shall be taken to indicate that he would plead not guilty.

(9) Subject to sub-section (6) above, the following shall not for any purpose be taken to constitute the taking of a plea:

(a) asking the accused under this section whether (if the offence were to proceed to trial) he would plead guilty or not guilty;

(b) an indication by the accused under this section of how he would plead.

Section 17B: Intention as to plea – absence of accused

(1) This section shall have effect where:

(a) a person who has attained the age of 18 years appears or is brought before a magistrates' court on an information charging him with an offence triable either way;

(b) the accused is represented by a legal representative;

(c) the court considers that by reason of the accused's disorderly conduct before the court it is not practicable for proceedings under section 17A above to be conducted in his presence; and

(d) the court considers that it should proceed in the absence of the accused.

(2) In such a case:

(a) the court shall cause the charge to be written down, if this has not already been done, and to be read to the representative;

(b) the court shall ask the representative whether (if the offence were to proceed to trial) the accused would plead guilty or not guilty;

(c) if the representative indicates that the accused would plead guilty the court shall proceed as if the proceedings constituted from the beginning the summary trial of the information, and as if section 9(1) above was complied with and the accused pleaded guilty under it;

(d) if the representative indicates that the accused would plead not guilty section 18(1) below shall apply.

(3) If the representative in fact fails to indicate how the accused would plead, for the purposes of this section and section 18(1) below he shall be taken to indicate that the accused would plead not guilty.

(4) Subject to sub-section (2)(c) above, the following shall not for any purpose be taken to constitute the taking of a plea:

(a) asking the representative under this section whether (if the offence were to proceed to trial) the accused would plead guilty or not guilty;

(b) an indication by the representative under this section of how the accused would plead.

Section 17C: Intention as to plea – adjournment

A magistrates' court proceeding under section 17A or 17B above may adjourn the proceedings at any time, and on doing so on any occasion when the accused is present may remand the accused, and shall remand him if:

(a) on the occasion on which he first appeared, or was brought, before the court to answer to the information he was in custody or, having been released on bail, surrendered to the custody of the court; or

(b) he has been remanded at any time in the course of proceedings on the information,

and where the court remands the accused, the time fixed for the resumption of proceedings shall be that at which he is required to appear or be brought before the court in pursuance of the remand or would be required to be brought before the court but for section 128(3A) below.[2]

Section 18: Initial procedure on information against adult for offence triable either way

(1) Sections 19 to 23 below shall have effect where a person who has attained the age of 18 appears or is brought before a magistrates' court on an information charging him with an offence triable either way and:

(a) he indicates under section 17A above that (if the offence were to proceed to trial) he would plead not guilty; or

(b) his representative indicates under section 17B above that (if the offence were to proceed to trial) he would plead not guilty.

(2) Without prejudice to section 11(1) above, everything that the court is required to do under sections 19 to 22 below must be done before any evidence is called and, subject to sub-section (3) below and section 23 below, with the accused present in court.

(3) The court may proceed in the absence of the accused in accordance with such of the provisions of sections 19 to 22 below as are applicable in the circumstances if the court considers that by reason of his disorderly conduct before the court it is not practicable for the proceedings to be conducted in his presence; and sub-sections (3) to (5) of section 23 below, so far as applicable, shall have effect in relation to proceedings conducted in the absence of the accused by virtue of this sub-section (references in those sub-sections to the person representing the accused being for this purpose read as references to the person, if any, representing him).

(4) A magistrates' court proceeding under sections 19 to 23 below may adjourn the proceedings at any time, and on doing so on any occasion when the accused is present may remand the accused, and shall remand him if:

(a) on the occasion on which he first appeared, or was brought, before the court to answer to the information he was in custody or, having been released on bail, surrendered to the custody of the court; or

(b) if he has been remanded at any time in the course of proceedings on the information,

---

2 Section 51 of the Crime (Sentences) Act 1997 inserts a new s 38A into the Magistrates' Courts Act 1980 as a consequence of the new 'indication as to plea' procedure.

and where the court remands the accused, the time fixed for the resumption of the proceedings shall be that at which he is required to appear to be brought before the court in pursuance of the remand or would be required to be brought before the court but for section 128(3A) below.

(5) The functions of a magistrates' court under sections 19 to 23 below may be discharged by a single justice, but the foregoing provision shall not be taken to authorise the summary trial of an information by a magistrates' court composed of less than two justices.

Section 19: Court to begin by considering which mode of trial appears more suitable

(1) The court shall consider whether, having regard to the matters mentioned in sub-section (3) below and any representations made by the prosecutor or the accused, the offence appears to the court more suitable for summary trial or for trial on indictment.

(2) Before so considering, the court:

(a) [repealed];

(b) shall afford first the prosecutor and then the accused an opportunity to make representations as to which mode of trial would be more suitable.

(3) The matters to which the court is to have regard under sub-section (1) above are the nature of the case; whether the circumstances make the offence one of serious character; whether the punishment which a magistrates' court would have power to inflict for it would be adequate; and any other circumstances which appear to the court to make it more suitable for the offence to be tried in one way rather than the other.

(4) If the prosecution is being carried on by the Attorney General, the Solicitor General or the Director of Public Prosecutions and he applies for the offence to be tried on indictment, the preceding provisions of this section and sections 20 and 21 below shall not apply, and the court shall proceed to inquire into the information as examining justices.

(5) The power of the Director of Public Prosecutions under sub-section (4) above to apply for an offence to be tried on indictment shall not be exercised except with the consent of the Attorney General.

Section 20: Procedure where summary trial appears more suitable

(1) If, where the court has considered as required by section 19(1) above, it appears to the court that the offence is more suitable for summary trial, the following provisions of this section shall apply (unless excluded by section 23 below).

(2) The court shall explain to the accused in ordinary language:

(a) that it appears to the court more suitable for him to be tried summarily for the offence, and that he can either consent to be so tried or, if he wishes, be tried by a jury; and

    (b) that if he is tried summarily and is convicted by the court, he may be committed for sentence to the Crown Court under section 38 below if the convicting court is of such opinion as is mentioned in sub-section (2) of that section.

(3) After explaining to the accused as provided by sub-section (2) above the court shall ask him whether he consents to be tried summarily or wishes to be tried by a jury, and:

    (a) if he consents to be tried summarily, shall proceed to the summary trial of the information;

    (b) if he does not consent, shall proceed to inquire into the information as examining justices.

Section 21: Procedure where trial on indictment appears more suitable

If, where the court has considered as required by section 19(1) above, it appears to the court that the offence is more suitable for trial on indictment, the court shall tell the accused that the court has decided that it is more suitable for him to be tried for the offence by a jury, and shall proceed to inquire into the information as examining justices.

Section 22: Certain offences triable either way to be tried summarily if value involved is small

(1) If the offence charged by the information is one of those mentioned in the first column of Schedule 2 of this Act (in this section referred to as 'scheduled offences'),[3] then the court shall, before proceeding in accordance with section 19 above, consider whether, having regard to any representations made by the prosecutor or the accused, the value involved (as defined by sub-section (10) below) appears to the court to exceed the relevant sum.

For the purposes of this section, the relevant sum is £5,000.

(2) If, where sub-section (1) above applies, it appears to the court clear that, for the offence charged, the value involved does not exceed the relevant sum, the court shall proceed as if the offence were triable only summarily, and sections 19 to 21 above shall not apply.

(3) If, where sub-section (1) above applies, it appears to the court clear that, for the offence charged, the value involved exceeds the relevant sum, the court

---

3   Schedule 2 defines the following as 'scheduled offences': 'Offences under section 1 of the Criminal Damage Act 1971 (destroying or damaging property), excluding any offence committed by destroying or damaging property by fire'; aiding, abetting, counselling or procuring such an offence; attempting to commit such an offence; inciting another to commit such an offence; and 'offences under section 12A of the Theft Act 1968 (aggravated vehicle taking) where no allegation is made under sub-section (1)(b) other than of damage, whether to the vehicle or other property or both.'

shall thereupon proceed in accordance with section 19 above in the ordinary way without further regard to the provisions of this section.

(4) If, where sub-section (1) above applies, it appears to the court for any reason not clear whether, for the offence charged, the value involved does or does not exceed the relevant sum, the provisions of sub-sections (5) and (6) below shall apply.

(5) The court shall cause the charge to be written down, if this has not already been done, and read to the accused, and shall explain to him in ordinary language:

   (a) that he can, if he wishes, consent to be tried summarily for the offence and that if he consents to be so tried, he will definitely be tried in that way; and

   (b) that if he is tried summarily and is convicted by the court, his liability to imprisonment or a fine will be limited as provided in section 33 below.[4]

(6) After explaining to the accused as provided by sub-section (5) above the court shall ask him whether he consents to be tried summarily and:

   (a) if he so consents shall proceed in accordance with sub-section (2) above as if that sub-section applied;

   (b) if he does not so consent, shall proceed in accordance with sub-section (3) above as if that sub-section applied.

(7) [Repealed.]

(8) Where a person is convicted by a magistrates' court of a scheduled offence, it shall not be open to him to appeal to the Crown Court against the conviction on the ground that the convicting court's decision as to the value involved was mistaken.

(9) If, where sub-section (1) above applies, the offence charged is one with which the accused is charged jointly with a person who has not attained the age of 18, the reference in that sub-section to any representations made by the accused shall be read as including any representations made by the person under 18.

---

4   Section 33 (maximum penalties on summary conviction in pursuance of s 22):

   (1) Where in pursuance of sub-section (2) of section 22 above a magistrates' court proceeds to the summary trial of an information, then, if the accused is summarily convicted of the offence:

      (a) subject to sub-section (3) below the court shall not have power to impose on him in respect of that offence imprisonment for more than 3 months or a fine greater than level 4 on the standard scale [£2,500]; and

      (b) section 3 of the Powers of Criminal Courts (Sentencing) Act 2000 [committal for sentence] shall not apply as regards that offence.

   (2) In sub-section (1) above 'fine' includes a pecuniary penalty but does not include a pecuniary forfeiture or pecuniary compensation.

   (3) Paragraph (a) of sub-section (1) above does not apply to an offence under section 12A of the Theft Act 1968 (aggravated vehicle taking).

(10) In this section 'the value involved', in relation to any scheduled offence, means the value indicated in the second column of Schedule 2 to this Act,[5] measured as indicated in the third column of that Schedule;[6] and in that Schedule 'the material time' means the time of the alleged offence.

(11) Where:

(a) the accused is charged on the same occasion with two or more scheduled offences and it appears to the court that they constitute or form part of a series of two or more offences of the same or a similar character; or

(b) the offence charged consists of incitement to commit two or more scheduled offences,

---

5 (a) For offences under s 1 of the Criminal Damage Act 1971 and aiding, abetting, counselling, procuring, attempting or inciting such offences: as regards property alleged to have been destroyed, its value; as regards property alleged to have been damaged, the value of the alleged damage.

(b) For offences under s 12A of the Theft Act 1968: the total value of the damage alleged to have been caused.

6 (a) *Offences under s 1 of the Criminal Damage Act 1971 and aiding, abetting, counselling, procuring, attempting or inciting such offences.*

(i) Where property is alleged to have been destroyed, the value of that property is measured thus: 'What the property would probably have cost to buy in the open market at the material time.'

(ii) Where property is alleged to have been damaged, the value of that damage is calculated thus:

'(a) If immediately after the material time the damage was capable of repair:

(i) what would probably then have been the market price for the repair of the damage; or

(ii) what the property alleged to have been damaged would probably have cost to buy in the open market at the material time,

whichever is the less; or

(b) if immediately after the material time the damage was beyond repair, what the said property would probably have cost to buy in the open market at the material time.'

(b) *Offences under s 12A of the Theft Act 1968.* the total value of the damage alleged to have been caused is calculated thus:

'(1) In the case of damage to any property other than the vehicle involved in the offence, as for [offences under section 1 of the Criminal Damage Act 1971], substituting a reference to the time of the accident concerned for any reference to the material time.

(2) In the case of damage to the vehicle involved in the offence:

(a) if immediately after the vehicle was recovered the damage was capable of repair:

(i) what would probably then have been the market price for the repair of the damage; or

(ii) what the vehicle would probably have cost to buy in the open market immediately before it was unlawfully taken,

whichever is the less; or

(b) if immediately after the vehicle was recovered the damage was beyond repair, what the vehicle would probably have cost to buy in the open market immediately before it was unlawfully taken.'

this section shall have effect as if any reference in it to the value involved were a reference to the aggregate of the values involved.

(12) Sub-section (8) of section 12A of the Theft Act 1968 (which determines when a vehicle is recovered) shall apply for the purposes of paragraph 3 of Schedule 2 to this Act as it applies for the purposes of that section.

Section 23: Power of court, with consent of legally represented accused, to proceed in his absence

(1) Where:

(a) the accused is represented by a legal representative who in his absence signifies to the court the accused's consent to the proceedings for determining how he is to be tried for the offence being conducted in his absence; and

(b) the court is satisfied that there is good reason for proceeding in the absence of the accused,

the following provisions of this section apply.

(2) Subject to the following provisions of this section, the court may proceed in the absence of the accused in accordance with such of the provisions of sections 19 to 22 above as are applicable in the circumstances.

(3) If, in a case where sub-section (1) of section 22 above applies, it appears to the court as mentioned in sub-section (4) of that section, sub-sections (5) and (6) of that section shall not apply and the court:

(a) if the accused's consent to be tried summarily has been or is signified by the person representing him, shall proceed in accordance with sub-section (2) of that section as if that sub-section applied; or

(b) if that consent has not been and is not so signified, shall proceed in accordance with sub-section (3) of that section as if that sub-section applied.

(4) If, where the court has considered as required by section 19(1) above, it appears to the court that the offence is more suitable for summary trial then:

(a) if the accused's consent to be tried summarily has been or is signified by the person representing him, section 20 above shall not apply, and the court shall proceed to the summary trial of the information; or

(b) if that consent has not been and is not so signified, section 20 above shall not apply and the court shall proceed to inquire into the information as examining justices and may adjourn the hearing without remanding the accused.

(5) If, where the court has considered as required by section 19(1) above, it appears to the court that the offence is more suitable for trial on indictment, section 21 above shall not apply, and the court shall proceed to inquire into the information as examining justices and may adjourn the hearing without remanding the accused.

Section 25: Power to change from summary trial to committal proceedings, and *vice versa*

(1) Sub-sections (2) to (4) below shall have effect where a person who has attained the age of 18 appears or is brought before a magistrates' court on an information charging him with an offence triable either way.

(2) Where the court has (otherwise than in pursuance of section 22(2) above)[7] begun to try the information summarily, the court may, at any time before the conclusion of the evidence for the prosecution, discontinue the summary trial and proceed to inquire into the information as examining justices and, on doing so, shall adjourn the hearing.

(3) Where the court has begun to inquire into the information as examining justices, then, if at any time during the inquiry it appears to the court, having regard to any representations made in the presence of the accused by the prosecutor, or made by the accused, and to the nature of the case, that the offence is after all more suitable for summary trial, the court may, after doing as provided in sub-section (4) below, ask the accused whether he consents to be tried summarily and, if he so consents, may subject to sub-section (3A) below proceed to try the information summarily.

(3A) Where the prosecution is being carried on by the Attorney General or the Solicitor General, the court shall not exercise the power conferred by sub-section (3) above without his consent and, where the prosecution is being carried on by the Director of Public Prosecutions, shall not exercise that power if the Attorney General directs that it should not be exercised.

(4) Before asking the accused under sub-section (3) above whether he consents to be tried summarily, the court shall in ordinary language:

   (a) explain to him that it appears to the court more suitable for him to be tried summarily for the offence, but that this can only be done if he consents to be so tried; and

   (b) unless it has already done so, explain to him, as provided in section 20(2)(b) above, about the court's power to commit to the Crown Court for sentence.

(5) Where a person under the age of 18 appears or is brought before a magistrates' court on an information charging him with an indictable offence other than homicide, and the court:

   (a) has begun to try the information summarily on the footing that the case does not fall within paragraph (a) or (b) of section 24(1) above and must therefore be tried summarily as required by the said section 24(1); or

   (b) has begun to inquire into the information as examining justices on the footing that the case does so fall,

   sub-section (6) or (7) below, as the case may be, shall have effect.

(6) If, in a case falling with sub-section (5)(a) above, it appears to the court at any time before the conclusion of the evidence for the prosecution that the

---

7   The special provisions relating to criminal damage, etc.

case is after all one which under the said section 24(1) ought not to be tried summarily, the court may discontinue the summary trial and proceed to inquire into the information as examining justices and, on doing so, shall adjourn the hearing.

(7) If, in a case falling with sub-section (5)(b) above, it appears to the court at any time during the inquiry that the case is after all one which under the said section 24(1) ought to be tried summarily, the court may proceed to try the information summarily.

(8) If the court adjourns the hearing under sub-section (2) or (6) above it may (if it thinks fit) do so without remanding the accused.

Section 26: Power to issue summons to accused in certain circumstances

(1) Where:

    (a) in the circumstances mentioned in section 23(1)(a) above the court is not satisfied that there is good reason for proceeding in the absence of the accused; or

    (b) sub-section (4)(b) or (5) of section 23 or sub-section (2) or (6) of sub-section 25 above applies, and the court adjourns the hearing in pursuance of that sub-section without remanding the accused,

the justice or any of the justices of which the court is composed may issue a summons directed to the accused requiring his presence before the court.

(2) If the accused is not present at the time and place appointed:

    (a) in a case within sub-section (1)(a) above, for the proceedings under section 19(1) or 22(1) above, as the case may be; or

    (b) in a case within sub-section (1)(b) above, for the resumption of the hearing,

the court may issue a warrant for his arrest.

...

(28) [Repealed.]

Sections 19 to 22 of the Magistrates' Courts Act 1980 as proposed to be amended by the Criminal Justice (Mode of Trial) Bill:

CRIMINAL JUSTICE (MODE OF TRIAL) (NO 2) BILL

Determination of mode of trial

The following shall be substituted for sections 19 to 22 of the Magistrates' Courts Act 1980 (offences triable either way: determination of mode of trial):

19 Court to consider mode of trial

(1) The court shall consider whether the offence ought to be tried summarily or on indictment.

(2) For the purpose of sub-section (1) above the court shall consider:

   (a) the nature of the case;

   (b) any of the circumstances of the offence (but not of the accused) which appears to the court to be relevant; and

   (c) whether, having regard to the matters to be considered under paragraph (b), the punishment which a magistrates' court would have power to impose for the offence would be adequate.

(3) For the purpose of sub-section (1) above the court:

   (a) shall permit the prosecutor and the accused to make representations about the matters to be considered under sub-section (2); and

   (b) shall have regard to any representations made under paragraph (a) above.

20. Determination of mode of trial.

(1) Following consideration of mode of trial under section 19 above the court shall inform the accused of:

   (a) its decision, and

   (b) the reasons for its decision.

(2) Where the court decides that the offence ought to be tried summarily then, subject to the outcome of any appeal under sub-section (4) below, the accused shall be tried summarily.

(3) Where the court decides that the offence ought to be tried on indictment the information shall be inquired into by examining justices.

(4) The accused may appeal to the Crown Court against a decision of a magistrates' court that he ought to be tried summarily if:

   (a) he made representations under section 19(3) above that he ought to be tried on indictment; and

   (b) he complies with any applicable condition imposed by rules under section 144 below.

(5) If the appeal is allowed the information shall be inquired into by examining justices.

21 Prosecutions by Attorney General, &c

(1) This section applies where a prosecution is being carried on by:

   (a) the Attorney General;

   (b) the Solicitor General; or

   (c) the Director of Public Prosecutions.

(2) If the person carrying on the prosecution applies for the accused to be tried on indictment:

(a) sections 19 and 20 above shall not apply; and

(b) the information shall be inquired into by examining justices.

(3) The Director of Public Prosecutions may not make an application under sub-section (2) above without the consent of the Attorney General.

22 Summary trial for certain small-value property offences

(1) This section applies where the offence charged by the information is an offence listed in the first column of Schedule 2 to this Act (a 'scheduled offence').

(2) Before proceeding in accordance with section 19 above, the court shall consider whether the value involved in relation to the offence exceeds the relevant sum.

(3) For the purposes of sub-section (2) above:

(a) the relevant sum is £5,000;

(b) 'the value involved' means the value identified in the relevant entry in the second column of Schedule 2;

(c) the value shall be measured in accordance with the third column of that Schedule;

(d) the material time mentioned in that Schedule shall be taken to be the time when the offence was alleged to have been committed; and

(e) the court shall permit the prosecutor and the accused to make representations and shall have regard to any representations made by either of them.

(4) If the court is satisfied that the value involved in relation to the offence exceeds the relevant sum, sections 19 to 21 above shall apply.

(5) In any other case:

(a) those sections shall not apply; and

(b) the offence shall be treated as if it were triable only summarily.

(6) Where a person is convicted by a magistrates' court of a scheduled offence, it shall not be open to him to appeal to the Crown Court against the conviction on the ground that the convicting court's decision as to the value involved was mistaken.

(7) If the offence charged is one with which the accused is charged jointly with a person who has not attained the age of 18:

(a) that person shall be entitled to make representations for the purposes of sub-section (2) above; and

(b) the court shall have regard to those representations.

(8) If:

(a) the accused is charged on one occasion with two or more scheduled offences and the court considers that they constitute or form part of a series of two or more offences of the same or a similar character; or

(b) the offence charged consists in incitement to commit two or more scheduled offences,this section shall have effect as if a reference to the value involved were a reference to the aggregate of the values involved.

(9) Section 12A(8) of the Theft Act 1968 (which determines when a vehicle is recovered) shall apply for the purposes of paragraph 3 of Schedule 2 to this Act as it applies for the purposes of that section.

SUMMARY OFFENCES IN THE CROWN COURT

CRIMINAL JUSTICE ACT 1988

Section 40: Power to join in indictment count for common assault, etc

(1) A count charging a person with a summary offence to which this section applies may be included in an indictment if the charge:

(a) is founded on the same facts or evidence as a count charging an indictable offence; or

(b) is part of a series of offences of the same or similar character as an indictable offence which is also charged,

but only if (in either case) the facts or evidence relating to the offence were disclosed in an examination or deposition taken before a justice in the presence of the person charged.

(2) Where a count charging an offence to which this section applies is included in an indictment, the offence shall be tried in the same manner as if it were an indictable offence; but the Crown Court may only deal with the offender in respect of it in a manner in which a magistrates' court could have dealt with him.

(3) The offences to which this section applies are:

(a) common assault;

(aa) an offence under section 90(1) of the Criminal Justice Act 1991 (assaulting a prisoner custody officer);

(ab) an offence under section 13(1) of the Criminal Justice and Public Order Act 1994 (assaulting a secure training centre custody officer);

(b) an offence under section 12(1) of the Theft Act 1968 (taking a motor vehicle or other conveyance without authority, etc);

(c) an offence under 103(1)(b) of the Road Traffic Act 1988 (driving a motor vehicle while disqualified);

(d) an offence mentioned in the first column of Schedule 2 to the Magistrates' Courts Act 1980 (criminal damage, etc) which would otherwise be triable only summarily by virtue of section 22(2) of that Act; and

(e) any summary offence specified under sub-section (4) below.

(4) The Secretary of State may by order made by statutory instrument specify for the purposes of this section any summary offence which is punishable with imprisonment or involves obligatory or discretionary disqualification from driving.

...

Section 41: Power of Crown Court to deal with summary offence where person committed for either way offence

(1) Where a magistrates' court commits a person to the Crown Court for trial on indictment for an offence triable either way or a number of such offences, it may also commit him for trial for any summary offence with which he is charged and which:

(a) is punishable with imprisonment or involves obligatory or discretionary disqualification from driving; and

(b) arises out of circumstances which appear to the court to be the same as or connected with those giving rise to the offence, or one of the offences, triable either way, whether or not evidence relating to that summary offence appears in the depositions or written statements in the case,

and the trial of the information for the summary offence shall then be treated as if the magistrates' court had adjourned it under section 10 of the Magistrates' Courts Act 1980 and had not fixed the time and place for its resumption.

(2) Where a magistrates' court commits a person to the Crown Court for trial on indictment for a number of offences triable either way and exercises the power conferred by sub-section (1) above in respect of a summary offence, the magistrates' court shall give the Crown Court and the person who is committed for trial a notice stating which of the offences triable either way appears to the court to arise out of circumstances which are the same as or connected with those giving rise to the summary offence.

(3) A magistrates' court's decision to exercise the power conferred by sub-section (1) above shall not be subject to appeal or liable to be questioned in any court.

(4) The committal of a person under this section in respect of an offence to which section 40 above applies shall not preclude the exercise in relation to the offence of the power conferred by that section; but where he is tried on indictment for such an offence, the functions of the Crown Court under this section in relation to the offence shall cease.

(5) If he is convicted on the indictment, the Crown Court shall consider whether the conditions specified in sub-section (1) above were satisfied.

(6) If it considers that they were satisfied, it shall state to him the substance of the summary offence and ask him whether he pleads guilty or not guilty.

(7) If he pleads guilty, the Crown Court shall convict him, but may deal with him in respect of that offence only in a manner in which a magistrates' court could have dealt with him.

(8) If he does not plead guilty, the powers of the Crown Court shall cease in respect of the offence except as provided by sub-section (9) below.

(9) If the prosecution inform the court that they would not desire to submit evidence on the charge relating to the summary offence, the court shall dismiss it.

(10) The Crown Court shall inform the clerk of the magistrates' court of the outcome of any proceedings under this section.

(11) Where the Court of Appeal allows an appeal against conviction of an offence triable either way which arose out of circumstances which were the same as or connected with those giving rise to a summary offence of which the appellant was convicted under this section:

(a) it shall set aside his conviction of the summary offence and give the clerk of the magistrates' court notice that it has done so; and

(b) it may direct that no further proceedings in relation to the offence are to be undertaken,

and the proceedings before the Crown Court in relation to the offence shall thereafter be disregarded for all purposes.

(12) A notice under sub-section (11) above shall include particulars of any direction given under paragraph (b) of that sub-section in relation to the offence.

...

OTHER MATERIALS

NATIONAL MODE OF TRIAL GUIDELINES[8]

The purpose of these guidelines is to help magistrates decide whether or not to commit 'either way' offences for trial in the Crown Court. Their object is to provide guidance not direction. They are not intended to impinge upon a magistrates' duty to consider each case individually and on its own particular facts.

These guidelines apply to all defendants aged 18 and above.

---

8 Issued in 1995 with the authority of the Lord Chief Justice.

[Summary of Magistrates' Courts Act 1980, s 19.]

Certain general observations can be made:

(a) the court should never make its decision on the grounds of convenience or expedition;

(b) the court should assume for the purpose of deciding mode of trial that the prosecution version of the facts is correct;

(c) the fact that the offences are alleged to be specimens is a relevant consideration; the fact that the defendant will be asking for other offences to be taken into consideration, if convicted, is not;

(d) where cases involve complex questions of fact or difficult questions of law, including difficult issues of disclosure of sensitive material, the court should consider committal for trial;

(e) where two or more defendants are jointly charged with an offence each has an individual right to elect his mode of trial;

(f) In general, except where otherwise stated, either way offences should be tried summarily unless the court considers that the particular case has one or more of the features set out in the following pages [not reprinted here] and that its sentencing powers are insufficient;

(g) The court should also consider its power to commit an offender for sentence, under section 3 of the Powers of Criminal Courts (Sentencing) Act 2000 ... if information emerges during the course of the hearing which leads them to conclude that the offence is so serious, or the offender such a risk to the public, that their powers to sentence him are inadequate ...

[The Guidelines then deal with a number of specific offences.]

CHAPTER 4

SUMMARY TRIAL

In this chapter, we look at the procedure for trying cases in the magistrates' court.

4.1   TERRITORIAL JURISDICTION

The rules regarding territorial jurisdiction are set out in ss 1 and 2 of the Magistrates' Courts Act 1980.

A magistrates' court can try a summary offence which is alleged to have been committed in the county served by that court. The court may try a summary offence not committed in its county if the defendant is already appearing before that court in respect of another offence or the accused is to be tried jointly with someone who is already appearing before that court.

It can try an offence which is triable either way, no matter where in England or Wales the offence was allegedly committed.

In *R v Croydon Magistrates' Court ex p Morgan* (1998) 162 JP 521, the defendant was charged with 10 either way offences and two summary offences. The summary offences were committed outside the commission area for that magistrates' court. The defendant was committed for trial in respect of the either way offences. The Divisional Court held that, since the Croydon magistrates had committed the defendant for trial of the either way offences rather than trying those offences themselves, that magistrates' court did not have jurisdiction to try the two summary offences committed outside its area.

4.2   TIME LIMITS

There are no time limits applicable to indictable (including either way) offences. However, an information alleging a summary offence must be laid within six months of the commission of the offence unless the statute creating the offence provides otherwise (s 127 of the Magistrates' Courts Act 1980). Where a statute creates a continuing summary offence, a prosecution can be brought at any time until six months have elapsed from the date when the offence ceased to be committed: *British Telecommunications plc v Nottinghamshire CC* [1999] Crim LR 217 (here, the offence was that of failing to reinstate the highway after street works had been carried out; the last date when the offence ceased to be committed was when the reinstatement of the road was completed satisfactorily).

There is no specific time limit within which the summons must be served once the information has been laid, although excessive delay in serving the summons could amount to an abuse of process giving the court the power to dismiss the case. This would only arise where the prosecution ask the court not to post the summons to the defendant or where the police were dilatory in serving a summons on a defendant personally where postal service had proved ineffective (see Chapter 2, 2.15.2).

4.3   A CHARGE EQUIVALENT TO AN INFORMATION

The rules of procedure which apply to summary trial refer to the trial of an information. The same rules apply where proceedings are commenced by arrest and charge, as a charge is regarded as an information for these purposes.

4.4   THE DUPLICITOUS INFORMATION

Rule 12 of the Magistrates' Courts Rules 1981 (as amended by r 3 of the Magistrates' Courts (Miscellaneous Amendments) Rules 1993) provides that an information should allege only one offence. If an information alleges more than one offence, the court must call upon the prosecution to decide which offence to proceed with. The other offence will then be struck out. If the prosecution fail to choose between the offences, the court must strike out the entire information.

In *Carrington Carr v Leicestershire County Council* [1993] Crim LR 938, it was held that there are five situations where informations may be duplicitous:

- where two or more discrete offences are charged conjunctively in one information, for example a single information alleges both dangerous driving and careless driving;
- where two offences are charged disjunctively or in the alternative in one information, for example a single information alleges dangerous driving or careless driving;
- where an offence was capable of being committed in more ways than one, for example driving under the influence of drink or drugs and both ways are referred to in one information;
- where a single offence was charged in respect of an activity but the activity involved more than one act; and
- where a single activity was charged but a number of particulars are relied on by the prosecution to prove the offence, for example, a single act of obtaining by deception where the deception involved several misrepresentations.

In the latter two instances, a single information may well be appropriate. However, if the defendant wishes to admit some but not other allegations, or wishes to raise different defences to different allegations, separate informations will be necessary.

An information would be duplicitous if, for example, the defendant were charged with receiving stolen goods and another form of handling stolen goods in the same information. Note, however, that a series of acts may amount to a single offence if those acts constitute a course of conduct (for example, stealing a number of items from a supermarket would be charged in one information under a single allegation of theft) (*Heaton v Costello* [1984] Crim LR 485).

It was also held in *Ministry of Agriculture, Fisheries and Food v Nunn* [1990] Crim LR 268 that an information will be duplicitous if it alleges more than one victim of the alleged offence. Whilst this will usually be the case (separate victims should be dealt with in separate informations as separate offences have been committed), there may be circumstances where a single offence can be committed against more than one victim; reference should be made to Chapter 8, which examines the equivalent rules in the Crown Court.

4.5 TRYING MORE THAN ONE OFFENCE OR MORE THAN ONE DEFENDANT

Where several defendants are charged with the same offence, they will be tried together.

Where an accused faces more than one information or there are several defendants charged in separate informations, a joint trial is possible.

More than one information may be tried at the same time if the magistrates feel that there is a sufficient link between the offences charged. This is a matter for the discretion of the justices, who should ask themselves whether the interests of justice are best served by a joint trial or separate trials, balancing convenience for the prosecution against the risk of any prejudice to the defendant. *Per* Lord Roskill in *Chief Constable of Norfolk v Clayton* [1983] 2 AC 473; [1983] 1 All ER 984:

> The justices should always ask themselves whether it would be fair and just to the defendant or defendants to allow a joint trial.

If the magistrates decide against a single trial where the defendant is accused of more than one offence, those justices should not hear any of the cases as a magistrate trying a case should be unaware that the defendant faces other charges (*R v Liverpool Justices ex p Topping* [1983] 1 WLR 119; [1983] 1 All ER 490). Each case would thus have to be heard by a different Bench.

4.6 DISMISSING CASE WITHOUT HEARING EVIDENCE

Section 15 of the Magistrates' Courts Act 1980 empowers the court to adjourn the case or dismiss the information if the prosecution fails to appear at the time and place fixed for the summary trial. Where a magistrates' court dismisses an information under s 15 without consideration of the merits of the case because of the non-attendance of the prosecutor, there is no rule of law which prevents the court from dealing with an identical information subsequently laid against the same defendant; the question to be decided is whether the new information amounts to an abuse of process, and so the court must consider what prejudice would be caused to the defendant by the preferment of the new information (*Holmes v Cambell* (1998) 162 JP 655).

A case can also be dismissed without a hearing if there has been delay. The circumstances where a case may be dismissed because of delay are considered in Chapter 2, 2.15.

However, in *R v Watford Justices ex p DPP* [1990] RTR 374; [1990] Crim LR 422, it was held that the justices cannot dismiss an information on the ground that the case is too trivial to justify the continuance of the proceedings. If the prosecution wish to adduce evidence, the magistrates must hear that evidence unless the prosecution are guilty of abuse of process.

4.7 PLEADING GUILTY BY POST

Section 12 of the Magistrates' Courts Act 1980 applies only to summary offences which have a maximum sentence of no more than three months' imprisonment. It provides that the defendant may be offered the opportunity of pleading guilty by post. The defendant will be sent a special form along with the summons. On the form, the defendant can indicate a plea of guilty and can also draw to the court's attention any mitigating circumstances which may persuade the court to impose a more lenient sentence.

At court, neither the prosecution nor the defence are represented. In open court, the clerk will read out the statement of facts which is sent out to the defendant along with the summons and whatever the defendant has written on the form or in an accompanying letter. The court then proceeds to pass sentence.

Note, however, that a sentence of imprisonment, or disqualification from driving, cannot be imposed in the absence of the defendant. If the court is minded to impose such a sentence, the defendant will be summoned to attend on a later occasion.

A specimen of the notice sent to the defendant (together with the standard form for the statement of facts) appears at the end of this chapter (4.15 and 4.16 below).

Section 12A of the Magistrates' Courts Act 1980 makes provision for the application of s 12 of the Magistrates' Courts Act 1980 where the defendant appears in court. If the accused has indicated that he wishes to plead guilty by post but nevertheless appears before the court, the court may (if the accused consents) proceed as if the defendant were absent. Similarly, if the accused has not indicated that he wishes to plead guilty by post but, when he attends court, indicates that he wishes to plead guilty, the court may (if the accused consents) proceed as if he were absent and he had indicated an intention to plead guilty by post. Where the court proceeds as if the defendant were absent, the prosecution summary of the facts of the case must not go beyond the statement served on the defendant when he was given the option of pleading guilty by post. However, if the accused is in fact present in court, he must be given the opportunity to make an oral submission with a view to mitigation of sentence.

A large number of defendants do not respond to the summons in which they are given the opportunity to plead guilty by post. The Magistrates' Courts (Procedure) Act 1998 allows for the police to prepare witness statements (rather than just a statement of facts) and to serve them along with the summons. The witness statements will be admissible as evidence unless the defendant objects. If the defendant fails to plead guilty by post or to attend court to plead not guilty, and so fails to object to the use of the witness statements as evidence, the court can proceed to try the defendant in his absence, the prosecution case being based upon the witness statements already served on the defendant.

The pleading guilty by post system is used most commonly for driving offences, and so the 1998 Act also makes provision for a print out from the Driver and Vehicle Licensing Agency to be admissible as evidence of previous convictions for traffic offences without the need to give the defendant advance notice of intention to refer to these previous convictions.

4.8   PRESENCE OF DEFENDANT

Where proceedings were commenced by summons (rather than by arrest and charge), the defendant is deemed to be present if his legal representative is in court (s 122 of the Magistrates' Courts Act 1980). The legal representative may enter a plea on behalf of the defendant if the latter is not in court.

Where proceedings were begun by summons, but s 122 is inapplicable, s 13 of the Magistrates' Courts Act 1980 says that a warrant for the defendant's arrest may be issued provided that:

(a) if the present hearing is the first hearing, it is proved that the summons was served on the defendant;

(b) if the present hearing is a second or subsequent hearing, the defendant was present on the last occasion and the date for the present hearing was fixed at that hearing.

In other words, it has to be proved that the defendant knew of the date of today's hearing.

However, where the defendant was originally arrested and charged, he must attend court personally or else is in breach of his bail, entitling the court to grant a bench warrant for his arrest under s 7 of the Bail Act 1976 (see Chapter 2, 2.11.3).

4.8.1   Trial in absence of defendant

Under s 11(1) of the Magistrates' Courts Act 1980, a defendant may be tried in his absence in the magistrates' court. However, if the offence charged is triable either way, the defendant can only be tried *in absentia* in the magistrates' court if, on an earlier occasion, he consented to summary trial.

In the year ending March 1996, the prosecution secured a conviction in the absence of the defendant in 10.4% of the cases brought by the Crown Prosecution Service.

Where an application for an adjournment is made on behalf of the defence on the ground that the defendant cannot attend court by reason of illness, and there is a medical certificate or doctor's letter to support this claim, but the magistrates think that the excuse is spurious, they should nevertheless give the defendant the chance to answer their doubts and not simply proceed with the trial (*R v Bolton Justices ex p Merna* [1991] Crim LR 848).

4.8.2   Setting aside conviction where the defendant did not know of proceedings (s 14 of the Magistrates' Courts Act 1980)

We saw in Chapter 1 that a summons could be served by posting it to the defendant's last known address or even by leaving it with someone at that address. There is therefore a risk that the summons will not in fact come to the attention of the defendant, and that the defendant will be tried and convicted in his absence under s 11 of the Magistrates' Courts Act 1980.

Section 14 of the Magistrates' Courts Act 1980 provides that in these circumstances the conviction may be set aside. The procedure to achieve this is as follows:

• The defendant must make a statutory declaration (a written statement under oath rather like an affidavit) averring that he did not know of the summons or the subsequent proceedings until after the court had begun to try the information. The declaration must also state the date on which the defendant first became aware of the proceedings.

- This statement must be served on the clerk to the justices who convicted the defendant within 21 days of the date when the defendant first knew of the proceedings.
- The effect of the declaration is to render void the summons and all subsequent proceedings. However, the information itself remains unaffected and so a fresh summons can be served on the basis of the original information.
- The defendant may attend the court in person to make the statutory declaration (in which case, it is sworn before a magistrate) or else he may swear the declaration before a solicitor or commissioner for oaths and then send it by post to the court.
- A magistrate or a clerk may allow a declaration to take effect even if it is served after the 21 day time limit if, in the circumstances of the case, it was not reasonable to expect the defendant to effect service of the declaration within that time.

The problem of a defendant not knowing about proceedings never arises where proceedings are commenced by arrest and charge: the charge sheet tells the defendant the date of his first court appearance.

4.9   SUMMARY TRIAL PROCEDURE

The first stage in a summary trial is for the plea to be taken. The clerk puts the allegation(s) to the defendant who has to plead guilty or not guilty. A separate plea should be entered in respect of each charge faced by the defendant.

4.9.1   Procedure where the defendant pleads guilty

The procedure where the defendant pleads guilty is as follows:
- The prosecution summarise the facts of the offence.

  It should be noted that if there is a significant difference between the prosecution version of the facts and the version to be put forward by the defence (for example, in the case of an offence of violence, there is a dispute as to whether a weapon was used), the court must either accept the defence version or else hear evidence on the question and then come to a decision on which version to believe (*R v Newton* (1982) 77 Cr App R 13). See Chapter 12, 12.1.1.
- The prosecutor hands the magistrates details of the defendant's previous convictions, if any. The prosecutor will have asked the defence to confirm that these details are correct. The magistrates will indicate which of the previous convictions they wish the prosecutor to read out loud on the basis that they are relevant to the sentence for the present offence; usually, it is

only the most recent convictions that are read out. The prosecutor will also tell the court what is known about the personal circumstances of the defendant (employment, housing, etc); this is based on what the defendant has told the police and will be very brief.

- Once the prosecution have summarised the facts, the magistrates may decide to adjourn for a pre-sentence report (see Chapter 12). If not, the defence will make a plea in mitigation in order to try to persuade the court to impose a lenient sentence. Having heard the plea in mitigation, the magistrates may then decide to adjourn for a pre-sentence report. The adjournment cannot be for more than four weeks if the defendant is on bail, and three weeks if he is in custody (s 10(3) of the Magistrates' Courts Act 1980).

- If there has been an adjournment for a pre-sentence report, it is unlikely that the same magistrates will be sitting on the next occasion, so the prosecution will have to summarise the facts of the offence and the defence will have to do a full plea in mitigation.

- Sentence is then passed.

4.9.2 Procedure where the defendant pleads not guilty

The procedure where the defendant pleads not guilty is as follows:

- The prosecution may make an opening speech, briefly setting out what they hope to prove.

- The prosecution witnesses give evidence (each one being examined-in-chief by the prosecution, cross-examined by the defence and, if necessary, re-examined by the prosecution).

- The written statements of any prosecution witnesses may be read to the court if the defence consent to this being done (as will be the case where the defence accept that the contents of the statement are true and so this evidence is not disputed) (s 9 of the Criminal Justice Act 1967).

- After the close of the prosecution case, the defendant may make a submission that there is no case to answer. This submission is considered more closely below.

- If the defence do not make a submission of no case to answer, or make a submission which is rejected by the magistrates, the defence may then call evidence.

- If there are defence witnesses in addition to the defendant, the defendant should give evidence first. Each defence witness is examined-in-chief by the defence, cross-examined by the prosecution and, if necessary, re-examined by the defence.

- After the defence witnesses have given evidence, the defence may make a closing speech.

- The magistrates consider their verdict. A Bench of lay magistrates usually retires to consider its decision, whereas a stipendiary magistrate usually announces his decision immediately. Reasons for the verdict are not given.

- If the defendant is convicted, the prosecution supply the court with details of any previous convictions recorded against the defendant, together with brief details of the defendant's personal circumstances. The court will either adjourn the case for a pre-sentence report to be obtained or hear a plea in mitigation on behalf of the defendant and then pass sentence. Again, the maximum period of the adjournment for reports to be prepared is four weeks if the defendant is on bail, three weeks if he is custody (s 10(3) of the Magistrates' Courts Act 1980).

4.9.3   Sentencing powers

The sentencing powers of the magistrates are dealt with in later chapters. In summary, a magistrates' court cannot impose a custodial sentence of more than six months unless the offender has been convicted of two or more offences which are triable either way, in which case, the maximum is 12 months.

4.10   SUMMARY TRIAL IN MORE DETAIL

Section 4.9 provides a thumbnail sketch of a summary trial. Several matters need to be considered in more detail.

4.10.1   Securing the attendance of witnesses

Under s 97 of the Magistrates' Courts Act 1980, a magistrate (or a clerk) may issue a summons requiring a person to attend court to give evidence or to produce a document or other item of evidence. This applies whether the summons is sought by the prosecution or the defence.

Before ordering a person to attend as a witness, the magistrate (or clerk) must be satisfied that the person will be able to give 'material evidence' and that the person will not attend voluntarily. Material evidence is evidence of some value to the party seeking the order. In *R v Marylebone Magistrates ex p Gatting and Emburey* [1990] Crim LR 578, the applicant was refused a witness order against two England cricketers as the motive for seeking the order was political rather than evidential.

Similarly, before the magistrate (or clerk) can issue a summons requiring the production of documents under s 97 of the Magistrates' Courts Act 1980, he must be satisfied that the respondent is likely to be able to produce the requested documents, and that the documents contain material evidence (that is, evidence which is both relevant and admissible). It is for the party who seeks the production of the documents to adduce evidence which satisfies the justices that there is a real possibility that the documents are material. Documents which are requested merely for the purpose of possible cross-examination are not material (see *R v Reading Justices ex p Berkshire County Council* [1996] 1 Cr App R 239).

If the witness fails to comply with the summons, a warrant for his arrest may be granted by a magistrate (s 97(3)).

A magistrate (but not a clerk) may issue a warrant rather than a summons if satisfied by evidence (on oath) that a summons would be ineffective (s 97(2)).

Under s 97(2B) of the Magistrates' Courts Act 1980, a witness summons may be refused if the application is not made as soon as reasonably practicable after the defendant has pleaded not guilty.

The standard forms for a witness summons and a warrant of arrest where the witness fails to attend are set out at the end of this chapter.

4.10.2   Defects in the information: amendment

Section 123 of the Magistrates' Courts Act 1980 says that no objection shall be allowed in respect of an information or summons where that objection is based on a defect in substance or form, or on any variance between it and the evidence adduced by the prosecution.

The practical effect of this provision is that all but the gravest of errors can be ignored or cured by amendment.

It appears from the case law that there are three categories of defect in the information.

(a) Minor defects

First, there are minor defects which do not require amendment. This would include a minor mis-spelling or other inconsequential error that has misled no one. In *R v Sandwell Justices ex p West Midlands Passenger Transport Executive* [1979] RTR 17; [1979] Crim LR 56, for example, the information alleged a defective rear nearside tyre, when in fact it was a near offside tyre which was defective; a conviction based on this unamended information was upheld.

(b) Defects requiring amendment

Secondly, there are defects which require amendment (which is possible under s 123 of the Magistrates' Courts Act 1980) but which are not so grave as to be incurable. If the defendant has been misled by the error, the court should remedy this by granting an adjournment to enable the defence to prepare their case in the light of the amendment.

An example of this sort of defect is where the information alleges an offence under a section of an Act which has been repealed and re-enacted in identical terms in a later statute (*Meek v Powell* [1952] 1 KB 164; [1952] 1 All ER 347).

Similarly, in *Wright v Nicholson* [1970] 1 WLR 142; [1970] 1 All ER 12, it was held that an information can be amended to show a different date for the alleged commission of the offence, provided that an adjournment is granted if the defence need more time to prepare their case in the light of the amendment. This was so even though the defendant had an alibi for the date originally alleged.

Indeed, in *R v Norwich Crown Court ex p Russell* [1993] Crim LR 518, the Divisional Court went even further. The information in that case alleged that the offence (criminal damage) had been committed on 19 February 1991. In fact, it was the prosecution's case that the offence was committed on 18 February. The discrepancy was not noticed until after the defendant had been convicted. The Divisional Court said that the justices had clearly ignored the confusion as to dates and there was no reason why the conviction could not stand, even though the information had not been amended.

In *R v Scunthorpe Justices ex p McPhee and Gallagher* (1998) 162 JP 635, the defendant was charged with robbery; the prosecution sought to amend the information to allege theft and common assault (a summary offence) instead. As we have seen in Chapter 4, 4.2, an information alleging a summary offence must be laid within six months of the commission of the alleged offence (s 127(1) of the Magistrates' Courts Act 1980). The Divisional Court held that an information laid within that time limit can be amended under s 123 even if the amendment is more than 6 months after the commission of the alleged offence. This is so even if the amendment involves alleging a different offence, provided that (i) the new offence alleges the 'same misdoing' as the original offence (in other words, 'the new offence should arise out of the same (or substantially the same) facts as gave rise to the original offence'); and (ii) the amendment can be made in the interests of justice. In considering whether it is in the interests of justice for the amendment to be made, the court should pay particular regard to the interests of the accused. If the amendment would result in the defendant facing a 'significantly more serious charge', it is likely to be against the interests of justice to allow such an amendment; similarly, the need for an adjournment would militate against the court granting leave for the amendment of the information. Similarly, in *R v Newcastle-upon-Tyne Justices ex p John Bryce (Contractors) Ltd* [1976] 1 WLR 517; [1976] 2 All ER 611, the prosecution were allowed to amend an information to allege 'use' rather than 'permitting use' of a vehicle, even though the effect was to charge a different summary offence and even though a new information could not have been laid because more than six months had elapsed from the date of the alleged offence. It was said that the defence were not prejudiced by this amendment as the true nature of the offence was clear from the statement of facts on the summons.

In *R v Thames Magistrates' Court ex p Stevens* (2000) 164 JP 164, the defendant was charged with assault occasioning actual bodily harm (s 47 of the Offences against the Persons Act 1861). The prosecution subsequently indicated that they wished to withdraw the s 47 charge and lay a charge alleging the summary offence of common of assault (s 39 of the Criminal Justice Act 1988) instead. However, it was more than six months since the commission of the offence. The Divisional Court held that the magistrate had correctly concluded that what was being sought by the prosecution was an amendment of the original charge, rather than a substitution or withdrawal of that charge. Section 127 of the Magistrates' Courts Act 1980 Act did not apply to prevent the court from dealing with the charge of common assault. The magistrate, in considering whether the amendment was in the interests of justice, had taken proper account of the fact that: (i) the offences had arisen out of the same facts; (ii) the applicant had not been misled or prejudiced by the amendment; (iii) she was not deprived by the amendment of any substantive defence that she had; (iv) the evidence to be adduced by the prosecution was not different after the amendment; and (v) the effect of the amendment was in fact to reduce the gravity of the original charge.

(c) Irremediable defencts

Thirdly, there are fundamental errors which cannot be corrected by amendment (despite the wide wording of s 123 of the Magistrates' Courts Act 1980). This would include an information which names the wrong person (for example, *Marco (Croydon) Ltd v Metropolitan Police* [1984] RTR 24; [1983] Crim LR 395 and *City of Oxford Tramway v Sankey* (1890) 54 JP 564). The only remedy for the prosecution in such a case is to lay a new information (which, in the case of a summary offence, is only possible if less than six months have elapsed since the commission of the offence). There must then be an adjournment so that a fresh summons can be served on the new defendant (*R v Greater Manchester Justices ex p Aldi GmbH & Co KG* (1995) 159 JP 717).

4.10.3   Withdrawal of summons/offering no evidence

If the defendant has not entered a plea, the prosecution can (with the agreement of the justices) withdraw the summons (*R v Redbridge Justices ex p Sainty* [1981] RTR 13). The prosecution may make such an application if one of their witnesses is not available but the court will not grant an adjournment because it takes the view that the prosecution should be in a position to proceed.

Withdrawal of a summons does not constitute an acquittal, so a fresh summons can be issued (*R v Grays Justices ex p Low* [1990] 1 QB 54; [1988] 3 All ER 834). Presumably, the same applies to charges, if proceedings were commenced by arrest and charge rather than by laying an information.

If the defendant has entered a plea of not guilty it is too late to withdraw the summons and so the prosecution must:

- proceed with the trial; or
- seek an adjournment; or
- offer no evidence.

The usual situations where the prosecution offer no evidence are where:

- the defendant has pleaded guilty to one offence and the prosecution do not wish to proceed with another (closely related) charge; or
- where new evidence exonerating the defendant has come to light; or
- where the Crown Prosecution Service review the evidence and decide that there is insufficient prospect of securing a conviction to merit continuing the proceedings.

If the prosecution offer no evidence, and an acquittal is recorded, fresh proceedings may be brought if (but only if) the defendant was never in jeopardy of conviction (*R v Dabhade* [1993] QB 329; [1992] 4 All ER 796). This application of the doctrine of *autrefois acquit* is discussed in greater detail in Chapter 9, 9.36.4.

In *Holmes v Campbell* (1998) 162 JP 655, a magistrates' court dismissed the information against the defendants when the prosecutor failed to appear at the hearing. The prosecutor subsequently laid a fresh information (containing the same allegations) but the magistrates' court declined to try that information on the ground that it would be an abuse of process. The Divisional Court held that by virtue of s 15 of the Magistrates' Courts Act 1980 (see Chapter 4, 4.6) the accused could not have been convicted at a hearing where the prosecutor was absent. They had therefore not be in jeopardy of conviction at that hearing and so, following *R v Dabhade* [1993] QB 329, the doctrine of *autrefois acquit* did not prevent the hearing of the fresh information. Furthermore, the magistrates were wrong to hold that the fresh information was an abuse of process, since before the hearing of the first information the defendants had indicated to the prosecution that they would be pleading guilty.

4.10.4 Making speeches in a summary trial

The making of speeches in a summary trial is governed by r 13 of the Magistrates' Courts Rules 1981.

The trial may begin with an opening speech by the prosecutor (unless the prosecutor waives his right to make an opening speech). Such speeches are generally very brief. Unlike a trial in the Crown Court, however, the prosecutor has no entitlement to make a closing speech.

The defence are entitled to make only one speech, and so they may make *either* an opening speech or a closing speech. Most defence advocates would invariably choose to make a closing speech, since that is the last chance to address the magistrates before they consider their verdict and it is useful to be able to draw together the threads of the defence case.

Rule 13(5) says that either party may, with the leave of the court, make a second speech. Thus, if the prosecutor wishes to make a closing speech or the defence wish to make a closing speech as well as an opening speech, an application must be made to the magistrates.

Where one party is allowed to make a second speech, the other party must also be allowed to make a second speech. Where the case is a complex one, the justices may well allow both parties to make two speeches. Rule 13(6) stipulates that where both parties address the court twice, the closing speech for the accused takes place after the closing speech for the prosecution. Thus, the defence always have the last word.

4.10.5   Pre-trial disclosure

The prosecution have to disclose to the defence any material not previously disclosed which might undermine the prosecution case against the accused. The defendant then has the chance to make voluntary disclosure of the nature of the defence case (setting out the matters where the defence take issue with the prosecution and giving particulars of any alibi the defence will rely on at trial). If the defence provide voluntary disclosure of their case, the prosecution then have to reveal any previously undisclosed material which might reasonably be expected to assist the defence case. These provisions are contained in the Criminal Procedure and Investigations Act 1996 and are dealt with in detail in Chapter 1, 1.19.

4.10.6   Witnesses prosecution must call

Where the prosecutor serves a bundle of witness statements on the defence prior to summary trial, the prosecution must call as witnesses all the people whose statements have been served (unless any of the exceptions which relate to Crown Court trials, as to which see Chapter 9, 9.12, are applicable (*R v Haringey Justices ex p DPP* [1996] 1 All ER 828).

4.10.7   Reading witness statements

Under s 9 of the Criminal Justice Act 1967, a written statement may be read aloud to the court as evidence (instead of the maker of the statement giving oral evidence) if:

- the statement is signed by its maker;

- the statement contains a declaration by the maker that it is true to the best of his knowledge and belief and that he makes it knowing that he is liable to prosecution if he has wilfully stated in it anything which he knows to be false or does not believe to be true;
- a copy of the statement has been served on all the other parties to the proceedings; and
- none of the parties on whom the statement is served objects within seven days of service to the statement being used as evidence.

The last two requirements do not apply if the parties agree immediately before or during the hearing that the statement may be used as evidence rather than the witness giving 'live' testimony.

If the maker of the statement is under 18 years of age, the statement must give her age.

If the maker of the statement cannot read it, it must be read to her and must contain a declaration that this has been done by the person who read it to her.

Where the statement refers to a document or other object as an exhibit, a copy of that document must accompany the statement when it is served on the other parties or the other parties must be told how they can inspect a copy of that document. When the statement is read out at the trial, any document or exhibit referred to in it becomes an exhibit just as if it has been produced by a witness giving oral evidence.

It is usually the statements of prosecution witness which are read out in this way, with the consent of the defence, on the basis that the defence concede that the evidence of that witness is uncontroversial and so the defence do not wish to cross-examine that witness. However, there is no reason why the evidence of a defence witness cannot be given in this way (if the prosecution agree).

4.10.8   Objecting to prosecution evidence in a summary trial

Objections to prosecution evidence are made under s 76 or s 78 of the Police and Criminal Evidence Act 1984.

If the defence invoke s 76 and allege that a confession has been obtained by oppression or in circumstances where anything said by the defendant is likely to be unreliable, the magistrates have to hold a *voir dire* or 'trial within a trial' (*R v Liverpool Juvenile Court ex p R* [1988] QB 1; [1987] 2 All ER 668).

This simply means that evidence has to be heard on the admissibility of the confession. The prosecution will have to call the police officers who were present when the defendant confessed and they can be cross-examined by the defence; the defendant may then give evidence (and be cross-examined by the prosecution). At this stage, it is only the admissibility of the confession, not its truth, which is in issue.

If the magistrates decide that the confession is inadmissible, the trial will continue (assuming there is other evidence against the accused) but no further mention may be made of the confession. If the confession is ruled admissible, the trial will resume with the police officer giving evidence of what the defendant said (unless this has already been done in the *voir dire*, in which case the evidence does not have to be repeated as the magistrates have already heard it).

Where the defendant asks for evidence to be excluded under s 78 of the Police and Criminal Evidence Act 1984 (that is, on the ground that its admission would be unfairly prejudicial to the defendant) the justices may either consider the admissibility of the evidence when that issue arises or postpone consideration of admissibility until the end of the hearing. Whereas the magistrates must allow evidence to be given on a *voir dire* if there is an application to exclude evidence under s 76, there is no such obligation where the application is under s 78 (*Vel v Owen; Vel v Chief Constable of North Wales* [1987] Crim LR 496; *Halawa v Federation Against Copyright Theft* [1995] Crim LR 409). In *Halawa*, the Divisional Court said that, in most cases, it is generally better for the magistrates to hear all the prosecution evidence (including the disputed evidence) before considering an application to exclude evidence under s 78.

In *Johnson v Leicestershire Constabulary* (1998) *The Times*, 7 October, it was held by the Divisional Court that, where magistrates wrongly become aware that a defendant has previous convictions, or has been before the court before, the test to be applied is whether there is any real danger of bias arising from the magistrates finding out something they should not have discovered. The court said that it has to be borne in mind that lay justices are capable of putting out of their minds matters which are irrelevant.

4.10.9 Dock identifications

Where the identity of the defendant as the person who committed the offence is in issue, the court will generally not allow a witness who has not previously identified the defendant at an identification parade to be asked 'do you see the person who committed the offence in court today?' (a so called 'dock identification'). The reason for not allowing this to be done is that the defendant is at a great disadvantage – the eyes of the witness are bound to go to the person sitting in the dock.

However, in *Barnes v DPP* [1997] 2 Cr App R 505, the defendant was charged with failing to provide a breath specimen. There had been no identity parade and the only evidence that the defendant was the person who refused to provide a specimen was a 'dock identification' by a police officer. The Divisional Court held that the justices had a discretion to allow a defendant to be identified in court even if there had not been a previous identification parade.

4.10.10 The submission of no case to answer

We have already seen that the defence may make a submission that there is no case to answer once the prosecution have called all their evidence. The principles to be applied to a submission of no case to answer in a magistrates' court are set out in a Practice Direction issued by the Lord Chief Justice in 1962.

A submission of no case to answer should succeed if either:

- there is no evidence to prove an essential element of the offence; or
- the prosecution evidence has been so discredited by cross-examination or is otherwise so manifestly unreliable that no reasonable bench could convict on it.

Thus, the basic question to be answered is whether or not there is sufficient evidence on which a reasonable bench of magistrates could convict. In other words, the submission should succeed if a conviction would be perverse, in the sense that no reasonable bench could convict.

It should be pointed out, however, that some justices may well take the view that even if there is just about enough evidence for there to be a case to answer, it is so unlikely that they will be able to convict that they might as well stop the case here and now.

The prosecution have the right to reply to the defence submission that there is no case to answer.

If the submission is successful, the defendant is acquitted. If it is unsuccessful, the trial continues.

In the Crown Court, the judge has to be careful not to trespass on the territory of the jury and so submissions should only succeed in the Crown Court where the prosecution evidence is clearly incredible. In *R v Barking & Dagenham Justices ex p DPP* [1995] Crim LR 953, the Divisional Court interpreted the 1962 Practice Direction in the light of *R v Galbraith* [1981] 1 WLR 1039; [1981] 2 All ER 1060, which deals with submissions of no case to answer in the Crown Court. The Divisional Court said that questions of credibility, except in the clearest of cases, should not normally result in a finding that there is no case to answer. Some magistrates, however, may take the pragmatic view that even if there is just about a case to answer it is unlikely that they will be able to convict the defendant at the end of the trial and so give him the benefit of the doubt and acquit him at this stage.

If a submission of no case to answer is made by the defence, it should be made clear to the magistrates that evidence will be called if the submission is unsuccessful. This avoids confusion, since the magistrates might otherwise think that the defence have simply chosen to make a closing speech without calling any evidence.

Where the justices are minded to dismiss a case prior to the start of the defence case (whether following a submission of no case to answer by the defence or of their own motion), the prosecution should be given the opportunity to address the court to show why the case should not be dismissed (*R v Barking and Dagenham Justices ex p DPP* [1995] Crim LR 953).

4.10.11   The defendant's evidence

If a submission of no case to answer is not made (or is unsuccessful), the defence then have the opportunity to present evidence to the court. If the defendant is going to call other witnesses as well as giving evidence himself, the defendant should give evidence first unless the court otherwise directs (see s 79 of the Police and Criminal Evidence Act 1984).

If the defendant decides not to give evidence, he runs the risk that the magistrates will be entitled to draw adverse inferences from his silence under s 35 of the Criminal Justice and Public Order Act 1994 (see, also, Chapter 9).

The magistrates should warn the defendant of the possible consequences of not testifying. However, in *Radford v Kent County Council* (1998) 162 JP 697, the magistrates failed to warn the defendant that adverse inferences could be drawn if he failed to testify (a warning they were required to give under s 35(2) of the Criminal Justice and Public Order Act 1994). However, in their stated case, the justices said that 'we drew no inferences whatsoever from the failure of the appellant to give evidence, but simply were aware that the evidence for the prosecution was not rebutted by evidence from or on behalf of the appellant'. The Divisional Court held that, although the warning of the consequences of not testifying is very important, the failure to give the warning in the present case did not render the appellant's conviction unsafe.

4.10.12   Re-opening the prosecution case

Rule 13(3) of the Magistrates' Courts Rules 1981 says that, after the close of the defence case, the prosecutor may call evidence to rebut the evidence called by the defence. In other words, the prosecution may be allowed to call further evidence even though the prosecution case has closed. Rebutting evidence under r 13(3) must be confined to a matter which has arisen unexpectedly (or, as it is sometimes put, *ex improviso*) during the defence case (*Price v Humphries* [1958] 2 QB 353). An example is *James v South Glamorgan County Council* [1993] RTR 312, where the main prosecution witness has not arrived but the trial proceeded; after the prosecution case had been closed and while the defendant was giving evidence, the witness arrived. It was accepted by the magistrates that the witness had a good reason for being late and the prosecution were allowed to call him as a witness. It was held by the Divisional Court that, since the evidence had not been available at the proper time and there was no unfairness to the defendant, the decision of the magistrates was correct.

4.10.13 Change of plea

The magistrates have a discretion to allow a defendant to change his plea from guilty to not guilty at any stage before sentence is passed (*S (an Infant) v Recorder of Manchester* [1971] AC 481; [1969] 3 All ER 1230). The question for the magistrates is whether the original plea was unequivocal and entered with a proper understanding of what the charge entailed.

If the defendant is allowed to change his plea to one of not guilty, he should also be allowed to re-consider his consent to summary trial (*R v Bow Street Magistrates ex p Welcombe* (1992) 156 JP 609).

Similarly, the magistrates can allow a defendant to change his plea from not guilty to guilty at any time before a verdict is returned.

4.10.14 Seeing the magistrates in private

It is open to the justices to hear representations from the parties in private, but they should do so only in exceptional cases. Steps must be taken to ensure that all parties are aware of the private hearing and are represented at it. The clerk must take a contemporaneous note of the hearing (see *R v Nottingham Justices ex p Furnell* (1995) 160 JP 201).

In *R v Faversham and Sittingbourne Justices ex p Stickings* (1996) 160 JP 801, the magistrates, during the course of a trial and acting on the advice of their clerk, ruled that certain prosecution evidence was inadmissible. During an adjournment, the prosecutor telephoned the clerk to say that the ruling was wrong in law. The clerk agreed that the ruling was wrong. The defence were not given notice of this until the court reconvened, whereupon the magistrates reversed their earlier ruling and ordered that case be retried by another bench. The Divisional Court said that it was procedurally unfair for a matter to be drawn to the clerk's attention by telephone. The proper method was to do so in writing, sending a copy to all other parties to the case. Furthermore, the general principle was that decisions reached by justices should not be reversed. Accordingly, a retrial should not have been ordered.

4.11   THE ROLE OF THE CLERK

Whereas lay justices receive only a very small amount of legal training, the clerk is a qualified lawyer. The functions of the clerk are set out in s 28(3) of the Justice of the Peace Act 1979 and in a Practice Direction (Justices: Clerk to Court) [1981] 1 WLR 1163.

Section 28(3) says that 'it is hereby declared that the functions of a justices' clerk include the giving to the justices to whom he is clerk or any of them, at the request of the justices or justice, of advice about law, practice or procedure on questions arising in connection with the discharge of their or his functions, including questions arising when the clerk is not personally attending on the justices or justice, and that the clerk may, at any time when he thinks he should do so, bring to the attention of the justices or justice any point of law, practice or procedure that is or may be involved in any question so arising'.

The Practice Direction summarises those functions as follows:

- to advise the justices on the law (this includes the elements of the offence(s) charged and the law relating to the admissibility of evidence, and the range of penalties available in the event of conviction);
- to advise the justices on practice and procedure;
- to remind the justices of the evidence that they have heard (to which end the clerk should keep a fairly comprehensive note of the evidence).

In *R v Chichester Justices ex p DPP* [1994] RTR 175, it was held (*obiter*) that, if the clerk who advises the justices is not the clerk who was present in court when the parties made their submissions on the point of law at issue, it is essential that the clerk should hear informal submissions on the relevant law from the parties before advising the justices.

What the clerk must not do is to express a view on questions of fact; these questions are for the magistrates. So, for example, the clerk should not say whether or not he believes a particular witness. (See *R v Stafford Justices ex p Ross* [1962] 1 WLR 456; [1962] 1 All ER 540, where a conviction was quashed because the clerk had passed a note to the bench suggesting that the defence case was implausible.) Nor should the clerk recommend a particular type of sentence in the event of the defendant being convicted.

When the clerk gives advice to the justices in the course of the hearing, this should be done in open court, so that the prosecution and defence can make submissions to the Bench on that advice.

If the clerk advises the justices after they have retired to consider their decision and the clerk cites authority which was not cited in open court, he should inform the advocates in the case and give them the opportunity to make further submissions to the magistrates (*W v W* (1993) *The Times*, 4 June).

The clerk should not leave the courtroom with the justices when they retire to consider their verdict. If the magistrates require assistance from the clerk, he should only join them when asked to do so and should return to the courtroom once the advice has been given (see *R v Eccles Justices ex p Farrelly* (1993) 157 JP 77 and *R v Birmingham Justices ex p Ahmed* [1995] Crim LR 503.)

Where the accused is unrepresented, the clerk may assist the defendant by asking any necessary questions of prosecution witnesses (although the clerk should not assume the role of defence counsel and cross-examine the prosecution witnesses).

4.12   THE DECISION OF THE JUSTICES

Usually, there are three lay magistrates. Their decision (whether to acquit or to convict) is by simple majority. The chairman does not have a second or casting vote.

If only two lay justices hear a case but cannot agree on a verdict, they have no option but to adjourn the case for re-trial in front of a bench with three justices (*R v Redbridge Justices ex p Ram* [1992] QB 384; [1992] 1 All ER 652).

In reaching their decision on a question of fact, it is open to magistrates to use their personal local knowledge, but they should inform the prosecution and the defence that they are doing so, so that those representing the parties have the opportunity of commenting upon the knowledge which the justices claim to have: *Bowman v DPP* [1991] RTR 263; *Norbrook Laboratories (GB) Ltd v Health and Safety Executive* [1998] EHLR 207.

The magistrates' decision is announced in open court by the chairman. Where the defendant is convicted the magistrates have to give brief reasons for their decision. This is because the right to a fair trial under Art 6 of the European Convention on Human Rights requires the court to give reasons for its judgement (*Hadjianastassiou v Greece* 16 EHRR 219). Whilst this requirement cannot apply to juries, it does apply to magistrates.

A record of the decision of the court is kept in the court's register, a specimen of which appears at the end of this chapter.

4.12.1   Alternative verdicts

Whereas a jury can sometimes convict the defendant of a lesser offence even though that offence is not on the indictment (for example, theft instead of robbery) under s 3 of the Criminal Law Act 1967, the magistrates have no such power (*Lawrence v Same* [1968] 2 QB 93; [1968] 1 All ER 1191). In that case, a conviction for common assault on an information alleging unlawful wounding was set aside by the Divisional Court because it was in excess of jurisdiction.

However, there are certain statutory exceptions to this rule, such as the power to convict of careless driving instead of dangerous driving (see s 24 of the Road Traffic Offenders Act 1988).

If the prosecution wish the justices to consider alternative offences, those offences must be charged (in separate informations). The informations can then be tried together. If the defendant only faces one charge to begin with, but the prosecution want the court to have the power to convict the defendant of a different offence, an information alleging the new offence may be laid in open court or the defendant may be 'further charged' by the police outside court. This course of action will be appropriate if the defendant is willing to plead guilty to an offence which is less serious than that originally charged and the prosecution are willing to accept that plea and drop the more serious charge. If the defendant is charged with alternative offences at the outset and pleads not guilty to both, and the magistrates convict the defendant of the more serious of the two offences, the magistrates should either adjourn the other information *sine die* (that is, with no date being set, the understanding being that the defendant will hear no more of that information) or else convict the defendant of the lesser offence too and impose only a nominal penalty in respect of it (*DPP v Gane* [1991] Crim LR 711).

4.12.2   Setting aside conviction or sentence

Section 142(2) of the Magistrates' Courts Act 1980 enables a defendant who was convicted in the magistrates' court (whether he pleaded guilty or was found guilty) to ask the magistrates to set the conviction aside. This application can be considered by the same magistrates who convicted the defendant or by a different bench. If the conviction is set aside, the case is re-heard by different magistrates from those who convicted the defendant. An application under s 142(2) may be appropriate if the magistrates made an error of law or there was some defect in the procedure which led to the conviction.

In *R v Dewsbury Magistrates ex p K* (1994) *The Times*, 16 March, the defendant (who was aware that the case was due to be heard) was convicted in his absence, but his failure to attend court was not intentional. He sought a re-hearing but the justices refused. This refusal was quashed by the Divisional Court, which said that any inconvenience to the court or to the prosecution should not outweigh the right of the defendant to have an opportunity of defending himself.

In *R v Gwent Magistrates' Court ex p Carey* (1996) 160 JP 613, the Divisional Court held that magistrates have a broad discretion in deciding whether or not to re-open a case under s 142. They are entitled to have regard to the fact that the defendant failed to attend the original hearing through his own fault and that witnesses would be inconvenienced if a re-trial were to be ordered. Henry LJ also said that the magistrates were entitled to take account of the apparent strength of the prosecution case, although little weight should be given to it, since an apparently strong case can collapse during the course of a trial. His Lordship also pointed out that the magistrates, by refusing to re-open the case, were not 'finally shutting out the defendant from the judgment seat' because he still had his unfettered right of appeal to the Crown Court.

Section 142(1) of the Magistrates' Courts Act 1980 empowers a magistrates' court to vary or rescind a sentence if it is in the interests of justice to do so. Again, this power may be exercised by a different bench from that which passed the original sentence. The main use of this power is to remedy the situation where an illegal sentence is inadvertently passed on an offender.

There is no time limit within which applications for the setting aside of a conviction or sentence under s 142 must be made.

However, where a defendant applies under s 142(2) for the trial to be re-heard, delay in making the application is a relevant consideration for the magistrates in deciding whether or not to grant that application (*R v Ealing Magistrates' Court ex p Sahota* (1998) 162 JP 73).

4.13   COMMITTAL FOR SENTENCE

Even if a defendant is tried and convicted by a magistrates' court, he may still in certain circumstances be sentenced by the Crown Court.

4.13.1   Section 3 of the Powers of Criminal Courts (Sentencing) Act 2000

The first type of committal for sentence is under s 3 of the Powers of Criminal Courts (Sentencing) Act 2000, which applies where a defendant is convicted in a magistrates' court of an offence which is triable either way. The 2000 Act is a consolidation Act. Section 3 replaces s 3 of the Magistrates' Courts Act 1980. The effect of a committal under s 38 is that the defendant will be sentenced by the Crown Court, whose sentencing powers are greater than those of the magistrates' court.

Section 3(2)(a) of the Powers of Criminal Courts (Sentencing) Act 2000 provides that where the magistrates take the view that the offence (or, where there is more than one offence, the combination of offences before the court) is so serious that greater punishment should be inflicted than the magistrates' court has power to impose, the magistrates' court can commit the defendant to the Crown Court to be sentenced.

Section 3(2)(b) allows committal for sentence for a violent or sexual offence (as defined in s 161 of the 2000 Act) where a longer sentence is necessary to protect the public from serious harm from the offender.

Where the defendant is committed for sentence, there is no presumption in favour of bail as s 4 of the Bail Act 1976 does not apply. The committal may be on bail or in custody (s 3(1)); it is usually in custody, since the defendant faces a relatively long custodial sentence (*R v Coe* [1968] 1 WLR 1950; [1969] 1 All ER 65).

In *R v Manchester Justices ex p Kaymanesh* (1994) 15 Cr App R(S) 838, the Divisional Court held that magistrates should normally exercise the power to commit the defendant for sentence under s 3 only if new information came to light which was not available to the magistrates when the decision to try the case summarily was reached.

However, it was held in *R v Dover Justices ex p Pamment* (1994) 15 Cr App R(S) 778, dismissing an application for judicial review of the decision of the magistrates to commit the defendant for sentence under s 3, that, if the justices do exercise their power to commit a defendant for sentence under s 3 having earlier accepted jurisdiction to try the case, the exercise of that power was unfettered.

Similarly, in *R v Sheffield Crown Court ex p DPP* (1994) 15 Cr App R(S) 768, it was held that where the magistrates commit a defendant for sentence under s 3, the Crown Court usually has no power to remit the case to the magistrates' court. If the order is plainly bad on its face (for example, s 3 is invoked by the magistrates in respect of an offence which is triable only summarily), the Crown Court could remit the case to the magistrates' court but the proper course of action is usually for the defendant to apply to the Divisional Court for judicial review.

R v Sheffield Crown Court ex p DPP and *R v Dover Justices ex p Pamment* were followed and approved in *R v North Sefton Justices ex p Marsh* (1995) 16 Cr App R(S) 401. In that case, the Divisional Court held that the discretion to commit for sentence under s 3 is unfettered. It was said that *Kaymanesh* was wrongly decided and should not be followed. It was said by the Divisional Court that the decision to commit for sentence under s 3 did not have to be based on information received by the court after the decision to try the defendant summarily. However, the court went on to say that magistrates should think carefully when deciding the appropriate mode of trial, since a defendant should be able to conclude that, once summary jurisdiction has been accepted, he will not be committed to the Crown Court on the same facts. Indeed, in the instant case, some of the information which caused the magistrates to commit for sentence had come to light after the mode of trial hearing. In *R v Southampton Magistrates Court ex p Sansome* [1999] 1 Cr App R (S) 112, the Divisional Court confirmed that the correct approach was that set out in *ex p Marsh* (above).

The revised mode of trial guidelines issued by the Lord Chief Justice in 1995 say that the magistrates should consider exercising their power to commit the defendant to the Crown Court under s 3 if information emerges during the course of the summary trial which leads them to conclude that their sentencing powers are inadequate.

In *R v Flax Burton Justices ex p Commissioners of Customs and Excise* (1996) 160 JP 481, the Divisional Court stressed the need for the justices to consider carefully whether their powers of sentencing are adequate to deal with an offence before accepting jurisdiction to try that offence.

Thus, in summary, magistrates should not normally commit a defendant for sentence under s 3 unless new information has come to light since the mode of trial decision was taken. However, if magistrates do commit a defendant for sentence on the basis of information which was already known to the court when the decision to try the case was reached, judicial review will not be granted since the magistrates have not acted beyond their powers.

The question of whether a s 3 committal can only be triggered by new information, or whether the magistrates can in effect simply change their minds about the adequacy of their sentencing powers, is now only relevant in those cases where the defendant indicates an intention to plead not guilty (or gives no indication as to plea) at the 'plea before venue' hearing described in Chapter 3, 3.3. Where the defendant indicates an intention to plead guilty, he will do so in the magistrates court, and so will be convicted by the magistrates, however serious the offence is and before the magistrates are given any information about the seriousness of the offence.

Home Office Circular 45/1997 deals with the situation where the defendant indicates a guilty plea and the magistrates, having heard the prosecution outline the brief facts of the case, immediately come to the view that their sentencing powers are insufficient to deal with the defendant. In such a case, the magistrates should allow the defence to make representations on the question of committal for sentence, or to put forward a plea in mitigation, but should not hesitate to make it clear that it is their firm intention to commit the defendant to the Crown Court for sentence. The Circular also makes the point that where the offence is obviously a serious one, a pre-sentence report will not be prepared before committal for sentence.

Guidance on several issues that may arise in this context was given by the Divisional Court in *R v Warley Magistrates' Court ex p DPP* [1999] 1 All ER 251. The court held as follows:

(1) Where a defendant indicates a guilty plea under the 'plea before venue' procedure in s 17A of the Magistrates' Courts Act 1980, the magistrates must take account of the discount to be granted for that guilty plea when deciding whether or not their sentencing powers are adequate to deal with the defendant.

(2) Where it is clear that the case is beyond the sentencing powers of the magistrates, they should be prepared to commit the defendant to the Crown Court for sentence without first seeking a pre-sentence report or hearing a plea in mitigation (although they should warn the defence that they have in this in mind so that the defence can make brief representations to oppose that course of action; if the magistrates are persuaded to change their minds, the prosecutor should be given a chance to reply).

(3) In other cases, the hearing should proceed as usual; if the question of whether or not to commit for sentence remains a live issue at the end of the hearing, the court should seek representations on this issue from the prosecution and the defence.

(4) Where there is a difference between the prosecution and defence versions of the facts of the offence (a 'Newton' dispute, as to which see Chapter 12, 12.1.1): (i) if the magistrates think that their sentencing powers will be

adequate however the dispute is resolved, they should adopt the procedure laid down in *R v Newton* (1982) 77 Cr App R 13; (ii) if they think that their sentencing powers will not be adequate however the dispute is resolved, they should simply commit for sentence, leaving the Crown Court to follow the Newton procedure; (iii) if the decision whether or not to commit turns or may turn on which version is found to be correct, the magistrates should follow the Newton procedure; if the offender is then committed for sentence, the Crown Court should adopt the findings of fact made by the magistrates at the Newton hearing unless the defendant can point to some significant development, such as the discovery of important new evidence in his favour.

Where the defendant indicates a not guilty plea (or gives no indication) at the 'plea before venue' hearing, and the court decides to accept jurisdiction at the mode of trial hearing, it may be that information emerges during the summary trial which makes the offence appear more serious than it did when the magistrates accepted jurisdiction. In such a case, it is open to magistrates to continue with the trial and, if they convict the defendant, to commit him for sentence under s 3; alternatively, they can terminate the summary trial and hold committal proceedings instead, so that the trial will start again in the Crown Court (s 25(2) of the Magistrates' Courts Act 1980).

If a defendant is aggrieved at a decision to commit him for sentence to the Crown Court, there is little that can be done about it. The decision to commit for sentence could be challenged by means of judicial review, but such a challenge would only succeed if the committal was perverse (in the sense that no reasonable bench of magistrates could have decided to commit the defendant for sentence). However, the defendant may derive some comfort from two points: firstly, it is by no means inevitable that the Crown Court will in fact impose a sentence which is more severe than the sentence which the magistrates' court could have imposed; secondly, if the Crown Court does impose a sentence which is greater than the sentence could have imposed, the Court of Appeal has jurisdiction to entertain an appeal against that sentence if it is in fact excessive (see Chapter 6, 6.8.1).

4.13.2 Procedure in Crown Court

The Crown Court when hearing a s 3 committal comprises a circuit judge or recorder (s 74 of the Supreme Court Act 1981).

The hearing takes the same form as the sentencing procedure in the magistrates' court, that is, the prosecution summarise the facts of the case and give details of the defendant's previous convictions (if any), followed by a defence plea in mitigation.

We have already seen that if there is a significant divergence between prosecution and defence versions, then there has to be a '*Newton*' hearing (see

4.9.1 above). In the context of a s 3 committal, if a *Newton* hearing took place at the magistrates' court, the Crown Court should adopt the outcome. If the divergence between prosecution and defence versions becomes apparent for the first time at the Crown Court (or no *Newton* hearing was held at the magistrates' court), the Crown Court should hold a *Newton* hearing to determine the issue (see *Munroe v Crown Prosecution Service* [1988] Crim LR 823).

Where the defendant is sentenced by the Crown Court following a s 3 committal, the maximum sentence which the Crown Court can impose is the same as if the defendant had just been convicted on indictment (so, the limit of six months' imprisonment for one offence, 12 months' for two or more offences, no longer applies) (s 5 of the 2000 Act).

Some sentences depend on the age of the offender (for example, imprisonment is only possible if the defendant has attained the age of 21). If the defendant's age has changed between the date he was committed for sentence under s 3 and the date the Crown Court passes sentence, he will be dealt with according to his age at the date of his Crown Court appearance (*Robinson* [1962] Crim LR 47).

4.13.3 Committal for breach of Crown Court order

The second form of committal for sentence is where a magistrates' court has convicted a defendant of any offence committed during the currency of a suspended sentence or a community order or conditional discharge imposed by the Crown Court. In such a case, the magistrates' court can commit the defendant to be dealt with by the Crown Court for the breach of the Crown Court order (which may mean the Crown Court re-sentencing the defendant for the offence originally dealt with by the Crown Court). The relevant provisions in the Powers of Criminal Courts (Sentencing) Act 2000 are: s 13(5) (breach of Crown Court conditional discharge); s 116(3)(b) (offence during period of early release from prison sentence imposed by Crown Court); s 120(2) (breach of Crown Court suspended sentence); para 4(4) of Sched 3 (breach of Crown Court probation, community service, combination or curfew orders).

Where the offender is committed for sentence because he is in breach of a Crown Court order, the Crown Court comprises a judge sitting alone.

4.13.4 Section 4 of the Powers of Criminal Courts (Sentencing) Act 2000

Section 4 of the Powers of Criminal Courts (Sentencing) Act 2000 replaces s 38A of the Magistrates' Courts Act 1980.

Section 4(1) and (2) provides that, where the defendant has indicated that he will plead guilty to an either way offence (and so is deemed to have pleaded guilty to it) and he is also committed for trial for one or more related offences, the magistrates may commit him to the Crown Court for sentence in respect of the either way offence to which he has pleaded guilty. For the purposes of these provisions, one offence is related to another if the charges for them could be joined (under r 9 of the Indictment Rules 1971, as to which see Chapter 8, 8.9) in the same indictment if both were to be tried in the Crown Court (s 4(7)). So, the two charges must be founded on the same facts or must be, or be part of, a series of offences of the same or similar character.

Section 4(3) provides that where the defendant has indicated that he will plead guilty to an either way offence (and so is deemed to have pleaded guilty to it) and there are committal proceedings in respect of other offences, the court must adjourn the proceedings on the first offence until the conclusion of the committal proceedings in respect of the others.

Section 4(4) provides that where the justices have committed a defendant for sentence pursuant to s 4(2), the Crown Court can only exceed the sentencing powers of the magistrates' court in respect of the either way offence to which the defendant indicated a plea of guilty if either:

(a) the magistrates stated that they considered their sentencing powers were inadequate to deal with the defendant for that offence (and so they also had power to commit him for sentence under s 3); or

(b) he is also convicted by the Crown Court of one or more of the related offences.

The relationship between s 3 and s 4 of the Powers of Criminal Courts (Sentencing) Act 2000 may seem rather confusing. The purpose of s 4 is to ensure that, if the defendant is to be tried in the Crown Court for an offence which is related to an offence to which the defendant has indicated a guilty plea at the plea before venue hearing, then the magistrates can commit him to the Crown Court for sentence for that later offence even if their sentencing powers are adequate to deal with that offence (and so a committal under s 3 would be inappropriate).

If the magistrates take the view that their sentencing powers are adequate to deal with the offence in respect of which the defendant has indicated a guilty plea, then only s 4 allows the justices to commit the defendant to the Crown Court for sentence for that offence. On the other hand, if the magistrates take the view that their sentencing powers are not adequate to deal with that offence, they have two options: they can either commit him for sentence for that offence under s 3, or they can commit him for sentence under s 4 but indicate that they took the view that their sentencing powers were inadequate and so could have invoked s 3.

Obviously, the best practice will be to use s 3 where the magistrates' sentencing powers are not adequate and to use s 4 where their powers are adequate. In any event, Home Office Circular 45/1997 says that when committing a defendant for sentence, the court should state whether it is doing so under s 3 or s 4. If the magistrates use s 4 but do not consider that their sentencing powers are adequate to deal with the offence, they should state (under s 4(4)) that they also had the power to commit the defendant for sentence under s 3, so as to avoid inadvertently fettering the powers of the Crown Court when dealing with the offence.

4.13.5 Section 6 of the Powers of Criminal Courts (Sentencing) Act 2000

Section 6 of the Powers of Criminal Courts (Sentencing) Act 2000 replaces s 56 of the Criminal Justice Act 1967. It provides that where the magistrates have exercised any of the following powers of committal:

- under s 3 of the Act; or

- under s 4 of the Act; or

- under s 13(5) of the Act (breach of Crown Court conditional discharge); or

- under s 116(3)(b) of the Act (offence during early release period of Crown Court prison sentence); or

- under s 120(2) of the Act (offence during operational period of Crown Court suspended sentence),

then they may also commit the defendant to the Crown Court to be sentenced for any other offence that the magistrates' court could sentence him for.

Therefore, if the defendant is committed to the Crown Court under s 3 of the 2000 Act for a triable either way offence, he can also be committed under s 6 of the Act in respect of any summary offence of which he has been convicted on the same occasion.

Similarly, if the defendant is committed to the Crown Court to be dealt with for the breach of a particular Crown Court order (see above), he can also be committed to be dealt with for the offence which gave rise to the breach.

Two examples may assist in illustrating the scope of s 6 of the 2000 Act:

(a) The defendant is charged with theft (triable either way) and common assault (a summary offence) and the magistrates convict him of both charges. The magistrates decide that their sentencing powers are inadequate to deal with the theft and so they commit the defendant to the Crown Court in respect of that offence under s 3 of the 2000 Act. This section does not apply to summary offences and so cannot be used to enable the magistrates to commit the defendant to the Crown Court for the common assault. However, s 6 of the 2000 Act enables the magistrates to commit the defendant to the Crown Court for the common assault, and so the Crown Court can sentence him for both offences.

(b) The defendant is charged with theft. The theft is a very minor offence and so the magistrates cannot invoke s 3 of the 2000 Act (since their sentencing powers are plainly adequate to deal with the theft). However, the defendant committed the theft while he was subject to a suspended sentence of imprisonment imposed by the Crown Court (see Chapter 13). If the magistrates want the Crown Court to deal with the defendant for the theft as well as dealing with him for the breach of the suspended sentence, they can commit him to the Crown Court under s 120(2) of the Act in respect of the suspended sentence and under s 6 of the Act in respect of the theft.

The sentencing powers of the Crown Court in respect of offences committed under s 6 are the same as those of the magistrates' court (s 7(1)). This is because the purpose of s 6 is for the defendant to be sentenced by one court in respect of all outstanding matters, not to increase the sentence which may be imposed.

4.14   TRANSFER OF CASES BETWEEN MAGISTRATES' COURTS

Suppose that the defendant faces charges in two different magistrates' courts. If he has not entered a plea in one court, the charge there can be withdrawn and he can be re-charged with that offence at the other court.

If he has entered a plea of not guilty in one court, the prosecution could discontinue those proceedings (either by serving a notice of discontinuance or by offering no evidence) and then institute fresh proceedings for the offence in the other court. This would only be done if it was likely that the magistrates would agree to try the offences together because of a link between them.

Furthermore, s 39 of the Magistrates' Courts Act 1980 provides that, if one magistrates' court convicts a defendant and then discovers that he has been convicted of another offence at another magistrates' court but has not yet been sentenced, he may be remitted to that other court to be sentenced for both offences so long as:

- the offence being remitted is imprisonable or carries disqualification from driving; and
- the other court consents.

4.15   NOTICE TO DEFENDANT: PLEA OF GUILTY IN ABSENCE

NOTICE TO DEFENDANT: PLEA OF GUILTY IN ABSENCE
(MC Act 1980, s 12(1)(a))
In the county of [   ] Petty Sessional Division of [   ].

To AB, of [address]

PLEASE READ THIS NOTICE CAREFULLY

If you admit the offence[s] referred to in the summons[es] served herewith and do not wish to appear before the court, it is open to you under section 12 of the Magistrates' Courts Act 1980, to inform the Clerk of the Court in writing that you wish to plead guilty to the charge[s] without appearing. If you decide to do this, you should write to the Clerk in time for him to receive your reply at least three days before the date fixed for the hearing in order to avoid the unnecessary attendance of witnesses. In writing to the Clerk you should mention any mitigating circumstances which you wish to have put before the Court .... A form which you can use for writing to the Clerk is enclosed. Please also complete the enclosed means inquiry form. This is to enable the court to take your income and outgoings into account should it decide to impose a fine for the offence.

If you send a written plea of guilty, the enclosed Statement[s] of Facts and your statement in mitigation will be read out in open Court before the Court decides whether to accept your plea and hear and dispose of the case in your absence. Unless the court adjourns the case after accepting your plea and before sentencing you (in which case you will be informed of the time and place of the adjourned hearing so that you may appear) the prosecution will not be permitted to make any statement with respect to any facts relating to the offence[s] other than the Statement[s] of Facts.

If you send in a written plea of guilty but the court decides not to accept the plea, the hearing will be adjourned and you will be informed of the time and place of the adjourned hearing. The case will then be heard as if you had not sent in a written plea of guilty.

If you send a written plea of guilty you may, if you wish, withdraw it by informing the Clerk of the withdrawal at any time before the hearing.

Neither this notice nor any reply you may send limits your right to appear before the Court at the time fixed for the hearing, either in person or by counsel or a solicitor, and then to plead guilty or not guilty as you may desire; if after sending in a written plea of guilty you do so appear, or if you inform the Clerk before the hearing of the withdrawal of your written plea, the case will be heard as if you had not sent it in. If after sending in a written plea of guilty you wish to appear and plead not guilty you will avoid delay and expense by informing the Clerk immediately of your change of intention: unless you do inform the Clerk in good time there will have to be an adjournment to allow the prosecution to bring their witnesses to Court.

Notes

1   If you want any more information you may get in touch with the Clerk of the court.

2   If you intend to consult a solicitor you would be well advised to do so before taking any action in response to this notice.

3   Address any letter to The Clerk of the [place]   Magistrates' Court at [address].

4.16   STATEMENT OF FACTS

STATEMENT OF FACTS
(MC Act 1980, s 12(1)(b))

To AB, of [address] [state age and occupation if known]

If you inform the Clerk of the court that you wish to plead guilty to the charge of [   ], set out in the summons served herewith, without appearing before the Court and the Court proceeds to hear and dispose of the case in your absence under section 12 of the Magistrates' Courts Act 1980, the following Statement of Facts will be read out in open Court before the Court decides whether to accept your plea. If your plea of guilty is accepted the Court will not, unless it adjourns the case after convicting you and before sentencing you, permit any other statement to be made by or on behalf of the prosecutor with respect to any fact relating to the charge.

Statement of Facts

Signed ....
[On behalf of the Prosecutor]

4.17   SUMMONS TO WITNESS

SUMMONS TO WITNESS
(MC Act 1980, s 97; MC Rules 1981, r 98)

.... Magistrates' Court (Code:)

Date:

To: [Name]

of: [Address]

You are hereby summoned to appear on [date] at [time] am/pm before the [place] magistrates' court to [give evidence] [and] [produce the document[s] or thing[s] specified in the Schedule hereto] at the hearing of the following case:

Informant: [Name of prosecutor]

against

Defendant: [Name of accused]

for

Alleged offence:

Justice of the Peace
[Justices' Clerk]

4.18   WARRANT FOR ARREST OF WITNESS ON FAILURE TO APPEAR TO SUMMONS

WARRANT FOR ARREST OF WITNESS ON FAILURE TO APPEAR TO SUMMONS

(MC Act 1980, ss 97, 117; MC Rules 1981, rr 95, 96)

.... Magistrates' Court (Code:)

Date:

Witness:

Address:

The witness having been summoned to appear before this court on [date] at [time] am/pm to [give evidence] [and] [produce the document[s] or thing[s] specified in the Schedule to the summons] at the hearing of the following case:
Informant:

against

Defendant:

for

Alleged offence:

And the witness having failed to answer the summons.

Direction: You the constables of [County] Police Force are hereby required to arrest the witness and bring the witness before the [place] magistrates' court [immediately] [on [date] at [time] am/pm] [unless the witness is released on bail as directed below].

*Bail   On arrest the witness shall be released on bail on entering into a recognizance in the sum of £ with suret[y][ies] in the sum of £ [each] for the witness's appearance before the above magistrates' court on [date] at [time].

Justice of the Peace
[or By order of the Court Clerk of the Court]

*Delete if bail is not granted

4.19   REGISTER

REGISTER

(MC Rules 1981, r 66)

In the [county of ....Petty Sessional Division of ....]
Register of the ....Magistrates' Court sitting at ....
....

The ...... day of .... 20 ....

Number	Name of informant or complainant	Name of defendant Age if known	Nature of offence or matter of complaint	Date of offence or matter of complaint	Plea or consent to order	Minute of adjudication	Time allowed for payment and instalments

Signature ....
Justice of the Peace for the [county] of [   ]   A justice adjudicating
[or Clerk of the Court present during these proceedings]

TABLE OF STATUTORY AND OTHER MATERIALS

STATUTORY MATERIALS

JURISDICTION OF MAGISTRATES' COURT

MAGISTRATES' COURTS ACT 1980

Section 2: Jurisdiction to deal with charges

(1) A magistrates' court for a commission area[1] shall have jurisdiction to try all summary offences committed within the commission area.

(2) Where a person charged with a summary offence appears or is brought before a magistrates' court in answer to a summons issued under paragraph (b) of section 1(2) above, or under a warrant issued under that paragraph, the court shall have jurisdiction to try the offence.

(3) A magistrates' court for a commission area shall have jurisdiction as examining justices over any offence committed by a person who appears or is brought before the court, whether or not the offence was committed within the commission area.

(4) Subject to sections 18 to 22 below and any other enactment (wherever contained) relating to the mode of trial of offences triable either way, a magistrates' court shall have jurisdiction to try summarily an offence triable either way in any case in which under sub-section (3) above it would have jurisdiction as examining justices.

(5) A magistrates' court shall, in the exercise of its powers under section 24 below [juveniles], have jurisdiction to try summarily an indictable offence in any case in which under sub-section (3) above it would have jurisdiction as examining justices.

(6) A magistrates' court for any area by which a person is tried for an offence shall have jurisdiction to try him for any summary offence for which he could be tried by a magistrates' court for any other area.

(7) Nothing in this section shall affect any jurisdiction over offences conferred on a magistrates' court by any enactment not contained in this Act.

Section 3: Offences committed on boundaries, etc

(1) Where an offence has been committed on the boundary between two or more areas to which this section applies, or within 500 yards of such a boundary, or in any harbour, river, arm of the sea or other water lying between two or more such areas, the offence may be treated for the

---

1   Defined by s 1 of the Justices of the Peace Act 1979 as a county, a London commission area or the City of London.

purposes of the preceding provisions of this Act as having been committed in any one of those areas.

(2) An offence begun in one area to which this section applies and completed in another may be treated for the purposes of the preceding provisions of this Act as having been wholly committed in either.

(3) Where an offence has been committed on any person, or on or in respect of any property, in or on a vehicle or vessel engaged in any journey or voyage through two or more areas to which this section applies, the offence may be treated for the purposes of the preceding provisions of this Act as having been committed in any one of those areas; and where the side or any part of a road or any water along which the vehicle or vessel passed in the course of the journey or voyage forms the boundary between two or more areas to which this section applies, the offence may be treated for the purposes of the preceding provisions of this Act as having been committed in any of those areas.

(4) The areas to which this section applies are commission areas.

Section 44: Aiders and abettors

(1) A person who aids, abets, counsels or procures the commission by another person of a summary offence shall be guilty of the like offence and may be tried (whether or not he is charged as a principal) either by a court having jurisdiction to try that other person or by a court having by virtue of his own offence jurisdiction to try him.

(2) Any offence consisting in aiding, abetting, counselling or procuring the commission of an offence triable either way (other than an offence listed in Schedule 1 to this Act) shall by virtue of this sub-section be triable either way.

Section 45: Incitement

(1) Any offence consisting in the incitement to commit a summary offence shall be triable only summarily.

...

(3) On conviction of an offence consisting in the incitement to commit a summary offence a person shall be liable to the same penalties as he would be liable to on conviction of the last-mentioned offence.

INFORMATIONS:
THE RULE AGAINST DUPLICITY

MAGISTRATES' COURTS RULES 1981

Rule 12: Information to be for one offence only

(1) ... [A] magistrates' court shall not proceed to the trial of an information that charges more than one offence.

(2) Nothing in this rule shall prohibit 2 or more informations being set out in one document.

(3) If, notwithstanding paragraph (1) above, it appears to the court at any stage in the trial of an information that the information charges more than one offence, the court shall call upon the prosecutor to elect on which offence he desires the court to proceed, whereupon the offence or offences on which the prosecutor does not wish to proceed shall be struck out of the information; and the court shall then proceed to try that information afresh.

(4) If a prosecutor who is called upon to make an election under paragraph (3) above fails to do so, the court shall dismiss the information.

(5) Where, after an offence has or offences have been struck out of the information under paragraph (3) above, the accused requests an adjournment and it appears to the court that he has been unfairly prejudiced, it shall adjourn the trial.

AMENDING THE INFORMATION

MAGISTRATES' COURTS ACT 1980

Section 123: Defect in process

(1) No objection shall be allowed to any information or complaint, or to any summons or warrant to procure the presence of the defendant, for any defect in substance or in form, or for any variance between it and the evidence adduced on behalf of the prosecutor or complainant at the hearing of the information or complaint.

(2) If it appears to a magistrates' court that any variance between a summons or warrant and the evidence adduced on behalf of the prosecutor or complainant is such that the defendant has been misled by the variance, the court shall, on the application of the defendant, adjourn the hearing.

SECURING ATTENDANCE OF WITNESSES

MAGISTRATES' COURTS ACT 1980

Section 97: Summons to witness and warrant for his arrest

(1) Where a justice of the peace for any commission area is satisfied that any person in England or Wales is likely to be able to give material evidence, or produce any document or thing likely to be material evidence at the summary trial of an information ... by a magistrates' court for that commission area and that that person will not attend voluntarily as a witness or will not voluntarily produce the document or thing, the justice shall issue a summons directed to that person requiring him to attend before the court at the time and place appointed in the summons to give evidence or to produce the document or thing.

(2) If a justice of the peace is satisfied on oath of the matters mentioned in sub-section (1) above, and also that it is probable that a summons under that sub-section would not procure the attendance of the person in question, the justice may instead of issuing a summons issue a warrant to arrest that person and bring him before such a court, as aforesaid at a time and place specified in the warrant; but a warrant shall not be issued under this sub-section where the attendance is required for the hearing of a complaint.

(2A) A summons may also be issued under sub-section (1) above if the justice is satisfied that the person in question is outside the British Islands but no warrant shall be issued under sub-section (2) above unless the justice is satisfied by evidence on oath that the person in question is in England or Wales.

(2B) A justice may refuse to issue a summons under sub-section (1) above in relation to the summary trial of an information if he is not satisfied that an application for the summons was made by a party to the case as soon as reasonably practicable after the accused pleaded not guilty.

(2C) In relation to the summary trial of an information, sub-section (2) above shall have effect as if the reference to the matters mentioned in sub-section (1) above included a reference to the matter mentioned in sub-section (2B) above.

(3) On the failure of any person to attend before a magistrates' court in answer to a summons under this section, if:

    (a) the court is satisfied by evidence on oath that he is likely to be able to give material evidence or produce any document or thing likely to be material evidence in the proceedings; and

    (b) it is proved on oath, or in such other manner as may be prescribed, that he has been duly served with the summons, and that a reasonable sum has been paid or tendered to him for costs and expenses; and

(c) it appears to the court that there is no just excuse for the failure,

the court may issue a warrant to arrest him and bring him before the court at a time and place specified in the warrant.

(4) If any person attending or brought before a magistrates' court refuses without just excuse to be sworn or give evidence, or to produce any document or thing, the court, may commit him to custody until the expiration of such period not exceeding one month as may be specified in the warrant or until he sooner gives evidence or produces the document or thing or impose on him a fine not exceeding £2,500, or both.

...

MAGISTRATES' COURTS RULES 1981

Rule 107: Application for summons to witness or warrant for his arrest

(1) An application for the issue of a summons or warrant under section 97 of the Magistrates' Courts Act 1980 may be made by the applicant in person or by his counsel or solicitor.

(2) An application for the issue of such a summons may be made by delivering or sending the application in writing to the clerk to the magistrates' court.

THE TRIAL

MAGISTRATES' COURTS ACT 1980

Section 9: Procedure on trial

(1) On the summary trial of an information, the court shall, if the accused appears, state to him the substance of the information and ask him whether he pleads guilty or not guilty.

(2) The court, after hearing the evidence and the parties, shall convict the accused or dismiss the information.

(3) If the accused pleads guilty, the court may convict him without hearing evidence.

MAGISTRATES' COURTS RULES 1981

Rule 13: Order of evidence and speeches

(1) On the summary trial of an information, where the accused does not plead guilty, the prosecutor shall call the evidence for the prosecution, and before doing so may address the court.

(2) At the conclusion of the evidence for the prosecution, the accused may address the court, whether or not he afterwards calls evidence.

(3) At the conclusion of the evidence, if any, for the defence, the prosecutor may call evidence to rebut that evidence.

(4) At the conclusion of the evidence for the defence and the evidence, if any, in rebuttal, the accused may address the court if he has not already done so.

(5) Either party may, with the leave of the court, address the court a second time, but where the court grants leave to one party it shall not refuse leave to the other.

(6) Where both parties address the court twice the prosecutor shall address the court for the second time before the accused does so.

MAGISTRATES' COURTS ACT 1980

Section 10: Adjournment of trial

(1) A magistrates' court may at any time, whether before or after beginning to try an information, adjourn the trial, and may do so, notwithstanding anything in this Act, when composed of a single justice.

(2) The court may when adjourning either fix the time and place at which the trial is to be resumed, or, unless it remands the accused, leave the time and place to be determined later by the court; but the trial shall not be resumed at that time and place unless the court is satisfied that the parties have had adequate notice thereof.

(3) A magistrates' court may, for the purpose of enabling inquiries to be made or of determining the most suitable method of dealing with the case, exercise its power to adjourn after convicting the accused and before sentencing him or otherwise dealing with him; but, if it does so, the adjournment shall not be for more than 4 weeks at a time unless the court remands the accused in custody and, where it so remands him, the adjournment shall not be for more than 3 weeks at a time.

(3A) A youth court shall not be required to adjourn any proceedings for an offence at any stage by reason only of the fact:

   (a) that the court commits the accused for trial for another offence; or

   (b) that the accused is charged with another offence.

(4) On adjourning the trial of an information the court may remand the accused and, where the accused has attained the age of 18, shall do so if the offence is triable either way and:

(a) on the occasion on which the accused first appeared, or was brought before the court to answer to the information he was in custody or, having been released on bail, surrendered to the custody of the court; or

(b) the accused has been remanded at any time in the course of the proceedings on the information,

and, where the court remands the accused, the time fixed for the resumption of the trial shall be at which he is required to appear or be brought before the court in pursuance of the remand or would be required to be brought before the court but for section 128(3A) below.

Section 11: Non-appearance of accused – general provisions

(1) Subject to the provisions of this Act, where at the time and place appointed for the trial or adjourned trial of an information the prosecutor appears but the accused does not, the court may proceed in his absence.

(2) Where a summons has been issued, the court shall not begin to try the information in the absence of the accused unless either it is proved to the satisfaction of the court, on oath or in such other manner as may be prescribed, that the summons was served on the accused within what appears to the court to be a reasonable time before the trial or adjourned trial or the accused has appeared on a previous occasion to answer the information.

(3) A magistrates' court shall not in a person's absence sentence him to imprisonment or detention ... or make a secure training centre order or an order under section 119 of the Powers of Criminal Courts (Sentencing) Act 2000 of the Powers of Criminal Courts Act 1973 that a suspended sentence passed on him shall take effect.

(4) A magistrates' court shall not in a person's absence impose any disqualification on him, except on resumption of the hearing after an adjournment under section 10(3) above; and where a trial is adjourned in pursuance of this sub-section the notice required by section 10(2) above shall include notice of the reason for the adjournment.

...

Section 13: Non-appearance of accused – issue of warrant

(1) Subject to the provisions of this section, where the court, instead of proceeding in the absence of the accused, adjourns or further adjourns the trial, the court may, if the information has been substantiated on oath, issue a warrant for his arrest.

(2) Where a summons has been issued, the court shall not issue a warrant under this section unless the condition in sub-section (2A) below or that in sub-section (2B) below is fulfilled.

(2A) The condition in this sub-section is that it is proved to the satisfaction of the court, on oath or in such other manner as may be prescribed, that the summons was served on the accused within what appears to the court to be a reasonable time before the trial or adjourned trial.

(2B) The condition in this sub-section is that:

(a) the adjournment now being made is a second or subsequent adjournment of the trial;

(b) the accused was present on the last (or only) occasion when the trial was adjourned; and

(c) on that occasion the court determined the time for the hearing at which the adjournment is now being made.

(3) A warrant for the arrest of any person who has attained the age of 18 shall not be issued under this section unless:

(a) the offence to which the warrant relates is punishable with imprisonment; or

(b) the court, having convicted the accused, proposes to impose a disqualification on him.

(4) This section shall not apply to an adjournment on the occasion of the accused's conviction in his absence under sub-section (5) of section 12 [pleading guilty by post] or to an adjournment required by sub-section (9) of that section.

(5) Where the court adjourns the trial:

(a) after having, either on that or on a previous occasion, received any evidence or convicted the accused without hearing evidence on his pleading guilty under section 9(3) above; or

(b) after having on a previous occasion convicted the accused without hearing evidence on his pleading guilty under section 12(5) above,

the court shall not issue a warrant under this section unless it thinks it undesirable, by reason of the gravity of the offence, to continue the trial in the absence of the accused.

Section 14: Proceedings invalid where accused did not know of them

(1) Where a summons has been issued under section 1 above and a magistrates' court has begun to try the information to which the summons relates, then, if:

(a) the accused, at any time during or after the trial, makes a statutory declaration that he did not know of the summons or the proceedings until a date specified in the declaration, being a date after the court has begun to try the information; and

(b) within 21 days of that date the declaration is served on the clerk to the justices,

without prejudice to the validity of the information, the summons and all subsequent proceedings shall be void.

(2) For the purposes of sub-section (1) above a statutory declaration shall be deemed to be duly served on the clerk to the justices if it is delivered to him, or left at his office, or is sent in a registered letter or by the recorded delivery service addressed to him at his office.

(3) If on the application of the accused it appears to a magistrates' court (which for this purpose may be composed of a single justice) that it was not reasonable to expect the accused to serve such a statutory declaration as is mentioned in sub-section (1) above within the period allowed by that sub-section, the court may accept service of such a declaration by the accused after that period has expired; and a statutory declaration accepted under this sub-section shall be deemed to have been served as required by that sub-section.

(4) Where any proceedings have become void by virtue of sub-section (1) above, the information shall not be tried again by any of the same justices.

Section 15: Non-appearance of prosecutor

(1) Where at the time and place appointed for the trial or adjourned trial of an information the accused appears or is brought before the court and the prosecutor does not appear, the court may dismiss the information or, if evidence has been received on a previous occasion, proceed in the absence of the prosecutor.

(2) Where, instead of dismissing the information or proceeding in the absence of the prosecutor, the court adjourns the trial, it shall not remand the accused in custody unless he has been brought from custody or cannot be remanded on bail by reason of his failure to find sureties.

Section 16: Non-appearance of both parties

Subject to section 11(3) and (4) and to section 12 above, where at the time and place appointed for the trial or adjourned trial of an information neither the prosecutor nor the accused appears, the court may dismiss the information or, if evidence has been received on a previous occasion, proceed in their absence.

Section 27: Effect of dismissal of information for offence triable either way

Where on the summary trial of an information for an offence triable either way the court dismisses the information, the dismissal shall have the same effect as an acquittal on indictment.

Section 121: Constitution and place of sitting of court

(1) A magistrates' court shall not try an information summarily ... except when composed of at least 2 justices ...

(6) Subject to the provisions of sub-section (7) below, the justices composing the court before which any proceedings take place shall be present during the whole of the proceedings; but, if during the course of the proceedings any justice absents himself, he shall cease to act further therein and, if the remaining justices are enough to satisfy the requirements of the preceding provisions of this section, the proceedings may continue before a court composed of those justices.

(7) Where the trial of an information is adjourned after the accused has been convicted and before he is sentenced or otherwise dealt with, the court which sentences or deals with him need not be composed of the same justices as that which convicted him; but, where among the justices composing the court which sentences or deals with an offender there are any who were not sitting when he was convicted, the court which sentences or deals with the offender shall before doing so make such inquiry into the facts and circumstances of the case as will enable the justices who were not sitting when the offender was convicted to be fully acquainted with those facts and circumstances.

...

Section 122: Appearance by a legal representative

(1) A party to any proceedings before a magistrates' court may be represented by a legal representative.

(2) Subject to sub-section (3) below, any absent party so represented shall be deemed not to be absent.

(3) Appearance of a party by a legal representative shall not satisfy any provision of any enactment or any condition of a recognizance expressly requiring his presence.[2]

READING WITNESS STATEMENTS

CRIMINAL JUSTICE ACT 1967

Section 9: Proof by written statement

(1) In any criminal proceedings, other than committal proceedings, a written statement by any person shall, if such of the conditions mentioned in the

---

2   Where D has been granted bail, he must attend personally.

next following sub-section as are applicable are satisfied, be admissible as evidence to the like extent as oral evidence to the like effect by that person.

(2) The said conditions are:

    (a) the statement purports to be signed by the person who made it;

    (b) the statement contains a declaration by that person to the effect that it is true to the best of his knowledge and belief and that he made the statement knowing that, if it were tendered in evidence, he would be liable to prosecution if he wilfully stated in it anything which he knew to be false or did not believe to be true;

    (c) before the hearing at which the statement is tendered in evidence, a copy of the statement is served, by or on behalf of the party proposing to tender it, on each of the other parties to the proceedings; and

    (d) none of the other parties or their solicitors, within seven days from the service of the copy of the statement, serves a notice on the party so proposing objecting to the statement being tendered in evidence under this section.

Provided that the conditions mentioned in paragraphs (c) and (d) of this sub-section shall not apply if the parties agree before or during the hearing that the statement shall be so tendered.

(3) The following provisions shall also have effect in relation to any written statement tendered in evidence under this section, that is to say:

    (a) if the statement is made by a person under the age of 18, it shall give his age;

    (b) if it is made by a person who cannot read it, it shall be read to him before he signs it and shall be accompanied by a declaration by the person who so read the statement to the effect that it was so read; and

    (c) if it refers to any other document as an exhibit, the copy served on any other party to the proceedings under paragraph (c) of the last foregoing sub-section shall be accompanied by a copy of that document or by such information as may be necessary in order to enable the party on whom it is served to inspect that document or a copy thereof.

(4) Notwithstanding that a written statement made by any person may be admissible as evidence by virtue of this section:

    (a) the party by whom or on whose behalf a copy of the statement was served may call that person to give evidence; and

    (b) the court may, of its own motion or on the application of any party to the proceedings, require that person to attend before the court and give evidence.

    ...

(6) So much of any statement as is admitted in evidence by virtue of this section shall, unless the court otherwise directs, be read aloud at the hearing and where the court so directs an account shall be given orally of so much of any statement as is not read aloud.

(7) Any document or object referred to as an exhibit and identified in a written statement tendered in evidence under this section shall be treated as if it

had been produced as an exhibit and identified in court by the maker of the statement.

...

OTHER MATERIALS

Practice Direction (Submission of No Case) [1962] 1 WLR 227

A submission that there is no case to answer may properly be made and upheld: (a) when there has been no evidence to prove an essential element in the alleged offence; (b) when the evidence adduced by the prosecution has been so discredited as a result of cross-examination or is so manifestly unreliable that no reasonable tribunal could safely convict upon it.

Apart from these two situations a tribunal should not in general be called upon to reach a decision as to conviction or acquittal until the whole of the evidence which either side wishes to tender has been placed before it. If however a submission is made that there is no case to answer, the decision should depend not so much on whether the adjudicating tribunal (if compelled to do so) would at that stage convict or acquit but on whether the evidence is such that a reasonable tribunal might convict. If a reasonable tribunal might convict on the evidence so far laid before it, there is a case to answer.

Practice Direction (Justices: Clerk to the Court) [1981] 1 WLR 1163

1 A justices' clerk is responsible to the justices for the performance of any of the functions set out below by any member of his staff acting as court clerk and may be called in to advise the justices even when he is not personally sitting with the justices as clerk to the court.

2 It shall be the responsibility of the justices' clerk to advise the justices as follows:

   (a) on questions of law or of mixed law and fact;

   (b) as to matters of practice and procedure.

3 If it appears to him necessary to do so, or if he is so requested by the justices, the justices' clerk has the responsibility to:

   (a) refresh the justices' memory as to any matter of evidence and to draw attention to any issues involved in the matters before the court;

   (b) advise the justices generally on the range of penalties which the law allows them to impose and on any guidance relevant to the choice of penalty provided by the law, the decisions of the superior courts or other authorities.

If no request for advice has been made by the justices, the justices' clerk shall discharge his responsibility in court in the presence of the parties.

4   The way in which the justices' clerk should perform his functions should be stated as follows.

(a) The justices are entitled to the advice of their clerk when they retire in order that the clerk may fulfil his responsibility outlined above.

(b) Some justices may prefer to take their own notes of evidence. There is, however, no obligation on them to do so. Whether they do so or not, there is nothing to prevent them from enlisting the aid of their clerk and his notes if they are in any doubt as to the evidence which has been given.

(c) If the justices wish to consult their clerk solely about the evidence or his notes of it, this should ordinarily, and certainly in simple cases, be done in open court. The object is to avoid any suspicion that the clerk has been involved in deciding issues of fact.

...

STATUTORY MATERIALS: COMMITTAL FOR SENTENCE

POWERS OF CRIMINAL COURTS (SENTENCING) ACT 2000

Section 3: Committal for sentence on summary trial of offence triable either way

(1) Subject to sub-section (4) below, this section applies where on the summary trial of an offence triable either way a person aged 18 or over is convicted of the offence.

(2) If the court is of the opinion-

(a) that the offence or the combination of the offence and one or more offences associated with it was so serious that greater punishment should be inflicted for the offence than the court has power to impose, or

(b) in the case of a violent or sexual offence, that a custodial sentence for a term longer than the court has power to impose is necessary to protect the public from serious harm from him,

the court may commit the offender in custody or on bail to the Crown Court for sentence in accordance with section 5(1) below.

(3) Where the court commits a person under sub-section (2) above, section 6 below (which enables a magistrates' court, where it commits a person under this section in respect of an offence, also to commit him to the Crown Court to be dealt with in respect of certain other offences) shall apply accordingly.

(4) This section does not apply in relation to an offence as regards which this section is excluded by section 33 of the Magistrates' Courts Act 1980 (certain offences where value involved is small).

(5) The preceding provisions of this section shall apply in relation to a corporation as if:

    (a) the corporation were an individual aged 18 or over; and

    (b) in sub-section (2) above, paragraph (b) and the words 'in custody or on bail' were omitted.

Section 4: Committal for sentence on indication of guilty plea to offence triable either way

(1) This section applies where:

    (a) a person aged 18 or over appears or is brought before a magistrates' court ('the court') on an information charging him with an offence triable either way ('the offence');

    (b) he or his representative indicates that he would plead guilty if the offence were to proceed to trial; and

    (c) proceeding as if section 9(1) of the Magistrates' Courts Act 1980 were complied with and he pleaded guilty under it, the court convicts him of the offence.

(2) If the court has committed the offender to the Crown Court for trial for one or more related offences, that is to say, one or more offences which, in its opinion, are related to the offence, it may commit him in custody or on bail to the Crown Court to be dealt with in respect of the offence in accordance with section 5(1) below.

(3) If the power conferred by sub-section (2) above is not exercisable but the court is still to inquire, as examining justices, into one or more related offences:

    (a) it shall adjourn the proceedings relating to the offence until after the conclusion of its inquiries; and

    (b) if it commits the offender to the Crown Court for trial for one or more related offences, it may then exercise that power.

(4) Where the court:

    (a) under sub-section (2) above commits the offender to the Crown Court to be dealt with in respect of the offence; and

    (b) does not state that, in its opinion, it also has power so to commit him under section 3(2) above, section 5(1) below shall not apply unless he is convicted before the Crown Court of one or more of the related offences.

(5) Where section 5(1) below does not apply, the Crown Court may deal with the offender in respect of the offence in any way in which the magistrates' court could deal with him if it had just convicted him of the offence.

(6) Where the court commits a person under sub-section (2) above, section 6 below (which enables a magistrates' court, where it commits a person under this section in respect of an offence, also to commit him to the Crown

Court to be dealt with in respect of certain other offences) shall apply accordingly.

(7) For the purposes of this section one offence is related to another if, were they both to be prosecuted on indictment, the charges for them could be joined in the same indictment.

Section 5: Power of Crown Court on committal for sentence under sections 3 and 4

(1) Where an offender is committed by a magistrates' court for sentence under section 3 or 4 above, the Crown Court shall inquire into the circumstances of the case and may deal with the offender in any way in which it could deal with him if he had just been convicted of the offence on indictment before the court.

(2) In relation to committals under section 4 above, sub-section (1) above has effect subject to section 4(4) and (5) above.

Section 6: Committal for sentence in certain cases where offender committed in respect of another offence

(1) This section applies where a magistrates' court ('the committing court') commits a person in custody or on bail to the Crown Court under any enactment mentioned in sub-section (4) below to be sentenced or otherwise dealt with in respect of an offence ('the relevant offence').

(2) Where this section applies and the relevant offence is an indictable offence, the committing court may also commit the offender, in custody or on bail as the case may require, to the Crown Court to be dealt with in respect of any other offence whatsoever in respect of which the committing court has power to deal with him (being an offence of which he has been convicted by that or any other court).

(3) Where this section applies and the relevant offence is a summary offence, the committing court may commit the offender, in custody or on bail as the case may require, to the Crown Court to be dealt with in respect of:

(a) any other offence of which the committing court has convicted him, being either:

(i) an offence punishable with imprisonment; or

(ii) an offence in respect of which the committing court has a power or duty to order him to be disqualified under section 34, 35 or 36 of the Road Traffic Offenders Act 1988 (disqualification for certain motoring offences); or

(b) any suspended sentence in respect of which the committing court has under section 120(1) below power to deal with him.

(4) The enactments referred to in sub-section (1) above are:

(a) the Vagrancy Act 1824 (incorrigible rogues);

(b) sections 3 and 4 above (committal for sentence for offences triable either way);

(c) section 13(5) below (conditionally discharged person convicted of further offence);

(d) section 116(3)(b) below (offender convicted of offence committed during currency of original sentence); and

(e) section 120(2) below (offender convicted during operational period of suspended sentence).

Section 7: Power of Crown Court on committal for sentence under section 6

(1) Where under section 6 above a magistrates' court commits a person to be dealt with by the Crown Court in respect of an offence, the Crown Court may after inquiring into the circumstances of the case deal with him in any way in which the magistrates' court could deal with him if it had just convicted him of the offence.

(2) Sub-section (1) above does not apply where under section 6 above a magistrates' court commits a person to be dealt with by the Crown Court in respect of a suspended sentence, but in such a case the powers under section 119 below (power of court to deal with suspended sentence) shall be exercisable by the Crown Court.

(3) Without prejudice to sub-sections (1) and (2) above, where under section 6 above or any enactment mentioned in sub-section (4) of that section a magistrates' court commits a person to be dealt with by the Crown Court, any duty or power which, apart from this sub-section, would fall to be discharged or exercised by the magistrates' court shall not be discharged or exercised by that court but shall instead be discharged or may instead be exercised by the Crown Court.

(4) Where under section 6 above a magistrates' court commits a person to be dealt with by the Crown Court in respect of an offence triable only on indictment in the case of an adult (being an offence which was tried summarily because of the offender's being under 18 years of age), the Crown Court's powers under sub-section (1) above in respect of the offender after he attains the age of 18 shall be powers to do either or both of the following:

(a) to impose a fine not exceeding £5,000;

(b) to deal with the offender in respect of the offence in any way in which the magistrates' court could deal with him if it had just convicted him of an offence punishable with imprisonment for a term not exceeding six months.

CHAPTER 5

JUVENILE OFFENDERS – THE YOUTH COURT

5.1   INTRODUCTION

In this chapter, we look at the way in which young offenders are dealt with by the courts. We look at the jurisdiction of the youth court and at what happens if the juvenile has committed a really serious offence or is jointly charged with an adult offender.

5.2   TERMINOLOGY

The youth court has jurisdiction to deal with juvenile offenders, that is offenders aged 10 to 17 years (inclusive). Ten to 13 year olds are called 'children' and 14 to 17 year olds are called 'young persons'. This distinction is relevant as sentencing powers differ to some extent according to whether the juvenile is a child or a young person.

5.3   THE AGE OF CRIMINAL RESPONSIBILITY

There used to be a rebuttable presumption that a child aged between 10 and 14 was incapable of committing an offence. This presumption was abolished by s 34 of the Crime and Disorder Act 1998.

However, it remains the case that there is a conclusive presumption that a child under 10 cannot commit an offence and so is outside the jurisdiction of the criminal courts. Note, however, that, if a child is beyond the control of her parents and is therefore at risk of harm, a family proceedings court can make a care or supervision order under s 31 of the Children Act 1989.

5.4   JUVENILES AND BAIL

The Bail Act 1976 (with the presumption in favour of bail) applies to juveniles.

The criteria for granting bail are virtually the same as for adults. Two differences are that a juvenile can be refused bail where this is necessary for her own welfare (not just if necessary for her own protection, as is the case with adults) and that a parent or guardian may be asked to act as a surety not only for the juvenile's attendance at court (the function of the surety in the case of adult defendants) but also for her compliance with any conditions of bail which the court may impose (s 3(7) of the Bail Act).

The most significant difference between adults and juveniles is in what happens to a juvenile under the age of 17 if bail is withheld, whether before or after conviction.

Where a juvenile is refused bail, she is remanded to local authority accommodation unless the criteria laid down in s 23(5) of the Children and Young Persons Act 1969 (set out below) are satisfied.

Section 23(7) provides that where a juvenile is remanded to local authority accommodation, the court can impose such conditions as it would be able to impose on a adult offender under s 3(6) of the Bail Act 1976.

Section 23A of the Children and Young Persons Act 1969 provides that where a juvenile has been remanded to local authority accommodation and conditions have been imposed under s 23(7), the juvenile may be arrested without a warrant if the police have reasonable grounds for suspecting that she has broken any of the conditions.

Section 23(5) provides that a juvenile may be remanded to a remand centre or prison if he:

(a) has attained the age of 15;[1] and

(b) either:

    (i)   is charged with or has been convicted of a violent or sexual offence or an offence punishable in the case of an adult offender with at least 14 years' imprisonment; or

    (ii)   has a recent history of absconding while remanded to local authority accommodation, and is charged with or has been convicted of an imprisonable offence alleged or found to have been committed while he was so remanded; and

(c) the court is of the opinion that remand to a remand centre or prison is the only way of protecting the public from serious harm from the juvenile.

These provisions are transitional and will in due course be replaced by a new version of s 23. In the new version, all remands of juveniles who are not granted bail will be to local authority accommodation. However, the court will be empowered (after consultation with the local authority) to require the local authority to place and keep the juvenile in 'secure accommodation' (run by the local authority). The power to impose such a security requirement will be confined to cases where the juvenile has attained at the age of 15, and:

---

1   The Secretary of State has power under s 20 of the Criminal Justice and Public Order Act 1994 to lower the age to 12, 13 or 14.

(a) either:

    (i)   he is charged with or has been convicted of a violent or sexual offence or an offence punishable in the case of an adult offender with at least 14 years' imprisonment; or

    (ii)   he has a recent history of absconding while remanded to local authority accommodation, and is charged with or has been convicted of an imprisonable offence alleged or found to have been committed while he was so remanded; and

(b) the court is of the opinion that imposing a security requirement is the only way to protect the public from serious harm from the juvenile.

In deciding whether the public needs to be protected from the juvenile, it is necessary for the court to assess the risk of serious harm to the public by reference to the nature of the offences in respect of which the young person has been charged or convicted, and the manner in which these offences have been carried out (or are alleged to have been carried out if the defendant has not yet been convicted); it is not enough to consider only the risk that such offences might be repeated (*R v Croydon Youth Court ex p G (a minor)* (1995) *The Times*, 3 May).

5.5   YOUTH COURTS

A youth court must consist of justices from the youth court panel, which comprises a number of magistrates who have received extra training to equip them to deal with juveniles (Youth Court (Constitution) Rules 1954, r 11).

Where the youth court comprises a bench of lay magistrates, there should be no more than three justices and there should (unless a properly constituted court is not available and it is inexpedient to adjourn) be at least one male and one female (r 12 of the 1954 Rules). Alternatively (under s 48 of the Crime and Disorder Act 1998), the court may comprise a stipendiary magistrate (District Judge) sitting alone.

The distinction between indictable, triable either way and summary offences does not apply to juvenile defendants. Thus, a bench of justices in the youth court may try an offence which, in the case of an adult defendant, would be triable only in the Crown Court. Furthermore, a juvenile has no right to elect Crown Court trial in any case where an adult defendant would have such a right. The justices in the youth court may, however, decline jurisdiction in respect of certain indictable offences: see 5.12.1 below.

5.6 DIFFERENCES BETWEEN YOUTH COURT AND ADULT MAGISTRATES' COURT

There is less formality in the youth court than in an adult magistrates' court. For example:

- the juvenile sits on a chair, not in a dock, and usually has a parent or guardian sitting next to her;
- the juvenile and any juvenile witnesses are addressed by their first names;
- the oath taken by witnesses is to promise (not swear) to tell the truth;
- the terminology differs slightly, for example, a 'finding of guilt' (not a 'conviction') and an 'order made upon a finding of guilt' (not a 'sentence'). Note, however, that the juvenile pleads guilty or not guilty.

5.6.1 Exclusion of public

The public are excluded from the courtroom (s 47(2) of the Children and Young Persons Act 1933). The only people entitled to be present in the youth court apart from the accused, her parents and the justices and their clerk are:

- the lawyers representing the juvenile or the prosecution in the present case; the lawyers cannot enter the courtroom if a case they are appearing in is not yet being dealt with;
- court officials (for example, the usher);
- reporters (but note the reporting restrictions set out below);
- probation officers and social workers;
- witnesses giving evidence (and they are allowed to remain in court once they have given evidence);
- anyone else directly concerned in the case;
- anyone whom the magistrates allow to be present (for example, law students).

Note that, if a juvenile is appearing as an accused or as a witness in the adult magistrates' court or the Crown Court, the public have the right to be present unless the court takes the exceptional step of sitting 'in camera'.

5.7 REPORTING RESTRICTIONS

Section 49 of the Children and Young Persons Act 1933 imposes automatic reporting restrictions. This section applies to newspaper reports and to broadcast programmes. The essence of the restrictions is that details should not be published or broadcast which would enable the accused or any juvenile witness in the case to be identified. Nor should any picture of the accused, or of any juvenile witness, be published or broadcast.

Breach of the reporting restrictions is punishable, on summary conviction, by a fine not exceeding level 5 (£5,000).

It should be noted that if a juvenile appears in the adult magistrates' court there are no reporting restrictions unless they are ordered by the court under s 39 of the Children and Young Persons Act 1933. Again, breach of an order under s 39 is punishable with a fine not exceeding level 5 (£5,000). In *R v Central Criminal Court ex p S* (1999) 163 JP 776, the Divisional Court held that there has to be a good reason for making an order under s 39 preventing identification of a juvenile who appears before an adult court. The court said that in deciding whether or not to make such an order, the weight which the court should attach to the various factors relevant to the decision might be different at differing stages of the proceedings. After the juvenile has been convicted, it might be appropriate to place greater weight on the interest of the public in knowing the identity of those who have committed serious crimes.

In *R v Tyne Tees TV Ltd* (1997) *The Times*, 20 October, the defendant published material in breach of an order under s 39 of the Children and Young Persons Act 1933. The judge dealt with this as a contempt of court. The Court of Appeal said that the proper course would have been for the judge to report the matter so that proceedings for the summary offence created by s 39 could be taken, not to treat it as a contempt of court.

5.7.1   Lifting the restrictions

The court does, however, have a discretion to lift the restrictions if it is appropriate to do so in order to avoid injustice (for instance, where the defence wish to make an appeal for potential witnesses to come forward).

Furthermore, s 49(5)(b) provides that where the young person is charged with a violent or sexual offence, or with an offence which carries at least 14 years' imprisonment in the case of an adult offender, the reporting restrictions may be lifted if that person is unlawfully at large and it is necessary to dispense with the restrictions for the purpose of apprehending him.

The power to lift the reporting restrictions may be exercised by a single justice.

Section 45 of the Crime (Sentences) Act 1997 adds sub-ss (4A) and (4B) to s 49 of the Children and Young Persons Act 1933. These provide that the court, if it considers it would be in the public interest to do so, may order that restrictions on the publication of reports of proceedings in a youth court be lifted in relation to a child or young person who has been convicted of an offence. The parties to the proceedings must be given an opportunity to make representations before such an order is made.

In *McKerry v Teesdale Justices* (2000) 97(11) LSG 36, the Divisional Court said that the statutory provisions on the welfare of juveniles involved in criminal proceedings, and on the imposition and removal of reporting restrictions in such cases, have to be read against the background of international law and practice on the topic. The power to dispense with anonymity has to be exercised with great care. It would be wholly wrong to dispense with a juvenile's *prima facie* right to anonymity as an additional punishment. The court said that it is difficult to see any place for 'naming and shaming'. The court has to be satisfied that it is in the public interest to dispense with the reporting restrictions. It is open to the court to hear representations from a representative of the press (even from a reporter with no formal right of audience).

The power to lift the restrictions applies both to the automatic restrictions under s 49 of the 1933 Act and to the order for restrictions under s 39 of the 1933 Act (so, after a s 39 order has been made, it is open to the court to discharge the order). In *R v Central Criminal Court ex p S* (above), the Divisional court declined to follow *R v Leicester Crown Court ex p S* (1992) 94 Cr App R 153 and held that it is not the case that a s 39 order should only be discharged in rare and exceptional circumstances.

5.8   ATTENDANCE OF PARENT OR GUARDIAN

Section 34A of the Children and Young Persons Act 1933 provides that if the juvenile is under 16 the court *must* (or if the juvenile is 16 or 17 the court *may*) require a parent or guardian to attend court during all stages of the proceedings unless and to the extent that the court is satisfied that it would be unreasonable to require such attendance. This was intended by the government to underline parental responsibility for the wrong-doings of their children.

If the juvenile is not legally represented, the parent or guardian may assist in her defence, for example, in cross-examination of prosecution witnesses.

5.9   YOUTH COURT TRIAL PROCEDURE

Apart from the attempt to make the atmosphere less forbidding, the procedure for a trial in the youth court is the same as the procedure for summary trial in the adult magistrates' court, which is described in Chapter 4.

5.9.1   Evidence by television link

If a juvenile aged 14 or under is to testify as a witness (not a defendant), the court may give permission for her to do so via a live television link (s 32 of the Criminal Justice Act 1988). The case must involve either:

- an assault on, or injury or threat of injury to a person (not necessarily the witness in question or another juvenile); or
- a specified offence involving cruelty to, or sexual misconduct with, juveniles (again not necessarily the witness in question).

This power was originally available only to the Crown Court (and is dealt with in more detail in Chapter 9), but s 55 of the Criminal Justice Act 1991 extends it to youth courts.

5.9.2   Pre-recorded interviews

In those cases where a juvenile witness could give evidence via a television link, s 32A of the Criminal Justice Act 1988 (inserted by s 54 of the Criminal Justice Act 1991) enables the court (including the youth court) to give leave for an interview pre-recorded on video to be admitted into evidence. The child should be available for live cross-examination if the court does give leave for the recording to be tendered in evidence.

5.9.3   Cross-examination of a child

If the evidence of a child is admitted under s 32 or 32A of the Criminal Justice Act, the defendant is not allowed to cross-examine the child in person, although he can do so through a solicitor or barrister.

5.10   SENTENCING JUVENILES

Sentencing of young offenders is dealt with in detail in Chapters 16 and 17. This section merely summarises some of the differences between sentencing juveniles and adult offenders.

5.10.1   The youth court: sentencing options

The youth court has a wide range of sentencing options available to it. These options are described in Chapters 16 and 17. It is worth noting at this stage that a sentence of detention in a young offender institution is only possible if the juvenile has attained the age of 15. The youth court can impose six months detention for an offence which is, in the case of an adult, an indictable offence. For two or more indictable offences, the youth court can impose a maximum aggregate sentence of 12 months. The maximum fine which a youth court can impose is £1,000 for a juvenile who has attained the age of 14 and £250 for a juvenile under 14 (s 24(3), (4) of the Magistrates' Courts Act 1980).

5.10.2   The youth court: sentencing procedure

The sentencing procedure is the same as in the adult magistrates' court, described in Chapter 4.

Under r 10 of the Magistrates' Courts (Children and Young Persons) Rules 1992, before passing sentence on a juvenile, the court must give a parent or guardian the chance to address the court and must consider all available information as to the juvenile's general conduct, home surroundings, school record and medical history.

There will usually be a pre-sentence report, written by a social worker (rather that a probation officer, as in the case of adult offenders), and also a school report.

Where a juvenile has been tried in the youth court, that court has no power to commit the juvenile to the Crown Court for sentence (indeed the Crown Court has no greater powers of sentence in respect of a juvenile convicted by the youth court).

5.11   PLACE OF FIRST APPEARANCE

The juvenile's first court appearance in respect of an offence will be in the youth court unless the case is one of the exceptional ones where the first appearance is in the adult magistrates' court. The exceptional cases are:

- the juvenile is jointly charged with an adult; or
- the juvenile is charged with aiding and abetting an adult to commit an offence (or *vice versa*); or
- the juvenile is charged with an offence which arises out of circumstances which are the same as (or connected with) those which resulted in the charge faced by an adult accused.

These exceptions exist because no one who is 18 or older at the time of their first court appearance should ever appear in the youth court.

5.12   PLACE OF TRIAL

We have already seen that a juvenile may be tried in the youth court for an offence which is triable only on indictment in the case of an adult offender and that a juvenile never has a right to elect trial on indictment.

In this section, we consider the circumstances in which a juvenile may be tried in the Crown Court or in an adult magistrates' court.

There are three circumstances in which the trial of a juvenile may take place in the Crown Court.

5.12.1   Murder and manslaughter

The first instance where a juvenile will be tried in the Crown Court is where he is charged with murder or manslaughter. In such a case, the trial must take place in the Crown Court (s 24(1) of the Magistrates' Courts Act 1980).

5.12.2   Section 91 of the Powers of Criminal Courts (Sentencing) Act 2000

The second situation where a juvenile may be tried in the Crown Court is where the provisions of s 91 of the Powers of Criminal Courts (Sentencing) Act 2000 apply. See, also, Chapter 16, 16.2. Section 91, which empowers the Crown Court to order that a juvenile be detained for a period not exceeding the maximum sentence of imprisonment which may be imposed on an adult offender for the offence in question, applies only in the following cases:

- where a juvenile who has attained the age of 10 is charged with an offence which carries at least 14 years' imprisonment in the case of an adult offender;
- where a juvenile who has attained the age of 10 is charged with indecent assault on a woman contrary to s 14 of the Sexual Offences Act 1956 or indecent assault on a man contrary to s 15 of the 1956 Act;
- where a juvenile who has attained the age of 14 is charged with causing death by dangerous driving (contrary to s 1 of the Road Traffic Act 1988) or with causing death by careless driving while under the influence of drink or drugs (contrary to s 3A of the Road Traffic Act 1988).

The power to commit a juvenile for trial in the Crown Court if the juvenile is charged with one or more of these offences is contained in s 24(1)(a) of the Magistrates' Courts Act 1980. Magistrates in the youth court should only commit a juvenile for trial in the Crown Court if, on its facts, the case is sufficiently serious to justify a sentence of detention under s 91 of the 2000 Act rather than the form of custodial sentence which would normally be applicable (that is, a detention and training order).

In *R v Inner London Youth Court ex p DPP* (1996) 161 JP 178, the Divisional Court said that the proper question for magistrates to ask themselves when deciding whether or not to commit a juvenile to the Crown Court for trial under s 24 of the Magistrates' Courts Act 1980 is this: 'If this defendant were convicted of the offence with which he stands charged, would it be proper for a Crown Court when sentencing to exercise its powers under [s 91]?' If the answer is 'yes', the juvenile should be committed to the Crown Court for trial. The same approach was taken in *R v AM* [1998] 1 WLR 63; [1998] 1 All ER 874, where the Court of Appeal said that magistrates should commit a juvenile for Crown Court trial in any case where a sentence under s 91 might be merited.

So, when might a sentence under s 91 be merited? Detailed guidance was handed down by Lord Bingham CJ in *R v AM* [1998] 1 WLR 63; [1998] 1 All ER 874. In that case, the Court of Appeal held as follows. In a case where a sentence of detention under s 91 of the 2000 Act is available, the court should impose whatever sentence it thinks appropriate, even if the appropriate sentence is not much longer than the two year maximum detention and training order. In other words, the court should decide upon the right length of detention; if the appropriate period is two years or less, then the appropriate order is a detention and training order; if the appropriate period exceeds two years, then the appropriate sentence is one of detention under s 91.

In *R v AM* (above), the Court of Appeal also confirmed that, where a juvenile is charged with more than one offence, and s 91 of the 2000 Act applies to one or some, but not all, of those offences, the court may, when considering the seriousness of the offence(s) to which s 91 applies, consider the seriousness of the combination of all offences, since they are 'associated offences' within the meaning of s 161(1) of the Powers of Criminal Courts (Sentencing) Act 2000.

The decision to commit a juvenile for trial under s 24(1)(a) of the Magistrates' Courts Act 1980 is based on representations made by the prosecution and the defence. No evidence is called (*R v South Hackney Juvenile Court ex p RB and CB* (1983) 77 Cr App R 294).

It used to be the case that the youth court should not be told of any previous findings of guilt recorded against the juvenile (*R v Hammersmith Juvenile Court ex p O* (1987) 86 Cr App R 843); however, now that rule appears to have been relaxed in the case of adult defendants (see Chapter 3, 3.5.1), the same presumably applies to juveniles.

If the magistrates decide to proceed by way of summary trial in a case where committal for trial under s 24 of the Magistrates' Courts Act 1980 is possible (that is, it is a case where detention under s 91 of the Powers of Criminal Courts (Sentencing) Act 2000 is possible following conviction in the Crown Court), the prosecution may seek judicial review to quash that decision if it is unreasonable (*R v Inner London Youth Court ex p DPP* (1996) 161 JP 178).

If the youth court decides to try the case, it has power under s 25(2) of the Magistrates' Courts Act 1980 to terminate the trial and send the case to the Crown Court for trial. In *R v Herefordshire Youth Court ex p J* (1998) 95(20) LSG 34, the juvenile was charged with indecent assault (an offence for which he could have been committed for trial to the Crown Court with a view to a sentence of detention being imposed in the event of conviction under s 91 of the Powers of Criminal Courts (Sentencing) Act 2000). The charge was put and he pleaded guilty. At the next hearing, the justices purported to commit the juvenile for Crown Court trial. The Divisional Court held that the justices had the power to discontinue summary trial in favour of Crown Court trial only where a summary trial, in the sense of determining the defendant's guilt or innocence, had actually started. In the instant case, as a plea of guilty had been entered by a defendant who had been properly represented, no trial could be said to be in progress.

In *R v Fareham Youth Court and Morey ex p CPS* (1999) 163 JP 812, the defendant was charged with indecent assault and attempted rape. The magistrates decided that, although the offences fell within s 91 of the Powers of Criminal Courts (Sentencing) Act 2000, it would not be necessary to sentence the defendant under that section in the event of conviction and that he should therefore be tried summarily. The applicant then pleaded guilty to the indecent assault but not guilty to the attempted rape. At a later hearing, CPS asked a differently constituted bench to reconsider the question of the appropriate penalty in the event of conviction. The court concluded that all the offences should be dealt with by the Crown Court and transferred the case to the Crown Court. The defendant challenged the validity of that transfer. The Divisional Court held that once the justices had concluded that there should be a summary trial, the matter cannot be reopened as a result of new circumstances or because existing circumstances were not brought to the justices' attention at the earlier hearing. The court added that attempted rape ought to be tried in the Crown Court, not the youth court.

What if the juvenile is charged with several offences? Where a juvenile appears before a youth court charged with a number of offences and is committed to the Crown Court in respect of some of them, the youth court is not required to adjourn proceedings in respect of the other offences (s 10(3A) of the Magistrates' Courts Act 1980, inserted by s 47(5) of the Crime and Disorder Act 1998).

Section 24(1A) of the Magistrates' Courts Act 1980 (inserted by s 47(6) of the Crime and Disorder Act 1998 and confirming the effect of *R v Stephenson* [1999] 1 Cr App R 1) provides that where a magistrates' court commits a juvenile to the Crown Court for trial for an offence of homicide or for a 'grave' offence under s 91 of the Powers of Criminal Courts (Sentencing) Act 2000, the court may also commit him for trial for any other indictable offence with which he is charged at the same time even if the other indictable offence is not within the ambit of s 91, provided that the charges for both offences can properly be joined in the same indictment (see Chapter 8, 8.9 for details of the rules on joinder of counts in an indictment). So, to use the facts of *Stephenson* as an example: the juvenile was charged with five offences; three (indecent assault) fell within the scope s 91 but the other two (actual bodily harm) did not. Under s 24(1A), all five indictable offences can appear on the same indictment (so long as there is a sufficient link between the offences). Obviously, in the event of conviction, the Crown Court could only order long term detention in respect of those offences to which s 91 applied.

Even if a juvenile is tried and convicted in the Crown Court, the Crown Court is not obliged to pass a sentence of detention under s 91 of the 2000 Act. The court retains the power to deal with the offender in any way that the youth court could have done. It would generally be undesirable for the Crown Court to remit the case to the youth court for sentence under s 8 of the 2000 Act, since the youth court will already have expressed the view that the case is too serious for its powers (see *R v Allen and Lambert* (1999) 163 JP 841).

5.12.3   Joint charge with adult to be tried in Crown Court

The third situation where a juvenile may be tried in the Crown Court is where the juvenile is jointly charged with an adult. Where a juvenile and an adult are jointly charged, their first court appearance will be in an adult magistrates' court (not a youth court, which would be an inappropriate forum for a case involving an adult defendant).

Section 24(1)(b) of the Magistrates' Courts Act 1980 provides that a juvenile may be sent to the Crown Court to be tried jointly with an adult if:

- the juvenile is jointly charged with the adult (in practice this will include cases where one aids and abets the other, since both will usually be charged as principal offenders); and

- the adult is going to be tried in the Crown Court (either because the offence is triable only on indictment in the case of an adult or else the mode of trial hearing resulted in a decision in favour of trial on indictment rather than summary trial); and

- the justices decide that it is in the interests of justice that the juvenile should be tried in the Crown Court alongside the adult.

In deciding whether or not it is in the interests of justice to send the juvenile to the Crown Court under s 24(1)(b), the court has to balance what may well be conflicting interests. On one hand, it is desirable that there should be a joint trial, to avoid prosecution witnesses having to give their evidence twice, to avoid the risk of inconsistent verdicts, and to avoid the risk of disparity in the sentences which are passed in the event of conviction. On the other hand, a juvenile may well find appearing in the Crown Court an unduly traumatic experience.

Generally speaking, the younger the juvenile and the less serious the charge, the more reluctant the justices should be to send the juvenile to the Crown Court.

Also relevant are the likely plea of the juvenile and the degree of his involvement in the offence. If the juvenile is likely to plead guilty and it is accepted by the prosecution that he played only a minor role in the offence, it is likely to be appropriate to deal with him separately.

It should also be noted that if a juvenile is sent for trial in the Crown Court because he is jointly charged with an adult, he may also be tried in the Crown Court for any other indictable offence which is charged at the same time, provided that it arises out of circumstances which are the same as or connected with those giving rise to the joint charge (s 24(2) of the Magistrates' Courts Act 1980).

Normally, s 24(1)(b) of the Magistrates' Courts Acts 1980 will be relevant where a juvenile and an adult appear together in an adult magistrates' court. However, in *R v Coventry City Magistrates ex p M* [1992] Crim LR 810, it was held that the power to send a juvenile for trial in the Crown Court under s 24(1)(b) is not confined to an adult magistrates' court in which the adult and the juvenile appear together. A youth court can also exercise this power in a case where a juvenile before it is to be jointly indicted with an adult who has been sent for trial by an adult magistrates' court.

In *R v Tottenham Youth Court ex p Fawzy* [1998] 1 All ER 365, the Divisional Court held that, where an adult and juvenile are jointly charged (and so make their first appearance in an adult magistrates' court) and the justices, following an application under s 6(1) of the Magistrates' Courts Act 1980, hold that there is no case to answer against the adult, the adult magistrates' court should take a plea from the juvenile. If the offence is one to which s 91 of the Powers of Criminal Courts (Sentencing) Act 2000 applies, the adult magistrates' court must consider whether the case is one in which such a sentence might be justified. If so, they should commit the juvenile to the Crown Court for trial; if not, they should take a plea from the juvenile.

5.12.4   Special arrangements where a juvenile is tried in the Crown Court

Special arrangements have to be made for the Crown Court trial of young defendants in order to take account of the judgement of the European Court of Human Rights in *V v UK; T v UK* (1999) *The Times*, 17 December. These arrangements are set out in some detail in *Practice Note (Crown Court: Trial of Children and Young Persons)* [2000] 2 All ER 285. This says that the steps to be taken must take account of the age, maturity and development (intellectual and emotional) of the young defendant. The trial process should not expose the young defendant to avoidable intimidation, humiliation or distress. All possible steps should be taken to assist the young defendant to understand and participate in the proceedings. If a young defendant is indicted jointly with an adult defendant, the court should consider (at the plea and directions hearing) whether the young defendant should be tried alone; the court should ordinarily so order unless a joint trial would be in the interests of justice and would not unduly prejudice the welfare of the young defendant.

Special arrangements to be made for the trial of young defendants include:

- the young defendant should be allowed to visit the courtroom out of court hours to familiarise himself with it;

- appropriate reporting restrictions should be imposed;

- a courtroom should be used where all the participants are on the same, or almost the same, level;

- the young defendant should be allowed to sit with his family and in a place that permits easy informal communication with his lawyers;

- the proceedings should be explained to the young defendant in terms that he can understand, and it should be ensured that the trial is conducted in language which the young defendant can understand;

- a timetable should be adopted which takes full account of the young defendant's inability to concentrate for long periods (frequent and regular breaks may be needed);

- wigs and robes should normally not be worn;

- where the young defendant is in custody, security staff should not be in uniform;

- there should be no recognisable police presence in the courtroom save for good reason;

- attendance at the trial should be restricted to those with an immediate and direct interest in the outcome;

- the number of reporters attending the trial should be restricted (if necessary, arrangements should be made for the proceedings to be relayed to another room in the building to which the media would have unrestricted access).

5.12.5   Sentencing juveniles after Crown Court trial

If a juvenile is convicted at the Crown Court following joint trial with an adult, the Crown Court should remit the juvenile to the youth court for sentence unless it is undesirable to do so (s 8 of the Powers of Criminal Courts (Sentencing) Act 2000).

In *R v Lewis* (1984) 79 Cr App R 94, it was held that remission to the youth court would generally be undesirable because:

- the Crown Court judge is better informed on the facts of the case (having presided over the trial);
- there would otherwise be a risk of disparity in the sentences passed on the adult and the juvenile;
- there would be unnecessary duplication of proceedings (causing unnecessary delay and public expense).

5.12.6 Procedure where juvenile not to be tried in Crown Court

If the justices decide that it is not in the interests of justice to send the juvenile to the Crown Court, even though the adult co-accused is to be tried by the Crown Court, the charge will be put to the juvenile in the adult magistrates' court and a plea taken from him.

If the juvenile pleads guilty, the magistrates will consider whether their sentencing powers in respect of the juvenile are adequate. Those powers are to make any one or more of the following orders:

- absolute discharge (that is, no action is taken against the juvenile);
- conditional discharge (that is, no action is taken against the juvenile unless he re-offends);
- a fine (up to £1,000 for a juvenile who has attained the age of 14; up to £250 for one who has not (s 135 of the Powers of Criminal Courts (Sentencing) Act 2000));
- requiring the juvenile's parents to enter into a recognisance to keep proper control of him.

If these powers, which are contained in s 8(8) of the 2000 Act, are not sufficient, the justices will remit the juvenile to the youth court to be sentenced (s 8(6) of the 2000 Act).

If the juvenile pleads not guilty: the adult magistrates' court may try him under s 29(2) of the Magistrates' Courts Act 1980 but, in the absence of a good reason to the contrary (for example, the prosecution wish to offer no evidence), he should normally be remitted to the youth court for trial.

5.12.7 Trial of juvenile in adult magistrates' court – joint charge

Now, we turn to the one situation where a juvenile may be tried in an adult magistrates' court. Where the juvenile is jointly charged with an adult who is to be tried summarily (that is, it is a summary offence or else an either way offence where the adult defendant and the justices agree to summary trial):

- *If the adult pleads not guilty*

  The adult magistrates' court will ask the juvenile to plead (guilty or not guilty). If she pleads not guilty, the adult court must try her (s 46(1)(a) of the Children and Young Persons Act 1933). If he pleads or is found guilty, the magistrates must remit him to the youth court for sentence if the sentences which the adult court can impose (see above) are inappropriate.

- *If the adult pleads guilty*

  If the juvenile pleads not guilty, the adult magistrates' court may try him under s 29(2) of the Magistrates' Courts Act 1980 or remit him to the youth court for trial. Although the magistrates could theoretically try the juvenile (even though the adult has pleaded guilty, so that there will be no trial of the adult) in fact they are likely to remit him to the youth court for trial. There is little justification for trying a juvenile on his own in the magistrates' court. If the juvenile pleads guilty (or is found guilty), the adult court will remit him to the youth court if none of the sentences which the adult court can impose are appropriate.

- *Aiding and abetting, etc*

  If the juvenile is charged with aiding and abetting the adult or the adult is charged with aiding and abetting the juvenile, the adult magistrates' court has a discretion to try them both if they both plead not guilty (s 46(1)(b) of the Children and Young Persons Act 1933; s 18(a) of the Children and Young Persons Act 1963). If the adult and juvenile are charged with offences which arise out of the same circumstances and both plead not guilty, the adult magistrates' court may either try the juvenile or remit him to the youth court for trial (s 18(b) of the Children and Young Persons Act 1963). If the adult pleads guilty and the juvenile not guilty, the magistrates are likely to remit the juvenile to the youth court for trial; if the adult magistrates' court tries the juvenile and convicts him, she will be remitted to the youth court for sentence if the magistrates' sentencing powers (see above) are inappropriate.

Where one offender is charged with taking a conveyance without the owner's consent and another is charged with allowing himself to be carried in a conveyance which has been taken without the owner's consent, although these are in reality separate offences, they are to be regarded as jointly charged for the purposes of s 24 of the Magistrates' Courts Act 1980 (see *R v Peterborough Justices ex p Allgood* (1995) 159 JP 627).

5.12.8   Mistake in age

If an adult magistrates' court starts to deal with a defendant believing him to be 18 or over and it then transpires that he is a juvenile, the court can continue to hear the case or remit it to the youth court, whichever seems most appropriate in the circumstances (s 46(1)(c) of the Children and Young Persons Act 1933).

5.13   RELEVANT DATE – AGE

The youth court has jurisdiction if the accused is under 18 when the proceedings are begun (s 29 of the Children and Young Persons Act 1963). In *R v Uxbridge Youth Court ex p H* (1998) 162 JP 327, the defendant was 17 when arrested and charged, but by the time he made his first appearance at the youth court, he had turned 18. The Divisional Court held that (construing s 29) that proceedings are begun when the defendant first appears before the justices; it followed that the youth court did not have jurisdiction to deal with this defendant.

What happens if a 17 year old has his 18th birthday during the course of proceedings in the youth court?

The House of Lords held in *R v Islington North Juvenile Court ex p Daley* [1983] 1 AC 347; [1982] 2 All ER 974, which was followed in *R v Nottingham Justices ex p Taylor* [1992] QB 557; [1991] 4 All ER 860 (Divisional Court), that:

> ... the only appropriate date at which to determine whether an accused person has attained an age which entitles him to elect to be tried by jury is the date of his appearance before the court on the occasion when the court makes its decision as to mode of trial.

In other words (as there is no mode of trial hearing as such in the youth court) the date when the juvenile pleads guilty or not guilty is the relevant date.

Section 9(1) of the Powers of Criminal Courts (Sentencing) Act 2000 provides that where a juvenile appearing before a youth court subsequently attains the age of 18, the youth court may, at any time either before the start of the trial, or after conviction and before sentence, remit the person for trial or, as the case may be, sentence to the magistrates' court. There is no right of appeal against the order of remission (s 9(4)).

Section 9(2)(b) provides that the magistrates' court may deal with the case in any way in which it could have dealt with the case if all proceedings relating to the offence had taken place before it.

5.14   APPEALS FROM THE YOUTH COURT

For discussion on appeals from the youth court, see Chapter 6, which deals with appeals from magistrates' courts.

TABLE OF STATUTORY AND OTHER MATERIALS

JUVENILES – BAIL

CHILDREN AND YOUNG PERSONS ACT 1969

Section 23: Remands and committals to local authority accommodation

(1) Where:

   (a) a court remands a child or young person charged with or convicted of one or more offences or commits him for trial or sentence; and

   (b) he is not released on bail,

   the remand or committal shall be to local authority accommodation; and in the following provisions of this section, any reference (however expressed) to a remand shall be construed as including a reference to a committal.

(2) A court remanding a person to local authority accommodation shall designate the local authority who are to receive him; and that authority shall be:

   (a) in the case of a person who is being looked after by a local authority, that authority; and

   (b) in any other case, the local authority in whose area it appears to the court that he resides or the offence or one of the offences was committed.

   ...

(4) Subject to sub-sections (5) and 5(A) below, a court remanding a person to local authority accommodation may, after consultation with the designated authority, require that authority to comply with a security requirement, that is to say, a requirement that the person in question be placed and kept in secure accommodation [that is, accommodation which is provided in a community home, a voluntary home or a registered children's home for the purpose of restricting liberty, and approved by the Secretary of State].

(5) A court shall not impose a security requirement except in respect of a child who has attained the age of 12 or a young person [of age and/or sex as prescribed by the Secretary of State], and then only if:

   (a) he is charged with or has been convicted of a violent or sexual offence, or an offence punishable in the case of an adult with imprisonment for a term of 14 years or more; or

   (b) he has a recent history of absconding while remanded to local authority accommodation, and is charged with or has been convicted of an imprisonable offence alleged or found to have been committed while he was so remanded,

   and (in either case) the court is of opinion that only such a requirement would be adequate to protect the public from serious harm from him.

(5A) A court shall not impose a security requirement in respect of a child or young person who is not legally represented in the court unless:

(a) he was granted a right to representation funded by the Legal Services Commission as part of the Criminal Defence Service but the right was withdrawn because of his conduct; or

(b) having been informed of his right to apply for such representation and had the opportunity to do so. he refused or failed to apply.

(6) Where a court imposes a security requirement in respect of a person, it shall be its duty:

(a) to state in open court that it is of such opinion as is mentioned in sub-section (5) above; and

(b) to explain to him in open court and in ordinary language why it is of that opinion.

...

(7) A court remanding a person to local authority accommodation without imposing a security requirement may, after consultation with the designated authority, require that person to comply with any such conditions as could be imposed under section 3(6) of the Bail Act 1976 if he were then being granted bail.

(8) Where a court imposes on a person any such conditions as are mentioned in sub-section (7) above, it shall be its duty to explain to him in open court and in ordinary language why it is imposing those conditions ...

(9) A court remanding a person to local authority accommodation without imposing a security requirement may, after consultation with the designated authority, impose on that authority requirements:

(a) for securing compliance with any conditions imposed on that person under sub-section (7) above; or

(b) stipulating that he shall not be placed with a named person.

...

Section 23A: Liability to arrest for breaking conditions of remand

(1) A person who has been remanded or committed to local authority accommodation and in respect of whom conditions under sub-section (7) or (10) of section 23 of this Act have been imposed may be arrested without warrant by a constable if the constable has reasonable grounds for suspecting that that person has broken any of those conditions.

(2) A person arrested under sub-section (1) above:

(a) shall, except where he was arrested within 24 hours of the time appointed for him to appear before the court in pursuance of the remand or committal, be brought as soon as practicable and in any event within 24 hours after his arrest before a justice of the peace for the petty sessions area in which he was arrested; and

(b) in the said excepted case shall be brought before the court before which he was to have appeared.

In reckoning for the purposes of this sub-section any period of 24 hours, no account shall be taken of Christmas Day, Good Friday or any Sunday.

(3) A justice of the peace before whom a person is brought under sub-section (2) above:

(a) if of the opinion that that person has broken any condition imposed on him under sub-section (7) or (10) of section 23 of this Act shall remand him; and that section shall apply as if he was then charged with or convicted of the offence for which he had been remanded or committed;

(b) if not of that opinion shall remand him to the place to which he had been remanded or committed at the time of his arrest subject to the same conditions as those which had been imposed on him at that time.

JUVENILES: PLACE OF TRIAL

CHILDREN AND YOUNG PERSONS ACT 1933

Section 46: Assignment of certain matters to youth courts

(1) Subject as hereinafter provided, no charge against a child or young person, and no application whereof the hearing is by rules made under this section assigned to youth courts, shall be heard by a court of summary jurisdiction which is not a youth court:

Provided that:

(a) a charge made jointly against a child or young person and a person who has attained the age of 18 years shall be heard by a court of summary jurisdiction other than a youth court; and

(b) where a child or young person is charged with an offence, the charge may be heard by a court of summary jurisdiction which is not a youth court if a person who has attained the age of 18 years is charged at the same time with aiding, abetting, causing, procuring, allowing or permitting that offence; and

(c) where in the course of any proceedings before any court of summary jurisdiction other than a youth court, it appears that the person to whom the proceedings relate is a child or young person, nothing in this sub-section shall be construed as preventing the court, if it thinks fit so to do, from proceeding with the hearing and determination of those proceedings.

CHILDREN AND YOUNG PERSONS ACT 1963

Section 18: Jurisdiction of magistrates' courts in certain cases involving children and young persons

Notwithstanding section 46(1) of the Children and Young Persons Act 1933 a magistrates' court which is not a youth court may hear an information against a child or young person if he is charged:

(a) with aiding, abetting, causing, procuring, allowing or permitting an offence with which a person who has attained the age of 18 is charged at the same time; or

(b) with an offence arising out of circumstances which are the same as or connected with those giving rise to an offence with which a person who has attained the age of 18 is charged at the same time.

MAGISTRATES' COURTS ACT 1980

Section 24: Summary trial of information against child or young person for indictable offence

(1) Where a person under the age of 18 appears or is brought before a magistrates' court on an information charging him with an indictable offence other than homicide, he shall be tried summarily unless:

(a) the offence is such as is mentioned in sub-sections (1) or (2) of section 91 of the Powers of Criminal Courts (Sentencing) Act 2000 (under which young persons convicted on indictment of certain grave crimes may be sentenced to be detained for long periods) and the court considers that if he is found guilty of the offence it ought to be possible to sentence him in pursuance of sub-section (3) of that section; or

(b) he is charged jointly with a person who has attained the age of 18 years and the court considers it necessary in the interests of justice to commit them both for trial,

and accordingly in a case falling within paragraph (a) or (b) of this sub-section the court shall commit the accused for trial if either it is of opinion that there is sufficient evidence to put him on trial or it has power under section 6(2) above so to commit him without consideration of the evidence.

(1A) Where a magistrates' court:

(a) commits a person under the age of 18 for trial for an offence of homicide; or

(b) in a case falling within sub-section (1)(a) above, commits such a person for trial for an offence,

the court may also commit him for trial for any other indictable offence with which he is charged at the same time if the charges for both offences could be joined in the same indictment.

(2) Where, in a case falling within sub-section (1)(b) above, a magistrates' court commits a person under the age of 18 for trial for an offence with which he is charged jointly with a person who has attained that age, the court may also commit him for trial for any other indictable offence with which he is charged at the same time (whether jointly with the person who has attained that age or not) if the charges for both offences could be joined in the same indictment.

...

Section 29: Power of magistrates' court to remit a person under 18 for trial to a youth court in certain circumstances

(1) Where:

    (a) a person under the age of 18 ('the juvenile') appears or is brought before a magistrates' court other than a youth court on an information jointly charging him and one or more other persons with an offence; and

    (b) that other person, or any of those other persons, has attained that age,

sub-section (2) below shall have effect notwithstanding proviso (a) in section 46(1) of the Children and Young Persons Act 1933 (which would otherwise require the charge against the juvenile to be heard by a magistrates' court other than a youth court).

In the following provisions of this section 'the older accused' means such one or more of the accused as have attained the age of 18.

(2) If:

    (a) the court proceeds to the summary trial of the information in the case of both or all of the accused, and the older accused or each of the older accused pleads guilty; or

    (b) the court:

        (i) in the case of the older accused or each of the older accused, proceeds to inquire into the information as examining justices and either commits him for trial or discharges him; and

        (ii) in the case of the juvenile, proceeds to the summary trial of the information,

then, if in either situation the juvenile pleads not guilty, the court may before any evidence is called in his case remit him for trial to a youth court acting for the same place as the remitting court or for the place where he habitually resides.

(3) A person remitted to a youth court under sub-section (2) above shall be brought before and tried by a youth court accordingly.

(4) Where a person is so remitted to a youth court:

    (a) he shall have no right of appeal against the order of remission; and

    (b) the remitting court may subject to section 25 of the Criminal Justice and Public Order Act 1994 give such directions as appear to be necessary with respect to his custody or for his release on bail until he can be brought before the youth court.

...

YOUTH COURT PROCEDURE

CHILDREN AND YOUNG PERSONS ACT 1933

Section 47: Procedure in youth courts

(2) No person shall be present at any sitting of a youth court except:

    (a) members and officers of the court;

    (b) parties to the case before the court, their solicitors and counsel, and witnesses and other persons directly concerned in that case;

    (c) *bona fide* representatives of news gathering or reporting organisations;

    (d) such other persons as the court may specially authorise to be present.

Schedule 2

2   A justice shall not be qualified to sit as a member of a youth court unless he is a member of a youth court panel, that is to say, a panel of justices specially qualified to deal with juvenile cases.

YOUTH COURTS (CONSTITUTION) RULES 1954 (SI 1954/1711) (AS AMENDED)

2   Where a stipendiary magistrate exercises jurisdiction in a petty sessions area he shall be a member of the [youth court] panel therefor by virtue of his office.

12

(1) Subject to the following provisions of these Rules, each youth court shall consist of either:

    (a) a stipendiary magistrate sitting alone;

    (b) not more than three justices who shall include a man and a woman.

(2) If at any sitting of a youth court other than one constituted in accordance with paragraph (1)(a) of this rule no man or no woman is available owing to circumstances unforeseen when the justices to sit were chosen under rule 11 of these Rules, or if the only man or woman present cannot properly sit as a member of the court, and in any such case the other members of the

panel present think it inexpedient in the interests of justice for there to be an adjournment, the court may be constituted without a man or, as the case may be, without a woman.

(3) Nothing in paragraph (1) of this Rule shall be construed as requiring a [youth court] to include both a man and a woman in any case in which a single justice has by law jurisdiction to act.

ATTENDANCE OF PARENT/GUARDIAN

CHILDREN AND YOUNG PERSONS ACT 1933

Section 34A: Attendance at court of parent or guardian

(1) Where a child or young person is charged with an offence or is for any other reason brought before a court, the court:

(a) may in any case; and

(b) shall in the case of a child or a young person who is under the age of 16 years,

require a person who is a parent or guardian of his to attend at the court during all the stages of the proceedings, unless and to the extent that the court is satisfied that it would be unreasonable to require such attendance, having regard to the circumstances of the case.

REPORTING RESTRICTIONS

CHILDREN AND YOUNG PERSONS ACT 1933

Section 39: Power to prohibit publication of certain matters in newspapers[2]

(1) In relation to any proceedings in any court ... the court may direct that:

(a) no newspaper report of the proceedings shall reveal the name, address, or school, or include any particulars calculated to lead to the identification, of any child or young person concerned in the proceedings, either as being the person by or against or in respect of whom the proceedings are taken, or as being a witness therein;

---

2   This section, with necessary modifications, applies to sound and television broadcasts: s 57(4) of the Children and Young Persons Act 1963.

(b) no picture shall be published in any newspaper as being or including a picture of any child or young person so concerned in the proceedings as aforesaid,

except in so far (if at all) as may be permitted by the direction of the court.

Section 49: Restrictions on reports of proceedings in which children or young persons are concerned

(1) The following prohibitions apply (subject to sub-section (5) below) in relation to any proceedings to which this sections applies, that is to say:

(a) no report shall be published which reveals the name, address or school of any child or young person concerned in the proceedings or includes any particulars likely to lead to the identification of any child or young person concerned in the proceedings; and

(b) no picture shall be published or included in a programme service as being or including a picture of any child or young person concerned in the proceedings.

(2) The proceedings to which this section applies are:

(a) proceedings in a youth court;

(b) proceedings on appeal from a youth court (including proceedings by way of case stated);

(c) proceedings under section 15 or 16 of the Children and Young Persons Act 1969 (proceedings for varying or revoking supervision orders); and

(d) proceedings on appeal from a magistrates' court arising out of proceedings under section 15 or 16 of that Act.

(3) The reports to which this section applies are reports in a newspaper and reports included in a programme service; and similarly as respects pictures.

(4) For the purposes of this section a child or young person is 'concerned' in any proceedings whether as being the person against or in respect of whom the proceedings are taken or as being a witness in the proceedings.

[(4A) If a court is satisfied that it is in the public interest to do so, it may, in relation to a child or young person who has been convicted of an offence, by order dispense to any specified extent with the requirements of this section in relation to any proceedings before it to which this section applies by virtue of sub-section (2)(a) or (b) above, being proceedings relating to:

(a) the prosecution or conviction of the offender for the offence;

(b) the manner in which he, or his parent or guardian, should be dealt with in respect of the offence;

(c) the enforcement, amendment, variation, revocation or discharge of any order made in respect of the offence;

(d) where an attendance centre order is made in respect of the offence, the enforcement of any rules made under section 16(3) of the Criminal Justice Act 1982; or

(e) where a secure training order is so made, the enforcement of any requirements imposed under section 3(7) of the Criminal Justice and Public Order Act 1994.

(4B) A court shall not exercise its power under sub-section (4A) above without:

(a) affording the parties to the proceedings an opportunity to make representations;

(b) taking into account any representations which are duly made.][3]

(5) Subject to sub-section (7) below, a court may, in relation to proceedings before it to which this section applies, by order dispense to any specified extent with the requirements of this section in relation to a child or young person who is concerned in the proceedings if it is satisfied:

(a) that it is appropriate to do so for the purpose of avoiding injustice to the child or young person; or

(b) that, as respects a child or young person to whom this paragraph applies who is unlawfully at large, it is necessary to dispense with those requirements for the purpose of apprehending him and bringing him before a court or returning him to the place in which he was in custody.

(6) Paragraph (b) of sub-section (5) above applies to any child or young person who is charged with or has been convicted of:

(a) a violent offence;

(b) a sexual offence; or

(c) an offence punishable in the case of a person aged 21 or over with imprisonment for 14 years or more.

...

MAGISTRATES' COURTS (CHILDREN AND YOUNG PERSONS) RULES 1992 (SI 1992/2071)

5   *Assistance in conducting case*

(1) Except where the relevant minor is legally represented, the court shall allow his parent or guardian to assist him in conducting his case.

...

6   *Duty of court to explain nature of proceedings, etc*

(1) The court shall explain to the relevant minor the nature of the proceedings and, where he is charged with an offence, the substance of the charge.

(2) The explanation shall be given in simple language suitable to his age and understanding.

---

3   Sub-sections (4A) and (4B) were added by s 45 of the Crime (Sentences) Act 1997.

7   *Duty of court to take plea to charge*

Where the relevant minor is charged with an offence the court shall, after giving the explanation required by rule 6, ask him whether he pleads guilty or not guilty to the charge.

8   *Evidence in support of charge or application*

(1) Where:

    (a) the relevant minor is charged with an offence and does not plead guilty; or

    (b) the proceedings are [variation or discharge of a supervision order; breach of requirements of, or revocation or amendment of, a probation order, community service order, combination order or curfew order; or discharge or variation of an attendance centre order],

the court shall hear the witnesses in support of the charge or, as the case may be, the application.

(2) Except where:

    (a) the proceedings are [variation or discharge of a supervision order; breach of requirements of, or revocation or amendment of, a probation order, community service order, combination order or curfew order; or discharge or variation of an attendance centre order]; and

    (b) the relevant minor is the applicant,

each witness may at the close of his evidence-in-chief be cross-examined by or on behalf of the relevant minor.

(3) If in any case where the relevant minor is not legally represented or assisted as provided by rule 5, the relevant minor, instead of asking questions by way of cross-examination, makes assertions, the court shall then put to the witness such questions as it thinks necessary on behalf of the relevant minor and may for this purpose question the relevant minor in order to bring out or clear up any point arising out of such assertions.

9   *Evidence in reply*

If it appears to the court after hearing evidence in support of the charge or application that a *prima facie* case is made out, the relevant minor shall, if he is not the applicant and is not legally represented, be told that he may give evidence or address the court, and the evidence of any witnesses shall be heard.

SENTENCING JUVENILES

MAGISTRATES' COURTS ACT 1980

Section 24: Summary trial of information against child or young person for indictable offence

(3) If on trying a person summarily in pursuance of sub-section (1) above, the court finds him guilty, it may impose a fine not exceeding £1,000 or may exercise the same powers as it could have exercised if he had been found guilty of an offence for which, but for section 89(1) of the said Act of 2000, it could have sentenced him to imprisonment for a term not exceeding:

    (a) the maximum term of imprisonment for the offence on conviction on indictment; or

    (b) six months,

    whichever is the less.

(4) In relation to a person under the age of 14 sub-section (3) above shall have effect as if for the words '£1,000' there were substituted the words '£250'.

MAGISTRATES' COURTS (CHILDREN AND YOUNG PERSONS) RULES 1992 (SI 1992/2071)

10 *Procedure after finding against minor*

(1) This rule applies where:

    (a) the relevant minor is found guilty of an offence, whether after a plea of guilty or otherwise; or

    (b) in proceedings [for variation or discharge of a supervision order; breach of requirements of, or revocation or amendment of, a probation order, community service order, combination order or curfew order; or discharge or variation of an attendance centre order] the court is satisfied that the case for the applicant:

        (i) if the relevant minor is not the applicant, has been made out; or

        (ii) if the relevant minor is the applicant, has not been made out.

(2) Where this rule applies:

    (a) the relevant minor and his parent or guardian, if present, shall be given an opportunity of making a statement;

    (b) the court shall take into consideration all available information as to the general conduct; home surroundings, school record and medical history of the relevant minor and, in particular, shall take into consideration such information as aforesaid which is provided in pursuance of section 9 of the Children and Young Persons Act 1969;[4]

(c) if such information as aforesaid is not fully available, the court shall consider the desirability of adjourning the proceedings for such inquiry as may be necessary;

(d) any written report of a probation officer, local authority, local education authority, educational establishment or registered medical practitioner may be received and considered by the court without being read aloud; and

(e) if the court considers it necessary in the interests of the relevant minor, it may require him or his parent or guardian, if present, to withdraw from the court.

(3) The court shall arrange for copies of any written report before the court to be made available to:

(a) the legal representative, if any, of the relevant minor;

(b) any parent or guardian of the relevant minor who is present at the hearing; and

(c) the relevant minor, except where the court otherwise directs on the ground that it appears to it impracticable to disclose the report having regard to his age and understanding or undesirable to do so having regard to potential serious harm which might thereby be suffered by him.

(4) In any case in which the relevant minor is not legally represented and where a report which has not been made available to him in accordance with a direction under paragraph (3)(c) has been considered without being read aloud in pursuance of paragraph (2)(d) or where he or his parent or guardian has been required to withdraw from the court in pursuance of paragraph (2)(e), then:

(a) the relevant minor shall be told the substance of any part of the information given to the court bearing on his character or conduct which the court considers to be material to the manner in which the case should be dealt with unless it appears to it impracticable so to do having regard to his age and understanding; and

(b) the parent or guardian of the relevant minor, if present, shall be told the substance of any part of such information which the court considers to

---

4   Section 9(1) of the Children and Young Persons Act 1969 provides that 'where a local authority or a local education authority ... are notified that ... proceedings [for an offence alleged to have been committed by a [child or] young person] are being brought, it shall be the duty of the authority, unless they are of opinion that it is unnecessary to do so, to make such investigations and provide the court before which the proceedings are heard with such information relating to the home surroundings, school record, health and character of the person in respect of whom the proceedings are brought as appear to the authority likely to assist the court'. Section 9(2) provides that 'if the court mentioned in sub-section (1) of this section requests the authority aforesaid to make investigations and provide information or to make further investigations and provide further information relating to the matters aforesaid, it shall be the duty of the authority to comply with the request'.

be material as aforesaid and which has reference to his character or conduct or to the character, conduct, home surroundings or health of the relevant minor,

and if such person, having been told the substance of any part of such information, desires to produce further evidence with reference thereto, the court, if it thinks the further evidence would be material, shall adjourn the proceedings for the production thereof and shall, if necessary in the case of a report, require the attendance at the adjourned hearing of the person who made the report.

YOUNG OFFENDERS – REMISSION FOR SENTENCE

POWERS OF CRIMINAL COURTS (SENTENCING) ACT 2000

Section 8: Power and duty to remit young offenders to youth courts for sentence

(1) Sub-section (2) below applies where a child or young person (that is to say, any person aged under 18) is convicted by or before any court of an offence other than homicide.

(2) The court may and, if it is not a youth court, shall unless satisfied that it would be undesirable to do so, remit the case:

(a) if the offender was committed for trial or sent to the Crown Court for trial under section 51 of the Crime and Disorder Act 1998, to a youth court acting for the place where he was committed for trial or sent to the Crown Court for trial;

(b) in any other case, to a youth court acting either for the same place as the remitting court or for the place where the offender habitually resides;

but in relation to a magistrates' court other than a youth court this sub-section has effect subject to sub-section (6) below.

(3) Where a case is remitted under sub-section (2) above, the offender shall be brought before a youth court accordingly, and that court may deal with him in any way in which it might have dealt with him if he had been tried and convicted by that court.

(3) A court by which an order remitting a case to a youth court is made under sub-section (2) above:

(a) may, subject to section 25 of the Criminal Justice and Public Order Act 1994 (restrictions on granting bail), give such directions as appear to be necessary with respect to the custody of the offender or for his release on bail until he can be brought before the youth court; and

(b) shall cause to be transmitted to the justices' chief executive for the youth court a certificate setting out the nature of the offence and stating:

(i) that the offender has been convicted of the offence; and

(ii) that the case has been remitted for the purpose of being dealt with under the preceding provisions of this section.

(5) Where a case is remitted under sub-section (2) above, the offender shall have no right of appeal against the order of remission, but shall have the same right of appeal against any order of the court to which the case is remitted as if he had been convicted by that court.

(6) Without prejudice to the power to remit any case to a youth court which is conferred on a magistrates' court other than a youth court by sub-sections (1) and (2) above, where such a magistrates' court convicts a child or young person of an offence it must exercise that power unless the case falls within sub-section (7) or (8) below.

(7) The case falls within this sub-section if the court would, were it not so to remit the case, be required by section 16(2) below to refer the offender to a youth offender panel (in which event the court may, but need not, so remit the case).

(8) The case falls within this sub-section if it does not fall within sub-section (7) above but the court is of the opinion that the case is one which can properly be dealt with by means of:

(a) an order discharging the offender absolutely or conditionally; or

(b) an order for the payment of a fine; or

(c) an order (under section 150 below) requiring the offender's parent or guardian to enter into a recognizance to take proper care of him and exercise proper control over him,

with or without any other order that the court has power to make when absolutely or conditionally discharging an offender.

...

Section 9: Power of youth court to remit offender who attains age of 18 to magistrates' court other than youth court for sentence

(1) Where a person who appears or is brought before a youth court charged with an offence subsequently attains the age of 18, the youth court may, at any time after conviction and before sentence, remit him for sentence to a magistrates' court (other than a youth court) acting for the same petty sessions area as the youth court.

(2) Where an offender is remitted under sub-section (1) above, the youth court shall adjourn proceedings in relation to the offence, and:

(a) section 128 of the Magistrates' Courts Act 1980 (remand in custody or on bail) and all other enactments, whenever passed, relating to remand or the granting of bail in criminal proceedings shall have effect, in relation to the youth court's power or duty to remand the offender on that adjournment, as if any reference to the court to or before which the person remanded is to be brought or appear after remand were a reference to the court to which he is being remitted; and

(b) subject to sub-section (3) below, the court to which the offender is remitted ('the other court') may deal with the case in any way in which it would have power to deal with it if all proceedings relating to the offence which took place before the youth court had taken place before the other court.

(3) Where an offender is remitted under sub-section (1) above, section 8(6) above (duty of adult magistrates' court to remit young offenders to youth court for sentence) shall not apply to the court to which he is remitted.

(4) Where an offender is remitted under sub-section (1) above he shall have no right of appeal against the order of remission (but without prejudice to any right of appeal against an order made in respect of the offence by the court to which he is remitted).

(5) In this section:

(a) 'enactment' includes an enactment contained in any order, regulation or other instrument having effect by virtue of an Act; and

(b) 'bail in criminal proceedings' has the same meaning as in the Bail Act 1976.

CHAPTER 6

APPEALS FROM MAGISTRATES' COURTS AND YOUTH COURTS

6.1   INTRODUCTION

In this chapter, we look at the mechanisms which exist for appealing against the decisions of a magistrates' court or a youth court. We examine the appellate jurisdiction of the Crown Court (completely different to its jurisdiction as a court of first instance when defendants are tried on indictment) and we also consider the supervisory jurisdiction which the High Court exercises over magistrates' courts and youth courts by means of the appeal by way of case stated and by means of judicial review.

Thus, there are three forms to appeal against the decisions of a magistrates' court or a youth court.

6.2   APPEAL TO CROWN COURT

The most common form of appeal from the magistrates' court and youth court is to the Crown Court. This is governed by s 108 of the Magistrates' Courts Act 1980. If the defendant pleaded guilty, he can appeal against sentence only (unless the plea was equivocal – see 6.2.5 below). If he pleaded not guilty, he can appeal against conviction and/or sentence.

6.2.1   Procedure

The procedure for appeal is as follows:
- notice of appeal is given to the clerk of the magistrates' court and to the prosecutor within 21 days of passing of sentence (r 7 of the Crown Court Rules 1982);
- leave to appeal is not required;
- grounds of appeal need not be given;
- the Crown Court can extend the 21 day period but will take account of the merits of the case as well as the reason for the delay if asked to extend the time limit (r 7(5), (6)).

The 21 day period for giving notice of appeal runs from the date when sentence is passed even if the appeal is against conviction only.

6.2.2   Bail pending appeal

Where the defendant is given a custodial sentence, bail pending appeal may be granted by the magistrates who passed sentence (though there is no presumption in favour of bail as s 4 of the Bail Act 1976 does not apply) (s 113 of the Magistrates' Courts Act 1980). If the magistrates do not grant bail, the Crown Court may do so (under s 81(1) of the Supreme Court Act 1981), or the defendant could apply to a High Court judge in chambers under s 22(1) of the Criminal Justice Act 1967. On bail, see Chapter 2.

The strongest argument that can be advanced in support of bail pending the hearing of the appeal is that a short sentence may have been served before the appeal is heard.

6.2.3   The hearing

The appeal is heard by a circuit judge or recorder and at least two lay justices.

An appeal against conviction takes the form of a complete re-hearing (so the procedure is the same as the trial in the magistrates' court or youth court) (s 79(3) of the Supreme Court Act 1981).

Because an appeal against conviction is a re-hearing, the parties are not limited to evidence which was called at the original trial. This has the important consequence that either party can call witnesses who were not called in the magistrates' court trial, or refrain from calling witnesses who did give evidence in the magistrates' court. Note, however, that the Crown Court cannot amend the information on which the appellant was convicted (*Garfield v Maddocks* [1974] QB 7; [1973] 2 All ER 303); *R v Swansea Crown Court ex p Stacey* [1990] RTR 183).

An appeal against sentence similarly mirrors the sentencing procedure in the magistrates' court or youth court, with the prosecution summarising the facts and the defence making a plea in mitigation. In *R v Swindon Crown Court ex p Murray* (1998) 162 JP 36, the Divisional Court held that, when dealing with an appeal against sentence, the Crown Court should not ask itself whether the sentence was within the discretion of the magistrates (the test which would be appropriate in judicial review) but should consider whether, in the light of all the matters which the Crown Court had heard, the sentence passed by the magistrates was the correct one.

In *Bussey v Director of Public Prosecutions* [1999] 1 Cr App R (S) 125, the defendant pleaded guilty to the offence of driving whilst disqualified. He maintained that he only drove because his wife had been taken ill and he had to take her to hospital. The Crown disputed this version of events, but the magistrates decided (without hearing evidence) to accept the defendant's version. The defendant felt that the sentence imposed was nonetheless excessive and he appealed to the Crown Court. It was held that, since the Crown Court is not bound by findings of fact made by a magistrates' court in a way that could limit the Crown Court's sentencing powers, where a defendant appeals against sentence to the Crown Court, the court is entitled to decide the appeal on a different factual basis from that accepted by the magistrates' court. However, where the Crown Court rejects the view taken by the magistrates' court, the court should make the position plain to the appellant and give him an opportunity, under the *Newton* principle (see Chapter 12, 12.1.1), to challenge the factual basis adopted by the court.

6.2.4   Decision

The decision of the Crown Court is a majority decision, so the lay justices can out-vote the judge. The lay justices must, however, accept any decisions on questions of law made by the judge.

Where the Crown Court dismisses an appeal against conviction, the judge must give reasons; judicial review can be sought to compel the judge to do so if necessary (*R v Warwick Crown Court ex p Patel* [1992] COD 143; *R v Harrow Crown Court ex p Dave* [1994] 1 WLR 98; [1994] 1 All ER 315). In *R v Snaresbrook Crown Court ex p Input Management Ltd* (1999) 163 JP 533, the Divisional Court defined the obligation to give reasons: the reasons given by the Crown Court should enable the defendant: (i) to see the nature of the criminality found to exist by the Court; and (ii) to consider properly whether there are grounds for a further appeal to the Divisional Court by way of case stated.

6.2.5   Equivocal pleas

If the plea of guilty was 'equivocal', the defendant can appeal against conviction despite having pleaded guilty. There are two main types of equivocal plea:

- The plea which is equivocal in court (that is, becomes equivocal because of something said prior to the passing of sentence).

   This will be the case if either:

   (i)   when the charge is put, the defendant says 'Guilty but ...', that is, some form of words raising a defence, for example, 'guilty of theft but I thought the property was mine'; or

   (ii)   when the charge is put, the defendant says only 'Guilty' but this straightforward plea is followed by a plea in mitigation which raises a defence and so is inconsistent with the guilty plea (for example, *R v Durham Quarter Sessions ex p Virgo* [1952] 2 QB 1; [1952] 1 All ER 466).

- The plea which is made equivocal not because of anything the defendant says in court but because the defendant pleaded guilty as a direct result of threats from a third party. Then, at some time after the passing of sentence, the defendant alleges that he only pleaded guilty as a result of duress and now maintains that he is innocent (for example, *R v Huntingdon Crown Court ex p Jordan* [1981] QB 857; [1981] 2 All ER 872).

In the case of the first type of equivocal plea, the problem should be dealt with at the original hearing. The charge should be put again by the magistrates' court once the relevant law has been explained to the defendant. If the plea remains equivocal, a not guilty plea should be entered by the court on the defendant's behalf.

If this does not occur, or if the plea is equivocal because of duress, the defendant should apply to the Crown Court to declare the plea equivocal. If the Crown Court decides that the plea was indeed equivocal, it will remit the case to the magistrates' court for trial.

Provided the Crown Court conducts a proper inquiry into what happened in the magistrates' court (the clerk or the chairman of the bench which convicted the defendant may have to supply an affidavit to assist the Crown Court in that inquiry) a direction from the Crown Court regarding remission for trial is binding on the magistrates' court (*R v Plymouth Justices ex p Hart* [1986] QB 950; [1986] 2 All ER 452).

There are no other grounds for going behind a plea of guilty and so no other cases where a defendant can appeal to the Crown Court after pleading guilty (*R v Marylebone Justices ex p Westminster London Borough Council* [1971] 1 WLR 567; [1971] 1 All ER 1025). It is therefore not sufficient for the defendant merely to show that he regrets pleading guilty and that he has an arguable defence.

6.2.6   Powers of Crown Court

Section 48 of the Supreme Court Act 1981 allows the Crown Court to:

- quash the conviction;
- remit the case to the magistrates' court (for example, in the case of an equivocal plea);
- vary the sentence imposed by the magistrates (this includes the power to increase the sentence, but not beyond the maximum sentence which the magistrates' court could have passed).

If the defendant appeals against part of the decision of the magistrates' court, every aspect of the magistrates' decision can be reconsidered by the Crown Court (s 48(2) of the Supreme Court Act). For example:

- even if the defendant appeals only against conviction, the Crown Court can still vary the sentence;

- if the defendant was convicted of two offences and appeals against only one conviction the Crown Court could allow the appeal but vary the sentence for the other offence;

- if the defendant was convicted by the magistrates of one offence but acquitted of another and he now appeals against the conviction, the Crown Court could convict the defendant of the offence of which the magistrates' court acquitted him.

6.2.7   Abandonment of appeal

Under rule 11 of the Crown Court Rules 1982, the appellant may abandon his appeal by giving written notice to the magistrates' court, the Crown Court and the prosecution. Notice should be given at least three days before the appeal is due to be heard. It is open to the Crown Court to allow an appeal to be abandoned even if these requirements are not satisfied. In *R v Gloucester Crown Court ex p Betteridge* (1997) *The Times*, 4 August, the Divisional Court held that once the Crown Court gives leave to an appellant to abandon his appeal from the decision of the magistrates' court, the Crown Court does not have the power to increase the sentence imposed by the magistrates.

6.2.8   Further appeal from Crown Court

The decision of the Crown Court on an appeal from a magistrates' court or youth court can only be challenged by means of an appeal to the Divisional Court by way of case stated or judicial review (see below). There is no appeal to the Court of Appeal.

6.3   APPEAL TO THE DIVISIONAL COURT BY WAY OF CASE STATED

This is possible under s 111 of the Magistrates' Courts Act 1980. Unlike the appeal to the Crown Court, it is available to the prosecution as well as the defence. It applies where the decision of the magistrates' court or youth court is:

- wrong in law; or

- in excess of jurisdiction.

It only applies where there has been a final determination of the case in the magistrates' court, so it excludes, for example, committal proceedings and the decision to commit for sentence (*Streames v Copping* [1985] QB 920; [1985] 2 All ER 122 and *Loade v DPP* [1990] 1 QB 1052; [1990] 1 All ER 36).

In *McKnight v Sheppard* [1999] 1 WLR 1333; [1999] 3 All ER 491, it was held that on an appeal by way of case stated a party is not entitled to take a new point the decision of which might be affected by evidence which could have been, but was not, adduced before the tribunal of fact. Similarly, where a defendant has been convicted by the magistrates and appeals to the Divisional Court, it is not possible to raise the issue that certain prosecution evidence should have been excluded under s 78 of the Police and Criminal Evidence Act 1984 if the defence had not asked the magistrates to exclude the evidence under s 78. In other words, the matter cannot be raised for the first time in the Divisional Court (*Braham v DPP* (1995) 159 JP 527).

The appellant makes an application to the magistrates to state a case. This application must be made within 21 days of conviction (or sentence, if later) identifying the question of law or jurisdiction at issue. This 21 day period cannot be extended (*Michael v Gowland* [1977] 1 WLR 296; [1977] 2 All ER 328; *R v Clerkenwell Magistrates' Court ex p DPP* [1984] QB 821). It should be noted, however, that where the final termination of proceedings is a decision on an application for costs, the 21 day time limit for asking the magistrates to state a case under s 111 of the Magistrates' Courts Act 1980 begins to run from the date of the decision on costs (*Liverpool City Council v Worthington* [1999] EHLR 225).

6.3.1   Refusal to state a case

The justices may refuse to state a case if they regard the application as frivolous and issue a certificate to that effect (s 111(5) of the Magistrates' Courts Act 1980). If they do refuse to state a case, the appellant can apply for judicial review of this refusal (s 111(6)).

The test of whether a request to state a case is frivolous is whether the application raises an arguable point of law (*R v City of London Justices ex p Ocansey* (1995), unreported, and *R v East Cambridgeshire Justices ex p Stephenson* (1995), unreported).

So, in *R v Mildenhall Magistrates' Court ex p Forest Heath District Council* (1997) 161 JP 401, it was held that the word 'frivolous' in this context means that the justices consider the application to be 'futile, misconceived, hopeless, or academic'. The court went on say that such a conclusion will be reached only rarely: it is not enough that the justices consider that their original decision was correct. Furthermore, where justices do refuse to state a case, they should give brief reasons explaining why they have done so. The court went on to say that a finding of fact may be challenged if it is perverse (see *Bracegirdle v Oxley* [1947] KB 349, p 353, *per* Lord Goddard CJ), for example, if it has no evidential foundation. However, a decision (even if mistaken) is not perverse if the justices prefer A's evidence to that of B and resolve the question of fact on the basis of A's evidence.

Where the magistrates refuse to state a case and the appellant seeks judicial review of that refusal, the usual remedy is for the Divisional Court to quash the refusal to state a case, so the magistrates have to state a case. However, it is open to the Divisional Court, when considering the application for judicial review of the refusal to state a case, to regard the affidavit evidence as the case stated (see *R v Reigate Justices ex p Counsell* (1983) 148 JP 193) and to treat the application for judicial review as if it were an appeal by way of case stated. In this way, the Divisional Court can, for example, quash a conviction without waiting for the case to go back to the magistrates to state a case (see, for example, *R v Ealing Justices ex p Woodman* [1994] Crim LR 372).

Furthermore, s 114 of the Magistrates' Courts Act 1980 empowers the magistrates to require the appellant to enter into a recognisance (that is, promise to pay a specified sum of money if the condition is not complied with) to pursue the appeal without delay. If this power is invoked, a case will not be stated until the appellant has entered into a recognisance.

The fact that the applicant's defence is publicly funded does not, of itself, mean that the justices cannot require him to enter in a recognizance; the defendant must satisfy the court that he has no means of raising sufficient capital to comply with the condition (*R v Croydon Magistrates' Court ex p Morgan* (1997) 161 JP 169).

In *R v Crown Court at Blackfriars ex p Sunworld Ltd* [2000] 2 All ER 837, the Divisional Court gave guidance on the approach to be adopted by that court in a case where the magistrates' court (or indeed the Crown Court, on appeal from the magistrates' court) has refused to state a case. Where a magistrates' court or Crown Court refuses to state a case, the aggrieved party should, without delay, apply for permission to bring judicial review (either seeking mandatory order to require the court to state a case or a quashing order to quash the order sought to be appealed). If the court below has already given a reasoned judgement containing all the necessary findings of fact and/or has explained its refusal to state a case in terms which clearly raise the true point of law in issue, the single judge should, if he thinks the point properly arguable, grant permission for judicial review which directly challenges the order complained of, thereby avoiding the need for a case to be stated at all. If the court below has stated a case but in respect of some questions only, the better course may be to apply for the case stated to be amended, unless there already exists sufficient material to enable the Divisional Court to deal with all the properly arguable issues in the case. The Divisional Court will adopt whatever course involves the fewest additional steps and the least expense, delay and duplication of proceedings. Whether (as in *R v Thames Magistrates Court ex p Levy* (1997) *The Times*, 17 July) it will be possible to proceed at once to a substantive determination of the issues must inevitably depend in part upon whether all interested parties are represented and prepared and on the availability of court time.

6.3.2   Statement of case

The statement of the case should set out:

- the charge(s) being tried by the magistrates;
- the facts as found by the magistrates (but not the evidence upon which those findings of fact were based, unless the basis of the appeal is that the decision of the justices was entirely unsupported by the evidence which they had heard);
- any submissions (including names of any authorities cited in argument) made to the magistrates by the prosecution and defence (see *DPP v Kirk* [1993] COD 99), and the magistrates' decision on those submissions;
- the question(s) for determination by the High Court.

The magistrates' clerk prepares a draft case and sends it to the prosecution and defence for comment. A properly drafted question should not be altered without the party who framed the original question being given the opportunity to commit on the changes (*R v Waldie* (1995) 159 JP 514). The final version (amended in the light of any comments made by prosecution or defence and signed by the clerk or by two of the magistrates whose decision is under appeal) is sent to the appellant.

The appellant should lodge the stated case at the Crown Office (in the Royal Courts of Justice) within 10 days of receiving it from the clerk (r 78 of the Magistrates' Courts Rules 1981).

The standard form for the statement of a case appears at the end of this chapter.

It should be borne in mind that when magistrates are asked to state a case, it is not open to them to put forward reasons why the respondent should not be able to challenge their decision where those reasons were not part of their original decision (*Kent County Council v Curtis* (1998) 95(25) LSG 34).

6.3.3   Bail pending appeal

If the defendant was given a custodial sentence, the magistrates may grant bail pending appeal under s 113 of the Magistrates' Courts Act 1980. If the magistrates refuse, the defendant can apply to a High Court judge in chambers under s 37(1)(b) of the Criminal Justice Act 1948.

6.3.4   The hearing

The appeal is heard by a Divisional Court (that is, two or more High Court judges in open court). If a two judge court hears the appeal but cannot agree on the outcome, the appeal fails (*Flannagan v Shaw* [1920] 3 KB 96).

No evidence is heard. The appeal takes the form of legal argument based on the facts stated in the case; no evidence is called, and so there are no witnesses.

6.3.5 Powers of the Divisional Court

The powers of the Divisional Court on an appeal by way of case stated are contained in s 112 of the Magistrates' Courts Act 1980.

Where the appellant was convicted, the Divisional Court may replace the conviction with an acquittal.

Where the appellant was acquitted after a full trial (that is, not after a successful submission of no case to answer at the close of the prosecution case), the Divisional Court may remit the case back to the magistrates' court with a direction to convict and proceed to sentence (or if it is plain what sentence should be passed, the Divisional Court may itself convict and proceed to sentence the appellant).

In some cases, it would not be fair to the prosecution simply to direct an acquittal; and it would breach the rules of natural justice to replace an acquittal which took place before the defence case had been heard with a conviction. Thus in some cases, a re-trial will be appropriate.

The Divisional Court cannot quash only part of an order and leave the rest intact. So, in *R v Old Street Magistrates ex p Spencer* (1994) *The Times*, 8 November, a costs order for £930 had been made. The Divisional Court felt that £150–250 was the appropriate bracket. However, the Divisional Court lacked the power to substitute a different amount. All it could do was to quash the original order and remit the case to the magistrates.

In *Griffith v Jenkins* [1992] 2 AC 76; [1992] 1 All ER 65, the House of Lords held that the Divisional Court had power to remit the case for a re-hearing before the same or a different bench of magistrates. Thus, it does not matter if the original court cannot be reconstituted for some reason (for example, one of the justices has retired or died). A re-hearing will only be ordered if a fair trial is still possible given the lapse of time since the alleged offence.

6.3.6 Abandonment of appeal

An appellant who has made an appeal by way of case stated is entitled to withdraw that appeal without the leave of the High Court (*Collett v Bromsgrove District Council* (1996) 160 JP 593).

6.3.7 Effect on right of appeal to Crown Court

The making of an application to the magistrates to state a case removes the defendant's right to appeal to the Crown Court (s 111(4) of the Magistrates' Courts Act 1980). It is therefore tactically wise to appeal to the Crown Court first and, if that appeal is not allowed, to appeal against the decision of the Crown Court to the Divisional Court.

6.4 APPEAL BY JUDICIAL REVIEW

Like appeal by way of case stated, judicial review is available to the prosecution as well as the defence. However, an acquittal will not be quashed unless the trial was a nullity and so the defendant was not in danger of a valid conviction (for example, the purported summary trial of an indictable only offence or where the magistrates acquit without hearing any prosecution evidence (*R v Dorking Justices ex p Harrington* [1984] AC 743; [1984] 2 All ER 474).

For judicial review to be available, there does not have to have been a final determination of the case.

Where the defendant pleaded guilty, the court will only entertain an application for judicial review of the conviction where the prosecution has acted in a way which has misled the defendant (*R v Burton-on-Trent Justices ex p Woolley* (1995) 159 JP 165, following *R v Home Secretary ex p Al Mehdawi* [1990] 1 AC 876; [1989] 3 All ER 843).

6.4.1 Grounds

The grounds for seeking judicial review are:

- error of law on the face of record (that is, an error disclosed in the court records). This would include passing a sentence in excess of the relevant statutory maximum for that offence;

- excess of jurisdiction (that is, the decision was *ultra vires*). In *R v Kent Justices ex p Machin* [1952] 2 QB 355; [1952] 1 All ER 1123, for example, the defendant was asked to agree to summary trial without first being warned that if he did so he could be committed for sentence to the Crown Court; the summary trial was therefore void;

- breach of the rules of natural justice (for example, bias or failing to allow both sides to put their case).

    Where bias is alleged, the court will apply the test laid down in *R v Liverpool Justices ex p Topping* [1983] 1 WLR 119; [1983] 1 All ER 490: would a reasonable and fair minded person sitting in court and hearing all the relevant facts have a reasonable suspicion that a fair trial of the appellant was not possible?

Breach of natural justice has been widely construed. It includes, for example:

(i) failing to give the accused adequate time to prepare a defence (*R v Thames Magistrates' Court ex p Polemis* [1974] 1 WLR 1371; [1974] 2 All ER 1219);

(ii) failing to allow an adjournment where a witness could not attend on the day of the trial (*R v Bracknell Justices ex p Hughes* [1990] Crim LR 266);

(iii) failure by the prosecution to notify the defence of the existence of a witness who could support the defence case (*R v Leyland Justices ex p Hawthorn* [1979] QB 283; [1979] 1 All ER 209);

(iv) failure by the prosecution to inform the defence in a shoplifting case that the key prosecution witness had a previous conviction for wasting police time, arising out of a false allegation of theft (*R v Knightsbridge Crown Court ex p Goonatilleke* [1986] QB 1; [1985] 2 All ER 498 (1986));

(v) ordering a defendant to pay costs without considering his means to pay them (*R v Newham Justices ex p Samuels* [1991] COD 412).

However, there are some restrictions on the use of judicial review to challenge decisions of magistrates. For example, in *R v Greater Manchester Justices ex p Aldi GmbH & Co KG* (1995) RTR 207, it was held that it is inappropriate to challenge interlocutory decisions of magistrates by way of judicial review. The exception to this is where the magistrates allow the information to be amended to show a different defendant and adjourn in order for the summons to be served on the new defendant.

Furthermore, in *R v Dolgellau Justices ex p Cartledge; R v Penrith Justices ex p Marks* (1995) *The Times*, 8 August, the Divisional Court held that it has no jurisdiction to quash a summary conviction following an unequivocal plea of guilty where no complaint is made of the conduct of the tribunal and the conduct of the prosecution cannot fairly be categorised as analogous to fraud.

In *R v Peterborough Justices ex p Dowler* [1996] 2 Cr App R 561, where the appellant claimed that his conviction for careless driving should be set aside because the prosecution had failed to disclose a witness statement which might have helped his case, it was held that it is unnecessary to grant judicial review of a conviction by magistrates where the procedural unfairness complained of could be rectified by a fair hearing before the Crown Court.

In *R v Hereford Magistrates' Court ex p Rowlands* [1997] 2 WLR 854, the Divisional Court held that the decision of the QBD in *R v Peterborough Justices ex p Dowler* (1996) 2 Cr App R 561, although correct on its facts, should not be treated as authority that a party complaining of procedural unfairness in a magistrates' court should invariable exercise his right of appeal to the Crown

Court rather than seek judicial review. The existence of a right of appeal to the Crown Court, particularly if it has not been exercised, should not ordinarily weigh against the grant of permission to seek judicial review or the grant of substantive relief once leave has been granted. However, leave to seek judicial review should only be granted if the applicant can show an apparently plausible complaint which, if upheld, might vitiate the proceedings in the magistrates' court. The Divisional Court should be slow to intervene, and should only do so when good (or arguably good) grounds are shown. It follows that the Divisional Court will not intervene if there have been only minor deviations from best practice.

6.4.2   Procedure

There are two stages to an application for judicial review (set out in Ord 53 of the Rules of Supreme Court, to be found in the Supreme Court Practice, colloquially know as the 'White Book').

6.4.3   Application for permission to apply for judicial review

A notice of application setting out the relief which is sought and the grounds upon which that relief is sought, supported by an affidavit verifying the contents of the application, is sent by the applicant to the Administrative Court Office.

There is a strict time limit of three months from the date of the decision complained of (and the applicant must act promptly even within the three months).

Usually, a High Court judge peruses the papers in private (though a hearing can be requested by the applicant) to see if there is a *prima facie* case for judicial review. The test is whether the application has a reasonable prospect of success.

If permission is refused by the judge, the applicant may renew the application before a Divisional Court (whether or not the refusal followed a hearing in front of a judge). Notice of intention to do so must be given within 10 days.

6.4.4   If permission is granted

If the applicant is granted permission to proceed, the application for judicial review is made, by means of a document known as an originating motion, to the Divisional Court. Notice of the motion is served (along with a copy of the applicant's affidavit on the basis of which leave was granted) on the respondent and on the clerk of the court below. They both have the chance to file affidavits in response to the applicant's affidavit.

6.4.5 Bail

Where the defendant was given a custodial sentence by the magistrates and is applying to the Divisional Court for a quashing order to quash the conviction, the magistrates do not have the power to grant bail pending the hearing of the application for judicial review. An application for bail should be made to a single High Court judge in chambers under s 37(1)(d) of the Criminal Justice Act 1948.

6.4.6 Hearing

A Divisional Court (that is, two or more High Court judges sitting in an open court) receives evidence in the form of the affidavits, and hears legal argument.

6.4.7 Remedies

The main judicial review remedies are:

- *Quashing order (formerly called certiorari)*

  This has the effect of quashing the original decision; where a conviction is quashed, the defendant stands acquitted of the offence.

- *Mandatory order (formerly called mandamus)*

  This requires the lower court to do something, for example, to go through the mode of trial procedure again or to re-hear an application for legal aid.

- *Prohibiting order (formerly called prohibition)*

  This prevents the lower court from doing something which it should not do, for example, committal proceedings where there have been several previous attempts to have the defendant committed for trial and so further attempts amount to an abuse of process.

It should be noted that these remedies are all discretionary. Even if the applicant is able to succeed on the merits, the High Court may decide that it is inappropriate to grant a remedy (see, for example, *R v Oxford City Justices ex p Berry* [1988] QB 507; [1987] 1 All ER 1244).

Delay is a fairly common ground for withholding relief. In *R v Neath and Port Talbot Justices ex p DPP* (2000) 97(9) LSG 41, the Divisional Court said that the circumstances to be taken into account when the court is exercising its discretion in criminal proceedings whether to grant relief in a judicial review application (or indeed an appeal by way of case stated) where there has been delay include: the seriousness of the offence; the nature of the evidence in the case (particularly the extent to which its quality would be affected by the delay); the extent, if any, to which the defendant had contributed to the magistrates' error; the extent, if any, to which the defendant had contributed to the delay in hearing the challenge; how far the complainant would be justifiably aggrieved by the proceedings being abandoned; how far the defendant would be justifiably aggrieved by the proceedings being continued.

6.5   APPEAL AGAINST SENTENCE

Although it would theoretically be possible to appeal by way of case stated (or to seek judicial review), if the magistrates impose a sentence which is beyond their powers, it is quicker and easier simply to appeal to the Crown Court against sentence.

Where the appeal is on the basis that the sentence is wrong in law (or outside jurisdiction) because it is so severe that no reasonable bench could impose such a sentence, the proper appeal is to the Crown Court rather than to the Divisional Court (*Tucker v DPP* [1992] 4 All ER 901; *R v Battle Justices ex p Shepherd* (1983) 5 Cr App R(S) 124).

6.6   CASE STATED OR JUDICIAL REVIEW?

The grounds on which judicial review can be sought and an appeal by way of case stated made are virtually the same: an error of law or jurisdiction.

In *R v Oldbury Justices ex p Smith* (1994) 159 JP 316, it was said that where appeal by way of case stated is available it is preferable to challenge a decision of a magistrates' court by means of appeal by way of case stated rather than judicial review. This is because judicial review is a remedy of last resort and because on an appeal by way of case stated the Divisional Court is presented with all the findings of fact made by the magistrates. In other words, judicial review applications should be confined to cases where there has not been a final determination of the case, such as committal for sentence (*R v Ipswich Crown Court ex p Baldwin* [1981] 1 All ER 596).

It should also be added that judicial review is particularly appropriate where the procedure adopted by the lower court is being questioned. On the other hand (provided that there has been a final determination), if the magistrates have misconstrued a statutory provision, appeal by way of case stated is preferable as it enables the question at issue to be set out more clearly.

6.7   APPEALS FROM THE YOUTH COURT

Appeal from the youth court against conviction and/or sentence lies to the Crown Court. The only difference from appeals from magistrates' courts is that, in the case of an appeal from the youth court, the Crown Court comprises a circuit judge or recorder and lay justices drawn from the youth court panel.

Appeal by way of case stated and judicial review are also available.

If a juvenile is convicted in the Crown Court (having been committed for the trial there because he was jointly charged with an adult or with a view to a sentence of long-term detention under s 53 of the Children and Young Persons Act 1933 being imposed in the event of conviction) appeal lies to the Court of Appeal (Criminal Division), as is always the case with conviction on indictment (see Chapter 10).

6.8   FURTHER APPEALS

If the initial appeal is unsuccessful, a further appeal may be possible.

6.8.1   From the Crown Court

There are two situations in which the Crown Court may be dealing with a case where the trial took place in a magistrates' court (or youth court). The rights of appeal differ according to why the Crown Court came to be dealing with the case.

- Where the Crown Court was hearing an appeal from the magistrates' court:

  Where the Crown Court is sitting in an appellate capacity from the magistrates' court, the appellant may appeal against the decision of the Crown Court to the Divisional Court by way of case stated, or seek judicial review, but only where the Crown Court has made an error of law or jurisdiction (ss 28(1) and 29(1) of the Supreme Court Act 1981).

  In *R v Gloucester Crown Court ex p Chester* [1998] COD 365, it was held by the Divisional Court that where a person is convicted by a magistrates' court and appeals to the Crown Court, further appeal against conviction to the High Court on a point of law should be by way of case stated, not judicial review.

  An application to the Crown Court to state a case for the opinion of the Divisional Court (following the Crown Court's determination of an appeal from a magistrates' court) must be made within 21 days of the decision complained of (r 26(1) of the Crown Court Rules 1982). Unlike the time limit applicable to challenging the decision of a magistrates' court, r 26(14) allows any time limit (including the initial 21 day period) under r 26 to be extended by the Crown Court. The decision to extend time can be taken by a judge alone (that is, without lay justices); the respondent must be given the chance to make representations; extensions of time should only be granted for cogent reasons (*DPP v Coleman* [1998] 1 WLR 1708; [1998] 1 All ER 912).

- Where the Crown Court passed sentence following committal for sentence under s 3 of the Powers of Criminal Courts (Sentencing) Act 2000:

Where the Crown Court is dealing with a committal for sentence under s 3 of the Powers of Criminal Courts (Sentencing) Act 2000, the defendant may appeal against the sentence imposed by the Crown Court to the Court of Appeal (Criminal Division) if, and only if, the Crown Court imposes a sentence in excess of six months (that is, imposes a sentence which was beyond the powers of the magistrates) (s 10 of the Criminal Appeal Act 1968) (see Chapter 10). The rationale behind this is that if the defendant is sentenced by the magistrates' court, he can appeal to the Crown Court but cannot appeal any further. So, if the Crown Court, on a s 3 committal, imposes a sentence which the magistrates could have imposed, he should be in the same position regarding appeals as the defendant who was originally sentenced in the magistrates' court and for whom the highest level of appeal would have been the Crown Court.

6.8.2   From the Divisional Court

Appeal from the Divisional Court lies direct to the House of Lords, by-passing the Court of Appeal (s 1(1)(a) of the Administration of Justice Act 1960). The Divisional Court must certify that there is a point of law of general public importance involved and either the Divisional Court or the House of Lords must give leave to appeal.

6.9   CASE STATED

CASE STATED

(MC Act 1980, s 111; MC Rules 1981, rr 78, 81)

In the High Court of Justice
Queen's Bench Division

Between   AB,
Appellant

                                        and

                 CD,
Respondent

Case stated by Justices for the [county of   , acting in and for the petty Sessional Division of   ], in respect of their adjudication as a magistrates' court sitting at [   ]

CASE

1. On the   day of   , 20   , an information [or complaint] was pre-ferred by the appellant [or respondent] against the respondent [or appel-lant] that he/she (state shortly particulars of information or complaint and refer to any relevant statutes).
2. We heard the said information [or complaint] on the day of   , 20   , and found the following facts:- (set out in separate lettered paragraphs).

*   [The following is a short statement of the evidence:- (set out so as to show relevant evidence given by each witness)].

†3. It was contended by the appellant that
†4. It was contended by the respondent that
5. We were referred to the following cases
6. We were of opinion that (state grounds of decision) and accordingly (state decision including any sentence or order).

Question

7. The question for the opinion of the High Court is

Dated the   day of   , 20

EF,

GH,

Justices of the peace for the [county] aforesaid
[on behalf of all the Justices adjudicating].

* Insert only if the opinion of the High Court is sought whether there was evidence upon which the magistrates' court could come to its decision.

† Only a brief summary should be given.

TABLE OF STATUTORY MATERIALS

STATUTORY MATERIALS

REVIEW OF DECISIONS BY MAGISTRATES' COURTS

MAGISTRATES' COURTS ACT 1980

Section 142: Power of magistrates' court to re-open cases to rectify mistakes, etc

(1) A magistrates' court may vary or rescind a sentence or other order imposed or made by it when dealing with an offender if it appears to the court to be in the interests of justice to do so; and it is hereby declared that this power extends to replacing a sentence or order which for any reason appears to be invalid by another which the court has power to impose or make.

(1A) The power conferred on a magistrates' court by sub-section (1) above shall not be exercisable in relation to any sentence or order imposed or made by it when dealing with an offender if:

    (a) the Crown Court has determined an appeal against:

        (i) that sentence or order;

        (ii) the conviction in respect of which that sentence or order was imposed or made; or

        (iii) any other sentence or order imposed or made by the magistrates' court when dealing with the offender in respect of that conviction (including a sentence or order replaced by that sentence or order; or

    (b) the High Court has determined a case stated for that opinion of that court on any question arising in any proceeding leading to or resulting from the imposition or making of the sentence or order.

(2) Where a person is convicted by a magistrates' court and it subsequently appears to the court that it would be in the interests of justice that the case should be heard again by different justices, the court may so direct.

(2A) The power conferred on a magistrates' court by sub-section (2) above shall not be exercisable in relation to a conviction if:

    (a) the Crown Court has determined an appeal against:

        (i) the conviction; or

        (ii) any sentence or order imposed or made by the magistrates' court when dealing with the offender in respect of the conviction; or

    (b) the High Court has determined a case stated for the opinion of that court on any question arising in any proceeding leading to or resulting from the conviction.

(3) Where a court gives a direction under sub-section (2) above:

    (a) the conviction and any sentence or other order imposed or made in consequence thereof shall be of no effect; and

    (b) section 10(4) above shall apply as if the trial of the person in question had been adjourned.

(4) [Repealed.]

(5) Where a sentence or order is varied under sub-section (1) above, the sentence or other order, as so varied, shall take effect from the beginning of the day on which it was originally imposed or made, unless the court otherwise directs.

APPEAL TO THE CROWN COURT

MAGISTRATES' COURTS ACT 1980

Section 108: Right of appeal to the Crown Court

(1) A person convicted by a magistrates' court may appeal to the Crown Court:

    (a) if he pleaded guilty, against his sentence;

    (b) if he did not, against the conviction or sentence.

(1A) Section 14 of the Powers of Criminal Courts (Sentencing) Act 2000 (under which a conviction of an offence for which an order for conditional or absolute discharge is made is deemed not to be a conviction except for certain purposes) shall not prevent an appeal under this section, whether against conviction or otherwise.

(2) A person sentenced by a magistrates' court for an offence in respect of which a probation order or an order for conditional discharge has been previously made may appeal to the Crown Court against the sentence.

(3) In this section 'sentence' includes any order made on conviction by a magistrates' court, not being:

    ...

    (b) an order for the payment of costs;

    ...

Section 109: Abandonment of appeal

(1) Where notice to abandon the appeal [from the magistrates' court to the Crown Court] has been duly given by the appellant:

    (a) the court against whose decision the appeal was brought may issue process for enforcing that decision, subject to anything already suffered or done under it by the appellant; and

(b) the said court may, on the application of the other party to the appeal, order the appellant to pay to that party such costs as appear to the court to be just and reasonable in respect of expenses properly incurred by that party in connection with the appeal before notice of abandonment was given to that party.

...

Section 110: Enforcement of decision of Crown Court

After the determination by the Crown Court of an appeal from a magistrates' court the decision appealed against as confirmed or varied by the Crown Court or any decision of the Crown Court substituted for the decision appealed against, may, without prejudice to the powers of the Crown Court to enforce the decision, be enforced:

(a) by the issue by the court by which the decision appealed against was given of any process that it could have issued if it had decided the case as the Crown Court decided it;

(b) so far as the nature of any process already issued to enforce the decision appealed against permits, by that process,

and the decision of the Crown Court shall have effect as if it has been made by the magistrates' court against whose decision the appeal is brought.

SUPREME COURT ACT 1981

Section 48: Appeals to Crown Court

(1) The Crown Court may, in the course of hearing any appeal, correct any error or mistake in the order or judgment incorporating the decision which is the subject of the appeal.

(2) On the termination of the hearing of an appeal the Crown Court:

(a) may confirm, reverse or vary any part of the decision appealed against, including a determination not to impose a separate penalty in respect of an offence; or

(b) may remit the matter with its opinion thereon to the authority whose decision is appealed against; or

(c) may make any such other order in the matter as the court thinks just, and by such order exercise any power which the said authority might have exercised.

...

(4) If the appeal is against a conviction or a sentence, the preceding provisions of this section shall be construed as including power to award any punishment, whether more or less severe than that awarded by the magistrates' court whose decision is appealed against, if that is a punishment which that magistrates' court might have awarded.

(5) This section applies whether or not the appeal is against the whole of the decision.

...

APPEAL BY WAY OF CASE STATED

MAGISTRATES' COURTS ACT 1980

Section 111: Statement of case by magistrates' court

(1) Any person who was a party to any proceeding before a magistrates' court or is aggrieved by the conviction, order, determination or other proceeding of the court may question the proceeding on the ground that it is wrong in law or is in excess of jurisdiction by applying to the justices composing the court to state a case for the opinion of the High Court on the question of law or jurisdiction involved ...

(2) An application under sub-section (1) above shall be made within 21 days after the day on which the decision of the magistrates' court was given.

(3) For the purpose of sub-section (2) above, the day on which the decision of the magistrates' court is given shall, where the court has adjourned the trial of an information after conviction, be the day on which the court sentences or otherwise deals with the offender.

(4) On the making of an application under this section in respect of a decision any right of the applicant to appeal against the decision to the Crown Court shall cease.

(5) If the justices are of opinion that an application under this section is frivolous, they may refuse to state a case, and, if the applicant so requires, shall give him a certificate stating that the application has been refused; but the justices shall not refuse to state a case if the application is made by or under the direction of the Attorney General.

(6) Where justices refuse to state a case, the High Court may, on the application of the person who applied for the case to be stated, make an order of *mandamus* requiring the justices to state a case.

Section 112: Effect of decision of High Court on case stated by magistrates' court

Any conviction, order, determination, or other proceeding of a magistrates' court varied by the High Court on appeal by case stated, and any judgment or order of the High Court on such an appeal may be enforced as if it were a decision of the magistrates' court from which the appeal was brought.

Section 114: Recognizances and fees on case stated

Justices to whom application has been made to state a case for the opinion of the High Court on any proceeding of a magistrates' court shall not be required to state the case until the applicant has entered into a recognizance, with or without sureties, before the magistrates' court, conditioned to prosecute the appeal without delay and to submit to the judgment of the High Court and pay such costs as that court may award ...

MAGISTRATES' COURTS RULES 1981

Rule 76: Application to state case

(1) An application under section 111(1) of the Magistrates' Courts Act 1980 shall be made in writing and signed by or on behalf of the applicant and shall identify the question or questions of law or jurisdiction on which the opinion of the High Court is sought.

(2) Where one of the questions on which the opinion of the High Court is sought is whether there was evidence on which the magistrates' court could come to its decision, the particular finding of fact made by the magistrates' court which it is claimed cannot be supported by the evidence before the magistrates' court shall be specified in such application.

(3) Any such application shall be sent to the clerk of the magistrates' court whose decision is questioned.

Rule 77: Consideration of draft case

(1) Within 21 days after receipt of an application made in accordance with rule 76, the clerk of the magistrates' court whose decision is questioned shall, unless the justices refuse to state a case under section 111(5) of the Magistrates' Courts Act 1980, send a draft case in which are stated the matters required under rule 81 to the applicant or his solicitor and shall send a copy thereof to the respondent or his solicitor.

(2) Within 21 days after receipt of the draft case under paragraph (1), each party may make representations thereon. Any such representations shall be in writing and signed by or on behalf of the party making them and shall be sent to the clerk.

(3) Where the justices refuse to state a case under section 111(5) of the Act and they are required by the High Court by order of *mandamus* under section 111(6) to do so, this rule shall apply as if in paragraph (1):

(a) for the words 'receipt of an application made in accordance with rule 76' there were substituted the words 'the date on which an order of *mandamus* under section 111(6) of the Act of 1980 is made'; and

(b) the words 'unless the justices refuse to state a case under section 111(5) of the Magistrates' Courts Act 1980' were omitted.

Rule 78: Preparation and submission of final case

(1) Within 21 days after the latest day on which representations may be made under rule 77, the justices whose decision is questioned shall make such adjustments, if any, to the draft case prepared for the purposes of that rule as they think fit, after considering any such representations, and shall state and sign the case.

(2) A case may be stated on behalf of the justices whose decision is questioned by any 2 or more of them and may, if the justices so direct, be signed on their behalf by their clerk.

(3) Forthwith after the case has been stated and signed the clerk of the court shall send it to the applicant or his solicitor, together with any statement required by rule 79.

Rule 79: Extension of time limits

(1) If the clerk of a magistrates' court is unable to send to the applicant a draft case under paragraph (1) of rule 77 within the time required by that paragraph, he shall do so as soon as practicable thereafter and the provisions of that rule shall apply accordingly; but in that event the clerk shall attach to the draft case, and to the final case when it is sent to the applicant or his solicitor under rule 78(3), a statement of the delay and the reasons therefore.

(2) If the clerk of a magistrates' court receives an application in writing from or on behalf of the applicant or the respondent for an extension of the time within which representations on the draft case may be made under paragraph (2) of rule 77, together with reasons in writing therefore, he may by notice in writing sent to the applicant or respondent as the case may be extend the time and the provisions of that paragraph and of rule 78 shall apply accordingly; but in that event the clerk shall attach to the final case, when it is sent to the applicant or his solicitor under rule 78(3), a statement of the extension and the reasons therefore.

(3) If the justices are unable to state a case within the time required by paragraph (1) of rule 78, they shall do so as soon as practicable thereafter and the provisions of that rule shall apply accordingly; but in that event the clerk shall attach to the final case, when it is sent to the applicant or his solicitor under rule 78(3), a statement of the delay and the reasons therefore.

...

Rule 81: Content of case

(1) A case stated by the magistrates' court shall state the facts found by the court and the question or questions of law or jurisdiction on which the opinion of the High Court is sought.

(2) Where one of the questions on which the opinion of the High Court is sought is whether there was evidence on which the magistrates' court could come to its decision, the particular finding of fact which it is claimed cannot be supported by the evidence before the magistrates' court shall be specified in the case.

(3) Unless one of the questions on which the opinion of the High Court is sought is whether there was evidence on which the magistrates' court could come to its decision, the case shall not contain a statement of evidence.

SUPREME COURT ACT 1981

Section 28: Appeals from Crown Court and inferior courts

(1) Subject to sub-section (2), any order, judgment or other decision of the Crown Court may be questioned by any party to the proceedings, on the ground that it is wrong in law or is in excess of jurisdiction, by applying to the Crown Court to have a case stated by that court for the opinion of the High Court.

(2) Sub-section (1) shall not apply to:

(a) a judgment or other decision of the Crown Court relating to trial on indictment; or

...

Section 28A: Proceedings on case stated by magistrates' court

(1) The following provisions apply where a case is stated for the opinion of the High Court under section 111 of the Magistrates' Courts Act 1980 (case stated on question of law or jurisdiction).

(2) The High Court may, if it thinks fit, cause the case to be sent back for amendment, whereupon it shall be amended accordingly.

(3) The High Court shall hear and determine the question arising on the case (or the case as amended) and shall:

(a) reverse, affirm or amend the determination in respect of which the case has been stated, or

(b) remit the matter to the justice or justices with the opinion of the court,

and may make such other order in relation to the matter (including as to costs) as it thinks fit.

(4) Except as provided by the Administration of Justice Act 1960 (right of appeal to House of Lords in criminal cases), a decision of the High Court made under this section is final and conclusive on all parties.

BAIL

MAGISTRATES' COURTS ACT 1980

Section 113: Bail on appeal or case stated

(1) Where a person has given notice of appeal to the Crown Court against the decision of a magistrates' court or has applied to a magistrates' court to state a case for the opinion of the High Court, then, if he is in custody, the magistrates' court may, subject to section 25 of the Criminal Justice and Public Order Act 1994, grant him bail.

(2) If a person is granted bail under sub-section (1) above, the time and place at which he is to appear (except in the event of the determination in respect of which the case is stated being reversed by the High Court) shall be:

(a) if he has given notice of appeal, the Crown Court at the time appointed for the hearing of the appeal;

(b) if he has applied for the statement of a case, the magistrates' court at such time within 10 days after the judgment of the High Court has been given as may be specified by the magistrates' court,

and any recognizance that may be taken from him or any surety for him shall be conditioned accordingly.

(3) Sub-section (1) above shall not apply where the accused has been committed to the Crown Court for sentence under section 37 or 38 above.

...

JUDICIAL REVIEW

SUPREME COURT ACT 1981

Section 29: Orders of mandamus, prohibition and certiorari

(1) The High Court shall have jurisdiction to make orders of mandamus, prohibition and certiorari in those classes of cases in which it had power to do so immediately before the commencement of this Act.

...

(3) In relation to the jurisdiction of the Crown Court, other than its jurisdiction in matters relating to trial on indictment, the High Court shall have all such jurisdiction to make orders of mandamus, prohibition or certiorari as the High Court possesses in relation to the jurisdiction of an inferior court.

...

CHAPTER 7

COMMITTAL PROCEEDINGS

7.1 INTRODUCTION

We have already seen that all criminal cases begin in the magistrates' court (either an information is laid and a summons is issued requiring the defendant to attend the magistrates' court, or else the defendant is arrested, charged and required to appear at the magistrates' court). If the offence of which the defendant is accused is to be tried in the Crown Court, either because it is triable only on indictment or because it was decided at the mode of trial hearing that it should be tried in the Crown Court, the magistrates have first to decide whether the prosecution are able to make out a *prima facie* case against the defendant. They do this by means of 'committal proceedings'. The object is to filter out cases where there is insufficient evidence against an accused to justify a trial.

When magistrates are conducting committal proceedings, they are known as 'examining justices'. They have jurisdiction to hold committal proceedings no matter where in England and Wales the offence was allegedly committed.

7.1.1 Background

The original version of the Magistrates' Courts Act 1980 provided two alternative methods for moving a case from the magistrates' court so that it could be tried in the Crown Court. The first, committal without consideration of the evidence under s 6(2) of the Magistrates' Courts Act 1980, remains in force and is described below.

The second was a version of committal with consideration of the evidence, which was significantly different from the version of committal under s 6(1) of the 1980 Act which is described below. Under the original version of s 6(1), the procedure for a committal with consideration of the evidence was very similar to that of an ordinary trial, with witnesses being subject to examination-in-chief, cross-examination and re-examination. A contemporaneous note of the evidence was taken down and when a witness had finished testifying the notes were read back to the witness, who was then given an opportunity to make any amendments. The witness then signed the notes (which became a 'deposition'). After the prosecution witnesses had given evidence, the defence had a chance to make a submission that there was no case to answer. If that submission was unsuccessful, the defence had the opportunity to call evidence and make a second submission of no case to answer (though it was very rare for the defence to call any evidence at this stage). If a submission of no case to answer was successful, the defendant was 'discharged'.

By the Criminal Justice and Public Order Act 1994, a new system, called transfer for trial, was set up to replace both forms of committal. The essence of the system was that the prosecution would serve a notice on the defendant and on the magistrates' court and that, following receipt of the notice, the magistrates would transfer the case to the Crown Court for trial. This procedure did not involve a hearing in court. It was, however, open to a defendant to make representations to the effect that the prosecution witness statements did not disclose a case to answer and in that case there could be a hearing. These provisions never came into force and were, by s 47 of the Criminal Procedure and Investigations Act 1996, replaced by a new system of committal proceedings set out in Sched 1 of the Criminal Procedure and Investigations Act 1996.

Under this new system, committal without consideration of the evidence remains in its original version, but committal with consideration of the evidence is amended so that witness statements are read out but witnesses do not attend the hearing.

A further change was made by the enactment of s 51 of the Crime and Disorder Act 1998, which effectively abolishes committal proceedings in the case of indictable only offences (see later, 7.13)

7.2   THE TWO FORMS OF COMMITTAL

Section 6 of the Magistrates' Courts Act 1980 (as amended by Sched 1, para 4 of the Criminal Procedure and Investigations Act 1996) provides for two methods of committing a defendant from the magistrates' court to the Crown Court. One method (under s 6(1) of the Magistrates' Courts Act 1980) involves a consideration of the evidence by the magistrates, the other (under s 6(2) of the 1980 Act) does not. Each of these is examined in more detail later in this chapter. First, however, some preliminary matters have to be considered.

7.3   DISCHARGE WITHOUT COMMITTAL PROCEEDINGS

The defendant may be discharged (that is, the case against him may be stopped by the magistrates) without committal proceedings taking place in two situations:

(1) the prosecution have deliberately manipulated the criminal process so as to take unfair advantage of the defendant (for example, causing delay in the hope that a potential defence witness will no longer be available); or

(2) there has been delay, and although this delay is not deliberate on the part of the prosecution, it is nevertheless unjustifiable and the defendant is likely to be prejudiced as a result of the delay:

R v Derby Crown Court ex p Brooks (1984) 80 Cr App R 164 and *R v Telford Justices ex p Badhan* [1991] 2 QB 78; [1991] 2 All ER 854. See, further, Chapter 1.

7.4   MORE THAN ONE DEFENDANT

If there is more than one defendant, and the defendants are jointly charged, there will be joint committal proceedings. If the defendants are not jointly charged, joint committal proceedings only take place if the charges against the defendants are sufficiently linked that it is likely that they will be tried together in the Crown Court (*R v Camberwell Green Magistrates ex p Christie* [1978] QB 602; [1978] 2 All ER 377. On joinder of counts on an indictment, see Chapter 8).

7.5   PRESENCE OF DEFENDANT

Section 4(3) of the Magistrates' Courts Act 1980 provides that the defendant must be present at committal proceedings unless (under s 4(4)):

(a) his disorderly conduct makes it impracticable for him to remain in court; or

(b) he is unwell but is legally represented and consents to the proceedings taking place in his absence.

In *R v Liverpool City Magistrates' Court ex p Quantrell* [1999] 2 Cr App R 24, the defendant was unwell and wanted committal proceedings under s 6(2) of the Magistrates' Courts Act 1980 (that is, committal without consideration of the evidence) to take place in his absence. Because s 4(4) of the 1980 Act refers to examining justices hearing evidence in the absence of the defendant where he is ill but is legally represented and consents to the evidence being given in his absence, the magistrates held that they had no power to conduct a hearing without consideration of evidence in the absence of the defendant. The Divisional Court held that the magistrates were wrong and that it was open to a magistrates' court to commit a defendant under s 6(2) in his absence, although they were not obliged to do so.

If the defendant fails without good cause to attend the committal proceedings, a warrant for his arrest will be issued (see Chapter 2).

7.6 COMMITTAL WITHOUT CONSIDERATION OF THE EVIDENCE

The vast majority of committals are under s 6(2), and so we will consider them first. Section 6(2) of the Magistrates' Courts Act 1980 provides for committal without consideration of the evidence. This form of committal is only possible if all of the following requirements are satisfied.

7.6.1 Pre-conditions for a s 6(2) committal

First, under s 5A of the Magistrates' Courts Act 1980, the prosecution evidence must comprise:

(a) written statements which comply with s 5B of the Magistrates' Courts Act 1980. In order for a statement to comply with s 5B:

  (i) the statement must be signed by its maker;

  (ii) the statement must contain a declaration by the maker that 'it is true to the best of my knowledge and belief and I make it knowing that, if it is tendered in evidence, I shall be liable to prosecution if I have wilfully stated in it anything which I know to be false or do not believe to be true'.

  (iii) a copy of the statement must be served on the defendant (or, if there is more than one defendant, on all the defendants);

  and/or

(b) depositions (under s 5C of the Magistrates' Courts Act), that is, sworn statements taken before a magistrate under s 97A of the Magistrates' Courts Act;

  and/or

(c) statements made admissible by virtue of s 23 or s 24 of the Criminal Justice Act 1988 (see Chapter 9, 9.10.5): s 5D of the Magistrates' Courts Act 1980.

Secondly, under s 6(2)(a) of the Magistrates' Courts Act 1980, the defendant (or, if more than one defendant, each of them) must have a legal representative acting for him in the case.

Thirdly, under s 6(2)(b) of the Magistrates' Courts Act 1980, the defendant must not have requested the magistrates' court to consider a submission that there is insufficient evidence to put the defendant on trial by jury for the offence. If there is more than one defendant, committal under s 6(2) is not possible if any of them wishes to submit that there is no case to answer.

7.6.2 Procedure

The procedure for a committal under s 6(2) of the Magistrates' Courts Act 1980 is therefore as follows. Prior to the hearing, the prosecution will have served on the defendant(s) the bundle of prosecution witness statements (assuming these statements have not already been served on the defence pursuant to the advance information rules, as to which see Chapter 3, 3.12).

At the hearing, the bundle of witness statements will be handed to the magistrates. The magistrates will not read the witness statements but will check that there is no submission on behalf of the defendant(s) that there is no case to answer. Assuming there is no such submission, the defendant will be committed to stand trial at the Crown Court and will be told the date of his or her first appearance at the Crown Court (for the Plea and Directions Hearing, as to which see Chapter 9, 9.5).

At this hearing, the magistrates will also consider ancillary matters such as bail, legal aid and publicity.

Rule 4A of the Justices' Clerks Rules 1970 allows a clerk to commit a defendant for trial provided that the defendant is already on bail and is committed to the Crown Court on bail with the same conditions (if any) as before.

7.7 BAIL

The presumption in favour of bail continues to apply where the defendant has been committed for trial to the Crown Court. Where the defendant was on bail prior to committal, bail will be continued unless the prosecution can satisfy the magistrates that any of the statutory reasons for withholding bail now apply. Where the defendant is in custody at the time of the committal proceedings, the committal hearing may present an opportunity to make a bail application, not least because the strength of the prosecution case (something which the magistrates have to consider under the Bail Act 1976) may well be much clearer.

7.8 LEGAL AID

Where a defendant is legally aided, the magistrates at the committal hearing must consider whether to extend the grant of legal aid to cover the proceedings in the Crown Court (unless the original order was a 'through order', automatically covering both magistrates' court and Crown Court hearings). Where the defendant has been granted legal aid prior to committal, the extension to cover the Crown Court proceedings is more or less automatic unless the defendant's financial circumstances have changed.

7.9   PUBLICITY: REPORTING RESTRICTIONS

Section 8(1) of the Magistrates' Courts Act 1980 makes it unlawful to publish a report (written or broadcast) of any information other than that specified by s 8(4) of the Magistrates' Courts Act 1980. This allows the publication of only basic details about the case such as:

(a) the identity of the court;

(b) names of examining justices, counsel and solicitors;

(c) names, addresses, ages and occupations of parties and witnesses;

(d) charges against the accused and those on which he was committed for trial;

(e) decisions on grant of bail and legal aid.

These restrictions mean that any evidence read out, and any arguments put forward, at committal proceedings cannot be reported by the media. This is so that the people who eventually sit on the jury that tries the defendant will not be biased against the defendant because of unfavourable pre-trial publicity.

Breach of the restrictions is a summary offence carrying a maximum fine of £5,000.

Under s 8(3) of the Magistrates' Courts Act 1980, these restrictions apply to all stages of the case against the defendant prior to and including the committal and, unless lifted, also apply until the Crown Court trial is over. The restrictions automatically lapse if the committal proceedings result in the discharge of the defendant.

7.9.1   Lifting the restrictions

These statutory reporting restrictions can be lifted by the magistrates. An application for the restrictions to be lifted may be made at the committal proceedings or at any remand hearing before those proceedings take place.

If there is only one defendant and he asks for the reporting restrictions to be lifted, the magistrates must comply with this request and lift the restrictions (s 8(2)).

If there is more than one defendant and one defendant asks for the reporting restrictions to be lifted, but another defendant opposes this application, the defendant who wants the restrictions lifted must show that it is in the interests of justice for this to be done (s 8(2A); *R v Leeds Justices ex p Sykes* [1983] 1 WLR 132; [1983] 1 All ER 460).

To ensure that the application is dealt with fairly, all the defendants must be given a chance to make representations on the lifting of the restrictions (s 8(2A); *R v Wirral Justices ex p Meikle* (1990) 154 JP 1035).

A strong argument in favour of lifting the restrictions is that publicity is necessary in order to encourage potential witnesses to come forward.

7.9.2   Defining what can be reported

If the restrictions are lifted, then all of the restrictions have to be lifted: the justices cannot pick and choose which of the restrictions are lifted and which remain. Furthermore, once the restrictions are lifted, they cannot be reimposed (*R v Bow Street Magistrates ex p Kray* [1969] 1 QB 473; [1968] 3 All ER 892).

However, if the justices wish to lift the reporting restrictions which apply under s 8 of the Magistrates' Courts Act 1980 but nonetheless wish to prevent the full reporting of all the details of the case, they can lift the s 8 restrictions but then make an order under s 4 of the Contempt of Court Act 1981. This allows the court to order postponement of the contemporaneous reporting of some or all of any legal proceedings where such action is necessary to prevent a 'substantial risk of prejudice to the administration of justice'. Thus, if the s 8 restrictions have been lifted, the court can effectively define what may be reported by making an order under the Contempt of Court Act 1981.

Once the restrictions contained in s 8 of the Magistrates' Courts Act 1980 are removed, the powers of the court to prohibit or postpone publication of reports of court proceedings are wholly contained in the Contempt of Court Act 1981; the court has no further common law powers or inherent jurisdiction to make such an order. Furthermore, an order under s 4 of the Contempt of Court Act 1981 can *only* be made where necessary to avoid a substantial risk of prejudice to the administration of justice in those proceedings. Accordingly, it was held in *R v Newtonabbey Magistrates' Court ex p Belfast Telegraph Newspapers Ltd* (1997) *The Times*, 27 August (Queen's Bench Division of Northern Ireland) that a magistrate erred in prohibiting the publication of the name of a defendant charged with indecent assault on the ground of a possible physical attack on the defendant by ill intentioned persons.

Where the court is minded to make an order under the Contempt of Court Act 1981, it should listen to any representations made on behalf of the press (*R v Clerkenwell Magistrates ex p The Telegraph plc* [1993] 2 All ER 183).

7.10 COMMITTAL WITH CONSIDERATION OF THE EVIDENCE

As we have seen, committal without consideration of the evidence under s 6(2) is only possible if the defendant concedes that the prosecution witness statements disclose a case to answer against him. In those comparatively rare cases where the defendant does not concede that this is so, the magistrates have to consider the evidence against the defendant under s 6(1). Section 6(1) of the Magistrates' Courts Act 1980 provides that a '... magistrates' court inquiring into an offence as examining justices shall on consideration of the evidence:

(a) commit the accused for trial if it is of opinion that there is sufficient evidence to put him on trial by jury for any indictable offence;

(b) discharge him if it is not of that opinion and he is in custody for no other cause than the offence under inquiry'.

Sections 5B(4), 5C(4) and 5D(4) of the Magistrates' Courts Act 1980 each provide that, unless the committal is without consideration of the evidence under s 6(2), each statement or deposition must 'be read aloud at the hearing; and where the court so directs, an account shall be given orally of so much of any [statement or deposition, as the case may be] as is not read aloud'.

The effect of these provisions is as follows:

7.10.1 Procedure for a s 6(1) committal

The hearing at which the magistrates consider whether the witness statements disclose a case to answer against the defendant will begin with a short opening speech by the prosecutor. The prosecutor will then read out the written statements made by the witnesses upon whose evidence the prosecution case is based (or, with the permission of the court, the prosecutor will summarise the effect of any part of a statement which is not read out loud). No witnesses will be called to give oral evidence.

When the prosecution statements have been read to the court, the defence will have the opportunity to submit that there is no case to answer on the basis of those witness statements; the prosecutor will be entitled to reply to that submission in order to try to persuade the magistrates that there is a case to answer.

Having heard the submission of no case to answer from the defence and a reply from the prosecution, the examining justices consider whether there is sufficient evidence to justify committing the defendant to stand trial at the Crown Court. The test they have to apply is whether there is a *prima facie* case against the accused. In other words, they have to ask themselves whether there is sufficient evidence on which a reasonable jury *could* convict him (not whether they would convict the defendant).

In summary, then, the only evidence tendered at a s 6(1) committal is prosecution evidence, and all that evidence must be in writing. There is no defence evidence at all.

This new procedure for committal with consideration of the evidence will be of comparatively little use to defendants. It will not often be the case that the witness statements do not disclose a case to answer. Because the new procedure does not allow oral evidence to be heard, there is no possibility of cross-examining a prosecution witness to probe potential weaknesses in their evidence. Furthermore (under Sched 1, paras 25 and 26 of the Criminal Procedure and Investigations Act 1996), ss 76 and 78 of the Police and Criminal Evidence Act 1984 (which enable a court to exclude prosecution evidence as being inadmissible) do not apply to committal proceedings.

In *Wilkinson v CPS* (1998) 162 JP 591, CPS served a bundle of witness statements on the defendant. The defendant opted for committal proceedings with consideration of the evidence under s 6(1) of the Magistrates' Courts Act 1980. At the committal proceedings, CPS relied solely on the statement of the alleged victim of the offence. The defendant argued that part of that statement was inadmissible and that the decision not to read any of the other witness statements created a false picture. The Divisional Court held that there was plainly sufficient admissible evidence in the complainant's statement and so it did not matter that other parts of the statement might be inadmissible at trial and, more generally, the prosecution may choose which witnesses to rely on for the purposes of committal proceedings.

Under s 6(1), it is open to the magistrates to decide that there is insufficient evidence to justify the defendant being committed for trial in respect of the offence for which the prosecution seek committal but that there is sufficient evidence to justify committal for trial for another offence. Provided that the offence in respect of which the magistrates find a case to answer is an indictable offence (whether triable only in the Crown Court or triable either way), they may commit him for trial for that offence. An example would be where the prosecution seek committal for murder but the magistrates decide that there is only sufficient evidence to support a charge of manslaughter.

Where the justices are minded to hold that there is a case to answer on a charge other than the original one, the parties should be given the opportunity to address the bench before the magistrates have made up their minds (*R v Gloucester Magistrates Court ex p Chung* (1989) 153 JP 75).

7.10.2 Effect of discharge under s 6(1)

Where the magistrates decide that there is insufficient evidence to justify a Crown Court trial in respect of any indictable offence, they must discharge the defendant. Upon discharge, the defendant is free to leave court unless he is in custody in respect of an offence which is not being considered at the committal proceedings. (If the defendant has been charged with two completely unrelated offences, the two offences would not be dealt with at the same committal hearing. If committal proceedings for one of the offences result in the magistrates finding no case to answer, the defendant would remain in custody if bail had been withheld in respect of the offence not being considered at the present proceedings.)

A 'discharge' at committal proceedings does not have the same effect as an acquittal, since the prosecution can re-prosecute the defendant for the same offence (something which is impossible where the defendant has been acquitted following a trial).

If the prosecution wish to challenge a discharge, there are two ways of doing so:

(1) The prosecution can bring fresh committal proceedings alleging the same offence (*R v Manchester Justices ex p Snelson* [1977] 1 WLR 911; [1978] 2 All ER 62).

Normally, the prosecution will only bring fresh proceedings if, for example:

(a) the examining justices who discharged the defendant came to a clearly unreasonable decision;

or

(b) the examining justices did not consider the evidence before discharging the defendant (for example, a vital prosecution witness failed to attend so the prosecution were unable to proceed but the justices refused to grant an adjournment);

or

(c) new evidence against the accused comes to light.

If the prosecution behave oppressively by bringing fresh committal proceedings where the defendant has already been discharged, the Divisional Court may (on an application for judicial review) grant an order of prohibition to prevent further committal proceedings which amount to an abuse of process (*R v Horsham Justices ex p Reeves* (1980) 75 Cr App R 236).

(2) Instead of bringing fresh committal proceedings the prosecution may decide instead to seek a 'Voluntary Bill of Indictment', described below.

7.11 CHALLENGING THE DECISION TO COMMIT FOR TRIAL

In most cases, there will be no remedy for a defendant who thinks that he should not have been committed for trial; all he can do is wait for the Crown Court trial and make a submission that there is no case to answer at the close of the prosecution case.

If the defendant is committed for trial, there is no possibility of an appeal to the Divisional Court by way of case stated as there has been no final determination of the case (*Cragg v Lewes District Council* [1986] Crim LR 800; see, also, Chapter 6, 6.3).

In *Williams v Bedwellty Justices* [1996] 3 All ER 737, the House of Lords, following their earlier decision in *Neill v North Antrim Magistrates' Court* [1992] 1 WLR 1221; [1992] 4 All ER 846, held that the decision of a magistrates' court to commit a defendant for trial is susceptible to judicial review. In *Williams*, the only evidence relied on by the Crown was the fact that the defendant was implicated in statements made to the police by other people who were charged in the same proceedings: these statements (being out of court statements by co-defendants) were inadmissible against Williams. There was, therefore, no admissible evidence against her. The House of Lords held that, because examining justices are required by s 6(1) of the Magistrates' Courts Act 1980 to consider the evidence adduced by the prosecution, a committal should be quashed if there was no admissible evidence of the defendant's guilt. The House of Lords went on to hold that where there was *some* admissible evidence against the accused, but it was insufficient to amount to a *prima facie* case against him, the remedy of judicial review is available, but the Divisional Court should be slow to interfere with that decision. Presumably, a decision based on admissible evidence that there is a *prima facie* case against the accused would only be quashed if no reasonable bench of magistrates could have come to the view that there was sufficient evidence (that is, the decision to commit the accused for trial was perverse).

In *R v Manchester Magistrates ex p Birtles* (1994) *The Times*, 25 January, the justices said that they would not take 'any real notice' of some evidence which was inadmissible. Clearly, the justices should have completely disregarded the inadmissible evidence, but the Divisional Court held that judicial review would only be available if the applicant could show that the mis-receipt of evidence resulted in real injustice to the applicant; the present case was said to fall short of that and so the application failed.

7.12   OTHER METHODS OF SECURING TRIAL ON INDICTMENT

Committal proceedings are the usual way of making a defendant stand trial in the Crown Court. There are, however, two other ways: the voluntary bill of indictment and the notice of transfer procedure.

7.12.1   A voluntary bill of indictment

A 'voluntary bill of indictment' is an order made by a High Court judge that the defendant should stand trial in the Crown Court for the offence(s) specified in the order. The obtaining of a voluntary bill of indictment is governed by s 2(2)(b) of the Administration of Justice (Miscellaneous Provisions) Act 1933 and a Practice Direction of 1999.

To obtain a voluntary bill of indictment, the prosecution have to make a written application to a High Court judge. *The Practice Direction (Crime: Voluntary Bills)* [1999] 4 All ER 62 provides as follows:

- Applications for a voluntary bill of indictment have to be accompanied by (a) a copy of any charges on which the defendant has been committed for trial; (b) a copy of any charges on which his committal for trial was refused by the magistrates' court; (c) a copy of any existing indictment which has been preferred in consequence of his committal; (d) a summary of the evidence which (i) identifies the counts in the proposed indictment on which he has been committed for trial and (ii) in relation to each other count in the proposed indictment, identifies the pages in the accompanying statements and exhibits where the essential evidence said to support that count is to be found. These requirements should be complied with in relation to each defendant named in the indictment for which consent is sought, whether or not it is proposed to prefer any new count against him.

- The preferment of a voluntary bill is an exceptional procedure. Consent should only be granted where good reason to depart from the normal procedure is clearly shown and only where the interests of justice, rather than considerations of administrative convenience, require it.

- CPS have issued revised guidance to prosecutors on the procedures to be adopted in seeking a voluntary bill. This guidance requires prosecutors: (i) to give notice to the prospective defendant that such application has been made; (ii) to serve on the prospective defendant a copy of all the documents delivered to the judge, save to the extent that they have already been served on him; (iii) to inform the prospective defendant that he may make submissions in writing to the judge within nine working days of the giving of notice of the application. These procedures should be followed unless there are good grounds for not doing so, in which case prosecutors should inform the judge that the procedures have not been followed and seek permission to dispense with all or any of them. Judges should not give such permission unless good grounds are shown.

- The judge will consider the documents submitted by the prosecutor and any written submissions made by the prospective defendant. The judge may invite oral submissions from either party, or accede to a request for an opportunity to make such oral submissions, if he considers it necessary or desirable to receive such oral submissions in order to make a sound and fair decision on the application. Any such oral submissions should be made on notice to the other party, who should be allowed to attend.

If the judge directs that a voluntary bill of indictment be preferred (that is, orders the defendant to stand trial in the Crown Court), that decision cannot be challenged by judicial review (*R v Manchester Crown Court ex p Williams* [1990] Crim LR 654). Similarly, the judge who presides over the trial in the Crown Court cannot quash the indictment if he disagrees with the decision of the High Court judge (*R v Rothfield* (1937) 26 Cr App R 103; [1937] 4 All ER 320).

Even though the decision of a High Court judge to issue a voluntary bill of indictment is not subject to judicial review, the decision of a prosecutor to seek a voluntary bill is susceptible to review, but only on very limited grounds (such as alleged malice on the part of the prosecutor (*R v Inland Revenue Commissioners ex p Dhesi* (1995) *Independent*, 14 August)).

7.12.2   Uses of voluntary bill procedure

The Practice Direction of 1999 makes it clear that, if committal proceedings can be brought, the voluntary bill procedure should not be used unless there is very good reason to depart from normal procedure. The main uses of this procedure are as follows:

(a) Where committal proceedings have taken place and the defendant has been discharged, the voluntary bill procedure is an alternative to bringing fresh committal proceedings. However, in *Brooks v DPP of Jamaica* [1994] 1 AC 568; [1994] 2 All ER 231, the Privy Council said that a judge should only direct the preferment of a voluntary bill of indictment in a case where magistrates have discharged a defendant in exceptional circumstances.

(b) Where the defendant disrupts the committal proceedings but for some reason the justices decide not to use their power (under s 4 of the Magistrates' Courts Act 1980, see above) to proceed in his absence, the voluntary bill procedure can be used.

(c) Where one defendant has already been committed for trial and another suspect is arrested shortly before the trial of the first defendant, it is desirable that there be a joint trial. If there is insufficient time for committal proceedings to take place and it is undesirable to seek an adjournment of the first defendant's trial, the voluntary bill procedure is a speedy way of getting the second suspect to the Crown Court so that there can be a joint trial.

7.12.3 Notices of transfer

In certain cases, the prosecution can bypass the need for committal proceedings merely by serving a notice on the defendant transferring the case to the Crown Court.

This procedure applies in two cases:

(1) Section 4 of the Criminal Justice Act 1987

Cases involving serious or complex fraud where the prosecution is brought by the Director of Public Prosecutions (this includes Crown Prosecution Service cases as the Director of Public Prosecutions is head of the Crown Prosecution Service), the Serious Fraud Office, the Inland Revenue, Her Majesty's Customs and Excise.

(2) Section 53 of the Criminal Justice Act 1991

Specified offences of a violent or sexual nature where there is a child witness (either the victim of the offence or a witness to its commission) who will be called at the trial. In such a case the Director of Public Prosecutions (who can delegate this function to Crown Prosecutors) may use the transfer procedure if he is of the opinion that it is necessary to transfer the case direct to the Crown Court in order to avoid prejudice to the welfare of the child.

The specified offences under s 53 are:

(a) an offence involving assault on, or injury or threat of injury to, a person (not necessarily the witness or another juvenile);

(b) cruelty to a person under 16 (s 1 of the Children and Young Persons Act 1933);

(c) an offence under the Sexual Offences Acts 1956 and 1967, the Indecency with Children Act 1960, s 54 of the Criminal Law Act 1977 or the Protection of Children Act 1978.

In cases (a) and (b), a child witness means a witness who has not attained the age of 14; in (c), a child witness means a witness under 17.

To by-pass committal proceedings under either of these statutes, a notice of transfer is served on the clerk to the justices and on the defendant. The notice must be accompanied by the written witness statements which show there is sufficient evidence for the accused to be committed for trial.

In *R v Wrench* [1996] Crim LR 265, it was held that, if one of the offences of which the defendant is accused is one to which the transfer provisions apply, then the procedure can also be used in respect of any other offences which can validly be joined on the same indictment.

Under both statutes, proceedings are still commenced in the magistrates' court, and the magistrates still have jurisdiction in respect of matters such as bail and legal aid.

7.12.4   'No case to answer' in the transfer procedure

When a notice of transfer has been served, the defendant may apply to a Crown Court judge to dismiss the charge(s) on the ground that there is no case to answer (s 6 of the Criminal Justice Act 1987 and Sched 6, para 5 of the Criminal Justice Act 1991).

Section 6 of the Criminal Justice Act 1987 provides that, in fraud case transfers, oral evidence may only be given at the hearing of the application to dismiss the case with leave of the judge, which is very rarely given.

Schedule 6 of the Criminal Justice Act 1991 provides that, in child witness case transfers, the judge may give leave for oral evidence to be called at the hearing of the application to dismiss the case, but he must not hear oral evidence from the child in whose interests the notice of transfer was given in deciding whether there is a case to answer.

In either case, the judge must dismiss the case if it appears to him that the evidence against the applicant would not be sufficient for a jury properly to convict him. Further proceedings in respect of the dismissed charge may only be brought by way of an application for a voluntary bill of indictment.

7.13   INDICTABLE ONLY OFFENCES: NO COMMITTAL PROCEEDINGS

Section 51 of the Crime and Disorder Act 1998 abolishes the requirement of committal proceedings in the case of offences which are triable only on indictment (so committal proceedings are relevant only to offences that are triable either way). The provisions of s 51 are supplemented by detailed provisions contained in Sched 3 of the 1998 Act.

7.13.1   Transfer to the Crown Court

Section 51(1) provides that, where an adult appears before a magistrates' court charged with an offence which is triable only on indictment, the magistrates' court must immediately send him to the Crown Court for trial for that offence and for any either way or summary offence which (under s 51(11)) appears to the court to be related to the indictable only offence; however (again subs (11)) this only applies to summary offences which are punishable with imprisonment or disqualification from driving.

Under s 51(7), the magistrates' court must provide a notice, which is served on the defendant and on the relevant Crown Court, specifying the offence(s) for which the defendant has been sent for trial. Section 51(8) provides that, where there is more than one indictable only offence, and the defendant is also sent for trial in respect of an either way or summary offence, the notice must specify which indictable offence the either way or summary offence is linked to.

In selecting which location of the Crown Court to send the defendant to for trial, the magistrates' court must have regard to: the convenience of the defence, the prosecution and the witnesses; the desirability of expediting the trial; and directions given by the Lord Chief Justice on the allocation of Crown Court business (s 51(10)).

7.13.2   Submission of no case to answer

Para 1 of Sched 3 requires the defendant to be served with copies of the documents containing the evidence on which the charge(s) are based.

Paragraph 2(1) says that at any time after the service of these documents but before he has been arraigned, the defendant may apply orally or in writing to the Crown Court to which he has been sent for trial to apply for the charge(s) to be dismissed. The application is heard by a judge, who is required, under para 2(2), to dismiss a charge (and where the indictment has been preferred, to quash any count on the indictment relating to that charge) if it appears to him 'that the evidence against the applicant would not be sufficient for a jury properly to convict him'.

Paragraph 2(3) says that an oral application can only be made if the applicant has given written notice of his intention to make the application. Paragraph 4 says that oral evidence may only be given on such an application with the leave of the judge, and leave is only to be given where it is in the interests of justice to do so. Paragraph 2(4) also envisages the possibility of the judge making an order that oral evidence should be heard (again, only if in the interests of justice to do so). Under para 2(5), if the judge gives leave or makes an order for someone to give evidence, but that person fails to give evidence, the judge may disregard any document indicating the evidence which that witness might have given at the hearing of the application.

Paragraph 2(6) provides that, where a charge has been dismissed under para 2(2), further proceedings on that charge can only be brought by means of an application to a High Court judge for a voluntary bill of indictment.

7.13.3 Reporting restrictions

Paragraph 3 of Sched 3 imposes reporting restriction: they are the same as those applicable to committal proceedings under s 6 of the Magistrates' Courts Act 1980 (see above).

7.13.4 Linked offences

Paragraph 6 of Sched 3 deals with the powers of the Crown Court to deal with cases where summary offences are sent to the Crown Court under s 51. Only indictable and either way offences can actually appear on the indictment. If the defendant is convicted on that indictment, the Crown Court must first consider whether the summary offence is related to the indictable only offence(s). Paragraph 6(12) provides that an offence is related to another offence for these purposes 'if it arises out circumstances which are the same as or connected with those giving rise to the other offence'. If the summary offence is related to the indictable offence of which the defendant has been convicted, the court asks the defendant whether he pleads guilty or not guilty to the summary offence. If he pleads guilty, the Crown Court will proceed to sentence him for that offence (but may not impose a greater sentence than a magistrates' court could have imposed). If he pleads not guilty, the Crown Court has no further part to play in respect of that offence (unless the prosecution indicate that they do not wish to proceed with the offence, in which case, the Crown Court can formally dismiss it, with the effect that the defendant is acquitted of it). Paragraph 6(8) makes it clear that the provisions of para 6 do not apply where the summary offence is tried on indictment under s 40 of the Criminal Justice Act 1988 (see Chapter 3, 3.14).

This procedure is of course very similar to that set out in s 41 of the Criminal Justice Act 1988 (see Chapter 3, 3.15) and achieves the same objectives.

Paragraph 6(9) provides that, where the Court of Appeal quashes a conviction for an indictable only offence, it must also set aside any conviction for a summary offence where the accused was dealt with for that offence by the Crown Court following conviction for the indictable only offence.

Section 51(2) provides that, where an adult has already been sent for trial under s 51(1) and then appears before a magistrates' court charged with a related either way offence (or a related summary offence, provided that it carries imprisonment or disqualification from driving), the magistrates may send him to the Crown Court for trial for that either way or summary offence.

Paragraph 7 deals with the situation where the defendant is sent for trial for an indictable only offence but is not arraigned for such an offence. If the indictment still contains any either way offences, the Crown Court must go through the indication as to plea ('plea before venue') procedure (see Chapter 3, 3.3) and, where the defendant indicates a not guilty plea or gives no indication, the mode of trial procedure which would have been followed in the magistrates' court.

7.13.5 Other defendants

Section 51(3) provides that where an adult is sent to the Crown Court for trial under s 51(1), and another adult, either then or on a subsequent occasion, appears at the magistrates' court charged jointly with him with an either way offence which is related to the indictable only offence, the court must (if it is the same occasion) or may (if it is a subsequent occasion) send the other adult to the Crown Court for trial for the either way offence. Under s 51(4), the magistrates must also send him to the Crown Court for trial for any either way or summary offence (in the case of the latter, provided that it is imprisonable or carries disqualification from driving) which is related to the indictable offence.

Under s 51(5), where an adult is sent for trial under s 51(1) or (3) and a juvenile is charged jointly with the adult with the indictable offence for which the adult has been sent for trial, the magistrates' court should only send the juvenile to the Crown Court for trial for the indictable offence 'if it considers it necessary in the interests of justice'. Where a juvenile is sent for trial for an indictable offence under s 51(5), the court may also send him for trial for a related either way or summary offence (in the case of the latter, provided that it is imprisonable or carries disqualification from driving).

7.14 MOVING THE TRIAL

The justices will usually commit the defendant to the nearest location of the Crown Court which is competent to deal with the case (see Chapter 1, 1.16).

It may be, however, that there are reasons why this may not be appropriate. For example, the offence with which the defendant is charged may have aroused such ill feeling locally that a fair trial at the nearest location of the Crown Court may not be possible. In such a case, the magistrates may be asked to commit the defendant to a different Crown Court.

If the magistrates do not accede to this application, or if no such application is made, there are two other ways of moving the trial:

- para 76(2) of the Supreme Court Act 1981 empowers an officer of the Crown Court to alter the place of trial;

- if the transfer is not effected administratively, either party may make an application to the Crown Court, under s 76(3) of the Supreme Court Act 1981, for the venue of the trial to be altered. Such an application is heard by a High Court judge, sitting in open court (s 76(4)).

7.15 SUMMONS TO POTENTIAL PROSECUTION WITNESS TO MAKE DEPOSITION

The Criminal Procedure and Investigations Act 1996 added a s 97A to the Magistrates' Courts Act 1980. The section enables a magistrate, prior to committal proceedings, to issue a summons to a *potential* prosecution witness. The summons requires the potential witness to attend before a magistrate so that the magistrate can take a deposition from the witness. The requirements which have to be met are:

(a) the person is likely to be able to make, on behalf of the prosecution, a written statement containing material evidence (or to produce a document or other exhibit likely to be material evidence), for the purposes of committal proceedings which have not yet taken place; and

(b) the person would not make the statement (or produce the document or exhibit) voluntarily.

Where these matters are established on oath and the magistrate is satisfied that the person will not attend even if a summons is issued, then an arrest warrant can be issued instead.

The deposition is taken before a single magistrate. A court does not have to be convened for this to be done; indeed, the deposition does not have to be taken in a court building. The defendant and his legal representative have no right to attend the taking of the deposition, and if they do attend have no right to cross-examine the witness. Indeed the magistrate does not even have to notify the accused that a deposition is being taken (and would not notify the accused if the prosecution feared that the witness might be the subject of intimidation if the defence knew that a statement was being taken). The prosecutor questions the witness and a note is taken of the answers given by the witness. The witness is then asked to confirm the accuracy of the note. The magistrate must ensure that the questions asked by the prosecutor are relevant to the charge faced by the accused.

This procedure is not available to the defence, since its object is to facilitate the gathering of evidence for committal proceedings. It represents the first time that magistrates have become part of the criminal investigation process (along the lines of the examining magistrate on the Continent).

TABLE OF STATUTORY AND OTHER MATERIALS

STATUTORY MATERIALS

MAGISTRATES' COURTS ACT 1980

Section 4: General nature of committal proceedings

(1) The functions of examining justices may be discharged by a single justice.

(2) Examining justices shall sit in open court except where any enactment contains an express provision to the contrary and except where it appears to them as respects the whole or any part of committal proceedings that the ends of justice would not be served by their sitting in open court.

(3) Subject to sub-section (4) below, evidence tendered before examining justices shall be tendered in the presence of the accused.

(4) Examining justices may allow evidence to be tendered before them in the absence of the accused if:

  (a) they consider that by reason of his disorderly conduct before them it is not practicable for the evidence to be tendered in his presence; or

  (b) he cannot be present for reasons of health but is represented by a legal representative and has consented to the evidence being tendered in his absence.

Section 5: Adjournment of inquiry

(1) A magistrates' court may, before beginning to inquire into an offence as examining justices, or at any time during the inquiry, adjourn the hearing, and if it does so shall remand the accused.

(2) The court shall when adjourning fix the time and place at which the hearing is to be resumed; and the time fixed shall be that at which the accused is required to appear or be brought before the court in pursuance of the remand or would be required to be brought before the court but for section 128(3A) below.

Section 5A: Evidence which is admissible

(1) Evidence falling within sub-section (2) below, and only that evidence, shall be admissible by a magistrates' court inquiring into an offence as examining justices.

(2) Evidence falls within this sub-section if it:

  (a) is tendered by or on behalf of the prosecutor; and

  (b) falls within sub-section (3) below.

(3) The following evidence falls within this sub-section:

  (a) written statements complying with section 5B below;

(b) the documents or other exhibits (if any) referred to in such statements;

(c) depositions complying with section 5C below;

(d) the documents or other exhibits (if any) referred to in such depositions;

(e) statements complying with section 5D below;

(f) documents falling with section 5E below.

(4) In this section 'document' means anything in which information of any description is recorded.

Section 5B: Written statements

(1) For the purposes of section 5A above a written statement complies with this section if:

(a) the conditions falling within sub-section (2) below are met; and

(b) such of the conditions falling within sub-section (3) below as apply are met.

(2) The conditions falling within this sub-section are that:

(a) the statement purports to be signed by the person who made it;

(b) the statement contains a declaration by that person to the effect that it is true to the best of his knowledge and belief and that he made the statement knowing that, if it were tendered in evidence, he would be liable to prosecution if he wilfully stated in it anything which he knew to be false or did not believe to be true;

(c) before the statement is tendered in evidence a copy of the statement is given, by or on behalf of the prosecutor, to each of the other parties to the proceedings.

(3) The conditions falling within this sub-section are that:

(a) if the statement is made by a person under 18 years old, it gives his age;

(b) if it is made by a person who cannot read it, it is read to him before he signs it and is accompanied by a declaration by the person who so read the statement to the effect that it was so read;

(c) if it refers to any other document as an exhibit, the copy given to any other party to the proceedings under sub-section (2)(c) above is accompanied by a copy of that document or by such information as may be necessary to enable the party to whom it is given to inspect that document or a copy of it.

(4) So much of any statement as is admitted in evidence by virtue of this section shall, unless the court commits the accused for trial by virtue of section 6(2) below or the court otherwise directs, be read aloud at the hearing; and where the court so directs an account shall be given orally of so much of any statement as is not read aloud.

(5) Any document or other object referred to as an exhibit and identified in a statement admitted in evidence by virtue of this section shall be treated as if it had been produced as an exhibit and identified in court by the maker of the statement.

(6) In this section 'document' means anything in which information of any description is recorded.

Section 5C: Depositions

(1) For the purposes of section 5A above a deposition complies with this section if:

    (a) a copy of it is sent to the prosecutor under section 97A(9) below;

    (b) the condition falling within sub-section (2) below is met; and

    (c) the condition falling within sub-section (3) below is met, in a case where it applies.

(2) The condition falling within this sub-section is that before the magistrates' court begins to inquire into the offence concerned as examining justices a copy of the deposition is given, by or on behalf of the prosecutor, to each of the other parties to the proceedings.

(3) The condition falling within this sub-section is that, if the deposition refers to any other document as an exhibit, the copy given to any other party to the proceedings under sub-section (2) above is accompanied by a copy of that document or by such information as may be necessary to enable the party to whom it is given to inspect that document or a copy of it.

(4) So much of any deposition as is admitted in evidence by virtue of this section shall, unless the court commits the accused for trial by virtue of section 6(2) below or the court otherwise directs, be read aloud at the hearing; and where the court so directs an account shall be given orally of so much of any deposition as is not read aloud.

(5) Any document or other object referred to as an exhibit and identified in a deposition admitted in evidence by virtue of this section shall be treated as if it had been produced as an exhibit and identified in court by the person whose evidence is taken as the deposition.

(6) In this section 'document' means anything in which information of any description is recorded.

Section 5D: Statements

(1) For the purposes of section 5A above a statement complies with this section if the conditions falling within sub-sections (2) to (4) below are met.

(2) The condition falling within this sub-section is that, before the committal proceedings begin, the prosecutor notifies the magistrates' court and each of the other parties to the proceedings that he believes:

    (a) that the statement might by virtue of section 23 or 24 of the Criminal Justice Act 1988 (statements in certain documents) be admissible as evidence if the case came to trial; and

    (b) that the statement would not be admissible as evidence otherwise than by virtue of sections 23 or 24 of that Act if the case came to trial.

(3) The condition falling within this sub-section is that:

(a) the prosecutor's belief is based on information available to him at the time he makes the notification;

(b) he has reasonable grounds for his belief; and

(c) he gives the reasons for his belief when he makes the notification.

(4) The condition falling within this sub-section is that when the court or a party is notified as mentioned in sub-section (2) above a copy of the statement is given, by or on behalf of the prosecutor, to the court or the party concerned.

(5) So much of any statement as is in writing and is admitted in evidence by virtue of this section shall, unless the court commits the accused for trial by virtue of section 6(2) below or the court otherwise directs, be read aloud at the hearing; and where the court so directs an account shall be given orally of so much of any statement as is not read aloud.

Section 5E: Other documents

(1) The following documents fall within this section:

(a) any document which by virtue of any enactment is evidence in proceedings before a magistrates' court inquiring into an offence as examining justices;

(b) any document which by virtue of any enactment is admissible, or may be used, or is to be admitted or received, in or as evidence in such proceedings;

(c) any document which by virtue of any enactment may be considered in such proceedings;

(d) any document whose production constitutes proof in such proceedings by virtue of any enactment;

(e) any document by the production of which evidence may be given in such proceedings by virtue of any enactment.

(2) In sub-section (1) above:

(a) references to evidence include references to *prima facie* evidence;

(b) references to any enactment include references to any provision of this Act.

(3) So much of any document as is admitted in evidence by virtue of this section shall, unless the court commits the accused for trial by virtue of section 6(2) below or the court otherwise directs, be read aloud at the hearing; and where the court so directs an account shall be given orally of so much of any statement as is not read aloud.

(4) In this section 'document' means anything in which information of any description is recorded.

Section 5F: Proof by production of copy

(1) Where a statement, deposition or document is admissible in evidence by virtue of sections 5B, 5C, 5D or 5E above it may be proved by the production of:

    (a) the statement, deposition or document; or

    (b) a copy of it or the material part of it.

(2) Sub-section (1)(b) above applies whether or not the statement, deposition or document is still in existence.

(3) It is immaterial for the purposes of this section how many removes there are between a copy and the original.

(4) In this section 'copy", in relation to a statement, deposition or document, means anything onto which information recorded in the statement, deposition or document has been copied, by whatever means and whether directly or indirectly.

Section 6: Discharge or committal for trial

(1) A magistrates' court inquiring into an offence as examining justices shall on consideration of the evidence:

    (a) commit the accused for trial if it is of the opinion that there is sufficient evidence to put him on trial by jury for any indictable offence;

    (b) discharge him if it is not of that opinion and he is in custody for no other cause than the offence under inquiry;

but the preceding provisions of this sub-section have effect subject to the provisions of this and any other Act relating to the summary trial of indictable offences.

(2) If a magistrates' court inquiring into an offence as examining justices is satisfied that all the evidence tendered by or on behalf of the prosecutor falls within section 5A(3) above, it may commit the accused for trial for the offence without consideration of the contents of any statements, depositions or other documents, and without consideration of any exhibits which are not documents, unless:

    (a) the accused or one of the accused has no legal representative acting for him in the case; or

    (b) a legal representative for the accused or one of the accused, as the case may be, has requested the court to consider a submission that there is insufficient evidence to put that accused on trial by jury for the offence,

and sub-section (1) above shall not apply to a committal for trial under this sub-section.

(3) Subject to section 4 of the Bail Act 1976 and section 41 below, the court may commit a person for trial:

    (a) in custody, that is to say, by committing him to custody there to be safely kept until delivered in due course of law; or

(b) on bail in accordance with the Bail Act 1976, that is to say, by directing him to appear before the Crown Court for trial,

and where his release on bail is conditional on his providing one or more surety or sureties and, in accordance with section 8(3) of the Bail Act 1976, the court fixes the amount in which the surety is to be bound with a view to his entering into his recognizance subsequently in accordance with sub-sections (4), (5) or (6) of that section the court shall in the meantime commit the accused to custody in accordance with paragraph (a) of this sub-section.

(4) Where the court has committed a person to custody in accordance with paragraph (a) of sub-section (3) above, then, if that person is in custody for no other cause, the court may, at any time before his first appearance before the Crown Court, grant him bail in accordance with the Bail Act 1976 subject to a duty to appear before the Crown Court for trial.

...

Section 7: Place of trial on indictment

A magistrates' court committing a person for trial shall specify the place at which he is to be tried, and in selecting that place shall have regard to:

(a) the convenience of the defence, the prosecution and the witnesses;

(b) the expediting of the trial; and

(c) any direction given by or on behalf of the Lord Chief Justice with the concurrence of the Lord Chancellor under section 4(5) of the Courts Act 1971.

Section 8: Restrictions of reports of committal proceedings

(1) Except as provided by sub-sections (2), (3) and (8) below, it shall not be lawful to publish in Great Britain a written report, or to include in a relevant programme for reception in Great Britain a report, of any committal proceedings in England and Wales containing any matter other than that permitted by sub-section (4) below.

(2) Subject to sub-section (2A) below a magistrates' court shall, on an application for the purpose made with reference to any committal proceedings by the accused or one of the accused, as the case may be, order that sub-section (1) above shall not apply to reports of those proceedings.

(2A) Where in the case of two or more accused one of them objects to the making of an order under sub-section (2) above, the court shall make the order if, and only if, it is satisfied, after hearing the representations of the accused, that it is in the interests of justice to do so.

(2B) An order under sub-section (2) above shall not apply to reports of proceedings under sub-section (2A) above, but any decision of the court to make or not to make such an order may be contained in reports published or included in a relevant programme before the time authorised by sub-section (3) below.

(3) It shall not be unlawful under this section to publish or include in a relevant programme a report of committal proceedings containing any matter other than that permitted by sub-section (4) below:

(a) where the magistrates' court determines not to commit the accused, or determines to commit none of the accused, for trial, after it so determines;

(b) where the court commits the accused or any of the accused for trial, after the conclusion of his trial or, as the case may be, the trial of the last to be tried,

and where at any time during the inquiry the court proceeds to try summarily the case of one or more of the accused under section 25(3) or (7) below, while committing the other accused or one or more of the other accused for trial, it shall not be unlawful under this section to publish or include in a relevant programme as part of a report of the summary trial, after the court determines to proceed as aforesaid, a report of so much of the committal proceedings containing any such matter as takes place before the determination.

(4) The following matters may be contained in a report of committal proceedings published or included in a relevant programme without an order under sub-section (2) above before the time authorised by sub-section (3) above, that is to say:

(a) the identity of the court and the names of the examining justices;

(b) the names, addresses and occupations of the parties and witnesses and the ages of the accused and witnesses;

(c) the offence or offences, or a summary of them, with which the accused is or are charged;

(d) the names of the legal representatives engaged in the proceedings;

(e) any decision of the court to commit the accused or any of the accused for trial, and any decision of the court on the disposal of the case of any accused not committed;

(f) where the court commits the accused or any of the accused for trial, the charge or charges, or a summary of them, on which he is committed and the court to which he is committed;

(g) where the committal proceedings are adjourned, the date and place to which they are adjourned;

(h) any arrangements as to bail on committal or adjournment;

(i) whether legal aid was granted to the accused or any of the accused.

(5) [Penalty: fine up to £5,000]

(6) [Consent of Attorney General required to bring prosecution under this section]

...

(8) For the purposes of this section committal proceedings shall, in relation to an information charging an indictable offence, be deemed to include any proceedings in the magistrates' court before the court proceeds to inquire

into the information as examining justices; but where a magistrates' court which has begun to try an information summarily discontinues the summary trial in pursuance of section 25(2) or (6) below and proceeds to inquire into the information as examining justices, that circumstance shall not make it unlawful under this section for a report of any proceedings on the information which was published, or included in a relevant programme before the court determined to proceed as aforesaid to have been so published, or included in a relevant programme.

(9) [Repealed]

(10) In this section:

    (a) 'publish', in relation to a report, means publish the report, either by itself or as part of a newspaper or periodical, for distribution to the public;

    (b) 'relevant programme' means a programme included in a programme service (within the meaning of the Broadcasting Act 1990).

INDICTABLE ONLY OFFENCES

CRIME AND DISORDER ACT 1998

Section 51: No committal proceedings for indictable only offences

(1) Where an adult appears or is brought before a magistrates' court ('the court') charged with an offence triable only on indictment ('the indictable only offence'), the court shall send him forthwith to the Crown Court for trial:

    (a) for that offence; and

    (b) for any either way or summary offence with which he is charged which fulfils the requisite conditions (as set out in sub-section (11) below).

(2) Where an adult who has been sent for trial under sub-section (1) above subsequently appears or is brought before a magistrates' court charged with an either way or summary offence which fulfils the requisite conditions, the court may send him forthwith to the Crown Court for trial for the either way or summary offence.

(3) Where:

    (a) the court sends an adult for trial under sub-section (1) above;

    (b) another adult appears or is brought before the court on the same or a subsequent occasion charged jointly with him with an either way offence; and

    (c) that offence appears to the court to be related to the indictable only offence,

the court shall where it is the same occasion, and may where it is a subsequent occasion, send the other adult forthwith to the Crown Court for trial for the either way offence.

(4) Where a court sends an adult for trial under sub-section (3) above, it shall at the same time send him to the Crown Court for trial for any either way or summary offence with which he is charged which fulfils the requisite conditions.

(5) Where:

    (a) the court sends an adult for trial under sub-section (1) or (3) above; and

    (b) a child or young person appears or is brought before the court on the same or a subsequent occasion charged jointly with the adult with an indictable offence for which the adult is sent for trial,

the court shall, if it considers it necessary in the interests of justice to do so, send the child or young person forthwith to the Crown Court for trial for the indictable offence.

(6) Where a court sends a child or young person for trial under sub-section (5) above, it may at the same time send him to the Crown Court for trial for any either way or summary offence with which he is charged which fulfils the requisite conditions.

(7) The court shall specify in a notice the offence or offences for which a person is sent for trial under this section and the place at which he is to be tried; and a copy of the notice shall be served on the accused and given to the Crown Court sitting at that place.

(8) In a case where there is more than one indictable only offence and the court includes an

either way or a summary offence in the notice under sub-section (7) above, the court shall specify in that notice the indictable only offence to which the either way offence or, as the case may be, the summary offence appears to the court to be related.

(9) The trial of the information charging any summary offence for which a person is sent for trial under this section shall be treated as if the court had adjourned it under section 10 of the 1980 Act and had not fixed the time and place for its resumption.

(10) In selecting the place of trial for the purpose of sub-section (7) above, the court shall have regard to:

    (a) the convenience of the defence, the prosecution and the witnesses;

    (b) the desirability of expediting the trial; and

    (c) any direction given by or on behalf of the Lord Chief Justice with the concurrence of the Lord Chancellor under section 75(1) of the Supreme Court Act 1981.

(11) An offence fulfils the requisite conditions if:

    (a) it appears to the court to be related to the indictable only offence; and

    (b) in the case of a summary offence, it is punishable with imprisonment or involves obligatory or discretionary disqualification from driving.

(12) For the purposes of this section:

    (a) 'adult' means a person aged 18 or over, and references to an adult include references to a corporation;

(b) 'either way offence' means an offence which, if committed by an adult, is triable either on indictment or summarily;

(c) an either way offence is related to an indictable only offence if the charge for the either way offence could be joined in the same indictment as the charge for the indictable only offence;

(d) a summary offence is related to an indictable only offence if it arises out of circumstances which are the same as or connected with those giving rise to the indictable only offence.

SCHEDULE 3

PROCEDURE WHERE PERSONS ARE SENT FOR TRIAL UNDER SECTION 51

1

(1) The Attorney General shall by regulations provide that, where a person is sent for trial under section 51 of this Act on any charge or charges, copies of the documents containing the evidence on which the charge or charges are based shall:

(a) be served on that person; and

(b) be given to the Crown Court sitting at the place specified in the notice under sub-section (7) of that section,

before the expiry of the period prescribed by the regulations; but the judge may at his discretion extend or further extend that period.

(2) The regulations may make provision as to the procedure to be followed on an application for the extension or further extension of a period under sub-paragraph (1) above.

2   Applications for dismissal

(1) A person who is sent for trial under section 51 of this Act on any charge or charges may, at any time:

(a) after he is served with copies of the documents containing the evidence on which the charge or charges are based; and

(b) before he is arraigned (and whether or not an indictment has been preferred against him),

apply orally or in writing to the Crown Court sitting at the place specified in the notice under sub-section (7) of that section for the charge, or any of the charges, in the case to be dismissed.

(2) The judge shall dismiss a charge (and accordingly quash any count relating to it in any indictment preferred against the applicant) which is the subject of any such application if it appears to him that the evidence against the applicant would not be sufficient for a jury properly to convict him.

(3) No oral application may be made under sub-paragraph (1) above unless the applicant has given to the Crown Court sitting at the place in question written notice of his intention to make the application.

(4) Oral evidence may be given on such an application only with the leave of the judge or by his order; and the judge shall give leave or make an order only if it appears to him, having regard to any matters stated in the application for leave, that the interests of justice require him to do so.

(5) If the judge gives leave permitting, or makes an order requiring, a person to give oral evidence, but that person does not do so, the judge may disregard any document indicating the evidence that he might have given.

(6) If the charge, or any of the charges, against the applicant is dismissed:

   (a) no further proceedings may be brought on the dismissed charge or charges except by means of the preferment of a voluntary bill of indictment; and

   (b) unless the applicant is in custody otherwise than on the dismissed charge or charges, he shall be discharged.

   …

3   Reporting restrictions

(1) Except as provided by this paragraph, it shall not be lawful:

   (a) to publish in Great Britain a written report of an application under paragraph 2(1) above; or

   (b) to include in a relevant programme for reception in Great Britain a report of such an application,

   if (in either case) the report contains any matter other than that permitted by this paragraph.

(2) An order that sub-paragraph (1) above shall not apply to reports of an application under paragraph 2(1) above may be made by the judge dealing with the application.

(3) Where in the case of two or more accused one of them objects to the making of an order under sub-paragraph (2) above, the judge shall make the order if, and only if, he is satisfied, after hearing the representations of the accused, that it is in the interests of justice to do so.

(4) An order under sub-paragraph (2) above shall not apply to reports of proceedings under sub-paragraph (3) above, but any decision of the court to make or not to make such an order may be contained in reports published or included in a relevant programme before the time authorised by sub-paragraph (5) below.

(5) It shall not be unlawful under this paragraph to publish or include in a relevant programme a report of an application under paragraph 2(1) above containing any matter other than that permitted by sub-paragraph (8) below where the application is successful.

(6) Where:

   (a) two or more persons were jointly charged; and

   (b) applications under paragraph 2(1) above are made by more than one of them,

   sub-paragraph (5) above shall have effect as if for the words 'the application is' there were substituted the words 'all the applications are'.

(7) It shall not be unlawful under this paragraph to publish or include in a relevant programme a report of an unsuccessful application at the conclusion of the trial of the person charged, or of the last of the persons charged to be tried.

(8) The following matters may be contained in a report published or included in a relevant programme without an order under sub-paragraph (2) above before the time authorised by sub-paragraphs (5) and (6) above, that is to say:

(a) the identity of the court and the name of the judge;

(b) the names, ages, home addresses and occupations of the accused and witnesses;

(c) the offence or offences, or a summary of them, with which the accused is or are charged;

(d) the names of counsel and solicitors engaged in the proceedings;

(e) where the proceedings are adjourned, the date and place to which they are adjourned;

(f) the arrangements as to bail;

(g) whether a right to representation funded by the Legal Services Commission as part of the Criminal Defence Service was granted to the accused or any of the accused.

(9) The addresses that may be published or included in a relevant programme under sub-paragraph (8) above are addresses:

(a) at any relevant time; and

(b) at the time of their publication or inclusion in a relevant programme.

(10) If a report is published or included in a relevant programme in contravention of this paragraph, the following persons, that is to say:

(a) in the case of a publication of a written report as part of a newspaper or periodical, any proprietor, editor or publisher of the newspaper or periodical;

(b) in the case of a publication of a written report otherwise than as part of a newspaper or periodical, the person who publishes it;

(c) in the case of the inclusion of a report in a relevant programme, any body corporate which is engaged in providing the service in which the programme is included and any person having functions in relation to the programme corresponding to those of the editor of a newspaper,

shall be liable on summary conviction to a fine not exceeding level 5 on the standard scale.

(11) Proceedings for an offence under this paragraph shall not, in England and Wales, be instituted otherwise than by or with the consent of the Attorney General.

(12) Sub-paragraph (1) above shall be in addition to, and not in derogation from, the provisions of any other enactment with respect to the publication of reports of court proceedings.

(13) In this paragraph:

'publish', in relation to a report, means publish the report, either by itself or as part of a newspaper or periodical, for distribution to the public;

'relevant programme' means a programme included in a programme service (within the meaning of the Broadcasting Act 1990);

'relevant time' means a time when events giving rise to the charges to which the proceedings relate occurred.

4   Power of justice to take depositions, etc

(1) Sub-paragraph (2) below applies where a justice of the peace for any commission area is satisfied that:

    (a) any person in England and Wales ("the witness") is likely to be able to make on behalf of the prosecutor a written statement containing material evidence, or produce on behalf of the prosecutor a document or other exhibit likely to be material evidence, for the purposes of proceedings for an offence for which a person has been sent for trial under section 51 of this Act by a magistrates' court for that area; and

    (b) the witness will not voluntarily make the statement or produce the document or other exhibit.

(2) In such a case the justice shall issue a summons directed to the witness requiring him to attend before a justice at the time and place appointed in the summons, and to have his evidence taken as a deposition or to produce the document or other exhibit.

(3) If a justice of the peace is satisfied by evidence on oath of the matters mentioned insub-paragraph (1) above, and also that it is probable that a summons under sub-paragraph (2) above would not procure the result required by it, the justice may instead of issuing a summons issue a warrant to arrest the witness and to bring him before a justice at the time and place specified in the warrant.

(4) A summons may also be issued under sub-paragraph (2) above if the justice is satisfied that the witness is outside the British Islands, but no warrant may be issued under sub-paragraph (3) above unless the justice is satisfied by evidence on oath that the witness is in England and Wales.

(5) If:

    (a) the witness fails to attend before a justice in answer to a summons under this paragraph;

    (b) the justice is satisfied by evidence on oath that the witness is likely to be able to make a statement or produce a document or other exhibit as mentioned in sub-paragraph (1)(a) above;

    (c) it is proved on oath, or in such other manner as may be prescribed, that he has been duly served with the summons and that a reasonable sum has been paid or tendered to him for costs and expenses; and

    (d) it appears to the justice that there is no just excuse for the failure,

the justice may issue a warrant to arrest the witness and to bring him before a justice at the time and place specified in the warrant.

(6) Where:

    (a) a summons is issued under sub-paragraph (2) above or a warrant is issued under sub-paragraph (3) or (5) above; and

    (b) the summons or warrant is issued with a view to securing that the witness has his evidence taken as a deposition,

the time appointed in the summons or specified in the warrant shall be such as to enable the evidence to be taken as a deposition before the relevant date.

(7) If any person attending or brought before a justice in pursuance of this paragraph refuses without just excuse to have his evidence taken as a deposition, or to produce the document or other exhibit, the justice may do one or both of the following:

    (a) commit him to custody until the expiration of such period not exceeding one month as may be specified in the summons or warrant or until he sooner has his evidence taken as a deposition or produces the document or other exhibit;

    (b) impose on him a fine not exceeding £2,500.

(8) A fine imposed under sub-paragraph (7) above shall be deemed, for the purposes of any enactment, to be a sum adjudged to be paid by a conviction.

(9) If in pursuance of this paragraph a person has his evidence taken as a deposition, the clerk of [chief executive to] the justice concerned shall as soon as is reasonably practicable send a copy of the deposition to the prosecutor and the Crown Court.

(10) If in pursuance of this paragraph a person produces an exhibit which is a document, the clerk of [chief executive to] the justice concerned shall as soon as is reasonably practicable send a copy of the document to the prosecutor and the Crown Court.

(11) If in pursuance of this paragraph a person produces an exhibit which is not a document, the clerk of [chief executive to] the justice concerned shall as soon as is reasonably practicable inform the prosecutor and the Crown Court of that fact and of the nature of the exhibit.

(12) In this paragraph:

'prescribed' means prescribed by rules made under section 144 of the 1980 Act;

'the relevant date' has the meaning given by paragraph 1(2) above.

5   Use of depositions as evidence

(1) Subject to sub-paragraph (3) below, sub-paragraph (2) below applies where in pursuance of paragraph 4 above a person has his evidence taken as a deposition.

(2) Where this sub-paragraph applies the deposition may without further proof be read as evidence on the trial of the accused, whether for an offence for which he was sent for trial under section 51 of this Act or for any other offence arising out of the same transaction or set of circumstances.

(3) Sub-paragraph (2) above does not apply if:

    (a) it is proved that the deposition was not signed by the justice by whom it purports to have been signed;

    (b) the court of trial at its discretion orders that sub-paragraph (2) above shall not apply; or

    (c) a party to the proceedings objects to sub-paragraph (2) above applying.

(4) If a party to the proceedings objects to sub-paragraph (2) applying the court of trial may order that the objection shall have no effect if the court considers it to be in the interests of justice so to order.

6   Power of Crown Court to deal with summary offence

(1) This paragraph applies where a magistrates' court has sent a person for trial under section 51 of this Act for offences which include a summary offence.

(2) If the person is convicted on the indictment, the Crown Court shall consider whether the summary offence is related to the offence that is triable only on indictment or, as the case may be, any of the offences that are so triable.

(3) If it considers that the summary offence is so related, the court shall state to the person the substance of the offence and ask him whether he pleads guilty or not guilty.

(4) If the person pleads guilty, the Crown Court shall convict him, but may deal with him in respect of the summary offence only in a manner in which a magistrates' court could have dealt with him.

(5) If he does not plead guilty, the powers of the Crown Court shall cease in respect of the summary offence except as provided by sub-paragraph (6) below.

(6) If the prosecution inform the court that they would not desire to submit evidence on the charge relating to the summary offence, the court shall dismiss it.

(7) The Crown Court shall inform the clerk of [justices' chief executive for] the magistrates' court of the outcome of any proceedings under this paragraph.

(8) If the summary offence is one to which section 40 of the Criminal Justice Act 1988 applies, the Crown Court may exercise in relation to the offence the power conferred by that section; but where the person is tried on indictment for such an offence, the functions of the Crown Court under this paragraph in relation to the offence shall cease.

(9) Where the Court of Appeal allows an appeal against conviction of an indictable only offence which is related to a summary offence of which the appellant was convicted under this paragraph:

    (a) it shall set aside his conviction of the summary offence and give the clerk of the magistrates' court notice that it has done so; and

    (b) it may direct that no further proceedings in relation to the offence are to be undertaken;

    and the proceedings before the Crown Court in relation to the offence shall thereafter be disregarded for all purposes.

(10) A notice under sub-paragraph (9) above shall include particulars of any direction given under paragraph (b) of that sub-paragraph in relation to the offence.

(11) The references to the clerk of the magistrates' court in this paragraph shall be construed in accordance with section 141 of the 1980 Act.

(12) An offence is related to another offence for the purposes of this paragraph if it arises out of circumstances which are the same as or connected with those giving rise to the other offence.

7   Procedure where no indictable only offence remains

(1) Subject to paragraph 13 below, this paragraph applies where:

    (a) a person has been sent for trial under section 51 of this Act but has not been arraigned; and

    (b) the person is charged on an indictment which (following amendment of the indictment, or as a result of an application under paragraph 2 above, or for any other reason) includes no offence that is triable only on indictment.

(2) Everything that the Crown Court is required to do under the following provisions of this paragraph must be done with the accused present in court.

(3) The court shall cause to be read to the accused each count of the indictment that charges an offence triable either way.

(4) The court shall then explain to the accused in ordinary language that, in relation to each of those offences, he may indicate whether (if it were to proceed to trial) he would plead guilty or not guilty, and that if he indicates that he would plead guilty the court must proceed as mentioned in sub-paragraph (6) below.

(5) The court shall then ask the accused whether (if the offence in question were to proceed to trial) he would plead guilty or not guilty.

(6) If the accused indicates that he would plead guilty the court shall proceed as if he had been arraigned on the count in question and had pleaded guilty.

(7) If the accused indicates that he would plead not guilty, or fails to indicate how he would plead, the court shall consider whether the offence is more suitable for summary trial or for trial on indictment.

(8) Subject to sub-paragraph (6) above, the following shall not for any purpose be taken to constitute the taking of a plea:

    (a) asking the accused under this paragraph whether (if the offence were to proceed to trial) he would plead guilty or not guilty;

    (b) an indication by the accused under this paragraph of how he would plead.

8

(1) Subject to paragraph 13 below, this paragraph applies in a case where:

    (a) a person has been sent for trial under section 51 of this Act but has not been arraigned;

(b) he is charged on an indictment which (following amendment of the indictment, or as a result of an application under paragraph 2 above, or for any other reason) includes no offence that is triable only on indictment;

(c) he is represented by a legal representative;

(d) the Crown Court considers that by reason of his disorderly conduct before the court it is not practicable for proceedings under paragraph 7 above to be conducted in his presence; and

(e) the court considers that it should proceed in his absence.

(2) In such a case:

(a) the court shall cause to be read to the representative each count of the indictment that charges an offence triable either way;

(b) the court shall ask the representative whether (if the offence in question were to proceed to trial) the accused would plead guilty or not guilty;

(c) if the representative indicates that the accused would plead guilty the court shall proceed as if the accused had been arraigned on the count in question and had pleaded guilty;

(d) if the representative indicates that the accused would plead not guilty, or fails to indicate how the accused would plead, the court shall consider whether the offence is more suitable for summary trial or for trial on indictment.

(3) Subject to sub-paragraph (2)(c) above, the following shall not for any purpose be taken to constitute the taking of a plea:

(a) asking the representative under this section whether (if the offence were to proceed to trial) the accused would plead guilty or not guilty;

(b) an indication by the representative under this paragraph of how the accused would plead.

9

(1) This paragraph applies where the Crown Court is required by paragraph 7(7) or 8(2)(d) above to consider the question whether an offence is more suitable for summary trial or for trial on indictment.

(2) Before considering the question, the court shall afford first the prosecutor and then the accused an opportunity to make representations as to which mode of trial would be more suitable.

(3) In considering the question, the court shall have regard to:

(a) any representations made by the prosecutor or the accused;

(b) the nature of the case;

(c) whether the circumstances make the offence one of a serious character;

(d) whether the punishment which a magistrates' court would have power to impose for it would be adequate; and

(e) any other circumstances which appear to the court to make it more suitable for the offence to be dealt tried in one way rather than the other.

10

(1) This paragraph applies (unless excluded by paragraph 15 below) where the Crown Court considers that an offence is more suitable for summary trial.

(2) The court shall explain to the accused in ordinary language:

(a) that it appears to the court more suitable for him to be tried summarily for the offence, and that he can either consent to be so tried or, of if he wishes, be tried by a jury; and

(b) that if he is tried summarily and is convicted by the magistrates' court, he may be committed for sentence to the Crown Court under section 38 of the 1980 Act if the convicting court is of such opinion as is mentioned in sub-section (2) of that section.

(3) After explaining to the accused as provided by sub-paragraph (2) above the court shall ask him whether he wishes to be tried summarily or by a jury, and:

(a) if he indicates that he wishes to be tried summarily, shall remit him for trial to a magistrates' court acting for the place where he was sent to the Crown Court for trial;

(b) if he does not give such an indication, shall retain its functions in relation to the offence and proceed accordingly.

11

If the Crown Court considers that an offence is more suitable for trial on indictment, the court:

(a) shall tell the accused that it has decided that it is more suitable for him to be tried for the offence by a jury; and

(b) shall retain its functions in relation to the offence and proceed accordingly.

12

(1) Where the prosecution is being carried on by the Attorney General, the Solicitor General or the Director of Public Prosecutions and he applies for an offence which may be tried on indictment to be so tried:

(a) sub-paragraphs (4) to (8) of paragraph 7, sub-paragraphs (2)(b) to (d) and (3) of paragraph 8 and paragraphs 9 to 11 above shall not apply; and

(b) the Crown Court shall retain its functions in relation to the offence and proceed accordingly.

(2) The power of the Director of Public Prosecutions under this paragraph to apply for an offence to be tried on indictment shall not be exercised except with the consent of the Attorney General.

13

(1) This paragraph applies, in place of paragraphs 7 to 12 above, in the case of a child or young person who:

(a) has been sent for trial under section 51 of this Act but has not been arraigned; and

(b) is charged on an indictment which (following amendment of the indictment, or as a result of an application under paragraph 2 above, or for any other reason) includes no offence that is triable only on indictment.

(2) The Crown Court shall remit the child or young person for trial to a magistrates' court acting for the place where he was sent to the Crown Court for trial unless:

(a) he is charged with such an offence as is mentioned in sub-section (2) of section 53 of the 1933 Act (punishment of certain grave crimes) and the Crown Court considers that if he is found guilty of the offence it ought to be possible to sentence him in pursuance of sub-section (3) of that section; or

(b) he is charged jointly with an adult with an offence triable either way and the Crown Court considers it necessary in the interests of justice that they both be tried for the offence in the Crown Court.

(3) In sub-paragraph (2) above 'adult' has the same meaning as in section 51 of this Act.

14 Procedure for determining whether offences of criminal damage, etc, are summary offences

(1) This paragraph applies where the Crown Court has to determine, for the purposes of this Schedule, whether an offence which is listed in the first column of Schedule 2 to the 1980 Act (offences for which the value involved is relevant to the mode of trial) is a summary offence.

(2) The court shall have regard to any representations made by the prosecutor or the accused.

(3) If it appears clear to the court that the value involved does not exceed the relevant sum, it shall treat the offence as a summary offence.

(4) If it appears clear to the court that the value involved exceeds the relevant sum, it shall treat the offence as an indictable offence.

(5) If it appears to the court for any reason not clear whether the value involved does or does not exceed the relevant sum, the court shall ask the accused whether he wishes the offence to be treated as a summary offence.

(6) Where sub-paragraph (5) above applies:

(a) if the accused indicates that he wishes the offence to be treated as a summary offence, the court shall so treat it;

(b) if the accused does not give such an indication, the court shall treat the offence as an indictable offence.

(7) In this paragraph 'the value involved' and 'the relevant sum' have the same meanings as in section 22 of the 1980 Act (certain offences triable either way to be tried summarily if value involved is small).

15 Power of Crown Court, with consent of legally represented accused, to proceed in his absence

(1) The Crown Court may proceed in the absence of the accused in accordance with such of the provisions of paragraphs 9 to 14 above as are applicable in the circumstances if:

    (a) the accused is represented by a legal representative who signifies to the court the accused's consent to the proceedings in question being conducted in his absence; and

    (b) the court is satisfied that there is good reason for proceeding in the absence of the accused.

(2) Sub-paragraph (1) above is subject to the following provisions of this paragraph which apply where the court exercises the power conferred by that sub-paragraph.

(3) If, where the court has considered as required by paragraph 7(7) or 8(2)(d) above, it appears to the court that an offence is more suitable for summary trial, paragraph 10 above shall not apply and:

    (a) if the legal representative indicates that the accused wishes to be tried summarily, the court shall remit the accused for trial to a magistrates' court acting for the place where he was sent to the Crown Court for trial;

    (b) if the legal representative does not give such an indication, the court shall retain its functions and proceed accordingly.

(4) If, where the court has considered as required by paragraph 7(7) or 8(2)(d) above, it appears to the court that an offence is more suitable for trial on indictment, paragraph 11 above shall apply with the omission of paragraph (a).

(5) Where paragraph 14 above applies and it appears to the court for any reason not clear whether the value involved does or does not exceed the relevant sum, sub-paragraphs (5) and (6) of that paragraph shall not apply and:

    (a) the court shall ask the legal representative whether the accused wishes the offence to be treated as a summary offence;

    (b) if the legal representative indicates that the accused wishes the offence to be treated as a summary offence, the court shall so treat it,

if the legal representative does not give such an indication, the court shall treat the offence as an indictable offence.

CONTEMPT OF COURT ACT 1981

Section 4: Contemporary reports of proceedings

...

(2) In any such proceedings [that is, legal proceedings held in public: section 4(1)] the court may, where it appears to be necessary for avoiding a substantial risk of prejudice to the administration of justice in those proceedings, or in any other proceedings pending or imminent, order that

the publication of any report of the proceedings, or any part of the proceedings, be postponed for such period as the court thinks necessary for that purpose.

REQUIRING WITNESSES TO MAKE STATEMENTS

MAGISTRATES' COURTS ACT 1980

Section 97A: Summons or warrant as to committal proceedings

(1) Sub-section (2) below applies where a justice of the peace for any commission area is satisfied that:

    (a) any person in England or Wales is likely to be able to make on behalf of the prosecutor a written statement containing material evidence, or produce on behalf of the prosecutor a document or other exhibit likely to be material evidence, for the purposes of proceedings before a magistrates' court inquiring into an offence as examining justices;

    (b) the person will not voluntarily make the statement or produce the document or other exhibit; and

    (c) the magistrates' court mentioned in paragraph (a) above is a court for the commission area concerned.

(2) In such a case the justice shall issue a summons directed to that person requiring him to attend before a justice of the peace at the time and place appointed in the summons to have his evidence taken as a deposition or to produce the document or other exhibit.

(3) If a justice of the peace is satisfied by evidence on oath of the matters mentioned in sub-section (1) above, and also that it is probable that a summons under sub-section (2) above would not procure the result required by it, the justice may instead of issuing a summons issue a warrant to arrest the person concerned and bring him before a justice at the time and place specified in the warrant.

(4) A summons may also be issued under sub-section (2) above if the justice is satisfied that the person concerned is outside the British Islands, but no warrant shall be issued under sub-section (3) above unless the justice is satisfied by evidence on oath that the person concerned is in England or Wales.

(5) If:

    (a) a person fails to attend before a justice in answer to a summons under this section;

    (b) the justice is satisfied by evidence on oath that he is likely to be able to make a statement or produce a document or other exhibit as mentioned in sub-section (1)(a) above;

    (c) it is proved on oath, or in such other manner as may be prescribed, that he has been duly served with the summons, and that a reasonable sum has been paid or tendered to him for costs and expenses; and

(d) it appears to the justice that there is no just excuse for the failure,

the justice may issue a warrant to arrest him and bring him before a justice at a time and place specified in the warrant.

(6) Where:

(a) a summons is issued under sub-section (2) above or a warrant is issued under sub-section (3) or (5) above; and

(b) the summons or warrant is issued with a view to securing that a person has his evidence taken as a deposition,

the time appointed in the summons or specified in the warrant shall be such as to enable the evidence to be taken as a deposition before a magistrates' court begins to inquire into the offence concerned as examining justices.

(7) If any person attending or brought before a justice in pursuance of this section refuses without just excuse to have his evidence taken as a deposition, or to produce the document or other exhibit, the justice may do one or both of the following:

(a) commit him to custody until the expiration of such period not exceeding one month as may be specified in the summons or warrant or until he sooner has his evidence taken as a deposition or produces the document or other exhibit;

(b) impose on him a fine not exceeding £2,500.

(9)–(11) [sending copies of deposition, document or exhibit to prosecutor as soon as reasonably practicable]

PREFERRING THE BILL OF INDICTMENT

ADMINISTRATION OF JUSTICE (MISCELLANEOUS PROVISIONS) ACT 1933

Section 2

(2) Subject as hereinafter provided no bill of indictment charging any person with an indictable offence shall be preferred unless either:

(a) the person charged has been committed for trial for the offence; or

(aa) the offence is specified in a notice of transfer under section 4 of the Criminal Justice Act 1987 (serious or complex fraud); or

(ab) the offence is specified in a notice of transfer under section 53 of the Criminal Justice Act 1991 (violent or sexual offences against children); or

(b) the bill is preferred by the direction of the Criminal Division of the Court of Appeal or by the direction or with the consent of a judge of the

High Court.

Provided that:

(i)   where the person charged has been committed for trial, the bill of indictment against him may include, either in substitution for or in addition to counts charging the offence for which he was committed, any counts founded on facts or evidence disclosed to the magistrates' court inquiring into that offence as examining justices, being counts which may lawfully be joined in the same indictment;

(iA) in a case to which paragraph (aa) or (ab) above applies, the bill of indictment may include, either in substitution for or in addition to any count charging an offence specified in the notice of transfer, any counts founded on material that accompanied the copy of that notice which, in pursuance of regulations under the relevant provision, was given to the person charged, being counts which may lawfully be joined in the same indictment;

and in paragraph (iA) above 'the relevant provision' means section 5(9) of the Criminal Justice Act 1987 in a case to which paragraph (aa) above applies, and paragraph 4 of Schedule 6 to the Criminal Justice Act 1991 in a case to which paragraph (ab) above applies.

OTHER MATERIALS

STATEMENT OF WITNESS[1]

CJ Act 1967, s 9; MC Act 1980, ss 5A(3)(a) and 5B; MC Rules 1981, r 70

STATEMENT OF [NAME OF WITNESS]

Age of witness (if over 18 enter 'over 18'):

Occupation of witness:

This statement [,   consisting of   pages each signed by me,] is true to the best of my knowledge and belief and I make it know that, if it is tendered in evidence, I shall be liable to prosecution if I have wilfully stated in it anything which I know to be false or do not believe to be true.

Dated the   day of   20 .

---

1   Form 13 set out in the Magistrates' Courts (Forms) Rules 1981 as amended by the Magistrates' Courts (Forms) Rules 1997. Wherever possible, the statement should be on foolscap paper. If statements are typed, double spacing should be used. One side only of the paper should be used. A space should be left at the top of the first page for headings to be entered by the clerk of the court. Each page should have a wide margin on the left.

CHAPTER 8

INDICTMENTS

8.1 INTRODUCTION

In this chapter, we examine the rules which govern the form and content of the indictment upon which a Crown Court trial is based.

8.2 TERMINOLOGY

The indictment is the formal document setting out the charges which the defendant faces at the Crown Court. Each offence is known as a 'count'. An indictment is only valid when it is signed by an appropriate officer of the Crown Court. A draft indictment which has not yet been signed by an officer of the Crown Court is known as a 'bill of indictment'.

An indictment is set out as shown overleaf:

No. 01321

INDICTMENT

THE CROWN COURT AT CROYDON

THE QUEEN v VICTOR JAMES WARD

VICTOR JAMES WARD is charged as follows:

COUNT 1

Statement of Offence

Burglary, contrary to section 9(1)(b) of the Theft Act 1968.

Particulars of Offence

VICTOR JAMES WARD, on the 2nd April 2001, having entered as a trespasser a building known as 17 Maidwell Avenue, Croydon, stole therein a television set and a video recorder, the property of John Green.

COUNT 2

Statement of Offence

Unlawful wounding, contrary to section 20 of the Offences Against the Person Act 1861.

Particulars of Offence

VICTOR JAMES WARD, on the 2nd April 2001, unlawfully and maliciously wounded John Green.

B.R. SMITH
Officer of the Crown Court
Date: 1st September 2001

8.3   DRAFTING THE INDICTMENT

It used to be the case that an officer of the Crown Court would look through the witness statements used by the prosecution at committal proceedings to establish a *prima facie* case, and would decide what offences should appear on the indictment on the basis of those statements.

Nowadays, however, the Crown Prosecution Service will usually send a 'bill of indictment' (that is, a draft indictment) to the Crown Court and a proper officer of the court simply signs it.

In most cases, the drafting is done by a Crown Prosecutor, although in difficult cases the Crown Prosecution Service will instruct counsel to do the drafting.

Under s 2(1) of the Administration of Justice (Miscellaneous Provisions) Act 1933, a proper officer of the Crown Court must sign a bill of indictment before it can become an indictment. In *R v Morais* [1988] 3 All ER 161, it was held by the Court of Appeal that this requirement is a mandatory requirement. It followed that a bill of indictment which had been initialled by a High Court judge after giving leave to the prosecution to prefer a voluntary bill of indictment, but which had not been signed by the proper office of the court, was not a valid indictment.

8.4   TIME LIMIT

The bill of indictment should be 'preferred' (that is, delivered to the Crown Court) within 28 days of the committal proceedings.

This period may be extended by up to 28 days by an officer of the Crown Court and may be extended for any period by a Crown Court judge.

The application for an extension of time may be made after the time limit has expired: r 5 of the Indictment Rules 1971.

In any event, preferment out of time is not a ground of appeal against conviction as it does not constitute a material irregularity (*R v Sheerin* (1976) 64 Cr App R 68 and *R v Soffe* (1982) 75 Cr App R 133).

8.5   FORM OF INDICTMENT

The rules which govern the form and content of an indictment are to be found in the Indictment Rules.

Rule 6 of the Indictment Rules sets out the components of a count. Each count comprises:

- *Statement of offence*

  This is a brief description of the offence; if the offence is a statutory one, the relevant section will be given.

- *Particulars of offence*

  This must give such particulars as may be necessary to give the defendant reasonable information about the nature of the charge against him (r 5).

The particulars will therefore set out who is charged, the date of the alleged offence, the act allegedly done, an allegation of *mens rea* (that is, the mental element of the crime), and the identity of the alleged victim.

Where the date is not known for sure, it is usual to say either 'on or about [date]' or 'on a date unknown between [day before the earliest date when the offence could have been committed] and [day after the latest date when the offence could have been committed]'. If the date is incorrectly stated, that is not fatal to the prosecution case since the indictment can be amended, though the defendant may well be entitled to an adjournment if necessary to prepare his defence on the basis of the new date (cf *Wright v Nicholson* [1970] 1 WLR 142; [1970] 1 All ER 12).

In *R v Ike* [1996] STC 391, the defendant was charged with tax offences relating to VAT. On appeal against conviction, she argued that the indictment was defective because it failed to spell out the *mens rea* which the prosecution had to prove in relation to acts which she was alleged to have done (in this case, fraudulent intent or intent to deceive). The Court of Appeal held that the indictment should indeed have spelled out the necessary *mens rea* and that those words should have appeared before any reference to the conduct which was alleged (so each count should have alleged that, with the necessary *mens rea*, the defendant carried out the *actus reus*). However, the jury had been correctly directed on the mental element of the offences and so the conviction was not unsafe; the appeal was therefore dismissed.

8.5.1 Secondary parties

Secondary parties (that is, those who aid, abet, counsel or procure the commission of the offence) are usually charged as principal offenders (s 8 of the Accessories and Abettors Act 1861).

Thus, in a burglary case where one person enters the premises and another person stays outside as a look out, both will be charged with burglary contrary to s 9(1)(b) of the Theft Act 1968 and the particulars will allege that both entered the premises and stole. Similarly, the getaway driver in a robbery will be charged in the same count as the defendants who actually carry out the robbery.

The fact that a defendant is really alleged to have been a secondary party is thus not apparent from the indictment itself but is made clear to the jury when the prosecution make their opening speech.

Occasionally, a count will allege specifically aiding and abetting. This would be done, for example, where the secondary party could not commit the full offence. So, if a man rapes a woman and is aided and abetted by another woman, both perpetrators could be charged with rape but it is much more likely that the woman would be charged specifically with aiding and abetting (as a woman cannot rape another woman).

8.6   QUASHING THE INDICTMENT

It is open to the defence to make an application to 'quash' the indictment. Such an application would normally be made at the Plea and Directions Hearing which precedes the trial itself.

There are three grounds for quashing an indictment. Those grounds are:

(a) the indictment (or a count on the indictment) is bad on its face, as where it alleges an offence which is not known to the law or where a single count alleges more than one offence;

(b) the indictment (or one of its counts) has been preferred without authority, in that there have been no committal proceedings and no notice of transfer (in the cases where that is possible) and no voluntary bill of indictment;

(c) the indictment contains a count in respect of which the defendant was not committed for trial (and there was no notice of transfer or voluntary bill of indictment in respect of that count) and the prosecution witness statements do not disclose a case to answer on that count.

The distinction between (b) and (c) is that, in the case of (b), there were no committal proceedings at all (or an acceptable alternative to them); in the case of (c), there were committal proceedings (or an acceptable alternative) but the person drafting the indictment added a new offence in addition to the offence(s) in respect of which the defendant was originally sent for trial.

The only instance in which the trial judge is entitled to look at the prosecution witness statements to see if they disclose a case to answer is in case (c), the 'new' count (*R v Jones* (1974) 59 Cr App R 120). It follows that, if the offence is one in respect of which there was a committal for trial (or a valid alternative to committal), the judge cannot be asked to quash the indictment on the basis that there is insufficient evidence in respect of that offence (*R v London Quarter Sessions ex p Downes* [1954] 1 QB 1).

Motions to quash are of little practical importance since the grounds (set out above) are very limited and, in any event, most errors can be cured by the prosecution seeking to amend the defective indictment under s 5(1) of the Indictments Act 1915.

Furthermore, if the indictment is quashed, the defendant is not regarded as having been acquitted and so can be prosecuted again. However, if the whole indictment is quashed, the effect of the committal is spent and so the defendant can only be indicted for the same offence again if there are fresh committal proceedings (*R v Thompson* [1975] 1 WLR 1425).

8.7 RULE 4 INDICTMENT RULES: THE RULE AGAINST DUPLICITY

Rule 4 provides that each count on an indictment may allege only one offence.

The specimen indictment shown above has as its first count an allegation of burglary involving the theft of two items. This does not contravene r 4 as the activity of burglary can and usually will involve more than one act. Where the acts form part of 'the same transaction', they may properly be said to amount to a single offence (*DPP v Merriman* [1973] AC 584; [1972] 3 All ER 42).

This means that, if a defendant steals a number of items from the same person at more or less the same time, that is a single act of theft (*R v Wilson* (1979) 69 Cr App R 83). In that case the defendant was charged with stealing three jumpers, a pair of shorts, two pairs of trousers, four dimmer switches and a cassette tape from Debenhams (count 1) and stealing eight records and a bottle of aftershave from Boots (count 2). It was argued on behalf of Wilson that both counts were bad for duplicity as the items stolen came from different departments of the stores in question. The argument was rejected on the basis that each count alleged acts forming a single activity. Neither count was duplicitous, therefore. Where a series of acts in effect amounts to a single course of conduct, those acts can validly be regarded as amounting to a single offence. So, in *DPP v McCabe* [1992] Crim LR 885, it was held by the Divisional Court that an allegation that the defendant stole 76 library books between two specified dates was a single offence and so was not bad for duplicity.

Where there are several victims, it is usual to have a separate count for each victim (as in *R v Mansfield* [1977] 1 WLR 1102; [1978] 1 All ER 134) where the defendant was charged with seven different counts of murder arising from a single act of arson). This is so even though a single count would be valid in such a case, since only one act was involved.

However, a count which alleged that the defendant stole £200 from A one day and £200 from B the next would be duplicitous.

In *R v Levantiz* [1999] 1 Cr App R 465, several discrete acts of supplying a controlled drug were alleged in a single count in the indictment. The Court of Appeal held (following *R v Thompson* [1914] 2 KB 99) that, where a count in an indictment is duplicitous (that is, charges more than one offence), that count is not void. It follows that an appeal against conviction on that count can be dismissed if the Court of Appeal decides that the conviction is safe despite the irregularity in the indictment.

8.7.1 Rule 7 indictment rules

Rule 7 provides that, if a section of a statute creates one offence which may be committed in a number of ways, the alternatives may be charged in a single count. If, however, the section creates more than one offence, each offence the prosecution wish the jury to consider must be put in a separate count.

A good example of the operation of r 7 (in practice, if not in strict legal theory) is to be found in respect of handling stolen goods contrary to s 22 of the Theft Act 1968. Handling effectively comprises two offences. The first is that of dishonestly receiving stolen goods; the second comprises all the other ways of handling and these ways are all different ways of committing a single offence. The various ways of committing the second form of handling can, and usually will, be charged in a single count. However, a count which charged receiving and the other forms of handling together would be regarded as defective.

Thus, there are two basic handling counts; either:

- AB on [date] dishonestly received stolen goods, namely [description of goods], knowing or believing the same to be stolen goods; or

- AB on [date] dishonestly undertook or assisted in the retention, removal, disposal or realisation of stolen goods, namely [description of goods], by or for the benefit of another, or dishonestly arranged to do so, knowing or believing the same to be stolen goods.

8.7.2 Breach of r 4 or r 7

The defence may make an application to quash the indictment if a count is bad for duplicity, but the prosecution may defeat this application by asking for leave to amend the indictment under s 5(1) of the Indictments Act 1915 to split the duplicitous count into two separate counts.

8.8 CO-DEFENDANTS CHARGED IN ONE COUNT

Rules 4 and 7 apply whether the count in question alleges that one defendant or more than one defendant committed the offence. Thus, all the parties to an offence may be joined in a single count. The jury will be directed that they must consider each defendant separately, so where there are two defendants they may acquit both defendants, convict both defendants, or convict one and acquit the other (*Director of Public Prosecutions v Merriman* (1973)).

8.9 RULE 9 INDICTMENT RULES: JOINDER OF COUNTS

We now consider the indictment which contains more than one count.

Each indictment must comply with r 9. This requires that all the counts on the indictment must be either:

- founded on the same facts; or
- form or be part of a series of offences of the same or a similar character.

8.9.1 Same facts

Two offences may be said to be founded on the same facts if either:

- They arise from a single incident, for example, in the specimen indictment shown above the defendant wounds the householder in the course of committing the burglary. The same principles would apply where someone steals a car in order to use it as a getaway vehicle in a robbery: the theft of the car and the robbery would be charged in a single indictment. Similarly, someone who causes criminal damage in order to commit a burglary may be charged with both offences in a single indictment (the criminal damage being charged pursuant to s 40 of the Criminal Justice Act 1988 if the value of the damage is less than £5,000); or

- A later offence would not have been committed but for the commission of an earlier offence, for example, *R v Barrell and Wilson* (1979) 69 Cr App R 250, where a defendant was charged with affray and assault (both arising out of a single incident) and with attempting to pervert the course of justice. The defendant had tried to bribe witnesses to the affray and assault not to give evidence against him. This attempt at bribery would not have taken place but for the charges arising out of the affray, and so the charges all had a 'common factual origin' (*per* Shaw LJ). It was held, therefore, that all these charges could appear in a single indictment.

8.9.2 Contradictory counts

In *R v Bellman* [1989] AC 836; [1989] 1 All ER 22, the House of Lords held that counts can be joined in an indictment even if they are mutually contradictory. The defendant in that case was charged with conspiracy to evade the prohibition on the importation of controlled drugs and with obtaining property by deception. If the defendant had intended to import the drugs, he was guilty of the first offence; if he took the money from the buyers but did not intend to import the drugs to give to them, he was guilty of the second offence. These inconsistent allegations could properly appear in a single indictment.

Another example is *R v Shelton* (1986) 83 Cr App R 379, where the defendant was charged under two counts, one alleging theft, the other alleging the second form of handling. It did not matter that these allegations were contradictory.

It will generally be unusual for the prosecution to include inconsistent counts on an indictment. The jury will be directed to consider each count separately. A conviction in respect of a given count is only possible if the jury are satisfied beyond reasonable doubt that the defendant is guilty under that particular count. If the prosecution are making contradictory allegations, the jury may well think that the defendant is guilty of something but may not be satisfied so that they are sure that he is guilty of a particular offence.

8.9.3   Same or similar character

In *Ludlow v Metropolitan Police Commissioner* [1971] AC 29; [1970] 1 All ER 567, the House of Lords had to construe the second limb of r 9. Ludlow faced two allegations, one of attempted theft on 20 August 1968 (the theft allegedly taking place at a public house in Acton) and one of robbery on 5 September 1968 (the allegation arising out of an altercation with a barman in a public house in Acton). The House of Lords held that these two allegations could be made in the same indictment. In coming to this conclusion, the following points were made:

- two offences are capable of amounting to a 'series';
- for counts to be joined in an indictment, there must be a 'nexus' between them both in law and in fact. In other words, the offences must be both legally and factually similar;
- the evidence in respect of one count need not be admissible by way of similar fact evidence in respect of the other count(s).

In *R v Harward* (1981) 73 Cr App R 168, the defendant was charged with conspiracy to defraud and with handling stolen goods. Despite the legal similarity (dishonesty), there was no factual link between the offences (apart from the fact that the stolen goods were found when his home was being searched during the fraud investigation). The indictment was therefore defective.

In *R v Marsh* (1985) 83 Cr App R 165, the defendant was charged with criminal damage and reckless driving (the same victim) and assault (a different victim). It was held that criminal damage and reckless driving were validly joined as they arose out of single act (causing damage by using the car). However, there was an insufficient legal link between either of these offences and the assault, and the only factual link between those offences was the use of violence. The addition of the assault charge thus rendered the indictment defective.

In *R v McGlinchey* (1983) 78 Cr App R 282, it was held that two counts alleging handling stolen goods were correctly joined. The first alleged receiving photographic equipment on 19 July 1982 and the second receiving a stolen credit card on 2 September 1982. There was clearly a legal nexus. The only factual nexus was that they were committed two months apart, but that was held to be sufficient.

In *R v Mariou* [1992] Crim LR 511, the defendant was charged with burglary, robbery, aggravated burglary and possession of a firearm with intent to endanger life. The Court of Appeal upheld the joinder of these counts as the burglary and robbery charges were legally similar and were all linked by violent entry into a dwelling-house and the subsequent use or threat of violence. The firearms offence was validly joined as it arose on the same facts as the others – the gun was carried when the offences were being committed.

In *R v Baird* (1993) 97 Cr App R 308, the defendant was charged with indecent assault on two different boys. The alleged offences were separated by a period of nine years. The Court of Appeal held that the offences nevertheless formed a series and so could validly be joined in a single indictment.

In *R v Williams* [1993] Crim LR 533, the defendant was charged with indecently assaulting a 13 year old girl on 8 June 1991 and with false imprisonment of the same girl on 13 June 1991. It was held that, had these two offences been committed on the same occasion, they could have been joined in a single indictment; however, they were different incidents and so they could not be validly joined on the same indictment.

8.9.4   Joinder of defendants under r 9

The provisions of r 9 apply whether the counts are against the same defendant or different defendants; all that matters is that the offences themselves are sufficiently linked to satisfy the provisions of r 9. Thus, a number of defendants may be joined in the same indictment even if no count applies to all of them, provided that the counts are sufficiently linked for r 9 to be satisfied. For example, the person who is alleged to have handled the proceeds of a burglary could be charged in the same indictment as the alleged burglar.

In *R v Assim* [1966] 2 QB 249; [1966] 2 All ER 881, there were two defendants, a receptionist and a doorman at a night club. The receptionist was charged with wounding one person (s 20 of the Offences Against the Person Act 1861) and the doorman with assault occasioning actual bodily harm (s 47 of the same Act) against a different person. Even though there was no joint count in the indictment, the indictment was held to be valid as there was sufficient link in time and place: both victims had tried to leave without paying; Assim allegedly attacked one victim with a knife; the other victim intervened and was attacked by the co-defendant. Thus, there was sufficient legal and factual nexus for the two counts to be joined in the same indictment.

8.9.5 Joinder of summary offences under s 40 of the Criminal Justice Act 1988

The requirement of s 40 of the Criminal Justice Act 1988 that a summary offence can only be added to an indictment alongside an indictable offence if it is founded on the same facts as the indictable offence or forms or is part of a series of offences of the same or a similar character to the indictable offence (see Chapter 3, 3.13), mirrors the requirement of r 9 of the Indictment Rules.

In *R v Callaghan* (1992) 94 Cr App R 226, the appellant was charged with six offences: one count of arson (an indictable offence), two counts of theft (an indictable offence), two counts of taking a conveyance without the consent of the owner (a summary offence to which s 40 of the Criminal Justice Act 1988 applies) and one count of driving while disqualified (a summary offence to which s 40 applies). The two counts of taking a conveyance without the owner's consent were held to be properly joined since they were of the same or a similar character to the two theft charges (which both involved motor vehicles). However, the charge of driving while disqualified related to his driving of a vehicle which he had taken without consent (the subject of one of the other counts on the indictment). The Court of Appeal held that the charge of driving while disqualified should not have been included in the indictment, since that charge was not linked with an *indictable* offence. The only link was with a summary offence validly added under s 40, and that was not enough.

8.10 BREACH OF RULE 9

If an indictment contains counts which should not be joined together in the same indictment, two questions arise. First, how can the defect be cured before the trial proceeds. Secondly, what happens if no remedial steps are taken and the defendant is convicted on the basis of the defective indictment.

8.10.1 Curing the defect

What should the Crown Court do if faced with an indictment which breaches r 9?

In *R v Newland* [1988] QB 402; [1988] 2 All ER 891, the defendant was charged with a drugs offence and three counts alleging assault which were wholly unconnected with the drugs charge. The trial judge simply ordered separate trials, so that the drugs offence and the assault charges were tried separately. The Court of Appeal held that the judge had no power to 'sever the indictment' under s 5(3) of the Indictments Act (that is, order separate trials of the counts – see 8.11 below) as this power applies only to a valid indictment, and the indictment in the present case was invalid because it failed to comply with r 9 of the indictment rules. The court went on to say that the trial judge should have deleted from the indictment either the drugs charge or the assault charges, and proceeded with the trial on that indictment. The allegations deleted from the indictment could only be proceeded with if the prosecution brought fresh committal proceedings in respect of them or sought a voluntary bill of indictment (see Chapter 7, 7.12.1 above).

In *R v Follett* [1989] QB 338; [1989] 1 All ER 995, a differently constituted Court of Appeal accepted a rather simpler solution. In this case, the indictment was invalid because it contained counts which were not sufficiently linked. The Court of Appeal upheld the decision of the trial judge to stay proceedings on the indictment as drafted and to give the prosecution leave to prefer fresh indictments (each complying with r 9) out of time. The effect of this is that the invalid indictment remains in existence but becomes irrelevant. Two or more trials then follow, based on the new indictments, without the need for fresh committal proceedings or a voluntary bill of indictment.

In the light of the case law set out below, it seems that *Newland* and *Follett* are not correct in labelling an indictment 'invalid' because of misjoinder. However, there is no reason to suppose that the methods for curing the defect of misjoinder which these two cases suggest should not still be followed where the misjoinder becomes apparent at the Crown Court trial. Thus the 'cure' is either to delete sufficient counts to leave an indictment which complies with r 9 or else (with the leave of the court) to prefer fresh indictments, each of which must comply with r 9.

In *R v Jackson* [1997] Crim LR 755, the trial judge decided that counts on an indictment were improperly joined (in that there was insufficient nexus between them: r 9 of the Indictment Rules 1971) and ordered that the defendants be re-arraigned on two fresh indictments. The proper officer of the Crown Court, however, failed to sign the indictments. The Court of Appeal had to decide whether the indictment on which the appellant was convicted was invalid, because it had not been signed by the proper officer. The court distinguished *R v Morais* (see 8.3 above) on the basis that in the present case the judge was exercising the powers conferred on him by the proviso to s 2(1) of the 1933 Act when he directed, of his own motion, that the proper officer should sign fresh indictments. In those circumstances, the proper officer should be deemed to have signed the indictments and so the indictment on which the defendants were convicted was not a nullity.

8.10.2 Validity of indictment

There has been a plethora of case law on the exact status of proceedings on an indictment which contained counts that are improperly joined. The question which the Court of Appeal has had to consider on several occasions is this: if a person is convicted on the basis of an indictment which does not comply with r 9 of the Indictment Rules, should all the convictions on that indictment be quashed, or just the convictions on counts which were improperly joined.

In *R v Bell* (1984) 78 Cr App R 305, Lord Lane CJ said that it cannot be the law that an indictment could be made a complete nullity by the addition of a count or counts contrary to r 9.

In *Newland* (above), however, Watkins LJ said that although the indictment itself could not, in the light of *Bell*, properly be described as a nullity, 'the proceedings flowing from the arraignment of the appellant upon that indictment must surely be a nullity'. This was followed in *R v O'Reilly* (1989) 90 Cr App R 40.

In *R v Callaghan* (1992) 94 Cr App R 226, the Court of Appeal had to consider a case where a summary offence was added to an indictment pursuant to s 40 of the Criminal Justice Act 1988 but where the required link (which is in the same terms as r 9 of the Indictment Rules) between the summary offence and the indictable offence was missing. The Court of Appeal held cases such as *Newland* (above) and *Follett* (above) do not decide that an indictment becomes a nullity by the addition of a count which involves a breach of r 9. The result of this was that the misjoinder did not nullify all the proceedings on the indictment. It followed that only the conviction for the improperly joined count should be quashed.

R v Lewis (1992) 95 Cr App R 131 was another case involving the addition of a summary offence under s 40 of the Criminal Justice Act 1988. The defendant was arrested for a number of offences. While he was at the police station he spat at one of the police officers; this resulted in a charge of common assault (a summary offence to which s 40 of the Criminal Justice Act 1988 applies). The Court of Appeal held that the common assault could not be regarded as being founded on the same facts as the other offences. What occurred at the police station took place too long after the other offences to be founded on the same facts as those offences. The Court of Appeal, reaching the opposite conclusion to *R v Callaghan*, went on to hold that the indictment was invalid and so technically there had been no convictions. Thus, all the convictions on the defective indictment had to be quashed. A re-trial could only be ordered by means of a writ of *venire de novo* (see Chapter 10, 10.8 below).

In *R v Simon* [1992] Crim LR 444, the appellant took one car without authority. That car ran out of petrol. He then took another car without authority and used it to get to a place where he and another defendant committed a robbery. The Court of Appeal held that the taking of the first car was properly joined, since the whole evening's criminality needed to be looked at as a continuous series of events; thus there was no misjoinder. However, the court went on to say (*obiter*) that *Callaghan*, having been decided earlier than *Lewis*, was to be preferred.

In *R v Smith* [1997] 2 WLR 588, three summary offences were added to an indictment under s 40 of the Criminal Justice Act 1988; joinder of two of those summary offences was improper because there was no sufficient link with the indictable offence which was also on the indictment. The Court of Appeal followed *Callaghan* and the *obiter dictum* in *Simon* and held that convictions for offences which are correctly joined are valid convictions. Accordingly, the convictions on the indictable offence and the correctly joined summary offence stood; only the convictions for the two improperly joined summary offences were quashed.

In *R v Lockley and Sainsbury* [1997] Crim LR 455, the appellants were charged with conspiracy to commit burglary and dangerous driving (on the basis that the car they used in connection with the burglary was dangerously defective). Both offences are indictable offences and so only r 9 of the Indictment Rules had to be considered. The Court of Appeal held that the dangerous driving charge was improperly joined. The court confirmed that s 40 of the Criminal Justice Act 1988 and r 9 of the Indictment Rules are in all material respects in the same terms, and so the same principles regarding misjoinder and the consequences thereof must apply to both. The court went on to hold that misjoinder does not nullify the whole indictment. It followed that only the conviction on the wrongly joined count(s) should be quashed.

8.11   DISCRETION TO ORDER SEPARATE TRIALS

Where an indictment validly alleges that a defendant committed more than one offence or alleges that more than one defendant was involved in the offence(s), the judge may nevertheless order that separate trials take place.

8.11.1   Separate counts

Section 5(3) of the Indictments Act 1915 empowers a Crown Court judge to order separate trials of offences on an indictment. This power is sometimes known as 'severing the indictment'. It applies both to a defendant who seeks separate trials for a number of offences and to co-defendants who seek separate trials.

We have already seen that this power applies only to a valid indictment (that is, one which satisfies r 9) (*Newland*).

The power to sever applies if the defendant can show that he would be 'prejudiced or embarrassed in his defence' or there is some other good reason. In other words the defendant has to show that he will not receive a fair trial if all the counts are dealt with together.

In *Ludlow* (see above), the House of Lords said that, if the counts are validly joined under r 9, those counts should usually be tried together and the defendant must show a 'special feature' (*per* Lord Pearson) in the case if there are to be separate trials.

In *R v Christou* [1996] 2 WLR 620; [1996] 2 All ER 926, the House of Lords held that where the defendant is charged with sexual offences against more than one person, and the evidence of one complainant is not so related to that of the others as to render that evidence admissible on the other charges (under the similar fact evidence rule), the judge has a discretion to sever the indictment. The essential criterion for the exercise of this discretion is the achievement of a fair resolution of the issues in the case. Factors which might have to be considered include: how closely related are the facts upon which the various charges are based; the effect of having two or more trials on the defendant and his family and on the victims and their families; the effect of press publicity; whether the judge can give directions to the jury which will enable there to be a fair trial if the counts are tried together.

In *R v Trew* [1996] 2 Cr App R 138, the defendant was charged with attacks on four different women. Only one of the women (B) picked him out at an identification parade. The trial judge refused to sever the counts relating to the attack on B from the counts relating to the other attacks. The Court of Appeal said that the judge should have taken account of the fact that evidence relating to the attack on B was inadmissible as regards the other alleged attacks. It followed that the presence of all the counts in the same indictment would have the sole effect of making it more likely that the appellant would be convicted. Accordingly, the appeal was allowed and a re-trial ordered.

Arguments which may succeed in appropriate cases include:

- the jury may find it difficult to disentangle the evidence, with the risk that they will rely on evidence which does not relate to a particular count when considering that count;

- one count is of a nature likely to arouse hostility in the minds of the jurors, and so they may not approach the other counts with open minds;

- the evidence on one count is strong but on the other is weak, and there is a risk that the jury will assume the defendant is guilty of the second count merely because they find him guilty of the first;

- the evidence in respect of each count is weak, but the jury may convict on the basis that there is no smoke without fire, taking an overview of the allegations rather than considering each count individually;

- the number of counts and/or defendants is such that the jury will be overwhelmed by the sheer weight of evidence, and the interests of justice are therefore better served by having a number of shorter trials. See *R v Novac* (1976) 65 Cr App R 107, dealt with below.

If the trial judge refuses to order separate trials, the exercise of his discretion will not be interfered with by the Court of Appeal unless it is manifestly wrong (*R v Tickner* [1992] Crim LR 44 and *R v Mariou* [1992] Crim LR 511).

8.11.2　Co-defendants

Where two or more defendants are charged in a single count, the judge has a discretion to order separate trials. Such an order means that the witnesses have to give evidence twice and there is the risk of inconsistent verdicts, and so such orders are made only rarely.

In *R v Lake* (1976) 64 Cr App R 172, the trial judge's refusal to order separate trials was upheld by the Court of Appeal even though there was some evidence in the case which was admissible against one defendant but inadmissible against (and highly prejudicial to) the other. This will be the case if defendant 1 confesses to the police and in that confession implicates defendant 2. The Court of Appeal agreed with the trial judge that the danger of prejudice could be removed by an appropriate direction to the jury. Similarly, in *R v Crawford* [1998] 1 Cr App R 338, the Court of Appeal upheld the decision of the trial judge not to order separate trials in a case where D1 was going to give evidence against D2 and so D2 would be able to cross examine D1 on her previous convictions.

In *R v Grondkowski and Malinowski* [1946] KB 369; [1946] 1 All ER 559, separate trials were not ordered even though the defendants were blaming each other (the so called 'cut throat defence'), a defence which usually results in both defendants being convicted.

In *R v Kennedy* [1992] Crim LR 37, two defendants were charged with affray. One defendant indicated that he would be referring to the previous convictions of the other (one for an offence of violence and others for offences of dishonesty) in the hope of persuading the jury that he had been acting in self-defence. Even though this was evidence which the prosecution would not have been able to adduce, and was clearly prejudicial to the other defendant, the judge's decision not to order separate trials was upheld.

In *R v Johnson* [1994] Crim LR 949; (1994) 15 Cr App R(S) 827, it was held that, although there is no firm rule that where an indictment contains an allegation that A assaulted B, and a second count alleging that C assaulted A, it would often be appropriate to order separate trials. However, the Court of Appeal went on to say that if that had been the only ground of appeal it would not have been a sufficient basis for allowing the appeal.

In *R v Eriemo* [1995] 2 Cr App R 206, it was held that a judge was justified in refusing an application to sever an indictment where one defendant intends to argue that he as acting under the duress of another defendant.

Where the defence would prefer separate trials of the defendants (for example, where the confession of one defendant implicates the other), it is worth making an application for separate trials to the trial judge, but if the judge refuses, the Court of Appeal is unlikely to interfere with his decision unless it is manifestly unreasonable (*R v Josephs* (1977) 65 Cr App R 253 and *R v Kennedy* (above)).

8.12   DECIDING THE CONTENTS OF THE INDICTMENT

In most cases, the counts on the indictment are the same as the charges in respect of which the defendant was committed for trial.

However, s 2(2) of the Administration of Justice (Miscellaneous Provisions) Act 1933 states that, where a defendant has been committed for trial at the Crown Court, the bill of indictment against the person charged may include, either in substitution for or in addition to counts charging the offence(s) for which the defendant was committed for trial, any counts founded on the evidence contained in the witness statements relied on by the prosecution at the committal proceedings, provided that the various counts may lawfully be joined in the same indictment.

Section 2(2) effectively confers two powers: the power to indict an offender for offences in addition to those for which he has been committed for trial by the magistrates, and the power to replace the offences for which he has been committed for trial with different offences.

In *R v Biddis* [1993] Crim LR 392, it was held that there need not be conclusive evidence in the papers used at the committal proceedings supporting the new count(s); it is enough if there is *prima facie* evidence in respect of them.

8.12.1   Substituting offences

An example of the power in s 2 of the Administration of Justice (Miscellaneous Provisions) Act 1933 to substitute a different offence would be a case where the magistrates commit the defendant for trial on a charge of burglary (entering premises as a trespasser and then stealing). The prosecution, after the committal, decide that the evidence on the issue of trespass is very weak, but that they can prove that the defendant stole what he is alleged to have stolen during the course of the 'burglary'. The prosecution could indict the defendant for theft instead of burglary.

Similarly, if the magistrates commit the defendant for trial on a charge of theft but the prosecution subsequently decide that there is sufficient evidence to prove that the theft was committed in the course of a burglary, the prosecution could indict the defendant for burglary instead of theft.

The power to indict for offences which differ from those in respect of which the justices committed the defendant for trial applies even if the justices expressly refused to commit the defendant for trial in respect of a particular offence but committed him for trial in respect of another offence. In *R v Moloney* [1985] AC 905; [1985] 1 All ER 1025, for example, the justices refused to commit the defendant on a charge of murder but committed him on a charge of manslaughter instead; the prosecution charged murder in the indictment and this decision was upheld. Similarly, in *R v C* (1995) 159 JP 205, the magistrates had stayed certain charges on the ground of abuse of process but the defendant was committed for trial on other charges. Evidence of the charges which had been stayed was contained in the witness statements which formed the bundle of evidence relied on by the prosecution at committal. The prosecution sought leave from the Crown Court to add to the indictment the charges which had been stayed by the magistrate. Leave was given and the Court of Appeal upheld this decision.

8.12.2 Adding offences

Section 2(2) of the Administration of Justice (Miscellaneous Provisions) Act 1933 also enables the prosecution to indict the defendant for charges which are additional to those in respect of which he was committed for trial. The essential restriction on this power is that the resulting indictment must satisfy the requirements of r 9 of the Indictment Rules (*R v Lombardi* [1989] 1 WLR 73; [1989] 1 All ER 992).

An example of the operation of the power to add offences would be where the defendant is committed for trial on a single charge of robbery. The prosecution witness statements relied upon by the prosecution at the committal proceedings also disclose the fact that the defendant was in possession of a firearm when carrying out the robbery. The prosecution could add a firearms offence to the indictment. Even though there has been no committal in respect of the firearms charge, it is a charge which is sufficiently closely related to the charge in respect of which there has been a committal to permit joinder of the two charges under r 9.

An example of where it would not be open to the prosecution to add a count to the indictment would be where the defendant is committed for trial on a charge on burglary. The prosecution witness statements also reveal evidence which would support a completely unrelated drugs charge. However, there has been no committal in respect of that charge. The prosecution cannot add the drugs charge to the indictment which contains the burglary charge. The two charges are unrelated and so to put them on the same indictment would infringe r 9 of the Indictment Rules.

8.12.3 More than one indictment

In *Lombardi*, Lord Lane CJ said that where the magistrates have committed a defendant to the Crown Court on more than one charge, the prosecution are at liberty to prefer a number of separate indictments if they feel that it is appropriate to do so. Take, for example, the defendant who is committed for trial on a charge of burglary and a completely unrelated drugs charge. Although the two charges (being unrelated) cannot appear on the same indictment (because of r 9 of the Indictment Rules), the prosecution can prefer two separate indictments (one for the burglary and the other for the drugs offence), because the defendant has been committed for trial in respect of both offences.

However, what the prosecution *cannot* do is to prefer one indictment containing the charges in respect of which the defendant was committed for trial, and a second indictment containing only charges in respect of which there was no committal. Take, for example, a case where the defendant is committed to the Crown Court for trial on a charge of burglary, but the prosecution witness statements also reveal evidence of a drugs offence. The prosecution can prefer an indictment for burglary because there has been a committal in respect of that charge. They cannot add the unrelated drugs offence to that indictment, because that would contravene r 9 of the Indictment Rules; and they cannot prefer a separate indictment in respect of the drugs offence, because there has been no committal in respect of that offence and that offence is not being substituted for an offence in respect of which there has been a committal.

8.12.4 More than one defendant

If the magistrates commit two or more defendants for trial at the same time, it is open to the prosecution to draft separate indictments against them if the prosecution feel that it would be appropriate to do so or if the defendants are charged with different offences and joinder of the offences in one indictment would breach r 9 of the Indictment Rules (see *R v Groom* [1977] QB 6; [1976] 2 All ER 321).

If defendants are not committed for trial at the same time, it is nevertheless open to the prosecution to join those defendants in the same indictment (assuming r 9 is satisfied). This is so even if an indictment in respect of any of the earlier committals has already been signed (see *Practice Direction (Crime: Indictment)* [1976] 1 WLR 409; [1976] 2 All ER 326).

8.12.5 Alternative counts

In many cases, the prosecution will include alternative counts on the indictment. For instance, an allegation of wounding with intent (s 18 of the Offences Against the Person Act 1861) may be accompanied by a separate count alleging unlawful wounding (s 20 of the same Act). This would be appropriate where the prosecution are not sure that they can prove that the accused had the requisite intent to commit the s 18 offence. There is nothing on the indictment to show that these are alternatives (the word 'or' does not appear) but counsel for the prosecution, during the opening speech, will inform the jury that the prosecution seek a conviction on one or other of the two counts but not both.

8.12.6   Overloading the indictment

In *R v Novac* (1976) 65 Cr App R 107 and *R v Thorne* (1977) 66 Cr App R 6, the Court of Appeal warned against the danger of having too many counts or too many defendants in a single trial. Splitting the case into a series of shorter trials may in the long run be easier.

Note also that, if both conspiracy and a related substantive offence are alleged, the judge may ask the prosecution to justify charging both or choose to proceed with one or the other (Practice Direction (1977)).

8.13   AMENDING THE INDICTMENT

Section 5(1) of the Indictments Act 1915 allows the amendment of a defective indictment at any stage, provided the amendment can be made without causing injustice. Amendment may be necessary, for example, where the evidence at trial shows that the prosecution have charged the wrong offence.

The amendment may take the form of inserting a new count in the indictment, whether in addition to or instead of the original count (*R v Johal; R v Ram* [1972] 2 All ER 449).

In *R v Osieh* [1996] 1 WLR 1260; [1996] 2 Cr App R 145, prior to the start of the trial, the judge gave leave for the indictment to be amended to include a count of attempted theft. The appellant argued that the judge should not have allowed this to be done, since there was no evidence relating to the attempted theft in the committal papers (as is required by s 2(2) of the Administration of Justice (Miscellaneous Provisions) Act 1933). The Court of Appeal held that the 1933 Act and the Indictments Act 1915 are two entirely different statutory regimes. The Administration of Justice (Miscellaneous Provisions) Act 1933 governs the signing and preferment of the bill of indictment; the Indictments Act 1915 governs the indictment itself. Accordingly, the requirement in the Administration of Justice (Miscellaneous Provisions) Act 1933 that there must be evidence in the committal papers to support a count on the indictment does not apply to the power conferred by the Indictments Act 1915. The court went on to say that where the amendment relates to matters which are not foreshadowed in the committal papers, it may be appropriate for the judge to exercise his discretion against giving leave for the amendment (or else allowing the amendment but adjourning the case to enable the defence to review their case). The court went on to make the point that the 1915 Act confers a wide discretion; the Court of Appeal will not interfere lightly with the exercise of such a discretion.

The pre-trial hearing procedure should reduce the number of amendments which take place at the start of (or during) trials. If an amendment is made just before the start of the trial, and the amendment changes the nature of the prosecution case, the defence must be allowed an adjournment to enable them to review their case in the light of the new allegations (see s 5(4) of the Indictments Act 1915). If a jury has already been empanelled, it may be necessary for the judge to discharge that jury and order a re-trial (see s 5(5)(a) of the Indictments Act 1915).

It is permissible (subject to the possible need for an adjournment) for the indictment to be amended in the course of the trial (although if the amendment is a fundamental one, so that defence would need a long adjournment, it may be appropriate for the judge to discharge the jury and order a re-trial).

In *R v Pople* [1951] 1 KB 53; [1950] 2 All ER 679, the judge allowed the amendment of the indictment at the close of the prosecution case to allege the obtaining by deception of a cheque instead of the original allegation, the obtaining of the sum of money for which the cheque was drawn. The Court of Appeal upheld this decision since, in substance, the allegation which the defendant had to meet was unchanged.

Such an amendment was even permitted after the jury had retired to consider their verdict in *R v Collison* (1980) 71 Cr App R 249. In that case, the jury wanted to convict of a lesser offence but as they could not agree on an acquittal of the offence on the indictment, they could not simply return a verdict of guilty to the lesser offence as s 6(3) of the Criminal Law Act 1967 only applies where the jury first acquit of the offence on the indictment (see Chapter 9, 9.24). It was to get round this problem that the lesser offence was added to the indictment and the Court of Appeal said that no injustice was caused by doing so.

The important question in deciding whether or not to allow an amendment once the trial has started is whether the defence case would have been conducted differently had the amendment taken place at the outset. In *R v Harris* (1993) *The Times*, 22 March, the defendant was charged with rape but at the close of the defence case, the prosecution applied to add an alternative count alleging attempted rape to the indictment. The judge allowed this amendment but the Court of Appeal held that this decision was wrong, since the defence case would have been put differently (different cross-examination of prosecution witnesses and different defence evidence).

Similarly, in *R v Thomas* [1983] Crim LR 619, the Court of Appeal quashed a conviction where a count of receiving stolen property was added to an indictment which hitherto alleged only theft. This amendment took place after the close of the prosecution case and the defence would have cross-examined differently if both allegations had been made at the outset.

In *R v Piggott and Litwin* [1999] 2 Cr App R 320, the defendants were charged with a single count of conspiracy to steal motor vehicles between May

1993 and May 1996. At the close of the prosecution case, the defendants submitted that there was no case to answer. The submission made on behalf of L was that the conspiracy count was bad, as the evidence adduced did not show one overall conspiracy but a number of different conspiracies. The trial judge ruled that the count was defective but allowed the prosecution to amend the indictment by adding a number of substantive counts against L, each alleging handling stolen goods, and a tenth count alleging a conspiracy between L and P. Due to the admission of irrelevant and highly prejudicial evidence, the judge discharged the jury and ordered a fresh trial. The appellants argued that the second trial was an abuse of process. The Court of Appeal held that the test to determine whether an amendment should be permitted is whether the trial itself can be continued without injustice. The power to amend does not affect the principle that the defendant is entitled to know the case he has to meet and the right to a fair trial. Accordingly, the prosecution are not entitled to present the case to the jury in one way and hope that leave to amend will be given if there is a successful submission of no case to answer. The amendment in the present case should not have been permitted and, so, the second trial was an abuse of process.

Once an indictment has been signed and preferred following the granting of a voluntary bill of indictment, the indictment is like any other indictment. It follows that the trial judge can give leave for that indictment to be amended if it is defective (for example, it does not include offences disclosed in the witness statements which were considered by the High Court judge (*R v Wells* [1995] 2 Cr App R 417)).

Where the Court of Appeal orders a re-trial under s 7 of the Criminal Appeal Act 1968 (see Chapter 10, 10.8.2), the trial judge has power under s 5(1) of the Indictments Act 1915 to allow the indictment to be amended, even if the amendment results in the defendant being tried for offences for which the Court of Appeal had no power to order a retrial. However, this is only permissible so long as the amendment does not put the defendant in a worse position than he was in after the original trial (*R v Hemmings* [2000] 2 All ER 155).

TABLE OF STATUTORY AND OTHER MATERIALS

STATUTORY MATERIALS

INDICTMENTS ACT 1915

Section 3

(1) Every indictment shall contain, and shall be sufficient if it contains, a statement of the specific offence or offences with which the accused person is charged, together with such particulars as may be necessary for giving reasonable information as to the nature of the charge.

(2) Notwithstanding any rule or law or practice, an indictment shall, subject to the provisions of this Act, not be open to objection in respect of its form or contents if it is framed in accordance with the rules under this Act.

Section 5

(1) Where, before trial, or at any stage of a trial, it appears to the court that the indictment is defective, the court shall make such order for the amendment of the indictment as the court thinks necessary to meet the circumstances of the case, unless, having regard to the merits of the case, the required amendments cannot be made without injustice.

...

(3) Where, before trial, or at any stage of a trial, the court is of opinion that a person accused may be prejudiced or embarrassed in his defence by reason of being charged with more than one offence in the same indictment, or that for any other reason it is desirable to direct that the person should be tried separately for any one or more offences charged in an indictment, the court may order a separate trial of any count or counts of such indictment.

(4) Where, before trial, or at any stage of a trial, the court is of opinion that the postponement of the trial of a person accused is expedient as a consequence of the exercise of any power of the court under this Act to amend an indictment or to order a separate trial of a count, the court shall make such order as to the postponement of the trial as appears necessary.

(5) Where an order of the court is made under this section for the postponement of a trial:

(a) if such an order is made during a trial the court may order that the jury are to be discharged from giving a verdict on the count or counts the trial of which is postponed or on the indictment, as the case may be; and

(b) the procedure on the separate trial of a count shall be the same in all respects as if the count had been found in a separate indictment, and the procedure on the postponed trial shall be the same in all respects (if the jury has been discharged) as if the trial had not commenced; and

(c) the court may make such order as to granting the accused person bail and as to the enlargement of recognizances and otherwise as the court thinks fit.

INDICTMENT RULES 1971 (SI 1971/1253)

Rule 4

(1) An indictment shall be in the form in Schedule 1 to these rules or in a form substantially to the like effect.

(2) Where more than one offence is charged in an indictment, the statement and particulars of each offence shall be set out in a separate paragraph called a count, and rules 5 and 6 of these rules shall apply to each count in the indictment as they apply to an indictment where one offence is charged.

(3) The counts shall be numbered consecutively.

Rule 5

(1) Subject only to the provisions of rule 6 of these rules, every indictment shall contain, and shall be sufficient if it contains, a statement of the specific offence with which the accused person is charged describing the offence shortly, together with such particulars as may be necessary for giving reasonable information as to the nature of the charge.

...

Rule 6

Where the specific offence with which an accused person is charged in an indictment is one created by or under an enactment, then (without prejudice to the generality of rule 5 of these rules):

(a) the statement of offence shall contain a reference to:

(i) the section of, or the paragraph of the schedule to, the Act creating the offence in the case of an offence created by a provision of an Act;

(ii) the provision creating the offence in the case of a subordinate instrument;

(b) the particulars shall disclose the essential elements of the offence.

Provided that an essential element need not be disclosed if the accused person is not prejudiced or embarrassed in his defence by the failure to disclose it;

(c) it shall not be necessary to specify or negative an exception, proviso excuse or qualification.

Rule 7

Where an offence created by or under an enactment states the offence to be the doing or the omission to do any one of any different acts in the alternative, or the doing or the omission to do any act in any one of any different capacities, or with any one of any different intentions, or states any part of the offence in the alternative, the acts, omissions, capacities or intentions, or other matters stated in the alternative in the enactment or subordinate instrument may be stated in the alternative in an indictment charging the offence.

Rule 8

It shall be sufficient in an indictment to describe a person whose name is not known as a person unknown.

Rule 9

Charges for any offences may be joined in the same indictment if those charges are founded on the same facts, or form or are a part of a series of offences of the same or a similar character.

ADMINISTRATION OF JUSTICE (MISCELLANEOUS PROVISIONS) ACT 1933

Section 2

(1) Subject to the provisions of this section, a bill of indictment charging any person with an indictable offence may be preferred by any person before the Crown Court, and where a bill of indictment has been so preferred the proper officer of the court shall, if he is satisfied that the requirements of the next following sub-section have been complied with, sign the bill, and it shall thereupon become an indictment and be proceeded with accordingly:

Provided that if the judge of the court is satisfied that the said requirements have been complied with, he may, on the application of the prosecutor or of his own motion, direct the proper officer to sign the bill and the bill shall be signed accordingly.

CHAPTER 9

TRIAL ON INDICTMENT

9.1 INTRODUCTION – PRELIMINARIES

In this chapter, we follow the course of a Crown Court trial and examine some of the preliminary matters which are dealt with before the trial takes place.

9.2 DISCLOSURE OF EVIDENCE TO THE DEFENCE

It is a vital principle that the defence are entitled to know in advance what case they have to meet. It is also wholly inappropriate for the prosecution to suppress evidence which might assist the defence.

9.2.1 Witness to be called by the prosecution

The prosecution may only call as witnesses at the Crown Court people whose written statements have been served on the defence.

9.2.2 Witnesses relied on at committal

Most of these witness statements will have been served on the defence prior to the committal proceedings, because committal proceedings cannot take place until the prosecution witness statements have been handed over to the defence. In some cases the witness statements will have been handed to the defence prior to the mode of trial hearing, under the advance information rules (see Chapter 3, 3.12).

9.2.3 Notice of additional evidence

If the prosecution wish to adduce the evidence of a witness whose statement was not used at the committal proceedings, a notice of additional evidence (including a copy of the written statement by the witness) must first be served on the defence. There is no specified time by which the notice must have been served on the defence; however, if the notice is served just before (or even during) the trial, so that there is insufficient time for the defence to consider the effect which the extra evidence has on the defence case, the judge should grant an adjournment.

9.2.4 Editing prosecution evidence

Some of the prosecution witness statements may contain matters upon which the prosecution do not wish to rely.

To ensure that editing of prosecution evidence does not result in non-disclosure to the defence, a Practice Direction (1986) provides that either:

- the maker of the original statement produces a new statement (both statements would have to be disclosed to the defence); or
- the prosecution may bracket or lightly strike out the material upon which they do not intend to rely, but in such a way that the original words remain visible.

Editing may also be necessary in the case of evidence which the jury will see. For example, the accused might make a statement to the police from which it becomes apparent that he has previous convictions or is accused of other offences. The transcript of this interview may well become an exhibit in the case which the jury will see. Such a document would have to be edited so that the material which is deleted is no longer visible.

9.2.5 Witnesses whom the prosecution do not intend to call: unused material

The prosecution have a duty to disclose to the defence any material which has not already been disclosed but which might undermine the prosecution case against the defendant. Furthermore, once the defendant has informed the prosecution of the nature of his defence and the matters on which he takes issue with the prosecution, the prosecution must disclose to the defence any previously undisclosed material which might reasonably be expected to assist the defence case. These statutory requirements, which are contained in the Criminal Procedure and Investigations Act 1996, are considered in detail in Chapter 1, 1.19.

9.2.6 Previous convictions of prosecution witnesses

If a prosecution witness has previous convictions, the prosecution must inform the defence that this is the case (*R v Collister* (1955) 39 Cr App R 100 and *R v Paraskeva* (1982) 76 Cr App R 162).

9.3   DISCLOSURE BY THE DEFENCE

The defence also have a duty of disclosure.

9.3.1   Disclosure of defence case

Under the Criminal Procedure and Investigations Act 1996, the defence have a duty to give the prosecution a written statement of the nature of the defence case and to set out the matters upon which the defence take issue with the prosecution. In particular, the defence must give full particulars of any alibi which is going to be raised at trial. Failure to comply with these requirements enables adverse inferences to be drawn by the jury. Full details of these provisions are contained in Chapter 1, 1.19 above.

9.3.2   Expert evidence

The other specific duty of pre-trial disclosure which the defence have to comply with is under s 81 of the Police and Criminal Evidence Act 1984 and the Crown Court (Advance Notice of Expert Evidence) Rules 1987. The Rules apply to the prosecution as well as the defence but the prosecution have to disclose all the evidence they wish to rely on anyway (at committal or by way of notice of additional evidence).

9.4   SECURING THE ATTENDANCE OF WITNESSES

Section 2 of the Criminal Procedure (Attendance of Witnesses) Act 1965 enables the Crown Court to grant a witness summons requiring the attendance at the Crown Court of a person who is likely to be able to give material evidence but who will not attend voluntarily. An application for a witness summons must be made as soon as reasonably practicable after the defendant has been committed for trial.

Under s 2C of the Criminal Procedure (Attendance of Witnesses) Act 1965, a person against whom a witness summons was made and who was not present or represented when the order was made, may apply to the Crown Court for the order to be discharged provided that he can show that he cannot give any evidence which is likely to be material evidence.

If the person who is the subject of the summons fails to attend court, and there are reasonable grounds for believing that there is no just excuse for this non-attendance, a warrant for the arrest of the witness may be issued by the judge. Otherwise, a notice is served on the witness requiring him to attend court on a specified date (and if he fails to do so, a warrant for his arrest may be issued). Someone arrested under such a warrant will be taken before the Crown Court and may be remanded in custody or on bail until the time his evidence is required (s 4(2) of the 1965 Act).

Failure to comply with a witness summons is punishable summarily by the Crown Court as a contempt of court (s 3(2) of the Criminal Procedure (Attendance of Witnesses) Act 1965).

If a witness summons has been obtained and there are grounds to believe that the person will not attend court, a Crown Court judge may issue a warrant for that person's arrest (s 4(1) of the Criminal Procedure (Attendance of Witnesses) Act 1965).

9.5 PREPARATORY AND PRE-TRIAL HEARINGS; PLEA AND DIRECTIONS HEARINGS

The Criminal Procedure and Investigations Act 1996 makes provision for preliminary hearings to take place prior to Crown Court trials. The Act supplements the existing practice of the Crown Court, which is to hold a 'plea and directions' hearing.

9.5.1 Preparatory hearings

Section 29(1) of the Criminal Procedure and Investigations Act 1996 empowers a Crown Court judge to order that a 'preparatory hearing' be held; such power may be exercised where the indictment reveals a case of such complexity, or a case whose trial is likely to be of such length, that substantial benefits are likely to accrue from such a hearing. These provisions do not apply to serious fraud cases, as these have their own system of preparatory hearings (s 29(3)).

Section 29(2) sets out the purposes of the preparatory hearing:
- (a) identifying issues which are likely to be material to the verdict of the jury;
- (b) assisting their comprehension of any such issues;
- (c) expediting the proceedings before the jury;
- (d) assisting the judge's management of the trial.

Section 30 says that the arraignment will take place at the start of the preparatory hearing, unless it has taken place before then.

Section 31 sets out the powers which the judge may exercise at the preparatory hearing. They are:
- (a) to rule on any question as to the admissibility of evidence;
- (b) to rule on any other question of law relevant to the case;

(c) to order the prosecutor to give the court and the defendant(s) a written case statement setting out:

   (i) the principal facts of the case for the prosecution;

   (ii) the witnesses whom the prosecution will be calling;

   (iii) any proposition of law on which the prosecution propose to rely;

(d) to order the prosecutor to prepare the prosecution evidence and any explanatory material in such a form as appears to the judge to be likely to aid comprehension by the jury;

(e) to order the prosecutor to give to the court and to the defendant(s) a written notice setting out matters which the prosecutor thinks ought to be agreed;

(f) where the prosecution have supplied a written case statement, the judge may order the defendant(s):

   (i) to give to the court and the prosecution a written statement setting out in general terms the nature of the defence and indicating the principal matters on which the defence take issue with the prosecution;

   (ii) to give to the court and the prosecution written notice of any objections that the defence have to the prosecution case statement;

   (iii) to give to the court and the prosecution written notice of any point of law (including admissibility of evidence) which the defence propose to take and any authority the defence propose to rely on;

(g) where the judge has ordered the prosecutor to say what matters he thinks ought to be agreed, the judge can order the defence to indicate in writing the extent to which they agree with the prosecutor's view and the reasons for any disagreement.

Under s 31(11), orders or rulings made at a preparatory hearing are effective throughout the trial unless it appears to the judge, on an application being made by the prosecution or the defence, that the interests of justice require him to vary or discharge it.

Section 34(1) provides that a party may depart from the case disclosed under s 31. However, s 34(2) provides that if a party departs from the case disclosed under s 31, or fails to comply with a requirement imposed under s 31, the judge may allow the jury to draw such inferences as appear proper, taking account of the extent of the failure or departure and whether there is any justification for it.

9.5.2 Appeals from preparatory hearings

Section 35(1) allows for an appeal to the Court of Appeal against a ruling on admissibility of evidence or other point of law relating to the case, but only with the leave of the judge or the Court of Appeal. Under s 35(2), the judge may continue with a preparatory hearing even though leave to appeal has been granted, but no jury can be empanelled until the appeal has been determined or abandoned.

The procedure for such an appeal is set out in the Criminal Procedure and Investigations Act (Preparatory Hearings) (Interlocutory Appeals) Rules 1997 (SI 1997/1053). Where the judge at the preparatory hearing does not give leave to appeal, an application for leave is made to a single judge of the Court of Appeal. The single judge also has the power to extend the time within which notice of application for leave to appeal must be given and the power to give leave for the defendant to be present at the hearing of the appeal if the defendant is in custody. If the single judge refuses leave to appeal, there is provision for a renewal of that application to the full Court of Appeal.

Section 37 of the Act imposes reporting restrictions very similar to those contained in s 8 of the Magistrates' Courts Act 1980 (see Chapter 7, 7.9).

9.5.3 Pre-trial hearings

The procedure that we have just looked at is concerned only with complex or lengthy trials. Section 39 of the Criminal Procedure and Investigations Act 1996 provides for pre-trial hearings in other cases to be tried in the Crown Court. These hearings take place before the jury is empanelled. At the hearing, the judge may rule on any question as to the admissibility of evidence, or any other question of law relevant to the case (s 40(1)). Any ruling is binding for the whole of the trial unless the judge (upon application by the prosecution or the defence, or of his own motion) varies or discharges that ruling (s 40(3), (4)). No application may be made for a ruling to be discharged or varied unless there has been a change in circumstances since the ruling was made (s 40(5)). These provisions apply whether or not the pre-trial hearing and the trial itself are presided over by the same judge (s 40(6)).

Again, there are similar reporting restrictions to those contained in s 8 of the Magistrates' Courts Act 1980 (s 41).

9.5.4 Plea and directions hearings

In 1995, the Lord Chief Justice issued Practice Rules requiring a plea and directions hearing to take place prior to all Crown Court trials. The powers conferred by s 39 of the Criminal Procedure and Investigations Act 1996, which we examined in 9.5.3 above, essentially give statutory effect to the plea and directions hearing rules. These rules apply to all cases (except serious fraud cases which have their own provisions for a preliminary hearing under s 7 of the Criminal Justice Act 1987).

The Rules stipulate that at the plea and directions hearing ('PDH'), the defendant must be asked to enter a plea to the offence(s) on the indictment (sometimes called 'arraigning' the defendant). The indictment is read out by the clerk of the court and after each count the defendant says 'guilty' or 'not guilty'. Each count must be 'put' to the defendant separately and a separate plea must be entered on each count.

If the defendant pleads guilty, the judge should proceed to sentencing whenever possible (although it may be necessary to adjourn in order for a pre-sentence report to be prepared).

In cases where the defendant pleads not guilty, the prosecution and defence will be expected to inform the court of:

- the issues in the case;
- whether the defendant or any witness is suffering from a mental or medical condition;
- whether the prosecution will agree to defence witnesses who are ill giving written evidence;
- the number of witnesses who will be giving evidence orally or in writing;
- any additional witnesses likely to be called by the prosecution and the evidence they are expected to give;
- any formal admissions under s 10 of the Criminal Justice Act 1967 (see 9.10.1 below);
- any alibi which the defendant will rely on (see Chapter 1, 1.19.3);
- any point of law or question of admissibility which is likely to arise in the trial;
- any applications for leave to give evidence via live television links or pre-recorded interviews (see 9.10.3 below) or for the use of screens so that the identity of the witness remains secret (see 9.10.6 below);
- estimated length of trial;
- availability of witnesses and advocates;
- whether there is a need for any further directions.

In the case of class 1 and class 2 offences (see Chapter 1, 1.16), the directions judge can deal only with matters necessary to see that the case is prepared conveniently for trial. This includes identifying any issues suitable for a preliminary hearing before the trial judge.

The rules envisage that the PDH will normally be conducted by the trial judge.

The PDH is normally held in open court and all defendants should be present unless the court otherwise directs.

The PDH should normally take place within six weeks of committal for trial to the Crown Court if the defendant is on bail, four weeks if he is in custody. When the magistrates commit the case to the Crown Court, they should (after consultation with the Crown Court listing officer) specify the date on which the PDH should take place.

The defence should inform the prosecution, the court, and the probation service as soon as it is known that the defendant intends to plead guilty to all or part of the indictment.

Finally, the rules require the defence solicitors to apply to the court for the case to be listed for mention if they are unable to obtain instructions from the defendant. If the defendant fails to attend this hearing, the judge is likely to issue a warrant for his arrest.

A copy of the questionnaire which should be completed by the barristers in the case prior to the plea and directions hearing appears at the end of this chapter.

9.6   THE TRIAL

Now, we start to examine in detail the course of a trial on indictment.

9.6.1   Presence of defendant

The defendant must be present at the start of the trial in order to enter the plea. In the magistrates' court, a trial can in some circumstance take place in the absence of the defendant; in the Crown Court, the defendant must be present at least at the start of the trial.

If, having entered a plea, the defendant then absconds (or misbehaves and disrupts the proceedings), the trial judge has a discretion to continue the trial in the defendant's absence. In practice, this would only occur if there was another defendant being tried at the same time and it would be unfair on that defendant to postpone the trial (*R v Jones (No 2)* [1972] 1 WLR 887; [1972] 2 All ER 731).

If a defendant is taken ill during the course of the trial and cannot attend court, the trial can only continue in his absence if the defendant consents. If the defendant does not consent to the trial continuing in his absence, and the illness is likely to last more than a few days, the jury will be discharged and a new trial will begin when the defendant is well enough to attend court.

9.6.2   Bail

If the defendant is remanded in custody prior to his trial, he will remain in custody during the trial itself (unless the trial judge grants bail, which is very unlikely).

In *R v Central Criminal Court ex p Guney* [1996] AC 616; [1996] 2 All ER 705, the question the House of Lords had to decide was the effect of a situation where a defendant who had not previously surrendered to the custody of the Crown Court was arraigned (that is, the indictment was read to him and he was asked to plead guilty or not guilty). The House of Lords held that when a defendant who has not previously surrendered to the custody of the court is arraigned, he thereby surrenders to the custody of the court at that moment. The result is that the Crown Court judge then has to decide whether or not to grant him bail; unless the judge grants bail, the defendant will remain in custody pending and during the trial.

Guney was followed by the Divisional Court in *R v Maidstone Crown Court ex p Jodka* (1997) 161 JP 638. In that case, the court held that bail granted by magistrates ceases when the defendant surrenders to the custody of the Crown Court, whether or not the defendant is arraigned at the hearing at which he surrenders. Where the magistrates grant bail subject to a surety, the responsibility of that surety under the magistrates' court order ceases once the defendant surrenders to the custody of the Crown Court. If the Crown Court wishes to grant bail subject to the same surety, the court must consider the position of that surety before imposing such a condition.

It follows from this that the question of bail will have to be considered at the pre-trial hearing. In any event, if the defendant is on bail before the trial, his bail effectively expires at the start of the trial. It is therefore a matter for the trial judge whether or not bail is granted to the defendant for lunch time and/or overnight adjournments.

Some judges usually withhold bail at lunch-time; some grant bail on the condition that the defendant remain in the company of his solicitor; others are happy to grant unconditional bail unless there seems to be a risk of the defendant absconding. Bail might be withdrawn if, for example, the likelihood of the defendant absconding increases because the case starts to go badly for him. If a custodial sentence is likely in the event of conviction, bail is normally withheld once the judge has begun the summing up (*Practice Direction (Crime: Bail During Trial)* [1974] 1 WLR 770; [1974] 2 All ER 794).

Applications for bail during the course of the trial should be made in the absence of the jury (who might otherwise be prejudiced against the accused if bail is not granted as they might take this as an indication of the judge's view that the defendant is guilty).

9.6.3 Unrepresented defendants

Where the defendant is unrepresented: (i) the trial judge should ask such questions as he sees fit to test the reliability of the prosecution witnesses and may ask the defendant whether there are certain matters he wishes to be put to the witnesses; (ii) the jury should be instructed (at the start of the trial and in the summing up) that the defendant is entitled to represent himself and they should also be warned of the difficulty of his doing so properly; (iii) the judge should prevent repetitious questioning of prosecution witnesses by the defendant.

Section 34 of the Youth Justice and Criminal Evidence Act 1999 provides that no person charged with a sexual offence may cross-examine the complainant, either in connection with that offence, or in connection with any other offence (of whatever nature) with which that person is charged in the proceedings. Under s 35 of the Act, unrepresented defendants are not allowed to cross-examine in person a child who is either the complainant of, or a witness to the commission of, an offence of kidnapping, false imprisonment or abduction. Section 36 gives courts the power to prohibit unrepresented defendants from cross-examining witnesses in cases where a mandatory ban does not apply under ss 34 and 35, but where the court is satisfied that the circumstances of the witness and the case merit a prohibition, and that it would not be contrary to the interests of justice.

Article 6(3)(c) of the European Convention on Human Rights guarantees the right to legal representation and legal aid. However, the European Court of Human Rights has held that a court may place restrictions on right of a defendant to appear without a lawyer (*Croissant v Germany* 16 EHRR 135). The provisions of the 1999 Act seem to be within Art 6.

9.7 THE JURY

In this section, we examine the composition of the jury, and how the jury to try a defendant is chosen.

9.7.1 Who can serve on a jury?

Jurors are drawn from the electoral register. Subject to exceptions, anyone on the register and aged between 18 and 70 can be summoned for jury service (s 1 of the Juries Act 1974).

The main exceptions are:

- *Those ineligible to serve*

  This category includes the judiciary (including lay magistrates), lawyers, those concerned in the administration of justice (for example, police officers, prison officers, probation officers), the clergy, and the mentally disordered (Sched 1, Pt I, of the Juries Act 1974).

- *Those disqualified from service*

  Someone sentenced to life imprisonment is disqualified for life from jury service; someone who has received any other custodial sentence (including a suspended sentence) is disqualified for 10 years; someone who has been ordered to perform community service is disqualified for 10 years; someone who has been subject to a probation order is disqualified for five years (Sched 1, Pt II of the Juries Act 1974). Furthermore, any person who is on bail at the time they would be serving on a jury is also disqualified.

• *Those who have the right to be excused*

This category includes those aged 65 or over, those who have served on a jury within the last two years, Members of Parliament, full time serving members of the armed forces, and medical personnel (such as doctors, dentists, nurses and vets) (s 8 and Sched 1, Pt III of the Juries Act 1974).

9.7.2 Excusal from jury service

Anyone outside these three groups is required to attend for jury service if summoned. However, if someone summoned for jury service believes that they have a good reason to be excused, they may apply to be excused by the officer of the Crown Court who summons them (s 9(2) of the Juries Act 1974). If that officer refuses, the unwilling juror could ask a judge to excuse him from service.

A Practice Direction (*Practice Direction (Excusal from Jury Service)* [1988] 1 WLR 1162) on excusal from jury service states that a person may be excused from service on the grounds (*inter alia*) of personal hardship and conscientious objection to jury service.

Section 9B of the Juries Act 1974 empowers the trial judge to excuse from jury service a person who is not capable of acting effectively as a juror because of a physical disability.

Section 42 of the Criminal Justice and Public Order Act gives statutory effect to the decision of the Divisional Court in *R v Guildford Crown Court ex p Siderfin* [1990] 2 QB 683; [1989] 3 All ER 7, by enabling the excusal from jury service of a practising member of a religious society or order the tenets or beliefs of which are incompatible with jury service.

Someone who is summoned for jury service at a time when they will be on holiday or away on business may ask the summoning officer at the Crown Court to defer their service (s 9A of the Juries Act 1974).

A person who is summoned for jury service and is not excused must attend. Failure to attend without reasonable cause is an offence punishable with a fine of up to £1,000 (s 20 of the Juries Act 1974).

9.7.3 Empanelling a jury

The term 'jury panel' is used to describe the body of people who have been summoned for jury service at a particular Crown Court.

Where a defendant has pleaded not guilty to an indictment, at least 12 members of the jury panel are brought into the court room, and are then known as the 'jury in waiting'. The clerk of the court calls out the names of 12 of them, chosen at random.

Once 12 people are in the jury box, the clerk says to the defendant, 'the names that you are about to hear are the names of the jurors who are to try you. If you wish to object to them or to any of them, you must do so as they come to the book to be sworn, and before they are sworn, and your objection shall be heard'. The nature of the objection referred to is considered below when we examine challenges to jurors.

Each of the jurors (one after the other (s 11(3))) takes the juror's oath, reading the words from a card and holding in her right hand the appropriate Holy Book (New Testament for Christians, Old Testament for Jews, Koran for Muslims). The oath is:

I swear by almighty God that I will faithfully try the defendant(s) and give (a) true verdict(s) according to the evidence.

Jurors who do not wish to swear may affirm instead, saying:

I [name] promise that I will faithfully try …

Once all 12 have taken the oath (or affirmed), the clerk reads out the indictment and then says, 'To this indictment the defendant has pleaded not guilty. It is your charge, having heard the evidence, to say whether he be guilty or not'. Note that if the defendant has pleaded guilty to some of the counts on the indictment, but not guilty to the others, the jury will not be told about the guilty pleas.

In some cases, there have been attempts to 'nobble' the jury. If the police fear that such an attempt is likely, an application may be made for the jurors to receive special protection. In *R v Comerford* [1998], 1 WLR 191; [1998] 1 All ER 823, it was held that an application for jury protection should normally be made in the presence of the defendant, and should be supported by evidence of the need for such protection (which the defendant can cross-examine). Any departure from this approach is only possible if the trial judge is satisfied that it is necessary and would not render the trial process unfair. Furthermore, the jury must be directed not to hold it against the defendant that protective measures have been taken. In the present case, the clerk in the Crown Court did not reveal the names of the jurors. The Court of Appeal held that, although the defendant is entitled under s 5(2) of the Juries Act 1974, if he wishes, to know the names of all the people on the jury panel (that is, all those summoned for jury service at that court), it is permissible, in an appropriate case, for the clerk not to follow the usual practice of calling out the names of the individual jurors as they enter the jury box.

9.8 CHALLENGES TO JURORS

The clerk tells the defendant that he can challenge the jury, or individual jurors. In this section, we consider the challenges which can be made to the jury as a whole and to individual jurors.

9.8.1 Challenging the whole jury

Theoretically, it is open to the defendant to challenge the way in which the jury panel was selected; this is known as challenging the array. In practice, this never occurs. The only basis for objecting to the entire jury panel would be that the population of the area served by that particular Crown Court would be hostile to the defendant because of the notoriety of the case. In such a case, the appropriate course of action would be to try to secure a change in the location of the trial. As to the ways for achieving this, see Chapter 7, 7.13.

9.8.2 Challenging individual jurors

- *Challenging for cause*

  Both the prosecution and the defence can challenge a potential juror on the ground that he may be biased for or against the accused. The party who alleges that a juror is biased bears the burden of proving bias.

  To challenge for cause, counsel says 'challenge' just before the juror takes his oath. The reason for the challenge is then explained to the judge. In a straightforward case, the judge will ask the juror to leave the jury box, having heard submissions from counsel. Otherwise, jurors who have already been sworn and the rest of the 'jury in waiting' will be asked to leave the court room and evidence will be called to substantiate the challenge.

  Unlike the position in the United States (where jurors are questioned at length on their suitability), the challenger must provide *prima facie* evidence in support of the challenge before being allowed to question the juror (*R v Chandler (No 2)* [1964] 2 QB 322; [1964] 1 All ER 761).

  An example of this taking place is *R v Kray* (1969) 53 Cr App R 412. The activities of the accused had been the subject of sensational reporting in a newspaper; counsel for the accused persuaded the trial judge that anyone who had read the graphic and inaccurate material would be predisposed to convict the accused. Once the judge was satisfied of this, he allowed the defence to ask each potential juror if they had read the offending press reports.

Questioning of potential jurors can only take place in exceptional cases. In *R v Andrews* [1999] Crim LR 156, the appellant claimed that her conviction for murder was unsafe because of adverse pre-trial publicity. It was argued on her behalf that potential jurors should have been asked whether they had read or heard the reports in question. It was held that such questioning of jurors (whether done orally or by means of a questionnaire) is of doubtful efficacy and may even be counter-productive (by reminding the jurors of the publicity); it should therefore only be done in the most exceptional circumstances.

In any event, whilst the names of the jury panel are available to the defence before the trial, it is unlikely that the defence will have the resources to investigate each one of the potential jurors.

If the challenge is successful the juror cannot try this case but, depending on the nature of the challenge (is she unsuitable to be a juror or just biased in this particular case?) may be called upon to try another case.

In *R v Brown* [1992] Crim LR 586, the judge was informed that one of the jurors was distantly related to one of the police officers in the case. The judge did not investigate the matter very fully and allowed the trial to continue. It was held by the Court of Appeal that the judge should have questioned the juror. The test for potential bias was held to be whether a reasonable and fair-minded person sitting in the court and knowing all the relevant facts would have a reasonable suspicion that a fair trial is not possible.

In *R v Gough* [1993] AC 646; [1992] 4 All ER 481, a juror realised at the end of the trial that the defendant was a neighbour of hers. The House of Lords dismissed an appeal against conviction on the ground that the juror may have been biased. The test requires there to be a real danger of bias.

See, also, *R v Wilson* (1979) 69 Cr App R 83, where convictions were quashed (and retrials ordered) because one of the jurors was the wife of a prison officer serving at the prison where the appellants had been held on remand. The Court of Appeal said that the test is one of possibility of bias rather than probability of bias and so it was not necessary to inquire into the juror's actual state of mind. There was a real danger that, consciously or not, she may have been biased against the appellants.

- *The prosecution stand by*

It used to be the case that each defendant could challenge up to three potential jurors peremptorily (that is, without giving a reason). This right was abolished in 1988, and the only challenge the defence can now make is the challenge for cause described above.

The prosecution, however, have retained their right to challenge a juror without giving reasons; this is known as the prosecution right to stand a juror by. To exercise this right, prosecuting counsel says 'stand by' just before the juror takes her oath. It is then explained to the juror that he cannot sit on this jury, but will go back to the jury panel and may be called on to try another case.

- *The Attorney General's guidelines*

As it may be seen as unfair that the prosecution should be able to challenge a juror without giving any reason but the defence do not have such a right, the Attorney General has issued guidelines which make it clear that the right of stand by should only be used in exceptional cases.

In cases involving national security or terrorism, the jury panel will be 'vetted' extensively to ensure that they are suitable to try such a sensitive case.

In other cases, the only check likely to be carried out is to see which members of the jury panel have previous convictions. Some may have convictions which disqualify them from jury service (and this would be the subject of a challenge for cause); others may not be disqualified from service but may be unsuitable to try a particular case (for example, someone who has just been fined for theft may not be the best person to try a theft case).

Finally, the prosecution may stand a juror by, if the defence agree to this, if the juror is manifestly unsuitable to try the case (for example, clearly has difficulty in reading the words on the card when trying to take the oath and is therefore unsuited to try a case where a number of documents have to be read).

- *The judge's right of stand by*

The judge has an inherent power to stand a juror by. This power is hardly ever exercised and would only be appropriate where a juror is manifestly unsuitable to try a particular case.

In *R v Ford* [1989] QB 89, the Court of Appeal held that a judge must not use his power to stand jurors by in order to try to ensure a racially balanced jury. The statutory procedure for selecting jurors is intended to ensure random selection and the judge should not interfere with this randomness. *Ford* was followed in *R v Tarrant* [1998] Crim LR 342, where the Court of Appeal repeated that a judge cannot use his discretion to discharge individual jurors in order to interfere with the composition of the jury panel (in the present case, to select jurors from outside the court's catchment area in order to minimise the risk of intimidation).

9.8.3 Discharge of individual jurors during the trial

A jury always starts off with 12 jurors. However, under s 16 of the Juries Act 1974 up to three jurors may be discharged during the course of the trial in case of illness or other necessity (for example, bereavement).

What constitutes necessity is a matter for the trial judge. In *R v Hambery* [1977] QB 924; [1977] 3 All ER 561, a juror was discharged because the trial went on longer than expected and she would otherwise have had to cancel a holiday.

If more than three jurors can no longer serve, the trial has to be abandoned; a fresh trial will take place later.

9.8.4   Discharge of entire jury

The entire jury may be discharged if, for example:

- the jury hears evidence which is inadmissible and prejudicial to the defendant and the judge decides that a direction to ignore this evidence would not be sufficient (where something prejudicial to the defendant has inadvertently been admitted in evidence, it is not necessarily the case that the jury should be discharged; whether or not the jury should be discharged is a matter for the discretion of the trial judge (*R v Weaver and Weaver* (1967) 51 Cr App R 77); the test to be applied is the test for bias (see *R v Gough* [1993] AC 646), namely whether there is real danger of injustice occurring because the jury, having heard the prejudicial matter, may be biased (*R v Docherty* [1999] 1 Cr App R 274)).

- the jury cannot agree on a verdict (see below);

- an individual juror has to be discharged and there is a risk that he may have contaminated the rest of the jury (for example, he happens to know that the defendant has previous convictions or is facing further trials for other offences) (*R v Hutton* [1990] Crim LR 875).

If members of the jury misbehave during the course of the trial, the jury should be discharged if there is a 'real danger of prejudice' to the accused (*R v Spencer* [1987] AC 128; [1986] 3 All ER 928). In *R v Sawyer* (1980) 71 Cr App R 283, for example, some jurors were seen in conversation with prosecution witnesses during an adjournment. The trial judge questioned them and it transpired that the conversation had been on subjects unconnected with the trial. The decision of the judge not to discharge the jury was upheld by the Court of Appeal. Where a juror has specialised knowledge of something relevant to the case against the defendant, and has communicated that knowledge to the rest of the jury, the judge is obliged to discharge the jury if this comes to light at a stage of the trial such that the defendant has had no opportunity to challenge what amounts to new evidence or to put forward his own explanation (*R v Fricker* (1999) 96(30) LSG 29).

In *R v Blackwell* (1995) 2 Cr App R 625, the Court of Appeal gave guidance on the approach to be taken by a judge where there is a suspicion that a member of the public has tried to influence members of the jury. The member of the public should be questioned by the judge (or by court officials or police at the direction of the judge) and, if it appears that there has been an attempt to influence the jurors, the jurors should be questioned to establish if their independence has been compromised. Only after a full investigation has been completed does the judge have sufficient information to decide whether any or all of the jurors should be discharged.

Where the jury is discharged from giving a verdict, the defendant can be re-tried, as he is not regarded as having been acquitted.

9.8.5 Composition of jury as a ground of appeal

Composition of jury as a ground of appeal is dealt with in Chapter 10, 10.6.2.

9.9 THE START OF THE TRIAL

Once the jury has been empanelled, the prosecution present their case. Counsel for the prosecution begins by making an opening speech.

9.9.1 Content of prosecution opening speech

In the opening speech, the prosecution remind the jury of the offences to which the defendant has pleaded not guilty. If those offences are complicated, the prosecution will summarise the relevant legal principles (making it clear that the judge is the final arbiter of the law). It should also be made clear at this stage that the prosecution bear the burden of proof and that the jury must be satisfied so that they are sure in order to convict. Prosecutors normally indicate who they will be calling as witnesses and how these witnesses fit in to the overall story. The purpose of the opening speech is to enable the jury to make sense of the evidence that they will now be hearing.

If counsel for the defence has indicated to the prosecution before the start of the trial that the defence will be challenging the admissibility of some of the prosecution evidence, the opening speech by the prosecution should make no mention of that evidence.

If, however, the evidence in dispute is so crucial to the prosecution case that an opening speech cannot be made without referring to it, the jury will be sent out of the court room and the admissibility of this evidence will be determined before the trial begins. Usually, where such crucial evidence is ruled inadmissible at the outset, the prosecution would have little choice but to abandon the case.

9.10 THE PROSECUTION CASE

If the defendant pleads not guilty, the prosecution are put to proof of their entire case, and so must adduce evidence on all the elements of the alleged offence(s).

The only exception to this rule is where the defence make a formal admission so that something which would otherwise be in issue is no longer an issue.

9.10.1 Formal admissions

Under s 10 of the Criminal Justice Act 1967, the prosecution or the defence (in practice, usually the defence) may admit any fact which would otherwise be in issue; this admission is conclusive evidence of the fact admitted. If, for example, the defendant is charged with causing death by dangerous driving, he might admit that he was driving the car at the time of the accident.

In the Crown Court, the admission may be made in writing (in which case, it will be signed by the person making it) or orally in court by counsel. In the magistrates' court, a formal admission must be made in writing.

Formal admissions are not made very frequently. It is usually apparent from questions asked in cross-examination if some of what the witness says is accepted by the defence. If all of the evidence of a particular witness is accepted by the defence, the defence will consent to that witness's statement being read to the court (see 9.10.4 below).

9.10.2 Prosecution witnesses

The prosecution witnesses whose written statements the defence do not allow to be read to the court each give evidence. Evidence is given under oath, the witness saying 'I swear by almighty God that the evidence I shall give shall be the truth, the whole truth, and nothing but the truth'. A witness who does not wish to take the oath may affirm instead, promising to tell the truth.

Each witness is examined-in-chief by the prosecution (who are not allowed to ask leading questions, that is, questions which suggest their own answer), then cross-examined by the defence, and (if necessary) re-examined by the prosecution (the rule against leading questions applying to re-examination as well).

Where a witness made a contemporaneous note of the matters on which he is about to give evidence, it is open to the party calling that witness to apply to the judge for the witness to be given permission to refresh his memory by referring to those notes (*R v Da Silva* [1990] 1 WLR 31). This is invariably done to enable police officers to refer to their notebooks while giving evidence. In *R v South Ribble Stipendiary Magistrate ex p Cochrane* (1996) 2 Cr Ap R 544, the Divisional Court held that the court also has a discretion to permit a witness to refresh his memory from a non-contemporaneous document; judges (and magistrates) must consider the requirements of fairness and justice in exercising that discretion.

9.10.3   Evidence through television link/pre-recorded video

Section 32 of the Criminal Justice Act 1988 allows evidence to be given via a live television link if either (a) the witness is outside the UK or (b) the witness is under 14 and the offence charged is one in respect of which a notice of transfer may be given under s 53 of the Criminal Justice Act 1991 (see Chapter 7, 7.12.3).

Section 54 of the Criminal Justice Act 1988 also provides for the admissibility of pre-recorded video evidence of child witness (that is, under the age of 14), again where the offence charged is one to which the s 53 notice of transfer provisions apply.

In both cases, the leave of the court is required.

9.10.4   Reading witness statements

Under paras 1 and 2 of Sched 2 to the Criminal Procedure and Investigations Act 1996, a witness statement or deposition which was tendered in evidence at committal proceedings is admissible in evidence at the subsequent Crown Court trial unless:

(a) the Crown Court exercises its discretion to exclude the statement or deposition; or

(b) the accused (or, if more than one, any of the accused) objects to the statement or deposition being used as evidence.

Where an accused wishes to object to the use of a written statement or deposition, the objection must be made in writing to the Crown Court and to the prosecution within 14 days of the date when the accused was committed for trial (see r 8 of the Magistrates' Courts Rules 1981, as amended).

However, if the accused does object to the statement or deposition being used as evidence, the Crown Court 'may order that the objection shall have no effect if the court considers it to be in the interests of justice so to order' (para 1(4) and para 2(4)). It is unlikely that the court will overrule a defence objection if the defence appear to have a cogent reason for wanting to cross-examine the maker of the statement.

This will be the case, for example, where the defence in a theft case is not that the property was not stolen but that the defendant was not the thief: the statement of the loser of the property saying that he gave no one permission to take it will not therefore be disputed by the defence.

9.10.5   Section 23 of the Criminal Justice Act 1988

Section 23 of the Criminal Justice Act 1988 allows a written statement to be used in place of oral evidence without the consent of the defence in any of the following instances:

- the maker of the statement is dead or cannot attend court because of his bodily or mental condition; or

- the maker of the statement is outside the UK and it is not reasonably practicable to secure his attendance; or

- all reasonable steps have been taken to find the maker of the statement but he cannot be found; or

- the statement was made to the police and the maker does not give oral evidence 'through fear or because he is kept out of the way'.

It should be noted that where fear is relied on, that fear must be proved by admissible evidence. Thus, in *Neill v North Antrim Magistrates' Court* [1992] 1 WLR 1221; [1992] 4 All ER 846, the House of Lords held that this provision could not be relied upon to admit the written statements of two boys where a police officer gave evidence that the mother of the boys had told him that they were in fear; it would have been different if the officer had been able to give evidence that the boys themselves had told him that they were in fear. Similarly, in *R v Belmarsh Magistrates Court ex p Gilligan* [1998] 1 Cr App R 14, the Divisional Court held that, in order to satisfy the requirements of s 23 of the Criminal Justice Act 1988, the court must hear oral evidence (for example, from a police officer) as to the fear of the witness. The fear cannot be proved by a written statement made by the witness who claims to be in fear.

In *R v Ricketts* [1991] Crim LR 915, it was said that the jury must not be told that a statement is being read to them on the ground that the maker of the statement is absent because of fear for his personal safety resulting from threats by the accused. Obviously this would be extremely prejudicial.

In *R v Waters* (1997) 161 JP 249, the victim of an assault made a statement to the police in which he identified the appellant as one of his assailants. At the appellant's trial, the witness started to give evidence but then ceased to give evidence through fear, saying that he could not now remember what had happened and could not identify his assailants. The Court of Appeal (following *R v Ashford Justices ex p Hilden* [1993] QB 555; [1993] 2 All ER 154) upheld the decision of the trial judge to allow the witness's earlier statement to be read to the jury under s 23 of the Criminal Justice Act 1988. The court said that what mattered was whether or not there was, at the time when s 23 was invoked, any relevant oral evidence which the witness was still expected to give. If there was such evidence, and it was proved beyond reasonable doubt that he did not give that evidence through fear, s 23 was satisfied.

Section 25 of the Criminal Justice Act 1988 gives the court a discretion to exclude evidence which would otherwise be admissible under s 23 of that Act. In *R v Radak* [1999] 1 Cr App R 187, the trial judge allowed a witness statement to be read to the jury under s 23 on the basis that the maker of the statement was in America and would not come to court to give evidence through fear. The Court of Appeal held that this decision was wrong. The witness's evidence was an essential link in the prosecution case and the defence had little or no evidence to controvert the contents of the statement; it would therefore be unfair to admit that evidence without the defence being able to cross-examine the witness. Furthermore, the prosecution had known from the outset that the witness might not attend voluntarily, and so should have taken steps to have his evidence taken on commission in the US (under s 3 of the Criminal Justice (International Co-operation) Act 1990). The witness statement should therefore not have been admitted.

Where a statement is read to the jury without the consent of the defence, the jury should be warned that the evidence needs to be viewed in the light of the fact that the defence have not had the opportunity to cross-examine the witness. It is not sufficient simply to draw the jury's attention to the fact that evidence has been given by way of a witness statement. The jury should be warned to use particular care when considering the witness statement, since the maker of the statement was not in court to be cross-examined as to its contents. Where the witness statement is vital to the prosecution case, failure to give such a direction will be render any subsequent conviction unsafe (*R v Curry* (1998) *The Times*, 23 March).

Article 6(3)(d) of the European Convention on Human Rights guarantees the right to examine and call witnesses. The admission of hearsay evidence without an opportunity for the defence to cross-examine may render the trial unfair if the conviction is based wholly or mainly on such evidence (*Unterpertinger v Austria* 13 EHRR 175). This may cause problems where s 23 is relied on, though the judge's discretion to exclude the evidence may be held to be a sufficient safeguard.

9.10.6 Screens

Where a witness fears reprisals for giving evidence, the court may allow that witness to remain anonymous and may allow the witness to give evidence from behind a screen (so that the jury can see the witness but the defendant cannot). Such precautions are obviously liable to prejudice the jury against the accused (and natural justice requires that the accused know the identity of his accusers) and so may only be used in very exceptional circumstances (*R v Schaub* [1994] Crim LR 531).

9.10.7   Real evidence

Real evidence means tangible evidence such as the murder weapon or the stolen goods. An item of real evidence has to be produced (that is, identified and its relevance established) by a witness. Once this has been done, counsel says to the judge 'may this be exhibit [number]' and the item then becomes an exhibit. Exhibits are numbered sequentially.

9.11   CHALLENGING THE ADMISSIBILITY OF PROSECUTION EVIDENCE

If the defence object to some of the prosecution evidence, arguing that it is inadmissible, this matter may be dealt with at the pre-trial hearing (at which the judge is empowered to give binding rulings on the admissibility of evidence (see 9.5.3 above). Otherwise, the objection is made (in the absence of the jury) during the course of the trial. If the objection is made during the course of the trial, the prosecution evidence is called in the usual way until the part of the evidence to which there is objection is reached. At that point the jury is invited to retire to the jury room.

Although s 82 of the Police and Criminal Evidence Act 1984 expressly preserved the common law rules on the admissibility of evidence, objections to prosecution evidence are usually made under s 76 or s 78 of the Police and Criminal Evidence Act 1984.

9.11.1   Section 76 of the Police and Criminal Evidence Act 1984

Where the defence allege that a confession has been obtained by oppression or in circumstances likely to render it unreliable, the prosecution must prove beyond reasonable doubt that the confession was not so obtained. The requirement for the prosecution to prove this means that they must call evidence on the point and so a *voir dire* ('trial within a trial') takes place.

Unless the witness is in the middle of giving (or has already given) evidence in the course of the trial, a witness giving evidence on a *voir dire* takes a special form of oath: 'I swear by almighty God that I will answer truthfully all such questions as the court may ask.'

Each prosecution witness called in the *voir dire* may be cross-examined by the defence. When the relevant prosecution witnesses have given evidence, the defence may call evidence (including the evidence of the defendant himself); each defence witness may be cross-examined by the prosecution.

After the evidence has been called, both counsel may address the judge and the judge then rules on the admissibility of the confession.

The only question to be determined under s 76 is *how* the confession was obtained. It is wholly irrelevant whether the confession was true or not.

If the defence case is simply that the police have fabricated the confession, that is a matter for the jury to decide and not a question of admissibility. However, there are cases where the defence allege that the confession has been fabricated but also argue that, even if that was not so, the confession is inadmissible anyway. In *Thongjai v The Queen* [1998] AC 54, the Privy Council (following *Ajodha v The State* [1982] AC 204) said that, if the defendant denies making an oral admission and also alleges that he was ill treated by the police before or at the time of the alleged admission, the two issues are not mutually exclusive. The judge has to assume that the admission was made and decide whether it is admissible; if (and only if) the judge decides that the evidence is admissible, it is for the jury to decide whether the admission was in fact made.

Where a judge conducts a *voir dire* and holds that a confession is admissible, the judge should not tell the jury of the ruling (the trial should simply continue with the prosecution leading evidence of the confession). If the judge indicates that he has ruled against the accused, this might lead the jury to think that the judge does not believe the accused (*Mitchell v The Queen* [1998] AC 695).

9.11.2 Section 78 of the Police and Criminal Evidence Act 1984

Where the defence object to prosecution evidence on the ground that its admission would be unfairly prejudicial, this objection is made in the absence of the jury but need not involve the judge hearing evidence. In other words, a *voir dire* need not take place if the judge is able to decide the question of admissibility under s 78 just by hearing legal argument from counsel and without hearing evidence. This will be the case, for example, where the breach of provisions of the Codes of Practice are apparent from the custody record and/or the committal statements and the judge merely has to decide the effect of those breaches (*R v Keenan* [1990] 2 QB 54; [1989] 3 All ER 598).

9.11.3 The European Convention on Human Rights

Under the European Convention on Human Rights, there is no absolute requirement that illegally obtained evidence should be excluded, but use of such evidence may give rise to unfairness in a particular case (*Schenck v Switzerland* 13 EHRR 242). Section 78 of the Police and Criminal Evidence appears to accord with this principle.

Admission of a confession which was obtained through maltreatment will inevitably violate Art 6. Section 76 of the 1984 Act accords with this principle.

9.12 WITNESSES WHOM THE PROSECUTION MUST CALL

The prosecution must call all the witnesses whose statements were served on the defence in the committal proceedings (*R v Balmforth* [1992] Crim LR 825). The exceptions to this rule are as follows:

- the defence consent to the written statement of the witness being read to the court (under Sched 1, para 1 or 2 of the Criminal Procedure and Investigations Act 1996); or

- the prosecution take the view that the witness is no longer credible (*R v Oliva* [1965] 1 WLR 1028; [1965] 3 All ER 116); or

- the witness would so fundamentally contradict the prosecution case that it would be better for that witness to be called by the defence (*R v Nugent* [1977] 1 WLR 789; [1977] 3 All ER 662).

These principles were restated in *R v Armstrong* [1995] Crim LR 831 and *R v Russell-Jones* [1995] 3 All ER 239.

9.12.1 Tendering witnesses for cross-examination

If a witness simply duplicates the evidence of another witness, the prosecution may simply 'tender' that witness, that is call him, establish his identity and relevance to the case, and then invite the defence to cross-examine.

9.13 SUBMISSION OF NO CASE TO ANSWER

After the close of the prosecution case, the defence may make a submission that there is no case to answer. This submission is made in the absence of the jury (who might otherwise be prejudiced against the defendant if the submission fails) (*R v Smith* (1986) 85 Cr App R 197; *Crosdale v R* [1995] 2 All ER 500).

9.13.1 Principles applied to submission of no case to answer

The principles governing this submission are to be found in *R v Galbraith* [1981] 1 WLR 1039; [1981] 2 All ER 1060:

- if the judge comes to the conclusion that the prosecution evidence, taken at its highest, is such that a jury properly directed could not properly convict upon it, it is his duty to stop the case if the defendant makes a submission of no case;

- if the strength or weakness of the prosecution evidence depends on the view to be taken of a witness's reliability and on one possible view there is evidence on which a jury could properly convict, the judge should allow the matter to be tried by the jury.

Thus, a judge should only accept a submission of no case to answer in a clear case, otherwise he is trespassing on the function of the jury. However, a judge may take account of the credibility of the prosecution evidence if no reasonable jury could believe that evidence.

In *R v Shippey* [1988] Crim LR 767, for example, Turner J found no case to answer in a rape trial because of 'really significant inherent inconsistencies' in the complainant's uncorroborated evidence, which his Lordship found 'frankly incredible'.

Thus, the judge can have regard:

- to the sheer improbability of what a witness says;
- to internal inconsistencies in the testimony of a particular witness; and
- to inconsistencies between one prosecution witness and another.

It should be noted that where identification is in issue, special rules apply. In *R v Turnbull* [1977] QB 224; [1976] 3 All ER 549, the Court of Appeal said that a judge should withdraw an identification case from the jury if the quality of the identification is poor (taking into account the circumstances of the identification – length of view, distance, lighting, etc) and there is no other evidence supporting the correctness of the identification.

If the submission succeeds in respect of all the counts being tried, the judge directs the jury to acquit the defendant on all those counts. If the submission fails on all counts, the trial proceeds and the jury know nothing about the submission.

If the submission succeeds on some counts but fails on others the jury are told that they are to consider only the counts that are left. A formal acquittal on those counts where the submission succeeded will be directed when the jury give their verdict on the remaining counts (*R v Plain* [1976] 1 WLR 565; [1967] 1 All ER 614).

If the judge wrongly holds that there is a case to answer, evidence called after the submission will not be considered by the Court of Appeal as no further evidence would have been called had the submission been upheld. Thus, an appeal against conviction would succeed even if the defendant was clearly incriminated by evidence given on behalf of the defence (see *R v Abbott* [1955] 2 QB 497; [1955] 2 All ER 899 and *R v Juett* [1981] Crim LR 113).

In *R v S; R v C* [1996] Crim LR 346, the Court of Appeal said that it assists the Court of Appeal if a trial judge gives reasons for rejecting a submission of no case to answer. Those reasons can either be given when the submission is rejected or, if the judge prefers, after the jury has retired or after the verdict. If the judge does not give reasons, defence counsel may ask him to do so.

Section 34(2)(c) of the Criminal Justice and Public Order Act 1994 provides that adverse inferences can be drawn from failure to answer police questions when the court is considering a submission of no case to answer. However, s 34(2)(c) can only be relied upon to take the case past half time if a fact has been relied on by the defence which brings s 34 into play. This would be the case where, for example, the defence cross-examine prosecution witnesses on the basis of facts that were not mentioned by the defendant when he was questioned by the police.

9.13.2 Power of the jury to acquit at any time after the close of the prosecution case

Not to be confused with the right of the defence to seek a ruling from the judge that there is no case to answer, the jury themselves have the power to stop the case and acquit the defendant at any time after the close of the prosecution case. Jurors are, of course, generally unaware that they have this power and it is only in exceptional cases that they will be told of this power. In *R v Kemp* [1995] 1 Cr App R 151, the Court of Appeal said that where the judge does remind the jury that they may acquit the defendant without hearing further evidence, he should be cautious not to do anything other than merely inform them of their right to stop the case. Thus, the judge should not in effect invite the jury to acquit the defendant. If the judge considers that the case against the defendant is too weak to be left to the jury, then the judge should stop the case himself.

9.14 THE DEFENCE CASE

If there is no submission of no case to answer, or a submission is made and the judge finds a case to answer in respect of some or all of the counts, evidence may then be adduced on behalf of the defendant.

Counsel for the defence may begin the defence case by making an opening speech if he proposes to call one or more witnesses (other than the defendant) as to the facts. If the only witness as to the facts is the defendant (that is, only the defendant gives evidence or there is evidence only from the defendant and character witnesses) there will be no defence opening speech.

Where there is more than one defence witness including the defendant, the defendant must give evidence first unless the court otherwise directs (s 79 of the Police and Criminal Evidence Act 1984).

9.14.1 Adverse inferences

There is no obligation on the defence to call any evidence: counsel for the defence could simply address the jury and ask them to find that the prosecution have failed to prove the guilt of the accused beyond reasonable doubt. However, s 35 of the Criminal Justice and Public Order Act 1994, although it does not render the accused compellable to give evidence on his own behalf, does enable the magistrates or jury to draw such inferences as appear proper from the failure of the accused to give evidence or from his refusal, without good cause, to answer any question.

Where the accused has taken the oath but then refuses to answer a question, he will only be regarded as having good cause not to answer the question if either he is entitled to refuse to answer by virtue of an Act of Parliament or on the ground of privilege, or the court, in the exercise of its general discretion, excuses him from answering it.

Section 35 requires the defendant to be warned that adverse inferences may be drawn from his silence unless he (or his barrister) has informed the court that he will give evidence. The details of what the judge should say are set out in *Practice Direction (Crown Court: Defendant's Evidence)* [1995] 1 WLR 657 and are as follows:

- If the defendant is represented but his lawyer has not indicated that the defendant will be giving evidence, the judge should ask the lawyer (in the presence of the jury): 'Have you advised your client that the stage has now been reached at which he may give evidence and, if he chooses not to do so or, having been sworn, without good cause refuses to answer any question, the jury may draw such inferences as appear proper from his failure to do so?'

- Where the accused is not legally represented, the judge (again, in the presence of the jury) should, at the close of prosecution case, say to the accused: 'You have heard the evidence against you. Now is the time for you to make your defence. You may give evidence on oath, and be cross-examined like any other witness. If you do not give evidence or, having been sworn, without good cause refuse to answer any question, the jury may draw such inferences as appear proper. That means they may hold it against you. You may also call any witness or witnesses whom you have arranged to attend court. Afterwards you may also, if you wish, address the jury by arguing your case from the dock. But you cannot at that stage give evidence. Do you now intend to give evidence?'

In *R v Bevan* (1993) 98 Cr App R 354, the Court of Appeal said that if the defendant chooses not to give evidence in his own defence, counsel should make sure that this decision is recorded (usually, this will be done by an endorsement on the brief); the record should be signed by the defendant and should indicate that he has made the decision of his own free will, bearing in mind the advice of counsel regarding the possible consequences of not testifying.

9.14.2   Defence evidence

Each defence witness (including the defendant himself, if he chooses to give evidence) is liable to be cross-examined by the prosecution and may then be re-examined by defence counsel, if necessary.

Where the defendant gives evidence, it must be borne in mind that he may be cross-examined as to any previous convictions he has if the nature or conduct of the defence case has involved 'imputations' on the character of prosecution witnesses (s 1(3)(ii) of the Criminal Evidence Act 1898). This will be the case if the defence cross-examine prosecution witnesses on the basis that they are lying, rather than mistaken, or if the defendant (or one of his witnesses) makes such an allegation. The judge has a discretion to refuse to allow such cross-examination to take place, and so the prosecutor should seek permission from the judge before embarking on such cross-examination. Leave may well be refused if there is a real risk that, because the previous convictions are for offences which are very similar to the present charges (but falling short of the similarity required for them to be admissible as similar fact evidence), the jury might use them as evidence of propensity despite a direction from the judge that they should not do so.

In *R v Taylor and Goodman* [1999] 2 Cr App R 163, the appellant was cross-examined on his previous convictions (he had cast imputations on the character of prosecution witnesses). On appeal, he argued that the judge had erred in allowing the prosecution to cross-examine him thus, as he had a very serious criminal record. The Court of Appeal held that to accept the argument that defendants with very bad criminal records should be protected against disclosure of those records would allow such defendants too much freedom to cast imputations against prosecution witnesses. However, the court said that where a defendant's criminal record was very serious, a judge was only likely to allow its admission where the allegations made by the defendant against the prosecution witnesses were equally serious.

A defendant who attacks the character of a prosecution witness is immune from questioning as to his own character under s 1(3)(ii) of the Criminal Evidence Act 1898 if he chooses not to give evidence, since that section is only concerned with cross-examination (*R v Butterwasser* [1948] 1 KB 4). However, where he elects to give evidence and has embarked on doing so, he cannot avoid evidence of his own character going before the jury simply by refusing to return to the witness box so that he cannot be cross-examined. In such circumstances, the Crown is entitled to adduce evidence as to his bad character (*R v Forbes* (1999) *The Times*, 5 May).

9.15   CLOSING SPEECHES

If the accused is unrepresented and either calls no evidence at all or else was himself the only witness as to the facts, then the prosecution have no right to make a closing speech.

Otherwise, once all the defence evidence has been called, both counsel may make a closing speech. The prosecution make the first speech (although prosecuting counsel may decide not to make a speech if the trial has been a very short one). Thus, the defence have the last word before the judge sums the case up to the jury.

9.16   VARIATION IN PROCEDURE WHERE MORE THAN ONE DEFENDANT

The procedure set out in 9.14 above varies slightly if there is more than one defendant.

9.16.1   Defendants separately represented

Where two or more defendants are charged in the same indictment and are separately represented, their cases are presented in the order in which their names appear on the indictment. So:

R v D1

  D2

Prosecution witnesses are cross-examined first on behalf of D1, then on behalf of D2.

The defence case is then presented as follows:

- opening speech on behalf of D1;
- D1 called as a witness (if he chooses to give evidence):

  examination in chief by his own counsel

  cross-examination on behalf of D2

  cross-examination by prosecution

  re-examination by his own counsel (if necessary);
- any witnesses called on behalf of D1 give evidence; the order of questioning is the same as above;
- opening speech on behalf of D2;
- D2 called as a witness (if he chooses to give evidence):

  examination in chief by his own counsel

cross-examination on behalf of D1

cross-examination by prosecution

re-examination by his own counsel (if necessary);

- any witnesses called on behalf of D2 give evidence; the order of questioning is the same as the point above;
- prosecution closing speech;
- closing speech on behalf of D1;
- closing speech on behalf of D2.

Whereas a defendant can ask the court to exclude prosecution evidence on the ground that it is unduly prejudicial, in *R v Myers* (1997) *The Times*, 31 July, Lord Hope said that the judge has no power to exclude relevant evidence given by or on behalf of a defendant on the ground that it might prejudice a co-defendant or because it was obtained by improper or unfair means.

It must be remembered that if one defendant (D1) gives evidence against a co-defendant (D2), D2 can cross-examine D1 as to any previous convictions recorded against him (s 1(f)(iii) of the Criminal Evidence Act 1898). The term 'evidence against' means evidence which supports the prosecution case against D2 in a material respect or which undermines D's defence (see *Murdoch v Taylor* [1965] AC 574 and *R v Crawford* [1997] 1 WLR 1329).

9.16.2 Defendants jointly represented

If the defendants are jointly represented, they are regarded as presenting a joint defence. Consequently, the defence case will be presented as follows:

- there will be a single opening speech on behalf of all the defendants;
- D1 gives evidence if he wishes to do so;
- D2 gives evidence if he wishes to do so;
- any other defence witnesses give evidence;
- prosecution closing speech;
- closing speech on behalf of all defendants.

9.17 RE-OPENING THE PROSECUTION CASE

In exceptional cases, the judge has a discretion to allow the prosecution to call additional evidence after the close of the prosecution case.

In *R v Munnery* (1991) 94 Cr App R 164, for example, the defendants were charged with shoplifting. When they were stopped by security staff, they were each carrying a carton of glassware. After the close of the prosecution case, the defence indicated that they wished to submit that there was no case to answer. The next morning, when the judge was to consider this submission, the prosecution stated that they wished to call a new witness, a shop assistant who would testify that two cartons of glassware were found to be missing from the shop. The Court of Appeal upheld the decision of the judge to allow this witness to be called. No injustice was done to the defendant as the defence case had not yet started.

In *R v Patel* [1992] Crim LR 739, further evidence against the defendant unexpectedly came to light in the context of an unrelated investigation. The prosecution were allowed to adduce this additional evidence even though closing speeches had already been made. The Court of Appeal said that judges should generally be reluctant to grant such late applications. However, the judge had invited the defence to seek an adjournment and to call fresh evidence if they wished and so no harm had been done.

If the judge takes the view that it would be unduly prejudicial to the defence to allow the prosecution to reopen their case, it is open to him to discharge the jury and a new trial will take place later.

9.18   THE JUDGE'S SUMMING UP

After the prosecution and defence counsel have made their closing speeches, the judge sums the case up to the jury. The judge must do this in all cases, however simple the case may seem. In the summing up, the judge should direct the jury on the following matters.

9.18.1   The respective functions of the judge and the jury

Matters of law are for the judge whereas matters of fact are for the jury. This means that the jury must accept what the judge says about the law whether they agree or not. The judge should be careful not to express an opinion on the facts and should make it clear to the jury that if he does express an opinion on the facts the jury are free to come to a different conclusion. The direction approved in *R v Jackson* [1992] Crim LR 214 was:

> It is my job to tell you what the law is and how to apply it to the issues of fact that you have to decide and to remind you of the important evidence on these issues. As to the law, you must accept what I tell you. As to the facts, you alone are the judges. It is for you to decide what evidence you accept and what evidence you reject or of which you are unsure. If I appear to have a view of the evidence or of the facts with which you do not agree, reject my view. If I mention or emphasise evidence that you regard as unimportant, disregard that evidence. If I do not mention what you regard as important, follow your own view and take that evidence into account.

9.18.2   Burden and standard of proof

- Burden of proof

  It is for the prosecution to prove the defendant's guilt, it is not for the defendant to prove his innocence.

- Standard of proof

  In describing the standard of proof, the judge should tell the jury that the prosecution have to prove the defendant's guilt beyond reasonable doubt; the jury have to be satisfied so that they are sure of the defendant's guilt (*Ferguson v The Queen* [1979] 1 WLR 94; [1979] 1 All ER 877 and *R v McVey* [1988] Crim LR 127).

Exceptionally, the defendant may bear a burden of proof. For example, if the defendant is charged with possession of an offensive weapon (s 1 of the Prevention of Crime Act 1953), it is open to him to show that he had lawful authority or reasonable excuse. In such a case, it must be made clear to the jury that the defendant can satisfy this burden of proof on the balance of probabilities (that is, showing that it is more likely than not that he had lawful authority or reasonable excuse).

There is only a burden of proof on the defendant if statute clearly so provides; otherwise it is for the prosecution to disprove a defence. Thus, if the defendant raises the defence of self-defence, it is for the prosecution to prove beyond reasonable doubt that he was not so acting.

9.18.3   Explanation of the law involved and how it relates to the facts

Even in a straightforward case, directions on the ingredients of the offence are an essential part of the summing up (*R v McVey* (1988)). Thus, the judge must explain what the prosecution have to prove and must remind the jury of the evidence they have heard (*R v O'Meara* (1989) *The Times*, 15 December). The judge should remind the jury of the main features of the prosecution and defence evidence, even if the case is a straightforward one (*R v Gregory* [1993] Crim LR 623).

The jury should thus be able to relate the evidence which they have heard to the legal principles which they have to apply.

9.18.4   Such warnings as are appropriate

(a) Co-defendants or more than one count

Where there is more than one count and/or more than one defendant, the judge must direct the jury to consider each count and each defendant separately.

If one defendant implicated another in a police interview, the judge should instruct the jury to disregard the out-of-court statement of one defendant in so far as it relates to the other defendant (*R v Rhodes* (1959) 44 Cr App R 23). Note that, if a defendant implicated a co-defendant in the witness box when giving evidence on his own behalf, that evidence is admissible against the co-defendant (*R v Rudd* (1948) 32 Cr App R 138).

(b) Identification evidence

If the case rests on identification evidence, the judge must warn the jury that such evidence is notoriously unreliable and that they should examine very closely the circumstances in which the identification took place when assessing the weight of that evidence (*R v Turnbull* [1977] QB 224; [1976] 3 All ER 549).

(c) Adverse inferences

Given the fact that a jury is now entitled to draw adverse inferences from the failure of a defendant to answer police questions (s 34 of the Criminal Justice and Public Order Act 1994) or to testify in court (s 35)), the jury will have to be given some guidance on what this means.

In *R v Cowan* [1996] QB 373; [1995] 4 All ER 939, the Court of Appeal considered what should be said in the summing up if the case is one where adverse inferences might be drawn under s 35 from the defendant's failure to testify. The essential elements of the direction are as follows:

(a) the judge must remind the jury that the burden of proof remains on the prosecution throughout;

(b) (as provided by s 38(3) of the Criminal Justice and Public Order Act 1994) an inference from silence could not on its own prove guilt;

(c) the jury had to be satisfied (on the basis of the evidence called by the prosecution) that the prosecution had established a case to answer before inferences could be drawn from the accused's silence; and

(d) they could only draw an adverse inference from the accused's silence if they concluded that the silence could only sensibly be attributed to the accused having no answer to the charge or none that would stand up to cross-examination; where the defendant offers an explanation for his silence, the jury must reject that explanation before drawing adverse inferences from the silence.

In other words, the defendant's failure to answer police questions or testify cannot be the sole basis for his conviction and so the jury must be directed not to convict just because the defendant has not testified. Nevertheless, if the evidence adduced by the prosecution calls for an explanation which the defendant should be in a position to give, the jury may be rightly suspicious of a defendant who declines to give an explanation unless they accept any explanation for the silence. Where the silence was failure to answer police questions, it may be that the defendant will explain this silence when he gives evidence. If the silence is a failure to testify, any explanation could come from the questions asked during the cross-examination of the prosecution witnesses.

The same approach was followed in *R v Birchall* (1998) *The Times*, 10 February. In that case, the Court of Appeal held that where the defendant fails to testify, the judge must tell the jury that they should not start to consider whether to draw adverse inferences from the defendant's failure to testify until they have concluded that there is a case to answer, that is, that the prosecution case against him is sufficiently compelling to call for an answer by him. This is so even if there is plainly sufficient evidence to amount to a *prima facie* case against the defendant.

Thus there are two key steps before adverse inferences can be drawn under s 35: (i) is the jury satisfied that the prosecution have established a case to answer against the defendant?; (ii) has the jury rejected any explanation put forward by the defendant for his refusal to give evidence? If the answer to these questions is 'yes', the jury may draw adverse inferences from the defendant's silence.

In *R v Argent* [1997] 2 Cr App R 27, the Court of Appeal set out the conditions which have to be satisfied before adverse inferences can be drawn, under s 34 of the Criminal Justice and Public Order Act 1994, from a person's failure to answer police questions. The conditions include:

(i)   the alleged failure to mention a relevant fact must take place before the person has been charged;

(ii)   the alleged failure must occur during questioning under caution;

(iii) the questioning must be directed at trying to discover whether and by whom the alleged offence has been committed;

(iv) the alleged failure must be a failure to mention a fact relied on by the defendant in his defence;

(v)   the fact must be one which this particular defendant (not some hypothetical reasonable accused) could reasonably be expected to have mentioned when being questioned, taking account of all the circumstances existing at that time (for example, the time of day, the defendant's age, experience, mental capacity, state of health, sobriety, personality and access to legal advice).

In *R v Roble* [1997] Crim LR 346 and *R v Daniel* [1998] 2 Cr App R 373, it was said that legal advice to remain silent at a police interview is unlikely of itself to be an adequate explanation for refusal to answer questions. So, the fact that a defendant was following his solicitor's advice not to answer police questions does not prevent the judge from directing the jury that they could draw an adverse inference from the defendant's failure to answer questions.

An important issue here is whether the defendant waives legal professional privilege by saying that his solicitor has advised him not to answer questions. In *R v Condron* [1997] 1 WLR 827, the Court of Appeal held that where legal advice is given as the reason for not answering police questions, this will not amount to waiver of privilege. However, where the defendant goes a step further and asks for adverse inferences not to be drawn because his silence was based on legal advice, this might amount to a waiver of privilege. Much more detailed guidance on this point was given by the Court of Appeal in *R v Bowden* [1999] 1 WLR 823; [1999] 4 All ER 43. In that case, it was held that, where a defendant says (at his interview in the police station or at trial) that he refused to answer police questions because he was advised to remain silent by his solicitor, he does not thereby waive legal professional privilege. However, if the defendant or his solicitor (at the time of the interview or at trial) explains the basis for that advice, the defendant has waived privilege and it is open to the prosecution to cross-examine the defendant about the information he gave to his solicitor (that is, he can be cross-examined on the nature of that advice and the factual premises on which it had been based). Article 6 of the European Convention on Human Rights requires that the confidentiality of communications between accused and his solicitor must be respected (*S v Switzerland* 14 EHRR 670); the decision in *R v Bowden* may well be inconsistent with this principle.

Another issue is what it means for a defendant to 'rely' on a fact at trial. In *R v Bowers* (1999) 163 JP 33, the Court of Appeal confirmed that adverse inferences can be drawn under s 34 even if the defendant does not give evidence at trial. The court said that, for s 34 to operate, the defendant must rely on a particular fact at trial, and he must have failed to mention that fact when questioned by the police. However, the defendant may rely on a fact even if he does not himself give evidence of that fact: for example, a witness called on his behalf may testify to that fact, or a prosecution witness may be cross-examined on that basis of that fact.

In *R v McGarry* [1998] 3 All ER 805, the prosecution had accepted that the defendant had not relied on anything in his defence that he had not mentioned when interviewed, and so no inferences could be drawn from his failure to answer questions in those interviews. It was held that the trial judge should have given the jury a specific direction that no adverse inference should be drawn from the defendant's silence; otherwise, the jury might have been left in doubt as to whether or not it was proper to hold the defendant's silence against him.

The right to a fair trial guaranteed by Art 6 of the European Convention on Human Rights includes 'the right of anyone charged with a criminal offence to remain silent and not to contribute to incriminating himself' (*Funke v France* 16 EHRR 297)

Drawing adverse inferences from the suspect's silence was considered by the European Court of Human Rights in the context of Northern Ireland legislation in *Murray v UK* (1996) 22 EHRR 29. The legislation was held to comply with the Convention but the Court was influenced by the fact that, under the legislation in question, inferences were drawn by a judge who gave a reasoned judgment. In England and Wales, adverse inferences are drawn by the jury, who do not give reasons for their verdict.

The case of *Condron* went to the European Court of Human Rights (*Condron v UK* (2000) *The Times*, May 9). On the basis that the defendant had testified at trial and had offered an explanation for remaining silent during the police interview, the European Court held that the jury should have been directed that if it was satisfied that the defendant's silence at the police interview could not sensibly be attributed to his having no answer, or none that would stand up to cross-examination, it should not draw an adverse inference.

(d) Alibi evidence

Where the defendant puts forward an alibi, the judge must direct the jury that the burden of proof rests on the prosecution to disprove it (not on the defendant to prove it). Where the defendant relies on an alibi at trial but either failed to give particulars of that alibi to the prosecution or gave particulars which are inconsistent with the story told in court, the judge may direct the jury that they are entitled to draw adverse inferences against the defendant (see s 11(3) of the Criminal Procedure and Investigations Act 1996). A conviction cannot, however, be based solely on such an adverse inference (s 11(5)). Where the evidence in court is different from the particulars of alibi given to the prosecution, regard must be had to the degree of divergence in the stories and to any justification which the defence put forward for the divergence (s 11(4)). See Chapter 1, 1.19.9.

Where the defendant has relied on an alibi and the prosecution have sought to prove that the alibi was false, the judge should direct the jury to the effect that 'even if you conclude that the alibi was false, that does not entitle you to convict the defendant. The Crown must still make you sure of his guilt. An alibi is sometimes invented to bolster a genuine defence'. A failure to give such a direction does not automatically render a conviction unsafe. The Court of Appeal will consider whether the jury might have come to a different conclusion had the direction been given (*R v Harron* [1996] Crim LR 581; *R v Lesley* [1996] 1 Cr App R 39).

(e) Lies by defendant

Where there evidence before the jury that the defendant has lied about something, and there is a risk of the jury thinking that, because the defendant has lied, he must therefore be guilty of the offence with which he is charged, they should be directed that proof of lying is not proof of guilt (in that an innocent defendant might lie): *R v Lucas* [1981] 1 QB 720.

(f) Defendant's previous convictions

If the prosecution have been given leave to cross-examine the defendant on his previous convictions (s 1(f) of the Criminal Evidence Act 1898), the jury must be warned that these previous convictions are relevant only to the defendant's credibility as a witness and are not evidence of his guilt (*R v Vickers* [1972] Crim LR 101 and *R v France* [1978] Crim LR 48). In *R v McLeod* [1994] 1 WLR 1500; [1994] 3 All ER 254, the Court of Appeal reiterated that where a defendant is cross-examined on his previous convictions, it must be made clear that the previous convictions are relevant only to his credibility as a witness and not to show a propensity to commit offences of the type of which he is now accused.

(g) Defendant's good character

Where the defendant has no previous convictions, the jury should be directed that this is relevant both to his credibility as a witness and to the likelihood of his having committed the offence. If the defendant does not testify, then his previous good character goes to the credibility of any denial that he made to the police when interviewed as well as being relevant to the likelihood of his having committed the offence alleged (*R v Vye* [1993] 1 WLR 471; [1993] 3 All ER 241 and *R v Teasdale* [1993] 4 All ER 290). These principles were confirmed by the House of Lords in *R v Aziz* [1996] 1 AC 41; [1995] 3 All ER 149. In *Barrow v The Queen* [1998] AC 846, the Privy Council considered *R v Aziz* and held that the judge ought only to direct the jury on the relevance of the good character of the accused if the matter is raised by the defence (calling evidence or questioning prosecution witnesses with a view to establishing the defendant's good character).

Where a defendant has previously been cautioned by the police, it is proper for the trial judge to direct the jury as to relevance of the defendant's lack of previous convictions in relation to his credibility as a witness but not to give the second limb of the *Vye* direction in relation to the defendant's lack of propensity to commit the offence charged (*R v Martin* (2000) 164 JP 174).

(h) Corroboration

Where an accomplice testifies as a prosecution witness against a defendant, there is no duty to warn the jury about the dangers of convicting on the basis of that evidence (s 32 of the Criminal Justice and Public Order Act 1994 removed the mandatory corroboration warning). However, the trial judge nevertheless has a discretion to give such a warning: *R v Makanjuola; R v Easton* [1995] 1 WLR 1348; [1995] 3 All ER 730). The Court of Appeal will only rarely interfere with the exercise of this discretion. Under the European Convention on Human Rights, admitting evidence of an accomplice may not violate Art 6 provided that jury are made fully aware of the circumstances. It is open to question whether the removal of the mandatory corroboration warning by s 32 of the 1994 Act accords with this principle.

(i) Expert evidence

In a case involving expert evidence, it is important for the judge to direct the jury that they are not bound by the opinion of an expert witness: *R v Fitzpatrick* [1999] Crim LR 832; *R v Stockwell* (1993) 97 Cr App R 260.

(j) Separation of jury

In *R v Oliver* (1995) 2 Cr App R 514, the Court of Appeal gave guidance on the directions which should be given to a jury which was allowed to separate before delivering its verdict. The jury must be warned that;

  (a) they may only decide the case on the basis of the evidence and arguments they have seen and heard in court;

  (b) they must not seek further information about the case (for example, by going and having a look at the scene of the crime);

  (c) they must not talk to anyone about the case except other jurors and even discussions with other jurors may only take place while they are deliberating together in the retiring room.

9.18.5 Alternative counts

If the indictment contains alternative counts where one is more serious than the other (for example, ss 18 and 20 of the Offences Against the Person Act 1861), the judge will tell the jury to consider the more serious count first. If they convict on that count, they should not consider the other count; if they acquit on the more serious count, they should go on to consider the less serious charge.

If the alternative counts are of more or less equal gravity (for example, theft and handling), the jury will simply be told to consider both but to acquit on both or convict on only one.

9.18.6 Unanimous verdict

The jury must be directed to return a unanimous verdict; a majority verdict (see 9.22 below) is only possible after an appropriate direction given later. The judge will normally say something like this to the jury: 'You may well have heard of the majority verdicts. Well, until I give you a direction to the contrary I can only accept a verdict upon which you are all agreed. If a time comes when I can accept a verdict which is not the verdict of all of you, I will give you further directions. Until that time, you should put thoughts of majority verdicts from your minds and try to reach a verdict upon which you are all agreed.'

In *R v Guthrie* (1994) *The Times*, 23 February, the judge was asked by the jury, after it had been deliberating for a little over an hour, how long it would be before the judge could accept a majority verdict. The Court of Appeal said that the judge acted correctly in telling them how long in response to their direct question. However, it is only where there is such a direct question that the jury should be given this information before the judge actually gives a majority verdict direction.

The jury will also be advised to elect a foreman to chair their discussions and announce their verdict.

9.18.7 Summing up fairly

The judge must take care to sum up fairly. He must for example ensure that the defence case is put fully and fairly (*R v Gaughan* [1990] Crim LR 880). The judge should deal with the case impartially. Sarcastic and extravagant language disparaging the defence must be avoided. In the event of an appeal against conviction, the Court of Appeal will look at 'the impact of the summing up as a whole' when considering its fairness (*R v Berrada* (1990) 91 Cr App R 131).

In *R v Spencer* [1995] Crim LR 235, the defendant's conviction was held to be unsafe as a result of excessive and largely one sided comment made by the judge when directing the jury. It was said by Henry LJ that some comment is permissible, but not to the extent that the rehearsal of the evidence is interrupted and the jury's task made more difficult.

In *R v Reid* (1999) *The Times*, 17 August, the Court of Appeal made the point that, where the case against the defendant is strong, and his defence correspondingly weak, the judge has to be scrupulous to ensure that the defendant's defence is presented to the jury in an even-handed and impartial manner.

In *R v Farr* (1999) 163 JP 193, the Court of Appeal said that a judge summing up a case is under no obligation to recite all the evidence or arguments (see *McGreevy v DPP* [1973] 1 WLR 276 and *R v Wilson* [1991] Crim LR 838). In general, the longer the trial, the greater would be the jury's need for the judge's help with the evidence. Where a trial lasts for a few days or more, it would usually assist the jury if the judge were to summarise undisputed factual issues and identify any evidence in dispute, thereby focusing the jury's attention on the issues to be resolved. However, the Court of Appeal will not look favourably on appeals based simply on a judge's failure to refer to particular arguments or specific pieces of evidence. However, the summing up in the present case was defective, in that it failed to refer to a number of the key features of the defence case, and (instead of being fair and balanced) resembled a speech for the prosecution. The convictions were quashed and a retrial ordered.

It should be noted that it is generally inappropriate for the judge to comment on the failure of the defence to call a particular witness, as such comment can easily detract from what is said about the burden of proof (see *R v Wheeler* [1967] 1 WLR 1531, 1535; *R v Wright* [2000] Crim LR 510).

9.19   RETIREMENT OF JURY

After the summing up, the jury are delivered into the custody of the jury bailiff who takes an oath to take them to a private place to consider their verdict and to prevent anyone from communicating with them. The jury then go to the jury room to consider their verdict.

In a serious case (especially where there are several counts and/or several defendants), the judge should not send the jury out after 3 pm save in exceptional cases. It would be better for them to start their deliberations the following day (*R v Birch* (1992) *The Times*, 27 March).

9.19.1   Separation of the jury

During lunch time and overnight adjournments during the trial, the jury are allowed to go their separate ways. Formerly, the jury were only allowed to separate before the judge had finished the summing up. Section 13 of the Juries Act 1974 now enables the court to allow the jury to separate after (as well as before) they have been sent out to consider their verdict.

Before being allowed to separate, the jurors should be warned not to discuss the case with anyone who is not on the jury (*R v Prime* (1973) 57 Cr App R 632).

The jury should also be told not to continue their deliberations except when they are together in the jury room, otherwise there is a risk that discussions might take place without all jurors being present (*R v Tharakan* [1995] 2 Cr App R 368).

9.19.2   No further evidence

Once the jury has retired, no further evidence can be called (*R v Owen* [1952] 2 QB 362; [1952] 1 All ER 1040). In that case, the jury came out of retirement to ask whether the premises where an indecent assault was alleged to have taken place would have been occupied or not at the relevant time. The Court of Appeal held that no further evidence can be called after the jury has retired to consider its verdict.

The jury is, however, entitled to have with them in the jury room evidence which has been exhibited during the trial (*R v Wright* [1993] Crim LR 607). In *R v Tonge* [1993] Crim LR 876, following *R v Emmerson* (1991) 92 Cr App R 284 and *R v Aitken* (1992) 94 Cr App R 85, the Court of Appeal considered what should be done if the jury (after they have retired) ask to hear the tape-recording of the defendant's interview at the police station. It was said that, if the tape recording had not been played in open court during the trial and the jury ask to hear the tape, it should usually be played in open court. However, if the tape has already been played in court, the jury may be allowed to hear it again in the jury room.

9.19.3   Questions from the jury after retirement

If the jury wish to communicate with the judge (for example, they need further directions on the law or to be reminded of some of the evidence), they do so by means of a note sent via the jury bailiff. If the judge receives such a note, he should show it to both counsel in open court and should invite submissions from them before sending for the jury (*R v Gorman* [1987] 1 WLR 545; [1987] 2 All ER 435 and *R v Sipson Coachworks Ltd* [1992] Crim LR 666).

In *Ramstead v The Queen* [1999] AC 92, the Privy Council said that any communication between the judge and jury has to take place in open court in the presence of the entire jury, both counsel and the defendant (see, also, *R v McCluskey* (1993) 98 Cr App R 216). The Privy Council reiterated that where the judge receives a note from the jury he should follow the procedure laid down in *R v Gorman*.

In *R v McQuiston* [1998] 1 Cr App R 139, it was held that, where the judge reads substantial parts of the complainant's evidence to the jury after the jury have retired to consider their verdict (as may be the case if the jury ask for their memory of certain evidence to be refreshed), the judge must warn the jury not to give disproportionate weight to that evidence simply because it was repeated well after the other evidence had been heard; the judge must also remind the jury of the cross-examination of the complainant and of any relevant part of D's evidence.

9.20   RETURNING A VERDICT

When the jury come back into court, the clerk asks them 'Have you reached a verdict upon which you are all agreed?'. If the answer is 'yes', the foreman will be asked to announce the verdict on each count of the indictment.

If the answer is 'yes', and the defendant is acquitted on all counts, he is told that he is free to go.

Where the defendant is charged with a number of offences and the jury indicate that they have agreed on verdicts on some, but not all, of the offences, it is good practice to take the verdicts on those counts upon which the jury are agreed before they carry on considering the other counts (*R v F* [1994] Crim LR 377).

9.20.1   Guilty verdict

If the answer is 'yes', and the defendant is convicted on some or all of the counts, the prosecution will tell the judge if the defendant has any previous convictions and will say what else is known about him (education, family situation, employment, etc). The judge may hear a plea in mitigation or the case may be adjourned for a pre-sentence report. If there is an adjournment, the plea in mitigation will be delivered when the report has been prepared. The usual period of an adjournment for a report is three weeks if the defendant is remanded in custody, four weeks if he is on bail. Where the case is adjourned for a pre-sentence report to be prepared, the prosecution may ask to be excused from attending court on the next occasion since the judge will be aware of the facts of the case (and so there will be no need for the prosecution to summarise those facts) and the prosecution have no other part to play in the sentencing process.

9.20.2   Alternative counts

If the indictment contains counts which are in the alternative (see Chapter 8, 8.12.1), the usual practice is for the clerk to ask for a verdict on the more serious allegation first. If the verdict on that count is 'not guilty', the clerk will go on to ask for the verdict on the other count. If, on the other hand, the verdict on the more serious count is 'guilty', the jury should be discharged from giving a verdict on the less serious charge (*R v Harris* [1969] 1 WLR 745; [1969] 2 All ER 599).

This should not be confused with the power of the jury to return an alternative verdict, acquitting the defendant of the count on the indictment but convicting him of an offence which is not on the indictment, a power dealt with later in 9.24 below.

9.21   JURY UNABLE TO REACH A VERDICT

The answer to the question 'Have you reached a verdict upon which you are all agreed?' will be 'no' if the jury have asked the judge for further assistance or if they have been out for some time and cannot reach a verdict. In the latter case, a majority verdict direction may be appropriate.

9.22   MAJORITY VERDICTS

There is no minimum length of deliberation which is required before a unanimous verdict can be delivered. However, s 17 of the Juries Act 1974 provides that, after two hours, or such longer period as the judge considers necessary having regard to the nature and complexity of the case, a majority verdict may be accepted.

A Practice Direction (1970) says that a further 10 minutes should be allowed, to allow the jury to settle down in the jury room and elect a foreman.

If a majority verdict were to be accepted before two hours have elapsed from the time the jury left the court room to begin its deliberations, that verdict would be a nullity.

The only permissible majorities are:

- for 12 jurors: 11–1 or 10–2;
- where one juror has been discharged, leaving 11 jurors: 10–1;
- where two jurors have been discharged, leaving 10: 9–1.

As we have already seen, if more than three jurors have to be discharged, the trial has to be aborted and a retrial takes place later.

If the judge considers that the jury have had long enough to come to a verdict (subject to the two hour minimum set out in s 17), the judge can send for the jury and give a majority verdict direction. Sometimes, the jury will take the initiative and send a note to the judge saying that they are deadlocked; if at least two hours have elapsed, the judge may if he thinks it appropriate give a majority verdict direction.

9.22.1   Content of majority verdict direction

A majority verdict direction will be along these lines:

> Members of the jury, it is desirable for you to reach a verdict upon which you are all agreed if that is possible. However, the time has now come when I can accept a verdict which is the verdict of at least 10 of you. Please go back into the jury room and try once again to reach a unanimous verdict or, if you are unable to do that, a verdict upon which at least 10 of you are agreed.

9.22.2   Procedure after direction given

When the jury return to the court room after a majority verdict direction has been given, the clerk asks the foreman, 'Have you reached a verdict on which at least 10 of you are agreed?'.

If the answer is 'yes', the clerk asks the foreman whether the verdict is guilty or not guilty. If it is not guilty, no further question will be asked of the jury; if it is guilty the clerk will ask how many jurors find the defendant guilty (s 17(3) of the Juries Act). If the size of the majority in favour of conviction is not stated, the verdict is a nullity (*R v Barry* [1975] 1 WLR 1190; [1975] 2 All ER 760 and *R v Pigg* [1983] 1 WLR 6; [1983] 1 All ER 56). However, if the error is realised after the jury has been discharged, it is possible to reconvene the jury for this purpose (*R v Maloney* (1996) 2 Cr App R 303).

Thus, it will not be known whether an acquittal is unanimous or by majority. However, in the case of a conviction it is important to know whether it was unanimous or by majority, and if the latter the size of the majority, to ensure that the majority was a lawful one.

If the answer to the clerk's first question is 'no', the foreman will be asked by the judge if there is any prospect of the jury reaching a verdict. If there is a possibility, the judge will almost certainly give the jury more time. If there is no such possibility, the jury will be discharged and a fresh trial will probably take place later.

9.23   THE *WATSON* DIRECTION

The judge must not exert undue pressure on the jury to reach a verdict. In *R v McKenna* [1960] 1 QB 411; [1960] 1 All ER 326, for example, the judge told the jury that they would be 'kept all night' if they could not reach a verdict; it was felt that this could have been interpreted by some of them that they would have to stay in the jury room and the resulting conviction was quashed.

However, the judge can inquire if there is a reasonable prospect of a verdict being reached; the judge may tell the jury that if there is no reasonable prospect of them reaching a verdict they will be discharged and if there is then they can have as much time as they need (*R v Modeste* [1983] Crim LR 746).

In *R v Watson* [1988] QB 690; [1988] 1 All ER 897, the Court of Appeal said that a judge must not point out to the jury that if they do not reach a verdict there will have to be a retrial which will cause inconvenience and expense. However, the jury could be directed in the following terms:

Each of you has taken an oath to return a true verdict according to the evidence. No one must be false to that oath, but you have a duty not only as individuals but collectively ... Each of you takes into the jury box with you your individual experience and wisdom. Your task is to pool that experience and wisdom. You do that by giving your views and listening to the views of others. There must necessarily be discussion, argument and give and take within the scope of your oath. That is the way in which agreement is reached. If, unhappily, 10 of you cannot reach agreement you must say so.

In *R v Buono* (1992) 95 Cr App R 338, the Court of Appeal said that a *Watson* direction should not be given at the same time as a majority verdict direction. Thus, the judge should give the majority verdict direction and then wait to see if the jury can reach a majority verdict; if the jury is still unable to reach a verdict, a *Watson* direction may then be given.

In *Buono*, and again in *R v Morgan* (1997) *The Times*, 18 April, the Court of Appeal said that where it is necessary to direct a jury on the need to reach a verdict, the judge should follow the precise terms laid down in *R v Watson* [1988] 1 QB 690; [1988] 1 All ER 897, because a conviction will be rendered unsafe if the judge says anything which might be construed as putting improper pressure on the jury.

No other pressure must be brought to bear on the jury. In *R v Duggan and Others* [1992] Crim LR 513, for example, the jury informed the judge that they would rather deliberate into the night than have to return the following day. The trial judge indicated that they might have to go into an hotel if they could not reach a verdict by 5 pm. A verdict of guilty was returned at 4.55 pm. As some jurors had already indicated that they did not wish to spend the night in an hotel, the judge's words were held to amount to undue pressure and the convictions were quashed.

9.24 THE VERDICT OF GUILTY TO AN ALTERNATIVE OFFENCE

Under s 6(3) of the Criminal Law Act 1967, where the allegations in the indictment amount to or include (whether expressly or by implication) an allegation of another offence which may be tried on indictment, the jury may acquit on the offence charged and convict on the included offence.

9.24.1 Express inclusion

An offence is expressly included in the indictment if words can be deleted from the existing count so as to leave words alleging another offence. This is sometimes called the 'blue pencil' test (*R v Lillis* [1972] 2 QB 236; [1972] 2 All ER 1209).

Suppose that it is alleged that the defendant 'entered 4 Gray's Inn Place as a trespasser and stole therein a typewriter'. If the words 'entered 4 Gray's Inn Place as a trespasser and' and 'therein' are deleted, that leaves an allegation that the defendant 'stole a typewriter'. Therefore, theft (s 1 of the Theft Act 1968) is expressly included in an allegation of burglary (s 9(1)(b) of the Theft Act 1968).

Thus, if a jury decides that they are not sure that the defendant entered as a trespasser but are sure that he stole the goods alleged in the indictment, they can acquit of burglary but convict of theft.

9.24.2   Implied inclusion

The meaning of implied inclusion was considered by the House of Lords in *Metropolitan Police Commissioner v Wilson* [1984] AC 242; [1983] 3 All ER 448. Where the commission of the offence alleged in the indictment will, in the normal course of events (that is, in the great majority of cases) involve the commission of another offence, that other offence is impliedly included in the offence charged in the indictment.

In *Wilson*, for example, it was held that inflicting grievous bodily harm (s 20 of the Offences Against the Person Act 1861) usually involves assault occasioning actually bodily harm (s 47 of the Offences Against the Person Act 1861), and so the jury can acquit of grievous bodily harm but convict of actual bodily harm. It may well be possible to inflict grievous bodily harm without assaulting the victim (for example, by deliberately creating a panic in a crowded building intending that people are hurt in the rush to escape), but, in the normal course of events, grievous bodily harm will involve assault occasioning actual bodily harm.

The same would apply to an allegation of wounding under s 20 of the Offences Against the Person Act 1861, so s 47 is an alternative offence to that charge too (*R v Savage* [1992] 1 AC 699; [1991] 4 All ER 698).

A charge of causing grievous bodily harm with intent (s 18 of the Offences Against the Person Act 1861) includes a charge of inflicting grievous bodily harm (s 20 of the Offences Against the Person Act 1861) (*R v Mandair* [1994] 2 WLR 700; [1994] 2 All ER 715).

Likewise, indecent assault is an alternative to rape (*R v Hodgson* [1973] QB 565; [1973] 2 All ER 552) and theft is an alternative to robbery.

9.24.3   Other statutory provisions

There are also statutory provisions which set out alternative offences:

* Section 6(2) of the Criminal Law Act 1967

  The jury may acquit of murder but convict of (*inter alia*) manslaughter or causing grievous bodily harm with intent.

* Section 6(4) of the Criminal Law Act 1967

  The jury may acquit of the offence charged but convict of attempt to commit that offence or attempt to commit an offence which is expressly or implied included in the offence charged. Thus, if the indictment alleges robbery, the jury could acquit of robbery but convict of attempted robbery or attempted theft.

* Section 12(4) of the Theft Act 1968

  On a count of theft, the jury could acquit of theft but convict the defendant of taking a conveyance without the owner's consent (even though the latter is a summary offence).

- Section 24 of the Road Traffic Offenders Act 1988

  On a count alleging dangerous driving or causing death by dangerous driving, the jury may convict the defendant instead of careless driving (again, even though the latter is a summary offence).

9.24.4 Summary offences

Section 6(3) of the Criminal Law Act 1967 makes it clear that the included offence must be one which can be tried in the Crown Court. Hence the need for s 12(4) of the Theft Act 1968 and s 24 of the Road Traffic Offenders Act 1988. The two included offences are both summary offences, and but for statutory provision to the contrary, the jury would not be able to convict of those summary offences.

So, in *R v Mearns* [1991] 1 QB 82; [1990] 3 All ER 989, followed in *Bird v DPP* [1992] COD 351, it was held that the jury cannot convict a defendant of common assault as that is a summary offence. Note that common assault is one of the four offences to which s 40 of the Criminal Justice Act 1988 applies, and so if the jury indicated that they could not convict of, say, assault occasioning actual bodily harm (because they are not satisfied that injury occurred) but nonetheless find that an assault (which includes the threat of violence) took place, a count alleging common assault could be added to the indictment. Only then could the jury convict of common assault.

The position as regards criminal damage is a little more complicated. As we saw in Chapter 3, 3.11, where the value involved in a criminal damage charge is less than £5,000, a magistrates' court has to treat the offence as if it were a summary offence. In *R v Fennell* (2000) 97(22) LSG 43, the defendant was charged with racially aggravated criminal damage (contrary to s 30 of the Crime and Disorder Act 1998). The judge allowed the jury to acquit him of that offence but convict him instead (under s 6 of the Criminal Law Act 1967) of ordinary criminal damage. The value involved was less than £5,000. The court held that it is open to a judge to leave an alternative verdict of criminal damage for the jury's consideration even if the value involved is less than £5,000 and without invoking s 40 of the Criminal Justice Act 1980 to add that offence of criminal damage to the indictment. The court held that *R v Burt* (1996) 161 JP 77, where the contrary view was expressed, was wrongly decided.

9.24.5 Scope of s 6(3) of the Criminal Law Act 1967

Convicting of an alternative offence is only possible if the jury first agree to acquit on the offence on the indictment. If the jury cannot agree on an acquittal of the offence charged, the only way they can convict of another offence is if that offence is added to the indictment as a new count. See, for example, *R v Collison* (1980) 71 Cr App R 249, where a count was added to the indictment after the jury had been considering their verdict for some while for this very reason.

9.24.6 Directing the jury on alternative offences

The jury will only know about the possibility of convicting of an offence other than the offence on the indictment if they are told about this power. So, when should the judge direct the jury about the possibility of convicting on an alternative offence?

In *R v Fairbanks* [1986] 1 WLR 1202, it was said that the judge should direct the jury that it is possible for them to acquit of the offence charged but convict of an alternative offence if:

- the possibility that the defendant is guilty only of a lesser offence has fairly arisen on the evidence; and

- directing the jury about the possibility of convicting the defendant of an alternative offence will not unnecessarily complicate the case.

In *R v Wilson* [1984] Crim LR 173, CA, it was held that there must be no risk of injustice to the defendant; he must have had the opportunity of fully meeting the alternative in the course of his defence. In other words, if the possibility of an alternative offence is only canvassed at the end of the trial, would the defence have cross-examined prosecution witnesses differently or adduced different defence evidence had the alternative offence been mentioned at the start of the trial?

In *R v Hammett* [1993] RTR 275, for example, the possibility of convicting of an alternative offence was first mentioned in the judge's summing up. Even though the judge then gave counsel the opportunity of addressing the jury further, it was held by the Court of Appeal to be unfair to raise the issue of an alternative offence so late in the proceedings. See, also, *R v Salter* [1993] Crim LR 891 .

The question was looked at again by the House of Lords in *R v Maxwell* [1990] 1 WLR 401; [1990] 1 All ER 801. The defendant was charged with robbery. He indicated that he would have been willing to plead guilty to burglary. However, the prosecution did not wish to add a count alleging burglary to the indictment. Burglary is not an alternative to robbery, but theft (a constituent of one type of burglary) is an alternative to robbery (which comprises theft together with the use or threat of violence). The judge refused to allow the jury to consider convicting of theft instead of robbery. This refusal was upheld by the House of Lords. The essential issue, as defined by the prosecution, was whether the defendant had used violence; theft was trivial by comparison and would merely have distracted the jury from the main issue of the case.

The implication of *Maxwell* is that it is for the prosecution to define the main issue(s) in the case and the judge should not subvert their decision by directing the jury to consider an alternative offence. Note that, even if defence counsel takes the initiative and tells the jury that they can convict of an alternative offence, the judge could direct the jury that they are not to consider this possibility.

The arguments in favour of letting the jury consider an alternative and lesser offence were considered in *Fairbanks*. From the prosecution point of view, where the evidence is such that it is clear that the defendant ought to be convicted of the lesser offence, it would be wrong for the jury to have to acquit him altogether merely because they cannot be sure that he is guilty of the more serious offence. From the defence point of view, if the judge does not allow the jury to consider the lesser offence, it is possible that the jury will convict the defendant of the more serious offence not because they are sure that he is guilty of it but so as to convict him of something rather than allow him to escape without any penalty at all.

It would of course be inappropriate for the judge to leave a lesser offence to jury if it is inappropriate given the way the defence has been conducted (for example, where the defence is one of alibi).

Where a judge refuses to leave an alternative offence to the jury, the Court of Appeal will only quash a conviction for the offence charged on the indictment if satisfied that the jury convicted the defendant only because it was reluctant to allow him to get away completely with his misconduct (*R v O'Hadhmaill* [1996] Crim LR 509).

This approach was followed in *R v Bergman and Collins* [1996] 2 Cr App R 399, where the trial judge should have directed the jury about the possibility of convicting the defendants of a lesser offence but the convictions for the offence charged on the indictment were upheld since there was no evidence which tended to show that the jury's verdict would have been different if they had been directed on the possibility of convicting of a lesser offence.

In *R v Mandair* [1994] 2 WLR 700; [1994] 2 All ER 715, Lord Mackay LC said that the simpler (and better) course of action is to add a count to the indictment alleging the lesser offence.

9.24.7 Summary

For the judge to leave the alternative offence to the jury:

- it must be appropriate (for example, it would not be appropriate where the defence is one of alibi since it would distract the jury from the main issue in the case, namely the whereabouts of the defendant at the time of the alleged offence);

- it must have been at least implicit in the defence questioning of prosecution witnesses and the defence evidence (otherwise, it will be unfair to the defence);
- if the alternative is trivial in comparison with the offence charged, it must not be an unnecessary and undesirable complication.

9.25   DISCHARGE OF JURY

If the jury cannot reach a verdict within what the judge regards as a reasonable time, the jury will be discharged. This does not count as an acquittal and so the accused can be re-tried. There is no need for fresh committal proceedings. If the second jury is 'hung' (unable to reach a verdict) too, the prosecution are unlikely to insist on a third trial.

9.26   GUILTY PLEAS

If the defendant pleads guilty to all the counts on the indictment (or pleads guilty to some of the counts and the prosecution do not proceed with the others), no trial takes place.

9.26.1   Procedure where the defendant pleads guilty

The defendant is asked to enter a plea to each of the counts on the indictment, so the counts are put to him by the clerk one by one.

A plea of guilty must be entered by the defendant personally (and not by his legal representative) (*R v Ellis* (1973) 57 Cr App R 571; *R v Williams* [1978] QB 373; [1977] 1 All ER 847).

If the defendant pleads guilty to all the counts, the prosecution summarise the facts of the case. Details of the defendant's previous convictions (if any) are handed to the judge and he will indicate which (if any) he wishes prosecuting counsel to read aloud. Usually, it is only the most recent previous convictions that are read out. The prosecution will also tell the judge what is known about the defendant's personal circumstances (employment, housing, etc); this is based on what the defendant has told the police and will be very brief.

The defence then make a plea in mitigation. If a pre-sentence report is not available, the judge may adjourn the case until one is prepared. In that case there is a presumption in favour of bail as s 4 of the Bail Act 1976 still applies (see Chapter 2). When the case is resumed, the prosecution will again summarise the facts and the defence will make a plea in mitigation. The usual period for the adjournment is three weeks if the defendant is in custody, four weeks if he is on bail.

9.27   THE *NEWTON* HEARING

If the defence challenge the version of events put forward by the prosecution, and the difference is one which will affect the sentence that is passed, the court can only reject the defence version of events after hearing evidence as to what happened. Such a hearing is known as *Newton* hearing (from *R v Newton* (1982) 77 Cr App R 13) and is described more fully later, in Chapter 12, 12.1.1.

9.28   MIXED PLEAS

If the defendant pleads guilty to some counts but not guilty to others, sentence will be postponed until the trial on the counts to which the defendant has pleaded not guilty has been completed, assuming that the prosecution wish to proceed with the trial of the offences to which the defendant pleaded not guilty.

This raises the question of plea bargaining between the prosecution and the defence.

9.29   PLEA BARGAINING

The usual basis of a plea bargain is either:

* that if the defendant will plead guilty to some counts on the indictment, the prosecution will not proceed with the remainder; or
* that if the defendant will plead guilty to a lesser offence, the prosecution will not proceed with the more serious offence.

This form of plea bargaining is widely accepted as a way of saving time and money. From the prosecution point of view, it may well be better to have a conviction for something rather than risk a jury acquitting on all counts.

9.30   PLEADING GUILTY TO A LESSER OFFENCE

Pleading guilty to a lesser offence is possible in the following two circumstances.

9.30.1   Pleading guilty to an offence which is not on the indictment

Under s 6(1)(b) of the Criminal Law Act 1967, the defendant may plead not guilty to the count on the indictment but guilty to a lesser offence of which the jury would be able to convict him under s 6(3) of the Criminal Law Act 1967 (see 9.24 above). If this plea is accepted, the defendant stands acquitted of the offence charged but convicted of the lesser offence, for which he will then be sentenced.

If the plea of guilty to the lesser offence is not accepted by the prosecution (or the judge refuses to accept it), the trial will proceed on the basis of a not guilty plea to the offence on the indictment. The defendant's plea of guilty to the lesser offence is impliedly withdrawn (so, if the jury acquit the defendant of the offence on the indictment, and do not convict of the lesser offence under s 6(3), the defendant cannot then be sentenced for the lesser offence (*R v Hazeltine* [1967] 2 QB 857; [1967] 2 All ER 671). Note, however, that the prosecution could adduce evidence of the defendant's earlier plea of guilty to the lesser offence if they so wished.

9.30.2 Pleading guilty to an alternative count on the indictment

The indictment may contain alternative counts. The word 'or' does not appear, and so there is nothing on the face of the indictment to indicate that the counts are in the alternative. For example, there might be one count alleging s 18 offences under the Offences Against the Person Act 1861 and another alleging s 20.

If the defendant pleads not guilty to both counts, the trial will proceed on both counts and the prosecution will tell the jury in the opening speech that they do not seek a conviction on both counts.

If the defendant pleads not guilty to the more serious offence but guilty to the lesser offence, it is up to the prosecution whether to proceed with a trial of the count to which the defendant pleads not guilty. If a trial does follow and the defendant is acquitted of the more serious offence, he will then be sentenced for the lesser offence to which he pleaded guilty. If he is convicted of the more serious offence, the lesser offence will be ignored for sentencing purposes.

Normally, the prosecution will indicate to the defence beforehand whether a plea of guilty to the lesser offence will be acceptable. Where the plea to the lesser offence is acceptable, the lesser offence is put to the defendant first and (assuming he pleads guilty to it as anticipated) the second offence will either not be put to the defendant or it will be put and the prosecution will either offer no evidence or ask it to be left on file (see 9.33 below).

The acceptance of a plea of guilty to a lesser offence is subject to the agreement of the judge, but it would be very rare for the judge to insist on a trial of the more serious offence if the prosecution do not wish that to happen.

9.31   ADVISING THE DEFENDANT ON PLEA

Care must be taken that a plea of guilty is entered voluntarily. If it is not entered voluntarily, the Court of Appeal will quash the conviction and will usually order a re-trial.

In the next section, we look at safeguards to prevent pressure from the judge. However, pressure can also be exerted by the defendant's own lawyers. It would be wholly improper to advise a client to plead guilty if the defendant reveals facts amounting to a defence. If, however, the facts revealed by the defendant show that he is effectively admitting the offence then this should be made clear to her.

The decision as to plea must be that of the accused. The Bar's Code of Conduct (Annex H) says that counsel may express advice in strong terms but must make it clear that the defendant has complete freedom of choice.

It should be added that if the defendant confesses to the crime to his barrister, that barrister can only continue to represent him if he pleads guilty.

If the defendant insists on pleading guilty but insists to her barrister that she is in fact innocent, counsel may continue to represent her but cannot say anything in mitigation which is inconsistent with the plea of guilty. This should be made clear to the defendant. The client should be asked to write a signed note on counsel's brief saying that he wishes to plead guilty against the advice of counsel.

9.31.1   Seeing the judge in his chambers

When a solicitor or barrister is advising a defendant as to plea, the client will inevitably want to know the likely sentence in the event of a conviction. Experienced lawyers are usually able to predict sentences with a reasonable degree of accuracy.

Sometimes, however, the question arises whether the judge can give a preliminary indication of the sentence he is minded to impose (based on a view of the offence founded on the witness statements sent from the magistrates' court and a pre-sentence report if one is already available).

The leading case on this topic is *R v Turner* [1970] 2 QB 321; [1970] 2 All ER 281, where the judge told defence counsel that if the defendant pleaded guilty he would not be sent to prison but if he was convicted by the jury a prison sentence was a very real possibility. The Court of Appeal said that a judge must not say (or imply) that the sentence is likely to take one form if the defendant pleads guilty and a different form if the defendant is convicted following a not guilty plea. This could be construed as putting pressure on the defendant to plead guilty. All the judge is allowed to do is to say that, whether the defendant pleads guilty or is found guilty, the sentence will or will not take a particular form.

So, for example, in *R v Ryan* (1977) 67 Cr App R 177, the judge said that, if the defendant pleaded guilty, he would get a non-custodial sentence but, if was found guilty by the jury, he would get a custodial sentence. Not surprisingly, the defendant pleaded guilty. Equally unsurprisingly, the Court of Appeal quashed the conviction and ordered a re-trial.

It should be remembered that if the judge does give an indication of the likely sentence he cannot then change his mind. In *R v Atkinson* [1978] 1 WLR 425; [1978] 2 All ER 460, the judge indicated that he could see no reason why the defendant should go to prison. The defendant was convicted (following trial) and sentenced to six months' imprisonment. The Court of Appeal varied the sentence to enable the defendant's immediate release from custody. Similarly, in *R v Cullen* (1984) 81 Cr App R 17, the judge indicated that, whether the defendant pleaded guilty or was found guilty, he would receive a non-custodial sentence. The judge subsequently imposed a suspended sentence of imprisonment (which is regarded as a custodial sentence); this sentence was quashed by the Court of Appeal. Again, in *R v Johnson and Lorraine* (1990) 12 Cr App R(S) 219, the judge indicated that he would impose either probation or a suspended sentence but when he came to pass sentence, imposed immediate custody. The Court of Appeal said that even though the sentences were proper in themselves, a sense of injustice resulted from the earlier comments of the judge and so those sentences had to be quashed.

In *R v Smith* [1990] 1 WLR 1311; [1990] 1 All ER 434, the Court of Appeal said that a shorthand writer should be present if counsel see the judge in his chambers. This will prevent an 'unseemly dispute' arising later as to exactly what was said.

In *R v Harper-Taylor* [1991] RTR 76, the Court of Appeal emphasised that the judge should only see counsel in private if there is a very good reason; otherwise all proceedings should be conducted in open court.

These principles were re-affirmed in *R v Ryan* (1999) 163 JP 849. Counsel for the defendant went to see the trial judge in chambers to seek an indication as to sentence if the defendant were to change her plea to guilty. The judge gave an indication, and the defendant changed her plea to guilty. The same judge was unavailable when the case was listed for sentencing; the sentencing judge passed a more severe sentence than that indicated by the first judge. The Court of Appeal ruled: (i) approaches to a judge seeking an indication of the length of sentence which might be imposed in the event of a plea of guilty are to be deprecated; (ii) where such an indication is given and conveyed to a defendant, it will normally be binding not only on the judge who gave the indication but also on any other judge before whom a defendant might appear to be sentenced; (iii) where a defendant changes plea in the light of such an indication from the judge but had subsequently receives a more severe sentence than that indicated, the Court of Appeal would often (though not invariably) feel constrained to reduce the sentence to that indicated, even if the indicated sentence was lower than the offence merited in all the circumstances.

In *R v Dossetter* [1999] 2 Cr App R(S) 248, the Court of Appeal reiterated (i) that the judge cannot give an indication of sentence which implies a different form of sentence if the defendant is found guilty rather than pleading guilty and (ii) that there should be no visits to the judge save in exceptional circumstances, and that (iii) there should be a record of what was said in such visits.

9.32 CHANGE OF PLEA

The defendant may change his plea from not guilty to guilty at any stage before the verdict is given. Counsel for the defendant simply asks for the indictment to be put again, the defendant pleads guilty and the jury return a formal verdict of guilty on the judge's direction (*R v Heyes* [1951] 1 KB 29; [1950] 2 All ER 587).

The judge has a discretion to allow the defendant to change his plea of guilty to one of not guilty at any stage before sentence has been passed (*R v Dodd* (1981) 74 Cr App R 50). The defendant will obviously have to give a reason for his change of mind. Permission to withdraw the guilty plea is unlikely to be given unless the defendant did not realise that he had a defence when he pleaded guilty (*R v McNally* [1954] 1 WLR 933; [1954] 2 All ER 372).

9.33 ALTERNATIVES TO TRIAL: OFFERING NO EVIDENCE; LEAVING COUNTS ON THE FILE

We have already seen that there may be circumstances where the prosecution do not wish to proceed with the trial. It is too late to serve a notice of discontinuance under s 23 of the Prosecution of Offences Act 1985 (see Chapter 1, 1.14.1) but there are two other ways of achieving the same objective.

9.33.1 Offering no evidence

Section 17 of the Criminal Justice Act 1967 allows the prosecution to offer no evidence in respect of one or more counts on an indictment. This may be appropriate where a key prosecution witness refuses to testify or where evidence exonerating the defendant comes to light or where the defendant pleads guilty to one offence and the prosecution do not wish to proceed with another.

Section 17 says that the court may enter a finding of not guilty where the prosecution offer no evidence. The use of the word 'may' shows that the court can refuse and can empanel a jury. In practice, however, the judge would not force the prosecution to present its case.

Indeed, in *R v Grafton* [1992] QB 101; [1992] 4 All ER 609, the Court of Appeal said that, before the completion of the prosecution case, the decision whether or not to continue had to be that of the prosecution and that a trial judge therefore had no power to refuse to permit discontinuance of the prosecution. It is suggested that the same principles must necessarily apply where the prosecution do not even wish to open their case.

9.33.2 Leaving counts on the file

The prosecution may ask for one or more counts to be 'left on the file marked not to be proceeded with without leave of the Crown Court or the Court of Appeal'. This may be appropriate where the defendant pleads guilty to some counts but not guilty to others as leaving a count on the file does not amount to an acquittal. Thus, if for some reason the conviction is overturned on appeal, the prosecution can proceed with the other counts if the Crown Court or Court of Appeal gives permission. This could happen if the trial judge gives a preliminary ruling on the law adverse to the accused, so the accused then pleads guilty and challenges the judge's ruling by means of an appeal against conviction; the prosecution could then seek leave to proceed with the other counts.

9.33.3 Difference between offering no evidence and leaving counts on file

The main difference between offering no evidence and leaving counts on the file is that in the former case an acquittal is entered (so the defendant cannot be re-prosecuted for the same offence) whereas, in the latter case, it is possible (with the leave of the court) for the case against the defendant to be revived.

9.34 DIFFERENT PLEAS FROM DIFFERENT DEFENDANTS

If more than one defendant is charged in the same indictment, it may well be that one defendant will plead guilty and another will plead not guilty.

9.34.1 What to tell the jury

Where one defendant pleads guilty but another not guilty, counsel for the prosecution should only tell the jury which tries the defendant who pleads not guilty that '[name of defendant who pleads guilty], of whom you may hear mention in the course of this case, is not before you and is none of your concern'.

Reference to the guilty plea of a co-defendant is only possible with leave of the judge, which can only be given where the evidence of the plea of the former co-defendant is admissible in evidence (in the circumstances set out in s 74 of the Police and Criminal Evidence Act 1984) (*R v Kempster* [1989] 1 WLR 1125; (1990) 90 Cr App R 14).

For example, in *R v Manzur and Mahmood* (1996) 1 Cr App R 414, three people had been charged with rape. One defendant pleaded guilty; the other two pleaded not guilty, saying that the victim consented to sexual intercourse. The judge allowed the jury to be told of the third defendant's plea of guilty. The Court of Appeal accepted the argument that the jury might have taken the view, on the basis of the third defendant's guilty plea, that the two appellants must have known that the victim was not consenting and so not have given sufficient consideration to the evidence of the two appellants that they believed the woman to be consenting to intercourse. The admission of the evidence of the plea of the third defendant was therefore unduly prejudicial to the appellants and so a re-trial was ordered.

Admission of evidence that a co-defendant pleaded guilty (under s 74 of the 1984 Act) does not violate Art 6 of the European Convention on Human Rights (*MH v UK* [1997] EHRLR 279)

9.34.2 When should sentence be passed on the defendant who pleads guilty?

Where one defendant pleads guilty and the other not guilty, the usual procedure is to adjourn sentence of the defendant who pleads guilty until after the trial of the defendant who pleads not guilty. There is less risk of disparity between the sentences if the judge sentences them together and the judge is in a better position to sentence as he will have heard the evidence about the gravity of the offence and the respective roles played by the defendants during the course of the trial (*R v Payne* [1950] 1 All ER 102).

Where it is accepted by the prosecution that the defendant who pleads guilty played a very minor role in the offence, or where the other defendant absconds, he will be sentenced as soon as he has pleaded guilty.

9.34.3 Turning Queen's evidence

If the defendant who pleads guilty also indicates that he is willing to give evidence for the prosecution, the arguments are slightly different. This is because 'turning Queen's evidence' attracts a discount in sentence well beyond the one-third discount that a plea of guilty normally receives. Such a person becomes a competent witness for the prosecution once he has pleaded guilty.

If the defendant who pleads guilty is sentenced after he has given evidence against the other accused, it could be thought that the sentence is determined by the quality of his evidence for the Crown rather than by his involvement in the offence. If, on the other hand, he is sentenced before he gives his evidence, he will receive a substantial discount for his promise to give evidence for the Crown and if, having achieved a more lenient sentence, he then refuses to testify he cannot be re-sentenced (see *R v Stone* [1970] 1 WLR 1112; [1970] 2 All ER 594).

Ultimately, it is a matter for the trial judge whether he sentences the defendant who is expected to testify for the Crown after his plea of guilty or after the trial of the other defendant (*R v Sheffield Crown Court ex p Brownlow* [1980] QB 530; [1980] 2 All ER 444). However, in most cases, sentence will be postponed; see for example, *R v Potter* [1977] Crim LR 112, and *R v Woods* (1977) 25 October, unreported. In *R v Weekes* (1980) 74 Cr App R 161, the Court of Appeal confirmed that in such a case sentence should be postponed until after the trial of the defendant who pleads not guilty. Nevertheless, in *R v Clement* (1991) *The Times*, 12 December, it was held that the decision whether or not to postpone sentence on a defendant who pleaded guilty and indicated that he was willing to give evidence against a co-defendant until the end of the trial, was a matter for the discretion of the trial judge, and would not in itself give rise to a ground of appeal.

9.35   VARIATION OF SENTENCE

Section 155(1) of the Powers of Criminal Courts (Sentencing) Act 2000 enables the judge who imposed a sentence to vary or rescind that sentence within 28 days of the sentence being passed.

This power is rarely invoked. It would be appropriate where, for example, an unlawful sentence has inadvertently been passed (*R v Newsome* [1970] 2 QB 711; [1970] 3 All ER 455).

However, it can also be used to increase sentence in exceptional cases where the original sentence was imposed on an erroneous factual basis. In *R v Hart* (1983) 5 Cr App R(s) 25, for example, a defendant boasted to the press that he had invented a false story to trick the judge into passing a lenient sentence. The judge re-listed the case and replaced a suspended sentence of imprisonment with immediate custody. The Court of Appeal upheld this use of s 155.

The power to vary a sentence (which can only be exercised by the judge who imposed the original sentence (s 155(4)) can be used to substitute one form of sentence for another. In *R v Sodhi* (1978) 66 Cr App R 260, for example, a prison sentence was replaced with a hospital order under the Mental Health Act 1983.

In *R v Hadley* (1994) 16 Cr App R(S) 358, the judge thought that the maximum sentence for the offence of which the defendant had been convicted was lower than in fact it was. When the judge discovered his error, he increased the defendant's sentence. The Court of Appeal upheld the use of the power to vary the sentence, saying that where a judge decides that the original sentence is too low, in the sense that it is outside the bracket of sentences which could reasonably be imposed for a particular offence, the judge will be justified in increasing the sentence.

Before a sentence is varied (especially if the variation amounts to an increase), the offender and his legal representative should be given the chance to make representations (*R v May* [1981] Crim LR 729; *R v Shacklady* [1987] Crim LR 713). Sentence should only be varied in open court (*R v Dowling* (1988) 88 Cr App R 88).

The power to vary a sentence under s 155(1) can only be exercised within the period of 28 days from the passing of the sentence (*R v Menocal* [1980] AC 598; [1979] 2 All ER 510). This means that not only must the original sentence be rescinded but a new sentence must be imposed within the 28 day period (*R v Stillwell* (1991) 94 Cr App R 65).

9.36   OTHER PLEAS

In this section, we consider the case where the plea of the defendant is unclear and we look at the special situations where the accused may not be fit to plead or where he claims the benefit of the doctrine of *autrefois convict* or *autrefois acquit*.

9.36.1   The ambiguous plea

If the defendant pleads guilty but, either then or when addressing the court in mitigation, says something which shows that he may have a defence, the judge will explain to the defendant that he is putting forward a defence and the defendant will be asked to plead again. If the defendant confirms his plea of guilty but still tries to put forward a defence, a not guilty plea will be entered by the court.

9.36.2   If the defendant refuses to plead

If the defendant refuses to enter a plea of guilty or not guilty when the indictment is put to him, a not guilty plea will be entered on his behalf.

9.36.3   Fitness to plead

Either the prosecution or the defence may raise the issue of whether the accused is fit to plead.

A defendant is unfit to plead if he suffers from a disability which prevents him from being unable to understand the course of the proceedings and the evidence which is given. Such a defendant would not be able to give proper instructions to his lawyer. It is not enough for the accused to be mentally disturbed or to be suffering from amnesia so that he cannot remember the events in question (see *R v Podola* [1960] 1 QB 325; [1959] 3 All ER 418).

The procedure to be followed in such a case is contained in the Criminal Procedure (Insanity) Act 1964 (as amended by the Criminal Procedure (Insanity and Unfitness to Plead) Act 1991).

The court may postpone consideration of the question of the defendant's fitness to be tried until any time up to the opening of the defence case if this is in the defendant's interests (s 4(2) of the Criminal Procedure (Insanity) Act 1964). This means that there is an opportunity for a submission of no case to answer to be made before the question of fitness is considered. If the submission of no case to answer is successful an acquittal is entered and the issue of fitness is not determined.

The issue of fitness to plead is determined by a jury and the evidence of at least two doctors (at least one of whom must specialise in mental disorder) is required.

If the issue of fitness is determined at the start of the trial and the defendant is found fit to plead, a fresh jury must be empanelled to try the case. If the issue of fitness is considered later, it can be considered either by the jury which is trying the defendant or by a separate jury (s 4(5) of the Criminal Procedure (Insanity) Act 1964). If the accused is found fit to plead, the trial will take its usual course.

Where the defendant is found unfit to plead, a jury has to consider whether the defendant committed the *actus reus* of the offence. If the issue of fitness was determined before arraignment, a fresh jury must be empanelled to decide whether the defendant committed the *actus reus* of the offence. If determination was postponed, the issue of fitness may be considered either by the jury trying the case or by a separate jury; however, if the defendant is found unfit to plead, the jury which was trying the case should determine whether the accused did the *actus reus*: s 4A(5) of the Criminal Procedure (Insanity) Act 1964. If the jury finds that he did not do the act alleged, then he must be acquitted (s 4A(4) of the Criminal Procedure (Insanity) Act 1964).

If the defendant is found unfit to plead and it is also found that he committed the *actus reus* of the offence, the court may order that the defendant be detained in a mental hospital, or make other orders appropriate to a mentally ill defendant, or order an absolute discharge (that is, impose no penalty) (s 5 of the Criminal Procedure (Insanity) Act 1964).

9.36.4 *Autrefois convict* and *autrefois acquit*

The basic principle of *autrefois convict* and *autrefois acquit* is that a person should not be tried twice for the same offence. In other words, a person should not be tried for a crime in respect of which he has already been acquitted or convicted (*Connelly v DPP* [1964] AC 1254; [1964] 2 All ER 401).

In *Connelly*, the House of Lords identified three other principles:

- the defendant cannot be tried for a crime in respect of which he could have been convicted on an earlier occasion, that is, cannot be convicted of an offence which was an alternative offence of which the jury could have convicted him under s 6(3) of the Criminal Law Act 1967 (see 9.24 above). Thus, if the defendant was earlier tried for robbery he cannot now be tried for the theft which comprised that robbery;

- the defendant cannot be tried for a crime, proof of which would necessarily entail proof of another crime of which he has already been acquitted, that is, the offence of which he has been acquitted is a necessary step towards establishing the second offence. Thus, if the defendant is acquitted of theft, he cannot later be charged with robbery alleging that same theft;

- the defendant cannot be tried for a crime which is in effect the same or substantially the same as one of which he has previously been acquitted or convicted or could have been convicted by way of a verdict of guilty to an alternative offence.

In *R v Beedie* [1997] 3 WLR 758; [1997] 2 Cr App R 167, a tenant died from carbon monoxide poisoning due to a defective gas fire. Her landlord was convicted of offences under health and safety legislation. He was subsequently charged with manslaughter, arising from the same facts. The Court of Appeal pointed out that in *Connelly v DPP* [1964] AC 1254; [1964] 2 All ER 401, the majority of the House of Lords confined the *autrefois convict* doctrine to cases where the second indictment charged the same offence as the first; in such a case, the later prosecution must be struck out as an abuse of process. In the other three situations identified in *Connelly*, the court has a discretion whether or not to strike out the later prosecution. In the present case, a stay should have been ordered because the manslaughter charge was based on substantially the same facts as the earlier prosecution and gave rise to a prosecution for an offence of greater gravity, no new facts having occurred.

In *R v Dabhade* [1993] QB 329; [1992] 4 All ER 796, the Court of Appeal confirmed the general principle that where a charge or count is dismissed without a hearing the prosecution may not thereafter institute fresh proceedings on the same or an essentially similar charge or count. However, if the summary dismissal of the charge or count is because it is defective or because the prosecution wish to reorganise their case as the charge is inappropriate given the evidence they have, it cannot properly be said that the defendant was ever in jeopardy of conviction. In *Dabhade*, the defendant was originally charged with obtaining property by deception but the prosecution offered no evidence on that charge which was then dismissed. The prosecution then brought proceedings on a charge of theft arising out of the same incident as this was felt to be more appropriate given the facts. The Court of Appeal rejected the argument that the defendant could plead *autrefois acquit* as the original charge was so fundamentally incorrectly framed that the prosecution had decided before a trial could take place that a different charge would have to be brought; the defendant was therefore never in any real sense in jeopardy of being convicted on the original charge.

Section 122 of the Criminal Justice Act 1988 provides that where the issue of *autrefois* is raised, it must be determined by a judge alone (that is, sitting without a jury).

9.36.5 Scope of the *autrefois* doctrine

The following situations do *not* amount to acquittal and so the defendant can be re-prosecuted:

- the quashing of an indictment (for example, because it is defective) (*R v Newland* [1988] QB 402; [1988] 2 All ER 891);

- the withdrawal of a summons in the magistrates' court at any time prior to the defendant entering a plea (*R v Grays Justices ex p Low* [1990] 1 QB 54; [1988] 3 All ER 834);

- the dismissal of an information by the magistrates where the prosecution failed to attend court or where the information is defective in a way that cannot be cured by amendment (*R v Dabhade* [1993] QB 329; [1992] 4 All ER 796);

- the prosecution serve a notice of discontinuance under s 23 of the Prosecution of Offences Act 1985; s 23(9) provides that where the prosecution serve a notice of discontinuance proceedings in respect of that offence may be instituted at a later date;

- the jury is discharged from giving a verdict.

In all of these cases, the defendant cannot be said to have been in jeopardy of a conviction. In *R v Old Street Magistrates' Court ex p Davies* [1995] Crim LR 629, it was held that in order for the *autrefois* doctrine to be applicable, the defendant must have been in jeopardy of a conviction.

Where a defendant asks for offences to be taken into consideration, the defendant is not in fact convicted of these offences and so could theoretically be prosecuted for them even though they were taken into account when he was sentenced for offences for which he had been convicted. However, in practice, offences which have been taken into consideration are never prosecuted.

9.36.6 Tainted acquittals

A further exception to the *autrefois convict* doctrine has been introduced by ss 54–57 of the Criminal Procedure and Investigations Act 1996. Section 54 provides that where:

(a) a person has been acquitted of an offence; and

(b) a person has been convicted of an administration of justice offence involving interference with, or intimidation of, a juror or witness (or potential witness) in any part of the proceedings which led to that acquittal,

the court before which the latter person was convicted may certify that:

   (i) there is a real possibility that, but for the interference or intimidation, the acquitted person would not have been acquitted; and

  (ii) that it is not contrary to the interests of justice (because of lapse of time or for any other reason) for the acquitted person to be re-prosecuted.

An application may then be made to the High Court for an order quashing the acquittal. The acquitted person may then be re-prosecuted for the offence of which he was acquitted.

Section 55 requires that four conditions must be satisfied before the High Court will quash the acquittal. They are:

(a) the High Court must agree that it is likely that, but for the interference or intimidation, the acquitted person would not have been acquitted;

(b) the High Court must agree that it is not contrary to the interests of justice for the acquitted person to be re-prosecuted;

(c) the acquitted person must be given a reasonable opportunity to make written representations to the High Court; and

(d) it must appear to the High Court that the conviction for the administration of justice offence will stand (and so there must not be an appeal against that conviction pending and the time limit for lodging such an appeal must have expired).

Under the Crown Court (Criminal Procedure and Investigations Act 1996) (Tainted Acquittals) Rules 1997 (SI 1997/1054), certification by the Crown Court under s 54 may be made at any time following the conviction for the administration of justice of offence but no later than immediately after the Crown Court has sentenced or otherwise dealt with the person convicted of that offence. Where the convicted person is under 18, and the Crown Court remits him to the youth court to be dealt with, the certification by the Crown Court must take place immediately after the order is made remitting him to the youth court. The Magistrates' Court (Criminal Procedure and Investigations Act 1996) (Tainted Acquittals) Rules 1997 (SI 1997/1055) provide that certification by a magistrates' court under s 54 must be made at any time following the conviction for the administration of justice of offence but no later than immediately after the court sentences or otherwise deals with the person convicted of that offence, or, where he is committed to the Crown Court for sentence, immediately after he is committed.

9.37 THE EFFECT OF THE EUROPEAN CONVENTION ON HUMAN RIGHTS

Article 6 of the Convention guarantees the right to a fair trial.

However, it has been held by the European Court of Human Rights that Art 6 does not apply to preliminary hearings concerning trial arrangements: *X v UK* 5 EHRR 273.

An important aspect of the operation of Art 6 is the principle of 'equality of arms'. This requires that the defendant should have a reasonable opportunity of presenting his case to the court under conditions which do not place him at a substantial disadvantage vis à vis his opponent' (*Foucher v France* (1997) 25 EHRR 234).

For example, handcuffing the accused during the trial may violate Art 6: *Kaj Raninen v Finland* [1998] EHRLR 344

The trial must take place before an unbiased tribunal. In the case of trial on indictment, that requirement applies to both the judge and the jury. There is a presumption that the court has acted impartially (*Hauschildt v Denmark* 12 EHRR 266; compare the UK case of *Locabail (UK) Ltd v Bayfield* [2000] 1 All ER 65). The test applied by the European Court is whether a legitimate doubt as to the impartiality of the tribunal can be objectively justified (*Hauschildt v Denmark* 12 EHRR 266). This seems very similar to the test applied by UK courts ('a real danger or possibility of bias': *R v Gough* [1993] 2 WLR 883).

9.38 PLEA AND DIRECTIONS HEARING QUESTIONNAIRE

For an example of a plea and directions hearing questionnaire, see Appendix 2 on p 863.

TABLE OF STATUTORY AND OTHER MATERIALS

STATUTORY AND OTHER MATERIALS

PRELIMINARY HEARINGS

CRIMINAL PROCEDURE AND INVESTIGATIONS ACT 1996

Section 28: Introduction

(1) This Part applies in relation to an offence if:

    (a) ... the accused is committed for trial for the offence concerned;

    (b) proceedings for the trial on the charge concerned are transferred to the Crown Court ...; or

    (c) a bill of indictment relating to the offence is preferred ... under the authority of section 2(2)(b) of the Administration of Justice (Miscellaneous Provisions) Act 1933.

    ...

Section 29: Power to order preparatory hearing

(1) Where it appears to a judge of the Crown Court that an indictment reveals a case of such complexity, or a case whose trial is likely to be of such length, that substantial benefits are likely to accrue from a hearing:

    (a) before the jury are sworn; and

    (b) for any of the purposes mentioned in sub-section (2),

    he may order that such a hearing (in this Part referred to as a preparatory hearing) shall be held.

(2) The purposes are those of:

    (a) identifying issues which are likely to be material to the verdict of the jury;

    (b) assisting their comprehension of any such issues;

    (c) expediting the proceedings before the jury;

    (d) assisting the judge's management of the trial.

(3) No order may be made under sub-section (1) where it appears to a judge of the Crown Court that the evidence on an indictment reveals a case of fraud of such seriousness or complexity as is mentioned in section 7(1) of the Criminal Justice Act 1987 (preparatory hearings in cases of serious or complex fraud).

(4) A judge may make an order under sub-section (1):

(a) on the application of the prosecutor;

(b) on the application of the accused or, if there is more than one, any of them; or

(c) of the judge's own motion.

Section 30: Start of trial and arraignment

If a judge orders a preparatory hearing:

(a) the trial shall start with that hearing; and

(b) arraignment shall take place at the start of that hearing, unless it has taken place before then.

Section 31: The preparatory hearing

(1) At the preparatory hearing the judge may exercise any of the powers specified in this section.

(2) The judge may adjourn a preparatory hearing from time to time.

(3) He may make a ruling as to:

(a) any question as to the admissibility of evidence;

(b) any other question of law relating to the case.

(4) He may order the prosecutor:

(a) to give the court and the accused or, if there is more than one, each of them a written statement (a case statement) of the matters falling within sub-section (5);

(b) to prepare the prosecution evidence and any explanatory material in such a form as appears to the judge to be likely to aid comprehension by the jury and to give it in that form to the court and to the accused or, if there is more than one, to each of them;

(c) to give the court and the accused or, if there is more than one, each of them written notice of documents the truth of the contents of which ought in the prosecutor's view to be admitted and of any other matters which in his view ought to be agreed;

(d) to make any amendments of any case statement given in pursuance of an order under paragraph (a) that appear to the judge to be appropriate, having regard to objections made by the accused or, if there is more than one, by any of them.

(5) The matters referred to in sub-section (4)(a) are:

(a) the principal facts of the case for the prosecution;

(b) the witnesses who will speak to those facts;

(c) any exhibits relevant to those facts;

(d) any proposition of law on which the prosecutor proposes to rely;

    (e) the consequences in relation to any of the counts in the indictment that appear to the prosecutor to flow from the matters falling within paragraphs (a) to (d).

(6) Where a judge has ordered the prosecutor to give a case statement and the prosecutor has complied with the order, the judge may order the accused or, if there is more than one, each of them:

    (a) to give the court and the prosecutor a written statement setting out in general terms the nature of his defence and indicating the principal matters on which he takes issue with the prosecution;

    (b) to give the court and the prosecutor written notice of any objections that he has to the case statement;

    (c) to give the court and the prosecutor written notice of any point of law (including any point as to the admissibility of evidence) which he wishes to take, and any authority on which he intends to rely for that purpose.

(7) Where a judge has ordered the prosecutor to give notice under sub-section (4)(c) and the prosecutor has complied with the order, the judge may order the accused or, if there is more than one, each of them to give the court and the prosecutor a written notice stating:

    (a) the extent to which he agrees with the prosecutor as to documents and other matters to which the notice under sub-section (4)(c) relates; and

    (b) the reason for any disagreement.

(8) A judge making an order under sub-section (6) or (7) shall warn the accused or, if there is more than one, each of them of the possible consequences under section 34 of not complying with it.

(9) If it appears to a judge that reasons given in pursuance of sub-section (7) are inadequate, he shall so inform the person giving them and may require him to give further or better reasons.

(10) An order under this section may specify the time within which any specified requirement contained in it is to be complied with.

(11) An order or ruling made under this section shall have effect throughout the trial, unless it appears to the judge on application made to him that the interests of justice require him to vary or discharge it.

Section 32: Orders before preparatory hearing

(1) This section applies where:

    (a) a judge orders a preparatory hearing; and

    (b) he decides that any order which could be made under section 31(4) to (7) at the hearing should be made before the hearing.

(2) In such a case:

    (a) he may make any such order before the hearing (or at the hearing); and

    (b) sections 31(4) to (11) shall apply accordingly.

Section 34: Later stages of trial

(1) Any party may depart from the case he disclosed in pursuance of a requirement imposed under section 31.

(2) Where:

    (a) a party departs from the case he disclosed in pursuance of a requirement imposed under section 31; or

    (b) a party fails to comply with such a requirement,

the judge or, with the leave of the judge, any other party may make such comment as appears to the judge or the other party (as the case may be) to be appropriate and the jury may draw such inference as appears proper.

(3) In deciding whether to give leave the judge shall have regard:

    (a) to the extent of the departure or failure; and

    (b) to whether there is any justification for it.

(4) Except as provided by this section no part:

    (a) of a statement given under section 31(6)(a); or

    (b) of any other information relating to the case for the accused or, if there is more than one, the case of any of them, which was given in pursuance of a requirement imposed under section 31,

may be disclosed at a stage in the trial after the jury have been sworn without the consent of the accused concerned.

Section 35: Appeals to Court of Appeal

(1) An appeal shall lie to the Court of Appeal from any ruling of a judge under section 31(3), but only with the leave of the judge or of the Court of Appeal.

(2) The judge may continue a preparatory hearing notwithstanding that leave to appeal has been granted under sub-section (1), but no jury shall be sworn until after the appeal has been determined or abandoned.

(3) On the termination of the hearing of an appeal, the Court of Appeal may confirm, reverse or vary the decision appealed against.

(4) [Appeal to lie to Criminal Division of Court of Appeal.]

PRE-TRIAL HEARINGS

CRIMINAL PROCEDURE AND INVESTIGATIONS ACT 1996

Section 39: Meaning of pre-trial hearing

(1) For the purposes of this Part a hearing is a pre-trial hearing if it relates to a trial on indictment and it takes place:

    (a) after the accused has been committed for trial for the offence concerned or after the proceedings for the trial have been transferred to the Crown Court; and

    (b) before the start of the trial.

(2) For the purposes of this Part a hearing is also a pre-trial hearing if:

    (a) it relates to a trial on indictment to be held in pursuance of a bill of indictment preferred under the authority of section 2(2)(b) of the Administration of Justice (Miscellaneous Provisions) Act 1933; and

    (b) it takes place after the bill of indictment has been preferred and before the start of the trial.

(3) For the purposes of this section the start of a trial on indictment occurs when a jury is sworn to consider the issue of guilt or fitness to plead or, if the court accepts a plea of guilty before a jury is sworn, when that plea is accepted; but this is subject to section 8 of the Criminal Justice Act 1987 and section 30 of this Act (preparatory hearings).

Section 40: Power to make rulings

(1) A judge may make at a pre-trial hearing a ruling as to:

    (a) any question as to the admissibility of evidence;

    (b) any other question of law relating to the case concerned.

(2) A ruling may be made under this section:

    (a) on an application by a party to the case; or

    (b) of the judge's own motion.

(3) Subject to sub-section (4), a ruling made under this section has binding effect from the time it is made until the case against the accused or, if there is more than one, against each of them is disposed of; and the case against an accused is disposed of if:

    (a) he is acquitted or convicted; or

    (b) the prosecutor decides not to proceed with the case against him.

(4) A judge may discharge or vary (or further vary) a ruling made under this section if it appears to him that it is in the interests of justice to do so, and a judge may act under this sub-section:

(a) on an application by a party to the case; or

(b) of the judge's own motion.

(5) No application may be made under sub-section (4)(a) unless there has been a material change of circumstances since the ruling was made or, if a previous application has been made, since the application (or last application) was made.

(6) The judge referred to in sub-section (4) need not be the judge who made the ruling or, if it has been varied, the judge (or any of the judges) who varied it.

(7) For the purposes of this section the prosecutor is any person acting as prosecutor, whether an individual or a body.

SECURING ATTENDANCE OF WITNESSES FOR CROWN COURT TRIAL

CRIMINAL PROCEDURE (ATTENDANCE OF WITNESSES) ACT 1965

Section 2: Issue of witness summons on application to Crown Court

(1) This section applies where the Crown Court is satisfied that:

(a) a person is likely to be able to give evidence likely to be material evidence, or produce any document or thing likely to be material evidence, for the purpose of any criminal proceedings before the Crown Court; and

(b) the person will not voluntarily attend as a witness or will not voluntarily produce the document or thing.

(2) In such a case the Crown Court shall, subject to the following provisions of this section, issue a summons (a witness summons) directed to the person concerned and requiring him to:

(a) attend before the Crown Court at the time and place stated in the summons; and

(b) give the evidence or produce the document or thing.

(3) A witness summons may only be issued under this section on an application; and the Crown Court may refuse to issue the summons if any requirement relating to the application is not fulfilled.

(4) Where a person has been committed for trial for any offence to which the proceedings concerned relate, an application must be made as soon as reasonably practicable after the committal.

(5) Where the proceedings have been transferred to the Crown Court, an application must be made as soon as is reasonably practicable after the transfer.

(6) Where the proceedings concerned relate to an offence in relation to which a bill of indictment has been preferred under the authority of section 2(2)(b) of the Administration of Justice (Miscellaneous Provisions) Act 1933, an application must be made as soon as is reasonably practicable after the bill was preferred.

...

Section 2A: Power to require advance production

A witness summons which is issued under section 2 above and which requires a person to produce a document or thing as mentioned in section 2(2) above may also require him to produce the document or thing:

(a) at a place stated in the summons; and

(b) at a time which is so stated and precedes that stated under section 2(2) above,

for inspection by the person applying for the summons.

...

Section 2C: Application to make summons ineffective

(1) If a witness summons issued under section 2 above is directed to a person who:

(a) applies to the Crown Court;

(b) satisfies the court that he was not served with notice of the application to issue the summons and that he was neither present nor represented at the hearing of the application; and

(c) satisfies the court that he cannot give any evidence likely to be material evidence or, as the case may be, produce any document or thing likely to be material evidence,

the court may direct that the summons shall be of no effect.

...

Section 3: Punishment for disobedience to witness summons, etc

(1) Any person who without just excuse disobeys a witness summons requiring him to attend before any court shall be guilty of contempt of that court and may be punished summarily by that court as if his contempt had been committed in the face of the court.

(1A) Any person who without just excuse disobeys a requirement made by any court under section 2A above shall be guilty of contempt of that court and may be punished summarily by that court as if his contempt had been committed in the face of the court.

(2) No person shall by reason of any disobedience mentioned in sub-section (1) or (1A) be liable to imprisonment for a period exceeding three months.

Section 4: Further process to secure attendance of witness

(1) If a judge of the Crown Court is satisfied by evidence on oath that a witness in respect of whom a witness summons is in force is unlikely to comply with the summons, the judge may issue a warrant to arrest the witness and bring him before the court before which he is required to attend:

Provided that a warrant shall not be issued under this sub-section unless the judge is satisfied by such evidence as aforesaid that the witness is likely to be able to give evidence likely to be material evidence or produce any document or thing likely to be material evidence in the proceedings.

(2) Where a witness who is required to attend before the Crown Court by virtue of a witness summons fails to attend in compliance with the summons that court may:

(a) in any case, cause to be served on him a notice requiring him to attend the court forthwith or at such time as may be specified in the notice;

(b) if the court is satisfied that there are reasonable grounds for believing that he has failed to attend without just excuse, or if he has failed to comply with a notice under paragraph (a) above, issue a warrant to arrest him and bring him before the court.

(3) A witness brought before a court in pursuance of a warrant under this section may be remanded by that court in custody or on bail (with or without sureties) until such time as the court may appoint for receiving his evidence or dealing with him under section 3 of this Act; and where a witness attends a court in pursuance of a notice under this section the court may direct that the notice shall have effect as if it required him to attend at any later time appointed by the court for receiving his evidence or dealing with him as aforesaid.

THE COURSE OF THE TRIAL

READING WITNESS STATEMENTS

CRIMINAL PROCEDURE AND INVESTIGATIONS ACT 1996

Schedule 2: Statements and Depositions

1 Statements

(1) Sub-paragraph (2) applies if:

    (a) a written statement has been admitted in evidence in proceedings before a magistrates' court inquiring into an offence as examining justices;

    (b) in those proceedings a person has been committed for trial;

    (c) for the purposes of section 5A of the Magistrates' Courts Act 1980 the statement complied with section 5B of that Act prior to the committal for trial;

    (d) the statement purports to be signed by a justice of the peace; and

    (e) sub-paragraph (3) does not prevent sub-paragraph (2) applying.

(2) Where this sub-paragraph applies the statement may without further proof be read as evidence on the trial of the accused, whether for the offence for which he was committed for trial or for any other offence arising out of the same transaction or set of circumstances.

(3) Sub-paragraph (2) does not apply if:

    (a) it is proved that the statement was not signed by the justice by whom it purports to have been signed;

    (b) the court of trial at its discretion orders that sub-paragraph (2) shall not apply; or

    (c) a party to the proceedings objects to sub-paragraph (2) applying.

(4) If a party to the proceedings objects to sub-paragraph (2) applying the court of trial may order that the objection shall have no effect if the court considers it to be in the interest of justice so to order.

2 Depositions

(1) Sub-paragraph (2) applies if:

    (a) in pursuance of section 97A of the Magistrates' Courts Act 1980 (summons or warrant to have evidence taken as a deposition, etc) a person has had his evidence taken as a deposition for the purposes of proceedings before a magistrates' court inquiring into an offence as examining justices;

(b) the deposition has been admitted in evidence in those proceedings;

(c) in those proceedings a person has been committed for trial;

(d) for the purposes of section 5A of the Magistrates' Courts Act 1980 the deposition complied with section 5C of that Act prior to the committal for trial;

(e) the deposition purports to be signed by the justice before whom it purports to have been taken; and

(f) sub-paragraph (3) does not prevent sub-paragraph (2) applying.

(2) Where this sub-paragraph applies the deposition may without further proof be read as evidence on the trial of the accused, whether for the offence for which he was committed for trial or for any other offence arising out of the same transaction or set of circumstances.

(3) Sub-paragraph (2) does not apply if:

(a) it is proved that the deposition was not signed by the justice by whom it purports to have been signed;

(b) the court of trial at its discretion orders that sub-paragraph (2) shall not apply; or

(c) a party to the proceedings objects to sub-paragraph (2) applying.

(4) If a party to the proceedings objects to sub-paragraph (2) applying the court of trial may order that the objection shall have no effect if the court considers it to be in the interest of justice so to order.

EXCLUDING PROSECUTION EVIDENCE

POLICE AND CRIMINAL EVIDENCE ACT 1984

Section 76: Confessions

(1) In any proceedings a confession[1] made by an accused person may be given in evidence against him in so far as it is relevant to any matter in issue in the proceedings and is not excluded by the court in pursuance of this section.

(2) If, in any proceedings where the prosecution proposes to give in evidence a confession made by an accused person, it is represented to the court that the confession was or may have been obtained:

(a) by oppression of the person who made it; or

---

1   That is, any statement wholly or partly adverse to the person who made it, whether made to a person in authority or not and whether made in words or otherwise (s 82 of the 1984 Act).

(b) in consequence of anything said or done which was likely, in the circumstances existing at the time, to render unreliable any confession which might be made by him in consequence thereof,

the court shall not allow the confession to be given in evidence against him except in so far as the prosecution proves to the court beyond reasonable doubt that the confession (notwithstanding that it may be true) was not obtained as aforesaid.

(3) In any proceedings where the prosecution proposes to give in evidence a confession made by an accused person, the court may of its own motion require the prosecution, as a condition of allowing it to do so, to prove that the confession was not obtained as mentioned in sub-section (2) above.

...

(8) In this section 'oppression' includes torture, inhuman or degrading treatment, and the use or threat of violence (whether or not amounting to torture).

(9) Where the proceedings mentioned in sub-section (1) above are proceedings before a magistrates' court inquiring into an offence as examining justices this section shall have effect with the omission of:

(a) in sub-section (1) the words 'and is not excluded by the court in pursuance of this section'; and

(b) sub-sections (2) to (6) and (8).

Section 78: Exclusion of unfair evidence

(1) In any proceedings the court may refuse to allow evidence on which the prosecution proposes to rely to be given if it appears to the court that, having regard to all the circumstances, including the circumstances in which the evidence was obtained, the admission of the evidence would have such an adverse effect on the fairness of the proceedings that the court ought not to admit it.

...

(3) This section shall not apply in the case of proceedings before a magistrates' court inquiring into an offence as examining justices.

CRIMINAL EVIDENCE ACT 1898

Section 1: Competency of witnesses in criminal cases

(1) A person charged in criminal proceedings shall not be called as a witness in the proceedings except upon his own application;

(2) A person charged in criminal proceedings who is called as a witness in the proceedings may be asked any question in cross-examination notwithstanding that it would tend to incriminate him as to any offence with which he is charged in the proceedings;

(3) A person charged in criminal proceedings who is called as a witness in the proceedings shall not be asked, and if asked shall not be required to answer, any question tending to show that he has committed or been convicted of or been charged with any offence other than one with which he is then charged, or is of bad character, unless:

    (i) the proof that he has committed or been convicted of such other offence is admissible evidence to show that he is guilty of an offence with which he is then charged; or

    (ii) he has personally or by his advocate asked questions of the witnesses for the prosecution with a view to establish his own good character, or has given evidence of his good character, or the nature or conduct of the defence is such as to involve imputations on the character of the prosecutor or the witnesses for the prosecution or the deceased victim of the alleged crime; or

    (iii) he has given evidence against any other person charged in the same proceedings.

(4) Every person charged in criminal proceedings who is called as a witness in the proceedings shall, unless otherwise ordered by the court, give his evidence from the witness box or other place from which the other witnesses give their evidence.

POLICE AND CRIMINAL EVIDENCE ACT 1984

Section 79: Time for taking accused's evidence

If at the trial of any person for an offence:

    (a) the defence intends to call two or more witnesses to the facts of the case; and

    (b) those witnesses include the accused,

the accused shall be called before the other witness or witnesses unless the court in its discretion otherwise directs.

CRIMINAL JUSTICE AND PUBLIC ORDER ACT 1994

Section 34: Effect of accused's failure to mention facts when questioned or charged

(1) Where, in any proceedings against a person for an offence, evidence is given that the accused:

    (a) at any time before he was charged with the offence, on being questioned under caution by a constable trying to discover whether or by whom the offence had been committed, failed to mention any fact relied on in his defence in those proceedings; or

   (b) on being charged with the offence or officially informed that he might be prosecuted for it, failed to mention any such fact,

being a fact which in the circumstances existing at the time the accused could reasonably have been expected to mention when so questioned, charged or informed, as the case may be, sub-section (2) below applies.

(2) Where this sub-section applies:

   (a) a magistrates' court inquiring into the offence as examining justices;

   (b) a judge, in deciding whether to grant an application made by the accused under:

      (i) section 6 of the Criminal Justice Act 1987 (application for dismissal of charge of serious fraud in respect of which notice of transfer has been given under section 4 of that Act); or

      (ii) paragraph 5 of Schedule 6 to the Criminal Justice Act 1991 (application for dismissal of charge of violent or sexual offence involving child in respect of which notice of transfer has been given under section 53 of that Act);

   (c) the court, in determining whether there is a case to answer; and

   (d) the court or jury, in determining whether the accused is guilty of the offence charged,

may draw such inferences from the failure as appear proper.

(2A) Where the accused was at an authorised place of detention at the time of the failure, sub-sections (1) and (2) above do not apply if he had not been allowed an opportunity to consult a solicitor prior to being questioned, charged or informed as mentioned in sub-section (1) above.

(3) Subject to any directions by the court, evidence tending to establish the failure may be given before or after evidence tending to establish the fact which the accused is alleged to have failed to mention.

(4) This section applies in relation to questioning by persons (other than constables) charged with the duty of investigating offences or charging offenders as it applies in relation to questioning by constables ...

    ...

Section 35: Effect of accused's silence at trial

(1) At the trial of any person who has attained the age of 14 years for an offence, sub-section (2) and (3) below apply unless:

   (a) the accused's guilt is not in issue; or

   (b) it appears to the court that the physical or mental condition of the accused makes it undesirable for him to give evidence,

but sub-section (2) below does not apply if, at the conclusion of the evidence for the prosecution, his legal representative informs the court that the accused will give evidence or, where he is unrepresented, the court ascertains from him that he will give evidence.

(2) Where this sub-section applies, the court shall, at the conclusion of the evidence for the prosecution, satisfy itself (in the case of proceedings on indictment, in the presence of the jury) that the accused is aware that the stage has been reached at which evidence can be given for the defence and that he can, if he wishes, give evidence and that, if he chooses not to give evidence, or having been sworn, without good cause refuses to answer any question, it will be permissible for the court or jury to draw such inferences as appear proper from his failure to give evidence or his refusal, without good cause, to answer any question.

(3) Where this sub-section applies, the court or jury, in determining whether the accused is guilty of the offence charged, may draw such inferences as appear proper from the failure of the accused to give evidence or his refusal, without good cause, to answer any question.

(4) This section does not render the accused compellable to give evidence on his own behalf, and he shall accordingly not be guilty of contempt of court by reason of a failure to do so.

(5) For the purposes of this section a person who, having been sworn, refuses to answer any question shall be taken to do so without good cause unless:

(a) he is entitled to refuse to answer the question by virtue of any enactment, whenever passed or made, or on the ground of privilege; or

(b) the court in the exercise of its general discretion excuses him from answering it.

(6) Where the age of any person is material for the purposes of sub-section (1) above, his age shall for those purposes be taken to be that which appears to the court to be his age.

...

Section 38: Interpretation, etc

(2) In sections 34(2) [and] 35(3) ... references to an offence charged include references to any other offence of which the accused could lawfully be convicted on that charge.

(3) A person shall not [be committed for trial], have a case to answer or be convicted of an offence solely on an inference drawn from such a failure or refusal as is mentioned in section 34(2) [or] 35(3) ...

(4) A judge shall not refuse to grant such an application as is mentioned in section 34(2)(b) ... solely on an inference drawn from such a failure as is mentioned in section 34(2) ...

...

PRACTICE DIRECTION (CROWN COURT: DEFENDANT'S EVIDENCE) [1995] 1 WLR 657

...

If the accused is legally represented

2   Section 35(1) [of the Criminal Justice and Public Order Act 1994] provides that section 35(2) does not apply if at the conclusion of the evidence for the prosecution the accused's legal representative informs the court that the accused will give evidence. This should be done in the presence of the jury. If the representative indicates that the accused will give evidence, the case should proceed in the usual way.

3   If the court is not so informed, or if the court is informed that the accused does not intend to give evidence, the judge should in the presence of the jury inquire of the representative in these terms:

'Have you advised your client that the stage has now been reached at which he may give evidence and, if he chooses not to do so or, having been sworn, without good cause refuses to answer any question, the jury may draw such inferences as appear proper from his failure to do so?'

4   If the representative replies to the judge that the accused has been so advised, then the case shall proceed. If counsel replies that the accused has not been so advised then the judge shall direct the representative to advise his client of the consequences set out in para 3 hereof and should adjourn briefly for this purpose before proceeding further.

If the accused is not legally represented

5   If the accused is not represented the judge shall at the conclusion of the evidence for the prosecution and in the presence of the jury say to the accused:

'You have heard the evidence against you. Now is the time for you to make your defence. You may give evidence on oath, and be cross-examined like any other witness. If you do not give evidence or, having been sworn, without good cause refuse to answer any question, the jury may draw such inferences as appear proper. That means they may hold it against you. You may also call any witness or witnesses whom you have arranged to attend court. Afterwards you may also, if you wish, address the jury by arguing your case from the dock. But you cannot at that stage give evidence. Do you now intend to give evidence?'

SUBMISSION OF NO CASE TO ANSWER

R v Galbraith [1981] 1 WLR 1039, p 1042, *per* Lord Lane CJ

How then should the judge approach a submission of 'no case'?

(1) If there is no evidence that the crime alleged has been committed by the defendant, there is no difficulty. The judge will of course stop the case.

(2) The difficulty arises where there is some evidence but it is of a tenuous character, for example because of inherent weakness or vagueness or because it is inconsistent with other evidence.

    (a) Where the judge comes to the conclusion that the Crown's evidence, taken at its highest, is such that a jury properly directed could not properly convict on it, it is his duty, on a submission being made, to stop the case.

    (b) Where however the Crown's evidence is such that its strength or weakness depends on the view to be taken of a witness's reliability, or other matters which are generally speaking within the province of the jury and where on one possible view of the facts there is evidence on which a jury could properly come to the conclusion that the defendant is guilty, then the judge should allow the matter to be tried by the jury
    ...

There will of course ... be borderline cases. They can safely be left to the discretion of the judge.

IDENTIFICATION CASES

R v Turnbull [1977] QB 224

Lord Widgery CJ: ... First, whenever the case against an accused depends wholly or substantially on the correctness of one or more identifications of the accused which the defence alleges to be mistaken, the judge should warn the jury of the special need for caution before convicting the accused in reliance on the correctness of the identification or identifications. In addition he should instruct them as to the reason for the need for such a warning and should make some reference to the possibility that a mistaken witness can be a convincing one and that a number of such witnesses can all be mistaken. Provided this is done in clear terms the judge need not use any particular form of words.

Secondly, the judge should direct the jury to examine closely the circumstances in which the identification by each witness came to be made. How long did the witness have the accused under observation? At what distance? In what light? Was the observation impeded in any way, as for example by passing traffic or a press of people? Had the witness ever seen the accused before? How often? If only occasionally, had he any special reason for remembering the accused? How long elapsed between the original observation and the subsequent identification to the police? Was there any material discrepancy between the description of the accused given to the police by the witness when first seen by them and his actual appearance? If in any case, whether it is being dealt with summarily or on indictment, the prosecution have reason to believe that there is such a material discrepancy they should supply the accused or his legal advisers with particulars of the description the police were first given.[2] In all cases if the accused asks to be given particulars of such descriptions, the prosecution should supply them. Finally, he should remind the jury of any specific weakness which had appeared in the identification evidence. Recognition may be more reliable than identification of a stranger; but, even when the witness is purporting to recognise someone whom he knows, the jury should be reminded that mistakes in recognition of close relatives and friends are sometimes made.

All these matters go to the quality of the identification evidence. If the quality is good and remains good at the close of the accused's case, the danger of a mistaken identification is lessened; but the poorer the quality, the greater the danger. In our judgment, when the quality is good, as for example when the identification is made after a long period of observation, or in satisfactory conditions by a relative, a neighbour, a close friend, a workmate and the like, the jury can safely be left to assess the value of the identifying evidence even though there is no other evidence to support it; provided always, however, that an adequate warning has been given about the special need for caution ...

When, in the judgment of the trial judge, the quality of the identifying evidence is poor, as for example when it depends solely on a fleeting glance or on a longer observation made in difficult conditions, the situation is very different. The judge should then withdraw the case from the jury and direct an acquittal unless there is other evidence which goes to support the correctness of the identification ...

The trial judge should identify to the jury the evidence which he adjudges is capable of supporting the evidence of identification. If there is any evidence or circumstance which the jury might think was supporting when it did not have this quality,[3] the judge should say so ...

Care should be taken by the judge when directing the jury about the support for an identification which may be derived from the fact that they have rejected an alibi. False alibis may be put forward for many reasons: an accused, for example, who has only his own truthful evidence to rely on

---

2   This would now be required under s 3 of the Criminal Procedure and Investigations Act 1996 which requires the prosecution to disclose material which might undermine the prosecution case against the accused.

3   For example, evidence which is inadmissible.

may stupidly fabricate an alibi and get lying witnesses to support it out of fear that his own evidence will not be enough. Further, alibi witnesses can make genuine mistakes about dates and occasions like any other witnesses can. It is only when the jury are satisfied that the sole reason for the fabrication was to deceive them and there is no other explanation for its being put forward, that fabrication can provide any support for identification evidence. The jury should be reminded that proving the accused has told lies about where he was at the material time does not by itself prove that he was where the identifying witness says he was.

...

A failure to follow these guidelines is likely to result in a conviction being quashed ...

ALTERNATIVE VERDICTS

CRIMINAL LAW ACT 1967

Section 6

(1) Where a person is arraigned on an indictment:

...

(b) he may plead not guilty of the offence specifically charged in the indictment but guilty of another offence of which he might be found guilty on that indictment;

(c) if he stands mute of malice or will not answer directly to the indictment, the court may order a plea of not guilty to be entered on his behalf, and he shall then be treated as having pleaded not guilty.

(2) On an indictment for murder a person found not guilty of murder may be found guilty:

(a) of manslaughter, or of causing grievous bodily harm with intent to do so; or

(b) of any offence of which he may be found guilty under an enactment specifically so providing, or under section 4(2) of this Act; or

(c) of an attempt to commit murder, or of an attempt to commit any other offence of which he might be found guilty,

but may not be found guilty of any offence not included above.

(3) Where, on a person's trial on indictment for any offence except treason or murder, the jury find him not guilty of the offence specifically charged in the indictment, but the allegations in the indictment amount to or include (expressly or by implication) an allegation of another offence falling within the jurisdiction of the court of trial, the jury may find him guilty of that

other offence or of an offence of which he could be found guilty on an indictment specifically charging that offence.

(4) For the purposes of sub-section (3) above any allegation of an offence shall be taken as including an allegation of attempting to commit that offence; and where a person is charged on indictment with attempting to commit an offence or with any assault or other act preliminary to an offence, but not with the completed offence, then (subject to the discretion of the court to discharge the jury with a view to the preferment of an indictment for the completed offence) he may be convicted of the offence charged notwithstanding that he is shown to be guilty of the completed offence.

(5) Where a person arraigned on an indictment pleads not guilty of an offence charged in the indictment but guilty of some other offence of which he might be found guilty on that charge, and he is convicted on that plea of guilty without trial for the offence of which he has pleaded not guilty, then (whether or not the two offences are separately charged in distinct counts) his conviction of the one offence shall be an acquittal of the other.

...

(7) Sub-sections (1) to (3) above shall apply to an indictment containing more than one count as if each count were a separate indictment.

MAJORITY VERDICTS

JURIES ACT 1974

Section 17

(1) Subject to sub-sections (3) and (4) below, the verdict of a jury in proceedings in the Crown Court ... need not be unanimous if:

   (a) in a case where there are not less than 11 jurors, 10 of them agree on the verdict; and

   (b) in a case where there are 10 jurors, nine of them agree on the verdict.

   ...

(3) The Crown Court shall not accept a verdict of guilty by virtue of sub-section (1) above unless the foreman of the jury has stated in open court the number of jurors who respectively agreed to and dissented from the verdict.

(4) No court shall accept a verdict by virtue of sub-section (1) ... above unless it appears to the court that the jury have had such a period of time for deliberation as the court thinks reasonable having regard to the nature and complexity of the case; and the Crown Court shall in any event not accept such a verdict unless it appears to the court that the jury have had at least two hours for deliberation.

PRACTICE DIRECTION (CRIME: MAJORITY VERDICTS) [1967] 1 WLR 1198

... Before the jury retire ... the judge should direct the jury in some such words as the following:

> As you may know, the law permits me in certain circumstances to accept a verdict which is not the verdict of you all. Those circumstances have not as yet arisen so that when you retire I must ask you to reach a verdict upon which each one of you is agreed. Should, however, the time come when it is possible for me to accept a majority verdict, I will give you a further direction.

Thereafter the practice should be as follows:

1. Should the jury return before the two hours (or such longer time as the judge thinks reasonable) has elapsed (see sub-section (3) [of the Juries Act]), they should be asked:

    (a) Have you reached a verdict upon which you are all agreed? Please answer yes or no.

    (b) (i) If *unanimous*: what is your verdict?

        (ii) If *not unanimous:* the jury should be sent out again for further deliberation with a further direction to arrive if possible at a unanimous verdict.

2. Should the jury return (whether for the first or second time) or be sent for *after* the two hours (or the longer period) has elapsed, questions (a) and (b)(i) in the preceding paragraph should be put to them and if it appears that they are not unanimous they should be asked to retire once more and told that they should continue to endeavour to reach a unanimous verdict but that if they cannot the judge will accept a majority verdict as in sub-section (1) [of the Juries Act].

3. When the jury finally return they should be asked:

    (a) Have at least 10 (or nine as the case may be) of you agreed upon your verdict? If yes;

    (b) What is your verdict? Please only answer 'Guilty' or 'Not guilty'.

    (c) (i)   If 'Not guilty': accept the verdict without more ado.

        (ii)   If 'Guilty': is it the verdict of you all or by a majority?

    (d) If 'Guilty' by a majority: how many of you agreed to the verdict and how many dissented?

Where there are several counts (or alternative verdicts) left to the jury the above practice will of course need to be adapted to the circumstances. The procedure will have to be repeated in respect of each count (or alternative verdict) the verdict being accepted in those cases where the jury are unanimous and the further direction in paragraph 2 being given in cases in which they are not unanimous.

Should the jury in the end be unable to agree on a verdict by the required majority (that is, if the answer to the question in paragraph 3(i) be in the negative) the judge in his discretion will either ask them to deliberate further or discharge them.

R v Watson [1988] QB 690, p 700, *per* Lord Lane CJ

Each of you has taken an oath to return a true verdict according to the evidence. No one must be false to that oath, but you have a duty not only as individuals but collectively. That is the strength of the jury system. Each of you takes into the jury-box with you your individual experience and wisdom. Your task is to pool that experience and wisdom. You do that by giving your views and listening to the views of others. There must necessarily be discussion, argument and give and take within the scope of your oath. That is the way in which agreement is reached. If, unhappily [10 of] you cannot reach agreement you must say so.

TAINTED ACQUITTALS

CRIMINAL PROCEDURE AND INVESTIGATIONS ACT 1996

Section 54

(1) This section applies where:

    (a) a person has been acquitted of an offence; and

    (b) a person has been convicted of an administration of justice offence involving interference with or intimidation of a juror or a witness (or potential witness) in any proceedings which led to the acquittal.

(2) Where it appears to the court before which the person was convicted that:

    (a) there is a real possibility that, but for the interference or intimidation, the acquitted person would not have been acquitted; and

    (b) sub-section (5) does not apply,

the court shall certify that it so appears.

(3) Where a court certifies under sub-section (2) an application may be made to the High Court for an order quashing the acquittal, and the Court shall make the order if (but shall not do so unless) the four conditions in section 55 are satisfied.

(4) Where an order is made under sub-section (3) proceedings may be taken against the acquitted person for the offence of which he was acquitted.

(5) This sub-section applies if, because of lapse of time or for any other reason, it would be contrary to the interests of justice to take proceedings against

the acquitted person for the offence of which he was acquitted.

(6) For the purposes of this section the following offences are administration of justice offences:

(a) the offence of perverting the course of justice;

(b) the offence under section 51(1) of the Criminal Justice and Public Order Act 1994 (intimidation etc of witnesses, jurors and others);

(c) an offence of aiding, abetting, counselling, procuring, suborning or inciting another person to commit an offence under section 1 of the Perjury Act 1911.

...

Section 55

(1) The first condition is that it appears to the High Court likely that, but for the interference or intimidation, the acquitted person would not have been acquitted.

(2) The second condition is that it does not appear to the Court that, because of lapse of time or for any other reason, it would be contrary to the interests of justice to take proceedings against the acquitted person for the offence of which he was acquitted.

(3) The third condition is that it appears to the Court that the acquitted person has been given a reasonable opportunity to make written representations to the Court.

(4) The fourth condition is that it appears to the Court that the conviction for the administration of justice offence will stand.

(5) In applying sub-section (4) the Court shall:

(a) take into account all the information before it; but

(b) ignore the possibility of new factors coming to light.

(6) Accordingly, the fourth condition has the effect that the Court shall not make an order under section 54(3) if (for instance) it appears to the Court that any time allowed for giving notice of appeal has not expired or that an appeal is pending.

CHAPTER 10

APPEALS FROM THE CROWN COURT

10.1   INTRODUCTION

In this chapter, we look at the procedure for appealing against conviction and/or sentence following trial on indictment and at the criteria applied by the Court of Appeal when disposing of such appeals.

Criminal appeals are governed by the Criminal Appeal Act 1968 and the Criminal Appeal Rules 1968. Reference may also be made to 'A Guide to the Proceedings of the Court of Appeal Criminal Division' (1983) to be found in 77 Cr App R.

Appeal against conviction and/or sentence lies from the Crown Court to the Court of Appeal (Criminal Division).

10.2   THE COURT OF APPEAL

The constitution of the Court of Appeal (Criminal Division) is governed by the Supreme Court Act 1981. The court is presided over by the Lord Chief Justice of England (although, of course, he will not hear every appeal). It comprises Lords Justices of Appeal, together with High Court Judges whom the Lord Chief Justice has asked to assist with the work of the Court of Appeal (ss 2, 3 and 9 of the Supreme Court Act 1981).

The number of judges requiring for a sitting of the Court of Appeal is governed by s 55 of the Supreme Court Act 1981:

- when determining an appeal against conviction, the Court of Appeal must comprise at least three judges; one or more of the judges must be a Lord Justice of Appeal. The decision is by majority (the presiding judge does not have a casting vote). Usually, only one judgment will be delivered;

- when determining an appeal against sentence, the Court of Appeal may consist of only two judges, but again one of them should be a Lord Justice of Appeal. Should an appeal be heard by a two-judge court (again, one would have to be a Lord Justice of Appeal) and the two judges disagree, the appeal will be reheard by a three judge court.

We shall see later that some of the powers of the Court of Appeal may be exercised by a single judge (for example, the granting of leave to appeal). The single judge may be a Lord Justice of Appeal or else a High Court judge whom the Lord Chief Justice has asked to assist with the work of the Court of Appeal.

Section 52 of the Criminal Justice and Public Order Act 1994 enables circuit judges who have been approved by the Lord Chancellor to sit in the Court of Appeal (Criminal Division). A sitting of the court will not be able to include more than one circuit judge. Circuit judges will not be permitted to exercise the powers of the single judge (see 10.4 below). A circuit judge will not be allowed to sit in the Court of Appeal if the original trial was presided over by a High Court judge.

The administrative work of the court is carried out by the Registrar of Criminal Appeals.

10.3 PROCEDURE

10.3.1 The need for leave to appeal

Under s 1(2) of the Criminal Appeal Act 1968 (as amended by the Criminal Appeal Act 1995), an appeal against conviction may only be made if either:

(a) the Court of Appeal gives leave to appeal; or

(b) the trial judge certifies that the case is fit for appeal.

Certificates from the trial judge are very rare and are only granted if the case has raised a point of law where there is no authority giving an answer or where there are conflicting decisions of the Court of Appeal. In *R v Williams* [1992] 1 WLR 380; [1992] 2 All ER 183, it was emphasised that a certificate should only be given by the trial judge if exceptional circumstances are present; it is not enough that the trial judge simply disagrees with the verdict.

Again, in *R v Bansal* [1999] Crim LR 484, the Court of Appeal said that a trial judge should only certify that a case is fit for appeal if there are exceptional features to the case; otherwise, the granting of leave to appeal is a matter for the Court of Appeal. It follows that leave (permission) to appeal is required in almost every case.

It should be noted that, although Art 6 of the European Convention on Human Rights does not necessarily require there to be a possibility of appeal against conviction or sentence, where there is a mechanism for appeal any appellate proceedings will be treated as an extension of the trial process and so will be subject to the requirements of Art 6 of the Convention, which guarantees the right to a fair trial (*Monnell and Morris v UK* 10 EHRR 205). It should also be borne in mind that, for the purposes of the European Convention on Human Rights, unfairness at first instance can be remedied by an effective appellate process: *Adolf v Austria* 4 EHRR 313

10.3.2   Appeal against conviction where defendant pleaded guilty

We saw in Chapter 6, 6.2 that a defendant who pleads guilty in the magistrates' court cannot appeal against conviction to the Crown Court if he pleaded guilty (s 108 of the Magistrates' Courts Act 1980). There is no such rule in s 1 of the Criminal Appeal Act 1968.

However, the Court of Appeal is very unwilling to give leave to appeal against conviction to a defendant who pleaded guilty in the Crown Court. In *R v Forde* [1923] 2 KB 400, Avory J said that leave should only be given in such a case if either the appellant did not appreciate the nature of the charge or did not intend to admit he was guilty of it, or else that upon the admitted facts he could not in law have been convicted of the offence charged. In *R v Eriemo* (1994) 2 Cr App R 206, the Court of Appeal reaffirmed its reluctance to entertain appeals where the defendant pleaded guilty. In that case, the applicant (who had changed his plea to guilty following the trial judge's refusal to sever the indictment on the basis that the applicant was going to allege that he committed the offence under the duress of the co-defendant) was refused leave to appeal. It was said by Glidewell LJ that, where a defendant pleads guilty, he is making an admission of the facts which form the basis of the offence with which he is charged and therefore loses his right to appeal against conviction.

There have, however, been a considerable number of cases where a defendant who has pleaded guilty was allowed to appeal against conviction. For example, if a defendant is pressurised (for example, by comments from the judge) into pleading guilty, he will be allowed to appeal (*R v Turner* [1970] 2 QB 321 [1970] 2 All ER 281). Similarly, in *R v Bane* [1994] Crim LR 134, the judge told counsel that he was not willing to leave the defence of self-defence to the jury. The defendant changed his plea to guilty. The conviction was quashed because of the pressure to plead guilty which was caused by the judge's refusal to allow the jury to consider Bane's defence. Again, in *R v Boal* [1992] QB 591; [1992] 3 All ER 177, the defendant pleaded guilty because of erroneous legal advice by his counsel and so the Court of Appeal entertained his appeal against conviction.

Another situation where the defendant might be able to appeal against conviction even though he pleaded guilty is where the plea of guilty was entered after the judge made an incorrect ruling on the law. In *R v Kenny* [1994] Crim LR 284, for example, the defendant changed his plea to guilty following a decision by the trial judge that a confession (the only evidence against him) was admissible.

However, in *R v Greene* [1997] Crim LR 659, the Court of Appeal took a tougher line. The defendant had changed his plea to guilty following the rejection by the trial judge of a submission that the confession should be excluded under s 78 of the Police and Criminal Evidence Act 1984. The Court of Appeal said that his plea of guilty was an acknowledgment of the truth of the confession and the commission of the offence. The court said that, had the defendant maintained his plea of not guilty and been convicted, he could then have complained on appeal about the judge's ruling under s 78.

In *R v Chalkley* [1998] QB 848; [1998] 2 All ER 155, the Court of Appeal returned to the vexed question of whether a defendant who pleads guilty in the Crown Court can appeal against conviction to the Court of Appeal. The defendants originally pleaded not guilty, but the judge ruled that certain evidence against them (covertly obtained tape recordings of conversations) was admissible; the defendants changed their pleas to guilty. The court held that s 2(1) of the Criminal Appeal Act 1968 entitles the Court of Appeal to quash as unsafe a conviction based on a guilty plea if that plea was mistaken or uninformed or without intention to admit the truth of the offence charged. Furthermore, said Auld LJ, a conviction would be unsafe where the effect of an incorrect ruling of law on admitted facts was to leave the defendant with no legal escape from a verdict of guilty on those facts (that is, on the basis of the ruling an acquittal would be legally impossible, for example where the judge rejects the defendant's submission that admitted facts do not in law amount to the offence charged, and so there is no issue of fact for the jury to try). However, a conviction will not normally be unsafe where the defendant is influenced to change his plea to guilty because he recognises that, as a result of the judge's ruling that compelling evidence is admissible against him, his case on the facts is hopeless. Pleading guilty would, in such a case, amount to acknowledgement of the truth of the facts constituting the offence charged (unless, of course, the plea was mistaken or made without intention to admit guilt of the offence charged).

It is therefore important to distinguish between two situations: (a) where, in the light of an erroneous ruling, the defendant is left with no legal basis for a verdict of not guilty (and so an appeal will be entertained despite the guilty plea); and (b) where the guilty plea is influenced by an erroneous ruling of law, for example, to admit strong evidence against the defendant (where, because of the guilty plea, no appeal would be entertained).

10.3.3 Procedure for obtaining leave to appeal

A barrister (usually the one who conducted the case in the Crown Court) will be asked to write an advice on the merits of an appeal. If the barrister advises that an appeal is appropriate, draft grounds of appeal will be attached to the advice.

As a matter of professional conduct, counsel should only advise in favour of an appeal if there are proper grounds for doing so (*R v Morson* (1976) 62 Cr App R 236).

A notice of application for leave to appeal is then lodged at the Crown Court where the defendant was convicted. This must be done within 28 days of conviction (s 18(2) of the Criminal Appeal Act 1968). The notice must be accompanied by grounds of appeal (r 2 of the Criminal Appeal Rules). These grounds should be particularised so that the matters relied upon are clearly identified and set out in some detail.

In *R v Long* [1998] 2 Cr App R 326, the Court of Appeal pointed out that, under s 18(2) of the Criminal Appeal Act 1968, a notice of application for leave to appeal against conviction must be lodged within 28 days of conviction even if there is lapse of time between conviction and sentence. In other words, time begins to run from the date of conviction, not the date of sentence.

The Crown Court then passes the papers to the Registrar of Criminal Appeals.

10.3.4 Transcript of evidence and summing up

The registrar (when he receives the grounds of appeal) decides whether a transcript is necessary and, if so, how extensive it should be (bearing in mind the cost!). Normally, the transcript is limited to the summing up and to any judgment given by the judge during the course of the trial. If counsel for the would be appellant wants a more extensive transcript, reasons for this request must be given. A transcript of the evidence should only be sought if genuinely essential, as it is an expensive and time consuming procedure (*R v Flemming* (1987) 86 Cr App R 32).

10.3.5 'Perfecting' the grounds of appeal

The transcript is sent to counsel for the would-be appellant (free of charge if the appellant is legally aided), who then has the chance to 'perfect' the grounds of appeal (that is, referring those grounds to specific passages of the transcript – for example, 'the learned trial judge erred in that at [specific page number] he ...'). The grounds of appeal, or the advice on appeal written by counsel which accompanies the grounds, should also cite any authorities upon which counsel for the appellant proposes to rely.

Once the grounds of appeal have perfected, the papers are referred to a single judge to decide the question of leave to appeal.

10.3.6 Granting of leave to appeal: the single judge

The single judge considers the papers (without a hearing) and decides whether the appeal has a sufficient prospect of success to justify the granting of leave of appeal (s 31(2)(a) of the Criminal Appeal Act 1968).

In most cases, a single judge granting leave to appeal will give leave to appeal generally. However, the single judge has the power to grant leave on some grounds and refuse leave on others. Where leave to appeal has been refused on particular grounds, those grounds can only be argued before the court with its leave (*R v Cox* [1999] 2 Cr App R 6; *R v Jackson* [1999] 1 All ER 572).

The determination of the application for leave to appeal without the applicant being present or represented is not incompatible with Art 6 of the European Convention on Human Rights (*Monnell and Morris v UK* 10 EHRR 205).

10.3.7 Challenging the decision of the single judge

If the single judge refuses leave to appeal the appellant has 14 days (which can only be extended if there is very good reason (*R v Doherty* [1971] 1 WLR 1454; [1971] 3 All ER 622) in which to renew the application for leave (r 12). If the appellant does renew the application it will be heard by two or three Court of Appeal judges sitting in open court (s 31(3) of the Criminal Appeal Act 1968). The risk the defendant runs in renewing his application is that a 'direction for loss of time' is likely to be made if the Court of Appeal confirms the refusal of leave to appeal.

10.3.8 The direction for loss of time

This is governed by s 29 of the Criminal Appeal Act 1968 and a Practice Direction (1980). It is only relevant if the appellant is serving a custodial sentence. The direction is that some or all of the sentence served by the appellant between the date of the commencement of the appeal proceedings and the date when the application for leave or (as the case may be) the renewed application for leave to appeal is dismissed does not count towards the service of the appellant's sentence.

According to the Practice Direction, there is a presumption that the Court of Appeal will make a direction for loss of time if the appellant renews an application for leave which was dismissed by the single judge as 'wholly devoid of merit'; this is so even if a barrister has advised the renewal of the application.

As noted above, the single judge has the power to make a direction for loss of time when he initially refuses leave to appeal. The Practice Direction says that this should not be done if a barrister has advised in writing that an application for leave to appeal be made and has drafted grounds of appeal.

Where the single judge gives leave to appeal (or the application is successfully renewed) but the Court of Appeal ultimately dismisses the appeal, a direction for loss of time cannot be made if the appeal is ultimately unsuccessful (s 29(2)(a) of the Criminal Appeal Act 1968).

A direction for loss of time under s 29 does not amount to arbitrary detention and so is compatible with the right to liberty under Art 5 of the European Convention on Human Rights (*Monnell and Morris v UK* 10 EHRR 205)

10.3.9 Procedure where leave not required

In the very few cases where leave to appeal is not required, the barrister who conducted the case still has to draft grounds of appeal. The only difference in procedure is that the registrar will not refer the papers to a single judge; instead, the case will be listed for a full hearing by the Court of Appeal.

10.3.10 Frivolous appeals

If the Registrar of Criminal Appeals takes the view that a notice of appeal or an application for leave to appeal is frivolous or vexatious, he can refer it to a sitting of the Court of Appeal for summary determination without a full hearing. If the Court of Appeal dismisses the application summarily, this decision cannot be challenged (s 20 of the Criminal Appeal Act 1968). The Court of Appeal may thus dispose summarily of appeals which are obviously without merit and have no reasonable prospect of success (*R v Taylor* [1979] Crim LR 649).

10.3.11 By-passing the single judge

If the registrar takes the view that an application for leave to appeal discloses grounds which make an appeal likely to succeed, he may refer the case to the Court of Appeal so that the court itself can give leave and then go on to hear the appeal itself. This would be appropriate, for example, where a number of other cases are awaiting trial and the present appeal will be a test case to clarify the law and needs to be dealt with urgently.

10.3.12 Other powers of the Registrar of Criminal Appeals

Under s 31A of the Criminal Appeal Act 1968 (as amended by the Criminal Appeal Act 1995), the Registrar of Criminal Appeals is empowered to:

(a) extend the time within which notice of appeal or of application for leave to appeal may be given: the 28 day time limit may be extended under s 18(3) of the Criminal Appeal Act 1968. The test to be applied in deciding whether to grant an extension of time is whether the case is an exceptional one (*R v Hawkins* (1996) 1 Cr App R 234) and so the applicant has to show a very good reason for missing the time limit (see *R v Ramsden* [1972] Crim LR 547; *R v Burley* (1994) *The Times*, 9 November);

(b) order a witness to attend for examination (see 10.8 below); and

(c) vary the conditions of bail granted to an appellant by the Court of Appeal (see 10.4.2 below) or the Crown Court (provided that the respondent does not object: s 31A(3)).

If the registrar refuses an application on behalf of an appellant to exercise any of these powers, the appellant is 'entitled to have the application determined by a single judge' (s 31A(4)).

10.4 OTHER POWERS OF THE SINGLE JUDGE

As well as granting leave to appeal, the single judge also has jurisdiction (under s 31 of the Criminal Appeal Act 1968) to deal with the following matters.

10.4.1 Presence of appellant

Where the appellant is not in custody, he may be present on any occasion when his appeal is being heard or where interlocutory applications in respect of his appeal are being made in open court.

However, an appellant who is in custody has no right to attend interlocutory applications in respect of his appeal or, if the appeal is on a ground of law alone, the hearing of the appeal itself. The single judge may make an order permitting the appellant to be present at the hearing of the appeal if the appellant does not have a right to attend. No order is needed, as the appellant has the right to attend, if the appeal involves questions of fact (s 22 of the Criminal Appeal Act 1968).

Where an appellant absconds before his appeal has been heard, the normal practice is to adjourn the appeal or, if the justice of the case permits, to dismiss the appeal. However, in exceptional cases, the court might allow the appeal to be heard in the absence of the appellant (*R v Gooch* [1998] 1 WLR 110; [1998] 4 All ER 402).

10.4.2 Bail

Bail may be granted to the appellant under s 19 of the Criminal Appeal Act 1968. The application for bail is considered by the single judge without a hearing.

If the single judge refuses bail, the appellant can renew his bail application in open court if he gives notice that he wishes to do so within 14 days of the single judge's decision.

Bail pending appeal will only be granted if there are exceptional circumstances which drive the court to the conclusion that justice can only be done by the granting of bail (*R v Watton* (1978) 68 Cr App R 293). The case where the grant of bail is most likely is where it is likely that the appellant will have served his sentence before the appeal is disposed of.

- *Restrictions on Crown Court granting bail pending appeal*

  It should be noted that the Crown Court only has jurisdiction to grant bail to someone who is appealing against conviction and/or sentence if the trial judge has certified that the case is fit for appeal (s 81 of the Supreme Court Act 1981). Such certificates are, as we have seen, very rare, and so in most cases it will only be the single judge of the Court of Appeal who can grant bail to an appellant.

- *Expedited appeals*

  If the single judge refuses to grant bail but the appellant may have served his sentence before the appeal is disposed of, the single judge may order an expedited appeal so that the appellant does not have to wait as long as usual for the appeal to be heard.

10.4.3 Legal aid

Legal aid is available to defendants who appeal to the Court of Appeal. The registrar may grant legal aid but not refuse it. So, if the registrar does not grant legal aid, he must refer the application for legal aid to the single judge. If the appellant's means are such that he needs assistance with the cost of representation legal aid will be granted, as it would be very difficult for an unrepresented appellant to present his case (s 20(2) of the Legal Aid Act 1988).

Note that, if the appellant was legally aided for the trial, that certificate covers advice on appeal and drafting grounds of appeal (s 2(4)(c) of the Legal Aid Act 1988).

10.4.4 Direction for loss of time

As we have already seen, where the appellant received a custodial sentence, the single judge may make a direction for loss of time, ordering that the time spent in custody since conviction shall not count towards the service of the appellant's sentence. Such an order should not be made if the appeal was supported by written advice from counsel and counsel drafted the grounds of appeal.

10.5   THE HEARING OF THE APPEAL

Prior to the hearing, the judges and all counsel will have received a summary of the case from the registrar. These case summaries are prepared by the registrar's staff.

Counsel for the appellant should also submit a skeleton argument in good time for the hearing.

The appeal takes the form of argument based on the grounds of appeal, the transcript of the summing up and any other documentary evidence.

Counsel for the appellant presents his case first and counsel for the respondent (the prosecution) then replies. Unless it is a case where the conviction is said to be unsafe because of fresh evidence (see 10.7 below), no oral evidence will be heard by the court.

10.6   GROUNDS OF APPEAL AGAINST CONVICTION

Under s 2(1) of the 1968 Act (as amended by the Criminal Appeal Act 1995), the Court of Appeal 'shall allow an appeal against conviction if they think that the conviction is unsafe'. Otherwise, they must dismiss the appeal. In other words, there is a single ground of appeal against conviction, that the conviction was 'unsafe'.

There is no statutory definition of the word 'unsafe'. However, it was said in Parliament that the new test was intended to restate the existing practice of the Court of Appeal. It follows that a conviction would be held to be 'unsafe' if the members of the Court of Appeal feel that there is 'some lurking doubt in our minds which makes us wonder whether an injustice has been done' (*R v Cooper* [1969] 1 QB 267; [1969] 1 All ER 32; *Stafford v DPP* [1974] AC 878; [1973] 3 All ER 762).

However, in *R v Farrow* [1999] Crim LR 306, the Court of Appeal deprecated the use of the 'lurking doubt' test for appeals against conviction and said that the court should focus on the wording of the statutory test of whether the conviction is unsafe.

The original version contained a 'proviso' to s 2(1) of the Criminal Appeal Act 1968. This was because there were other grounds of appeal (a material irregularity in the course of the trial or a wrong decision on a question of law). It was open to the Court of Appeal to decide that something had gone wrong during the trial but that there had been no miscarriage of justice, in that the conviction was safe. This proviso has been removed: under the new formulation, it is unnecessary, since a conviction could not be 'safe' if a miscarriage of justice has occurred.

10.6.1   Errors in the course of trial

Matters which are capable of rendering a conviction unsafe include the following:

(1) A decision by the judge that certain evidence against the defendant was admissible. If the Court of Appeal decides that the evidence in question ought to have been excluded, the judges will go on to consider what impact this mistake had on the trial: for example, how strong was the other (admissible) evidence against the accused.

(2) The wrongful rejection by the judge of a submission that there is no case to answer (for example, *R v Abbott* [1955] 2 QB 497; [1955] 2 All ER 899). Where a defendant appeals against conviction on the ground that the trial judge wrongly rejected a submission of no case to answer at the end of the prosecution case, the Court of Appeal should ignore any evidence admitted after the submission of no case. Therefore, if the defendant admits his guilt during cross-examination, the conviction should still be set aside if the submission of no case was rejected wrongly (*R v Cockley* (1984) 79 Cr App R 181; *R v Smith* [2000] 1 All ER 263; [1999] 2 Cr App R 23).

(3) Irregularities occurring during the course of the trial, for example misconduct on the part of a juror (as where a juror was seen in conversation with a prosecution witness during an adjournment). Another example of something going wrong in the course of the trial is provided by *R v Maguire* [1996] Crim LR 838. A witness called by the defendant repeatedly refused to answer certain questions regarding his own whereabouts at the time of the alleged offence. The judge, in the presence of the jury, ordered the witness to be arrested and taken down to the cells. The Court of Appeal accepted the argument that the jury might have been affected by seeing an important defence witness being arrested. The judge should have invited the jury to retire before ordering the arrest of the witness. The appeal was therefore allowed and a re-trial ordered.

(4) Errors in the summing up: see Chapter 9, 9.18 for details of what the summing up must contain and how the various components should be dealt with.

(5) The judge's conduct of the trial: in *R v Whybrow* (1994) 144 New LJ 124, the Court of Appeal expressed support for the recommendation of the 1993 Royal Commission on Criminal Justice that judges should be more interventionist in order to prevent trials becoming protracted. However, such intervention must not go beyond legitimate bounds. If, for example, a witness gives an ambiguous answer, the judge should have it clarified. If a witness gives a long answer, the judge may ask the witness to confirm the gist of that answer so that there is no misunderstanding. What the judge must not do is to become an advocate. The court approved a *dictum* of Cumming-Bruce LJ in *R v Gunning* (1980), reported (1994) 98 Cr App R 303,

comparing the function of the judge with that of an umpire in a cricket match:

> He is certainly not the bowler, whose business is to get the batsman out. If a judge ... descends into the forum and asks great numbers of pointed questions of the accused when he is giving his evidence-in-chief, the jury may well get the impression that the judge does not believe a word that the witness is saying and by putting these pointed questions, to which there is sometimes only a lame answer, he blows the evidence out of the water during the stage that counsel ought to be having the opportunity to bring the evidence of the accused to the attention of the jury in its most impressive pattern and shape.

In both cases, it was stressed that the opportunity to examine-in-chief without interruption is particularly important 'if the evidence emerging in chief is a story that takes a bit of swallowing'. In *R v Wiggan* (1999) *The Times*, 22 March, after the defendant had been re-examined by her counsel, the judge asked some 64 questions of a testing nature, suggesting scepticism of the defendant's evidence. The Court of Appeal held that, after a witness has been re-examined, it is open to the judge to ask questions to clear up uncertainties, to fill gaps, or to answer queries which might be lurking in the jury's mind. However, it is not appropriate for the judge to cross-examine the witness. Similarly, in *R v Tuegel* [2000] 2 All ER 872, the Court of Appeal held that although a judge should avoid asking a witness questions which appear to suggest that the judge is taking sides, he has a duty to ask questions which clarify ambiguities in answers previously given or which identify the nature of the defence, if that is unclear. Such questions should usually be asked at, or close to, the time when the ambiguity first becomes apparent. The court went on to say that although it might exceptionally be necessary for a judge, in the presence of the jury, to interrupt a speech by counsel, it is generally preferable for him not to do so. Ideally, interventions for the purpose of clarifying or correcting something said, either by judge or counsel, should be made in the first instance in the absence of the jury and at a break in the proceedings, so that, if necessary, the point could be dealt with before the jury in an appropriate fashion.

(6) Errors by defence counsel: in *R v Ullah* [2000] 1 Cr App R 351, defence counsel was aware of the existence of evidence that cast doubt on the veracity of the complainant's evidence; this evidence was not put before the court (possibly because its admissibility was rather doubtful). Had the jury known about this evidence, it would have seriously damaged the prosecution case. The Court of Appeal held (following *R v Clinton* (1993) 97 Cr App R 320) that a conviction will not be unsafe merely because defence counsel took a decision that another counsel might not have taken; the Court of Appeal will only have regard to 'significant' fault by trial counsel or solicitor. The court said that it may well be appropriate to apply the *Wednesbury Corporation* ([1948] 1 KB 223) test of unreasonableness: was the decision one that no reasonable advocate could have reached?

(7) Events before the trial: A conviction may be rendered unsafe by events which occurred before the trial started. In *R v Mullen* [1999] 3 WLR 777, for example, the appellant's deportation to this country had been procured by unlawful means. There was no complaint about the conduct of the trial but it was argued that the trial should never have taken place, since there had been abuse of process by the prosecution prior to the trial. The Court of Appeal confirmed that a conviction can be 'unsafe' under s 2 of the Criminal Appeal Act 1968 as a result of matters occurring prior to the trial itself.

In *R v Davis, Rowe and Johnson* (2000) *The Times*, 25 July, the Court of Appeal had to decide how to deal with the fact that the European Court of Human Rights had held that there had been a breach of Art 6.1 of the Convention (the right to a fair trial) during the trial of these defendants, and that this had not been cured by the appeal process. The court had to consider the effect of this ruling on the application of the Criminal Appeal Act 1968 to the defendants' convictions. The court held that the Court of Appeal is concerned only with the safety of a conviction. A conviction can never be safe if there is doubt about the appellant's guilt. However, a conviction might be unsafe even if there is no doubt about the appellant's guilt but the trial process was vitiated by serious unfairness or significant legal misdirection (see *R v Smith (Patrick Joseph)* (1999) *The Times*, 31 May and *R v B (Attorney General's Reference No 3 of 1999)*; *R v Weir* (2000) *The Times*, 16 June). Usually, the court should apply the test in *Stirland v DPP* [1944] AC 315 and ask itself: 'Assuming the wrong decision on law or the misdirection had not occurred and the trial had been free from legal error, would the only reasonable and proper verdict have been one of guilty?' The European Court of Human Rights is charged with inquiring into whether there has been a breach of a Convention right; the Court of Appeal is concerned with the safety of the conviction. Obviously, the first question might intrude upon the second, but the extent to which it did so would depend upon the circumstances of the particular case. A finding of a breach of Art 6.1 of the Convention would not lead inexorably to the quashing of a conviction. The effect of any unfairness upon the safety of a conviction would vary according to its nature and degree. The court went on to hold that the unfairness in the present case did cast doubt of the safety of the convictions, which were accordingly quashed.

10.6.2   Appeals relating to the jury

Apart from instances of misconduct by jurors, there are special rules which deal with appeals which are based on complaints about the jury. Those rules are contained in s 18 of the Juries Act 1974. This provides that a conviction may not be quashed on any of the following grounds:

(a) that the provisions of the Act regarding the selection of the jury have not been complied with;

(b) that a juror was not qualified to serve (see Chapter 9, 9.7 for the rules on who can be a juror);

(c) that a juror was unfit to serve. In *R v Chapman and Lauday* (1976) 63 Cr App R 75, this was held to include an allegation that one of the jurors was partially deaf and so missed most of the evidence. The Court of Appeal did say in that case that, although such unfitness could not amount to a material irregularity, it could be used as one factor amongst others rendering the conviction unsafe.

On allegations that jurors were biased, see *R v Bean* [1991] Crim LR 843 and *R v Gough* [1993] AC 646; [1992] 4 All ER 481, discussed in Chapter 9, 9.8.2.

In addition to the statutory restriction contained in s 18, it is a strict rule that the Court of Appeal will not investigate what went on in the jury room while the jury were considering their verdict: *R v Bean* [1991] Crim LR 843, where the defence wanted to adduce evidence from the jury bailiff that he had overheard an exchange which could be regarded as one juror being pressurised into voting in favour of conviction. In *R v Thompson* [1962] 1 All ER 65, the Court of Appeal refused to hear evidence that most of the jury had been in favour of an acquittal until the foreman of the jury had read out a list of the defendant's previous convictions (which had not been referred to in court).

Likewise, in *R v Roads* [1967] 2 QB 108; [1967] 2 All ER 84, the Court of Appeal would not hear evidence that one of the jurors had in fact disagreed with the verdict announced by the foreman. In *R v Less* (1993) *The Times*, 30 March, the Court of Appeal disregarded letters from jurors saying that they disagreed with the verdict. Similarly, in *R v Scholfield* [1993] Crim LR 217, the Court of Appeal refused to entertain evidence of a conversation between a juror and the jury bailiff in which it became apparent that the jury did not understand the legal definition of the charge.

In *R v Miah; R v Akhbar* [1997] 2 Cr App R 12, the Court of Appeal reaffirmed the rule that it will not receive evidence of discussions which take place in the jury room.

In any event, it was pointed out in *R v Mickleburgh* [1995] 1 Cr App R 297 that taking a statement from a juror about the deliberations which took place in the jury room could well amount to contempt under s 8 of the Contempt of Court Act 1981. Following *R v McCluskey* (1993) 98 Cr App R 216, it was held that such inquiries should only take place with the consent of the Court of Appeal.

In *R v Millward* [1999] 1 Cr App R 61, after a majority verdict direction had been given, the jury later returned to court. They were asked if they had reached a verdict on which at least 10 of them were agreed. The foreman said that they had. The verdict was guilty. The clerk asked whether it was a verdict of all the jury or by a majority. The foreman replied 'all'. A juror subsequently wrote to the court saying that in fact it was a 10:2 majority verdict in favour of conviction. The Court of Appeal said that there had been a clear statement from the foreman that the verdict was unanimous, and so the court did not have to make the further inquiries required by s 17(3) of the Juries Act 1974 (see Chapter 9, 9.22.2). Furthermore, the Court of Appeal was not entitled to inquire into what went on in the jury room.

In *R v Young* [1995] 2 WLR 430, it was said by the Court of Appeal that s 8 of the Contempt of Court Act 1981 applies only to deliberations which take place in the jury room. Thus, it did not prevent the court from inquiring into what took place if the jury were not allowed to go home after they had retired to consider their verdict (see Chapter 9, 9.19.1) but had been sent to stay in an hotel overnight instead. In the present case (a murder trial), a re-trial was ordered because, during the overnight adjournment, some members of the jury had used an Ouija board to try to get in touch with the murder victim to ask him who had committed the murder.

10.7   FRESH EVIDENCE IN THE COURT OF APPEAL

One reason for a conviction being unsafe is that new evidence has come to light which casts doubt on the conviction. Another reason is that the trial judge wrongly declared certain evidence to be inadmissible. In either case, the Court of Appeal has a discretion to receive evidence which was not adduced at the trial.

Section 23(1) of the Criminal Appeal Act 1968 empowers the Court of Appeal to receive fresh evidence. Section 23(2) of the Criminal Appeal Act 1968 says that the:

Court of Appeal shall, in considering whether to receive any evidence, have regard in particular to:

(a) whether the evidence appears to the court to be capable of belief;

(b) whether it appears to the court that the evidence may afford any ground for allowing the appeal;

(c) whether the evidence would have been admissible in the proceedings from which the appeal lies on an issue which is the subject of the appeal; and

(d) whether there is a reasonable explanation for the failure to adduce the evidence in those proceedings.

To assess the credibility of the witness for the purpose of s 23(2)(a), the court should either be provided with an affidavit or a written witness statement or else the registrar must have been asked to arrange for an out-of-court deposition to be taken by an examiner appointed by the court. In *R v Gogana* (1999) *The Times*, 12 July, the Court of Appeal emphasised the importance of this requirement, particularly where it is suggested that a witness who has previously made a statement is now prepared to give different evidence. In such a case, the court must be supplied with affidavit evidence from all those involved in the taking of the new statement (since the circumstances in which that new statement came into existence are highly relevant to its potential credibility).

In assessing credibility, the court will consider whether the evidence is intrinsically credible and whether it fits in with at least some of the evidence adduced at trial (*R v Parks* [1961] 1 WLR 1484; [1961] 3 All ER 633).

As far as s 23(2)(b) is concerned, in *R v Gilfoyle* [1996] 3 All ER 883, Beldam LJ said 'We are satisfied that the interests of justice are not simply confined to receiving evidence which would result in an appeal being allowed, particularly when the court is being asked to review as unsafe ... the verdict of a jury after an impeccable summing up on the ground that it has a lurking doubt' (*per* Beldam LJ at p 898). The court is therefore empowered to receive admissible evidence which reinforces or dispels a lurking doubt.

Section 23(2)(c) simply requires that the evidence be admissible (for example, not hearsay). Where the trial judge ruled that certain evidence was inadmissible, it is open to the Court of Appeal, if it rules that the evidence was in fact admissible, to receive that evidence itself.

The fact that counsel for the defence took a tactical decision not to call a particular witness is not a reasonable explanation for the failure to adduce the evidence at trial for the purpose of s 23(2)(d), and so the Court of Appeal is unlikely to hear the evidence of that witness (*R v Shields and Patrick* [1977] Crim LR 281). In *R v Ahluwalia* [1992] 4 All ER 889, however, the Court of Appeal received evidence of the appellant's diminished responsibility, which evidence had been available for use at the trial but which had not been used as the appellant had relied instead on the defence of provocation. The Court of Appeal made it clear that this was an exceptional case and that it would not ordinarily receive evidence which was available at trial but not used.

Where evidence could not have been obtained with 'reasonable diligence' in time for the trial (for example, a relevant witness has only just come forward), there is a reasonable explanation for not adducing that evidence at the trial (*R v Beresford* (1971) 56 Cr App R 143). In *Beresford*, the appellant wished to rely on the evidence of alibi witnesses who had not been called at the trial. The defence solicitors had not been given the names and addresses of the potential witnesses. However, as the appellant could have supplied this information to his solicitors before the trial, the Court of Appeal held that there was not a reasonable explanation for the failure to adduce the evidence at trial.

Even if there is no reasonable explanation for the failure to adduce particular evidence at trial, it might nevertheless be expedient in the interests of justice to receive that fresh evidence (provided that it would have been admissible at the trial, is capable of belief, and might afford a ground for allowing the appeal): see *R v Sale* (2000) *The Times*, 14 June and *R v Cairns* [2000]

Crim LR 473, where the Court of Appeal noted that it is possible for the court to receive fresh evidence under s 23 of the Criminal Appeal Act 1968 even if all of the four criteria in sub-ss 2(a)–(d) are not satisfied.

Where an appellant wishes the Court of Appeal to receive fresh evidence under s 23 of the Criminal Appeal Act 1968 and the circumstances give rise to the need for a lengthy or complex explanation of why the evidence was not adduced at the original trial, an affidavit or signed statement from the appellant or his solicitor, setting out the grounds relied on, should be usually be supplied to the Court.

In *R v Jones* [1997] 1 Cr App R 86, the Court of Appeal considered the position of expert witnesses. As far as s 23(2)(d) is concerned, the requirement of a reasonable explanation for the failure to adduce the evidence at trial, this applies more aptly to factual evidence of which a party was unaware or could not adduce at the trial. Expert witnesses, unlike factual witnesses, are interchangeable, even though they may vary in standing. A defendant who is unable to call a particular expert at the trial should either apply for a postponement of the trial or else should try to find a different expert witness. Having said that, the Court of Appeal decided that it was in the interests of justice in the present case to receive the evidence of the three expert witnesses upon whom the appellant wishes to rely.

In *R v Garner* [1997] *Archbold News*, 13 March, the Court of Appeal drew a distinction between cases involving (on one hand) the new discovery of an earlier suppression or mistake, or evidence dealing with an area hitherto unknown, or unappreciated, scientific or technical advance, or a confession of error or change of opinion by an expert who was called at the trial, and (on the other hand) on the facts which were known at the trial, opinion within the relevant profession as represented by the experts called at (or consulted before) the trial was broadly agreed, but the defence have since found an expert who is in significant disagreement with such opinion. In the latter case, the court should think long and hard before permitting the evidence to be adduced on appeal.

As we have seen, the Court of Appeal decides whether or not to receive fresh evidence on the basis of written witness statements. If the Court of Appeal decides to receive the evidence, the witnesses have to attend court to give their evidence unless the court regards the written statement it has already seen as sufficient. Each witness is usually examined-in-chief on behalf of the appellant and cross-examined on behalf of the Crown.

10.8   RESULT OF APPEAL AGAINST CONVICTION

The Court of Appeal has a number of options open to it when disposing of an appeal against conviction.

10.8.1   Appeal dismissed

If the Court of Appeal decides that the appellant's conviction was safe, it will dismiss the appeal and the appellant's conviction will stand.

10.8.2   Successful appeal

If the Court of Appeal decides that one or more of the statutory grounds of appeal is made out, the Court of Appeal has up to four options:

*   *To quash the conviction*

    The appellant is regarded for all purposes as if he had been acquitted by the jury. The doctrine of *autrefois acquit* applies, so the appellant cannot be re-prosecuted for the same offence.

    If the Court of Appeal allows the appellant's appeal on some counts of an indictment but not others, the Court of Appeal may also review the sentence. However, if the sentence is altered, it must not be more severe than that imposed by the Crown Court.

*   *To order a re-trial*

    Section 7 of the Criminal Appeal Act 1968 provides that the Court of Appeal may order a re-trial if the interests of justice so require.

    If the appeal is allowed after the Court of Appeal has heard fresh evidence, a re-trial will usually be ordered so that a jury can hear all the evidence. If, on the other hand, the fresh evidence clearly establishes that the appellant is innocent of the charge, the Court of Appeal will simply quash the conviction.

    No re-trial will be ordered if the original trial took place so long ago that the memories of the witnesses would have faded, making a fair trial impossible (*R v Saunders* (1973) 58 Cr App R 248). Furthermore, if the appellant has already spent time in custody so that he has, in effect, already served whatever sentence would be appropriate were he to be found guilty on a re-trial, no re-trial will be ordered (*R v Newland* [1988] QB 402; [1988] 2 All ER 891).

    Section 8 of the Criminal Appeal Act 1968 says that where a re-trial has been ordered a fresh indictment must be preferred within two months of the order; if it is not preferred within that time, the defendant may apply to the Court of Appeal for the order to be set aside. Such an application will succeed unless the prosecution can show that they have acted with all due expedition (that is, all reasonable promptness) and there is good and sufficient cause for a re-trial despite the delay.

*   *To order a venire de novo*

    There will be some rare cases where the statutory power to order a re-trial will not be available. This will be the case where the proceedings at the trial were a nullity. Examples of this are where some irregularity of procedure has occurred so that no trial was validly commenced (an extreme instance of this would be if a defendant were to be tried in the Crown Court without there having been committal proceedings or a valid alternative to committal proceedings) or where the trial comes to an end without a properly constituted jury ever having returned a valid verdict (an instance of this would be where the number of jurors remaining falls below the statutory minimum of nine but the judge nevertheless allows the trial to continue and accepts a 'verdict' from the remaining jurors). In such a case, if the Court of Appeal wishes to order a re-trial, it does so by means of a writ of *venire de novo* (see *R v Rose* [1982] 2 All ER 731).

In *R v O'Donnell* [1996] 1 Cr App R 286, for example, the question arose as to the defendant's fitness to plead. The judge decided to postpone consideration of this issue until the completion of the prosecution case. At the end of the prosecution case, the judge empanelled a different jury to determine whether the defendant was fit to plead. That jury decided that the defendant was not fit to plead. In breach of s 4A(2) of the Criminal Procedure (Insanity) Act 1964, the judge then recalled the first jury and carried on with the trial. That jury subsequently found the defendant guilty of the offence. Because the trial should not have continued after the finding that the defendant was unfit to plead, the conviction was a nullity; thus, there was no conviction for the defendant to appeal against for the purposes of s 2 of the Criminal Appeal Act 1968. Nonetheless, the Court of Appeal used its inherent jurisdiction to set aside and annul the 'conviction' and then exercised its discretion to order a *venire de novo*.

Where the Court of Appeal allows an appeal on the ground that there has been an irregularity which vitiates the whole trial but decides not to grant an order for re-trial (*venire de novo*), the proper form of order is that the conviction 'be set aside and annulled and that there be no new trial'. There is no conviction to quash (since the purported conviction is a nullity) and so there is no power to grant a statutory acquittal under the Criminal Appeal Act 1968 (*R v Booth* [1999] 1 Cr App R 457).

- *To substitute a conviction for an alternative offence*

Section 3 of the Criminal Appeal Act 1968 provides that if:

(a) the jury could on the indictment have found the appellant guilty of some other offence; and

(b) the jury must have been satisfied of facts which proved him guilty of the other offence,

the Court of Appeal may quash the conviction appealed against but replace it with a conviction for that other offence.

For example, in *R v Spratt* [1980] 1 WLR 554; [1980] 2 All ER 269, a conviction for manslaughter was substituted for the conviction of murder and, in *R v Blackford* (1989) 89 Cr App R 239, a conviction for possession of cannabis with intent to supply was replaced by a conviction for possession of cannabis.

The first requirement in s 3 of the Criminal Appeal Act 1968 means that the Court of Appeal must consider whether the jury could, on the indictment they were trying, have found the appellant guilty of some other offence (under s 6 of the Criminal Law Act 1967 or other statutory provisions dealing with specific offences).

The second requirement in s 3 means that the Court of Appeal has to consider the evidence which was put before the jury. In *R v Graham* (1997) 1 Cr App R 302, the Court of Appeal said that in considering this requirement, the court would have regard to whether or not the jury had been given a proper direction on the other offence and to the question whether there were reasonable grounds for concluding that the conduct of the defence would have been materially affected if the appellant had been charged with that other offence.

If the Court of Appeal does quash the conviction appealed against but substitutes a conviction for a different offence, it must then go on to review the sentence imposed by the Crown Court, although, if the Court of Appeal alters the sentence, it must not impose a sentence which is more severe than the original sentence.

In *R v Horsman* [1997] 3 All ER 385, the Court of Appeal held that where the defendant pleads guilty in the Crown Court to an offence and then appeals against that conviction, and the Court of Appeal quashes the conviction, the Court of Appeal has no power under s 3 of the Criminal Appeal Act 1968 to substitute a conviction for an alternative offence. That power applies only where the defendant was convicted by the jury of the offence which gives rise to the appeal against conviction.

10.9   APPEAL AGAINST SENTENCE

Section 9 of the Criminal Appeal Act 1968 provides that a person sentenced following conviction on indictment may appeal against that sentence to the Court of Appeal.

Sentence includes an order to pay prosecution costs (*R v Hayden* [1975] 1 WLR 852; [1975] 2 All ER 558) and a compensation order (*R v Vivian* [1979] 1 WLR 291; [1979] 1 All ER 48).

Section 10 of the Criminal Appeal Act 1968 states that a person who was convicted by a magistrates' court but was sentenced by the Crown Court following committal for sentence may appeal to the Court of Appeal if:

- the Crown Court imposed a sentence in excess of the sentence which the magistrates could have imposed (that is, more than six months' imprisonment for a single offence or the sentence is otherwise in excess of the power of the magistrates (in the rare cases where a maximum of less than six months is applicable)); or

- the Crown Court disqualifies the defendant from driving; or
- the Crown Court activates a suspended sentence because the offence for which he was committed for sentence was in breach of that suspended sentence.

10.9.1 Leave to appeal

Section 11 of the Criminal Appeal Act 1968 provides that leave is always required in order to appeal against sentence unless the trial judge certifies the sentence fit for appeal. Certificates are hardly ever given and are discouraged by the Court of Appeal. In *R v Grant* (1990) 12 Cr App R(S) 441, for example, it was said that, if the judge has second thoughts about a sentence he has imposed, he should use his power under s 155 of the Powers of Criminal Courts (Sentencing) Act 2000 to vary the sentence (provided that no more than 28 days have elapsed since the sentence was imposed) or else allow the case to proceed through the ordinary process of appeal; he should not grant a certificate that the sentence is fit for appeal.

It should be emphasised that leave to appeal is needed even if the sentence is wrong in law.

10.9.2 Procedure

The procedure for obtaining leave to appeal is virtually identical to that for obtaining leave to appeal against conviction. Within 28 days of sentence, the appellant has to lodge notice of application for leave to appeal against sentence at the Crown Court which passed the sentence. Grounds of appeal (usually drafted by counsel), based on the remarks made by the judge when passing sentence, are drafted. The papers are sent to the Registrar of Criminal Appeals, who refers them to a single judge to decide whether leave to appeal should be given. Again, the test is whether the appeal has a reasonable prospect of success. The appellant has 14 days to renew the application for leave to appeal if the single judge refuses leave.

10.9.3 The hearing

At the hearing of the appeal (assuming leave is granted), the appellant will usually be represented by counsel (and the single judge will grant legal aid for this purpose if the appellant's means are insufficient). The Crown will not usually be represented, however, as it is not part of the role of the prosecution to advocate for a higher sentence.

10.10 GROUNDS OF APPEAL AGAINST SENTENCE

Unlike appeals against conviction, the Criminal Appeal Act 1968 does not specify grounds for appeal against sentence. However, the following grounds may be derived from case law.

10.10.1 Sentence wrong in law

If the judge imposes a sentence which he has no jurisdiction to impose, that sentence can be set aside by the Court of Appeal. This would apply if the judge imposed a sentence of three years' imprisonment for an offence which carries a maximum of two years' imprisonment. In *R v Corcoran* (1986) 8 Cr App R(S) 118, for example, a Crown Court judge imposed a sentence of long term detention on a juvenile who had been committed for sentence following conviction in a youth court; thus the offender had not been convicted on indictment, and so a sentence under s 53(2) of the Children and Young Persons Act 1933 was clearly unlawful.

Such cases are, of course, very rare as most judges know the extent of their sentencing power. Furthermore, it is the duty of both prosecuting and defence counsel to make themselves aware of the sentencing options that are available and to draw the judge's attention to any mistake he makes (*R v Clarke* (1974) 59 Cr App R 298; *R v Kennedy* [1976] Crim LR 508; *R v Komsta* (1990) 12 Cr App R(S) 63; *R v Hartrey* (1993) 14 Cr App R(S) 507).

10.10.2 Sentence wrong in principle

A sentence which is wrong in principle occurs where the Crown Court judge imposes the wrong form of sentence. For example, an appellant who receives a custodial sentence argues that the offence was not so serious that only a custodial sentence was appropriate (s 1 of the Criminal Justice Act 1991).

In *R v Nuttall* (1908) 1 Cr App R 180, it was said that the appellant must show that he was dealt with in a way which was outside the broad range of penalties appropriate to the case.

10.10.3 Sentence manifestly excessive

This is where the Crown Court judge imposed the correct form of sentence but nevertheless imposed too severe a sentence. For example, the judge imposes a sentence of three years' imprisonment in a case where 18 months would be more appropriate.

In *R v Gumbs* (1926) 19 Cr App R 74, Lord Hewart CJ said:

This court never interferes with the discretion of the court below merely on the ground that this court might have passed a somewhat different sentence; for this court to revise a sentence there must be some error in principle.

10.10.4   Wrong approach to sentencing

The Court of Appeal will interfere with a sentence if the judge adopted the wrong approach to the sentencing process. This occurs where the judge ignores relevant factors or takes account of irrelevant factors. In *R v Skone* (1965) 51 Cr App R 165, for example, the judge incorrectly penalised the defendant for casting imputations on the veracity of the prosecution witnesses. Similarly, in *R v Doab* [1983] Crim LR 569, the judge wrongly increased the sentence because the defendant had chosen Crown Court trial for an offence which could have been tried in the magistrates' court.

10.10.5   Procedural errors

The Court of Appeal will also interfere if there has been a procedural error. An example of a procedural error is where the judge failed to hold a *Newton* hearing where defence and prosecution versions of events differ significantly where the defendant has pleaded guilty (see Chapter 9, 9.27).

10.10.6   Legitimate sense of grievance

If a judge gives an indication that a custodial sentence will not be imposed, the Court of Appeal will interfere if a custodial sentence is subsequently imposed for that offence (*R v Moss* (1984) 5 Cr App R(S) 209).

If a court adjourns for pre-sentence reports, it should be made clear to the defendant that the court is nevertheless keeping all its sentencing options open (*R v Gillam* (1980) 2 Cr App R(S) 267; *R v Horton* (1985) 7 Cr App R(S) 299).

10.10.7   Disparity

In *Attorney General's Reference (Nos 62, 63 and 64 of 1995)* [1996] 2 Cr App R(S) 223, the Court of Appeal pointed out that it is wrong to pass the same sentence on two defendants when one has strong personal mitigation and the other does not; in such a case, disparity is to be encouraged.

Where two offenders are sentenced for an offence which they have committed jointly, any difference in sentence should only result from differing degrees of involvement in the offence or from personal mitigating circumstances. Even if a difference cannot be so justified, an appeal on the basis of disparity will only succeed in rare cases.

If the heavier of the two sentences is the correct one, the Court of Appeal will not generally reduce it to bring it in line with the more lenient sentence: this would convert one right sentence and one wrong sentence into two wrong sentences. The main question is whether the appellant's sentence is excessive in itself (*R v Stroud* (1977) 65 Cr App R 150; *R v Nooy* (1982) 4 Cr App R(S) 308).

An appeal will only succeed on the ground of disparity if the appellant would otherwise be left with a justifiable and burning sense of grievance (*R v Potter* [1977] Crim LR 112, unreported, and *R v Dickinson* [1977] Crim LR 303). As Lawton LJ put it in *R v Fawcett* (1983) 5 Cr App R(S) 158, would right thinking members of the public, with full knowledge of the facts and circumstances, hearing of this sentence consider that something has gone wrong with the administration of justice?

10.11   EFFECT OF APPEAL AGAINST SENTENCE

If the appeal is dismissed, the original sentence stands.

If the Court of Appeal allows the appeal it may quash the sentence and replace it with the appropriate sentence.

Section 11(3) of the Criminal Appeal Act 1968 provides that, taking the case as a whole, the appellant should not be dealt with more severely by the Court of Appeal than he was dealt with by the Crown Court.

Two examples may assist in interpreting the restrictions imposed by s 11(3):

- An appellant is sentenced to two years' imprisonment on count 1 and 12 months' imprisonment on count 2 and the judge ordered the terms to run consecutively, making a total of three years. The Court of Appeal could substitute sentences of 12 months on count 1 (a reduction) and two years on count 2 (an increase), to run consecutively: the original total of three years is not exceeded.

- An appellant is sentenced to two years on count 1 and three years on count 2, these terms to run consecutively (making a total of five years). The Court of Appeal could theoretically substitute sentences of five years on each count to run concurrently, as the total of five years is not exceeded.

Note that the Court of Appeal cannot replace a suspended sentence of imprisonment with a sentence of immediate custody, even if the term is the same as or less than the original term that was suspended (*R v Peppard* (1990) 12 Cr App R(S) 88). However, where a term of imprisonment is reduced the

Court of Appeal may impose a fine as well (*R v Walton* (1989) 29 August, unreported).

10.12   APPEALS BY THE PROSECUTION

If a person is acquitted by the Crown Court, that acquittal cannot be challenged. Unlike cases which were tried by a magistrates' court, the prosecution cannot appeal against an acquittal even if the acquittal was based on a mistaken understanding of the law. However, the prosecution can ask the Court of Appeal to clarify the law. The prosecution can also, in certain cases, challenge an excessively lenient sentence imposed by the Crown Court.

10.12.1   Attorney General's reference

Where a defendant has been acquitted following trial on indictment and the Attorney General thinks that the trial judge misdirected the jury on a point of law, he may refer the case to the Court of Appeal. This power is contained in s 36 of the Criminal Justice Act 1972.

The acquittal is not in jeopardy as the Court of Appeal cannot reverse an acquittal, but the reference does enable the Court of Appeal to clarify the law. Thus, judges in subsequent trials will not make the same mistake (*Attorney General's Reference (No 1 of 1975)* [1975] QB 773; [1975] 2 All ER 684).

The acquitted defendant cannot be named unless he gives his permission.

This power is only relevant to acquittal following trial on indictment. Where the defendant was acquitted following summary trial and there was an error of law, the prosecution can challenge the acquittal by asking the magistrates to state a case for the opinion of the High Court (s 111 of the Magistrates' Courts Act 1980) and the High Court has power to quash the acquittal (see Chapter 6, 6.3).

10.12.2   Attorney General's reference: excessively lenient sentences

Sections 35 and 36 of the Criminal Justice Act 1988 enable the Attorney General to appeal against excessively lenient sentences imposed by the Crown Court. Three restrictions apply:

• this power only applies in respect of offences which are triable only on indictment or which are triable either way and have been prescribed by statutory instrument (currently the latter category comprises only indecent assault, making threats to kill, cruelty to or neglect of children and serious fraud cases);

- the Attorney General requires leave from a single judge of the Court of Appeal in order to bring such an appeal;
- the Court of Appeal may increase the sentence (but not beyond the maximum which the Crown Court could have imposed) only if it holds that the original sentence was excessively lenient.

Section 36(3) of the Criminal Justice Act 1988 and s 10(4) of the Criminal Appeal Act 1968, taken together, provide that if the Crown Court sentences the defendant for two offences, one triable only on indictment and the other triable either way and not listed on the 1994 Order, the Attorney General may refer both sentences to the Court of Appeal provided that either:

- the sentences were imposed on the same day by the Crown Court; or
- the Crown Court, in passing sentence, said that it was treating the two sentences as a single sentence. The Court of Appeal can then increase the sentence on both offences, if it thinks it appropriate to do so.

In *Attorney General's Reference (No 4 of 1989)* [1990] 1 WLR 41, the Court of Appeal gave guidance on the use of such references:

- a sentence is unduly lenient if it falls outside the range of sentences which the judge could reasonably consider appropriate;
- even if the Court of Appeal does consider the original sentence to be unduly lenient, it does not have to increase that sentence. It may be that the sentence can be justified in the light of events since the trial or that increasing the sentence would be unfair to the offender or detrimental to others for whose well-being the court should be concerned;
- if the Attorney General is given leave to refer a sentence to the Court of Appeal on the ground that it is unduly lenient, the court's powers are not confined to increasing the sentence. In theory, the sentence could be reduced.

Where a sentence is referred to the Court of Appeal by the Attorney General (under s 36 of the Criminal Justice Act 1988), the Court of Appeal will not inquire into the facts of the offence but will base its decision on the findings made by the Crown Court (*Attorney General's Reference (No 95 of 1998)*; *R v Highfield* (1999) *The Times*, 21 April).

In *Attorney General's Reference (No 17 of 1998)*; *R v Stokes* [1999] 1 Cr App R(S) 407, a judge gave an indication that he was not minded to impose a sentence of immediate custody. The defendant pleaded guilty (and received a suspended sentence). The prosecution sought to appeal against the sentence as unduly lenient (s 36 of the Criminal Justice Act 1988). The Court of Appeal rejected the argument that it should not increase the sentence because the defendant had pleaded guilty on the basis of the judge's indication as to likely sentence.

An order deferring sentence (s 1 of the Powers of Criminal Courts (Sentencing) Act 2000) is a sentence within the meaning of s 36 of the Criminal Justice Act 1988 and so the Attorney General can seek leave to refer that order to the Court of Appeal as unduly lenient (*R v L; R v Jones* (1999) 163 JP 97).

The prosecution can also use this procedure to appeal against sentence where the sentencer fails to impose a mandatory sentence under the Crime (Sentences) Act 1997.

10.13   APPEALS TO THE HOUSE OF LORDS

Under ss 33 and 34 of the Criminal Appeal Act 1968, either the prosecution or the defence can appeal to the House of Lords against a decision of the Court of Appeal. This is subject to two conditions:

- the Court of Appeal must certify that a point of law of general public importance is involved; and

- leave to appeal is given by the Court of Appeal or by the Appeals Committee of the House of Lords.

Given the ability of the prosecution to appeal, it should be noted that even if a conviction is quashed by the Court of Appeal that conviction could be reinstated by the House of Lords.

10.14   THE ROLE OF THE DIVISIONAL COURT

Section 29(3) of the Supreme Court Act 1981 provides that the High Court may judicially review a decision of the Crown Court provided the decision is not in respect of a matter relating to trial of indictment. In *DPP v Manchester Crown Court and Huckfield* [1993] 1 WLR 1524, the House of Lords held that any decision which arises in the issue between the Crown and the defendant formulated in the indictment is likely to be outside the scope of judicial review. In that case, the decision of a Crown Court judge to quash an indictment was held to be incapable of judicial review. This followed the earlier decision of the House of Lords in *DPP v Manchester Crown Court and Ashton* [1993] 2 All WLR 846; [1993] 2 All ER 663, where it was held by the House of Lords that an order to stay proceedings because they amounted to an abuse of process could not be the subject of judicial review.

A decision as to the date the trial of an indictment would commence (in the present case, the decision at issue was the order in which indictments against the same defendant were to be tried) is not susceptible to judicial review (*R v Southwark Crown Court ex p Ward* [1996] Crim LR 123).

In *R v Leeds Crown Court ex p Hussain* [1995] 3 All ER 527; [1995] 1 WLR 1329, the Divisional Court declined to follow *R v Maidstone Crown Court ex p Clark* [1995] 1 WLR 831; [1995] 3 All ER 513 and *R v Maidstone Crown Court ex p Hollstein* [1995] 3 All ER 503, holding that the decision when to arraign a defendant (and indeed the conduct of the plea and directions hearing generally) is sufficiently closely related to the trial on indictment that s 29(3) of the Supreme Court Act 1981 operates to exclude judicial review of the decision.

The Divisional Court has jurisdiction to entertain an application for judicial review of an order made by the Crown Court lifting reporting restrictions imposed under s 39 of the Children and Young Persons Act 1933: *R v Manchester Crown Court ex p H* [2000] 1 WLR 760; [2000] 2 All ER 166 (*R v Harrow Crown Court ex p Perkins* (1998) 162 JP 527 followed; *R v Winchester Crown Court ex p B* [1999] 1 WLR 788 not followed).

10.15 FREE PARDONS

It is open to the Home Secretary to advise the Queen to pardon someone who has been convicted of an offence. This may be the only remedy if the Court of Appeal (usually after a reference by the Home Secretary under s 36 of the Criminal Justice Act 1972) has failed to secure the quashing of the conviction.

This exercise of the royal prerogative of mercy does not, however, have the effect of quashing the conviction (*R v Foster* [1985] QB 115; [1984] 2 All ER 679); only a successful appeal to the Court of Appeal (or House of Lords, on further appeal) can achieve that.

10.16 THE CRIMINAL CASES REVIEW COMMISSION

Section 8(1) of the Criminal Appeal Act 1995 creates a new body called the Criminal Cases Review Commission ('the Commission'). Its function is to investigate possible miscarriages of justice.

10.16.1 Membership

The Commission is to consist of at least 11 members (s 8(3)). The members are appointed by the Queen on the recommendation of the Prime Minister (s 8(4)). At least one third of the members should be legally qualified and at least two thirds of the members should have 'knowledge or experience of any aspect of the criminal justice system' (s 8(5), (6)).

10.16.2 References

Section 9(1) of the Criminal Appeal Act 1995 says that, where a person has been convicted by the Crown Court, the Commission may at any time refer the conviction and/or the sentence to the Court of Appeal.

Section 11(1) of the Criminal Appeal Act 1995 says that where a person has been convicted by a magistrates' court, the Commission may at any time refer the conviction and/or the sentence to the Crown Court. The power to refer a conviction to the Crown Court applies whether or not the defendant pleaded guilty (s 11(2)). Section 11(6) says that, on a reference under s 11, the Crown Court may not impose a more severe punishment than that inflicted by the magistrates' court. Section 11(7) empowers the Crown Court to grant bail to someone whose conviction or sentence has been referred to the Crown Court under s 11.

Section 13(1)(a)–(c) sets out the three conditions which have to be satisfied before a reference can be made:

(a) the Commission consider that there is a 'real possibility' that the conviction or sentence 'would not be upheld were the reference to be made';

(b) the Commission so consider:

   (i) in the case of a conviction, 'because of an argument, or evidence, not raised in the proceedings which led to it or on any appeal or application for leave to appeal against it';

   (ii) in the case of a sentence, 'because of an argument on a point of law, or information, not so raised';

(c) an appeal against the conviction or sentence has been dismissed or leave to appeal has been refused.

Section 13(2) says that 'nothing in sub-s 1(b)(i) or (c) shall prevent the making of a reference if it appears to the Commission that there are exceptional circumstances which justify making it'.

Section 14(1) says that a reference may be made whether or not the person to whom it relates has applied for a reference to be made.

10.16.3 References by the Home Secretary

Section 3 of the Criminal Appeal Act 1995 repeals s 17 of the Criminal Appeal Act 1968, which empowered the Secretary of State to refer cases tried on indictment to the Court of Appeal. This power is effectively replaced by the Criminal Cases Review Commission.

10.16.4 Power to order investigations

Section 5(1) of the Criminal Appeal Act 1995 inserts s 23A into the Criminal Appeal Act 1968. Section 23A(1) states that, on an appeal against conviction, the Court of Appeal may direct the Criminal Cases Review Commission to investigate and report to the court on any matter if it appears to the court that:

(a) the matter is relevant to the determination of the case and ought, if possible, to be resolved before the case is determined;

(b) an investigation of the matter by the Commission is likely to result in the court being able to resolve it; and

(c) the matter cannot be resolved by the court without an investigation by the Commission.

The court may make the Commission's report available to the appellant and the respondent (s 23A(4)).

Section 15(1) of the 1995 Act says that where such a direction is given by the Court of Appeal, the Commission must investigate the matter in such manner as the Commission thinks fit. Section 15(2) provides that where, in investigating a matter pursuant to a direction from the Court of Appeal, it appears to the Commission that another matter 'which is relevant to the determination of the case by the Court of Appeal ought, if possible, to be resolved before the case is determined by that court' and an investigation of that other matter 'is likely to result in the court's being able to resolve it', the Commission may investigate the related matter.

10.16.5 Investigative powers of the Commission

Section 17 of the Criminal Appeal Act 1995 empowers the Commission to order 'a person serving in a public body' to produce documents or other material which may assist the Commission. A 'public body' is defined in s 22 as meaning a police force, any government department, or local authority, or any other body whose members are appointed by the Queen or whose revenue comes from the government.

Section 19 of the Criminal Appeal Act 1995 enables the Commission to require the appointment of an 'investigating officer' to carry out inquiries which the Commission believe are necessary. This may be an appropriate official of a public body or a police officer.

TABLE OF STATUTORY AND OTHER MATERIALS

STATUTORY MATERIALS

CRIMINAL APPEAL ACT 1968

Section 1: Right of appeal

(1) Subject to sub-section (3) below a person convicted of an offence on indictment may appeal to the Court of Appeal against his conviction.

(2) An appeal under this section lies only:

    (a) with the leave of the Court of Appeal; or

    (b) if the judge of the court of trial grants a certificate that the case is fit for appeal.

    ...

Section 2: Ground for allowing an appeal under section 1

(1) Subject to the provisions of this Act, the Court of Appeal:

    (a) shall allow an appeal against conviction if they think that the conviction is unsafe; and

    (b) shall dismiss such an appeal in any other case.

(2) In the case of an appeal against conviction the court shall, if they allow the appeal, quash the conviction.

(3) An order of the Court of Appeal quashing a conviction shall, except when under section 7 below the appellant is ordered to be re-tried, operate as a direction to the court of trial to enter, instead of the record of conviction, a judgment and verdict of acquittal.

Section 3: Power to substitute conviction of alternative offence

(1) This section applies on an appeal against conviction, where the appellant has been convicted of an offence and the jury could on the indictment have found him guilty of some other offence, and on the finding of the jury it appears to the Court of Appeal that the jury must have been satisfied of facts which proved him guilty of the other offence.

(2) The court may, instead of allowing or dismissing the appeal, substitute for the verdict found by the jury a verdict of guilty of the other offence, and pass such sentence in substitution for the sentence passed at the trial as may be authorised by law for the other offence, not being a sentence of greater severity.

Section 4: Sentence when appeal allowed on part of an indictment

(1) This section applies where, on an appeal against conviction on an indictment containing two or more counts, the Court of Appeal allow the appeal in respect of part of the indictment.

(2) Except as provided by sub-section (3) below, the Court of Appeal may in respect of any count on which the appellant remains convicted pass such sentence, in substitution for any sentence passed thereon at the trial, as they think proper and is authorised by law for the offence of which he remains convicted on that count.

(3) The court shall not under this section pass any sentence such that the appellant's sentence on the indictment as a whole will, in consequence of the appeal, be of greater severity than the sentence (taken as a whole) which was passed at the trial for all the offences of which he was convicted on the indictment.

Section 7: Power to order re-trial

(1) Where the Court of Appeal allow an appeal against conviction and it appears to the court that the interests of justice so require, they may order the appellant to be re-tried.

(2) A person shall not under this section be ordered to be re-tried for any offence other than:

    (a) the offence of which he was convicted at the original trial and in respect of which his appeal is allowed as mentioned in sub-section (1) above;

    (b) an offence of which he could have been convicted at the original trial on the indictment for the first-mentioned offence; or

    (c) an offence charged in an alternative count of the indictment in respect of which the jury were discharged from giving a verdict in consequence of convicting him of the first-mentioned offence.

Section 9: Appeal against sentence following conviction on indictment

(1) A person who has been convicted of an offence on indictment may appeal to the Court of Appeal against any sentence[1] (not being a sentence fixed by law) passed on him for the offence, whether passed on his conviction or in subsequent proceedings.

(2) A person who on conviction on indictment has also been convicted of a summary offence under section 41 of the Criminal Justice Act 1988 (power of the Crown Court to deal with summary offence where person committed for either way offence) may appeal to the Court of Appeal against any sentence passed on him for the summary offence (whether on his conviction or in subsequent proceedings) under sub-section (7) of that section.

Section 10: Appeal against sentence in other cases

(1) This section has effect for providing rights of appeal against sentence when a person is dealt with by the Crown Court (otherwise than on appeal from a magistrates' court) for an offence of which he was not convicted on indictment.

(2) The proceedings from which an appeal against sentence lies under this section are those where an offender convicted of an offence by a magistrates' court:

---

1   Section 50 of the Act defines the term 'sentence'.

Section 50: Meaning of 'sentence'

(1) In this Act, 'sentence', in relation to an offence, includes any order made by a court when dealing with an offender including, in particular:

(a) a hospital order under Part III of the Mental Health Act 1983, with or without a restriction order;

(b) an interim hospital order under that part;

(bb) a hospital direction and a limitation direction under that Part;

(c) a recommendation for deportation;

(cc) a direction under section 20(3) or 21(3) of the Crime (Sentences) Act 1997 (extended supervision for sexual or violent offenders);

(d) a confiscation order under the Drug Trafficking Act 1994 other than one made by the High Court;

(e) a confiscation order under Part VI of the Criminal Justice Act 1988;

(f) an order varying a confiscation order of a kind which is included by virtue of paragraph (d) or (e) above;

(g) an order made by the Crown Court varying a confiscation order which was made by the High Court by virtue of section 19 of the Act of 1994; and

(h) a declaration of relevance under the Football Spectators Act 1989.

(1A) Section 14 of the Powers of Criminal Courts (Sentencing) Act 2000 (under which a conviction of an offence for which an order for conditional or absolute discharge is made is deemed not to be a conviction except for certain purposes) shall not prevent an appeal under this Act, whether against conviction or otherwise.

...

(a) is committed by the court to be dealt with for his offence at the Crown Court; or

(b) having been made the subject of an order for conditional discharge or a community order within the meaning of of the Powers of Criminal Courts (Sentencing Act 2000 (other than a supervision order within the meaning of that Part) or given a suspended sentence, appears or is brought before the Crown Court to be further dealt with for his offence.

(3) An offender dealt with for an offence at the Crown Court in a proceeding to which sub-section (2) of this section applies may appeal to the Court of Appeal against sentence in any of the following cases::

(a) where either for that offence alone or for that offence and other offences for which sentence is passed in the same proceeding, he is sentenced to imprisonment or to detention in a young offender institution for a term of six months or more; or

(b) where the sentence is one which the court convicting him had not power to pass; or

(c) where the court in dealing with him for the offence makes in respect of him:

(i) a recommendation for deportation; or

(ii) an order disqualifying him for holding or obtaining a licence to drive a motor vehicle under Part II of the Road Traffic Offenders Act 1988; or

(iii) an order under section 119 of the Powers of Criminal Courts (Sentencing) Act 2000 (orders as to existing suspended sentence when person subject to the sentence is again convicted); or

(iv) a restriction order under section 15 of the Football Spectators Act 1989; or

(v) a declaration of relevance under the Football Spectators Act 1989.

(4) For the purposes of sub-section (3)(a) of this section and section 11 of this Act, any two or more sentences are to be treated as passed in the same proceeding if:

(a) they are passed on the same day; or

(b) they are passed on different days but the court in passing any one of them states that it is treating that one together with the other or others as substantially one sentence,

and consecutive terms of imprisonment and terms which are wholly or partly concurrent are to be treated as a single term.

Section 11: Supplementary provisions as to appeal against sentence

(1) Subject to sub-section (1A) below, an appeal against sentence, whether under section 9 or section 10 of this Act, lies only with the leave of the Court of Appeal.

(1A) If the judge who passed the sentence grants a certificate that the case is fit for appeal under section 9 or 10 of this Act, an appeal lies under this section without the leave of the Court of Appeal.

...

(3) On an appeal against sentence the Court of Appeal, if they consider that the appellant should be sentenced differently for an offence for which he was dealt with by the court below may:

(a) quash any sentence or order which is the subject of the appeal; and

(b) in place of it pass such sentence or make such order as they think appropriate for the case and as the court below had power to pass or make when dealing with him for the offence;

but the court shall so exercise their powers under this sub-section that, taking the case as a whole, the appellant is not more severely dealt with on appeal than he was dealt with by the court below.

(4) The power of the Court of Appeal under sub-section (3) of this section to pass a sentence which the court below had power to pass for an offence shall, notwithstanding that the court below made no order under section 119(1) of the Powers of Criminal Courts (Sentencing) Act 2000 ... in respect of a suspended ... sentence previously passed on the appellant for another offence, include power to deal with him in respect of that sentence where the court below made no order in respect of it.

...

Section 19: Bail

(1) The Court of Appeal may, subject to section 25 of the Criminal Justice and Public Order Act 1994, if they think fit:

(a) grant an appellant bail pending the determination of his appeal; or

(b) revoke bail granted to an appellant by the Crown Court under paragraph (f) of section 81(1) of the Supreme Court Act 1981 or paragraph (a) above; or

(c) vary the conditions of bail granted to an appellant in the exercise of the power conferred by either of those paragraphs.

(2) The powers conferred by sub-section (1) above may be exercised:

(a) on the application of an appellant; or

(b) if it appears to the registrar of criminal appeals of the Court of Appeal ... that any of them ought to be exercised, on a reference to the court by him.

Section 20: Disposal of groundless appeal or application for leave to appeal

If it appears to the registrar that a notice of appeal or application for leave to appeal does not show any substantial ground of appeal, he may refer the appeal or application for leave to the court for summary determination; and where the case is so referred the court may, if they consider that the appeal or application for leave is frivolous or vexatious, and can be determined without adjourning it for a full hearing, dismiss the appeal or application for leave summarily, without calling on anyone to attend the hearing or to appear for the Crown thereon.

Section 22: Right of appellant to be present

(1) Except as provided by this section, an appellant shall be entitled to be present, if he wishes it, on the hearing of his appeal, although he may be in custody.

(2) A person in custody shall not be entitled to be present:

(a) where his appeal is on some ground involving a question of law alone; or

(b) on an application by him for leave to appeal; or

(c) on any proceedings preliminary or incidental to an appeal;

...

unless the Court of Appeal give him leave to be present.

(3) The power of the Court of Appeal to pass sentence on a person may be exercised although he is for any reason not present.

Section 23: Evidence

(1) For the purposes of this Part of this Act the Court of Appeal may, if they think it necessary or expedient in the interests of justice:

(a) order the production of any document, exhibit or other thing connected with the proceedings, the production of which appears to them necessary for the determination of the case;

(b) order any witness who would have been a compellable witness in the proceedings from which the appeal lies to attend for examination and be examined before the court, whether or not he was called in those proceedings; and

(c) receive any evidence which was not adduced in the proceedings from which the appeal lies.

(2) The Court of Appeal shall, in considering whether to receive any evidence, have regard in particular to:

(a) whether the evidence appears to the Court to be capable of belief;

(b) whether it appears to the Court that the evidence may afford any ground for allowing the appeal;

(c) whether the evidence would have been admissible in the proceedings from which the appeal lies on an issue which is the subject of the appeal; and

(d) whether there is a reasonable explanation for the failure to adduce the evidence in those proceedings.

...

Section 29: Effect of appeal on sentence

(1) The time during which an appellant is in custody pending the determination of his appeal shall, subject to any direction which the Court of Appeal may give to the contrary, be reckoned as part of the term of any sentence to which he is for the time being subject.

(2) Where the Court of Appeal give a contrary direction under sub-section (1) above, they shall state their reasons for doing so; and they shall not give any such direction where:

(a) leave to appeal has been granted; or

(b) a certificate has been given by the judge of the court of trial under:

(i) section 1 or 11(1A) of this Act.

...

Practice Direction (Crime: Sentence: Loss of Time)
 [1980] 1 WLR 270

... It may expected that such a direction will normally be made unless the grounds are not only settled and signed by counsel, but also supported by the written opinion of counsel ... Counsel should not settle grounds, or support them with written advice, unless he considers that the proposed appeal is properly arguable. It would, therefore, clearly not be appropriate to penalise the appellant in such a case, even if the single judge considered that the appeal was quite hopeless.

It is also necessary to stress that, if an application is refused by the single judge as being wholly devoid of merit, the full court has power, in the event of renewal, both to order loss of time, if the single judge has not done so, and to increase the amount of time ordered to be lost if the single judge has already made a direction, whether or not grounds have been settled and signed by counsel. It may be expected that this power too will ... normally be exercised.

CHAPTER 11

LEGAL AID AND COSTS

11.1 INTRODUCTION

In this chapter, we see how State funds can be available to pay for the defence of people who cannot afford to pay for their own representation. We go on to look at the various orders for costs which can be made when a case has been disposed of.

11.2 LEGAL AID – DUTY SOLICITOR SCHEME

Part III of the Legal Aid Act 1988 (ss 3–7) and the Legal Advice and Assistance Regulations 1989 (SI 1989/340) as amended, together with the Legal Advice and Assistance (Scope) Regulations 1989 (SI 1989/550), create a 'duty solicitor' scheme. There are essentially two parts to this scheme.

11.2.1 Regulation 6 of the Advice and Assistance Regulations

Regulation 6 of the Advice and Assistance Regulations makes provision for the giving of advice and assistance to people who have been arrested and are being held at a police station. A rota scheme means that a solicitor should always be available to attend a police station (to advise a suspect who does not have their own solicitor and, if necessary, to be present when the suspect is interviewed by the police). Provision of aid does not depend on the suspect's means and no contribution towards the costs of the assistance is payable.

11.2.2 Regulation 7 of the Advice and Assistance Regulations

Regulation 7 of the Advice and Assistance Regulations makes provision for advice by way of representation ('ABWOR'). A duty solicitor scheme means that a solicitor should be available at the magistrates' court to advise and, if necessary, represent a defendant. The representation is limited to:

(a) making a bail application;

(b) making a plea in mitigation if the suspect is in custody and wishes to plead guilty so that his case can be dealt with forthwith;

(c) making a plea in mitigation for a defendant who is not in custody but who wishes to plead guilty so that his case can be dealt with forthwith, provided that the solicitor is of the opinion that representation under the scheme is appropriate.

Pleas (b) and (c) will only be possible in the case of relatively minor offences where little preparation time is required by the prosecution or the defence and so both sides are ready to proceed.

It should be noted that the scheme does not extend to representation in committal proceedings, summary trials where the defendant pleads not guilty, or to proceedings for a non-imprisonable offence.

Unless the case is one which can be disposed of immediately, the duty solicitor will simply make a bail application (if necessary) and assist the defendant in making a legal aid application to enable him to be represented under the ordinary legal aid scheme.

ABWOR is not subject to the means of the accused and no contribution to the costs may be required.

11.3   LEGAL AID IN CRIMINAL PROCEEDINGS

Legal aid in criminal cases is governed by Pt V of the Legal Aid Act 1988 (ss 19–26) and by the Legal Aid in Criminal and Care Proceedings (General) Regulations 1989 (SI 1989/344), as amended.

11.4   WHICH COURT?

Section 20 of the Legal Aid Act 1988 sets out the jurisdiction of criminal courts to grant legal aid.

11.4.1   The magistrates' court

The magistrates' court can grant legal aid for its own proceedings and for Crown Court proceedings.

In the case of offences which are triable only on indictment, the magistrates' court may make a 'through order' at the start of the case granting legal aid for the appearances in the magistrates' court and also for the Crown Court trial itself. Usually, however, the magistrates grant legal aid to cover proceedings up to and including committal, and if the defendant is committed for trial, that order will be extended at the end of the committal proceedings to cover the Crown Court trial.

11.4.2   The Crown Court

The Crown Court can only grant legal aid in respect of its own proceedings. This means that if the magistrates refuse to grant legal aid for the mode of trial hearing, for committal proceedings or for summary trial, the Crown Court has no jurisdiction to review this refusal. If, on the other hand, the magistrates refuse legal aid for trial on indictment or for representation in the Crown Court following committal for sentence (s 38 of the Magistrates' Courts Act 1980) or for an appeal against summary conviction and/or sentence then the Crown Court may itself grant legal aid.

11.5   PROCEDURE FOR APPLYING FOR LEGAL AID IN THE MAGISTRATES' COURT

The usual method is for the defendant's solicitors to file a standard application form at the magistrates' court. This form contains a statement saying why legal aid should be granted and also a statement of the defendant's means. The application should be accompanied by documentary evidence of means (for example, pay slips, bank statements, etc) or else explain why the applicant is unable to produce such evidence. The application will then be considered by a clerk, who may grant or refuse legal aid.

If there is insufficient time to file the application beforehand, the completed forms may be handed to the court clerk before the hearing, and the clerk may grant legal aid there and then. Alternatively, or if the clerk refuses legal aid, an application may be made in open court to the magistrates. The magistrates will not examine the defendant's means but, if they think legal aid appropriate, will grant legal aid subject to means (that is, the order is only effective if, when the defendant provides a statement of means, his resources are such that he is eligible for legal aid).

11.6   RETROSPECTIVE EFFECT OF LEGAL AID ORDERS

Usually, a legal aid order applies only in respect of costs incurred after the order has been made. However, under reg 44 of the 1989 General Regulations, where representation is given in the magistrates' court before legal aid has been granted, it is deemed to be covered by a subsequent legal aid order if:

- the interests of justice required that representation be provided as a matter of urgency; and
- there was no undue delay in applying for legal aid; and
- the representation was given by the solicitor named in the legal aid order.

See, also, *R v Newham Justices ex p Mumtaz* [1990] Crim LR 589.

In *R v Highbury Corner Magistrates' Court ex p Sonn* [1995] 4 All ER 57, legal aid was applied for only after the conclusion of the summary trial because the defendant had not supplied a statement of means prior to the conclusion of the hearing. The Divisional Court held that, if the conditions set out in reg 44(7) of the Legal Aid in Criminal and Care Proceedings (General) Regulations 1989 are satisfied, a legal aid order in respect of proceedings in a magistrates' court can be made after the proceedings have been completed, enabling payment to be made for representation and advice already given.

11.7 PROCEDURE FOR APPLYING FOR LEGAL AID IN THE CROWN COURT

If the magistrates refuse legal aid for Crown Court proceedings (or if no application was made to the magistrates), the defendant may apply for legal aid by submitting a written application to the Chief Clerk at the Crown Court (using the same forms as in the magistrates, namely a statement of why it is in the interests of justice to grant legal aid and a statement of means) or else an oral application may be made to the Crown Court.

11.8 THE CRITERIA FOR GRANTING LEGAL AID

The grant of legal aid depends on a merit test and a means test.

11.8.1 The merits of the case – mandatory legal aid

Under s 21(3) of the Legal Aid Act 1988, legal aid must (subject to the means test described below) be granted if either:

- the accused is committed for trial on a charge of murder; or
- the accused is unrepresented and is in custody following a remand hearing at which he was unrepresented and is at risk of a further remand in custody.

In the latter case, legal aid may be limited to the cost of representation on a bail application. The purpose is to prevent defendants from being remanded in custody merely because they have no one to speak on their behalf. In practice, however, the duty solicitor scheme (see 11.2.2 above) usually provides representation in such cases.

11.8.2 The merits of the case – discretionary legal aid

Section 21(2) of the Legal Aid Act 1988 provides that, in cases where legal aid is not mandatory, the applicant may be granted legal aid if it appears 'desirable to do so in the interests of justice'.

Section 22(2) sets out the factors which are considered in deciding whether it is in the interests of justice to grant legal aid:

- whether, in the event of conviction, the court is likely to impose a sentence which would:

  (a) deprive the accused of his liberty; or

  (b) lead to the loss of his livelihood; or

  (c) seriously damage his reputation.

  This requirement is obviously satisfied if the accused is at risk of a custodial sentence. However, in *R v Liverpool City Magistrates ex p McGhee* [1993] Crim LR 609, the Divisional Court rejected the argument that a community service order, which places constraints on the offender's freedom, is to be regarded as a sentence which deprives the offender of his liberty (under s 22(2)(a) of the Legal Aid Act 1988). Those words are, said the Divisional Court, to be construed as meaning only a custodial sentence. However, the Divisional Court went on to hold that the list of factors in s 22(2) is not exhaustive and that 'the possibility of a community service order being made might be a factor to be considered when considering whether or not to grant legal aid' (*per* Rose LJ).

- whether the case involves a substantial (that is, complex) question of law;

- whether the accused may have difficulty in understanding the proceedings or in presenting his case, either because of lack of knowledge of English or because of mental or physical disability;

- whether the nature of the defence case involves the tracing and interviewing of potential defence witnesses or the expert cross-examination of prosecution witnesses (in *McGhee* (above), it was held that the latter provision means expertly conducted cross-examination, not just the cross-examination of expert witnesses);

- whether it is in the interests of someone other than the accused that he be legally represented (for example, it is undesirable in a case involving a sexual offence that the victim should have to face cross-examination by the alleged perpetrator).

For an example of a case requiring expert cross-examination (and a point of law), see *R v Scunthorpe Justices ex p S* (1998) *The Times*, 5 March. The defendant was charged with assaulting a police officer (s 89(2) of the Police Act 1996); his defence was that the police officer was not acting in the execution of his duty. This defence required expert cross-examination and so the refusal of legal aid was held by the Divisional Court to be irrational.

11.8.3   The means test

All legal aid is means tested. Section 21(5) of the Legal Aid Act 1988 says that the applicant's disposable income and disposable capital must be such that he requires assistance to meet the costs of the proceedings. Regulations are published each year, setting out the relevant figures for deciding whether the applicant is eligible for legal aid. Some people are simply ineligible because of their means; others qualify for all their legal costs to be met; others are granted legal aid subject to making a contribution towards their own costs.

11.8.4   Legal aid and custodial sentences

These provisions should be seen in the light of the provisions which apply where the court is minded to impose a custodial sentence. Under s 83 of the Powers of Criminal Courts (Sentencing) Act 2000, a custodial sentence may not be passed on an offender who is not legally represented in court unless either: (a) he was granted a right to representation funded by the Legal Services Commission as part of the Criminal Defence Service (the new form of criminal legal aid under the Access to Justice Act 1999; see 11.13 below) but the right was withdrawn because of misconduct on the part of the offender; or (b) he was informed of his right to apply for legal representation but, despite having the opportunity to do so, has refused or failed to apply.

If a magistrates' court passes a custodial sentence where such a sentence is forbidden by s 83 of the 2000 Act, that custodial sentence will be a nullity and if the offender appeals to the Crown Court, that court will have to replace the sentence with a non-custodial sentence (*R v Birmingham Justices ex p Wyatt* [1976] 1 WLR 260; [1975] 3 All ER 897).

If the Crown Court fails to comply with either of these provisions, the Court of Appeal may uphold the custodial sentence if it considers that a custodial sentence was, in fact, appropriate (*R v McGinlay* (1975) 62 Cr App R 156; *R v Hollywood* (1990) 12 Cr App R(S) 324).

In *R v Wilson* (1995) 16 Cr App R(S) 997, the defendant, who was legally aided, pleaded guilty to arson. She dismissed the firm of solicitors who were representing her; a second firm was assigned but they subsequently indicated that they were no longer able to act for her. She asked for another firm of solicitors to be assigned to her under the legal aid order, but the judge refused to do so. She received a custodial sentence. The Court of Appeal said that a person was only to be regarded as legally represented for the purposes of s 83 of the 2000 Act if he had the assistance of counsel or a solicitor to represent him in the proceedings in that court after he was convicted of the offence and before sentence was passed. The court went on to say that s 83 would have been complied with if, at some time between conviction and sentence, the defendant had received advice from her lawyers, even if she rejected that advice and dismissed them. However, this defendant had been granted legal aid and so she had the right to be represented by solicitors and counsel selected by her and who were willing to represent her, unless and until the legal aid order was withdrawn. In the present case, the legal aid order had not been withdrawn and so the defendant was entitled to representation pursuant to that order. Accordingly, the custodial sentence was unlawful.

11.9   CONTRIBUTION ORDERS

If, according to the figures set out in the regulations, the defendant is deemed able to pay a contribution towards his legal costs (but is not sufficiently wealthy as to be ineligible for legal aid at all), then the grant of legal aid will be subject to a contribution order (s 23(1) of the Legal Aid Act 1988).

Note that a person who is receiving income support, family credit or disability working allowance cannot be required to make a contribution to their legal costs.

11.9.1   Payment of the contribution

The contribution may be payable as a lump sum if it can be paid out of the applicant's disposable capital. More usually, it is paid by instalments out of the applicant's disposable income. The usual period for payment of the instalments is 26 weeks.

11.9.2   Non-payment of contribution: revocation of legal aid

Sometimes, the court will direct that the contribution has to be paid before the legal aid order is effective (s 24(1) of the Legal Aid Act 1995). Otherwise, the legal aid order may be revoked if the defendant fails to pay the amount required under the contribution order (s 24(2)). The order can only be revoked if the court takes the view that the accused could afford to pay the contribution ordered (and the accused must be given the opportunity to make representations to the court on this issue) (s 24(3)).

If the legal aid order is revoked because of non-payment of contributions, the defendant cannot simply re-apply to the clerk of the justices to renew his legal aid (*R v Liverpool Magistrates ex p Shacklady and Pender* [1993] 2 All ER 929). However, the defendant may still apply to the court for legal aid for the trial itself and for pre-trial proceedings, such as remands, bail applications, committal proceedings (*R v Liverpool Justices ex p Pender (No 2)* [1994] 1 WLR 964; [1994] 2 All ER 897).

11.9.3   Change of means

If the defendant's means change for the better after legal aid has been granted, he must inform the court, which may then make a contribution order (if one is not already in existence) or increase the amount payable under an existing contribution order, or even revoke the order.

11.9.4   Defendant acquitted

Regulation 35 of the 1989 General Regulations provides that if the defendant was granted legal aid subject to payment of a contribution but is acquitted of the charge:

- contributions which have already been paid should be returned to him; and

- contributions which have not been paid or which have not yet fallen due should be remitted.

According to a Practice Direction (1991), where a defendant is acquitted on all charges or successfully appeals against conviction, the court should normally order the repayment of any contribution already paid and the remission of any future instalments. However, the court retains a discretion not to do so if, for example, the defendant was acquitted on a technicality.

11.9.5   Defendant convicted

Under reg 35 of the 1989 General Regulations, if the defendant was granted legal aid subject to payment of a contribution and is convicted, then the court may remit payment of any instalments which have not yet fallen due. Future payments are automatically remitted if a custodial sentence is passed (reg 37).

11.10   CO-DEFENDANTS

A legal aid order will provide for joint representation of legally aided co-defendants (so they will have the same solicitor and, where appropriate, barrister) unless the interests of justice required separate representation (for example, they present inconsistent defences) (reg 49 of the 1989 General Regulations).

11.11   REPRESENTATION UNDER A LEGAL AID ORDER

The legal aid order will contain a provision regarding the level of representation it covers.

11.11.1   Magistrates' court

Regulation 44 of the 1989 General Regulations provides that the legal aid certificate for proceedings in front of the magistrates' court should be limited to representation by a solicitor, unless the case involves an indictable offence and it is an unusually grave or difficult case. It is of course open to the solicitor to instruct counsel, but the legal aid fund will only pay on the basis that representation was provided by a solicitor.

11.11.2   Crown Court

Legal aid for the Crown Court is normally for a solicitor and counsel. In cases of exceptional difficulty, there may be legal aid for two counsel in the Crown Court.

11.12   CHALLENGING REFUSAL OF LEGAL AID

If legal aid is refused, there are a number of ways of challenging that refusal.

11.12.1   Apply again to magistrates' court

If legal aid is refused by a magistrates' clerk, a further application may be made to the magistrates themselves in open court. It would not be worth doing this unless the refusal was on the grounds that it was not in the interests of justice to grant legal aid (that is, legal aid was not refused on the ground of means).

Although further applications can then be made if legal aid is still not granted, there is little point in doing so unless there is a change in circumstances.

11.12.2   Apply to Crown Court

If the magistrates refuse legal aid in respect of Crown Court proceedings (trial on indictment, committal for sentence following summary conviction, appeal to Crown Court against summary conviction and/or sentence), an application may be made to the Crown Court for the grant of legal aid.

11.12.3   Apply to area committee

If the magistrates or their clerk have refused legal aid in respect of an indictable offence (triable only on indictment or triable either way), the defendant may apply for legal aid from the area committee of the Legal Aid Board. This review is only possible where legal aid was originally refused on the ground that it was not in the interests of justice to grant it (that is, it was not refused because of the defendant's means). The application must be made at least 21 days before summary trial or committal proceedings (regs 15–17 of the General Regulations).

11.12.4   Judicial review

The only other way of challenging the refusal of legal aid is to apply for judicial review by the Divisional Court. This would only be appropriate in very rare cases where the original decision is perverse, or where relevant factors were ignored or irrelevant ones taken into account (*R v Derby Justices ex p Kooner* [1971] 1 QB 147; [1970] 3 All ER 399 and *R v Highgate Justices ex p Lewis* [1977] Crim LR 611).

11.13   THE CRIMINAL DEFENCE SERVICE: THE ACCESS TO JUSTICE ACT 1999

Section 12 of the Access to Justice Act 1999 requires the newly-established Legal Services Commission to establish, maintain and develop the Criminal Defence Service for the purpose of 'securing that individuals involved in criminal investigations or criminal proceedings have access to such advice, assistance and representation as the interests of justice require'.

The Legal Services Commission will be empowered to secure these services through contracts with lawyers in private practice, or by providing them through salaried defenders (employed directly by the Commission or by non-profit making organisations established for the purpose). This will necessarily mean that suspects and defendants will be limited in their choice of representative: the choice will be limited to contracted or salaried defenders. However, the government's intention is to offer a choice between contracted or salaried defenders in all but exceptional cases. All contractors will be expected to meet quality assurance standards; and contracts will, wherever possible, cover the full range of services from arrest until the case is completed.

There will, of course, have to be a transitional period while contracts are being developed and extended to cover the full range of services. In the meantime, the Commission will be able to pay lawyers on a case by case basis for representation provided on a non-contractual basis, according to remuneration scales set by Statutory Instrument (very similar to the current criminal legal aid scheme).

The Commission will gradually take over the functions currently undertaken by the higher courts in respect of criminal legal aid. At first, Court Service staff will continue to determine costs in most Crown Court cases; but the number of cases dealt with like this will diminish as the Commission increases the proportion of cases covered by contracts.

As with the present system of legal aid, the courts will grant representation under the scheme to defendants, applying the interests of justice test. However, the courts will no longer have to conduct a means test as well before granting representation. Instead, at the end of a case before any court other than a magistrates' court, the judge will have power to order a defendant to pay some or all of the cost of his or her defence. The Commission may investigate the defendant's means in order to assist the judge. The government's intention is to abolish the system of means testing every defendant, while nonetheless ensuring that, in the more expensive cases, defendants continue to pay towards the cost of their defence if they can afford to do so.

Regulations will be produced to provide for advice and assistance in more or less the same categories as those currently applicable to people subject to criminal investigations or proceedings. These categories include advice and assistance provided by duty solicitors at a magistrates' court, at a solicitor's office, or at a police station.

Schedule 3 of the Access to Justice Act 1999 deals with the grant of rights of representation. Paragraph 1 provides that a right may be granted to individuals involved in criminal proceedings; para 1(2) provides that a right may also be granted to private prosecutors to resist appeals to the Crown Court by people they had prosecuted in a magistrates' court.

Paragraph 2 provides that a right may be granted by the court hearing the proceedings and by other courts prescribed in regulations. In most cases, a right will be granted by a magistrates' court and will also cover the case if it goes on to the Crown Court (as under s 20(4) of the Legal Aid Act 1988.)

Paragraph 2(5) provides for regulations prescribing when a court must consider withdrawing a right to representation. The prescribed circumstances will include situations where the charges are reduced so that imprisonment is no longer likely, and where the defendant has refused to co-operate with an inquiry into his or her means.

Paragraph 5 provides that a right to representation should be granted where the interests of justice require it, and sets out the factors to be considered in assessing the interests of justice. The factors mirror those in s 22(2) of the 1988 Act. Paragraph 5(3) allows the Lord Chancellor to make an order amending the criteria, and para 4 provides for regulations about appeals. Paragraph 5(4) allows for cases in which a right must always be granted; this power will be used to mirror s 21(3) of the 1988 Act.

It is expected that contracts with solicitors' firms will cover both initial advice and assistance (at a police station or elsewhere) and any subsequent representation at court. Section 15(2)(b) provides that, in prescribed circumstances, a defendant may be deemed to have chosen as representative the person who had previously advised him or her (to ensure continuity of representation wherever possible in order to minimise delay and avoid the extra cost of instructing a different representative). This power only applies where a suspect chose the duty solicitor or another firm to advise him or her. Suspects advised by a duty solicitor because their chosen adviser was not available at the time will be allowed to use their original choice as representative in court. Regulations under s 15(4) will provide that suspects who do not express any preference will be deemed to have chosen the duty solicitor. Regulations under s 15(2)(f) will say that defendants may not subsequently change their representative without good reason.

In certain types of complex case (for example, serious fraud trials), the defendant's choice may be limited to representatives from panels of firms and advocates specialising in such cases. Membership of a panel will depend on meeting pre-determined criteria.

Section 15(5) provides for regulations prescribing when the Commission may stop funding a defendant's chosen representative (in effect, requiring that defendant to make a fresh choice). This might be necessary, for example, in cases that turned out to be more complex than originally expected, making it appropriate to require the defendant to change to a specialist panel member.

Section 15(2)(a) enables the Lord Chancellor to make regulations defining circumstances where a defendant will not have a right to choose a representative, but will instead have a representative assigned to them. This power might be used, for example, to assign an advocate to an otherwise unrepresented defendant charged with a serious sexual offence against a child.

Section 15(3) secures that regulations under s 15(2) may not provide for defendants' choice of representative to be restricted to employees of the Commission or any bodies it establishes to employ salaried defenders. The intention is that in most cases there should be a choice between several contracted firms and possibly a salaried defender. In some circumstances, for example, when a representative is assigned under s 15(2)(a), it may be that the only person available at the time is an employee of the Commission; s 15(3) would not prevent that employee providing representation; but it would preclude regulations saying that the representative in such circumstances must always or whenever possible be an employee.

Section 16 provides that salaried defenders employed by the Legal Services Commission, or by any bodies established by the Commission to provide criminal defence services, should be subject to a code of conduct. The code must include duties to avoid discrimination and to protect the interests of the individuals for whom services are provided; plus a duty to the court; a duty to avoid conflicts of interest; a duty of confidentiality; and a duty to act in accordance with professional rules.

Section 17 provides that suspects and defendants do not have to pay towards the cost of services provided as part of the Criminal Defence Service, except where the court orders them to pay some or all of the cost of their representation. Section 17(2) provides that magistrates' courts do not have the power to make such orders. This means that only defendants in the more expensive cases that go to the higher courts may be ordered to repay their defence costs, but such an order could include the cost of any representation before a magistrates' court.

Section 17(3) empowers the Lord Chancellor to make regulations about how this new power should be used. It will generally only apply to convicted defendants able to make a substantial repayment. Defendants may be required to provide information about their means to inform a decision, and it will be possible to freeze their assets while their means are being investigated (s 17(3)(d) and (e)).

11.14 COSTS

The power of the criminal courts to award costs is contained in ss 16–21 of the Prosecution of Offences Act 1985 and the Costs in Criminal Cases (General) Regulations 1986 (as amended). These provisions are considered in a Practice Direction (1991).

Three types of order have to be considered: an order that the defendant's costs be paid out of central funds, an order that the prosecution costs be paid out of central funds, and an order that the defendant pay the prosecution costs.

11.15 DEFENDANT'S COSTS ORDER

Section 16 makes provision for the award of defence costs out of central funds (that is, government funds pay some or all of the defendant's legal bill). Such an order may be made in any of the following circumstances:

- the prosecution decide not to proceed with an information;
- the defendant is discharged when the magistrates find no case to answer in committal proceedings;

- the defendant is acquitted following summary trial;
- the prosecution at the Crown Court offer no evidence or ask that all counts remain on the file marked not to be proceeded with without leave;
- the defendant is acquitted following trial on indictment;
- the defendant successfully appeals against conviction and/or sentence.

Unless the defendant is legally aided (see 11.16 below), there is a strong presumption that a defendant who has been acquitted should recover his costs. *Practice Direction (Crime: Costs)* [1991] 1 WLR 498 (as amended by *Practice Direction (Crime: Costs in Criminal Proceedings)* [1999] 4 All ER 436) cites only one instance where it would be appropriate for costs to be withheld from a defendant, namely, that the defendant's own conduct has brought suspicion on himself and misled the prosecution into thinking that the case against him was stronger than it was.

On an application for a defendant's costs order (under s 16 of the Prosecution of Offences Act 1985), the court is entitled to rely on a statement of facts from the prosecution when concluding that the defendant brought the prosecution on himself. Thus, the court does not have to hear oral evidence on this matter (*Mooney v Cardiff Justices* (2000) 164 JP 220).

A defendant's costs order (under s 16 of the Prosecution of Offences Act 1985) does not have to be made by the bench which acquits the defendant, and so a differently constituted court (for example, the bench which sentences the defendant for other offences) can make such an order regarding an earlier acquittal (*R v Clerk to Liverpool Justices ex p Abiaka* (1999) 163 JP 497).

The court should not refuse to make an order that the defence recover their costs from central funds merely because the prosecution acted properly in bringing the case (*R v Birmingham Juvenile Court ex p H* (1992) 156 JP 445).

11.16   LEGALLY AIDED DEFENDANT

A defendant's costs order will not be made in respect of costs covered by a legal aid order, as these costs are being paid by the Legal Aid Board anyway. If the defendant has incurred costs which were not covered by the legal aid order (this does not include any contributions paid under a contribution order), he may recover those costs from central funds (s 21(4A)(a) of the Prosecution of Offences Act 1985), provided that the costs are reasonable.

As we have already seen, any contributions which the defendant has already paid will normally be repaid to him and any future contributions remitted if he is acquitted.

11.17 PROSECUTION COSTS FROM CENTRAL FUNDS

An order that the prosecutor's costs be paid out of central funds may be made under s 17 of the Prosecution of Offences Act 1985. It applies only to private prosecutors, and so excludes the Crown Prosecution Service and any other public authority (for example, Customs and Excise, local authorities, etc). Furthermore, this section applies only to the prosecution of indictable offences (whether triable only on indictment or triable either way). According to the Practice Direction, an order should be made unless, for example, 'proceedings have been instituted or continued without good cause'. Such an order can be made even though the defendant was acquitted.

11.18 AMOUNT OF ORDERS FOR COSTS FROM CENTRAL FUNDS

Where the court orders that the costs of a defendant, appellant or private prosecutor be paid out of central funds, the amount of the order should be the amount the court considers reasonably sufficient to compensate the party in whose favour the order is made for expenses properly incurred in the proceedings. The order cannot include expenses that do not relate directly to the proceedings themselves, such as loss of earnings.

In *R v Dudley Magistrates' Court ex p Power City Stores Ltd* (1990) 154 JP 654, where the defendant wanted to recover the cost of employing leading counsel (that is, a QC), the Divisional Court held that in calculating the amount of costs to be paid under s 16 of the Prosecution of Offences Act 1985, the taxing officer has to carry out a two stage test. First, he has to consider whether the expenses claimed were properly incurred by the defendant. If so, the second step is to ask what amount would be reasonably sufficient to compensate the defendant for those costs.

Section 16(7) allows the court to make a defendant's costs order in respect of only part of the costs incurred. If the defendant is convicted of some offences but acquitted of others, it may be appropriate to award him some costs, or none at all.

11.19 DEFENDANT TO PAY PROSECUTION COSTS

Section 18 of the Prosecution of Offences Act 1985 allows the court to order a defendant who has been convicted (or whose appeal against conviction and/or sentence has been dismissed) to pay the prosecution costs. Section 18(3) provides that the amount of the order is whatever sum the court considers just and reasonable.

In *R v Northallerton Magistrates' Court ex p Dove* (1999) 163 JP 657, the Divisional Court held that a costs order against a defendant (under s 18 of the Prosecution of Offences Act 1985) should never exceed the sum which, having regard to his means and any other financial order imposed on him, he is able to pay. Where a fine is imposed as well, a costs order should not be grossly disproportionate to the fine. The court should begin by deciding on the appropriate fine (taking account of the seriousness of the offence and the offender's means) and should then consider what costs he should be ordered to pay. If the offender cannot afford to pay both, the fine has priority. It is for the defendant to disclose such information as is necessary for the court to decide what he can reasonably afford to pay; in the absence of such disclosure, the court can draw reasonable inferences as to his means from evidence they have heard and from all the circumstances of the case.

When seeking an order for costs against a defendant, the prosecution must give notice to the defendant of its intention to apply for such an order (*R v Emmett* (1999) *The Times*, 15 October).

In *R v Associated Octel Co Ltd* [1996] 1 WLR 1543; [1996] 4 All ER 846, the Court of Appeal held that where a defendant is ordered to pay costs under s 18 of the Prosecution of Offences Act 1985, the amount can include the cost of investigating the offence (as well as the costs of preparing and presenting the prosecution).

In *R v Bow Street Stipendiary Magistrate ex p Multimedia Screen Ltd* (1998) *The Times*, 28 January, the defendant sought judicial review of a costs order requiring him to pay £15,000 although he had made only a tiny profit from the offence of which he was convicted. The Divisional Court held that the prosecution had had to do a lot of research and so the order was appropriate.

11.19.1 Relevant factors

- Defendant's means

  Such an order will only be made if the defendant has sufficient means to enable him to pay some or all of the prosecution costs.

  In *R v Newham Justices ex p Samuels* [1991] COD 412, the Divisional Court quashed a costs order which had been made without proper account being taken of the defendant's means.

  In *R v Ghadami* [1997] Crim LR 606, it was held that mortgage debts must be taken into account in deciding whether it is appropriate to make a costs order against a defendant.

  In the case of a juvenile, the amount of the costs order cannot exceed the amount of any fine imposed on him (s 18(5)). It should be borne in mind that a compensation order in favour of the victim of the offence has first priority on the defendant's means.

- Co-defendants

  Where costs are awarded against several defendants and one of them lacks the means to pay costs, the court should divide the total amount payable between the number of defendants (not just those who are able to pay) so that each defendant pays only his own share of the costs and does not subsidise the defendant who cannot pay (*R v Ronson* (1992) 13 Cr App R(S) 153). In that case, there were four defendants of whom one could not afford to pay costs. It was held by the Court of Appeal that the defendants who could afford to pay costs should each pay one quarter of the total, not one third.

In *R v Harrison* (1993) 14 Cr App R(S) 419, however, the Court of Appeal upheld an order that only one defendant was the principal defendant (the other defendants had played relatively minor roles in the offences) and he had the means to pay the amount ordered.

11.19.2   Choice of Crown Court trial

A judge in the Crown Court should not use a costs order as a means of penalising a defendant for electing Crown Court trial of an offence which could have been dealt with in the magistrates' court (*R v Hayden* [1975] 1 WLR 852; [1975] 2 All ER 558). Nevertheless, it has been recognised by the Court of Appeal that trial on indictment is necessarily more expensive than summary trial and this will inevitably be reflected in the costs order (*R v Bushell* (1980) 2 Cr App R(S) 77; *R v Boyle* (1995) 16 Cr App R(S) 927).

11.19.3   Strength of prosecution case

A costs order is more likely to be made against a defendant where the prosecution case is manifestly strong and the defendant must have known all along that he was guilty (*R v Singh* (1982) 4 Cr App R(S) 38, following *R v Mountain* (1978) 68 Cr App R 4).

11.19.4   Attitude of prosecution

If the prosecution in the Crown Court accept a plea of guilty to an offence to which the defendant would have pleaded guilty in the magistrates' court if the prosecution had not at that stage wanted to proceed with a more serious offence, the defendant will only be ordered to pay the costs appropriate to a guilty plea in the magistrates' court (*R v Hall* (1988) 10 Cr App R(S) 456). In that case, the defendant was willing to plead guilty to careless driving but the prosecution insisted on proceeding with a charge of reckless (now known as dangerous) driving. At the Crown Court, the prosecution offered no evidence on the reckless driving and the defendant pleaded guilty to careless driving (made possible even though careless driving is a summary offence by what is now s 24 of the Road Traffic Offenders Act 1988). On appeal, the costs order was reduced to the figure he would have had to pay had his plea been accepted in the magistrates' court.

11.19.5 Plea

A costs order may (and, subject to means, usually will) be made where the defendant pleads guilty. However, the order will be for less than would be the case upon conviction following a not guilty plea, not least because less expense will probably have been incurred, especially if a plea of guilty is intimated at the earliest opportunity (see *R v Maher* (1983) 5 Cr App R(S) 39, CA).

11.20   APPEALS ON COSTS

Neither party has a right of appeal to the Crown Court in respect of a costs order made by a magistrates' court: the prosecution have no right of appeal to the Crown Court, and s 108(3)(b) of the Magistrates' Courts Act 1980 precludes a defence appeal to the Crown Court against a costs order. However, it was held in *Johnson v RSPCA* (2000) 164 JP 345 that the Crown Court does have jurisdiction to make an order as to costs incurred before the conclusion of the magistrates' court proceedings (either under s 18(1) of the Prosecution of Offences Act 1985 or s 48(2) of the Supreme Court Act 1981). Usually, following an unsuccessful appeal against conviction, the Crown Court should hesitate to modify the magistrates' costs order. If the prosecutor wishes to seek an increase in the costs the defendant has to pay, he should give written notice to this effect to the defendant, so that the defendant is aware of the possible consequences of pursuing an appeal against conviction.

11.21   WASTED COSTS ORDERS

Section 19A of the Prosecution of Offences Act 1985 empowers the court to make a 'wasted costs order' against a lawyer acting for a party to criminal proceedings. It was held in *Re a Barrister (Wasted Costs Order) (No 9 of 1999)* (2000) *The Times*, 18 April (following the civil case of *Ridehalgh v Horsefield* [1994] Ch 205) that such an order is only appropriate where the lawyer has made an error that no reasonably well informed and competent lawyer could have made.

A wasted costs order against a solicitor is not appropriate where the solicitor relied on the advice of experienced counsel. Such a solicitor cannot be said to have acted in a way that no reasonably competent solicitor could have acted (*Re Hickman and Rose (Wasted Costs Order) (No 10 of 1999)* (2000) *The Times*, 3 May).

TABLE OF STATUTORY AND OTHER MATERIALS

STATUTORY MATERIALS

COSTS

PROSECUTION OF OFFENCES ACT 1985

Section 16: Defence costs

(1) Where:

    (a) an information laid before a justice of the peace for any area, charging any person with an offence, is not proceeded with;

    (b) a magistrates' court inquiring into an indictable offence as examining justices determines not to commit the accused for trial;

    (c) a magistrates' court dealing summarily with an offence dismisses the information,

that court, or in a case falling within paragraph (a) above, a magistrates' court for that area, may make an order in favour of the accused for a payment to be made out of central funds in respect of his costs (a 'defendant's costs order').

(2) Where:

    (a) any person is not tried for an offence for which he has been indicted or committed for trial; or

    (aa) a notice of transfer is given under a relevant transfer provision but a person in relation to whose case it is given is not tried on a charge to which it relates; or

    (b) any person is tried on indictment and acquitted on any count in the indictment,

the Crown Court may make a defendant's costs order in favour of the accused.

(3) Where a person convicted of an offence by a magistrates' court appeals to the Crown Court under section 108 of the Magistrates' Courts Act 1980 (right of appeal against conviction or sentence) and, in consequence of the decision on appeal:

    (a) his conviction is set aside; or

    (b) a less severe punishment is awarded,

the Crown Court may make a defendant's costs order in favour of the accused.

(4) Where the Court of Appeal:

    (a) allows an appeal under Part I of the Criminal Appeal Act 1968 against:

        (i) conviction;

      (ii) a verdict of not guilty by reason of insanity; or

      (iii) a finding under section 4 of the Criminal Procedure (Insanity) Act 1964 that the appellant is under disability or that he did the act or made the omission charged against him; or

    (aa) directs under section 8(1B) of the Criminal Appeal Act 1968 the entry of a judgment and verdict of acquittal;

   (b) on an appeal under that Part against conviction:

      (i)   substitutes a verdict of guilty of another offence;

      (ii) in a case where a special verdict has been found, orders a different conclusion on the effect of that verdict to be recorded; or

      (iii) is of the opinion that the case falls within paragraph (a) or (b) of section 6(1) of that Act (cases where the court substitutes a finding of insanity or unfitness to plead); or

   (c) on an appeal under that Part against sentence, exercises its powers under section 11(3) of that Act (powers where the court considers that the appellant should be sentenced differently for an offence for which he was dealt with by the court below),

the court may make a defendant's costs order in favour of the accused.

(4A) The court may also make a defendant's costs order in favour of the accused on an appeal under section 9(11) of the Criminal Justice Act 1987 (appeals against orders or rulings at preparatory hearings).

 (5) Where:

   (a) any proceedings in a criminal cause or matter are determined before a Divisional Court of the Queen's Bench Division;

   (b) the House of Lords determines an appeal, or application for leave to appeal, from such a Divisional Court in a criminal cause or matter;

   (c) the Court of Appeal determines an application for leave to appeal to the House of Lords under Part II of the Criminal Appeal Act 1968; or

   (d) the House of Lords determines an appeal, or application for leave to appeal, under Part II of that Act,

the court may make a defendant's costs order in favour of the accused.

 (6) A defendant's costs order shall, subject to the following provisions of this section, be for the payment out of central funds, to the person in whose favour the order is made, of such amount as the court considers reasonably sufficient to compensate him for any expenses properly incurred by him in the proceedings.

 (7) Where a court makes a defendant's costs order but is of the opinion that there are circumstances which make it inappropriate that the person in whose favour the order is made should recover the full amount mentioned in sub-section (6) above, the court shall:

   (a) assess what amount would, in its opinion, be just and reasonable; and

   (b) specify that amount in the order.

 (8) [Repealed]

(9) Subject to sub-section (7) above, the amount to be paid out of central funds in pursuance of a defendant's costs order shall:

    (a) be specified in the order, in any case where the court considers it appropriate for the amount to be so specified and the person in whose favour the order is made agrees the amount; and

    (b) in any other case, be determined in accordance with regulations made by the Lord Chancellor for the purposes of this section.

(10) Sub-section (6) above shall have effect, in relation to any case falling within sub-section (1)(a) or (2)(a) above, as if for the words 'in the proceedings' there were substituted the words 'in or about the defence'.

(11) Where a person ordered to be re-tried is acquitted at his re-trial, the costs which may be ordered to be paid out of central funds under this section shall include:

    (a) any costs which, at the original trial, could have been ordered to be so paid under this section if he had been acquitted; and

    (b) if no order was made under this section in respect of his expenses on appeal, any sums for the payment of which such an order could have been made.

(12) In sub-section (2)(aa) 'relevant transfer provision' means:

    (a) section 4 of the Criminal Justice Act 1987; or

    (b) section 53 of the Criminal Justice Act 1991.

Section 17: Prosecution costs

(1) Subject to sub-section (2) below, the court may:

    (a) in any proceedings in respect of an indictable offence; and

    (b) in any proceedings before a Divisional Court of the Queen's Bench Division or the House of Lords in respect of a summary offence,

order the payment out of central funds of such amount as the court considers reasonably sufficient to compensate the prosecutor for any expenses properly incurred by him in the proceedings.

(2) No order under this section shall be made in favour of:

    (a) a public authority; or

    (b) a person acting:

        (i) on behalf of a public authority; or

        (ii) in his capacity as an official appointed by such an authority.

(3) Where a court makes an order under this section but is of the opinion that there are circumstances which make it inappropriate that the prosecution should recover the full amount mentioned in sub-section (1) above, the court shall:

    (a) assess what amount would, in its opinion, be just and reasonable; and

    (b) specify that amount in the order.

(4) Subject to sub-section (3) above, the amount to be paid out of central funds in pursuance of an order under this section shall:

    (a) be specified in the order, in any case where the court considers it appropriate for the amount to be so specified and the prosecutor agrees the amount; and

    (b) in any other case, be determined in accordance with regulations made by the Lord Chancellor for the purposes of this section.

(5) Where the conduct of proceedings to which sub-section (1) above applies is taken over by the Crown Prosecution Service, that sub-section shall have effect as if it referred to the prosecutor who had the conduct of the proceedings before the intervention of the Service and to expenses incurred by him up to the time of intervention.

(6) In this section 'public authority' means:

    (a) a police force within the meaning of section 3 of this Act;

    (b) the Crown Prosecution Service or any other government department;

    (c) a local authority or other authority or body constituted for the purposes of:

        (i) the public service or of local government; or

        (ii) carrying on under national ownership any industry or undertaking or part of an industry or undertaking; or

    (d) any other authority or body whose members are appointed by Her Majesty or by any Minister of the Crown or government department or whose revenues consist wholly or mainly of money provided by Parliament.

Section 18: Award of costs against accused

(1) Where:

    (a) any person is convicted of an offence before a magistrates' court;

    (b) the Crown Court dismisses an appeal against such a conviction or against the sentence imposed on that conviction; or

    (c) any person is convicted of an offence before the Crown Court,

the court may make such order as to costs to be paid by the accused to the prosecutor as it considers just and reasonable.

(2) Where the Court of Appeal dismisses:

    (a) an appeal or application for leave to appeal under Part I of the Criminal Appeal Act 1968; or

    (b) an application by the accused for leave to appeal to the House of Lords under Part II of that Act; or

    (c) an appeal or application for leave to appeal under section 9(11) of the Criminal Justice Act 1987,

it may make such order as to the costs to be paid by the accused, to such persons as may be named in the order, as it considers just and reasonable.

(3) The amount to be paid by the accused in pursuance of an order under this section shall be specified in the order.

(4) Where any person is convicted of an offence before a magistrates' court and:

(a) under the conviction the court orders payment of any sum as a fine, penalty, forfeiture or compensation; and

(b) the sum so ordered to be paid does not exceed £5,

the court shall not order the accused to pay any costs under this section unless in the particular circumstances of the case it considers it right to do so.

(5) Where any person under the age of eighteen is convicted of an offence before a magistrates' court, the amount of any costs ordered to be paid by the accused under this section shall not exceed the amount of any fine imposed on him.

(6) Costs ordered to be paid under sub-section (2) above may include the reasonable cost of any transcript of a record of proceedings made in accordance with rules of court made for the purposes of section 32 of the Act of 1968.

CHAPTER 12

PROCEDURE BETWEEN
CONVICTION AND SENTENCE

In this chapter, we examine the procedure which takes place between conviction and the passing of sentence and at the factors which affect the sentence passed.

12.1 PROCEDURE FOLLOWING A PLEA OF GUILTY

Where the defendant pleads guilty, the first step is for the court to ascertain the facts of the case. The prosecution therefore summarise the facts of the offence so that the court is able to form a view of how serious the offence was.

The prosecution adopt a neutral stance when it comes to sentencing. It is considered wrong for a prosecutor to try to persuade the court to impose a heavy sentence. The prosecutor should therefore summarise the facts fairly.

All the allegations which are made by the prosecution should be based on admissible evidence and should be apparent from the written witness statements which have been disclosed to the defence. In *R v Hobstaff* (1993) 14 Cr App R(S) 605, for example, the Court of Appeal criticised prosecuting counsel for making allegations about the effect of the offence on the victim because he used emotive language and made allegations which were not contained in the witness statements which had been supplied to the defence.

12.1.1 The *Newton* hearing

In cases where the defendant pleads guilty but does so on a factual basis which is different from the prosecution version of what took place, the conflict must be resolved in accordance with the rules laid down by the Court of Appeal in *R v Newton* (1982) 77 Cr App R 13.

In *R v Newton* (1982) 77 Cr App R 13, the defendant was charged with buggery of his wife. He claimed that she consented to this (at that time not a defence, but relevant to sentence) but the prosecution alleged that she had not consented. The judge wrongly accepted the prosecution version without hearing evidence on the issue of consent. The Court of Appeal held that if, on a plea of guilty, there is a substantial conflict between the prosecution and the defence (that is, there is sharp divergence between the prosecution version of the facts and the defence version of the facts), the judge must either:

- accept the defence version and sentence accordingly; or
- hear evidence on what happened and then make a finding of fact as to what happened, and sentence accordingly.

In other words, where there is a substantial divergence between the two stories (that is a divergence which will have a material effect on the sentence imposed), the judge can only reject the defence version after he has heard evidence on what happened.

If the judge hears evidence, then he sits alone (that is, a jury is not empanelled). The parties are given the opportunity to call such evidence as they wish and to cross-examine witnesses called by the other side.

An example of a situation where a *Newton* hearing was appropriate is to be found in *R v McFarlane* (1995) 16 Cr App R(S) 315: the defendant was charged with assault occasioning actual bodily harm. The prosecution case was that he had jabbed his wife in the face with a fork and repeatedly punched her about the face. The defendant pleaded guilty but claimed that he had not jabbed her in the face with a fork and that he had slapped her (and had not punched her).

The judge cannot compel the prosecution or the defence to call evidence or cross-examine witnesses. However, if a party refuses to cooperate, the judge is entitled to draw the appropriate adverse inferences. In *R v Mirza* (1993) 14 Cr App R(S) 64, for example, the trial judge directed that a *Newton* hearing should take place. The defendant refused to give evidence, however. The judge accepted the prosecution version of events, and the defendant appealed on the ground that a *Newton* hearing had not taken place. Not surprisingly, the Court of Appeal dismissed the appeal.

If the defendant wants to plead guilty on the basis that he committed the offence but not in the way alleged by the prosecution (for example, he might admit the offence but deny the presence of aggravating features alleged by prosecution witnesses), the defence should warn the prosecution that this is so, to enable the prosecution to ensure that the relevant witnesses attend court on the relevant date (see *R v Mohun* (1993) 14 Cr App R(S) 5). That way, a *Newton* hearing can take place without the need for an adjournment.

As we have seen, a *Newton* hearing takes the form of the judge himself hearing evidence and deciding issues of the fact. However, in *R v Newton*, it was suggested that there may be cases where the difference between the versions put forward by the prosecution and the defence ought to be resolved by use of a jury. This can only be done where the difference in stories amounts to an allegation that the defendant committed an additional offence. For example, in a robbery case, if the offender admits threatening the use of violence but denies brandishing a weapon, one way of resolving this dispute would be to add a count alleging possession of an offensive weapon (s 1 of the Prevention of Crime Act 1953).

Another example of where it might have been appropriate to empanel a jury comes from the case of *R v Gandy* (1989) 11 Cr App R(S) 564. The defendant pleaded guilty to a charge of violent disorder. The prosecution alleged that the defendant threw a glass which caused serious injury to the victim. The defendant denied that this was the case. The judge held a *Newton* hearing, but the Court of Appeal said that it would have been more appropriate to add a count alleging wounding with intent (s 18 of the Offences Against the Person Act 1861) or alternatively a count alleging unlawful wounding (s 20 of the Offences Against the Person Act 1861); this would have enabled a jury to determine whether the defendant threw the glass.

In fact, cases where this method of resolving the difference between the two versions of events will be quite rare. The jury should not be empanelled needlessly. In *R v Dowdall* (1992) 13 Cr App R(S) 441, for example, the defendant was charged with stealing a pension book from a bag carried by a woman in a supermarket. He offered to plead guilty to theft on the basis that he had found the book and subsequently dishonestly appropriated it, but he denied that he had taken the book from the loser's bag. The judge allowed the prosecution to amend the indictment so that it contained a count alleging theft by finding as an alternative alleging theft from the woman's bag. The Court of Appeal said that the judge erred in allowing the prosecution to amend the indictment in this way. He should have accepted the defendant's plea of guilty and then held a *Newton* hearing (without empanelling a jury) to determine the circumstances in which the defendant stole the pension book. It is only appropriate to empanel a jury where the prosecution allege one offence and the defence admit a different offence; in the present case, the only offence alleged was theft. See, also, *R v Young* (1990) 12 Cr App R(S) 279.

12.1.2   Exceptions to the rule

The only exception where a *Newton* hearing need not be held is the case where the defendant's story is manifestly false or implausible (see *R v Hawkins* (1985) 7 Cr App R(S) 351; *R v Walton* (1987) 9 Cr App R(S) 279); and *Attorney General's References (Nos 3 and 4 of 1996)* [1997] 1 Cr App R(S) 29.

12.1.3   Standard of proof

The judge, in making findings of fact on a *Newton* hearing, should apply the criminal standard of proof; in other words, he must be satisfied so that he is sure that the prosecution version is correct before sentencing on that basis (*R v Kerrigan* (1993) 14 Cr App R(S) 179).

In *R v Gandy* (1989) 11 Cr App R(S) 564, it was stressed by the Court of Appeal that where the judge holds a *Newton* hearing, the rules of evidence must be followed strictly and the judge must direct himself in the same terms as he would direct a jury. In that case, for example, the Court of Appeal rejected the finding of the fact made by the judge that it was the defendant that had caused injury to the victim because the judge had not taken proper account of the weaknesses in the identification evidence against the accused (cf *R v Turnbull* [1977] QB 224; [1976] 3 All ER 549).

12.1.4   Appeals

In *R v Wood* [1991] Crim LR 926, the Court of Appeal said that it would not interfere with the judge's findings of fact in a *Newton* hearing unless no reasonable jury could have reached the conclusion reached by the judge.

If the judge wrongly fails to conduct a *Newton* hearing, the Court of Appeal will allow an appeal against sentence and will impose the sentence which would be appropriate on the basis that the defendant's version of events is the correct one (*R v Mohun* (1993) 14 Cr App R(S) 5).

12.1.5   Responsibility of the sentencer and of counsel

In *Attorney General's Reference Nos 3 and 4 of 1996* [1997] 1 Cr App R(S) 29, the defendants pleaded guilty to robbery but, when speaking to the probation officer, denied some of the allegations made by the victim. These denials were set out in the pre-sentence reports. Counsel for the defendants, when addressing the court in mitigation, referred to the pre-sentence reports but did not make specific reference to the fact that the defendants denied some of the allegations made by the prosecution. The Court of Appeal said that it was the duty of defence counsel to make it known to the prosecution, and to the court, that there was a dispute so that a *Newton* hearing could be held. The Court of Appeal went on to consider the dispute (since it had not been considered in the Crown Court) but upheld the sentence on the basis that a *Newton* hearing need not be held if the defendant's story is manifestly false or implausible.

However, in *R v Oakley* [1997] Crim LR 607, it was said that the court must itself be alert to differences between the prosecution case and the defence case. In that case, sentence was passed on a factual basis which was inconsistent with the defence version of what had happened as set out in the pre-sentence report. Defence counsel did not invite the judge to hold a *Newton* hearing. The Court of Appeal held that the judge should have been alert to the conflict and should have resolved the conflict with the *Newton* hearing whether or not the defence or prosecution asked for such a hearing.

In *R v Tolera* [1999] 1 Cr App R 29, the Court of Appeal gave further guidance on this issue. The court preferred the approach taken in *Attorney General's Reference (Nos 3 and 4 of 1996)*, above, and re-emphasised that it is not enough for the defence version to be set out in the pre-sentence report. It was said that, while the judge will normally read that part of the report, he will not ordinarily pay attention, for the purposes of sentence, to any account of the crime given by the offender to the probation officer where it conflicts with the prosecution case. If the defendant wants to rely on such an account, the defence must expressly draw those paragraphs to the court's attention and ask that sentence be passed on that basis.

Tolera also gives guidance on what should be done where the defendant puts forward a version of events which is inconsistent with the prosecution case but which the prosecutor is unable to challenge by adducing evidence to contradict what the defendant is saying. This might be the case if, for example, the defendant alleges the existence of mitigating circumstances relating to the commission of the offence. If the court is unwilling to accept the defence version, the court should make its views known so that a *Newton* hearing can take place before sentence is passed. That will normally involve the defendant giving evidence; the prosecutor should ask appropriate questions to test the defendant's evidence rather than simply leaving it to the court to question the defendant.

12.2 PROCEDURE FOLLOWING CONVICTION AFTER A NOT GUILTY PLEA

Where the defendant was convicted following a plea of not guilty, the facts of the offence will have emerged during the evidence. However, the prosecution may have to summarise the facts of the case where there has been an adjournment after conviction, as will usually be the case where a pre-sentence report has to be prepared. In the Crown Court, it is usually the judge who presided over the trial who passes sentence and it is likely that he will use his note of the evidence to refresh his memory, and so will not need the prosecution to remind him of the facts. In magistrates' courts, however, it is very common for a bench other than the bench which convicted the defendant to pass sentence, and so the bench which passes sentence will need a summary of the facts from the prosecution.

12.3 PROCEDURE AFTER PROSECUTION SUMMARY OF FACTS (IF GIVEN)

After the prosecution have summarised the facts of the case (if the defendant pleaded guilty), or after the defendant has been found guilty, the prosecution supply the court with details of the defendant's character and antecedents.

The way in which the court is made aware of the defendant's previous convictions is dealt with in *Practice Direction (Crime: Antecedents)* [1997] 4 All ER 350 (which replaces the earlier *Practice Direction* [1993] 1 WLR 1459). The new *Practice Direction* makes provision for information relating to a defendant's previous convictions to be provided by the police directly from the Police National Computer (PNC).

In cases being dealt with by either the magistrates' court or the Crown Court, the antecedents form will contain:

(a) personal details (domestic circumstances, financial commitments, employment, etc; this is based on information provided by the defendant to the police following arrest and no action will be taken by the police to verify this information);

(b) a list of previous convictions (showing, for each conviction, the date of the conviction, the court, the offence, and the sentence imposed);

(c) details of any cautions recorded against the offender.

In cases being dealt with in the Crown Court, the antecedents form should also:

(a) show the circumstances of the last three similar convictions; and

(b) set out the circumstances of the offence leading to any community order which is still in force.

The *Practice Direction* goes on to give details about the preparation and use of these forms. Those details are as follows.

In the Crown Court, the police will provide brief details of the circumstances of the last three similar convictions, and/or of convictions likely to be of interest to the court. That information should be supplied separately and attached to the form which sets out the defendant's antecedents. Where the current alleged offence is within the term of an existing community order which is still in force, brief details of the circumstances (including the date) of the offence leading to the community order should be included in the antecedents form (in case the Crown Court decides to revoke the community order and re-sentence for the earlier offence).

In Crown Court cases, seven copies of the antecedents of each defendant should be prepared by police as soon as the defendant is committed for trial or sentence. Within 21 days, the police should sent two copies to CPS, and the remaining five to the court; the court should then send one copy to the defence, and one to the Probation Service; the rest are for the court's use. Seven days before the hearing date, the police should check the record of previous convictions. Details of any additional convictions should be sent to CPS and the Court. Details of any additional outstanding cases should also be provided at this stage.

Where the defendant disputes the accuracy of the information provided by the police, this matter should, where possible, be raised at least seven days before the date of the hearing.

In the magistrates' court, antecedents are prepared by the police and five copies of the antecedents of each defendant are to be submitted to CPS in the case file. Unless there is a local agreement between CPS and the court, CPS is responsible for distributing the copies: two to the court, one to the defence and one to the Probation Service (when appropriate). Where the antecedents were provided some time before the hearing, the police should, if requested to do so by CPS, check the record of convictions. Details of any additional convictions, and of any additional outstanding cases, should be provided at this stage.

It used to be the practice, at least in the Crown Court, for a police officer to give sworn evidence about the defendant's antecedents. However, this information is now given by the prosecutor, who simply reads details from the standard forms.

Where the offender has a large number of previous convictions, the court will indicate which of those convictions should be referred to by the prosecutor; it is only the convictions referred to by the prosecutor that the court will take into account in passing sentence for the present offence.

If the offender disputes the accuracy of the list of previous convictions, the convictions which he disputes have to be proved. Section 73 of the Police and Criminal Evidence Act 1984 enables proof of previous convictions to be by way of a certificate of conviction from the convicting court. Alternatively, s 39 of the Criminal Justice Act 1948 enables a previous conviction to be proved by showing that the fingerprints of the defendant are the same as those of the person previously convicted.

A further option is for someone (for example, a police officer) to give evidence that he was present in court when the defendant was convicted of the offence on the earlier occasion and that that person is the defendant in the present proceedings. However, a previous conviction can be proved by any admissible evidence; for example, if the defendant admits the previous conviction to the police (*R v Derwentside Magistrates' Court ex p Swift* (1996) 160 JP 468).

If the present conviction means that the offender is in breach of a previous order (for example, suspended sentence or conditional discharge), it is necessary to ask the defendant whether he admits that he is in breach of the earlier order. If the defendant denies the breach, the breach has to be proved by means of admissible evidence that the earlier order was made.

12.4 REPORTS ON THE OFFENDER

As well as considering the prosecution summary of the facts (if given) and the defendant's antecedents, the court will usually have to consider a pre-sentence report.

12.4.1 Pre-sentence report

Section 81(1) of the Powers of Criminal Courts (Sentencing) Act 2000 requires the court to obtain and consider a pre-sentence report before imposing a custodial sentence unless the court takes the view that a report is unnecessary.

Section 36(4) of the Act requires the court to obtain and consider a pre-sentence report before imposing a community service order, a combination order, or a probation or supervision order with additional requirements (again, unless the court takes the view that a report is unnecessary).

Where the court which passes sentence does not obtain a pre-sentence report and there is an appeal against sentence, the court hearing the appeal need not obtain a report itself if either it decides that the court below was justified in deciding that a report was unnecessary or the court hearing the appeal decides that, even though the court below should have obtained a report, it is unnecessary to obtain one now.

In the case of offenders who have attained the age of 18, pre-sentence reports are compiled by probation officers.

The court is not bound to accept the conclusions in a pre-sentence report. So, for example, if the report says that the offender is suitable for probation, the court does not have to accept that view. In *R v Smith* [1998] 1 Cr App R(S) 138, for example, the defendant was convicted following trial of causing actual bodily harm by stalking his victim. A psychiatric report said that the defendant did not represent a continuing threat to the victim. The judge rejected that view. The Court of Appeal held that the judge was entitled to take the view that he did and to sentence accordingly.

12.4.2 Disclosure of pre-sentence report

The present practice is that the defence advocate invariably has sight of a copy of the pre-sentence report. It is good practice to ask the defendant if he has seen a copy of the report. If he has not, then he should be asked to read through it and check its accuracy (or the advocate should summarise its contents).

At the moment, it is rare for the prosecutor to have sight of a copy of the pre-sentence report. This is no doubt because the traditional view is that the prosecutor has no further part to play once a conviction has been recorded (apart from ensuring that the court does not exceed its sentencing powers).

Section 156 of the Powers of Criminal Courts (Sentencing) Act 2000 requires the pre-sentence report to be disclosed to the offender or his legal representative and to the prosecutor. Where the offender is under 17 and is not legally represented, the report is to be disclosed to his parent or guardian (if present in court) instead.

Section 156(5) stipulates that the prosecutor can only use information gleaned from the report for the purpose of deciding whether to make representations to the court about the content of the report and for making any such representations.

The disclosure of the report to the prosecutor under s 156 means that prosecutors will have a chance to check that any factual information contained in the report agrees with information contained in the prosecution file. Any representations made by the prosecutor under sub-section (5) are likely to be confined to drawing the attention of the court to any factual inaccuracies in the report.

12.4.3   Juveniles

If the offender is under 18, the court (that is, the youth court or the Crown Court) may only dispense with a pre-sentence report if it is considering a custodial sentence, or one of the community sentences to which the need for a report applies, if either the offence is triable only on indictment or there exists a pre-sentence report in respect of an earlier (though presumably fairly recent) offence. See s 81(7) and s 36(9) of the Powers of Criminal Courts (Sentencing) Act 2000.

For offenders who are under 13, reports are prepared by local authority social workers. In the case of young offenders who have attained the age of 13, reports are prepared either by social workers or probation officers. Such reports are usually prepared by a social worker, but the report would be prepared by a probation officer if, for example, the probation service was already having dealings with a member of the offender's family.

Before passing sentence on a juvenile, the court must give the juvenile and her parent or guardian a chance to make representations about the appropriate sentence. The court must also consider all available information about the offender's general conduct, home environment, school record and medical history. In addition to the report from a local authority social worker (or a probation officer), there will also be a report from the juvenile's school (and, if appropriate, her doctor) (see rr 10 and 11 of the Magistrates' Courts (Children and Young Persons) Rules 1992 and s 9 of the Children and Young Persons Act 1969).

12.4.4   Adjournments prior to sentence

Section 10(3) of the Magistrates' Courts Act 1980 empowers a magistrates' court to adjourn before passing sentence in order to enable inquiries to be made as to the most suitable method of dealing with the offender.

Section 10(3) stipulates that adjournments between conviction and sentence should be for no more than four weeks at a time if the offender is on bail (note that the presumption in favour of bail created by s 4 of the Bail Act 1976 applies to such an offender) and for no more than three weeks at a time if the offender is in custody.

The Crown Court has inherent jurisdiction to adjourn and there is no statutory limit on the length of the adjournment. However, the Crown Court will usually adopt the same periods as magistrates' courts.

12.4.5 Other reports

Before the court can make a hospital order or a probation order with a requirement for medical treatment, a psychiatric report is required (see s 37 of the Mental Health Act 1983; para 5, Sched 2, of the Powers of Criminal Courts (Sentencing) Act 2000.

12.4.6 Keeping sentencing options open

When the court adjourns the case so that a report can be prepared, great care must be exercised when the court explains to the defendant what is happening.

In *R v Gillam* (1980) 2 Cr App R(S) 267, the judge adjourned the case so that a report could be prepared to assess whether the defendant was suitable for community service. The circumstances were such that the defendant was led to believe that if the report was favourable he would receive community service rather than a custodial sentence. In the event, the report was favourable but a custodial sentence was passed nonetheless. The Court of Appeal said that the judge should have imposed a non-custodial sentence; otherwise a feeling of injustice is aroused.

Similarly, in *R v Howard* (1989) 11 Cr App R(S) 583, the court adjourned for a pre-sentence report and the defendant was told that the court was minded to deal with the case by means of a community service order. A custodial sentence was subsequently imposed and this sentence was quashed by the Court of Appeal.

In *R v Keily* (1989) 11 Cr App R(S) 273, a judge at a pre-trial review said that if the defendant were to plead guilty a custodial sentence would not be imposed. The case was later tried by a different judge; the defendant pleaded not guilty but was convicted and was sent to prison. The Court of Appeal quashed the custodial sentence on the grounds that the first judge had erred in giving an indication which put pressure on the defendant to plead guilty (infringing the rule set out in *R v Turner* [1970] 2 QB 321 [1970] 2 All ER 281; see Chapter 9, 9.31.1) and that the second judge was bound by the indication given by the first judge that an immediate custodial sentence would not be imposed (following *R v Wilkinson* (1988) 9 Cr App R(S) 468).

This principle only applies if there was something 'in the nature of a promise, express or implied, that, if a particular proposal is recommended, it will be adopted' (*R v Moss* (1984) 5 Cr App R(S) 209, *per* Croom-Johnson LJ).

Thus, if the court makes it clear that it is not committing itself to a non-custodial sentence even if the pre-sentence report recommends a non-custodial sentence, no sense of injustice is created if a custodial sentence is passed even if the court rejects a recommendation for a non-custodial sentence contained in the report (*R v Horton* (1985) 7 Cr App R(S) 299).

Thus, in *R v Renan* (1994) 15 Cr App R(S) 722, the judge granted the defendant bail pending the preparation of a pre-sentence report but said nothing about sentencing options. It was held that this did not, in the circumstances of the particular case, create an expectation that a custodial sentence would not be passed. A custodial sentence was, accordingly, upheld.

12.5   THE PLEA IN MITIGATION

A plea in mitigation usually comprises a speech by the barrister or solicitor appearing for the defence. If the defendant is unrepresented, he will be asked if there is anything he wishes to say before sentence is passed.

Occasionally, witnesses will be called to show the good character of the offender or to explain why he acted out of character by committing an offence.

The matters which the prosecution will draw to the courts attention will be matters which relate to the seriousness of the offence; the plea in mitigation by the defence may address the seriousness of the offence, together with mitigating factors relating to the offender. In the next section, we consider factors which make an offence more or less serious.

12.6   AGGRAVATING AND MITIGATING FACTORS

The decision as to what sentence to pass involves a two stage process:

- the court first has to decide what sentence is appropriate given the seriousness of the offence committed by the defendant;
- the court then goes on to consider whether that sentence should be reduced in the light of any mitigating circumstances which relate to the defendant.

Thus, the court looks first at the offence and then at the offender.

12.7   THE OFFENCE ITSELF

Relevant factors relating to the offence include the following:

- In a case involving money, the amount is an important factor in determining the seriousness of the offence. The greater the sum stolen or the greater the value of the property damaged, the more serious the offence.
- Using or threatening the use of violence makes the offence more serious, and the use or threatened use of a weapon makes it more serious still.

- The offence is more serious if the victim is vulnerable. The term vulnerable includes not only the aged and infirm (as in *Attorney General's Reference (No 13 of 1991)* (1993) 14 Cr App R(S) 756), but also those whose work brings them into contact with the public and so places them at greater risk (for example, police officers, taxi drivers, bus drivers, milkmen and, as in *R v Rigg* (1997) *The Times*, 4 July, a publican).

- Where an offence is committed in breach of trust, the offence is made more serious by that breach (see, for example, *R v Barrick* (1985) 81 Cr App R 78 and *R v Clark* [1998] 2 Cr App R 137). This includes the employee who steals from his employer and the postman who steals or destroys the mail. In a case involving breach of trust, a custodial sentence may be appropriate even if the sum involved is small (*R v McCormick* (1995) 16 Cr App R(S) 134).

- If the offence was committed on impulse, that is a mitigating factor. On the other hand, an offence is made more serious if it is premeditated. The greater the degree of planning and sophistication, the more serious the offence. See, for example, *Attorney General's Reference (No 13 of 1991)* (1993).

- Where more than one person is involved in the commission of an offence, the fact that more than one person was involved may make the offence more serious. A mugging by a gang is worse than a mugging carried out by one person.

- Where more than one person is involved, the level of a particular person's involvement affects the seriousness of the offence as regards that offender. The look-out and the get-away driver will be dealt with more leniently than those who actually carry out the burglary or the robbery as the case may be.

- If the offender is able to show that the offence was committed out of something approaching necessity (but the necessity falls short of being a defence) that offence is less serious than one committed for purely personal gain.

- Provocation is only a defence to murder but may be used as a mitigating circumstance for any offence. Usually, of course, the question of provocation arises only in offences of violence. See, for example, *R v Brookin* (1994).

- Section 151(2) of the Powers of Criminal Courts (Sentencing) Act 2000 provides that, if an offence is committed whilst the offender is on bail in respect of another offence, that is an aggravating factor as far as the later offence is concerned. This would appear to be the case even if the two offences are different in nature or relative seriousness.

- The fact that an offence was 'racially aggravated' must be treated as an aggravating factor which increases the seriousness of the offence (s 153 of the Powers of Criminal Courts (Sentencing) Act 2000. In *R v Saunders* [2000]

1 Cr App R 458, the Court of Appeal said that, where an offence involves racial aggravation, a term of up to two years' custody may be added to the sentence. The presence of racial aggravation may make a custodial sentence appropriate for an offence which would otherwise have merited a non-custodial sentence.

- The effect of the offence on the victim: the government is keen for the views of victims to be given greater prominence in the sentencing process and is likely to introduce legislation on the topic. The common law position was summarised in *R v Perks* (2000) *The Times*, 5 May. The Court of Appeal (following *R v Hobstaff* (1993) 14 Cr App R(S) 605) laid down guidelines where the court, at the sentencing stage, wishes to take account of a statement from the victim as to impact of the offence on the victim. The court must not make assumptions, unsupported by evidence, about the effects of an offence on the victim. However, if an offence has had a particularly damaging or distressing effect on the victim, that should be known to, and be taken into account by, the court when passing sentence. Evidence of the effect of an offence on the victim must be in the form of a witness statement complying with the requirements of s 9 of the Criminal Justice Act 1967 (signed by the maker and containing a declaration of truth) or an expert's report, duly served on the defence prior to sentence. Evidence of the victim alone should be approached with care, especially if it relates to matters which the defence cannot realistically be expected to investigate. The court went on to say that the opinions of the victim or the victim's close relatives on the appropriate level of sentence should not be taken into account.

12.8   MITIGATION RELATING TO THE OFFENDER

After consideration of the seriousness of the offence itself, the court goes on to examine any mitigation which relates to the offender.

12.8.1   A plea of guilty

Section 152 of the Powers of Criminal Courts (Sentencing) Act 2000 gives statutory effect to the already well established principle that credit should be given for pleading guilty. Section 152 requires the court to take account of the stage in the proceedings at which the offender indicated his intention to plead guilty and the circumstances in which this indication was given. It is difficult to see what this statutory provision adds to the existing law. The reasons for this credit are:

- it shows contrition on the part of the accused;
- it saves court time, in that no trial takes place;

- if the defendant admitted the offence when first questioned by the police (or, better still, surrendered himself to police custody), police time is saved, in that unnecessary enquiries do not have to be made;

- in cases where the experience of giving evidence would be traumatic to a witness (for example, a rape victim), the plea of guilty spares the witness this trauma.

The usual credit for pleading guilty in a case where a custodial sentence is imposed is a one third reduction in that sentence (*R v Buffery* (1993) 14 Cr App R(S) 511). This credit may be withheld if, for example, it is clear that the offender is only pleading guilty because the prosecution case against him is overwhelming. See, also, Chapter 13, 13.1.6.

Section 152 requires the court to have regard to when the defendant pleads guilty. In the case of an offence which is triable only on indictment, the earliest point at which the defendant can plead guilty is when he is arraigned in the Crown Court; however, the defendant can nevertheless give an informal indication that he intends to plead guilty. In the case of an offence which is triable either way, the earliest stage at which the defendant can effectively enter a plea of guilty is at the 'plea before venue' hearing (see Chapter 3, 3.3). If the defendant indicates an intention to plead not guilty (or give no indication of likely plea) at the plea before venue hearing, but then (at the trial) enters a plea of guilty, he may forfeit some of the credit which he would otherwise have earned for pleading guilty.

Credit should also be given if the offender has assisted the police, perhaps by helping them to trace stolen property or to arrest other offenders. Where an accomplice pleads guilty and gives evidence for the prosecution against his erstwhile co-defendants, substantial credit should be given. In *R v Wood* [1997] 1 Cr App R(S) 347, the Court of Appeal said that the discount for someone who 'turns Queen's evidence' (that is, gives evidence against an accomplice) should reflect the seriousness of the offence, the importance of the evidence, and the effect which giving the evidence will have on the future circumstances of the witness (for example, placing him in danger of retribution).

In *R v A (Informer: Reduction of Sentence)* [1999] 1 Cr App R(S) 52, the Court of Appeal reiterated that, where an offender gives information which is accurate, detailed, useful and hitherto unknown to the authorities, enabling serious criminal activity to be stopped and serious criminals brought to book, a substantial discount in sentence may be appropriate. Where, by supplying such valuable information, the offender exposes himself or his family to personal jeopardy, this should be taken into account. However, where the offender gives information to the authorities after he has been sentenced, the Court of Appeal will not normally take account of that information. On the other hand, if the offender expresses willingness to help prior to sentence but the value of the help is not fully appreciated at that stage, or the help thereafter given greatly exceeds the help anticipated by the sentencer, the Court of Appeal can adjust the sentence to reflect the value of the help given after sentence.

It is also very good mitigation, because it is a sign of remorse, if the offender has tried to compensate the victim of the crime.

The other side of the coin is that the defendant should not be penalised for pleading not guilty. In *R v Blaize* (1997) *The Times*, 12 June, for example, the Court of Appeal said that a defendant ought to be sentenced for the offence of which he or she has been convicted, not for the manner in which the defence was conducted. By contesting the charge, the defendant loses the benefit of the discount which a plea of guilty usually earns but, by pleading not guilty the defendant does not run the risk of the sentence being increased. It followed, said the Court of Appeal, that false accusations of racial prejudice made in the course of the defence case should not serve to increase the sentence imposed on conviction.

12.8.2   Previous convictions

Section 151(1) of the Powers of Criminal Courts (Sentencing) Act 2000 states that:

> In considering the seriousness of any offence, the court may take into account any previous convictions of the offender or any failure of his to respond to previous sentences.

The statute is, unfortunately, silent on what effect previous convictions should have. The best view appears to be that expressed in *R v Carlton* [1993] Crim LR 981, namely, that s 151(1) preserves the common law principle that in fixing the sentence to be imposed, the starting point is to assess the seriousness of the offence. A more lenient sentence can be imposed than that justified by the seriousness of the offence if the defendant is of previous good character. The effect of previous convictions is that the offender is deprived of what would otherwise be the very strong mitigation that he has no previous convictions. Thus, a defendant who has previous convictions will not receive the discount in sentence which a person who does not have previous convictions will receive. It would, however, be wrong in principle to impose a sentence greater than that appropriate to the seriousness of the offence merely because the offender has previous convictions.

Thus, the more previous convictions recorded against an offender, the greater the loss of 'good character' mitigation. This effect is sometimes called 'progressive loss of mitigation'. What the court must not do is to impose a sentence greater than that justified by the seriousness of the offence merely because the offender has previous convictions. To do so is, in effect, to sentence the defendant again for his previous misdemeanours (see *R v Queen* (1981) 3 Cr

App R(S) 245). So, to take a case where the custody threshold has been met, if the appropriate sentence is between six and nine months, an offender with previous convictions might receive a sentence closer to nine months than six. However, it would be wrong in such a case to impose 12 months.

If the offender has previous convictions, but those convictions were some time ago, this conviction-free period should be taken into account when sentence is passed.

It has frequently been recognised (for example, in *R v Bowles* [1996] 2 Cr App R(S) 248) that there are occasions when, in the case of persistent offenders, it is appropriate to make a probation order, rather than impose a custodial sentence, provided that there is sufficient reason to think that it might be possible to break his cycle of offending once and for all. To take such a course of action, the court should be satisfied that the offender is highly motivated to change his ways.

It is also very strong mitigation to have good character that goes beyond merely the absence of previous convictions. For example, in *R v Clark (Joan)* (1999) *The Times*, 27 January, the defendant had defrauded the public of a total of £18,000 over a period of six years (a very serious offence, almost certain to carry a lengthy prison sentence). However, there was a moving tribute from the nephews and nieces whom she had brought up following the death of their mother, and her parish priest gave evidence of a number of local community and charitable activities with which she had been involved. The Court of Appeal held (maybe a little surprisingly) that the judge should have placed greater weight on her positive good character (that is, good character going beyond the legal sense of an absence of convictions); the sentence of six months' imprisonment was reduced to seven days.

12.8.3 Failures to respond

The provision in s 151(1) of the Powers of Criminal Courts (Sentencing) Act 2000 which entitles the court to take account of failure to respond to previous sentences operates in this way: if the sentence appropriate to the seriousness of the offence is a custodial sentence but it is argued on behalf of the defendant that a non-custodial sentence should be imposed, that argument can be rejected if the offender has previously been given a sentence such as community service or probation but has nonetheless re-offended. Re-offending may be taken as showing that non-custodial sentences do not prevent this offender from re-offending (see *R v Oliver and Little* [1993] 1 WLR 177; [1993] 2 All ER 9).

This argument is strongest where the offender has committed offences whilst being on probation or subject to a community service order.

If some time has elapsed since the offender's last conviction, some credit may be given for the conviction-free period in determining the effectiveness of non-custodial sentences in preventing the offender from re-offending.

In *R v Southwark Crown Court ex p Ager* (1990) 91 Cr App R 322, it was held (interpreting earlier legislation) that a failure to respond can only be established by the existence of at least two previous sentences.

Under the Criminal Justice Act 1991, conditional discharges, fines, community orders are all regarded as sentences for these purposes.

12.8.4   Other factors

Mitigation may be derived from the personal circumstances of the offender. The courts tend to look more favourably on people who have stable homes and secure jobs, partly by giving credit for a past contribution to society and partly because such people have more to lose as a result of acquiring a criminal record.

In appropriate cases, a plea in mitigation should try to explain why the offender has turned to crime. For example, it may well be that a person with no previous convictions suddenly starts committing offences at a time when she is suffering stress at work or as a result of a family break up. A related argument is that, if the source of the stress has been removed, the risk of re-offending is negligible. See, for example, *R v Khan* (1994) *The Times*, 24 February and *R v Edney* (1994) 15 Cr App R(S) 889.

The age of the offender may be relevant. Account is taken particularly of the youth of an offender, perhaps because the young are more easily led astray. However, in *R v Dodds* (1997) *The Times*, 28 January, the Court of Appeal said that, in a serious case, such as aggravated burglary involving the use of violence, a substantial reduction in sentence should no longer be given because of the offender's youth.

Account is also taken of any mental disorder from which the offender is suffering. Specific orders for mentally ordered offenders are considered in Chapter 18.

The fact that the offender was acting under the influence of drink or drugs is regarded by some as a mitigating factor on the basis that the offender did not know what she was doing. Others, however, regard it as an aggravating factor that the offender deprived herself of self-control.

In some cases, it will be appropriate to consider the likely effect of a particular sentence on people other than the offender. For example, if a single parent is sent to prison, the children may well have to go into the care of the local authority.

12.8.5 Associated offences

In assessing seriousness where there is more than one offence, the court looks at the seriousness of the combination of associated offences.

Section 161(1) of the Powers of Criminal Courts (Sentencing) Act 2000 provides that an offence is an associated offence with another offence (which we may call the main offence) if:

- it is an offence of which the defendant has been convicted, or for which he is to be sentenced, in the same proceedings as the main offence; or
- it is an offence which the offender has asked the court to take into consideration (see 12.9.1 below) when passing sentence for the main offence.

In *R v Godfrey* (1993) 14 Cr App R(S) 804, it was held that, if the defendant is being re-sentenced for an offence in respect of which a conditional discharge was imposed at the same time as he is being sentenced for the offence which put him in breach of the conditional discharge, the earlier offence is an associated offence with the later one. The same would apply where the offender is re-sentenced following the revocation of a community sentence.

In *R v Crawford* (1993) 14 Cr App R(S) 782 and *R v McQuillan* [1993] Crim LR 893, it was held that, where an offence is committed in breach of a suspended sentence, the present offence and the offence for which the suspended sentence was imposed are not 'associated offences'. This is because the court is not imposing a sentence for the earlier offence, it is merely activating a sentence imposed on an earlier occasion.

12.9 RULE THAT DEFENDANT SHOULD BE SENTENCED ONLY FOR OFFENCES OF WHICH HE HAS BEEN CONVICTED AND EXCEPTIONS TO THAT RULE

It is an important principle of sentencing that the offender should only be sentenced for offences to which he has pleaded guilty or been found guilty. For example, if the offender is charged with an indictment containing a count alleging wounding with intent (s 18 of the Offences Against the Person Act 1861) and an alternative count alleging unlawful wounding (s 20), and the jury acquits the offender of the s 18 offence but convicts him of the s 20 offence, the judge must ensure that the sentence reflects the fact that the offender is guilty only of the lesser offence. The same applies where the prosecution agree to accept a plea of guilty to a lesser offence and the more serious offence is left on the file or the prosecution offer no evidence in respect of it (see *R v Booker* (1982) 4 Cr App R(S) 53; *R v Stubbs* (1988) 88 Cr App R 53).

A good example of the operation of this principle is to be found in *R v Lawrence* (1981) 3 Cr App R(S) 49. The defendant was charged with two offences under the Misuse of Drugs Act 1971; he pleaded guilty to cultivating cannabis and the prosecution did not proceed with a count alleging possession of cannabis with intent to supply. The Court of Appeal reduced his sentence because it was apparent that the judge had sentenced him on the basis that he was growing cannabis in order to sell it.

Moreover, the judge must not sentence the offender on the basis that he has committed similar offences on other occasions, even if the circumstances of the offence of which the defendant has been convicted (or even admissions made by the defendant to the police) suggest that the offence of which the defendant has been convicted is just part of a course of criminal conduct (*R v Ayensu* (1982) 4 Cr App R(S) 248; *R v Reeves* (1983) 5 Cr App R(S) 292).

In *R v Perkins* (1994) 15 Cr App R(S) 402, the defendant was accused of breaching a notice under the Town and Country Planning Act 1971 preventing him from tipping waste onto certain land. The summons alleged a breach of the notice on one particular day. However, the judge imposed a fine on the basis not of one incident but on the basis that breaches of the notice had been taking place over an extensive period of several months. The Court of Appeal said that since the basis of the appellant's conviction was a single breach of the notice, that should be the basis of the sentence. The appellant had not admitted other breaches of the notice and so should only have been sentenced for the offence of which he had actually been convicted.

The same principle applies to compensation orders. In *R v Crutchley and Tonks* (1994) 15 Cr App R(S) 627, the offenders pleaded guilty to specimen offences arising out of a social security fraud; the appellants accepted that the charges to which they had pleaded guilty were sample counts representing a substantial number of other offences. However, no other offences were taken into consideration. The compensation order made by the Crown Court reflected the whole amount lost as a result of the fraud, not just the offences to which the appellants had pleaded guilty. The Court of Appeal held that there was no power to make such an order since it was not open to the court to make a compensation order in respect of loss or damage arising from offences which, even though admitted by the defendant, have not been subject of a conviction and have not been taken into consideration.

There is, however, a very important exception to the general rule: 'offences taken into consideration'.

12.9.1 Offences taken into consideration

It is very common for an offender to ask for offences with which he is not charged to be taken into consideration when he is sentenced for offences with which he is charged and to which he pleads guilty. These other offences are colloquially known as 't.i.c.s'.

Suppose that a person is arrested for an offence and when he is interviewed by the police admits that he has committed a large number of similar offences.

In such a case, the defendant is usually charged with a number of the offences which he has admitted. The prosecution also draw up a list of the other offences which the offender has admitted to the police. The offender is asked to sign the list to confirm that he wishes those offences to be taken into consideration. Any offences which he subsequently denies should be deleted from the list.

When the prosecution summarise the facts of the case, they will refer to the list of 't.i.c.s' and the court will ask the offender to confirm that he wishes the offences to be taken into consideration.

The offender does not stand convicted of offences which are taken into consideration. This means that the maximum sentence which the court may impose is fixed by the offences to which the offender has pleaded guilty or of which he has been found guilty.

It follows from this that no separate penalty can be imposed in respect of an offence which has been taken into consideration. However, 't.i.c.s' are regarded as associated offences under s 31(2)(b) of the Criminal Justice Act 1991 and, so, the presence of 't.i.c.s' may result in an increase in the sentence imposed for the offences of which the defendant actually stands convicted.

Because the offender does not stand convicted of offences which have been taken into consideration, the doctrine of *autrefois convict* (see Chapter 9, 9.36.4) does not apply to those offences (*R v Nicholson* [1947] 2 All ER 535). Thus, in theory, the offender could subsequently be prosecuted for offences which have been taken into consideration. However, such action would only be taken in exceptional circumstances.

There is no statutory basis for the practice of taking offences into consideration. However, it enables the police to close their files on the offences which have been dealt with in this way (which has a good effect on that force's 'clear up rate'); although the existence of 't.i.c.s' will result in a slightly increased sentence, the defendant is able to 'wipe the slate clean', which is a good indicator of remorse.

The court has a discretion whether or not to comply with the defendant's request to take offences into consideration. There is very little authority on the subject, but it is regarded as inappropriate for offences to be taken into consideration if they are of a different type to the offence(s) of which the defendant actually stands convicted.

In *R v Simons* [1953] 1 WLR 1014, it was held that magistrates should not take into consideration offences which are triable only on indictment.

In *R v Collins* [1947] KB 560; [1947] 1 All ER 147, it was held that a court should not take into consideration offences which carry endorsement or disqualification from driving unless the offences of which the offender stands convicted also carry such penalty.

12.9.2 Specimen or sample counts

A 'specimen' (or 'sample') count is where the defendant is tried on a single charge alleging that he engaged in criminal conduct of a specified kind on a single specified occasion or on a single occasion within a specified period, but the prosecution allege that such conduct was representative of other criminal conduct of the same kind on other occasions which are not the subject of specific charges. Take, for example, the case of a defendant who dishonestly receives a stolen cheque book and then dishonestly obtains property using each of the 20 cheques: if the indictment contains one count of receiving (the cheque book itself) and, say, three counts of obtaining property by deception (the use of three of the 20 cheques), those three counts would be sample counts.

In a number of cases, such as *R v Huchison* [1972] 1 WLR 398; [1972] 1 All ER 936, *R v McKenzie* (1984) 6 Cr App R(S) 99, and *R v Burfoot* (1990) 12 Cr App R(S) 252, the Court of Appeal made it clear that the offender could only be sentenced on the basis that the counts of which he stood convicted were sample counts, illustrative of an overall course of conduct (rather than being sentenced on the basis that he had only committed the offences of which he stood convicted), if the offender accepted that the convictions represented an overall course of conduct. Thus, in *R v Clark* [1996] 2 Cr App R(S) 351, the appellant was convicted of a single count of indecent assault. This single count was said by the prosecution to reflect a series of offences committed over a two year period. However, the appellant did not admit committing any offence. The judge passed sentence on the basis that D had committed a series of offences. The Court of Appeal said that, having been convicted on a single count particularising a single act and not having admitted any offence beyond that, the appellant could only be sentenced on the basis of that single act.

However, in *R v Kidd* [1998] 1 W LR 604; [1998] 1 All ER 42, the Court of Appeal went further and effectively put a stop to the practice of using counts as 'specimen counts'. The court held that the defendant can only be sentenced for an offence which has been proved against him (that is, where he pleads guilty to it or is found guilty of it) or which he has asked the court to take into consideration when passing sentence. Therefore, when passing sentence, the court must not take account of the fact that the charges are said by the prosecution to be 'specimen' or 'sample' charges. Thus, if the prosecution want other incidents to be taken account of, those other incidents must be the subject of individual charges (or offences 'taken into consideration' under the procedure set out in the previous section).

In *R v Rosenburg* [1999] 1 Cr App R(S) 365 and *R v T (Michael Patrick)* [1999] 1 Cr App R(S) 419, the Court of Appeal repeated that a defendant should not be sentenced for offences of which he has not been convicted (whether by pleading guilty or being found guilty) and which he has not asked the court to take into consideration under the 't.i.c.' procedure.

12.10   SENTENCING POWERS OF MAGISTRATES' COURTS

The sentence which may be imposed by a magistrates' court often depends on whether the offence is summary or triable either way.

12.10.1 Summary offences

The statute creating a summary offence indicates whether or not the offence is punishable with imprisonment.

If the summary offence is an imprisonable offence, the maximum sentence is six months or that prescribed by the statute which creates the offence, whichever is less (s 78(1) of the Powers of Criminal Courts (Sentencing) Act 2000). If the statute creating the offence expressly overrides the limit of six months, then the statute creating the offence prevails (s 78(2)).

The maximum fine for an offence is that prescribed by the statute which creates the offence. Most enactments refer to a level on the standard scale of fines (see Chapter 15), rather than to a specific sum of money.

12.10.2 Offences which are triable either way

The maximum sentence for an offence which is triable either way because it is listed in Sched 1 of the Magistrates' Courts Act 1980 is six months' imprisonment or a fine not exceeding £5,000 (s 32(1)).

Where the offence is triable either way because the statute creating it gives alternative penalties for summary conviction and conviction on indictment, the maximum penalty is six months' imprisonment or the term specified in the statute creating the offence, whichever is the less (s 78(1) of the 2000 Act). If the statute creating the offence expressly overrides the six month limit, the statute creating the offence prevails (s 78(2)). The maximum fine which may be imposed is a fine not exceeding £5,000 or the amount prescribed by the statute, whichever is greater (s 32(2) of the 1980 Act).

12.10.3   Consecutive sentences of imprisonment

Section 133(1) of the Magistrates' Courts Act 1980 empowers a magistrates' court to order that custodial sentences which it imposes may run concurrently or consecutively. However, the maximum aggregate sentence which may be imposed is six months (s 133(1)) unless the court is dealing with the offender for two or more offences which are triable either way; in that case, the maximum aggregate sentence is 12 months (s 133(2)).

Thus, if an offender is convicted of three summary offences each of which is punishable with three months' imprisonment, the magistrates could, for example, impose a sentence of three months on each offence but one of the terms would have to be concurrent so that the maximum does not exceed six months; alternatively, they could impose a sentence of two months on each to run consecutively.

If the offender is being dealt with for one either way offence and a number of summary offences, the maximum aggregate sentence is six months. It is only where the court is dealing with an offender for at least two either way offences that a total of up to 12 months' imprisonment may be imposed.

It should be noted that, where a magistrates' court activates a suspended sentence (which it can only do if that sentence was imposed by a magistrates' court), the provisions of s 133 do not apply; the effect of this is that, whilst the sentence(s) for the present offence(s) must not exceed the limit set by s 133, the suspended sentence may be activated even if doing so has the effect of imposing a total term in excess of the limit set by s 133 (*R v Chamberlain* (1992) 13 Cr App R(S) 525).

12.10.4   Aggregate fines

Although there is a limit to the amount of a fine for an individual offence, there is no limit on the aggregate fine which may be imposed. Thus, if the court is dealing with an offender for 10 offences which are triable either way, it could impose a fine of £5,000 on each, making a total of £50,000.

12.10.5   Criminal damage

Chapter 3, 3.11 sets out the special procedure to be followed in criminal damage cases. Where the value of the criminal damage is less than £5,000, the maximum sentence which may be imposed is three months' imprisonment or a fine not exceeding level 4 (£2,500).

12.10.6 Compensation orders

Compensation orders are considered in Chapter 18, 18.1. The maximum compensation order which can be made by a magistrates' court is £5,000 per offence, and this applies whether the offence is summary or triable either way (s 131(1) of the Powers of Criminal Courts (Sentencing) Act 2000).

Apart from the limit of £5,000 per offence, there is no limit on the aggregate amount of compensation which may be awarded.

Where the offender asks for offences to be taken into consideration (see 12.9.1 above), compensation may be ordered in respect of offences taken into consideration but the total amount of the order must not exceed the maximum which could be ordered for the offence(s) of which the offender has actually been convicted (s 131(2)). Thus, if the offender is convicted of three offences and asks for six others to be taken into consideration, the maximum compensation order is £15,000.

12.10.7 Other sentences

In respect of other sentences (for example, community sentences), the powers of the magistrates' courts are identical to those of the Crown Court.

12.10.8 Offenders aged 18 to 20

Where a magistrates' court is dealing with an offender aged between 18 and 20, all of the principles set out above apply, save that references to imprisonment should read detention in a young offender institution.

12.10.9 Sentencing juveniles in the magistrates' court

In Chapter 5, we saw that there are circumstances in which a person under the age of 18 may be tried in an adult magistrates' court.

If an adult magistrates' court convicts an offender who is under 18, the following options are available to the court under s 8(8) of the Powers of Criminal Courts (Sentencing) Act 2000:

- discharge the offender absolutely or conditionally;
- impose a fine not exceeding £1,000 (£250 if the offender is under 14);
- order a parent or guardian to enter into a recognisance to take proper care of, and exercise proper control over, the offender.

In addition, the court may disqualify the offender from driving and make ancillary orders such as orders to pay compensation and costs.

If none of these powers is appropriate, the adult magistrates' court will remit the offender to the youth court to be dealt with under s 8(2) of the 2000 Act.

Note that an adult magistrates' court dealing with a juvenile cannot impose a custodial sentence or a community sentence; nor can it commit the juvenile to the Crown Court for sentence.

12.10.10 Sentencing the defendant in his absence

We saw in Chapter 4 that s 11 of the Magistrates' Courts Act 1980 empowers a magistrates' court to try a defendant in his absence in certain circumstances This power extends to sentencing a defendant who has been convicted in his absence. The power to sentence a defendant in his absence is subject to two restrictions:

- a person may not be sentenced to a custodial sentence in his absence (s 11(3)); and

- a person may not have any disqualification imposed on him in his absence (s 11(4)). Section 11(4) applies to any disqualification and so would include, for example, the most common disqualification, namely, disqualification from driving under the Road Traffic Offenders Act 1988 but would also include, for example, disqualification from keeping an animal under the Protection of Animals (Amendment) Act 1954.

If a custodial sentence or a disqualification is imposed in the absence of the defendant, the order is a nullity and would be quashed by the Divisional Court on an application for judicial review (*R v Llandrindod Wells Justices ex p Gibson* [1968] 1 WLR 598; [1968] 2 All ER 20).

Where the defendant has pleaded guilty by post under s 12 of the Magistrates' Courts Act 1980, the court will have to adjourn the case if it is minded to impose a custodial sentence or to make an order involving disqualification. There is no power to issue an arrest warrant against the defendant unless the court has adjourned once and the defendant fails to appear on the occasion of the adjourned hearing.

Where the defendant was tried in his absence under s 11, the court has the power to issue a warrant for the defendant's arrest under s 13(1) provided that the information is substantiated on oath. This power also applies if the defendant has been convicted of a non-imprisonable offence provided that the court is minded to impose a disqualification on the defendant (s 13(3)(b)).

12.11   SENTENCING POWERS OF YOUTH COURTS

Under ss 100 and 101 of the Powers of Criminal Courts (Sentencing) Act 2000, where the offender has attained the age of 12 at the date of conviction (which is the relevant date for determining the offender's age for sentencing purposes (*R v Danga* [1992] QB 476; [1992] 1 All ER 624), the youth court may impose a detention and training order for up to 24 months.

Note that the youth court cannot make an order for long term detention under s 91 of the Powers of Criminal Courts (Sentencing) Act 2000, as this power only arises where the offender has been convicted by the Crown Court.

The maximum fine which the youth court can impose is £1,000 per offence (£250 if the offender is under 14).

As regards other sentences, the powers of the youth court are identical to the Crown Court.

12.12   DUTIES OF COUNSEL

In *R v Hartrey* (1993) 14 Cr App R(S) 507 and in *R v Street* (1997) 161 JP 281, the Court of Appeal reiterated that it is the duty of both prosecution and defence counsel to acquaint themselves with the sentencing powers of the court in the particular case, so that they know what options are available to the judge, and to correct the judge if he passes a sentence which is unlawful. This principle applies equally in the magistrates' court.

12.13   DEFERRING SENTENCE

Section 1 of the Powers of Criminal Courts (Sentencing) Act 2000 empowers a court to defer passing sentence on an offender for up to six months (s 1(3)). The court may only defer sentence if the offender consents and if the court considers that it is in the interests of justice to do so, having regard to the nature of the offence and the character and circumstances of the offender (s 1(2)).

The purpose of deferring sentence is to enable the court to have regard to the offender's conduct after conviction (including, where appropriate, the making by him of reparation for the offence) or to any change in the offender's circumstances (s 1(1)).

When sentence is deferred, this does not count as a remand and so bail does not have to be granted in order that the offender remain at liberty (s 1(4)). However, if the defendant fails to appear on the date to which sentence is deferred, a bench warrant for his arrest may be issued (s 2(5)).

When the court eventually deals with the offender, it may deal with him in any way in which he could have been dealt with by the court which deferred sentence (s 1(5)(a)). Where sentence is deferred by a magistrates' court, the magistrates retain their power to commit the defendant for sentence to the Crown Court at the end of the period of deferment (s 1(5)(b)).

12.13.1 Principles governing deferment of sentence

The leading case on deferment of sentence is *R v George* [1984] 1 WLR 1082; [1984] 3 All ER 13. In that case, it was said that:

- deferring sentence is especially appropriate where there are improvements in the offender's conduct, or steps which the court wants him to take, which are not sufficiently specific to be requirements under a probation order. Sentence should not be deferred if the court's objective could be achieved by means of a probation order;

- the court should make it clear to the offender why sentence is being deferred and what conduct is expected of him during the period of deferment;

- a careful note should be made by the court of what the offender is told and, ideally, the offender should have a copy of that note;

- at the end of the period of deferment, the court which passes sentence should consider whether the offender has substantially conformed with what was required of him; if the defendant has conformed with what was required of him, a non-custodial sentence should be imposed. If the defendant has not conformed, a custodial sentence may be passed but the offender should be told in what respects he has failed to conform. A fresh pre-sentence report should be available to the sentencing court.

It will always be a requirement that the offender does not commit any further offences, but merely refraining from committing further offences will not be enough. In *R v Smith* (1976) 64 Cr App R 116, for example, sentence was deferred to see if the offender could find regular work and reduce his consumption of alcohol. He did not commit any further offences but failed to achieve either of the objectives set by the court and so a custodial sentence was upheld by the Court of Appeal.

In *Attorney General's Reference (No 22 of 1992)* [1994] 1 All ER 105, it was held that a deferred sentence is a sentence for the purposes of appeal and so the Attorney General may use his powers under s 36 of the Criminal Justice Act 1988 to appeal to the Court of Appeal on the ground that it is too lenient (see Chapter 10, 10.12.2).

12.13.2 Commission of further offence

Where the offender is convicted of a further offence which was committed during the period of the deferment, the court passing sentence on him for the later offence may also pass sentence on him in respect of the offence for which sentence was deferred. The only exception to this is that if sentence on the original offence was deferred by the Crown Court, a magistrates' court cannot deal with the original offence. If sentence on the original offence was deferred by a magistrates' court and the offender is being dealt with for the later offence by the Crown Court, the Crown Court may only impose a sentence which the magistrates could have imposed when it is dealing with the original offence (see s 2(3) of the Powers of Criminal Courts (Sentencing) Act 2000).

If the offender does re-offend during the period of the deferment, it is highly likely that a custodial sentence will be imposed for the original offence.

However, it may well be that the defendant is charged with a further offence allegedly committed during the period of the deferment but the offender has not been convicted of that offence before the date when the court passes sentence in respect of the original offence. In such a case, the allegation of a later offence should be ignored by the court dealing with the offence for which sentence was deferred. It is only where the offender is convicted of an offence committed during the period of deferment that account can be taken of the later offence when sentence is passed for the offence in respect for which sentence was deferred. An unproved allegation of a further offence should be disregarded (*R v Aquilina* (1989) 11 Cr App R(S) 431).

12.14 REHABILITATION OF OFFENDERS: SPENT CONVICTIONS

The Rehabilitation of Offenders Act 1974 allows a person who has been convicted of an offence to regard himself as rehabilitated after a period of time has elapsed and the conviction is deemed to be 'spent'. However, s 7(2) of the Rehabilitation of Offenders Act 1974 says that the provisions of the Act do not apply to criminal proceedings. Nevertheless, a Practice Direction (1975) provides that:

- spent convictions should be clearly marked as such; and

- no reference should be made in open court to any spent convictions without leave of the court; leave should only be given where the interests of justice so require.

Home Office Circular 98/1975 makes the same provision for magistrates' courts.

In some instances, a conviction can never become spent. Sentences which are outside the scope of the Rehabilitation of Offenders Act 1974 (and so never become spent) are:

- life imprisonment (custody for life or detention during Her Majesty's pleasure in the case of young offenders);
- imprisonment (detention in a young offender institution or detention under s 91 of the Powers of Criminal Courts (Sentencing) Act 2000 in the case of young offenders) for a period exceeding 30 months.

The Rehabilitation of Offenders Act 1974 applies to all other convictions. The rehabilitation period (that is, the time which must elapse before the conviction is regarded as spent) depends on the sentence imposed for the original offence. In some cases, the rehabilitation period is shortened if the offender was under 18 at the date of conviction.

The rehabilitation periods are as follows:

- Imprisonment (or detention in a young offender institution) for a term of more than six months but less than 30 months:

    10 years (five years if offender under 18 when convicted).

- Imprisonment (or detention in a young offender institution) for a term of six months or less:

    Seven years (five years if offender under 18 when convicted).

- Community service order:

    Five years.

- Probation order:

    Five years (two and a half if the offender was under 18 when convicted).

- Supervision order:

    Binding over when imposed as a sentence.

- Conditional discharge:

    The date when the order ceases to have effect, or one year, whichever is the longer.

- Attendance centre order:

    One year after completion of attendance.

- Hospital order:

    Five years from date of conviction, or two years after expiry of order, whichever is the longer.

- Absolute discharge:

    Six months.

The rehabilitation period for a sentence of imprisonment is the same whether the imprisonment is immediate or suspended.

In *Power v Provincial Insurance plc* (1997) 161 JP 556, it was held that, under the Rehabilitation of Offenders Act 1974, an endorsement on a driving licence is not a 'penalty' for the purposes of the 1974 Act and, so, the driver does not have to wait until he can apply for a 'clean' licence for the conviction to be spent. It follows that, once the rehabilitation period for the fine/disqualification has expired, the driver can lawfully say to an insurer that he has not been disqualified from driving.

12.14.1 Further offences

The rehabilitation periods listed above only apply if the offender is not convicted of a further offence during the rehabilitation period.

If the offender is convicted of a further offence during the rehabilitation period, the rehabilitation period for the first offence continues to run until the expiry of the rehabilitation period for the subsequent offence.

TABLE OF STATUTORY MATERIALS

STATUTORY MATERIALS

FACTORS TO BE TAKEN INTO ACCOUNT IN SENTENCING

POWERS OF CRIMINAL COURTS (SENTENCING) ACT 2000

Section 151: Effect of previous convictions and of offending while on bail

(1) In considering the seriousness of any offence, the court may take into account any previous convictions of the offender or any failure of his to respond to previous sentences.

(2) In considering the seriousness of any offence committed while the offender was on bail, the court shall treat the fact that it was committed in those circumstances as an aggravating factor.

(4) A conditional discharge order made after 30th September 1992 (which by virtue of section 1A of the Powers of Criminal Courts Act 1973 or section 12 above would otherwise not be a sentence for the purposes of this section) is to be treated as a sentence for those purposes.

(6) A conviction in respect of which an order discharging the offender absolutely or conditionally was made at any date (which by virtue of section 14 above would otherwise not be a conviction for the purposes of this section) is to be treated as a conviction for those purposes.

Section 152: Reduction in sentences for guilty pleas

(1) In determining what sentence to pass on an offender who has pleaded guilty to an offence in proceedings before that or another court, a court shall take into account:

(a) the stage in the proceedings for the offence at which the offender indicated his intention to plead guilty; and

(b) the circumstances in which this indication was given.

(2) If, as a result of taking into account any matter referred to in sub-section (1) above, the court imposes a punishment on the offender which is less severe than the punishment it would otherwise have imposed, it shall state in open court that it has done so.

(3) In the case of an offence the sentence for which falls to be imposed under sub-section (2) of section 110 or 111 above, nothing in that sub-section shall

prevent the court, after taking into account any matter referred to in sub-section (1) above, from imposing any sentence which is not less than 80 per cent of that specified in that sub-section.

Section 153: Increase in sentences for racial aggravation

(1) This section applies where a court is considering the seriousness of an offence other than one under sections 29 to 32 of the Crime and Disorder Act 1998 (racially-aggravated assaults, racially aggravated criminal damage, racially aggravated public order offences and racially aggravated harassment, etc).

(2) If the offence was racially aggravated, the court:

    (a) shall treat that fact as an aggravating factor (that is to say, a factor that increases the seriousness of the offence); and

    (b) shall state in open court that the offence was so aggravated.

(3) Section 28 of the Crime and Disorder Act 1998 (meaning of 'racially aggravated') applies for the purposes of this section as it applies for the purposes of sections 29 to 32 of that Act.

DEFINITION OF 'ASSOCIATED OFFENCE'

POWERS OF CRIMINAL COURTS (SENTENCING) ACT 2000

Section 161: Meaning of 'associated offence', etc

(1) For the purposes of this Act, an offence is associated with another if:

    (a) the offender is convicted of it in the proceedings in which he is convicted of the other offence, or (although convicted of it in earlier proceedings) is sentenced for it at the same time as he is sentenced for that offence; or

    (b) the offender admits the commission of it in the proceedings in which he is sentenced for the other offence and requests the court to take it into consideration in sentencing him for that offence.

DEFERRING SENTENCE

POWERS OF CRIMINAL COURTS (SENTENCING) ACT 2000

Section 1: Deferment of sentence

(1) The Crown Court or a magistrates' court may defer passing sentence on an offender for the purpose of enabling the court, or any other court to which it falls to deal with him, to have regard in dealing with him to:

    (a) his conduct after conviction (including, where appropriate, the making by him of reparation for his offence); or

    (b) any change in his circumstances;

    but this is subject to sub-sections (2) and (3) below.

(2) The power conferred by sub-section (1) above shall be exercisable only if:

    (a) the offender consents; and

    (b) the court is satisfied, having regard to the nature of the offence and the character and circumstances of the offender, that it would be in the interests of justice to exercise the power.

(3) Any deferment under this section shall be until such date as may be specified by the court, not being more than six months after the date on which the deferment is announced by the court; and, subject to section 2(7) below, where the passing of sentence has been deferred under this section it shall not be further so deferred.

(4) Notwithstanding any enactment, a court which under this section defers passing sentence on an offender shall not on the same occasion remand him.

(5) Where the passing of sentence on an offender has been deferred by a court under this section, the court's power under this section to deal with the offender at the end of the period of deferment:

    (a) is power to deal with him, in respect of the offence for which passing of sentence has been deferred, in any way in which it could have dealt with him if it had not deferred passing sentence; and

    (b) without prejudice to the generality of paragraph (a) above, in the case of a magistrates' court includes the power conferred by section 3 below to commit him to the Crown Court for sentence.

(6) Nothing in this section or section 2 below shall affect:

    (a) the power of the Crown Court to bind over an offender to come up for judgment when called upon; or

    (b) the power of any court to defer passing sentence for any purpose for which it may lawfully do so apart from this section.

Section 2: Further powers of courts where sentence deferred under section 1

(1) A court which under section 1 above has deferred passing sentence on an offender may deal with him before the end of the period of deferment if during that period he is convicted in Great Britain of any offence.

(2) Sub-section (3) below applies where a court has under section 1 above deferred passing sentence on an offender in respect of one or more offences and during the period of deferment the offender is convicted in England or Wales of any offence ('the later offence').

(3) Where this sub-section applies, then (without prejudice to sub-section (1) above and whether or not the offender is sentenced for the later offence during the period of deferment), the court which passes sentence on him for the later offence may also, if this has not already been done, deal with him for the offence or offences for which passing of sentence has been deferred, except that-

(a) the power conferred by this sub-section shall not be exercised by a magistrates' court if the court which deferred passing sentence was the Crown Court; and

(b) the Crown Court, in exercising that power in a case in which the court which deferred passing sentence was a magistrates' court, shall not pass any sentence which could not have been passed by a magistrates' court in exercising that power.

(4) Where:

(a) a court which under section 1 above has deferred passing sentence on an offender proposes to deal with him, whether on the date originally specified by the court or by virtue of sub-section (1) above before that date; or

(b) the offender does not appear on the date so specified, the court may issue a summons requiring him to appear before the court, or may issue a warrant for his arrest.

(5) In deferring the passing of sentence under section 1 above a magistrates' court shall be regarded as exercising the power of adjourning the trial conferred by section 10(1) of the Magistrates' Courts Act 1980, and accordingly sections 11(1) and 13(1) to (3A) and (5) of that Act (non-appearance of the accused) apply (without prejudice to sub-section (4) above) if the offender does not appear on the date specified under section (3) above.

(6) Any power of a court under this section to deal with an offender in a case where the passing of sentence has been deferred under section 1 above:

(a) is power to deal with him, in respect of the offence for which passing of sentence has been deferred, in any way in which the court which deferred passing sentence could have dealt with him; and

(b) without prejudice to the generality of paragraph (a) above, in the case of a magistrates' court includes the power conferred by section 3 below to commit him to the Crown Court for sentence.

(7) Where:

    (a) the passing of sentence on an offender in respect of one or more offences has been deferred under section 1 above; and

    (b) a magistrates' court deals with him in respect of the offence or any of the offences by committing him to the Crown Court under section 3 below,

the power of the Crown Court to deal with him includes the same power to defer passing sentence on him as if he had just been convicted of the offence or offences on indictment before the court.

CUSTODIAL SENTENCES: LIMITS ON POWERS OF MAGISTRATES

POWERS OF CRIMINAL COURTS (SENTENCING) ACT 2000

Section 78: General limit on magistrates' court's power to impose imprisonment or detention in a young offender institution

(1) A magistrates' court shall not have power to impose imprisonment, or detention in a young offender institution, for more than six months in respect of any one offence.

(2) Unless expressly excluded, sub-section (1) above shall apply even if the offence in question is one for which a person would otherwise be liable on summary conviction to imprisonment or detention in a young offender institution for more than six months.

(3) Sub-section (1) above is without prejudice to section 133 of the Magistrates' Courts Act 1980 (consecutive terms of imprisonment).

(4) Any power of a magistrates' court to impose a term of imprisonment for non-payment of a fine, or for want of sufficient distress to satisfy a fine, shall not be limited by virtue of sub-section (1) above.

(5) In sub-section (4) above 'fine' includes a pecuniary penalty but does not include a pecuniary forfeiture or pecuniary compensation.

(6) In this section 'impose imprisonment' means pass a sentence of imprisonment or fix a term of imprisonment for failure to pay any sum of money, or for want of sufficient distress to satisfy any sum of money, or for failure to do or abstain from doing anything required to be done or left undone.

(7) Section 132 of the Magistrates' Courts Act 1980 contains provision about the minimum term of imprisonment which may be imposed by a magistrates' court.

REMISSION OF CASES BETWEEN MAGISTRATES' COURTS

POWERS OF CRIMINAL COURTS (SENTENCING) ACT 2000

Section 10: Power of magistrates' court to remit case to another magistrates' court for sentence

(1) Where a person aged 18 or over ('the offender') has been convicted by a magistrates' court ('the convicting court') of an offence to which this section applies ('the instant offence') and:

   (a) it appears to the convicting court that some other magistrates' court ('the other court') has convicted him of another such offence in respect of which the other court has neither passed sentence on him nor committed him to the Crown Court for sentence nor dealt with him in any other way; and

   (b) the other court consents to his being remitted under this section to the other court, the convicting court may remit him to the other court to be dealt with in respect of the instant offence by the other court instead of by the convicting court.

(2) This section applies to:

   (a) any offence punishable with imprisonment; and

   (b) any offence in respect of which the convicting court has a power or duty to order the offender to be disqualified under section 34, 35 or 36 the Road Traffic Offenders Act 1988 (disqualification for certain motoring offences).

(3) Where the convicting court remits the offender to the other court under this section, it shall adjourn the trial of the information charging him with the instant offence, and:

   (a) section 128 of the Magistrates' Courts Act 1980 (remand in custody or on bail) and all other enactments, whenever passed, relating to remand or the granting of bail in criminal proceedings shall have effect, in relation to the convicting court's power or duty to remand the offender on that adjournment, as if any reference to the court to or before which the person remanded is to be brought or appear after remand were a reference to the court to which he is being remitted; and

   (b) subject to sub-section (7) below, the other court may deal with the case in any way in which it would have power to deal with it if all proceedings relating to the instant offence which took place before the convicting court had taken place before the other court.

(4) The power conferred on the other court by sub-section (3)(b) above includes, where applicable, the power to remit the offender under this section to another magistrates' court in respect of the instant offence.

(5) Where the convicting court has remitted the offender under this section to the other court, the other court may remit him back to the convicting court;

and the provisions of sub-sections (3) and (4) above (so far as applicable) shall apply with the necessary modifications in relation to any remission under this sub-section.

(6) The offender, if remitted under this section, shall have no right of appeal against the order of remission (but without prejudice to any right of appeal against any other order made in respect of the instant offence by the court to which he is remitted).

(7) Nothing in this section shall preclude the convicting court from making any order which it has power to make under section 148 below (restitution orders) by virtue of the offender's conviction of the instant offence.

(8) In this section:

(a) 'conviction' includes a finding under section 11(1) below (remand for medical examination) that the person in question did the act or made

the omission charged, and 'convicted' shall be construed accordingly;

(b) 'enactment' includes an enactment contained in any order, regulation or other instrument having effect by virtue of an Act; and

(c) 'bail in criminal proceedings' has the same meaning as in the Bail Act 1976.

PRE-SENTENCE REPORTS

POWERS OF CRIMINAL COURTS (SENTENCING) ACT 2000

Section 156: Disclosure of pre-sentence reports

(1) This section applies where a court obtains a pre-sentence report.

(2) Subject to sub-sections (3) and (4) below, the court shall give a copy of the report:

(a) to the offender or his counsel or solicitor; and

(b) to the prosecutor, that is to say, the person having the conduct of the proceedings in respect of the offence.

(3) If the offender is aged under 17 and is not represented by counsel or a solicitor, a copy of the report need not be given to him but shall be given to his parent or guardian if present in court.

(4) If the prosecutor is not of a description prescribed by order made by the Secretary of State, a copy of the report need not be given to the prosecutor if the court considers that it would be inappropriate for him to be given it.

(5) No information obtained by virtue of sub-section (2)(b) above shall be used or disclosed otherwise than for the purpose of:

(a) determining whether representations as to matters contained in the report need to be made to the court; or

(b) making such representations to the court.

CHAPTER 13

OFFENDERS OVER 21: CUSTODIAL SENTENCES

In this chapter, we examine the sentences of imprisonment (immediate and suspended) which may be imposed on an adult offender. Custodial sentences for young offenders are considered in Chapter 16. However, we begin by considering the statutory criteria which govern the imposition of custodial sentences; these statutory criteria apply to all custodial sentences and so are equally applicable to the sentences discussed in Chapter 16.

13.1 STATUTORY CRITERIA FOR IMPOSING CUSTODIAL SENTENCES

Section 79(2) of the Powers of Criminal Courts (Sentencing) Act 2000 provides that a court shall not pass a custodial sentence on an offender unless it is of the opinion:

(a) that the offence, or the combination of the offence and one or more offences associated with it, was so serious that only such a sentence can be justified for the offence; or

(b) where the offence is a violent or sexual offence, that only such a sentence would be adequate to protect the public from serious harm from him.

Section 79(3) of the Act sets out a third ground for imposing a custodial sentence, namely, where the offender fails to express his willingness to comply with a requirement which is proposed by the court to be included in a probation order or supervision order and which requires an expression of such willingness.

These pre-conditions apply to sentences of imprisonment (both immediate custody and suspended sentences) and to sentences of detention in a young offender institution, detention and training orders and detention under s 91 of the 2000 Act.

13.1.1 Seriousness of offence: s 79(2)(a) of the Powers of Criminal Courts (Sentencing) Act 2000

A very important case on the 'custody threshold' in s 79(2)(a) of the Powers of Criminal Courts (Sentencing) Act 2000 is *R v Howells* [1999] 1 All ER 50. In it, the Lord Chief Justice Lord Bingham CJ gave detailed guidance on the application of the test of whether an offence is so serious that only a custodial sentence can be justified. Lord Bingham described the problem of dealing with cases which are on the borderline of the custody threshold as 'one of the most elusive problems of criminal sentencing'.

Corresponding provisions in earlier legislation had been interpreted by Lawton LJ in *R v Bradbourn* (1985) 7 Cr App R(S) 180, 182 thus: 'The phrase "so serious that a non-custodial sentence cannot be justified" comes to this: the kind of offence which when committed by a young person would make right-thinking members of the public, knowing all the facts, feel that justice had not been done by the passing of any sentence other than a custodial one.' In *R v Cox* [1993] 1 WLR 188, this 'right thinking members of the public' test was held to apply to the slightly different criterion for custody set out in s 1(2)(a) of the Criminal Justice Act 1991 (now s 79(2)(a) of the Powers of Criminal Courts (Sentencing) Act 2000. However, in *Howells*, Lord Bingham said that this test is unhelpful, since the court has no means of ascertaining the views of right thinking members of the public.

In deciding which side of the custodial/non-custodial line a case falls, Lord Bingham said that the starting point should be a consideration of the 'nature and extent to the defendant's criminal intention and the nature and extent of any injury or damage caused to the victim'.

As regards the defendant's criminal intention, his Lordship re-stated the well established principle that a deliberate and premeditated offence will usually be regarded as more serious than a 'spur of the moment', unpremeditated, offence.

His Lordship went on to say that an offence which causes 'personal injury or mental trauma, particular if permanent, will usually be more serious than an offence which inflicts financial loss only'.

Lord Bingham also pointed out that under what is now s 151 of the Powers of Criminal Courts (Sentencing) Act 2000, the court *may* take into account any previous convictions of the offender or any failure of his to respond to previous sentences and *must*, where an offence is committed while the offender was on bail, treat that fact as an aggravating factor.

Lord Bingham then went on to list a number of matters which the court should normally take into account when deciding whether or not to impose a custodial sentence in a borderline case. Those factors are as follows:

(1) An admission of responsibility for the offence. Section 152 of the Powers of Criminal Courts (Sentencing) Act 2000 requires the court to take account of the fact of a guilty plea, and also of the stage at which that plea is entered. The best mitigation obviously comes from an early admission of responsibility when the offender is first questioned by the police, together with a guilty plea tendered at the earliest opportunity (in the case of an offence which is triable either way, the guilty plea should be entered at the

'plea before venue' hearing if the offender is to receive the maximum credit for that guilty plea: *R v Rafferty* (1998) 162 JP 353). Lord Bingham added that the court should also look for 'hard evidence of genuine remorse' (for example, an expression of regret to the victim of the offence and an offer to pay compensation).

(2) Where the offence is connected with addiction to drink or drugs, the court should look favourably on an offender who has already started to take practical steps which demonstrate a genuine and self-motivated determination to rid himself of the addiction.

(3) Youth and immaturity would often justify a less rigorous penalty than that appropriate to an adult offender. (This may be contrasted with *R v Dodds* (1997) *The Times*, 28 January, where the Court of Appeal said that in a serious case, such as aggravated burglary involving the use of violence, a substantial reduction in sentence should no longer be given because of the offender's youth.)

(4) Some measure of leniency should be extended to an offender who is of previous good character. More credit should be given to a person who can demonstrate 'positive good character' rather than just an absence of previous convictions. Lord Bingham gave examples of a 'solid employment record or faithful discharge of family duties'. The list could also include actions which have benefited the community or charitable deeds.

(5) There should be even greater than usual reluctance to impose a custodial sentence on someone who has never before served such a sentence. The reasoning behind this is that the most traumatic part of a custodial sentence is the first part of the offender's first custodial sentence (the effect of the so called 'clang of the prison gates'), and so the court should be reluctant to put someone through this.

Lord Bingham added that it was right for the court to bear in mind that the purpose of sentencing is to protect the public (by punishing the offender, by reforming him, or by deterring him and others from offending). (In *Attorney General's References (Nos 62 and 63 of 1997)*; *R v McMaster* [1998] 2 Cr App R(S) 300, for example, the Court of Appeal referred to the need for sentences to have a proper deterrent effect on those who embark on brutal attacks.)

In *R v Cunningham* [1993] 1 WLR 183; [1993] 2 All ER 15, it was held that the prevalence of a particular type of offence (and public concern about it) could be regarded as an aggravating factor.

In assessing the seriousness of the offence, the court should consider the facts of the case and not just the label which is attached to the offence. Thus, although most cases involving the burglary of a dwelling house will result in a custodial sentence, domestic burglary should not be regarded as automatically so serious that a custodial sentence is justified.

Where the offender is convicted of two or more offences, the court should consider the offences together and should decide whether the combination of offences is such that a custodial sentence is justified.

In *R v Oliver and Little* [1993] 1 WLR 177; [1993] 2 All ER 9, the Court of Appeal considered what should be done where an offender is convicted of a number of offences, some of which merit a custodial sentence and some of which do not. It was held to be permissible to impose custodial sentences for the lesser offences but those sentences should be concurrent with the sentences for the offences which do merit custody. See, also, *R v Jones* [1996] 1 Cr App R(S) 153.

In *R v Oliver and Little* [1993] 1 WLR 177; [1993] 2 All ER 9, the Court of Appeal also considered the approach to be taken where a court which is sentencing an offender for one offence is also re-sentencing him for an earlier offence. For example, the earlier offence may well have been dealt with by means of a probation order, and the court may now take the view that probation is ineffective to prevent this offender from re-offending. The Court of Appeal said that the fact that the earlier court dealt with the offence by means of a community order does not necessarily mean that the offence was not so serious that only a custodial sentence could be justified; it may well be that the earlier court found that the custody threshold had been passed but there was sufficient personal mitigation to allow the court to pass a more lenient sentence. If the offender commits a subsequent offence and is re-sentenced to the earlier offence, he will have deprived himself of much of the mitigation which led the earlier court to pass a non-custodial sentence for the original offence; the later court would therefore be entitled to impose a custodial sentence for that original offence.

In *R v Cox* [1993] 1 WLR 188; [1993] 2 All ER 19, following *R v Baverstock* [1993] 1 WLR 202; [1993] 2 All ER 32, the Court of Appeal pointed out that even if the court decides that an offence is sufficiently serious to justify the imposition of a custodial sentence, the court is not prevented from imposing a non-custodial sentence in the light of mitigating circumstances. Indeed, this is expressly permitted by s 158 of the Powers of Criminal Courts (Sentencing) Act 2000 .

13.1.2 Public protection: s 79(2)(b) of the Powers of Criminal Courts (Sentencing) Act 2000

Protecting the public from serious harm is the second ground for imposing a custodial sentence. It is only a relevant factor where the offender has been convicted of a 'violent or sexual offence'. These terms are defined in s 161 of the 2000 Act.

A violent offence is one 'which leads, or is intended or likely to lead, to a person's death or to physical injury to a person'.

In *R v Robinson* [1993] 1 WLR 168; [1993] 2 All ER 1, the Court of Appeal held that whether a particular offence is a violent offence depends on the individual facts of each case.

It was also held in *Robinson* that the phrase 'physical injury' does not require serious physical harm to be caused. See, also, *R v Joszbo* (1994) *The Times*, 11 August.

The term 'sexual offence' includes offences under the Sexual Offences Act 1956, the Indecency with Children Act 1960, the Sexual Offences Act 1967, s 54 of the Criminal Law Act 1977, or the Protection of Children Act 1978, as well as burglary with intent to commit rape and attempting to commit, conspiring to commit or inciting another to commit any of the specified offences.

Although there is nothing to stop a magistrates' court from invoking s 79(2)(b) of the 2000 Act, it will be rare for a magistrates' court to do so. Offences where the considerations set out in s 79(2)(b) are applicable will normally be regarded by the magistrates as too serious for summary trial and so the justices are likely to refuse jurisdiction at the mode of trial hearing.

13.1.3 Procedural requirements before imposing a custodial sentence

Section 81(1) of the Powers of Criminal Courts (Sentencing) Act 2000 requires that the court, in order to determine whether the criteria set out in s 79(2) of the Act are satisfied, 'shall obtain and consider a pre-sentence report', unless the court considers a report to be unnecessary (s 81(2)). Such a report is prepared by a probation officer (or, in the case of a young offender, by a probation officer or a local authority social worker).

Under s 79(4) of the 2000 Act, the court must explain to the offender in open court and in ordinary language why it is passing a custodial sentence on him.

A magistrates' court which imposes a custodial sentence must also make a written record of its reason for passing a custodial sentence.

Section 83(1) of the 2000 Act provides that a sentence of imprisonment (whether immediate or suspended) cannot be imposed on someone who has not previously served a sentence of imprisonment (that is, was sentenced on an earlier occasion to immediate custody or received a suspended sentence which was subsequently activated) unless he is legally represented, or has refused to apply for representation funded by the Criminal Defence Service.

In all cases where a court is contemplating sentencing a defendant to prison for the first time, other than for a very short period, it should be the invariable practice that a pre-sentence report should be obtained before such a sentence is passed (*R v Gillette* (1999) *The Times*, 3 December).

13.1.4 Determining length of sentence: s 80(2)(a) of the Powers of Criminal Courts (Sentencing) Act 2000

Section 80(2)(a) of the 2000 Act states that the length of the sentence, which must not exceed the maximum sentence prescribed for the offence(s) being dealt with, should be 'commensurate with the seriousness of the offence, or the combination of the offence and one or more offences associated with it'.

In *R v Cunningham* [1993] 1 WLR 183, the Court of Appeal considered the question of deterrence. Lord Taylor of Gosforth CJ said that the phrase 'commensurate with the seriousness of the offence' must mean 'commensurate with the punishment and deterrence which the seriousness of the offence requires'. However, his Lordship added the rider that s 80(2)(a) prohibits the court from adding any extra length to the sentence which is commensurate with the seriousness of the offence, simply to make a special example of the defendant. However, Lord Taylor then went on to hold that the prevalence of the kind of offence of which the offender has been convicted is a legitimate factor in determining the length of the custodial sentence to be passed (presumably with the implication that a stiff sentence on the present occasion might make it less prevalent in the future!)

In *R v Howells* (above), Lord Bingham CJ endorsed the observations of Rose LJ in *R v Ollerenshaw* [1999] 1 Cr App R(S) 65. In that case, it was said that where a court is considering a comparatively short custodial sentence (that is, a sentence of about 12 months or less), it should generally ask itself (especially if the offender has not served a custodial sentence before) whether custody for an even shorter period might be equally effective in protecting the public and punishing and deterring criminal behaviour. For example, said Rose LJ, six months might be just as effective as nine months, and two months just as effective as four months. This echoes observations made by Lord Lane CJ in *R v Bibi* [1980] 1 WLR 1193, where he said that a sentence should be 'as short as possible, consistent only with the duty to protect the interests of the public and to punish and deter the criminal'. This point will be of particular relevance where the offender has been remanded in custody prior to conviction and/or sentence: it may well be possible to mitigate on the basis that the period spent behind bars on remand is sufficient punishment.

The Court of Appeal has laid down guidelines as to the approach to be taken to particular offences (for example, *R v Barrick* (1985) 81 Cr App R 78, for theft involving breach of trust). In *R v Johnson* [1994] Crim LR 949; (1994) 15 Crim App R(S) 827, it was said that the decisions of the Court of Appeal are no more than guidelines and within those guidelines there is a great deal of flexibility. The Court of Appeal recognised that a judge has to take into account many factors when passing sentence, for example, it may be that a particular crime is too prevalent in that area, or the offence may have had a particularly distressing effect on the victim, or the offender may have behaved in an especially vicious manner. Nevertheless, judges must pay attention to the guidance given by the Court of Appeal and sentences should be broadly in line with guideline cases unless the particular case presents factors which allow the judge to depart from the tariff set by the Court of Appeal. What a judge must not do is to state that he is applying some personal tariff of his own because he feels that the range of sentences set by the Court of Appeal is wrong.

When considering earlier guidelines, cases on the level of sentence to be imposed for a particular offence where the statutory maximum for that offence has subsequently been increased, the court must take account of the increase in statutory maximum since the guideline case was decided and must adjust the guidelines accordingly (*R v L (Indecent Assault: Sentencing)* [1999] 1 Cr App R 117).

13.1.5 Violent or sexual offences: s 80(2)(b) of the Powers of Criminal Courts (Sentencing) Act 2000

In the case of a violent or sexual offence, the sentence must still not exceed the maximum sentence prescribed for the offence(s) being dealt with, but may be 'for such longer term ... as in the opinion of the court is necessary to protect the public from serious harm from the offender' (s 80(2)(b)).

Where the court invokes s 80(2)(b) to pass a sentence longer than that commensurate with the seriousness of the offence, it must state why it is of that opinion and must explain this to the offender in ordinary language (s 80(3)).

An example of the use of s 80(2)(b) is to be found in *R v Bowler* [1993] Crim LR 799. The defendant pleaded guilty to indecent assault on a six year old girl; he had put his hand up her skirt and touched her genitals through her knickers. The defendant had eight previous convictions for similar offences committed on adult women. The defendant had received drug treatment to curb his offending but was unwilling to undergo any further treatment. The Court of Appeal upheld a sentence of six years' imprisonment. Even though no physical harm had been caused to any of his previous victims, the court felt that if the offender were to re-offend by assaulting another young girl serious psychological harm could be caused to her.

Detailed guidance on the use of sentences under s 80(2)(b) was given by the Court of Appeal in *R v Fawcett* (1983) 5 Cr App R(S) 158. For a sentence under s 80(2)(b) to be appropriate, the offender must pose a danger to the public which is more than merely minimal. A medical report should be sought first, to ensure that a medical disposal would not be more appropriate. There must be a repetition of similar offending. A longer than normal sentence might be appropriate where there is a mixture of minor offending and a severe personality disorder or other mental abnormalities. The court should hear evidence of the facts of the previous convictions. Relevant considerations would include the irrationality of the behaviour, the selection of vulnerable people or particular classes of people, unexplained severe violence, unusual obsessions or delusions, any inability on the part of the offender to understand the consequences of his actions, or lack of remorse on his part, or unwillingness on the part of the offender to accept medication. The court must be satisfied beyond reasonable doubt that such a sentence is appropriate.

The danger of serious psychological injury to a potential future victim can trigger the power to impose a longer than normal sentence (*R v Kaye* [1996] Crim LR 129). However, there must be some basis in fact for the belief that future victims are likely to suffer serious psychological injury (*R v Fishwick* [1996] Crim LR 127).

In *R v Carpenter* [1997] 1 Cr App R(S) 4, the Court of Appeal accepted that a longer than normal sentence may be appropriate even if the offence itself is towards the lower end of the scale of seriousness, but only if other factors (in this case, which involved indecent assault, breach of trust, use of alcohol to achieve seduction, lack of remorse and past offences) show that the offender is a danger to the public.

In *R v Auger* [1996] 1 Cr App R(S) 431 and *R v Etchells* [1991] 1 Cr App R(S) 163, the Court of Appeal emphasised that there must be evidence that the risk of further offending on the part of the defendant is of such a nature that the applicant is likely to cause serious harm – whether physical or psychological – to members of the public.

Some of the sentencing guidelines handed down by the Court of Appeal for particular offences already include an element for the protection of the public (for example, rape). It follows that, where a court wishes to impose a longer than normal sentence in such an case, the correct starting point is to consider what the appropriate sentence would be without taking into account any increase for the protection of the public already included in the sentencing guidelines for that offence. Thus, where public protection is already included in the guidelines, the starting point should be lower than in a case where a longer than normal sentence is not being imposed. The second stage is then to increase the sentence in accordance with s 80(2)(b). See *R v Campbell* [1997] 1 Cr App R(S) 119.

In *R v Henshaw* [1996] 2 Cr App R(S) 310 and *R v Palmer* [1996] 2 Cr App R(S) 68, the Court of Appeal held that where the trial judge incorrectly passes a sentence under s 80(2)(b) (for example, where there is no evidence that the appellant is likely to commit violent offences in the future), the Court of Appeal is not obliged to interfere with the sentence if that court takes the view that the length of the sentence is proper.

In *R v Smith (Wayne Anthony)* (1999) *The Times*, 22 June, the Court of Appeal pointed out that the court may pass a 'longer than normal sentence' under s 80(2)(b) of the Powers of Criminal Courts (Sentencing) Act 2000 even if the defendant has no previous convictions.

13.1.6   Discount where offender pleads guilty

Where the offender pleads guilty, the length of the custodial sentence is usually reduced. In *R v Buffery* (1993) 14 Cr App R(S) 511, a serious fraud case, Lord Taylor CJ said that where a defendant pleads guilty, a discount of approximately one-third from the sentence which would have been imposed on conviction following a not guilty plea is usually appropriate.

However, it was held in *R v Costen* (1989) 11 Cr App R(S) 182, that this discount may be lost or reduced in any of the following circumstances:

- where the offender has been caught red-handed, and a plea of guilty was virtually inevitable (for example, *R v Landy* (1995) 16 Cr App R(S) 908);

- where the protection of the public makes a long sentence necessary (thus, the discount may not be applicable where s 80(2)(b) is invoked);

- where the offender does not plead guilty at the earliest opportunity;

The credit may also be increased. *R v Claydon* (1994) 15 Cr App R(S) 526, for example, concerned a defendant who voluntarily approached the police and admitted the offences to which he later pleaded guilty. Had he not done so, it was highly unlikely that he would have been caught. Where an offender who would otherwise have escaped detection gives himself up and confesses, a discount of 50% may be appropriate.

If the defendant pleads guilty but there is a significant difference between the defence version and prosecution version of events, and a *Newton* hearing takes place, the defendant may lose some of the credit which he would otherwise have received for pleading guilty if the judge, having heard evidence, rejects the defence version of events (*R v Stevens* (1986) 8 Cr App R(S) 291; *R v Jauncey* (1986) 8 Cr App R(S) 401). However, the defendant remains entitled to some credit for pleading guilty; even if the victim has not been spared the trauma of giving evidence, some court time has been saved (*R v Williams* [1992] 1 WLR 380; [1992] 2 All ER 183).

13.1.7   Concurrent and consecutive sentences

Where an offender is convicted of more than one offence, a separate sentence will usually be imposed for each offence. In the case of custodial sentences, prison terms may be concurrent or consecutive.

Sentences are concurrent if they are to be served simultaneously. In other words, a sentence of nine months on count 1 and three months concurrent on count 2 means that the offender receives a total sentence of nine months.

Sentences are consecutive if they have to served one after the other. In other words, a sentence of nine months on count 1 and three months consecutive on count 2 means that the offender receives a total sentence of 12 months.

It is possible to have a mixture of consecutive and concurrent sentences. For example, an offender could be sentenced to six months on count 1, nine months consecutive on count 2 and three months concurrent on count 3. The total sentence would be 15 months.

If the court fails to specify whether sentences are concurrent or consecutive, they are deemed to be concurrent.

Terms of imprisonment may be ordered to run consecutively even if the total sentence is greater than the maximum which could have been imposed for one of the offences (*R v Prime* (1983) 5 Cr App R(S) 127).

It would be wrong in principle to impose consecutive sentences if the two offences in question essentially amount to a single crime. In *R v Coker* [1984] Crim LR 184, the defendant was convicted of indecent assault and assault occasioning actual bodily harm. He had struck a young woman repeatedly about the face, removed most of her clothes and then indecently assaulted her. The judge imposed consecutive terms of imprisonment but the Court of Appeal held that the two offences were so inextricably linked that the sentences should have been concurrent.

Generally, concurrent sentences will be imposed where the offences arise out of the same transaction. For example, dangerous driving and driving while disqualified on the same occasion (*R v Skinner* (1986) 8 Cr App R(S) 166), driving with excess alcohol and driving while disqualified on the same occasion (*R v Jones* (1980) 2 Cr App R(S) 152). However, this is not an invariable rule. In *R v Wheatley* (1983) 5 Cr App R(S) 417, consecutive sentences were imposed for driving while disqualified and driving with excess alcohol on the same occasion on the ground that it would be wrong to lead the offender to believe that he could drive with excess alcohol and incur no extra penalty for driving while disqualified: though the offences were committed on the same occasion, they were in fact completely separate offences.

In *R v Ling* (1993) 157 JP 931, the defendant was convicted of burglary, affray, dangerous driving, driving while disqualified, refusing to provide a specimen, and making off without payment. It was said that his offending, which took place over a single (and rather eventful!) evening, was due to the effects of diabetes. The Court of Appeal held that these events should have been regarded as a single on-going offence.

In *R v Tutu Sikwabi* (1993) 157 JP 1182, the defendant was convicted of dangerous driving, driving while disqualified, taking a vehicle without the owner's consent and making off without payment. The offences had been committed over a period of three days (beginning with the taking of the car and ending with a police car chase). It was held that the offences arose out of a single series of incidents and that the sentences for the various parts of the series should be made concurrent.

Consecutive sentences are usually imposed where the offences are committed on different occasions, even if there is a link between the offences.

For example, in *Attorney General's Reference (No 1 of 1990)* (1990) 12 Cr App R(S) 245, consecutive sentences were imposed for indecent assault and attempting to pervert the course of justice, the latter offence arising out of an attempt to dissuade the victim of the assault from giving evidence. See, also, *Attorney General's Reference (No 4 of 1994)* (1995) 16 Cr App R(S) 81 where consecutive sentences were imposed for robbery and wounding with intent committed on separate occasions.

Consecutive sentences are also appropriate where, though the offences were committed on the same occasion, they are not part of the same transaction. Thus, a sentence for using violence to resist arrest or in an attempt to escape from the scene of the crime will normally lead to a consecutive sentence being imposed (*R v Fitter* (1983) 5 Cr App R(S) 168). Similarly, a sentence for a firearms offence will usually be consecutive to the sentence for the main offence where that offence involves the use or possession of a firearm (*R v French* (1982) 4 Cr App R(S) 57).

In *R v Gorman* (1993) 14 Cr App R(S) 120, the Court of Appeal said that where a custodial sentence of 12 months is passed and the court is also dealing with the offender for an offence for which a very short custodial sentence is appropriate (for example, failing to surrender to bail) the sentences should normally be concurrent rather than consecutive.

13.1.8 The principle of 'totality'

If the offender is being sentenced for a number of offences, and terms of imprisonment are ordered to run consecutively rather than concurrently, the court should ensure that the total sentence is commensurate with the overall seriousness of the offender's crimes. This is known as the principle of 'totality', a principle expressly preserved by s 158(2)(b) of the Powers of Criminal Courts (Sentencing) Act 2000.

13.1.9 Procedural requirements for determining length of sentence

In determining the length of the sentence, s 81(4)(a) of the Powers of Criminal Courts (Sentencing) Act 2000 requires the court to take into account all available information about the circumstances of the offence(s), including aggravating and mitigating factors, and s 158(1) enables the court to take into account any mitigation put forward on behalf of the offender.

Section 81(4)(b) provides that where s 80(2)(b) is relevant (violent or sexual offences) the court may take account of any information it has about the offender.

13.1.10   Effect of time spent on remand

Section 87 of the Powers of Criminal Courts (Sentencing) Act 2000 provides that, if an offender has spent time in custody awaiting trial and/or sentence, the length of time spent in custody counts towards the service of a custodial sentence passed in respect of that offence. This means that where an offender has been remanded in custody before conviction and/or sentence, the period for which he has already been detained is deducted from the sentence he has to serve.

Section 87 applies to sentences of imprisonment and to detention in a young offender institution or a sentence of long term detention under s 91 of the 2000 Act.

In *R v Governor of Haverill Prison ex p McMahon* (1997) *The Times*, 24 September, the Divisional Court held that where the defendant is remanded in custody at the same time for related offences but those offences are subsequently tried and dealt with separately, any time spent on remand for the first offence which exceeds the time the defendant has to serve for that offence is to be credited as service of the second sentence.

13.2   EARLY RELEASE

13.2.1   Relative to length of sentence

The length of time which a prisoner actually has to serve before early release can take place depends on the length of sentence imposed by the court:

- Where the offender was sentenced to a term of less than 12 months, he will automatically be released after he has served half of the sentence. The release is unconditional.

- Where the offender was sentenced to a term of 12 months or more but less than four years (a 'short term prisoner'), he will automatically be released after he has served half of the sentence. However, from the date of release until the three-quarter point of the sentence is reached, the offender will be on licence and will be under the supervision of a probation officer. If the offender fails to comply with the conditions of his licence, he may be punished (on summary conviction) with a fine.

- Where the offender was sentenced to a term of four years or more (a 'long term prisoner'), there is no automatic release. However, there is discretionary release (subject to the recommendation of the Parole Board) after half the sentence has been served. The release is on licence, again under the supervision of a probation officer. Once two thirds of the sentence has been served, a long term prisoner must be released on licence. If the offender fails to comply with the terms of the licence, there is no provision for a fine but the Home Secretary may revoke the licence, requiring the offender to return to prison.

Section 34A(3) of the Criminal Justice Act 1991, inserted by s 99 of the Crime and Disorder Act 1998, provides that, after a short term prisoner (that is, one serving less than 4 years) has served the requisite period for the term of his sentence, the Secretary of State may, subject to s 37A, release him on licence (rather than unconditional release). Section 34A(4)(c) says that, where the sentence imposed was three months or more but less than four months, that period is 30 days; where the sentence was four months or more but less than eight months, it is one quarter of the term; where it is more than eight months, it is one half of the term. Section 37A(1) of the 1991 Act, inserted by s 100 of the 1998 Act, provides that a person shall not be released under s 34A(3) unless the licence includes a condition ('the curfew condition') which (a) requires the released person to remain at a specified place and (b) includes requirements for securing the electronic monitoring of his whereabouts. Section 37A(3) provides that the curfew condition shall remain in force until the date when the released person would (but for his release) have served one half of his sentence.

In *R v Secretary of State for the Home Dept ex p Probyn* [1998] 1 WLR 809; [1998] 1 All ER 357, it was held that in determining whether a prisoner is a short term or long term prisoner, the relevant sentence is the sentence pronounced by the court (not the sentence as reduced by any time spent in custody while on remand).

In *R v Secretary of State for the Home Department ex p Francois* [1988] 1 All ER 929, the House of Lords held that where a person is sentenced to a term of imprisonment on one occasion and is subsequently sentenced to a further term of imprisonment for another offence, the two terms are to be treated as if they are one term for the purpose of calculating the prisoner's release date.

The Criminal Justice and Court Services Bill 2000 will provide powers to include, in the licence of any prisoner being released from a custodial sentence, a requirement to submit to electronic monitoring. The Secretary of State already has the statutory power to attach conditions to a release licence and so it is already possible to impose curfew conditions, non-contact or exclusion conditions. The Bill will enable these types of condition to have the additional requirement of electronic monitoring attached to them. At present, the only statutory basis for the use of electronic monitoring of curfew conditions in a release licence is under the Home Detention Curfew scheme, which applies only to prisoners serving sentences of less than four years. The new powers provided for by the Bill may be used as follows:

- where a licence requires the released person to observe a curfew or otherwise remain at a specified place, electronic monitoring could be used to determine whether the curfew is being observed;

- where a licence requires the released person not to enter a specified place or places, electronic monitoring could be used to determine whether that person has entered the restricted area.

Furthermore, the Bill proposes new powers to enable the 'tracking' of offenders released from prison on licence, by electronically monitoring their whereabouts, on a continuous basis, until the expiry of the licence or the removal of the condition, whichever happens first. The requisite technology to enable this sort of 'tracking' is not yet available, but is apparently under development.

13.2.2   Commission of further offences

Section 116 of the Powers of Criminal Courts (Sentencing) Act 2000 provides that, where a short term or long term prisoner is released and, before the date on which he would have served his sentence in full, he commits a further offence punishable with imprisonment, the court dealing with him for the new offence may, whether or not it passes any other sentence on him, order him to be returned to prison. The maximum period of the return to prison is equal to the length of time between the date of the offence and the date when he would have served his sentence in full (s 116(2)).

However, a magistrates' court cannot order a person's return to prison for more than six months but may commit the offender (in custody or on bail) to the Crown Court, which may make an order for any period up to the maximum set out in s 116(2) of the Criminal Justice Act 1991 (s 116(3)).

The order for return counts as a sentence of imprisonment and may be ordered to be served consecutively with, or concurrently to, any custodial sentence imposed for the new offence.

In *R v Worthing Justices ex p Varley* [1997] Crim LR 688, it was held that, where the justices impose the maximum custodial sentence, they can for the offences committed while the offender was on licence (six months, or, if two or more 'either way' offences, 12 months); the court can nonetheless order that the sentence(s) for the new offence(s) be served consecutively with the period of return order under s 116.

It was held by the Divisional Court in *R v Burton-on-Trent Justices ex p Smith* [1997] Crim LR 685 (following *R v Harrow Justices ex p Jordan* [1997] 1 WLR 84) that, where the defendant commits a new offence during his release from prison on licence, the magistrates must either (i) deal with both the question of the defendant's return to prison and the sentence for the new offence, or (ii) commit the defendant to the Crown Court for that court to determine both questions. This is so even if the new offence is a purely summary offence. Thus, it is not open to the magistrates to impose a sentence for the new offence and then to commit the offender to the Crown Court so that the Crown Court can decide whether to make an order for return to prison.

Thus, the options open to a magistrates' court in such a case are:

- to sentence for the new offence, but make no order for return to prison;
- to sentence for the new offence and make an order for return to prison for up to six months; or
- to commit the offender to the Crown Court to be sentenced for the new offence (even if the new offence is a summary offence), thus leaving it to the Crown Court to decide whether or not to make an order for return to prison.

In *R v Taylor* [1998] 1 All ER 357, the Court of Appeal held as follows: where an offender commits an offence while on licence from prison, the sentencing court must first decide what it is the appropriate sentence for the new offence (disregarding, at this stage, the possibility of an order for the offender's return to prison). Then, in considering whether an order for return should be made, the court should have regard to: (i) the nature and extent of any progress made by the offender since his release on licence; (ii) whether the new offence calls for a custodial sentence; (iii) the question of 'totality' (that is, whether the overall punishment reflects the seriousness of what the offender has done). The court may also have regard to the length of time between the offender's release on licence and the commission of the new offence.

In *R v Secretary of State for Home Dept ex p Probyn* [1998] 1 WLR 809; [1998] 1 All ER 357, it was held that where an offender commits an offence while on licence and the court orders his return to prison and also imposes a sentence of imprisonment for the later offence, the two terms are to be regarded as a single term for the purpose of deciding whether the offender is a short term prisoner or a long term prisoner (which affects whether he has to serve half or two thirds of his sentence before release).

13.2.3   Effect of early release on original sentence

In *Practice Statement (Crime: Sentencing)* [1992] 1 WLR 948; [1992] 4 All ER 307, Lord Taylor CJ pointed out that these early release provisions mean that some offenders (especially those serving between 12 months and four years) may well have to spend longer in prison than they would have done under the former system. Accordingly, said the Lord Taylor CJ, it will be necessary, when passing a custodial sentence in the Crown Court, to have regard to the actual period likely to be served. Furthermore, existing guideline judgments on the sentences which are appropriate for particular offences should be applied with these considerations in mind.

13.2.4 Life sentences

The early release provisions set out above apply only to prisoners who have received determinate sentences (that is, a specific number of months or years). Prisoners serving life sentences are treated differently.

13.2.5 Murder

A person convicted of murder must be sentenced to life imprisonment (s 1(1) of the Murder (Abolition of Death Penalty) Act 1965). In the case of an offender who is under 18, the appropriate sentence is one of detention during Her Majesty's pleasure under s 90 of the Powers of Criminal Courts (Sentencing) Act 2000.

Under s 1(2) of the Murder (Abolition of Death Penalty) Act 1965, the trial judge is empowered to make a recommendation as to the minimum period which should elapse before the offender is released on licence. This recommendation is communicated to the Home Secretary, along with the view of the Lord Chief Justice. The Home Secretary must inform the prisoner of the views of the judges and the prisoner has the right to make written representation as to the minimum period he should serve. The view of the judges does not bind the Home Secretary, who can shorten or lengthen the period. The prisoner's case will ultimately be reviewed by the Parole Board, which may recommend that the prisoner be released on licence. The Home Secretary is not bound by that recommendation.

13.2.6 Discretionary life sentences

Several offences carry a maximum sentence of life imprisonment (for example, rape, robbery, inflicting grievous bodily harm with intent).

In *R v Whittaker* (1996) *The Times*, 24 July (following *Attorney General's Reference (No 34 of 1992)* (1994) 15 Cr App R(S) 167), the Court of Appeal set out the conditions which must be satisfied before a discretionary life sentence can be imposed. First, the offender must have been convicted of a very serious offence. Secondly, it must be established that there are good grounds for believing that the offender might remain a serious danger to the public for a period that could not be estimated reliably at the time when the sentence was passed.

Further guidance on discretionary life sentences was given in *R v Chapman* [2000] 1 Cr App R 77. The offender was given a discretionary life sentence after pleading guilty to arson, being reckless whether life would be endangered. The offender, aged 19, had started a fire in the room he shared in an adult residential unit where it could be, and was, quickly discovered and extinguished. The property had not been extensively damaged; no personal injuries had been sustained, nor were they likely or intended to have been. The Court of Appeal held as follows: (a) a discretionary life sentence imposed for purposes of public protection and not for pure retribution or deterrence can only be passed under s 80(2)(b) of the Powers of Criminal Courts (Sentencing) Act 2000 (see 13.1.2 above). The pre-conditions for imposing an indeterminate life sentence for purposes of public protection are that: (i) the offender has committed an offence grave enough to merit an extremely long sentence and (ii) there are good grounds for believing that the offender might remain a serious danger to the public for a period which could not be reliably estimated at the date of sentence; (b) a longer than commensurate sentence under s 80(2)(b) should not be longer than judged necessary to achieve the object of protecting the public; but there is no necessary ratio between the part of the sentence intended to punish and that intended to protect. Thus, there was no objection in principle if the court regarded, for example, a term of two years as that necessary to punish and additionally, say, six to eight years as that necessary for protection purposes, making a total of eight to 10 years. A sentence so constructed, if justified by the grounds relied on in its support, is to be preferred to an indefinite life sentence which leaves a defendant uncertain when, if ever, he might hope for release and exposes him to the risk of extremely protracted incarceration; (c) the more likely it is that the offender will re-offend and the more grave such offending might be, the less emphasis the court might place on the gravity of the original offence. However, a life sentence should never be imposed unless the circumstances are such as to call for a serious sentence based on the offence committed. In the present case, the offence was not sufficiently grave to justify imposition of a life sentence. Despite the prospect of continuing risk, a life sentence was inappropriate and a determinate sentence under s 80(2)(b) was appropriate; the life sentence was replaced with a determinate sentence of three years to which seven years was added for purposes of public protection under s 80(2)(b), giving a total sentence of 10 years.

When imposing a discretionary life sentence, the trial judge is empowered to specify a minimum length of time which the offender should serve before release on licence (s 34(3) of the Criminal Justice Act 1991). *Practice Direction (Imposition of Discretionary Life Sentence)* (1993) says that a minimum recommendation should be made unless the case is an exceptional one, where the judge considers the offence to be so serious that detention for life is justified by the seriousness of the offence alone, irrespective of the risk to the public.

Release on licence is considered by the Parole Board. The prisoner has the right to attend the hearing and to be legally represented. The Parole Board should only recommend release if satisfied that it is no longer necessary for the protection of the public that the prisoner be detained (s 34(4)(b) of the Criminal Justice Act 1991). If the Board decide that the prisoner should be released, that decision is final and binds the Home Secretary (s 34(3)). If the Board does not decide to release the prisoner, he can require his case to be considered every two years (s 34(5)(b)).

Where a life prisoner is released on licence, he is liable to be recalled to prison at any time during the rest of his life (s 37(3) of the Criminal Justice Act 1991).

Section 28 of the Crime (Sentences) Act 1997 provides that where a person receives a discretionary life sentence (that is, in a case other than murder, where the life sentence is mandatory), the court which sentences him may order that this section should apply to him as soon as he has served a part of his sentence specified in the order. The time which the offender must serve before this section applies to him must take into account the seriousness of the offence(s) and the length of time the offender spent in custody while on remand. Once the prisoner has served the part of his sentence specified in the order and the Parole Board has directed his release, the Secretary of State must release him on licence. The Parole Board can only give such a direction if the Secretary of State has referred the case to it and the Board is satisfied that it is no longer necessary for the protection of the public that the prisoner remain in prison.

Section 31 stipulates that, where a life prisoner is released on licence, the licence (unless revoked) remains in force until his death. Section 32 enables the Secretary of State (subject to the approval of the Parole Board) to revoke the licence of a life prisoner who has been released on licence, thus recalling the offender to prison.

In *R v Secretary of State for the Home Department ex p Stafford* [1999] 2 AC 38; [1998] 4 All ER 7, the Court of Appeal considered the wide discretion conferred on the Home Secretary by s 29 of the Crime (Sentences) Act 1997 and held that he was entitled to refuse to release a mandatory life sentence prisoner after the expiry of the punitive term which had been fixed in his case on the ground that, if released, the lifer might commit some other imprisonable offence or fail to comply with the requirements of his licence.

As the European Court of Human Rights held in *V v UK; T v UK* (1999) *The Times*, 17 December that an independent and impartial tribunal – not the Secretary of State – should fix the tariff to be served by young offenders sentenced to detention during Her Majesty's pleasure, it is likely that new arrangements will have to be made in respect of adult lifers as well.

13.3   SUSPENDED SENTENCES OF IMPRISONMENT

Section 118(1), (2) of the Powers of Criminal Courts (Sentencing) Act 2000 provides that, where a court imposes a prison sentence of two years or less, it may order that the sentence is not to take effect unless, during a specified period of between one and two years from the date the sentence is imposed, the offender commits a further imprisonable offence and the court dealing with the later offence orders that the original sentence of imprisonment take effect.

The length of the original sentence imprisonment is known as the 'term' and the period during which it is to remain suspended is known as the 'operational period'.

Section 118(7) of the 2000 Act requires the court to warn the offender that he will be liable to serve the suspended sentence if he commits a further imprisonable offence during the operational period.

Only a sentence of imprisonment can be suspended. The power does not, therefore, apply to detention in a young offender institution or to long term detention under s 91 of the Act. It follows that a suspended sentence can only be imposed on an offender who has attained the age of 21.

Where an offender is being dealt with for more than one offence and consecutive sentences of imprisonment are imposed, those sentences can only be suspended if the aggregate total is two years or less (s 125(1) of the Act).

Where two suspended sentences are imposed on the same occasion, the court should indicate whether they are to run concurrently or consecutively if they are activated (*R v Wilkinson* [1970] 1 WLR 1319; [1970] 3 All ER 439). In *R v Gall* (1970) 54 Cr App R 292, it was held that if the sentences run consecutively, they constitute a single suspended sentence for the purpose of activation in the event of the commission of a later offence.

Section 118(2) of the 2000 Act stipulates that a suspended sentence may only be imposed if:

- '... a sentence of imprisonment would have been appropriate even without the power to suspend the sentence'; and
- the exercise of the power to suspend the sentence 'can be justified by the exceptional circumstances of the case'.

The fact that a suspended sentence may only be imposed if the court is satisfied that immediate custody would have been appropriate in the absence of the power to suspend the sentence serves to emphasise that s 79 of the Act applies equally to suspended sentences. In other words, the offence must be sufficiently serious to justify a custodial sentence (*R v Fletcher* (1991) 12 Cr App R(S) 671).

By requiring the presence of exceptional circumstances before a suspended sentence can be imposed, it is clearly the intention of Parliament that the suspended sentence 'should be used far more sparingly than it has been in the past' (*R v Lowery* (1993) 14 Cr App R(S) 485). There is no statutory definition of exceptional circumstances: in *R v Okinikan* [1993] 1 WLR 173; [1993] 2 All ER 5, Lord Taylor CJ declined to provide a judicial definition of the phrase, saying that it will depend on the facts of each individual case whether it can be said that exceptional circumstances are present.

In *Okinikan*, it was said that good character (that is, lack of previous convictions), youth, and an early plea of guilty cannot amount to exceptional circumstances. The rationale is that such factors are present in a large number of cases and so can hardly be described as exceptional.

The term 'exceptional circumstances' can include the poor health of the defendant (*R v Weston* [1995] Crim LR 900).

In *R v French* [1993] Crim LR 893, the defendant had experienced severe financial and emotional difficulties and was receiving psychiatric care for depression; there was evidence that a custodial sentence would impede her recovery. These factors were said to amount to exceptional circumstances justifying the suspension of the custodial sentence.

The decision in *R v Lowery* (1993) 14 Cr App R(S) 485, appears rather more harsh. The defendant was a police officer whose duties included collecting fines. He stole a total of just over £1,500. It was argued in the Court of Appeal that a suspended sentence was appropriate because the defendant's wife had become disabled and the money had been stolen to pay for adaptations to the family home for her benefit; as a result of the offence the defendant was unemployed and had lost much of his pension rights; the defendant was very depressed and had attempted suicide twice. The Court of Appeal held that these circumstances were not exceptional because theft in breach of trust will usually involve far reaching adverse consequences to the offender which go far beyond the immediate impact of any sentence which might be imposed on him. Accordingly, a suspended sentence was not appropriate. However, as an act of mercy, the Court of Appeal substituted a sentence of immediate custody of such length as would mean the offender's immediate release.

In *R v Brookin* (1994) 16 Cr App R(S) 78, provocation resulting in violence was said to be capable of amounting to exceptional circumstances.

In *R v Murti* [1996] 2 Cr App R(S) 152, the defendant was convicted of social security fraud. She was a postal worker and she allowed two women to cash DSS benefit vouchers which she knew were stolen. In mitigation, reliance was placed on her initial reluctance to become involved in the offence, the fact that she was suffering from post-natal depression, the fact that her husband had threatened to leave her, so that she would be the sole carer for two small children, the fact that her employer had re-engaged her and that she had pleaded guilty and testified against a co-defendant. The Court of Appeal rejected the argument that any of these factors amounted to exceptional circumstances. However, since the sentence was passed, she had attempted suicide in prison and her husband had left her, taking the children with him. The Court of Appeal, as an act of mercy, substituted a probation order for the prison sentence.

13.3.1   Combining suspended sentence with other orders

Section 118(5) of the Powers of Criminal Courts (Sentencing) Act 2000 requires the court to consider imposing a fine and/or making a compensation order in addition to imposing a suspended sentence.

In *R v Sapiano* (1968) 52 Cr App R 674, it was held to be wrong in principle to impose an immediate sentence of imprisonment and a suspended sentence of imprisonment on the same occasion.

Section 118(6) of the Powers of Criminal Courts (Sentencing) Act 2000 provides that, if the court imposes a suspended sentence, it may not impose a community sentence (probation, community service or a combination order) in respect of the same offence or for any other offence being dealt with by the court.

13.3.2   Suspended sentence supervision order

There is an indirect method of combining a form of probation with some suspended sentences. Section 122 of the Powers of Criminal Courts (Sentencing) Act 2000 states that, where a sentence of more than six months is suspended, the court may make a suspended sentence supervision order. The effect of such an order is to place the offender under the supervision of a probation officer for a specified period not exceeding the operational period of the suspended sentence.

This power only applies if there is a sentence of six months or more for one offence. It does not apply if sentences which are each shorter than six months are imposed but made to run consecutively so that the aggregate term exceeds six months (*R v Baker* (1988) 10 Cr App R(S) 409). This restriction has the effect that a magistrates' court (which cannot impose a sentence of more than six months' imprisonment for a single offence (s 78 of the 2000 Act) cannot make a suspended sentence supervision order.

If a supervision order is made, the offender is required to keep in touch with the probation officer in accordance with the probation officer's instructions and must notify the probation officer of any change of address. No other conditions may be added to the supervision order.

Failure without reasonable cause to comply with the requirements of the order is punishable with a fine of up to £1,000 (s 123(3)).

The supervision order ceases to have effect if either the suspended sentence is activated because of the commission of a later offence or else the supervision order is discharged (which is possible on the application of the offender or the probation officer) (s 124).

13.3.3   Length of suspended sentence

In *R v Mah-Wing* (1983) 5 Cr App R(S) 347, it was held that the court, when determining the length of a suspended sentence, must first consider what would be the appropriate sentence of immediate custody and then go on to consider whether there are grounds for suspending it. 'What the court must not do is pass a longer custodial sentence than it would otherwise do, because it is suspended' (*per* Griffiths LJ).

In determining the length of the sentence, the court must impose a term which is commensurate with the seriousness of the offence (cf s 80(2)(a) of the 2000 Act).

When fixing the term of the suspended sentence, the court should take into account any period which the offender has spent in custody on remand prior to being dealt with for the offence in respect of which the suspended sentence is to be imposed (*Practice Direction (Crime: Suspended Sentence)* (1970)).

13.4   ACTIVATION OF SUSPENDED SENTENCE

Section 119(2) of the Powers of Criminal Courts (Sentencing) Act 2000 creates a presumption that where an offender is convicted of an imprisonable offence committed during the operation period of a suspended sentence, the court dealing with him for the later offence should activate the suspended sentence.

Section 119(2) stipulates that the whole of the suspended sentence should be brought into effect unless the court takes the view that it would be unjust to do so. If the court does not activate the whole of the suspended sentence, it must give its reasons for not doing so.

Section 119(1) sets out the other options available to the court if it decides not to activate the whole of the suspended sentence. Those options are:

- To activate part of the suspended sentence. The effect of this is best illustrated by an example. Suppose that an offender is sentenced to nine months' imprisonment, suspended for two years, and during that two year period he commits a further offence. Suppose that, for the second offence, the defendant is sentenced to three months' imprisonment. It would be open to the court to take the view that it would be excessive to activate the whole of the nine months' suspended sentence consecutive to the three months for the later offence (which would make a total sentence of 12 months); the court could, for example, activate the suspended sentence but reduce its term to six months. Where part of a suspended sentence is activated, the rest lapses and the defendant can never be required to serve it.

- To vary the operational period of the original suspended sentence by replacing it with a new operational period of up to two years from the date of the variation. For example, if the court wishes to make a community service order in respect of the later offence, it would be inappropriate to activate any part of the suspended sentence (the offender could not do community service if he were in prison!) but if the court does not wish to ignore the breach of the suspended sentence, increasing the operational period may well be the appropriate solution.

Where the court varies the operational period, it may also make a suspended sentence supervision order (see above) provided that at least six months' imprisonment is suspended (s 122(8) of the 2000 Act).

• To take no action at all in respect of the breach of the suspended sentence.

Where the court activates all or part of a suspended sentence, it should be ordered to run consecutively to a prison sentence for the later offence unless there are exceptional circumstances (*R v Ithell* [1969] 1 WLR 272; [1969] 2 All ER 449).

In *R v Bocskei* (1970) 54 Cr App R 519, it was pointed out that the totality principle referred to in 13.1.8 above applies to the activation of suspended sentences. Therefore, if the activation of a suspended sentence to run consecutively with a custodial sentence for the present offence would result in a total sentence which is too harsh, the court may activate part of the suspended sentence and/or order that the two sentences be served concurrently.

It must be emphasised that a defendant is only in breach of a suspended sentence if he commits an imprisonable offence during the operational period of the suspended sentence. It follows from this that the defendant will be in breach of the suspended sentence even if he is convicted of the later offence after the expiry of the operational period provided that the offence was committed during the operational period. It is the date of the commission of the later offence, not the date when the defendant is convicted of that offence, which determines whether there is a breach of a suspended sentence or not.

Where an offender commits an offence during the operational period of a suspended sentence but is conditionally discharged for the later offence, it does not count as a conviction for the purpose of activating the suspended sentence and so the suspended sentence cannot be activated (*R v Moore* [1995] 2 WLR 728; [1995] 4 All ER 843).

13.4.1 Determining action to be taken for breach of suspended sentence

As we have seen, s 119(2) of the 2000 Act creates a presumption that the court will activate the suspended sentence in full in the event of a breach. In *R v Craine* (1981) 3 Cr App R(S) 198, it was emphasised that it is only in exceptional circumstances that a suspended sentence will not be activated if a further imprisonable offence is committed.

The mere fact that the later offence is of a different type to the offence for which the suspended sentence was imposed does not justify refraining from activating the suspended sentence (*R v Saunders* (1970) 54 Cr App R 247; *R v Craine* (1981) 3 Cr App R(S) 198; *R v Clitheroe* (1987) 9 Cr App R(S) 159).

In most cases (though not all), it will be inappropriate to activate a suspended sentence where the later offence is dealt with by means of a non-custodial sentence (*R v McElhorne* (1984); *R v Jagodzinski* (1986) 8 Cr App R(S) 150). This is so even if the later offence is of the same nature as the offence for which the suspended sentence was imposed (*R v Dobson* (1989) 11 Cr App R(S) 332).

Thus, in *R v Brooks* (1990) 12 Cr App R(S) 756, the defendant was convicted of possessing a small quantity of cannabis for his own use. This conviction placed him in breach of a suspended sentence for possession of cannabis with intent to supply. It was held by the Court of Appeal that the later offence was not sufficiently serious to justify a custodial sentence. The comparative triviality of the second offence, making a custodial sentence for that offence inappropriate, meant that it would be wrong to activate the suspended sentence for the earlier offence (see, also, *R v Bee* (1993) 14 Cr App R(S) 703).

Another argument in favour of leniency is that the later offence was committed when the operational period of the suspended sentence had almost expired (*R v Carr* (1979) 1 Cr App R(S) 53); *R v Fitton* (1989) 11 Cr App R(S) 350). In that case, the later offence was committed when the offender had completed 22 months of a two year suspended sentence. He was sentenced to two years' imprisonment for the later offence but the Court of Appeal ordered that the suspended sentence run concurrently with the sentence for the later offence. See, also, *R v Kilroy* (1979) 1 Cr App R(S) 179. An alternative in such a case may well be to activate only part of the suspended sentence.

In *R v Stacey* (1994) 15 Cr App R(S) 585, a non-custodial sentence was imposed for an offence committed in breach of a suspended sentence, but the suspended sentence was activated in full. The Court of Appeal affirmed the general principle that where a non-custodial sentence is imposed for the later offence, it is inappropriate to activate the suspended sentence unless there are exceptional circumstances. In the present case, however, the appellant had breached the suspended sentence shortly after its imposition (and had committed another offence while on bail for the present offence) and so the decision to activate the suspended sentence was justified (although, in fact, the Court of Appeal decided that, because of personal mitigation, only half the period of the suspended sentence should be activated). See, also, *R v Calladine* [1993] Crim LR 980.

13.5 MANDATORY SENTENCES

13.5.1 Life sentence for second serious offence

Section 109 of the Powers of Criminal Courts (Sentencing) Act 2000 provides for the imposition of a mandatory life sentence for an offender who commits a second serious offence. The section states that where:

(a) a person is convicted of a serious offence; and

(b) at the time when that offence was committed, the offender had attained the age of 18 years and had also been convicted in any part of the United Kingdom of another serious offence,

then the court must impose a sentence of imprisonment for life (custody for life in the case of an offender who is under 21) unless the court is of the opinion that there are exceptional circumstances (relating to either of the offences or of the offender) which justify it passing a lesser sentence.

Sub-section (5) defines the phrase 'serious offence' as meaning: attempted murder; conspiracy to murder; incitement to murder; soliciting murder (s 4 of the Offences Against the Person Act 1861); manslaughter; wounding or causing grievous bodily harm with intent (s 18 of the Offences Against the Person Act 1861); rape; attempted rape; intercourse with a girl under 13 (s 5 of the Sexual Offences Act 1956); possession of a firearm with intent to injure, use of a firearm to resist arrest, carrying a firearm with criminal intent (ss 16, 17 and 18 of the Firearms Act 1968); and robbery where, at some time during the commission of the offence, the offender had in his possession a firearm or imitation firearm. Sub-sections (6) and (7) specify the offences under the law of Scotland and Northern Ireland which are to be regarded as 'serious' for the purpose of s 2.

In the joined cases of *R v Kelly* and *Attorney General's Reference (No 53 of 1998)* [2000] 1 QB 198; [1999] 2 All ER 13, the Court of Appeal held that, to be exceptional, a circumstance need not be unique, or unprecedented or very rare, but it could not be one that was regularly or routinely or normally encountered. The court added that it is not enough that the circumstances are exceptional: they must also be such as to justify the court in not imposing the mandatory sentence. The court went on to hold that it is not enough that the offender does not present a serious threat to the safety of the public. Also, the offender's age when convicted of the first offence, the interval of time between the two offences, and the difference in nature between the two offences do not give rise to exceptional circumstances.

In *R v Buckland* [2000] 1 All ER 907, the Court of Appeal gave further guidance on the mandatory life sentence provisions. The court held that acute mental illness at the time of committing a 'serious offence' is not of itself an exceptional circumstance which justifies the court in not passing a life sentence. The court went to hold that the judgment whether exceptional circumstances exist is qualitative as well as quantitative: if the court finds that exceptional circumstances exist, it must go on to consider whether those exceptional circumstances justify not imposing a life sentence. The court added that in any case where it appears that the defendant presents a serious and continuing danger to public safety, it is hard to see how the court could consider itself justified in not imposing a life sentence even if exceptional circumstances are found to exist. However, if there are exceptional circumstances and the offender does not represent a serious and continuing danger to the safety of the public, the court may be justified in imposing a lesser penalty. The court also held that attempted robbery is not within the definition of a 'serious offence' for these purposes; and that firearms offences are within the definition of a 'serious offence' even if the offence involves only an imitation firearm.

In *R v Stephens* [2000] Crim LR 402, defence counsel had failed to inform the defendant that, if he were to be convicted of causing grievous bodily harm with intent (s 18 of the Offences Against the Person Act 1861), he faced a mandatory life sentence under s 109 of the Powers of Criminal Courts (Sentencing) Act 2000. If the defendant had been aware of this fact, he might have pleaded guilty of the alternative charge of inflicting grievous bodily harm (s 20), a plea that would have been acceptable to the prosecution (and which would not have attracted a mandatory life sentence). The Court of Appeal held that the lack of appropriate advice gave rise to exceptional circumstances justifying the court in not imposing a life sentence.

13.5.2 Minimum sentences for third class A drug trafficking offence

Section 110 of the Powers of Criminal Courts (Sentencing) Act 2000 provides for the imposition of a minimum sentence of seven years for conviction of a third Class A drug trafficking offence. The section states that where:

(a) a person is convicted of a Class A drug trafficking offence (as defined by the Drug Trafficking Act 1994); and

(b) at the time when that offence was committed the offender was 18 or over and had been convicted in any part of the United Kingdom of two other Class A drug trafficking offences; and

(c) one of those other offences was committed after he had been convicted of the other (so where the offender is convicted of more than one offence on a single occasion that only counts as one conviction for these purposes),

then the court must impose a custodial sentence of at least seven years unless the court takes the view that there are particular circumstances which relate to any of the offences or to the offender and which would make it unjust in all the circumstances to impose the minimum sentence.

In *R v Stenhouse* (2000) *The Times*, 11 April, the Court of Appeal decided that there were 'particular circumstances' making it unjust to impose the seven year minimum: the last of the offender's previous convictions had led to a probation order; that fact, together with other mitigating features, made the minimum sentence unjust in all the circumstances.

13.5.3   Minimum sentence for third domestic burglary

Section 111 of the Powers of Criminal Courts (Sentencing) Act 2000 prescribes a minimum sentence of three years for conviction of a third domestic burglary. It states that where:

(a) a person is convicted of a domestic burglary (that is, a burglary committed in respect of a building or part of a building which is a dwelling); and

(b) at the time when that offence was committed the offender had attained the age of 18 and had been convicted in England or Wales of two other domestic burglaries; and

(c) one of those other burglaries was committed after he had been convicted of the other, and both were committed after 30 November 1999,

then the court must impose a custodial sentence of at least 3 years unless the court takes the view that there are particular circumstances which relate to any of the offences or to the offender and which would make it unjust in all the circumstances to impose the minimum sentence.

Section 111(3) provides that where a person is charged with a domestic burglary which could otherwise be triable either way but the case is one to which s 4 applies, the burglary is to be regarded as triable only on indictment.

13.5.4   Discount for guilty plea

Where s 110 or s 111 of the 2000 Act is applicable, the court can still give credit for a guilty plea under s 152 of the Act. However, the amount of discount is limited by s 152(3). This provides that, in a case under s 110 or s 111, the court can take account of a guilty plea by passing a sentence which is not less than 80% of what would otherwise be the minimum sentence prescribed by the 2000 Act.

13.5.5   Mentally disordered offenders

Section 46 of the Crime (Sentences) Act 1997 provides that when imposing a sentence of imprisonment on an offender who is suffering from a psychopathic disorder, the court may direct that he be detained in hospital and subject to special conditions. The Secretary of State is empowered to extend these provisions to cover offenders suffering from other mental disorders. See Chapter 18, 18.9.

TABLE OF STATUTORY MATERIALS

STATUTORY MATERIALS

RESTRICTIONS ON IMPOSITION OF CUSTODIAL SENTENCES

POWERS OF CRIMINAL COURTS (SENTENCING) ACT 2000

Section 79: General restrictions on imposing discretionary custodial sentences

(1) This section applies where a person is convicted of an offence punishable with a custodial sentence other than one:

    (a) fixed by law; or

    (b) falling to be imposed under section 109(2), 110(2) or 111(2) below.

(2) Subject to sub-section (3) below, the court shall not pass a custodial sentence on the offender unless it is of the opinion:

    (a) that the offence, or the combination of the offence and one or more offences associated with it, was so serious that only such a sentence can be justified for the offence; or

    (b) where the offence is a violent or sexual offence, that only such a sentence would be adequate to protect the public from serious harm from him.

(3) Nothing in sub-section (2) above shall prevent the court from passing a custodial sentence on the offender if he fails to express his willingness to comply with:

    (a) a requirement which is proposed by the court to be included in a probation order or supervision order and which requires an expression of such willingness; or

    (b) a requirement which is proposed by the court to be included in a drug treatment and testing order or an order under section 52(4) above (order to provide samples).

(4) Where a court passes a custodial sentence, it shall:

    (a) in a case not falling within sub-section (3) above, state in open court that it is of the opinion that either or both of paragraphs (a) and (b) of sub-section (2) above apply and why it is of that opinion; and

    (b) in any case, explain to the offender in open court and in ordinary language why it is passing a custodial sentence on him.

(5) A magistrates' court shall cause a reason stated by it under sub-section (4) above to be specified in the warrant of commitment and to be entered in the register.

Section 80: Length of discretionary custodial sentences: general provision.

(1) This section applies where a court passes a custodial sentence other than one fixed by law or falling to be imposed under section 109(2) below.

(2) Subject to sections 110(2) and 111(2) below, the custodial sentence shall be:

(a) for such term (not exceeding the permitted maximum) as in the opinion of the court is commensurate with the seriousness of the offence, or the combination of the offence and one or more offences associated with it; or

(b) where the offence is a violent or sexual offence, for such longer term (not exceeding that maximum) as in the opinion of the court is necessary to protect the public from serious harm from the offender.

(3) Where the court passes a custodial sentence for a term longer than is commensurate with the seriousness of the offence, or the combination of the offence and one or more offences associated with it, the court shall:

(a) state in open court that it is of the opinion that sub-section (2)(b) above applies and why it is of that opinion; and

(b) explain to the offender in open court and in ordinary language why the sentence is for such a term.

(4) A custodial sentence for an indeterminate period shall be regarded for the purposes of sub-sections (2) and (3) above as a custodial sentence for a term longer than any actual term.

(5) Sub-section (3) above shall not apply in any case where the court passes a custodial sentence falling to be imposed under sub-section (2) of section 110 or 111 below which is for the minimum term specified in that sub-section.

Section 81: Pre-sentence reports and other requirements

(1) Subject to sub-section (2) below, a court shall obtain and consider a pre-sentence report before forming any such opinion as is mentioned in sub-section (2) of section 79 or 80 above.

(2) Sub-section (1) above does not apply if, in the circumstances of the case, the court is of the opinion that it is unnecessary to obtain a pre-sentence report.

(3) In a case where the offender is aged under 18 and the offence is not triable only on indictment and there is no other offence associated with it that is triable only on indictment, the court shall not form such an opinion as is mentioned in sub-section (2) above unless:

(a) there exists a previous pre-sentence report obtained in respect of the offender; and

(b) the court has had regard to the information contained in that report, or, if there is more than one such report, the most recent report.

(4) In forming any such opinion as is mentioned in sub-section (2) of section 79 or 80 above, a court:

(a) shall take into account all such information as is available to it about the circumstances of the offence or (as the case may be) of the offence and the offence or offences associated with it, including any aggravating or mitigating factors; and

(b) in the case of any such opinion as is mentioned in paragraph (b) of that sub-section, may take into account any information about the offender which is before it.

(5) No custodial sentence shall be invalidated by the failure of a court to obtain and consider a pre-sentence report before forming an opinion referred to in sub-section (1) above, but any court on an appeal against such a sentence:

(a) shall, subject to sub-section (6) below, obtain a pre-sentence report if none was obtained by the court below; and

(b) shall consider any such report obtained by it or by that court.

(6) Sub-section (5)(a) above does not apply if the court is of the opinion:

(a) that the court below was justified in forming an opinion that it was unnecessary to obtain a pre-sentence report; or

(b) that, although the court below was not justified in forming that opinion, in the circumstances of the case at the time it is before the court, it is unnecessary to obtain a pre-sentence report.

(7) In a case where the offender is aged under 18 and the offence is not triable only on indictment and there is no other offence associated with it that is triable only on indictment, the court shall not form such an opinion as is mentioned in sub-section (6) above unless:

(a) there exists a previous pre-sentence report obtained in respect of the offender; and

(b) he court has had regard to the information contained in that report, or, if there is more than one such report, the most recent report.

(8) Section 156 below (disclosure of pre-sentence report to offender, etc) applies to any pre-sentence report obtained in pursuance of this section.

Section 82: Additional requirements in case of mentally disordered offender

(1) Subject to sub-section (2) below, in any case where the offender is or appears to be mentally disordered, the court shall obtain and consider a medical report before passing a custodial sentence other than one fixed by law or falling to be imposed under section 109(2) below.

(2) Sub-section (1) above does not apply if, in the circumstances of the case, the court is of the opinion that it is unnecessary to obtain a medical report.

(3) Before passing a custodial sentence, other than one fixed by law or falling to be imposed under section 109(2) below, on an offender who is or appears to be mentally disordered, a court shall consider:

(a) any information before it which relates to his mental condition (whether given in a medical report, a pre-sentence report or otherwise); and

(b) the likely effect of such a sentence on that condition and on any treatment which may be available for it.

(4) No custodial sentence which is passed in a case to which sub-section (1) above applies shall be invalidated by the failure of a court to comply with that sub-section, but any court on an appeal against such a sentence:

(a) shall obtain a medical report if none was obtained by the court below; and

(b) shall consider any such report obtained by it or by that court.

(5) In this section, 'mentally disordered', in relation to any person, means suffering from a mental disorder within the meaning of the Mental Health 83.

(6) In this section, 'medical report' means a report as to an offender's mental condition made or submitted orally or in writing by a registered medical practitioner who is approved for the purposes of section 12 of the Mental Health Act 1983 by the Secretary of State as having special experience in the diagnosis or treatment of mental disorder.

(7) Nothing in this section shall be taken as prejudicing the generality of section 81 above.

Section 83: Restriction on imposing custodial sentences on persons not legally represented

(1) A magistrates' court on summary conviction, or the Crown Court on committal for sentence or on conviction on indictment, shall not pass a sentence of imprisonment on a person who:

(a) is not legally represented in that court; and

(b) has not been previously sentenced to that punishment by a court in any part of the United Kingdom,

unless he is a person to whom sub-section (3) below applies.

(2) A magistrates' court on summary conviction, or the Crown Court on committal for sentence or on conviction on indictment, shall not:

(a) pass a sentence of detention under section 90 or 91 below;

(b) pass a sentence of custody for life under section 93 or 94 below;

(c) pass a sentence of detention in a young offender institution; or

(d) make a detention and training order,

on or in respect of a person who is not legally represented in that court unless he is a person to whom sub-section (3) below applies.

(3) This sub-section applies to a person if either:

(a) he was granted a right to representation funded by the Legal Services Commission as part of the Criminal Defence Service but the right was withdrawn because of his conduct; or

(b) having been informed of his right to apply for such representation and having had the opportunity to do so, he refused or failed to apply.

(4) For the purposes of this section a person is to be treated as legally represented in a court if, but only if, he has the assistance of counsel or a solicitor to represent him in the proceedings in that court at some time after he is found guilty and before he is sentenced.

(5) For the purposes of sub-section (1)(b) above a previous sentence of imprisonment which has been suspended and which has not taken effect under section 119 below or under section 19 of the Treatment of Offenders Act (Northern Ireland) 1968 shall be disregarded.

(6) In this section 'sentence of imprisonment' does not include a committal for contempt of court or any kindred offence.

Section 161: Meaning of 'associated offence', 'sexual offence', 'violent offence' and 'protecting the public from serious harm'

(1) For the purposes of this Act, an offence is associated with another if:

(a) the offender is convicted of it in the proceedings in which he is convicted of the other offence, or (although convicted of it in earlier proceedings) is sentenced for it at the same time as he is sentenced for that offence; or

(b) the offender admits the commission of it in the proceedings in which he is sentenced for the other offence and requests the court to take it into consideration in sentencing him for that offence.

(2) In this Act, 'sexual offence' means any of the following:

(a) an offence under the Sexual Offences Act 1956, other than an offence under section 30, 31 or 33 to 36 of that Act;

(b) an offence under section 128 of the Mental Health Act 1959;

(c) an offence under the Indecency with Children Act 1960;

(d) an offence under section 9 of the Theft Act 1968 of burglary with intent to commit rape;

(e) an offence under section 54 of the Criminal Law Act 1977;

(f) an offence under the Protection of Children Act 1978;

(g) an offence under section 1 of the Criminal Law Act 1977 of conspiracy to commit any of the offences in paragraphs (a) to (f) above;

(h) an offence under section 1 of the Criminal Attempts Act 1981 of attempting to commit any of those offences;

(i) an offence of inciting another to commit any of those offences.

(3) In this Act, 'violent offence' means an offence which leads, or is intended or likely to lead, to a person's death or to physical injury to a person, and includes an offence which is required to be charged as arson (whether or not it would otherwise fall within this definition).

(4) In this Act any reference, in relation to an offender convicted of a violent or sexual offence, to protecting the public from serious harm from him shall be construed as a reference to protecting members of the public from death or serious personal injury, whether physical or psychological, occasioned by further such offences committed by him.

SUSPENDED SENTENCES

POWERS OF CRIMINAL COURTS (SENTENCING) ACT 2000

Section 118: Suspended sentences of imprisonment

(1) A court which passes a sentence of imprisonment for a term of not more than two years for an offence may (subject to sub-section (4) below) order that the sentence shall not take effect unless, during a period specified in the order, the offender commits in Great Britain another offence punishable with imprisonment and thereafter a court having power to do so orders under section 119 below that the original sentence shall take effect.

(2) The period specified in an order under sub-section (1) above must be a period of not less than one year nor more than two years beginning with the date of the order.

(3) In this Act:

'suspended sentence' means a sentence to which an order under sub-section (1) above relates; and

'operational period', in relation to such a sentence, means the period specified in the order under sub-section (1).

(4) A court shall not deal with an offender by means of a suspended sentence unless it is of the opinion:

  (a) that the case is one in which a sentence of imprisonment would have been appropriate even without the power to suspend the sentence; and

  (b) that the exercise of that power can be justified by the exceptional circumstances of the case.

(5) A court which passes a suspended sentence on any person for an offence shall consider whether the circumstances of the case are such as to warrant in addition the imposition of a fine or the making of a compensation order.

(6) A court which passes a suspended sentence on any person for an offence shall not impose a community sentence in his case in respect of that offence or any other offence of which he is convicted by or before the court or for which he is dealt with by the court.

(7) On passing a suspended sentence the court shall explain to the offender in ordinary language his liability under section 119 below if during the operational period he commits an offence punishable with imprisonment.

(8) Subject to any provision to the contrary contained in the Criminal Justice Act 1967, this Act or any other enactment passed or instrument made under any enactment after 31st December 1967:

(a) a suspended sentence which has not taken effect under section 119 below shall be treated as a sentence of imprisonment for the purposes of all enactments and instruments made under enactments except any enactment or instrument which provides for disqualification for or loss of office, or forfeiture of pensions, of persons sentenced to imprisonment; and

(b) where a suspended sentence has taken effect under section 119, the offender shall be treated for the purposes of the enactments and instruments excepted by paragraph (a) above as having been convicted on the ordinary date on which the period allowed for making an appeal against an order under that section expires or, if such an appeal is made, the date on which it is finally disposed of or abandoned or fails for non-prosecution.

Section 119: Power of court on conviction of further offence to deal with suspended sentence

(1) Where an offender is convicted of an offence punishable with imprisonment committed during the operational period of a suspended sentence and either he is so convicted by or before a court having power under section 120 below to deal with him in respect of the suspended sentence or he subsequently appears or is brought before such a court, then, unless the sentence has already taken effect, that court shall consider his case and deal with him by one of the following methods:

(a) the court may order that the suspended sentence shall take effect with the original term unaltered;

(b) the court may order that the sentence shall take effect with the substitution of a lesser term for the original term;

(c) the court may by order vary the original order under section 118(1) above by substituting for the period specified in that order a period ending not later than two years from the date of the variation; or

(d) the court may make no order with respect to the suspended sentence.

(2) The court shall make an order under paragraph (a) of sub-section (1) above unless it is of the opinion that it would be unjust to do so in view of all the circumstances, including the facts of the subsequent offence; and where it is of that opinion the court shall state its reasons.

(3) Where a court orders that a suspended sentence shall take effect, with or without any variation of the original term, the court may order that that sentence shall take effect immediately or that the term of that sentence shall commence on the expiry of another term of imprisonment passed on the offender by that or another court.

(4) The power to make an order under sub-section (3) above has effect subject to section 84 above (restriction on consecutive sentences for released prisoners).

(5) In proceedings for dealing with an offender in respect of a suspended sentence which take place before the Crown Court, any question whether the offender has been convicted of an offence punishable with imprisonment committed during the operational period of the suspended sentence shall be determined by the court and not by the verdict of a jury.

(6) Where a court deals with an offender under this section in respect of a suspended sentence, the appropriate officer of the court shall notify the appropriate officer of the court which passed the sentence of the method adopted.

(7) Where on consideration of the case of an offender a court makes no order with respect to a suspended sentence, the appropriate officer of the court shall record that fact.

(8) For the purposes of any enactment conferring rights of appeal in criminal cases, any order made by a court with respect to a suspended sentence shall be treated as a sentence passed on the offender by that court for the offence for which the suspended sentence was passed.

Section 120: Court by which suspended sentence may be dealt with

(1) An offender may be dealt with in respect of a suspended sentence by the Crown Court or, where the sentence was passed by a magistrates' court, by any magistrates' court before which he appears or is brought.

(2) Where an offender is convicted by a magistrates' court of an offence punishable with imprisonment and the court is satisfied that the offence was committed during the operational period of a suspended sentence passed by the Crown Court:

(a) the court may, if it thinks fit, commit him in custody or on bail to the Crown Court; and

(b) if it does not, shall give written notice of the conviction to the appropriate officer of the Crown Court.

(3) For the purposes of this section and of section 121 below, a suspended sentence passed on an offender on appeal shall be treated as having been passed by the court by which he was originally sentenced.

Section 121: Procedure where court convicting of further offence does not deal with suspended sentence

(1) If it appears to the Crown Court, where that court has jurisdiction in accordance with sub-section (2) below, or to a justice of the peace having jurisdiction in accordance with that sub-section:

(a) that an offender has been convicted in Great Britain of an offence punishable with imprisonment committed during the operational period of a suspended sentence; and

(b) that he has not been dealt with in respect of the suspended sentence,

that court or justice may, subject to the following provisions of this section, issue a summons requiring the offender to appear at the place and time specified in it, or a warrant for his arrest.

(2) Jurisdiction for the purposes of sub-section (1) above may be exercised:

(a) if the suspended sentence was passed by the Crown Court, by that court;

(b) if it was passed by a magistrates' court, by a justice acting for the area for which that court acted.

...

Section 122: Suspended sentence supervision orders

(1) Where a court passes on an offender a suspended sentence for a term of more than six months for a single offence, the court may make a suspended sentence supervision order, that is to say, an order placing the offender under the supervision of a supervising officer for a period which is specified in the order and does not exceed the operational period of the suspended sentence.

(2) A suspended sentence supervision order shall specify the petty sessions area in which the offender resides or will reside; and the supervising officer shall be a probation officer appointed for or assigned to the area for the time being specified in the order (whether under this sub-section or by virtue of section 124(3) below (power to amend order)).

(3) An offender in respect of whom a suspended sentence supervision order is in force shall keep in touch with the supervising officer in accordance with such instructions as he may from time to time be given by that officer and shall notify him of any change of address.

(4) On making a suspended sentence supervision order, the court shall explain its effect to the offender in ordinary language.

(5) The court by which a suspended sentence supervision order is made shall forthwith give copies of the order to a probation officer assigned to the court, and he shall give a copy to the offender and to the supervising officer.

(8) Where under section 119 above a court deals with an offender in respect of a suspended sentence by varying the operational period of the sentence or by making no order with respect to the sentence, the court may make a suspended sentence supervision order in respect of the offender:

(a) in place of any such order made when the suspended sentence was passed; or

(b) if the court which passed the sentence could have made such an order but did not do so; or

(c) if that court could not then have made such an order but would have had power to do so if sub-section (1) above had then had effect as it has effect at the time when the offender is dealt with under section 119.

Section 123: Breach of requirement of suspended sentence supervision order

(1) If, at any time while a suspended sentence supervision order is in force in respect of an offender, it appears on information to a justice of the peace acting for the petty sessions area for the time being specified in the order that the offender has failed to comply with any of the requirements of section 122(3) above, the justice may:

(a) issue a summons requiring the offender to appear at the place and time specified in it; or

(b) if the information is in writing and on oath, issue a warrant for his arrest.

(2) Any summons or warrant issued under this section shall direct the offender to appear or be brought before a magistrates' court acting for the petty sessions area for the time being specified in the suspended sentence supervision order.

(3) If it is proved to the satisfaction of the court before which an offender appears or is brought under this section that he has failed without reasonable cause to comply with any of the requirements of section 122(3) above, the court may, without prejudice to the continuance of the order, impose on him a fine not exceeding £1,000.

(4) A fine imposed under sub-section (3) above shall be deemed, for the purposes of any enactment, to be a sum adjudged to be paid by a conviction.

Section 124: Suspended sentence supervision orders: revocation, amendment and cessation

(1) A suspended sentence supervision order may be revoked on the application of the supervising officer or the offender:

(a) if it was made by the Crown Court and includes a direction reserving the power of revoking it to that court, by the Crown Court;

(b) in any other case, by a magistrates' court acting for the petty sessions area for the time being specified in the order.

(2) Where a suspended sentence supervision order has been made on appeal, for the purposes of sub-section (1) above it shall be deemed:

(a) if it was made on an appeal brought from a magistrates' court, to have been made by that magistrates' court;

(b) if it was made on an appeal brought from the Crown Court or from the criminal division of the Court of Appeal, to have been made by the Crown Court.

(3) If a magistrates' court acting for the petty sessions area for the time being specified in a suspended sentence supervision order is satisfied that the offender proposes to change, or has changed, his residence from that petty sessions area to another petty sessions area, the court may, and on the application of the supervising officer shall, amend the order by substituting the other petty sessions area for the area specified in the order.

(4) Where a suspended sentence supervision order is amended by a court under sub-section (3) above, the court shall send to the justices' chief executive for the new area specified in the order a copy of the order, together with such documents and information relating to the case as it considers likely to be of assistance to a court acting for that area in the exercise of its functions in relation to the order.

(5) A suspended sentence supervision order shall cease to have effect if before the end of the period specified in it:

(a) a court orders under section 119 above that a suspended sentence passed in the proceedings in which the order was made shall have effect; or

(b) the order is revoked under sub-section (1) above or replaced under section 122(8) above.

Section 125: Suspended sentences: supplementary

(1) For the purposes of any reference in this Chapter, however expressed, to the term of imprisonment to which a person has been sentenced, consecutive terms and terms which are wholly or partly concurrent shall, unless the context otherwise requires, be treated as a single term.

MANDATORY SENTENCES

POWERS OF CRIMINAL COURTS (SENTENCING) ACT 2000

Section 109: Life sentence for second serious offence

(1) This section applies where:

(a) a person is convicted of a serious offence committed after 30th September 1997; and

(b) at the time when that offence was committed, he was 18 or over and had been convicted in any part of the United Kingdom of another serious offence.

(2) The court shall impose a life sentence, that is to say:

    (a) where the offender is 21 or over when convicted of the offence mentioned in sub-section (1)(a) above, a sentence of imprisonment for life,

    (b) where he is under 21 at that time, a sentence of custody for life under section 94 above,

unless the court is of the opinion that there are exceptional circumstances relating to either of the offences or to the offender which justify its not doing so.

(3) Where the court does not impose a life sentence, it shall state in open court that it is of that opinion and what the exceptional circumstances are.

(4) An offence the sentence for which is imposed under sub-section (2) above shall not be regarded as an offence the sentence for which is fixed by law.

(5) An offence committed in England and Wales is a serious offence for the purposes of this section if it is any of the following, namely:

    (a) an attempt to commit murder, a conspiracy to commit murder or an incitement to murder;

    (b) an offence under section 4 of the Offences Against the Person Act 1861 (soliciting murder);

    (c) manslaughter;

    (d) an offence under section 18 of the Offences Against the Person Act 1861 (wounding, or causing grievous bodily harm, with intent);

    (e) rape or an attempt to commit rape;

    (f) an offence under section 5 of the Sexual Offences Act 1956 (intercourse with a girl under 13);

    (g) an offence under section 16 (possession of a firearm with intent to injure), section 17 (use of a firearm to resist arrest) or section 18 (carrying a firearm with criminal intent) of the Firearms Act 1968; and

    (h) robbery where, at some time during the commission of the offence, the offender had in his possession a firearm or imitation firearm within the meaning of that Act.

(6) An offence committed in Scotland is a serious offence for the purposes of this section if the conviction for it was obtained on indictment in the High Court of Justiciary and it is any of the following, namely:

    (a) culpable homicide;

    (b) attempted murder, incitement to commit murder or conspiracy to commit murder;

    (c) rape or attempted rape;

    (d) clandestine injury to women or an attempt to cause such injury;

    (e) sodomy, or an attempt to commit sodomy, where the complainer, that is to say, the person against whom the offence was committed, did not consent;

    (f) assault where the assault:

        (i) is aggravated because it was carried out to the victim's severe injury or the danger of the victim's life; or

        (ii) was carried out with an intention to rape or to ravish the victim;

    (g) robbery where, at some time during the commission of the offence, the offender had in his possession a firearm or imitation firearm within the meaning of the Firearms Act 1968;

    (h) an offence under section 16 (possession of a firearm with intent to injure), section 17 (use of a firearm to resist arrest) or section 18 (carrying a firearm with criminal intent) of that Act;

    (i) lewd, libidinous or indecent behaviour or practices; and

    (j) an offence under section 5(1) of the Criminal Law (Consolidation) (Scotland) Act 1995 (unlawful intercourse with a girl under 13).

(7) An offence committed in Northern Ireland is a serious offence for the purposes of this section if it is any of the following, namely:

    (a) an offence falling within any of paragraphs (a) to (e) of sub-section (5) above;

    (b) an offence under section 4 of the Criminal Law Amendment Act 1885 (intercourse with a girl under 14);

    (c) an offence under Article 17 (possession of a firearm with intent to injure), Article 18(1) (use of a firearm to resist arrest) or Article 19 (carrying a firearm with criminal intent) of the Firearms (Northern Ireland) Order 1981; and

    (d) robbery where, at some time during the commission of the offence, the offender had in his possession a firearm or imitation firearm within the meaning of that Order.

Section 110: Minimum of seven years for third class A drug trafficking offence

(1) This section applies where:

    (a) a person is convicted of a class A drug trafficking offence committed after 30th September 1997;

    (b) at the time when that offence was committed, he was 18 or over and had been convicted in any part of the United Kingdom of two other class A drug trafficking offences; and

    (c) one of those other offences was committed after he had been convicted of the other.

(2) The court shall impose an appropriate custodial sentence for a term of at least seven years except where the court is of the opinion that there are particular circumstances which:

    (a) relate to any of the offences or to the offender; and

    (b) would make it unjust to do so in all the circumstances.

(3) Where the court does not impose such a sentence, it shall state in open court that it is of that opinion and what the particular circumstances are.

(4) Where:

    (a) a person is charged with a class A drug trafficking offence (which, apart from this sub-section, would be triable either way); and

    (b) the circumstances are such that, if he were convicted of the offence, he could be sentenced for it under sub-section (2) above, the offence shall be triable only on indictment.

(5) In this section 'class A drug trafficking offence' means a drug trafficking offence committed in respect of a class A drug; and for this purpose:

'class A drug' has the same meaning as in the Misuse of Drugs Act 1971;

'drug trafficking offence' means a drug trafficking offence within the meaning of the Drug Trafficking Act 1994, the Proceeds of Crime (Scotland)Act 95 or the Proceeds of Crime (Northern Ireland) Order 1996.

(6) In this section 'an appropriate custodial sentence' means:

    (a) in relation to a person who is 21 or over when convicted of the offence mentioned in sub-section (1)(a) above, a sentence of imprisonment;

    (b) in relation to a person who is under 21 at that time, a sentence of detention in a young offender institution.

Section 111: Minimum of three years for third domestic burglary

(1) This section applies where:

    (a) a person is convicted of a domestic burglary committed after 30th November 1999;

    (b) at the time when that burglary was committed, he was 18 or over and had been convicted in England and Wales of two other domestic burglaries; and

    (c) one of those other burglaries was committed after he had been convicted of the other, and both of them were committed after 30th November 1999.

(2) The court shall impose an appropriate custodial sentence for a term of at least three years except where the court is of the opinion that there are particular circumstances which:

    (a) relate to any of the offences or to the offender; and

    (b) would make it unjust to do so in all the circumstances.

(3) Where the court does not impose such a sentence, it shall state in open court that it is of that opinion and what the particular circumstances are.

(4) Where:

    (a) a person is charged with a domestic burglary which, apart from this sub-section, would be triable either way; and

    (a) the circumstances are such that, if he were convicted of the burglary, he could be sentenced for it under sub-section (2) above,

the burglary shall be triable only on indictment.

(5) In this section 'domestic burglary' means a burglary committed in respect of a building or part of a building which is a dwelling.

(6) In this section 'an appropriate custodial sentence' means:

(a) in relation to a person who is 21 or over when convicted of the offence mentioned in sub-section (1)(a) above, a sentence of imprisonment;

(b) in relation to a person who is under 21 at that time, a sentence of detention in a young offender institution.

CHAPTER 14

OFFENDERS OVER 16: COMMUNITY SENTENCES

In this chapter, we look at the community sentences which may be imposed on adult offenders, namely, the probation order, the community service order, and the combination order. However, the statutory criteria which have to be met before any of these orders can be made also have to be met for supervision orders and attendance centre orders (which may be made in respect of young offenders).

14.1   STATUTORY CRITERIA FOR IMPOSING COMMUNITY ORDERS

A community order means:

- a community service order;
- a probation order;
- a combination order (which combines community service and probation);
- a supervision order;
- an attendance centre order;
- a curfew order;
- a drug treatment and testing order;
- an action plan order.

Before imposing a community sentence (that is, a sentence which consists of or includes one or more community orders), the court must be satisfied that 'the offence, or the combination of the offence and one or more offences associated with it, was serious enough to warrant such a sentence' (s 35(1) of the Powers of Criminal Courts (Sentencing) Act 2000).

As with custodial sentences, associated offences include offences which are taken into consideration (s 161(1) of the 2000 Act).

Furthermore, s 35(3) of the Act provides that:

- the community order(s) must be 'the most suitable for the offender'; and
- the restrictions on the offenders liberty imposed by the community order(s) must be commensurate with the seriousness of the offence(s).

Section 36(1) of the Act states that in deciding whether a community sentence is appropriate the court must take into account:

- information about the circumstances of the offence (including any aggravating or mitigating factors); and
- information about the offender.

Section 36(3) provides that a pre-sentence report must be obtained before any of the following community orders is imposed:

- a community service order;
- a probation order where additional requirements are imposed;
- a combination order;
- a supervision order where additional requirements are imposed;
- a drug treatment and testing order.

It follows that the obtaining of a pre-sentence report is not mandatory (although one will often be obtained) before any of the following sentences is imposed:

- a probation order which does not contain any additional requirements;
- a supervision order which does not contain any additional requirements;
- an attendance centre order;
- a curfew order.

14.2   COMMUNITY SERVICE ORDERS

Section 46 of the Powers of Criminal Courts (Sentencing) Act 2000 provides that, where a person who has attained the age of 16 is convicted of an offence which is punishable with imprisonment, the court may make a community service order. The effect of the order is to require the offender to perform unpaid work under the direction of a probation officer or, where the offender is under 18, a social worker or a member of a youth offending team.

The obligations imposed by a community service order are contained in s 47(1) of the Act, namely:

- to keep in touch with the probation officer and to notify the probation officer of any change of address; and
- to perform the number of hours of work specified in the order at such times as he may be instructed by the probation officer.

Section 47(2) says that the instructions given by the probation officer should, so far as practicable, be such as to avoid any conflict with the offender's religious beliefs and to avoid any interference with the times (if any) at which the offender normally works or attends a school or other educational establishment.

14.2.1   Requirements to be met before an order is made

Section 46 of the 2000 Act states that a community service order cannot be made unless the following requirements are satisfied:

- there must be a pre-sentence report (s 36(3)(b));
- there must be evidence before the court from a probation officer (usually part of the pre-sentence report procedure) that the offender is a suitable person to perform community service (s 46(4));
- the court must be satisfied that provision can be made for the offender to perform community service in the area in which he resides (s 46(6)).

Where the court adjourns the case so that a report can be prepared to assess the offender's suitability for community service, the court will usually warn the offender that the court may nonetheless impose a custodial sentence. The reason for this is that, if the court does not warn the defendant in this way, and the report shows that the offender is suitable for community service, the offender will be left with a legitimate sense of grievance if the court later imposes a custodial sentence. In such a case, the custodial sentence would almost certainly be overturned on appeal (see *R v Gillam* (1980) 2 Cr App R(S) 267; *R v Millwood* (1982) 4 Cr App R(S) 281; and *R v Stokes* [1983] RTR 59).

Section 46(10) of the Act provides that, before a court makes a community service order, it must explain to the offender:

- the purpose and effect of the order;
- the consequences of failing to comply with the order;
- that the court may review the order on the application of the offender or the probation officer.

It used to be a requirement that the offender had to give his consent before a community service order could be made, but that requirement was removed in 1997.

14.2.2   Number of hours

Section 46(3) of the 2000 Act provides that the aggregate number of hours of community service imposed under a community service order must be between 40 and 240.

Section 46(8) says that where a court makes community service orders in respect of two of more offences, the hours of work specified in the orders may be concurrent or cumulative, provided that the total does not exceed 240 hours.

Section 46(8) only applies where a court is imposing two or more community service orders on the same occasion. However, in *R v Siha* (1992) 13 Cr App R(S) 588, the defendant was sentenced in April 1990 to 180 hours' community service and in October 1990 to 90 hours for a separate offence. The

Court of Appeal held that, even though the legislation does not prevent a court from making a community service order where the offender is already subject to a community service order imposed on an earlier occasion, with the effect that orders imposing more than a total of 240 hours are in force against that offender, a court should not impose a consecutive community service order on an offender who is already subject to a community service order if the effect of the two orders is to impose a total of more than 240 hours.

The community service should normally be completed within one year of the making of the order. However, the order remains in force (unless revoked by the court) until the total number of hours specified in the order have been completed (see s 47(3) of the 2000 Act).

Note that, in *R v Porter* (1992) 13 Cr App R(S) 258, it was pointed out by the Court of Appeal that there is no hard and fast rule that where the offence is not sufficiently serious to justify the imposition of a custodial sentence, the number of hours of community service which the offender is ordered to perform should be small. The court should make sure that the number of hours ordered reflects the gravity of the offence.

14.2.3   Mixing community service with other orders

A community service order cannot be imposed with a probation order imposed for the same offence, although a combination order achieves the same effect. Furthermore, where an offender is convicted of more than one offence and is being sentenced for those offences at the same hearing, there is no power to impose a probation order for one offence and a community service order in respect of another offence (*Gilding v Director of Public Prosecutions* (1998) 162 JPN 523).

It would be wrong in principle to impose a community service order and a sentence of immediate imprisonment (even where the court is sentencing for two offences) as the two are clearly incompatible (*R v Starie* (1979) 69 Cr App R 239). By virtue of s 118(6) of the Powers of Criminal Courts (Sentencing) Act 2000, it is not permissible to impose a suspended sentence and make a community service order on the same occasion.

14.3   PROBATION ORDERS

Section 41(1) of the Powers of Criminal Courts (Sentencing) Act 2000 provides that a court which is dealing with an offender who has attained the age of 16 may make a probation order if the court is of the opinion that supervision of the offender by a probation officer (or member of a youth offending team if the offender is under 18) is desirable in the interests of:

- securing the rehabilitation of the offender; or
- protecting the public from harm from him or preventing the commission by him of further offences.

The minimum period of a probation order is six months; the maximum period is three years.

14.3.1 Effect of a probation order

The offender's principal duty under a probation order is to keep in touch with the probation officer in accordance with instructions given by the probation officer and to notify the probation officer of any change of address (s 41(11)).

14.3.2 Imposing additional requirements under a probation order

The court is empowered by s 42 of the Powers of Criminal Courts (Sentencing) Act 2000 to impose additional requirements in the probation order where it takes the view that these are necessary to secure the rehabilitation of the offender or to protect the public from harm from him or to prevent him from committing further offences.

Before imposing any additional requirements, the court must first obtain a pre-sentence report on the offender (s 36(3)(a) of the 2000 Act). In practice, courts are generally reluctant to make a probation order at all unless a pre-sentence report has been prepared.

The additional requirements which may be imposed are set out in Sched 2 of the 2000 Act. They are:

- *Requirements as to residence (para 1)*

  Before imposing such a requirement, the court must consider the home surroundings of the offender.

  Where the residence requirement is that the offender reside in an approved hostel, the period for which this requirement applies must be stated in the order.

- *Requirements as to activities (para 2)*

  The court may require the offender:

  (a) to present himself to a specified person at a specified place for up to a total of 60 days;

  (b) to participate (for up to 60 days) or to refrain from participating in specified activities.

  The probationer may be required to comply with instructions given by the person in charge of the place or activities in question.

Such requirements should avoid, so far as possible, interference with the times (if any) during which the probationer is normally at work or attends a school or other educational establishment.

- *Requirements as to attendance at a probation centre (para 3)*

A probation centre is a place at which non-residential facilities are provided for use in connection with the rehabilitation of offenders (para 3(8)).

A probation order may require the probationer to attend a probation centre for up to a total of 60 days. If the probationer was convicted of a sexual offence, then the 60 hours maximum does not apply (para 4).

Again, the requirement should avoid, so far as possible, interference with the times (if any) during which the probationer is normally at work or attends a school or other education establishment.

The probationer must comply with instructions given by staff at the probation centre.

- *Requirements as to treatment for mental condition (para 5)*

Where the court is satisfied, on the evidence of a duly qualified medical practitioner, that the mental condition of the offender is such that he requires (and may be susceptible to) treatment but is not such as to warrant the making of a hospital order or a guardianship order (under the Mental Health Act 1983), the court may impose a requirement that the offender submit to treatment with a view to improving his mental condition. This requirement can be imposed for the duration of the probation order or for such lesser period as may be specified in the order.

The treatment which may be required by a probation order must be one of the following:

(a) treatment as a resident patient in a mental hospital;

(b) treatment as a non-resident patient at a place specified in the order;

(c) treatment by a qualified medial practitioner.

However, the nature of the treatment to be administered cannot be specified in the order.

- *Requirements as to treatment for alcohol or drug dependency (para 6)*

If the court is satisfied that:

(a) the offender is dependent on drugs or alcohol or has a propensity towards the misuse of drugs or alcohol; and

(b) this dependency or propensity caused or contributed to the offence in respect of which the probation order is to be made; and

(c) the offender's dependency or propensity is such that it requires and may be susceptible to treatment, the court can impose a requirement that the offender attend a specified place for such treatment. This requirement may be imposed for the duration of the probation order or some shorter period specified in the order.

Section 42(3) of the 2000 Act specifically prohibits the court from imposing a requirement in a probation order that the offender pay compensation to the victim of the offence. The court may, however, make a compensation order under s 130 of the Act even if it imposes a probation order for the offence itself.

14.3.3   Procedure for making a probation order

Section 41(7) of the Powers of Criminal Courts (Sentencing) Act 2000 states that, before making a probation order, the court must explain the effect of the order (including the consequences of failing to comply with any additional requirements that have been imposed under the order) and must inform the offender that the court has power to review the order on the application of the offender or of the probation officer. The court may only include a requirement in a probation order that the offender undergo treatment for a mental condition, or for drug or alcohol dependency, if the offender expresses willingness to comply with such requirements.

14.3.4   Combining a probation order with other sentences

A probation order cannot be made if the offender receives an immediate custodial sentence on the same occasion (whether in respect of the same offence or separate offences) as the two forms of sentence are clearly incompatible (*R v Mullervy* (1986) 8 Cr App R(S) 41).

Furthermore, a probation order cannot be combined with a suspended sentence of imprisonment (s 118(6) of the 2000 Act). However, the 'suspended sentence supervision order' (see Chapter 13, 13.3.2) provides a means of achieving the same end.

A probation order cannot be combined with a community service order where the two sentences are imposed for a single offence (s 35(2) of the 2000 Act), although a combination order (14.4 below) will achieve the same effect.

If the offender is to be sentenced for two offences, there is power to impose a probation order for one and community service for another (*Gilding v Director of Public Prosecutions* (1998) 162 JPN 523). The court can, of course, make a combination order instead.

14.4   COMBINATION ORDERS

Although s 35(2) of the 2000 Act prevents the court imposing a probation order and a community service order for the same offence, the same effect can be achieved by means of a combination order.

Section 51(1) of the 2000 Act states that, where the court is dealing with an offender who has attained the age of 16 who has been convicted of an imprisonable offence, the court may make a combination order.

The effect of the order is that:

• the offender is under the supervision of a probation officer (or member of a youth offending team if the offender is under 18) for the period specified in the order, which must be between 12 months and three years; and

• the offender is required to perform unpaid work for the number of hours specified in the order, which must be between 40 and 100 hours.

A combination order can only be made if the court is of the opinion that it is desirable to do so in the interests of securing the rehabilitation of the offender or of protecting the public from harm by preventing him from committing further offences (s 51(3)).

Before making a combination order, the court must obtain a pre-sentence report (s 36(3)(c)).

Under s 51(4), the court may impose any additional requirements into the probation part of the order which it could impose if the order were merely a probation order.

14.5   CURFEW ORDERS

The power to make curfew orders is contained in s 37 of the Powers of Criminal Courts (Sentencing) Act 2000.

The effect of a curfew order is to require the offender to remain, for periods specified in the order, at a place or places specified in the order.

A curfew order can be made in respect of an offender of any age.

However, where the offender has not attained the age of 16, the maximum duration of the curfew order is three months. Where the offender has attained the age of 16, the maximum duration of the order is six months. In either case, the curfew order can only apply for between two and 12 hours per day.

Where the offender is under 16, the court must, before making a curfew order, obtain and consider information about his family circumstances and the likely effect of making such an order on those circumstances.

Whatever the age of the offender, the order should avoid conflict with the offender's religious beliefs and interference with the times he normally works or attends a school or other education establishment.

Before making a curfew order, the court must also seek information about the attitude of anyone likely to be affected by the enforced presence of the offender at the place specified in the order.

The effect of the order and the consequences of failing to comply with it must be explained to the offender by the court.

Section 38 of the 2000 Act provides for the imposition of a requirement for the electronic monitoring of the offender's whereabouts to assist in the enforcement of the curfew order.

14.6   DRUG TREATMENT AND TESTING ORDERS

Section 52 of the Powers of Criminal Courts (Sentencing) Act 2000 empowers the court to make a drug treatment and testing order where it convicts someone aged 16 or over of an offence, provided that the court is satisfied that he is dependent on (or has a propensity to misuse) drugs and that his dependency (or propensity) requires and may be susceptible to treatment (s 52(3)). An order cannot be made unless the offender expresses his willingness to comply with its requirements (s 52(7)).

The order is for a specified period of between six months and three years (s 52(1)). It includes a requirement that the offender must submit, during the period covered by the order, to treatment by a qualified person with a view to reducing or eliminating his dependency or propensity to misuse drugs (s 53(2)). The treatment may include a period of residential or non-residential treatment at a place specified in the order s 53(2). During this period, the offender can also be required to provide samples for the purpose of ascertaining whether he has any drugs in his body (s 53(4)).

Before making a drug treatment and testing order, the court must explain its effect to the offender and the consequences which may follow if he fails to comply with the order (s 52(6)).

During the period covered by the order, the offender is also under the supervision of a probation officer (s 54(2)).

Section 55 provides for periodic reviews by the court of the offender's progress. The court may amend the order, but only with the consent of the offender. If the offender withholds consent, the court may revoke the order and sentence the offender for the original offence as if the court had just convicted him of that offence (s 55(3)). In such a case, the court must take into account the extent to which the offender has complied with the order; a custodial sentence may be imposed notwithstanding the restrictions in s 79(2) of the 2000 Act (s 55(4)).

Schedule 3 of the 2000 Act deals with breach of drug treatment and testing orders.

14.7   ORDERS FOR PERSISTENT PETTY OFFENDERS

Section 59 of the Powers of Criminal Courts (Sentencing) Act 2000 applies where someone aged 16 or over is convicted of an offence in respect of which the court would be minded to impose a fine, but the offender has one or more unpaid fines imposed for previous convictions and, if a fine commensurate with the seriousness of the offence were to be imposed for the present offence, the offender would not have sufficient means to pay it. In such a case, the court may make a curfew order or community service order instead of imposing a fine.

14.8   ENFORCING COMMUNITY SENTENCES

Enforcement of community sentences is primarily a matter for the probation service and the offender's local magistrates' court.

14.8.1   Dealing with breaches of community orders

In this section, we examine what happens if a community order is not complied with. This will be the case, for example, if a person subject to a probation order fails to keep appointments with the probation officer or fails to comply with an additional requirement imposed by the court, or if a person subject to a community service order fails to perform the requisite number of hours.

The enforcement of community service orders, probation orders, combination orders, curfew orders and drug treatment and testing orders is dealt with by Sched 3 of the Powers of Criminal Courts (Sentencing) Act 2000.

No matter which court imposes a community order, enforcement proceedings are taken in the magistrates' court which serves the place where the offender resides. If a court in Newcastle-upon-Tyne imposes a community order on an offender who lives in Croydon, the offender will perform his obligations under the order in Croydon and if he fails to do so will have to appear before the Croydon magistrates' court.

If a person who is subject to a community order fails to comply with the terms of the order, a probation officer will lay an information at the local magistrates' court. A summons will then be issued requiring the offender to appear before the magistrates' court (Sched 3, para 2).

When the offender attends the court, he will be asked whether he admits or denies failing to comply with the order. If the offender denies the allegation, the court can only deal with him for breaching the order if that breach is proved by evidence (*R v Devine* (1956) 40 Cr App R 45).

Schedule 3, para 4 provides that, if it is proved to the satisfaction of the magistrates that the offender has failed without reasonable excuse to comply with any of the requirements of the relevant order, the court may either:

- impose a fine of up to £1,000; or
- impose a community service order for up to 60 hours' community service.

If the court takes the latter option, and the order breached was a community service order, the total number of hours of community service imposed under the two orders must not exceed 240 hours (para 7(3)(b)).

Paragraph 4 also provides that if the order breached is a probation order or combination order and the offender is under 21, or if the order is a curfew order and the offender is under 16, the court may make an attendance centre order instead of imposing a fine or community service order.

These powers apply whether the original order was made by a magistrates' court or a Crown Court. If the breach is dealt with by the imposition of a fine, a community service order or an attendance centre order, the original community order remains in force.

If the original order was made by a magistrates' court, the magistrates' court dealing with the breach may (instead of imposing a fine or community service order or, if appropriate, an attendance centre order) revoke the original order and impose a new sentence for the original offence (Sched 2, para 4(1)(d)).

If the original order was made by a Crown Court, the magistrates' court dealing with the breach may (instead of imposing a fine, a community service order or an attendance centre order) commit the offender (in custody or on bail) to the Crown Court (para 4(4)). The Crown Court may impose any of the punishments for non-compliance which the magistrates could have imposed or it may impose a new sentence for the original offence (see para (5)).

The important point to note is that a magistrates' court dealing with an offender for the breach of a community order imposed by the Crown Court can never revoke the community order and re-sentence the offender for the original offence.

If the original community order is revoked and the offender is re-sentenced for the original offence, para 4(2) (magistrates' court) or 5(2) (Crown Court) applies. This states:

- that the court must take into account the extent to which the offender has complied with the requirements of the original order; and

- where the offender has 'wilfully and persistently' failed to comply with the requirements of the community order, the court may impose a custodial sentence notwithstanding the restrictions contained in s 79(2) of the 2000 Act.

The power to impose a custodial sentence on the basis that refusal to consent to a community order can be deduced from the offenders non-compliance with the order only applies where that non-compliance is wilful and persistent. It follows that a custodial sentence could not be substituted for the community order merely on the basis of a single allegation of non-compliance.

In *Caton v Community Service Officer* (1995) 159 JP 444, the offender had twice threatened to hit a community service officer. It was held by the Divisional Court (dismissing an appeal against a finding that the offender was in breach of the order) that it was implicit in the concept of 'performing' community service that the offender was under an obligation to behave in a reasonable manner during the required performance; it followed that unacceptable (in this case, violent) behaviour could amount to a failure to comply with the requirements of the community service order.

14.8.2 Revocation of community orders on grounds other than breach

Schedule 3, para 10 of the Powers of Criminal Courts (Sentencing) Act 2000 enables a person subject to a community order made by a magistrates' court, or the probation officer concerned, to apply to the magistrates' court which serves the area where the offender resides on the ground that having regard to circumstances which have arisen since the order was made, it is in the interests of justice that:

- the original community order should be revoked; or

- the offender should be dealt with in some other manner for the original offence.

The magistrates' court to which the application is made may:

- revoke the order; or

- revoke the order and impose a different sentence for the original offence.

If the original order was made by the Crown Court, the application to revoke it is made to the Crown Court, which is similarly empowered to revoke the order or revoke the order and re-sentence the offender (para 11).

It should be noted that, if an order is revoked by a magistrates' court, the offender cannot afterwards be committed to the Crown Court to be dealt with for breach of the order (*R v Brent Justices ex p Ward* (1993) 157 JP 192).

Revocation under para 10 or 11 is on the basis that the circumstances have changed since the original order was made. For example, a probation order may be revoked if the offender has made such good progress that the order is no longer necessary; a community service order may be revoked if the offender is no longer physically capable of doing community service.

In *R v Fielding* (1993) 14 Cr App R(S) 494, for example, it was held inappropriate to impose a custodial sentence (even a suspended sentence) where the community service order is revoked because the offender is unable, through no fault of his own (for example, illness or injury) to carry out the work.

14.8.3 Commission of a subsequent offence

The commission of a subsequent offence does not amount to a breach of a community sentence. It follows that, if a magistrates' court convicts an offender of an offence committed during the currency of a probation order, they cannot revoke the probation order (even if it was made by a magistrates' court) and they cannot commit the offender to the Crown Court to be dealt with for breaching the probation order (see *R v Adams* (1994) 15 Cr App R(S) 417). The order can only be revoked (by a magistrates' court if the original order was made by a magistrates' court, by the Crown Court if the original order was made in the Crown Court) if there is an application by the probation service for its revocation (on the ground that it is not working).

However, Sched 3, para 11(1)(b) of the Powers of Criminal Courts (Sentencing) Act 2000 says that, where an offender is convicted by the Crown Court, or convicted by a magistrates' court but committed for sentence to the Crown Court, and the offence was committed during the currency of a community sentence, the Crown Court may revoke the community order and, if the Crown Court thinks it appropriate, re-sentence the offender. This power only applies if the community order is in force at the date when the Crown Court is sentencing the offender. If the community order has expired by the time the Crown Court is dealing with the offender, there is no power to revoke the order and re-sentence the offender for the original offence (*R v Bennett* (1994) 15 Cr App R(S) 213; *R v Cousin* (1994) 15 Cr App R(S) 516).

In *R v Kenny* [1996] 1 Cr App R(S) 397, the appellant was charged with burglary. While on bail for that offence, he committed a further burglary. For the first burglary, he was given a community service order. Having performed a few hours community service, he was tried in respect of the other burglary. Upon his conviction for that second burglary, the Crown Court judge revoked the community service order and substituted a short prison sentence (to be served consecutively to a custodial sentence for the burglary of which the appellant had just been convicted). The Court of Appeal said that the power conferred by Sched 3, para 11(1)(b), to revoke a community order and re-sentence an offender is not confined to cases where the offender has committed an offence during the currency of the community order. The judge was entitled to come to the view that it was in the interests of justice to revoke the community service order and re-sentence the appellant.

Where the Crown Court re-sentences an offender in a case where the original community order was imposed by a magistrates' court, the powers of the Crown Court are limited to those of the magistrates' court (see *R v Ogden* [1996] 2 Cr App R(S) 386 and *R v Kosser* (1996) 16 Cr App R(S) 737).

Even though the commission of a further offence during the currency of a probation order does not constitute a breach of the order, the fact that a further offence has been committed may be regarded by the court as evidence that the community sentence is ineffective as regards this offender. This can be regarded as a 'failure to respond' to a previous sentence (under s 151(1) of the 2000 Act), something which affects the seriousness of the subsequent offence.

However, in *R v Rowsell* (1988) 10 Cr App R(S) 411, the offender committed an offence within weeks of being put on probation. The court accepted the argument that the probation order had not had time to have any effect on the offender. It was thus premature to say that probation would not work for this offender and so the order should be left in place.

Also of relevance in such a situation is para 13 of Sched 3 of the Powers of Criminal Courts (Sentencing) Act 2000. This provides that, where a magistrates' court convicts someone of an offence and decides to impose a custodial sentence for that offence, and that person is currently subject to a community order imposed because of an earlier offence, the magistrates can revoke that community order (if it was imposed by a magistrates' court) or commit the offender to the Crown Court (if the order was made by the Crown Court).

14.8.4 Re-sentencing for the original offence

In *R v Hewitt* [1996] 2 Cr App R(S) 14, the Court of Appeal made the point that, in deciding what custodial sentence to pass in place of a community order, the offender must be given credit if he pleaded guilty to the offence for which community service was imposed and, where the original sentence was a community service order, he must also be given credit for the hours of community service which he has performed.

Furthermore, where the community order is replaced with a custodial sentence, the offender should be given credit for any time spend in custody on remand for the offence in respect of which the community order was made (see *R v Wiltshire* (1992) 13 Cr App R(S) 642 and *R v Henderson* [1997] 2 Cr App R(S) 266).

14.8.5   Age of offender

Where the offender is under 21 when the community order is made but is over 21 when the order is revoked and he is re-sentenced for the offence for which the community order was imposed, the replacement sentence must be one which is appropriate to the age of the offender at the date when the original order was made. So, such an offender is given a custodial sentence in place of the community order, it would have to be a sentence of detention in a young offender institution, not imprisonment (*R v Pesapane* (1992) 13 Cr App R(S) 438).

14.9   THE CRIMINAL JUSTICE AND COURT SERVICES BILL 2000

Under the Criminal Justice and Court Services Bill 2000, probation orders are re-named 'community rehabilitation orders', community service orders become 'community punishment orders', and combination orders become 'community punishment and rehabilitation orders'.

The Criminal Justice and Court Services Bill also introduces some new community orders:

14.9.1   Exclusion orders

Section 40A of the Powers of Criminal Courts (Sentencing) Act 2000 will enable the court to make an order prohibiting the offender from entering a place specified in the order for a specified period of up to one year (three months where the offender is under 16). The order may provide for the prohibition to operate only during the periods specified in the order, and may specify different places for different periods or days. The order may contain an additional requirement that the offender submit to electronic monitoring of his whereabouts to ensure compliance with the order.

The requirements of the order should avoid conflict with the offender's religious beliefs or with the requirements of any other community order to which he is subject, and should avoid interference with the times at which he attends work or school or any other educational establishment.

Where the offender is under 16, the court must first obtain and consider information about his family circumstances and the likely effect of the order on those circumstances. Before making an exclusion order, the court must always explain the effect of the order and the consequences of failing to comply with it.

Breach of an exclusion order is dealt with under the procedure set out in Sched 3 of the Powers of Criminal Courts (Sentencing) Act 2000.

14.9.2 Drug abstinence orders

Section 58A of the Powers of Criminal Courts (Sentencing) Act 2000 will enable the court to make a drug abstinence order against an offender aged 18 or over. The order requires the offender to abstain from misusing specified Class A drugs and to provide samples for the purpose of ascertaining whether he has any specified Class A drug in his body. The court cannot make a drug abstinence order unless satisfied that the offender is dependent on (or has a propensity to misuse) specified Class A drugs and either the offence in question is a trigger offence (as defined in Sched 5 of the Bill) or else the misuse by the offender of any specified Class A drug caused or contributed to the offence of which he has been convicted.

The list of 'trigger offences' in Sched 5 of the Bill encompasses:

(a) the following offences under the Theft Act 1968: theft, robbery, burglary, aggravated burglary, taking a motor vehicle or other conveyance without authority, aggravated vehicle taking, obtaining property by deception, going equipped for stealing, etc;

(b) the following offences under the Misuse of Drugs Act 1971 if committed in respect of a specified Class A drug: restriction on production and supply of controlled drugs, possession of a controlled drug, possession of a controlled drug with intent to supply.

The order can last for a specified period between six months and three years. Before making the order, the court must explain its effect and the consequences of non-compliance. Breach of a drug abstinence order is deal with under the procedure set out in Sched 3 of the Powers of Criminal Courts (Sentencing) Act 2000.

Section 42 of the Powers of Criminal Courts (Sentencing) Act 2000 is amended by the Criminal Justice and Court Services Bill 2000 to enable the court to add a 'drug abstinence requirement' to a community rehabilitation order. This is a requirement that the offender abstain from misusing specified Class A drugs and that he must provide samples for analysis to determine whether he has any specified Class A drug in his body. The offender must be aged 18 or over at the date of conviction. Such a requirement must be added where the offender is (in the opinion of the court) dependent on (or has a propensity to misuse) specified Class A drugs, and the offence of which he has been convicted is a trigger offence. The court may add such a requirement if (in the opinion of the court) he is dependent on (or has a propensity to misuse) specified Class A drugs, and misuse by him of any specified Class A drug caused or contributed to the offence of which he has been convicted. However, a community rehabilitation order cannot include a drug abstinence requirement if it includes a requirement of treatment for drug dependency (under para 2 of Sched 6 of the 2000 Act); also, a community sentence cannot

include a drug abstinence requirement if it includes a drug treatment and
testing order or a drug abstinence order.

14.9.3   More additional requirements under a community rehabilitation order

Schedule 2 of the Powers of Criminal Courts (Sentencing) Act 2000 will be
amended by the Criminal Justice and Court Services Bill 2000 to enable a
community rehabilitation order to include further additional requirements.

The first of the new additional requirements is the 'curfew requirement'.
This is a requirement that the offender remain, for periods specified in the
order, at a place specified in the order. The maximum duration of the
requirement is six months, and the curfew period must be for between two and
12 hours per day. The order may specify different curfew addresses or
different periods of curfew on different days.

Before imposing a curfew requirement, the court must obtain and consider
information about the curfew address and, in particular, must take account of
the attitude of anyone likely to be affected by the enforced presence of the
offender in the place to be specified in the order.

The second of the new additional requirements is the 'exclusion
requirement'. This is a requirement that prohibits the offender from entering a
place specified in the order for a specified period of up to one year. The order
may provide for the prohibition to operate continuously or only during the
periods specified in the order, and may specify different places for different
periods or days.

14.9.4   Breach of community orders

Section 36B of the Powers of Criminal Courts (Sentencing) Act 2000 will enable
a community order to include requirements for securing the electronic
monitoring of the offender's compliance with any requirement imposed by the
community order. Where the co-operation of someone other than the offender
is required in order for electronic monitoring of the offender to be practicable,
an electronic monitoring requirement cannot be imposed without that person's
consent.

Also, under the Criminal Justice and Court Services Bill 2000, Sched 3 of the
Powers of Criminal Courts (Sentencing) Act 2000 is amended to create a
warning scheme. The warning scheme will apply to curfew orders, exclusion
orders, community rehabilitation orders, community punishment orders,
community punishment and rehabilitation orders, and drug abstinence orders.

There is a duty on the probation service to issue a warning to an offender
who has unacceptably failed to comply with the requirements of the order if

the offender has not already been referred back to court for the failure. The warning must describe the circumstances of the failure, state that the failure is unacceptable, and inform the offender of the consequence of a further failure: namely, if there is a second unacceptable failure to comply within 12 months, or six months in the case of a curfew order, the offender must be referred back to court for breach proceedings. If two or more orders were imposed at the same time, they will be considered as one order to which the warning scheme applies, so only one warning in total can be given in any 12 month period.

Where the offender has attained the age of 18 and the matter is referred back to the court (whether a magistrates' court or the Crown Court), the court must, unless there are exceptional circumstances, impose a custodial sentence for the offence in respect of which the community order was imposed if he is found to be in breach of the order. The maximum sentence will be three months unless the court takes the view that it would be appropriate to impose a longer period of imprisonment (in which case, the longer period will apply). Where the court finds the circumstances of the case to be exceptional, or where the breach involves an offender under the age of 18, then the existing discretionary sanctions available to the court will apply without the new presumption of imprisonment.

These warning and punishment measures do not apply to any failure to abstain from misusing specified Class A drugs.

Finally, under the Criminal Justice and Court Services Bill 2000, the Crown Court will receive new powers to issue a summons or warrant in respect of an offender who fails to appear at the Crown Court to answer a summons issued by a justice of the peace in respect of an alleged breach of a community order.

14.9.5   Pre-sentence drug testing

Under the Criminal Justice and Court Services Bill 2000, s 36A of the Powers of Criminal Courts (Sentencing) Act 2000 will provide that, where a person aged 18 or over is convicted of an offence and the court is considering passing a community sentence, it may make a 'pre-sentence drug testing order' for the purpose of ascertaining whether the offender has any specified Class A drug in his body. The order requires the offender to provide samples for analysis. Failure without reasonable excuse to comply with the order will be an offence punishable with a fine of up to level 4 (£2,500).

TABLE OF STATUTORY MATERIALS

STATUTORY MATERIALS

STATUTORY CRITERIA
FOR IMPOSING COMMUNITY SENTENCES

POWERS OF CRIMINAL COURTS (SENTENCING) ACT 2000

Section 33: Meaning of 'community order' and 'community sentence'

(1) In this Act, 'community order' means any of the following orders:

    (a) a curfew order;

    (b) a probation order;

    (c) a community service order;

    (d) a combination order;

    (e) a drug treatment and testing order;

    (f) an attendance centre order;

    (g) a supervision order;

    (h) an action plan order.

(2) In this Act, 'community sentence' means a sentence which consists of or includes one or more community orders.

Section 35: Restrictions on imposing community sentences

(1) A court shall not pass a community sentence on an offender unless it is of the opinion that the offence, or the combination of the offence and one or more offences associated with it, was serious enough to warrant such a sentence.

(2) In consequence of the provision made by section 51 below with respect to combination orders, a community sentence shall not consist of or include both a probation order and a community service order.

(3) Subject to sub-section (2) above and to section 69(5) below (which limits the community orders that may be combined with an action plan order), where a court passes a community sentence:

    (a) the particular order or orders comprising or forming part of the sentence shall be such as in the opinion of the court is, or taken together are, the most suitable for the offender; and

    (b) the restrictions on liberty imposed by the order or orders shall be such as in the opinion of the court are commensurate with the seriousness of the offence, or the combination of the offence and one or more offences associated with it.

(4) Sub-sections (1) and (3)(b) above have effect subject to section 59 below (curfew orders and community service orders for persistent petty offenders).

Section 36: Procedural requirements for community sentences: pre-sentence reports, etc

(1) In forming any such opinion as is mentioned in sub-section (1) or (3)(b) of section 35 above, a court shall take into account all such information as is available to it about the circumstances of the offence or (as the case may be) of the offence and the offence or offences associated with it, including any aggravating or mitigating factors.

(2) In forming any such opinion as is mentioned in sub-section (3)(a) of that section, a court may take into account any information about the offender which is before it.

(3) The following provisions of this section apply in relation to:

(a) a probation order which includes additional requirements authorised by Schedule 2 to this Act;

(b) a community service order;

(c) a combination order;

(d) a drug treatment and testing order;

(e) a supervision order which includes requirements authorised by Schedule 6 to this Act.

(4) Subject to sub-section (5) below, a court shall obtain and consider a pre-sentence report before forming an opinion as to the suitability for the offender of one or more of the orders mentioned in sub-section (3) above.

(5) Sub-section (4) above does not apply if, in the circumstances of the case, the court is of the opinion that it is unnecessary to obtain a pre-sentence report.

(6) In a case where the offender is aged under 18 and the offence is not triable only on indictment and there is no other offence associated with it that is triable only on indictment, the court shall not form such an opinion as is mentioned in sub-section (5) above unless:

(a) there exists a previous pre-sentence report obtained in respect of the offender; and

(b) the court has had regard to the information contained in that report, or, if there is more than one such report, the most recent report.

(7) No community sentence which consists of or includes such an order as is mentioned in sub-section (3) above shall be invalidated by the failure of a court to obtain and consider a pre-sentence report before forming an opinion as to the suitability of the order for the offender, but any court on an appeal against such a sentence:

(a) shall, subject to sub-section (8) below, obtain a pre-sentence report if none was obtained by the court below; and

(b) shall consider any such report obtained by it or by that court.

(8) Sub-section (7)(a) above does not apply if the court is of the opinion:

(a) that the court below was justified in forming an opinion that it was unnecessary to obtain a pre-sentence report; or

(b) that, although the court below was not justified in forming that opinion, in the circumstances of the case at the time it is before the court, it is unnecessary to obtain a pre-sentence report.

(9) In a case where the offender is aged under 18 and the offence is not triable only on indictment and there is no other offence associated with it that is triable only on indictment, the court shall not form such an opinion as is mentioned in sub-section (8) above unless:

(a) there exists a previous pre-sentence report obtained in respect of the offender; and

(b) the court has had regard to the information contained in that report, or, if there is more than one such report, the most recent report.

(10) Section 156 below (disclosure of pre-sentence report to offender, etc) applies to any pre-sentence report obtained in pursuance of this section.

COMMUNITY SERVICE

POWERS OF CRIMINAL COURTS (SENTENCING) ACT 2000

Section 46: Community service orders

(1) Where a person aged 16 or over is convicted of an offence punishable with imprisonment, the court by or before which he is convicted may (subject to sections 34 to 36 above) make an order requiring him to perform unpaid work in accordance with section 47 below.

(2) An order under sub-section (1) above is in this Act referred to as a 'community service order'.

(3) The number of hours which a person may be required to work under a community service order shall be specified in the order and shall be in the aggregate:

(a) not less than 40; and

(b) not more than 240.

(4) A court shall not make a community service order in respect of an offender unless, after hearing (if the court thinks it necessary) an appropriate officer, the court is satisfied that the offender is a suitable person to perform work under such an order.

(5) In sub-section (4) above 'an appropriate officer' means:

    (a) in the case of an offender aged 18 or over, a probation officer or social worker of a local authority social services department; and

    (b) in the case of an offender aged under 18, a probation officer, a social worker of a local authority social services department or a member of a youth offending team.

(6) A court shall not make a community service order in respect of an offender unless it is satisfied that provision for him to perform work under such an order can be made under the arrangements for persons to perform work under such orders which exist in the petty sessions area in which he resides or will reside.

(7) Sub-section (6) above has effect subject to paragraphs 3 and 4 of Schedule 4 to this Act (transfer of order to Scotland or Northern Ireland).

(8) Where a court makes community service orders in respect of two or more offences of which the offender has been convicted by or before the court, the court may direct that the hours of work specified in any of those orders shall be concurrent with or additional to those specified in any other of those orders, but so that the total number of hours which are not concurrent shall not exceed the maximum specified in sub-section (3)(b) above.

(9) A community service order:

    (a) shall specify the petty sessions area in which the offender resides or will reside; and

    (b) where the offender is aged under 18 at the time the order is made, may also specify a local authority for the purposes of section 47(5)(b) below (cases where functions are to be discharged by member of a youth offending team),

and if the order specifies a local authority for those purposes, the authority specified must be the local authority within whose area it appears to the court that the offender resides or will reside.

(10) Before making a community service order, the court shall explain to the offender in ordinary language:

    (a) the purpose and effect of the order (and in particular the requirements of the order as specified in section 47(1) to (3) below);

    (b) the consequences which may follow (under Part II of Schedule 3 to this Act) if he fails to comply with any of those requirements; and

    (c) that the court has power (under Parts III and IV of that Schedule) to review the order on the application either of the offender or of the responsible officer.

(11) The court by which a community service order is made shall forthwith give copies of the order to:

    (a) if the offender is aged 18 or over, a probation officer assigned to the court; or

    (b) if the offender is aged under 18, a probation officer or member of a youth offending team so assigned,

and he shall give a copy to the offender and to the responsible officer.

(12) The court by which such an order is made shall also, except where it itself acts for the petty sessions area specified in the order, send to the clerk to the justices for that area:

(a) a copy of the order; and

(b) such documents and information relating to the case as it considers likely to be of assistance to a court acting for that area in the exercise of its functions in relation to the order.

(13) In this section and Schedule 3 to this Act 'responsible officer', in relation to an offender subject to a community service order, means the person mentioned in sub-section (4)(a) or (b) or (5)(b) of section 47 below who, as respects the order, is responsible for discharging the functions conferred by that section.

Section 47: Obligations of person subject to community service order

(1) An offender in respect of whom a community service order is in force shall:

(a) keep in touch with the responsible officer in accordance with such instructions as he may from time to time be given by that officer and notify him of any change of address; and

(b) perform for the number of hours specified in the order such work at such times as he may be instructed by the responsible officer.

(2) The instructions given by the responsible officer under this section shall, as far as practicable, be such as to avoid:

(a) any conflict with the offender's religious beliefs or with the requirements of any other community order to which he may be subject; and

(b) any interference with the times, if any, at which he normally works or attends school or any other educational establishment.

(3) Subject to paragraph 22 of Schedule 3 to this Act (power to extend order), the work required to be performed under a community service order shall be performed during the period of twelve months beginning with the date of the order; but, unless revoked, the order shall remain in force until the offender has worked under it for the number of hours specified in it.

(4) If the offender is aged 18 or over at the time when the order is made, the functions conferred by this section on 'the responsible officer' shall be discharged by:

(a) a probation officer appointed for or assigned to the petty sessions area specified in the order; or

(b) a person appointed for the purposes of this section by the probation committee for that area.

(5) If the offender is aged under 18 at that time, those functions shall be discharged by:

(a) a person mentioned in sub-section (4)(a) or (b) above; or

(b) a member of a youth offending team established by a local authority specified in the order.

(6) The reference in sub-section (4) above to the petty sessions area specified in the order and the reference in sub-section (5) above to a local authority so specified are references to the area or an authority for the time being so specified, whether under section 46(9) above or by virtue of Part IV of Schedule 3 to this Act (power to amend orders).

PROBATION ORDERS

POWERS OF CRIMINAL COURTS (SENTENCING) ACT 2000

Section 41: Probation orders

(1) Where a person aged 16 or over is convicted of an offence and the court by or before which he is convicted is of the opinion that his supervision is desirable in the interests of:

(a) securing his rehabilitation; or

(b) protecting the public from harm from him or preventing the commission by him of further offences,

the court may (subject to sections 34 to 36 above) make an order requiring him to be under supervision for a period specified in the order of not less than six months nor more than three years.

(2) An order under sub-section (1) above is in this Act referred to as a 'probation order'.

(3) A probation order shall specify the petty sessions area in which the offender resides or will reside.

(4) If the offender is aged 18 or over at the time when the probation order is made, he shall, subject to paragraph 18 of Schedule 3 to this Act (offender's change of area), be required to be under the supervision of a probation officer appointed for or assigned to the petty sessions area specified in the order.

(5) If the offender is aged under 18 at that time, he shall, subject to paragraph 18 of Schedule 3, be required to be under the supervision of:

(a) a probation officer appointed for or assigned to the petty sessions area specified in the order; or

(b) a member of a youth offending team established by a local authority specified in the order;

and if an order specifies a local authority for the purposes of paragraph (b) above, the authority specified must be the local authority within whose area it appears to the court that the offender resides or will reside.

(6) In this Act, 'responsible officer', in relation to an offender who is subject to a probation order, means the probation officer or member of a youth offending team responsible for his supervision.

(7) Before making a probation order, the court shall explain to the offender in ordinary language:

(a) the effect of the order (including any additional requirements proposed to be included in the order in accordance with section 42 below);

(b) the consequences which may follow (under Part II of Schedule 3 to this Act) if he fails to comply with any of the requirements of the order; and

(c) that the court has power (under Parts III and IV of that Schedule) to review the order on the application either of the offender or of the responsible officer.

(8) On making a probation order, the court may, if it thinks it expedient for the purpose of the offender's reformation, allow any person who consents to do so to give security for the good behaviour of the offender.

(9) The court by which a probation order is made shall forthwith give copies of the order to:

(a) if the offender is aged 18 or over, a probation officer assigned to the court; or

(b) if the offender is aged under 18, a probation officer or member of a youth offending team so assigned,

and he shall give a copy to the offender, to the responsible officer and to the person in charge of any institution in which the offender is required by the order to reside.

(10) The court by which such an order is made shall also, except where it itself acts for the petty sessions area specified in the order, send to the clerk to the justices for that area:

(a) a copy of the order; and

(b) such documents and information relating to the case as it considers likely to be of assistance to a court acting for that area in the exercise of its functions in relation to the order.

(11) An offender in respect of whom a probation order is made shall keep in touch with the responsible officer in accordance with such instructions as he may from time to time be given by that officer, and shall notify him of any change of address.

Section 42: Additional requirements which may be included in probation orders

(1) Subject to sub-section (3) below, a probation order may in addition require the offender to comply during the whole or any part of the probation period with such requirements as the court, having regard to the circumstances of the case, considers desirable in the interests of:

(a) securing the rehabilitation of the offender; or

(b) protecting the public from harm from him or preventing the commission by him of further offences.

(2) Without prejudice to the generality of sub-section (1) above, the additional requirements which may be included in a probation order shall include the requirements which are authorised by Schedule 2 to this Act.

(3) Without prejudice to the power of the court under section 130 below to make a compensation order, the payment of sums by way of damages for injury or compensation for loss shall not be included among the additional requirements of a probation order.

SCHEDULE 2

ADDITIONAL REQUIREMENTS WHICH MAY BE INCLUDED IN PROBATION ORDERS

Requirements as to residence

1

(1) Subject to sub-paragraphs (2) and (3) below, a probation order may include requirements as to the residence of the offender.

(2) Before making a probation order containing any such requirement, the court shall consider the home surroundings of the offender.

(3) Where a probation order requires the offender to reside in an approved hostel or any other institution, the period for which he is required to reside there shall be specified in the order.

Requirements as to activities, etc

2

(1) Subject to the provisions of this paragraph, a probation order may require the offender:

(a) to present himself to a person or persons specified in the order at a place or places so specified;

(b) to participate or refrain from participating in activities specified in the order:

(i) on a day or days so specified; or

(ii) during the probation period or such portion of it as may be so specified.

(2) A court shall not include in a probation order a requirement such as is mentioned in sub-paragraph (1) above unless:

(a) it has consulted:

(i) in the case of an offender aged 18 or over, a probation officer; or

(ii) in the case of an offender aged under 18, either a probation officer or a member of a youth offending team; and

(b) it is satisfied that it is feasible to secure compliance with the requirement.

(3) A court shall not include a requirement such as is mentioned in sub-paragraph (1)(a) above or a requirement to participate in activities if it would involve the co-operation of a person other than the offender and the offender's responsible officer, unless that other person consents to its inclusion.

(4) A requirement such as is mentioned in sub-paragraph (1)(a) above shall operate to require the offender:

(a) in accordance with instructions given by his responsible officer, to present himself at a place or places for not more than 60 days in the aggregate; and

(b) while at any place, to comply with instructions given by, or under the authority of, the person in charge of that place.

(5) A place specified in an order shall have been approved by the probation committee for the area in which the premises are situated as providing facilities suitable for persons subject to probation orders.

(6) A requirement to participate in activities shall operate to require the offender:

(a) in accordance with instructions given by his responsible officer, to participate in activities for not more than 60 days in the aggregate; and

(b) while participating, to comply with instructions given by, or under the authority of, the person in charge of the activities.

(7) Instructions given by the offender's responsible officer under sub-paragraph (4) or (6) above shall, as far as practicable, be such as to avoid:

(a) any conflict with the offender's religious beliefs or with the requirements of any other community order to which he may be subject; and

(b) any interference with the times, if any, at which he normally works or attends school or any other educational establishment.

Requirements as to attendance at probation centre

3

(1) Subject to the provisions of this paragraph, a probation order may require the offender during the probation period to attend at a probation centre specified in the order.

(2) A court shall not include in a probation order such a requirement as is mentioned in sub-paragraph (1) above unless it has consulted:

(a) in the case of an offender aged 18 or over, a probation officer; or

(b) in the case of an offender aged under 18, either a probation officer or a member of a youth offending team.

(3) A court shall not include such a requirement in a probation order unless it is satisfied:

(a) that arrangements can be made for the offender's attendance at a centre; and

    (b) that the person in charge of the centre consents to the inclusion of the requirement.

(4) A requirement under sub-paragraph (1) above shall operate to require the offender:

    (a) in accordance with instructions given by his responsible officer, to attend on not more than 60 days at the centre specified in the order; and

    (b) while attending there to comply with instructions given by, or under the authority of, the person in charge of the centre.

(5) Instructions given by the offender's responsible officer under sub-paragraph (4) above shall, as far as practicable, be such as to avoid:

    (a) any conflict with the offender's religious beliefs or with the requirements of any other community order to which he may be subject; and

    (b) any interference with the times, if any, at which he normally works or attends school or any other educational establishment.

(6) References in this paragraph to attendance at a probation centre include references to attendance elsewhere than at the centre for the purpose of participating in activities in accordance with instructions given by, or under the authority of, the person in charge of the centre.

(7) The Secretary of State may make rules for regulating the provision and carrying on of probation centres and the attendance at such centres of persons subject to probation orders; and such rules may in particular include provision with respect to hours of attendance, the reckoning of days of attendance and the keeping of attendance records.

(8) In this paragraph probation centre' means premises:

    (a) at which non-residential facilities are provided for use in connection with the rehabilitation of offenders; and

    (b) which are for the time being approved by the Secretary of State as providing facilities suitable for persons subject to probation orders.

Extension of requirements for sexual offenders

4   If the court so directs in the case of an offender who has been convicted of a sexual offence:

    (a) sub-paragraphs (4) and (6) of paragraph 2 above; and

    (b) sub-paragraph (4) of paragraph 3 above,

shall each have effect as if for the reference to 60 days there were substituted a reference to such greater number of days as may be specified in the direction.

Requirements as to treatment for mental condition, etc

5

(1) This paragraph applies where a court proposing to make a probation order is satisfied, on the evidence of a registered medical practitioner approved for the purposes of section 12 of the Mental Health Act 1983, that the mental condition of the offender:

(a) is such as requires and may be susceptible to treatment; but

(b) is not such as to warrant the making of a hospital order or guardianship order within the meaning of that Act.

(2) Subject to sub-paragraph (4) below, the probation order may include a requirement that the offender shall submit, during the whole of the probation period or during such part or parts of that period as may be specified in the order, to treatment by or under the direction of a registered medical practitioner or a chartered psychologist (or both, for different parts) with a view to the improvement of the offender's mental condition.

(3) The treatment required by any such order shall be such one of the following kinds of treatment as may be specified in the order, that is to say:

(a) treatment as a resident patient in a hospital or mental nursing home within the meaning of the Mental Health Act 1983, but not hospital premises at which high security psychiatric services within the meaning of that Act are provided;

(b) treatment as a non-resident patient at such institution or place as may be specified in the order;

(c) treatment by or under the direction of such registered medical practitioner or chartered psychologist (or both) as may be so specified,

but the nature of the treatment shall not be specified in the order except as mentioned in paragraph (a), (b) or (c) above.

(4) A court shall not by virtue of this paragraph include in a probation order a requirement that the offender shall submit to treatment for his mental condition unless:

(a) it is satisfied that arrangements have been or can be made for the treatment intended to be specified in the order (including arrangements for the reception of the offender where he is to be required to submit to treatment as a resident patient); and

(b) the offender has expressed his willingness to comply with such a requirement.

(5) While the offender is under treatment as a resident patient in pursuance of a requirement of the probation order, his responsible officer shall carry out the supervision of the offender to such extent only as may be necessary for the purpose of the revocation or amendment of the order.

(6) Where the medical practitioner or chartered psychologist by whom or under whose direction an offender is being treated for his mental condition in pursuance of a probation order is of the opinion that part of the treatment can be better or more conveniently given in or at an institution or place which:

(a) is not specified in the order; and

(b) is one in or at which the treatment of the offender will be given by or under the direction of a registered medical practitioner or chartered psychologist,

he may, with the consent of the offender, make arrangements for him to be treated accordingly.

(7) Such arrangements as are mentioned in sub-paragraph (6) above may provide for the offender to receive part of his treatment as a resident patient in an institution or place notwithstanding that the institution or place is not one which could have been specified for that purpose in the probation order.

(8) Where any such arrangements as are mentioned in sub-paragraph (6) above are made for the treatment of an offender:

(a) the medical practitioner or chartered psychologist by whom the arrangements are made shall give notice in writing to the offender's responsible officer, specifying the institution or place in or at which the treatment is to be carried out; and

(b) the treatment provided for by the arrangements shall be deemed to be treatment to which he is required to submit in pursuance of the probation order.

(9) Sub-sections (2) and (3) of section 54 of the Mental Health Act 1983 shall have effect with respect to proof for the purposes of sub-paragraph (1) above of an offender's mental condition as they have effect with respect to proof of an offender's mental condition for the purposes of section 37(2)(a) of that Act.

(10) In this paragraph, 'chartered psychologist' means a person for the time being listed in the British Psychological Society's Register of Chartered Psychologists.

Requirements as to treatment for drug or alcohol dependency

6

(1) Subject to sub-paragraph (2) below, this paragraph applies where a court proposing to make a probation order is satisfied:

(a) that the offender is dependent on drugs or alcohol;

(b) that his dependency caused or contributed to the offence in respect of which the order is proposed to be made; and

(c) that his dependency is such as requires and may be susceptible to treatment.

(2) If the court has been notified by the Secretary of State that arrangements for implementing drug treatment and testing orders are available in the area proposed to be specified in the probation order, and the notice has not been withdrawn, this paragraph shall have effect as if the words 'drugs or', in each place where they occur, were omitted.

(3) Subject to sub-paragraph (5) below, the probation order may include a requirement that the offender shall submit, during the whole of the probation period or during such part of that period as may be specified in the order, to treatment by or under the direction of a person having the necessary qualifications or experience with a view to the reduction or elimination of the offender's dependency on drugs or alcohol.

(4) The treatment required by any such order shall be such one of the following kinds of treatment as may be specified in the order, that is to say:

    (a) treatment as a resident in such institution or place as may be specified in the order;

    (b) treatment as a non-resident in or at such institution or place as may be so specified;

    (c) treatment by or under the direction of such person having the necessary qualifications or experience as may be so specified,

but the nature of the treatment shall not be specified in the order except as mentioned in paragraph (a), (b) or (c) above.

(5) A court shall not by virtue of this paragraph include in a probation order a requirement that the offender shall submit to treatment for his dependency on drugs or alcohol unless:

    (a) it is satisfied that arrangements have been or can be made for the treatment intended to be specified in the order (including arrangements for the reception of the offender where he is to be required to submit to treatment as a resident); and

    (b) the offender has expressed his willingness to comply with such a requirement.

(6) While the offender is under treatment as a resident in pursuance of a requirement of the probation order, his responsible officer shall carry out the offender's supervision to such extent only as may be necessary for the purpose of the revocation or amendment of the order.

(7) Where the person by whom or under whose direction an offender is being treated for dependency on drugs or alcohol in pursuance of a probation order is of the opinion that part of the treatment can be better or more conveniently given in or at an institution or place which:

    (a) is not specified in the order; and

    (b) is one in or at which the treatment of the offender will be given by or under the direction of a person having the necessary qualifications or experience,

he may, with the consent of the offender, make arrangements for him to be treated accordingly.

(8) Where any such arrangements as are mentioned in sub-paragraph (7) above are made for the treatment of an offender:

    (a) the person by whom the arrangements are made shall give notice in writing to the offender's responsible officer, specifying the institution or place in or at which the treatment is to be carried out; and

    (b) the treatment provided for by the arrangements shall be deemed to be treatment to which he is required to submit in pursuance of the probation order.

(9) In this paragraph, the reference to the offender being dependent on drugs or alcohol includes a reference to his having a propensity towards the misuse of drugs or alcohol; and references to his dependency on drugs or alcohol shall be construed accordingly.

COMBINATION ORDERS

POWERS OF CRIMINAL COURTS (SENTENCING) ACT 2000

Section 51: Combination orders

(1) Where a person aged 16 or over is convicted of an offence punishable with imprisonment and the court by or before which he is convicted is of the opinion mentioned in sub-section (3) below, the court may (subject to sections 34 to 36 above) make an order requiring him both:

    (a) to be under supervision for a period specified in the order, being not less than twelve months nor more than three years; and

    (b) to perform unpaid work for a number of hours so specified, being in the aggregate not less than 40 nor more than 100.

(2) An order under sub-section (1) above is in this Act referred to as a 'combination order'.

(3) The opinion referred to in sub-section (1) above is that the making of a combination order is desirable in the interests of:

    (a) securing the rehabilitation of the offender; or

    (b) protecting the public from harm from him or preventing the commission by him of further offences.

(4) Subject to sub-section (1) above, sections 41, 42, 46 and 47 above and Schedule 2 to this Act shall apply in relation to combination orders:

    (a) in so far as those orders impose such a requirement as is mentioned in paragraph (a) of sub-section (1) above, as if they were probation orders; and

    (b) in so far as they impose such a requirement as is mentioned in paragraph (b) of that sub-section, as if they were community service orders.

(5) Schedule 3 to this Act (which makes provision for dealing with failures to comply with the requirements of certain community orders, for revoking such orders with or without the substitution of other sentences and for amending such orders) shall have effect so far as relating to combination orders.

(6) Schedule 4 to this Act (which makes provision for and in connection with the making and amendment in England and Wales of certain community orders relating to persons residing in Scotland or Northern Ireland) shall have effect so far as relating to combination orders.

CURFEW ORDERS

POWERS OF CRIMINAL COURTS (SENTENCING) ACT 2000

Section 37: Curfew orders

(1) Where a person is convicted of an offence, the court by or before which he is convicted may (subject to sections 34 to 36 above) make an order requiring him to remain, for periods specified in the order, at a place so specified.

(2) An order under sub-section (1) above is in this Act referred to as a 'curfew order'.

(3) A curfew order may specify different places or different periods for different days, but shall not specify:

    (a) periods which fall outside the period of six months beginning with the day on which it is made; or

    (b) periods which amount to less than two hours or more than twelve hours in any one day.

(4) In relation to an offender aged under 16 on conviction, sub-section (3)(a) above shall have effect as if the reference to six months were a reference to three months.

(5) The requirements in a curfew order shall, as far as practicable, be such as to avoid:

    (a) any conflict with the offender's religious beliefs or with the requirements of any other community order to which he may be subject; and

    (b) any interference with the times, if any, at which he normally works or attends school or any other educational establishment.

(6) A curfew order shall include provision for making a person responsible for monitoring the offender's whereabouts during the curfew periods specified in the order; and a person who is made so responsible shall be of a description specified in an order made by the Secretary of State.

(7) A court shall not make a curfew order unless the court has been notified by the Secretary of State that arrangements for monitoring the offender's whereabouts are available in the area in which the place proposed to be specified in the order is situated and the notice has not been withdrawn.

(8) Before making a curfew order, the court shall obtain and consider information about the place proposed to be specified in the order (including information as to the attitude of persons likely to be affected by the enforced presence there of the offender).

(9) Before making a curfew order in respect of an offender who on conviction is under 16, the court shall obtain and consider information about his family circumstances and the likely effect of such an order on those circumstances.

(10) Before making a curfew order, the court shall explain to the offender in ordinary language:

   (a) the effect of the order (including any additional requirements proposed to be included in the order in accordance with section 38 below (electronic monitoring));

   (b) the consequences which may follow (under Part II of Schedule 3 to this Act) if he fails to comply with any of the requirements of the order; and

   (c) that the court has power (under Parts III and IV of that Schedule) to review the order on the application either of the offender or of the responsible officer.

(11) The court by which a curfew order is made shall give a copy of the order to the offender and to the responsible officer.

(12) In this Act, 'responsible officer', in relation to an offender subject to a curfew order, means the person who is responsible for monitoring the offender's whereabouts during the curfew periods specified in the order.

Section 38: Electronic monitoring of curfew orders

(1) Subject to sub-section (2) below, a curfew order may in addition include requirements for securing the electronic monitoring of the offender's whereabouts during the curfew periods specified in the order.

(2) A court shall not make a curfew order which includes such requirements unless the court:

   (a) has been notified by the Secretary of State that electronic monitoring arrangements are available in the area in which the place proposed to be specified in the order is situated; and

   (b) is satisfied that the necessary provision can be made under those arrangements.

(3) Electronic monitoring arrangements made by the Secretary of State under this section may include entering into contracts with other persons for the electronic monitoring by them of offenders' whereabouts.

Section 59: Curfew orders and community service orders for persistent petty offenders

(1) This section applies where:

   (a) a person aged 16 or over is convicted of an offence;

   (b) the court by or before which he is convicted is satisfied that each of the conditions mentioned in sub-section (2) below is fulfilled; and

   (c) if it were not so satisfied, the court would be minded to impose a fine in respect of the offence.

(2) The conditions are that:

   (a) one or more fines imposed on the offender in respect of one or more previous offences have not been paid; and

    (b) if a fine were imposed in an amount which was commensurate with the seriousness of the offence, the offender would not have sufficient means to pay it.

(3) The court may:

    (a) subject to sub-sections (5) and (7) below, make a curfew order under section 37(1) above; or

    (b) subject to sub-sections (6) and (7) below, make a community service order under section 46(1) above,

in respect of the offender instead of imposing a fine.

(4) Sub-section (3) above applies notwithstanding anything in sub-sections (1) and (3)(b) of section 35 above (restrictions on imposing community sentences).

...

POWERS OF CRIMINAL COURTS (SENTENCING) ACT 2000

Section 52: Drug treatment and testing orders

(1) Where a person aged 16 or over is convicted of an offence, the court by or before which he is convicted may (subject to sections 34 to 36 above) make an order which:

    (a) has effect for a period specified in the order of not less than six months nor more than three years ('the treatment and testing period'); and

    (b) includes the requirements and provisions mentioned in sections 53 and 54 below,

but this section does not apply in relation to an offence committed before 30th September 1998.

(2) An order under sub-section (1) above is in this Act referred to as a 'drug treatment and testing order'.

(3) A court shall not make a drug treatment and testing order in respect of an offender unless it is satisfied:

    (a) that he is dependent on or has a propensity to misuse drugs; and

    (b) that his dependency or propensity is such as requires and may be susceptible to treatment.

(4) For the purpose of ascertaining for the purposes of sub-section (3) above whether the offender has any drug in his body, the court may by order require him to provide samples of such description as it may specify; but the court shall not make such an order unless the offender expresses his willingness to comply with its requirements.

(5) A court shall not make a drug treatment and testing order unless it has been notified by the Secretary of State that arrangements for implementing such orders are available in the area proposed to be specified in the order under section 54(1) below and the notice has not been withdrawn.

(6) Before making a drug treatment and testing order, the court shall explain to the offender in ordinary language:

(a) the effect of the order and of the requirements proposed to be included in it;

(b) the consequences which may follow (under Part II of Schedule 3 to this Act) if he fails to comply with any of those requirements;

(c) that the order will be periodically reviewed at intervals as provided for in the order (by virtue of section 54(6) below); and

(d) that the order may be reviewed (under Parts III and IV of Schedule 3) on the application either of the offender or of the responsible officer,

and 'responsible officer' here has the meaning given by section 54(3) below.

(7) A court shall not make a drug treatment and testing order unless the offender expresses his willingness to comply with its requirements.

Section 53: The treatment and testing requirements

(1) A drug treatment and testing order shall include a requirement ('the treatment requirement') that the offender shall submit, during the whole of the treatment and testing period, to treatment by or under the direction of a specified person having the necessary qualifications or experience ('the treatment provider') with a view to the reduction or elimination of the offender's dependency on or propensity to misuse drugs.

(2) The required treatment for any particular period shall be:

(a) treatment as a resident in such institution or place as may be specified in the order; or

(b) treatment as a non-resident in or at such institution or place, and at such intervals, as may be so specified,

but the nature of the treatment shall not be specified in the order except as mentioned in paragraph (a) or (b) above.

(3) A court shall not make a drug treatment and testing order unless it is satisfied that arrangements have been or can be made for the treatment intended to be specified in the order (including arrangements for the reception of the offender where he is to be required to submit to treatment as a resident).

(4) A drug treatment and testing order shall include a requirement ('the testing requirement') that, for the purpose of ascertaining whether he has any drug in his body during the treatment and testing period, the offender shall during that period, at such times or in such circumstances as may (subject to the provisions of the order) be determined by the treatment provider, provide samples of such description as may be so determined.

(5) The testing requirement shall specify for each month the minimum number of occasions on which samples are to be provided.

Section 54: Provisions of order as to supervision and periodic review

(1) A drug treatment and testing order shall include a provision specifying the petty sessions area in which it appears to the court making the order that the offender resides or will reside.

(2) A drug treatment and testing order shall provide that, for the treatment and testing period, the offender shall be under the supervision of a probation officer appointed for or assigned to the petty sessions area specified in the order.

(3) In this Act 'responsible officer', in relation to an offender who is subject to a drug treatment and testing order, means the probation officer responsible for his supervision.

(4) A drug treatment and testing order shall:

(a) require the offender to keep in touch with the responsible officer in accordance with such instructions as he may from time to time be given by that officer, and to notify him of any change of address; and

(b) provide that the results of the tests carried out on the samples provided by the offender in pursuance of the testing requirement shall be communicated to the responsible officer.

(5) Supervision by the responsible officer shall be carried out to such extent only as may be necessary for the purpose of enabling him:

(a) to report on the offender's progress to the court responsible for the order;

(b) to report to that court any failure by the offender to comply with the requirements of the order; and

(c) to determine whether the circumstances are such that he should apply to that court for the revocation or amendment of the order.

(6) A drug treatment and testing order shall:

(a) provide for the order to be reviewed periodically at intervals of not less than one month;

(b) provide for each review of the order to be made, subject to section 55(6) below, at a hearing held for the purpose by the court responsible for the order (a 'review hearing');

(c) require the offender to attend each review hearing;

(d) provide for the responsible officer to make to the court responsible for the order, before each review, a report in writing on the offender's progress under the order; and

(e) provide for each such report to include the test results communicated to the responsible officer under sub-section (4)(b) above and the views of the treatment provider as to the treatment and testing of the offender.

(7) In this section references to the court responsible for a drug treatment and testing order are references to:

(a) where a court is specified in the order in accordance with sub-section (8) below, that court;

(b) in any other case, the court by which the order is made.

(8) Where the area specified in a drug treatment and testing order made by a magistrates' court is not the area for which the court acts, the court may, if it thinks fit, include in the order provision specifying for the purposes of sub-section (7) above a magistrates' court which acts for the area specified in the order.

(9) Where a drug treatment and testing order has been made on an appeal brought from the Crown Court or from the criminal division of the Court of Appeal, for the purposes of sub-section (7)(b) above it shall be deemed to have been made by the Crown Court.

Section 55: Periodic reviews

(1) At a review hearing (within the meaning given by sub-section (6) of section 54 above) the court may, after considering the responsible officer's report referred to in that sub-section, amend any requirement or provision of the drug treatment and testing order.

(2) The court:

(a) shall not amend the treatment or testing requirement unless the offender expresses his willingness to comply with the requirement as amended;

(b) shall not amend any provision of the order so as to reduce the treatment and testing period below the minimum specified in section 52(1) above, or to increase it above the maximum so specified; and

(c) except with the consent of the offender, shall not amend any requirement or provision of the order while an appeal against the order is pending.

(3) If the offender fails to express his willingness to comply with the treatment or testing requirement as proposed to be amended by the court, the court may:

(a) revoke the order; and

(b) deal with him, for the offence in respect of which the order was made, in any way in which it could deal with him if he had just been convicted by the court of the offence.

(4) In dealing with the offender under sub-section (3)(b) above, the court:

(a) shall take into account the extent to which the offender has complied with the requirements of the order; and

(b) may impose a custodial sentence (where the order was made in respect of an offence punishable with such a sentence) notwithstanding anything in section 79(2) below.

(5) Where the order was made by a magistrates' court in the case of an offender under 18 years of age in respect of an offence triable only on indictment in

the case of an adult, any powers exercisable under sub-section (3)(b) above in respect of the offender after he attains the age of 18 shall be powers to do either or both of the following:

(a) to impose a fine not exceeding £5,000 for the offence in respect of which the order was made;

(b) to deal with the offender for that offence in any way in which the court could deal with him if it had just convicted him of an offence punishable with imprisonment for a term not exceeding six months.

(6) If at a review hearing the court, after considering the responsible officer's report, is of the opinion that the offender's progress under the order is satisfactory, the court may so amend the order as to provide for each subsequent review to be made by the court without a hearing.

(7) If at a review without a hearing the court, after considering the responsible officer's report, is of the opinion that the offender's progress under the order is no longer satisfactory, the court may require the offender to attend a hearing of the court at a specified time and place.

(8) At that hearing the court, after considering that report, may:

(a) exercise the powers conferred by this section as if the hearing were a review hearing; and

(b) so amend the order as to provide for each subsequent review to be made at a review hearing.

(9) In this section any reference to the court, in relation to a review without a hearing, shall be construed:

(a) in the case of the Crown Court, as a reference to a judge of the court;

(b) in the case of a magistrates' court, as a reference to a justice of the peace acting for the commission area for which the court acts.

ENFORCEMENT OF COMMUNITY SENTENCES

SCHEDULE 3

BREACH, REVOCATION AND AMENDMENT OF CURFEW, PROBATION, COMMUNITY SERVICE, COMBINATION AND DRUG TREATMENT AND TESTING ORDERS

PART I

PRELIMINARY

Definitions

1

(1) In this Schedule 'relevant order' means any of the following orders:

   (a) a curfew order;

   (b) a probation order;

   (c) a community service order;

   (d) a combination order;

   (e) a drug treatment and testing order.

(2) In this Schedule 'the petty sessions area concerned' means:

   (a) in relation to a curfew order, the petty sessions area in which the place for the time being specified in the order is situated; and

   (b) in relation to a probation, community service, combination or drug treatment and testing order, the petty sessions area for the time being specified in the order.

(3) In this Schedule, references to the court responsible for a drug treatment and testing order shall be construed in accordance with section 54(7) of this Act.

(4) In this Schedule:

   (a) references to the probation element of a combination order are references to the order in so far as it imposes such a requirement as is mentioned in section 51(1)(a) of this Act (and in so far as it imposes any additional requirements included in the order by virtue of section 42); and

   (b) references to the community service element of such an order are references to the order in so far as it imposes such a requirement as is mentioned in section 51(1)(b).

Orders made on appeal

2

(1) Where a curfew, probation, community service or combination order has been made on appeal, for the purposes of this Schedule it shall be deemed:

    (a) if it was made on an appeal brought from a magistrates' court, to have been made by a magistrates' court;

    (b) if it was made on an appeal brought from the Crown Court or from the criminal division of the Court of Appeal, to have been made by the Crown Court.

(2) Where a drug treatment and testing order has been made on an appeal brought from the Crown Court or from the criminal division of the Court of Appeal, for the purposes of this Schedule it shall be deemed to have been made by the Crown Court.

PART II

BREACH OF REQUIREMENT OF ORDER

Issue of summons or warrant

3

(1) If at any time while a relevant order is in force in respect of an offender it appears on information to a justice of the peace acting for the petty sessions area concerned that the offender has failed to comply with any of the requirements of the order, the justice may:

    (a) issue a summons requiring the offender to appear at the place and time specified in it; or

    (b) if the information is in writing and on oath, issue a warrant for his arrest.

(2) Any summons or warrant issued under this paragraph shall direct the offender to appear or be brought:

    (a) in the case of a drug treatment and testing order, before the court responsible for the order;

    (b) in the case of any other relevant order which was made by the Crown Court and included a direction that any failure to comply with any of the requirements of the order be dealt with by the Crown Court, before the Crown Court; and

    (c) in the case of a relevant order which is neither a drug treatment and testing order nor an order to which paragraph (b) above applies, before a magistrates' court acting for the petty sessions area concerned.

Powers of magistrates' court

4

(1) If it is proved to the satisfaction of a magistrates' court before which an offender appears or is brought under paragraph 3 above that he has failed

without reasonable excuse to comply with any of the requirements of the relevant order, the court may deal with him in respect of the failure in any one of the following ways:

(a) it may impose on him a fine not exceeding £1,000;

(b) where the offender is aged 16 or over it may, subject to paragraph 7 below, make a community service order in respect of him;

(c) where:

(i) the relevant order is a curfew order and the offender is aged under 16; or

(ii) the relevant order is a probation order or combination order and the offender is aged under 21,

it may, subject to paragraph 8 below, make an attendance centre order in respect of him; or

(d) where the relevant order was made by a magistrates' court, it may deal with him, for the offence in respect of which the order was made, in any way in which it could deal with him if he had just been convicted by the court of the offence.

(2) In dealing with an offender under sub-paragraph (1)(d) above, a magistrates' court:

(a) shall take into account the extent to which the offender has complied with the requirements of the relevant order; and

(b) in the case of an offender who has wilfully and persistently failed to comply with those requirements, may impose a custodial sentence (where the relevant order was made in respect of an offence punishable with such a sentence) notwithstanding anything in section 79(2) of this Act.

(3) Where a magistrates' court deals with an offender under sub-paragraph (1)(d) above, it shall revoke the relevant order if it is still in force.

(4) Where a relevant order was made by the Crown Court and a magistrates' court has power to deal with the offender under sub-paragraph (1)(a), (b) or (c) above, it may instead commit him to custody or release him on bail until he can be brought or appear before the Crown Court.

(5) A magistrates' court which deals with an offender's case under sub-paragraph (4) above shall send to the Crown Court:

(a) a certificate signed by a justice of the peace certifying that the offender has failed to comply with the requirements of the relevant order in the respect specified in the certificate; and

(b) such other particulars of the case as may be desirable,

and a certificate purporting to be so signed shall be admissible as evidence of the failure before the Crown Court.

(6) A person sentenced under sub-paragraph (1)(d) above for an offence may appeal to the Crown Court against the sentence.

Powers of Crown Court

5

(1) Where under paragraph 3 or by virtue of paragraph 4(4) above an offender is brought or appears before the Crown Court and it is proved to the satisfaction of that court that he has failed without reasonable excuse to comply with any of the requirements of the relevant order, the Crown Court may deal with him in respect of the failure in any one of the following ways:

(a) it may impose on him a fine not exceeding £1,000;

(b) where the offender is aged 16 or over it may, subject to paragraph 7 below, make a community service order in respect of him;

(c) where:

    (i) the relevant order is a curfew order and the offender is aged under 16; or

    (ii) the relevant order is a probation order or combination order and the offender is aged under 21,

it may, subject to paragraph 8 below, make an attendance centre order in respect of him; or

(d) it may deal with him, for the offence in respect of which the order was made, in any way in which it could deal with him if he had just been convicted before the Crown Court of the offence.

(2) In dealing with an offender under sub-paragraph (1)(d) above, the Crown Court:

(a) shall take into account the extent to which the offender has complied with the requirements of the relevant order; and

(b) in the case of an offender who has wilfully and persistently failed to comply with those requirements, may impose a custodial sentence (where the relevant order was made in respect of an offence punishable with such a sentence) notwithstanding anything in section 79(2) of this Act.

(3) Where the Crown Court deals with an offender under sub-paragraph (1)(d) above, it shall revoke the relevant order if it is still in force.

(4) In proceedings before the Crown Court under this paragraph any question whether the offender has failed to comply with the requirements of the relevant order shall be determined by the court and not by the verdict of a jury.

Exclusions from paragraphs 4 and 5

6

(1) Without prejudice to paragraphs 10 and 11 below, an offender who is convicted of a further offence while a relevant order is in force in respect of him shall not on that account be liable to be dealt with under paragraph 4 or 5 above in respect of a failure to comply with any requirement of the order.

(2) An offender who:

    (a) is required by a probation order or combination order to submit to treatment for his mental condition, or his dependency on or propensity to misuse drugs or alcohol; or

    (b) is required by a drug treatment and testing order to submit to treatment for his dependency on or propensity to misuse drugs,

shall not be treated for the purposes of paragraph 4 or 5 above as having failed to comply with that requirement on the ground only that he has refused to undergo any surgical, electrical or other treatment if, in the opinion of the court, his refusal was reasonable having regard to all the circumstances.

Community service orders imposed for breach of relevant order

7

(1) Section 46(1) of this Act (community service orders) shall apply for the purposes of paragraphs 4(1)(b) and 5(1)(b) above as if for the words from the beginning to 'make' there were substituted 'Where a court has power to deal with an offender aged 16 or over under Part II of Schedule 3 to this Act for failure to comply with any of the requirements of a relevant order, the court may make in respect of the offender'.

(2) In this paragraph a 'secondary order' means a community service order made by virtue of paragraph 4(1)(b) or 5(1)(b) above.

(3) The number of hours which an offender may be required to work under a secondary order shall be specified in the order and shall not exceed 60 in the aggregate, and:

    (a) where the relevant order is a community service order, the number of hours which the offender may be required to work under the secondary order shall not be such that the total number of hours under both orders exceeds the maximum specified in section 46(3) of this Act; and

    (b) where the relevant order is a combination order, the number of hours which the offender may be required to work under the secondary order shall not be such that the total number of hours under:

        (i) the secondary order; and

        (ii) the community service element of the combination order,

exceeds the maximum specified in section 51(1)(b) of this Act.

(4) Section 46(4) of this Act and, so far as applicable:

    (a) section 46(5) to (7) and (9) to (13); and

    (b) section 47 and the provisions of this Schedule so far as relating to community service orders,

have effect in relation to a secondary order as they have effect in relation to any other community service order, subject to sub-paragraph (6) below.

(5) Sections 35 and 36 of this Act (restrictions and procedural requirements for community sentences) do not apply in relation to a secondary order.

(6) Where the provisions of this Schedule have effect as mentioned in sub-paragraph (4) above in relation to a secondary order:

(a) the power conferred on the court by each of paragraphs 4(1)(d) and 5(1)(d) above and paragraph 10(3)(b) below to deal with the offender for the offence in respect of which the order was made shall be construed as a power to deal with the offender, for his failure to comply with the original order, in any way in which the court could deal with him if that failure had just been proved to the satisfaction of the court;

(b) the references in paragraphs 10(1)(b) and 11(1)(a) below to the offence in respect of which the order was made shall be construed as references to the failure to comply in respect of which the order was made; and

(c) the power conferred on the Crown Court by paragraph 11(2)(b) below to deal with the offender for the offence in respect of which the order was made shall be construed as a power to deal with the offender, for is failure to comply with the original order, in any way in which a magistrates' court (if the original order was made by a magistrates' court) or the Crown Court (if the original order was made by the Crown Court) could deal with him if that failure had just been proved to its satisfaction,

and in this sub-paragraph 'the original order' means the relevant order the failure to comply with which led to the making of the secondary order.

Attendance centre orders imposed for breach of relevant order

8

(1) Section 60(1) of this Act (attendance centre orders) shall apply for the purposes of paragraphs 4(1)(c) and 5(1)(c) above as if for the words from the beginning to 'the court may', there were substituted 'Where a court:

(a) has power to deal with an offender aged under 16 under Part II of Schedule 3 to this Act for failure to comply with any of the requirements of a curfew order; or

(b) has power to deal with an offender aged under 21 under that Part of that Schedule for failure to comply with any of the requirements of a probation or combination order,

the court may'.

(2) The following provisions of this Act, namely:

(a) sub-sections (3) to (11) of section 60; and

(b) so far as applicable, Schedule 5,

have effect in relation to an attendance centre order made by virtue of paragraph 4(1)(c) or 5(1)(c) above as they have effect in relation to any other attendance centre order, but as if there were omitted from each of paragraphs 2(1)(b), 3(1) and 4(3) of Schedule 5 the words ', for the offence in respect of which the order was made,' and 'for that offence'.

(3) Sections 35 and 36 of this Act (restrictions and procedural requirements for community sentences) do not apply in relation to an attendance centre order made by virtue of paragraph 4(1)(c) or 5(1)(c) above.

...

PART III

REVOCATION OF ORDER

Revocation of order with or without re-sentencing: powers of magistrates' court

10

(1) This paragraph applies where a relevant order made by a magistrates' court is in force in respect of any offender and on the application of the offender or the responsible officer it appears to the appropriate magistrates' court that, having regard to circumstances which have arisen since the order was made, it would be in the interests of justice:

(a) for the order to be revoked; or

(b) for the offender to be dealt with in some other way for the offence in respect of which the order was made.

(2) In this paragraph 'the appropriate magistrates court' means:

(a) in the case of a drug treatment and testing order, the magistrates' court responsible for the order;

(b) in the case of any other relevant order, a magistrates' court acting for the petty sessions area concerned.

(3) The appropriate magistrates' court may:

(a) revoke the order; or

(b) both:

(i) revoke the order; and

(ii) deal with the offender, for the offence in respect of which the order was made, in any way in which it could deal with him if he had just been convicted by the court of the offence.

(4) The circumstances in which a probation, combination or drug treatment and testing order may be revoked under sub-paragraph (3)(a) above shall include the offender's making good progress or his responding satisfactorily to supervision or, as the case may be, treatment.

(5) In dealing with an offender under sub-paragraph (3)(b) above, a magistrates' court shall take into account the extent to which the offender has complied with the requirements of the relevant order.

(6) A person sentenced under sub-paragraph (3)(b) above for an offence may appeal to the Crown Court against the sentence.

(7) Where a magistrates' court proposes to exercise its powers under this paragraph otherwise than on the application of the offender, it shall summon him to appear before the court and, if he does not appear in answer to the summons, may issue a warrant for his arrest.

(8) No application may be made by the offender under sub-paragraph (1) above while an appeal against the relevant order is pending.

Revocation of order with or without re-sentencing: powers of Crown Court on conviction, etc

11

(1) This paragraph applies where:

(a) a relevant order made by the Crown Court is in force in respect of an offender and the offender or the responsible officer applies to the Crown Court for the order to be revoked or for the offender to be dealt with in some other way for the offence in respect of which the order was made; or

(b) an offender in respect of whom a relevant order is in force is convicted of an offence before the Crown Court or, having been committed by a magistrates' court to the Crown Court for sentence, is brought or appears before the Crown Court.

(2) If it appears to the Crown Court to be in the interests of justice to do so, having regard to circumstances which have arisen since the order was made, the Crown Court may:

(a) revoke the order; or

(b) both:

(i) revoke the order; and

(ii) deal with the offender, for the offence in respect of which the order was made, in any way in which the court which made the order could deal with him if he had just been convicted of that offence by or before the court which made the order.

(3) The circumstances in which a probation, combination or drug treatment and testing order may be revoked under sub-paragraph (2)(a) above shall include the offender's making good progress or his responding satisfactorily to supervision or, as the case may be, treatment.

(4) In dealing with an offender under sub-paragraph (2)(b) above, the Crown Court shall take into account the extent to which the offender has complied with the requirements of the relevant order.

Substitution of conditional discharge for probation or combination order

12

(1) This paragraph applies where a probation order or combination order is in force in respect of any offender and on the application of the offender or the responsible officer to the appropriate court it appears to the court that, having regard to circumstances which have arisen since the order was made, it would be in the interests of justice:

(a) for the order to be revoked; and

(b) for an order to be made under section 12(1)(b) of this Act discharging the offender conditionally for the offence for which the probation or combination order was made.

(2) In this paragraph 'the appropriate court' means:

(a) where the probation or combination order was made by a magistrates' court, a magistrates' court acting for the petty sessions area concerned;

(b) where the probation or combination order was made by the Crown Court, the Crown Court.

(3) No application may be made under paragraph 10 or 11 above for a probation order or combination order to be revoked and replaced with an order for conditional discharge under section 12(1)(b); but otherwise nothing in this paragraph shall affect the operation of paragraphs 10 and 11 above.

(4) Where this paragraph applies:

(a) the appropriate court may revoke the probation or combination order and make an order under section 12(1)(b) of this Act discharging the offender in respect of the offence for which the probation or combination order was made, subject to the condition that he commits no offence during the period specified in the order under section 12(1)(b); and

(b) the period specified in the order under section 12(1)(b) shall be the period beginning with the making of that order and ending with the date when the probation period specified in the probation or combination order would have ended.

(5) For the purposes of sub-paragraph (4) above, sub-section (1) of section 12 of this Act shall apply as if:

(a) for the words from the beginning to 'may make an order either' there were substituted the words 'Where paragraph 12 of Schedule 3 to this Act applies, the appropriate court may (subject to the provisions of sub-paragraph (4) of that paragraph) make an order in respect of the offender'; and

(b) paragraph (a) of that sub-section were omitted.

(6) An application under this paragraph may be heard in the offender's absence if:

(a) the application is made by the responsible officer; and

(b) that officer produces to the court a statement by the offender that he understands the effect of an order for conditional discharge and consents to the making of the application,

and where the application is so heard section 12(4) of this Act shall not apply.

(7) No application may be made under this paragraph while an appeal against the probation or combination order is pending.

(8) Without prejudice to paragraph 15 below, on the making of an order under section 12(1)(b) of this Act by virtue of this paragraph the court shall forthwith give copies of the order to the responsible officer, and the responsible officer shall give a copy to the offender.

(9) Each of sections 1(11), 2(9) and 66(4) of the Crime and Disorder Act 1998 (which prevent a court from making an order for conditional discharge in certain cases) shall have effect as if the reference to the court by or before which a person is convicted of an offence there mentioned included a reference to a court dealing with an application under this paragraph in respect of the offence.

Revocation following custodial sentence by magistrates' court unconnected with order

13

(1) This paragraph applies where:

(a) an offender in respect of whom a relevant order is in force is convicted of an offence by a magistrates' court unconnected with the order;

(b) the court imposes a custodial sentence on the offender; and

(c) it appears to the court, on the application of the offender or the responsible officer, that it would be in the interests of justice to exercise its powers under this paragraph, having regard to circumstances which have arisen since the order was made.

(2) In sub-paragraph (1) above 'a magistrates' court unconnected with the order' means:

(a) in the case of a drug treatment and testing order, a magistrates' court which is not responsible for the order;

(b) in the case of any other relevant order, a magistrates' court not acting for the petty sessions area concerned.

(3) The court may:

(a) if the order was made by a magistrates' court, revoke it;

(b) if the order was made by the Crown Court, commit the offender in custody or release him on bail until he can be brought or appear before the Crown Court.

(4) Where the court deals with an offender's case under sub-paragraph (3)(b) above, it shall send to the Crown Court such particulars of the case as may be desirable.

14 Where by virtue of paragraph 13(3)(b) above an offender is brought or appears before the Crown Court and it appears to the Crown Court to be in the interests of justice to do so, having regard to circumstances which have arisen since the relevant order was made, the Crown Court may revoke the order.

...

PART IV

AMENDMENT OF ORDER

Amendment by reason of change of residence

18

(1) This paragraph applies where, at any time while a relevant order (other than a drug treatment and testing order) is in force in respect of an offender, a magistrates' court acting for the petty sessions area concerned is satisfied that the offender proposes to change, or has changed, his residence from that petty sessions area to another petty sessions area.

(2) Subject to sub-paragraphs (3) to (5) below, the court may, and on the application of the responsible officer shall, amend the relevant order by substituting the other petty sessions area for the area specified in the order or, in the case of a curfew order, a place in that other area for the place so specified.

(3) The court shall not amend under this paragraph a probation or curfew order which contains requirements which, in the opinion of the court, cannot be complied with unless the offender continues to reside in the petty sessions area concerned unless, in accordance with paragraph 19 below, it either:

   (a) cancels those requirements; or

   (b) substitutes for those requirements other requirements which can be complied with if the offender ceases to reside in that area.

(4) Sub-paragraph (3) above applies also in relation to a combination order whose probation element contains requirements such as are mentioned in that sub-paragraph.

(5) The court shall not amend a community service order or combination order under this paragraph unless it appears to the court that provision can be made for the offender to perform work under the order under the arrangements which exist for persons who reside in the other petty sessions area to perform work under such orders.

(6) Where:

   (a) the court amends a probation, community service or combination order under this paragraph;

   (b) a local authority is specified in the order in accordance with section 41(5) or 46(9) of this Act; and

   (c) the change, or proposed change, of residence also is or would be a change of residence from the area of that authority to the area of another such authority,

   the court shall further amend the order by substituting the other authority for the authority specified in the order.

(7) In sub-paragraph (6) above 'local authority' has the meaning given by section 42 of the Crime and Disorder Act 1998, and references to the area of a local authority shall be construed in accordance with that section.

Amendment of requirements of probation, combination or curfew order

19

(1) Without prejudice to the provisions of paragraph 18 above but subject to sub-paragraphs (2) and (3) below, a magistrates' court acting for the petty sessions area concerned may, on the application of the offender or the responsible officer, by order amend a probation or curfew order or the probation element of a combination order:

(a) by cancelling any of the requirements of the probation or curfew order or of the probation element of the combination order; or

(b) by inserting in the probation or curfew order or probation element of the combination order (either in addition to or in substitution for any of its requirements) any requirement which the court could include if it were then making the order.

(2) A magistrates' court shall not under sub-paragraph (1) above amend a probation order or the probation element of a combination order:

(a) by reducing the probation period, or by extending that period beyond the end of three years from the date of the original order; or

(b) by inserting in it a requirement that the offender shall submit to treatment for his mental condition, or his dependency on or propensity to misuse drugs or alcohol, unless:

(i) the offender has expressed his willingness to comply with such a requirement; and

(ii) the amending order is made within three months after the date of the original order.

(3) A magistrates' court shall not under sub-paragraph (1) above amend a curfew order by extending the curfew periods beyond the end of six months from the date of the original order.

Amendment of treatment requirements of probation or combination order on report of practitioner

20

(1) Where the medical practitioner or other person by whom or under whose direction an offender is, in pursuance of any requirement of a probation or combination order, being treated for his mental condition or his dependency on or propensity to misuse drugs or alcohol:

(a) is of the opinion mentioned in sub-paragraph (2) below; or

(b) is for any reason unwilling to continue to treat or direct the treatment of the offender,

he shall make a report in writing to that effect to the responsible officer and that officer shall apply under paragraph 19 above to a magistrates' court acting for the petty sessions area concerned for the variation or cancellation of the requirement.

(2) The opinion referred to in sub-paragraph (1) above is:

    (a) that the treatment of the offender should be continued beyond the period specified in that behalf in the order;

    (b) that the offender needs different treatment;

    (c) that the offender is not susceptible to treatment; or

    (d) that the offender does not require further treatment.

Amendment of drug treatment and testing order

21

(1) Without prejudice to the provisions of section 55(1), (6) and (8) of this Act, the court responsible for a drug treatment and testing order may by order:

    (a) vary or cancel any of the requirements or provisions of the order on an application by the responsible officer under sub-paragraph (2) or (3)(a) or (b) below; or

    (b) amend the order on an application by that officer under sub-paragraph (3)(c) below.

(2) Where the treatment provider is of the opinion that the treatment or testing requirement of the order should be varied or cancelled:

    (a) he shall make a report in writing to that effect to the responsible officer; and

    (b) that officer shall apply to the court for the variation or cancellation of the requirement.

(3) Where the responsible officer is of the opinion:

    (a) that the treatment or testing requirement of the order should be so varied as to specify a different treatment provider;

    (b) that any other requirement of the order, or a provision of the order, should be varied or cancelled; or

    (c) that the order should be so amended as to provide for each subsequent periodic review (required by section 54(6)(a) of this Act) to be made without a hearing instead of at a review hearing, or vice versa,

he shall apply to the court for the variation or cancellation of the requirement or provision or the amendment of the order.

(4) The court:

    (a) shall not amend the treatment or testing requirement unless the offender expresses his willingness to comply with the requirement as amended; and

    (b) shall not amend any provision of the order so as to reduce the treatment and testing period below the minimum specified in section 52(1) of this Act, or to increase it above the maximum so specified.

(5) If the offender fails to express his willingness to comply with the treatment or testing requirement as proposed to be amended by the court, the court may:

    (a) revoke the order; and

    (b) deal with him, for the offence in respect of which the order was made, in any way in which it could deal with him if he had just been convicted by or before the court of the offence.

(6) In dealing with the offender under sub-paragraph (5)(b) above, the court:

    (a) shall take into account the extent to which the offender has complied with the requirements of the order; and

    (b) may impose a custodial sentence (where the order was made in respect of an offence punishable with such a sentence) notwithstanding anything in section 79(2) of this Act.

(7) Paragraph 9(3) above shall apply for the purposes of this paragraph as it applies for the purposes of paragraph 4 above, but as if for the words 'paragraph 4(1)(d) above' there were substituted 'paragraph 21(5)(b) below'.

Extension of community service or combination order

22 Where:

    (a) a community service order or combination order is in force in respect of any offender; and

    (b) on the application of the offender or the responsible officer, it appears to a magistrates' court acting for the petty sessions area concerned that it would be in the interests of justice to do so having regard to circumstances which have arisen since the order was made,

the court may, in relation to the order, extend the period of twelve months specified in section 47(3) of this Act.

Supplementary

23 No order may be made under paragraph 18 above, and no application may be made under paragraph 19 or 22 above or, except with the consent of the offender, under paragraph 21 above, while an appeal against the relevant order is pending.

24

(1) Subject to sub-paragraph (2) below, where a court proposes to exercise its powers under this Part of this Schedule, otherwise than on the application of the offender, the court:

    (a) shall summon him to appear before the court; and

    (b) if he does not appear in answer to the summons, may issue a warrant for his arrest.

(2) This paragraph shall not apply to an order cancelling a requirement of a relevant order or reducing the period of any requirement, or substituting a new petty sessions area or a new place for the one specified in a relevant order.

25

(1) On the making under this Part of this Schedule of an order amending a relevant order (other than a drug treatment and testing order), the justices' chief executive for the court shall forthwith:

  (a) if the order amends the relevant order otherwise than by substituting a new petty sessions area or a new place for the one specified in the relevant order, give copies of the amending order to the responsible officer;

  (b) if the order amends the relevant order in the manner excepted by paragraph (a) above, send to the chief executive to the justices for the new petty sessions area or, as the case may be, for the petty sessions area in which the new place is situated:

    (i) copies of the amending order; and

    (ii) such documents and information relating to the case as he considers likely to be of assistance to a court acting for that area in the exercise of its functions in relation to the order,

  and in a case falling within paragraph (b) above the chief executive to the justices for that area shall give copies of the amending order to the responsible officer.

(2) On the making under this Part of this Schedule of an order amending a drug treatment and testing order, the justices' chief executive for the court shall forthwith give copies of the amending order to the responsible officer.

(3) A responsible officer to whom in accordance with sub-paragraph (1) or (2) above copies of an order are given shall give a copy to the offender and to the person in charge of any institution in which the offender is or was required by the order to reside.

CHAPTER 15

FINES, DISCHARGES AND BINDING OVER TO KEEP THE PEACE

In this chapter, we consider fines, conditional and absolute discharges and the power to bind a person over. These powers apply irrespective of the age of the offender.

15.1 FINES

A fine may be imposed for any offence except murder and treason (which carry mandatory life imprisonment).

15.1.1 Crown Court fines

Section 127 of the Powers of Criminal Courts (Sentencing) Act 2000 empowers the Crown Court to impose a fine instead of, or in addition to, dealing with the offender in any other way. This power applies where the offender has been convicted on indictment and where the offender has been convicted summarily but then committed to the Crown Court for sentence under s 3 of the Powers of Criminal Courts (Sentencing) Act 2000.

There is no statutory limit on the amount of a fine imposed by the Crown Court following conviction on indictment or following a s 3 committal for sentence. Note, however, that where a Crown Court is dealing with an offence following committal under s 6 of the 2000 Act, the Crown Court cannot exceed the amount of the fine which the magistrates could have imposed.

Section 139(2) of the 2000 Act provides that where the Crown Court imposes a fine it must fix a term of imprisonment (if the offender is 21 or over) or detention in a young offenders institution (if the offender is aged between 18 and 20) in default.

Section 139(2) of the 2000 Act sets out the maximum term of imprisonment or detention which may be imposed under s 139:

Fine (£)	Term
1–200	7 days
201–500	14 days
501–1,000	28 days
1,001–2,500	45 days

2,501–5,000	3 months
5,001–10,000	6 months
10,001–20,000	12 months
20,001–50,000	18 months
50,001–100,000	2 years
100,001–250,000	3 years
250,001–1,000,000	5 years
over 1,000,000	10 years

15.1.2 Magistrates' courts fines for either way offences

Where a magistrates' court convicts a person of an offence which is triable either way because it is listed in Sched 1 of the Magistrates' Courts Act 1980, the court may impose a fine not exceeding the 'prescribed sum' (s 32(1) of the Magistrates' Courts Act, currently £5,000).

Where a magistrates' court convicts a person of an offence which is triable either way because the statute creating the offence specifies penalties for summary conviction and conviction on indictment, the court may impose a fine not exceeding the amount fixed in the statute creating the offence or the prescribed sum (that is, £5,000), whichever is greater (s 32(2)). Where the statute creating the offence states that the fine may not exceed 'the statutory maximum', the maximum referred to is the prescribed sum (that is, £5,000).

If the statute creating the offence refers only to imprisonment as a punishment, a fine on level 3 (£1,000) is deemed to be included (s 34(3)).

15.1.3 Magistrates' courts fines for summary offences

Fines for summary offences are expressed in terms of a standard scale (s 37(2) of the Criminal Justice Act 1982). The standard scale has five levels:

Level	Maximum fine (£)
1	200
2	500
3	1,000
4	2,500
5	5,000

15.1.4   Imprisonment in default (magistrates' court fines)

Section 82(1) of the Magistrates' Courts Act 1980 provides that a magistrates' court which imposes a fine may only fix a term of imprisonment (or detention in a young offenders institution) if:

- the offence is punishable with imprisonment and it appears to the court that the offender has sufficient means to pay the fine immediately; or
- it appears to the court that the offender is unlikely to remain long enough at an address where he can be found so that enforcement of the fine by other methods is possible; or
- the court also imposes a custodial sentence on the offender or the offender is already serving a custodial sentence.

Where a magistrates' court does fix a term of imprisonment in default of payment of a fine, the same periods apply as in the Crown Court (save that a magistrates' court cannot fix more than 12 months' imprisonment in default) (Sched 4 of the Magistrates' Courts Act 1980).

15.1.5   Fixing the amount of the fine

Section 128 of the Powers of Criminal Courts (Sentencing) Act 2000 sets out the procedure for fixing the amount of a fine.

Section 128(2) says that the amount fixed shall be such as, in the opinion of the court, reflects the seriousness of the offence. The court will also take account of any mitigating circumstances relating to the offender.

However, s 128(1) says that before fixing the amount of any fine the court must inquire into the financial circumstances of the offender. Section 128(3) requires the court to take into account the financial circumstances of the offender so far as they are known to the court. It should be noted that s 128(1) applies only where the offender is an individual (that is, not a company); s 128(3) applies both to individuals and to companies.

Section 128(4) states that the financial circumstances of the offender must be taken into account whether this has the effect of increasing or reducing the amount of the fine. In other words, the court first fixes an amount related to the seriousness of the offence and then considers whether that amount should be increased or reduced as a result of the offender's means. See, also, *R v Cowley* (1995) *The Times*, 2 February, where a fine was reduced because proper account had not been taken of the offender's means.

In *R v Chelmsford Crown Court ex p Birchall* [1990] RTR 80, the Divisional Court emphasised that where the offender is fined for a number of offences, the court must ensure that the total amount to be paid is proportionate to the totality of the offending.

If the offender does not have the means to pay a fine which adequately reflects the seriousness of the offence but the offence is not sufficiently serious to justify a custodial sentence, it is wrong in principle to impose a custodial sentence (*R v Reeves* (1972) 56 Cr App R 366). The same applies even if the sentence of imprisonment is to be suspended. On the other hand, if the seriousness of the offence does justify a custodial sentence, the offender should not escape custody merely because he has the means to pay a large fine (*R v Markwick* (1953) 37 Cr App R 125).

In *R v Warden* (1996) 160 JP 363, it was held that, in determining a non-custodial sentence, the offender should normally be given credit for any time spent in custody on remand. In the present case, a fine of £2,000 was reduced to £1,000 on that basis.

In *R v F Howe & Son Ltd* [1999] 2 All ER 249, the Court of Appeal gave some guidance on fines where the defendant is a company. The starting point should the company's annual accounts; these need to be scrutinised with some care to avoid reaching a superficial or erroneous conclusion. Where accounts or other financial information are deliberately not supplied, the court is entitled to conclude that the company can afford to pay any fine the court is minded to impose. The fine needs to be large enough to bring home the seriousness of the offending to the managers and to the shareholders. Where the defendant is a small company, with limited resources, it must be borne in mind that the fine (and costs) are not tax deductible and so the full burden will fall on the company.

In *R v Rollco Screw and Rivet Co Ltd* [1999] 2 Cr App R(S) 436, the Court of Appeal pointed out that, in a small company, the directors might also be the shareholders and so the court must be alert to this if a fine is imposed on both the directors and on the company; however, the penalties imposed should make it clear that there is personal responsibility on the part of the directors which cannot be shuffled off to the company. When deciding the period for payment of the fine, it is proper for the court to fix a longer period in the case of a company than would be appropriate in the case of an individual.

15.1.6   Obtaining information about the offenders' means

Section 126 of the Powers of Criminal Courts (Sentencing) Act 2000 empowers a court to make a 'financial circumstances order' against any person convicted by that court. The order requires the offender to provide a statement of his financial circumstances within the period specified in the order.

Failure to comply without reasonable excuse is a summary offence punishable with a fine not exceeding level 3 (£1,000): s 126(4).

Furthermore, s 128(5)(b) of the 2000 Act states that where the offender fails to comply with a s 126 order or otherwise fails to co-operate with the court's inquiry into his means, the court may make such determination as it thinks fit.

Under s 126(5) of the 2000 Act, where a financial circumstances order has been made under the Act, it is an offence to make a statement which is known to be false, or recklessly to furnish a statement which is false, or knowingly to fail to disclose a material fact. These offences are punishable with up to three months' imprisonment and/or a fine not exceeding level 4 (£2,500).

15.1.7 Summary

There are three stages to fixing a fine:

- what fine is appropriate to the seriousness of the offence?;
- is there personal mitigation which enables the fine to be reduced?;
- should the actual fine be higher or lower because of the means of the offender?

15.1.8 Enforcement of fines

Whether the fine was imposed by the Crown Court or a magistrates' court, enforcement is the responsibility of a magistrates' court. If the fine was imposed by a magistrates' court, enforcement is the responsibility of that court. If the fine was imposed by the Crown Court, responsibility for enforcement rests with the magistrates' court which committed the offender for trial or sentence (as the case may be). If the offender resides outside the area served by the enforcing magistrates' court, the order can be transferred to the offender's local magistrates' court.

Under s 75 of the Magistrates' Courts Act 1980, the court may allow time (or extend the time already allowed) for payment or may order payment by instalments.

Where a fine is to be paid by instalments, the instalments should usually be calculated so that the fine is paid off within 12 months. However, there is no rule of law to this effect and there may be cases where a period longer than a year may be appropriate (*R v Olliver* (1989) 11 Cr App R(S) 10)).

Where the court allows time (or further time), it may also set a date when the offender must attend court for an inquiry into his means if any part of the fine remains unpaid (s 86).

The offender's means are taken into account when the decision is taken to impose a fine. However, if the offender fails to pay some or all of the fine and an inquiry into her means shows that the default results from inability (rather than refusal) to pay, then the magistrates' court may remit the whole or part of the fine (s 129 of the 2000 Act).

Otherwise, the sanctions for non-payment of a fine are:

- to issue a 'distress warrant' (this authorises the seizure and sale of goods belonging to the offender; the proceeds of sale go to meet the outstanding fine);
- where the offender is in employment, to make an attachment of earnings order (this requires the offender's employer to deduct a regular sum from the offender's wages and to pay that sum direct to the court (Attachment of Earnings Act 1971));
- where the offender is in receipt of income support, to make an order for the deduction of regular sums from the offender's income support (under the Fines (Deduction from Income Support) Regulations 1992);
- where the offender is under 25, to make an attendance centre order;
- to commit the offender to prison. This is possible if either:
  - (a) the offence for which the fine was imposed was imprisonable and it appears to the court that the offender has the means to pay the outstanding amount forthwith; or
  - (b) the court is satisfied that the offender's failure to pay the fine is due to wilful refusal or culpable neglect, and no other method of enforcement would be effective.

Where a term of imprisonment is ordered, it must be for the term originally specified as the term in default (see above); if no term in default was specified when the fine was imposed, the court dealing with the default fixes a term which must not exceed the term which could have been fixed in the first place (see Sched 4 of the Magistrates' Courts Act 1980).

Prior to the issue of a distress warrant (authorising seizure of goods) where a fine remains unpaid, there is no need (indeed, there is no power) to hold a means inquiry. It is only where the court is considering issuing a warrant of committal (sending the defaulter to prison) that such an inquiry is required (*R v Hereford Magistrates' Court ex p MacRae* (1999) 163 JP 433).

Before an offender can be committed to prison for non-payment of a fine, all other methods of enforcing payment must have been considered or tried; where other methods have been considered inappropriate, reasons for that determination must be given (*R v St Helen's Justices ex p Jones* [1999] 2 All ER 73).

Where magistrates are considering a warrant of commitment to prison and the defendant is not present, the hearing should be adjourned if the justices are aware that the defendant has not received notice of the proceedings (*R v Doncaster Justices ex p Hannan* (1999) 163 JP 182).

15.1.9 Enforcement of fines under the Crime (Sentences) Act 1997

The Crime (Sentences) Act 1997 adds a number of additional ways of enforcing the fines.

Under s 35 of the Crime (Sentences) Act 1997, where the offender has attained the age of 16, the court may impose a community service order or a curfew order as a penalty for default in paying a fine.

Section 40 of the Crime (Sentences) Act 1997 enables a magistrates' court to disqualify an offender from driving for such period as it thinks fit (up to a maximum of 12 months) if the offender is in default in paying a sum adjudged to be by a conviction (for example, a fine or a compensation order) instead of sending him to prison for non-payment. Sub-section (4) provides for the disqualification to cease once full payment of the sum due has been made and for the *pro rata* reduction of the period of disqualification where part-payment is made. Sub-section (5) authorises the Secretary of State to alter the 12 month maximum period of disqualification.

15.1.10 Combining fines with other orders

A fine may be combined with any other sentence.

However, it will usually be wrong in principle to impose a fine and an immediate custodial sentence unless the object of the fine is to deprive the offender of the profit which he has made from committing the offence (*R v Savundranayagan* [1968] 1 WLR 1761; [1968] 3 All ER 439). Note that, in the case of drugs offences, there is specific provision for confiscating the proceeds of the crime and so there is no need to use a fine to achieve this objective (see Chapter 18, 18.4).

A fine may be imposed at the same time as a compensation order. However, s 130(12) of the 2000 Act provides that, if an offender has insufficient means to pay both a fine and a compensation order, the compensation order takes priority; thus, in such a case, the fine will be reduced or a different sentence altogether imposed.

A fine may be imposed in addition to an order to pay the costs incurred by the prosecution, but the court should ensure that the total sum is within the offender's means.

15.2 ABSOLUTE AND CONDITIONAL DISCHARGES

Section 12(1) of the Powers of Criminal Courts (Sentencing) Act 2000 provides that, where a court has convicted a person of an offence but is of the opinion, having regard to the nature of the offence and the character of the offender, that it is inexpedient to inflict punishment, the court may either:

- discharge the offender absolutely; or
- discharge the offender subject to a condition that he does not commit a further offence during the period (of up to three years) specified in the order.

15.2.1 Absolute discharge

The effect of an absolute discharge is that, apart from the fact that a conviction is recorded against the offender, no penalty is imposed.

An absolute discharge is appropriate where the court decides that it would be wrong to take any action against the accused. An absolute discharge may be ordered if the defendant is convicted of a very trivial offence or if the circumstances of the commission of the offence show little or no blame on the part of the defendant. In *R v O'Toole* (1971) 55 Cr App R 206, for example, an ambulance driver who collided with another vehicle while answering a 999 call received an absolute discharge.

15.2.2 Conditional discharge

The only condition of a conditional discharge is that the offender does not commit another offence during the period of the conditional discharge. No other condition can be imposed.

Before ordering a conditional discharge, the court must explain to the offender that if he commits another offence during the period of the conditional discharge she is liable to be sentenced for the original offence (as well as the subsequent offence) (s 12(4) of the Powers of Criminal Courts (Sentencing) Act 2000).

A conditional discharge may be appropriate instead of a fine where the offence is not sufficiently serious to justify a community sentence or there is sufficient personal mitigation to render a community sentence too harsh.

15.2.3 Breach of conditional discharge

If the offender commits an offence during the period of a conditional discharge, the court dealing with the breach may deal with the offender in any way in which the offender could have been dealt with when the conditional discharge was ordered (s 13(6) of the Powers of Criminal Courts (Sentencing) Act 2000).

A magistrates' court can only deal with the breach of a conditional discharge imposed by a magistrates' court; the Crown Court can deal with the breach of a conditional discharge imposed by a Crown Court or a magistrates' court (s 13(2) of the Powers of Criminal Courts (Sentencing) Act 2000).

In practice, little is usually done in respect of a breach of a conditional discharge. A custodial sentence can only be imposed in respect of the original offence if that offence was sufficiently serious to justify a custodial sentence; this will rarely be the case. Similarly, a community sentence can only be imposed if the original offence merited such a sentence but there was sufficient personal mitigation in respect of the offender for a conditional discharge to be imposed instead.

Thus, the breach of a conditional discharge is often ignored, or else a fine is imposed for the original offence.

15.2.4 Combining discharges with other orders

As a discharge is only to be imposed where it is inexpedient to inflict punishment (s 12(1) of the 2000 Act), it would be wrong in principle to combine a discharge with any other sentence for the same offence (*R v Savage* (1983) 5 Cr App R(S) 216). So, a conditional discharge cannot be combined with a fine (*R v Sanck* (1990) 12 Cr App R(S) 155).

Section 12(7) of the 2000 Act, however, enables the court to make an order for costs and/or compensation even if it discharges the offender.

15.2.5 Effect of conditional or absolute discharge

Section 14(1) of the Powers of Criminal Courts (Sentencing) Act 2000 provides that a conditional or absolute discharge only counts as a conviction for certain purposes.

It follows that, where an offence is dealt with by way of a discharge, conviction for that offence cannot amount to a breach of an earlier order. So, for example, if the offender commits an offence during the currency of a conditional discharge or during the operational period of a suspended sentence, but the later offence is dealt with by way of a discharge, the court cannot re-sentence the offender for the earlier offence or activate the suspended sentence.

However, an offence which is dealt with by way of conditional discharge does amount to a conviction where an offence is committed during the currency of the conditional discharge and the offender is re-sentenced for the offence for which the conditional discharge was imposed (s 14(2) of the Powers of Criminal Courts (Sentencing) Act 2000).

Furthermore, an offence dealt with by way of discharge appears on the offender's criminal record.

15.3   BINDING OVER TO KEEP THE PEACE

Section 1 of the Justices of the Peace Act 1968 declares that any 'court of record' with criminal jurisdiction (that is, a magistrates' court, the Crown Court, the Court of Appeal) has the power to bind a person over to be of good behaviour. This may be done by requiring the person to enter into his own recognizance or to find sureties, or both, and he may be committed to prison if he does not comply.

A similar power arises under s 115 of the Magistrates' Courts Act 1980 where the court has finished hearing a 'complaint' (a method of bringing proceedings of a civil or quasi-civil nature before magistrates).

The effect of the order is that the offender promises to pay a specified sum of money (or sureties promise to pay money on his behalf) if he misbehaves during a period specified by the court.

When exercising its power to bind over, the court must fix the period during which the bind over is to last (that is, the period during which misbehaviour will result in forfeiture of the recognizance) and must also fix the amount to be forfeited if the person breaches the order.

There is no statutory maximum for the amount of the recognizance. A person could, therefore, be convicted of an offence and bound over in a sum which exceeds the maximum fine that could be imposed for that offence (*R v Sandbach Justices ex p Williams* [1935] 2 KB 192).

Similarly, there is no statutory maximum for the length of time for which the order is to run.

The only conditions which may be imposed are that the person bound over must keep the peace and be of good behaviour. No other conditions may be imposed (*R v Randall* (1986) 8 Cr App R(S) 433).

A person may be bound over at any stage of criminal proceedings. It may be done, for example, where the prosecution discontinue the case, or offer no evidence.

The power to bind over arises 'not by reason of any offence having been committed, but as a measure of preventive justice' to prevent a future breach of the peace (*Veater v Glennon* [1981] 1 WLR 567; [1981] 2 All ER 304). It follows that:

- the power to bind over does not apply only to defendants. It also applies to a witness appearing before the court (see *Sheldon v Bromfield Justices* [1964] 2 QB 573; [1964] 2 All ER 131) and to the alleged victim of the defendant's wrongdoing (see *R v Wilkins* [1907] 2 KB 380);

- it does not depend on a conviction being recorded against the person to be bound over. So, a defendant who has been acquitted can be bound over (*R v Inner London Crown Court ex p Benjamin* (1986) 85 Cr App R 267).

In *R v Middlesex Crown Court ex p Khan* (1997) *The Times*, 24 January, the Divisional Court held that where a defendant is acquitted, he may only be bound over if the judge is satisfied beyond reasonable doubt that he is a potential threat to other people and a person of violence.

In *R v Lincoln Crown Court ex p Jude* [1997] 3 All ER 737, the Divisional Court held that where a court intends to bind a person over, there is no requirement that the person must consent to the order.

15.3.1   Procedure

Where the court is minded to bind over a person who has not been charged with an offence or a defendant who has been acquitted, that person should be given the opportunity to make representations (*R v Hendon Justices ex p Gorchein* [1973] 1 WLR 1502; [1974] 1 All ER 168; *R v Woking Justices ex p Gossage* [1973] QB 448; [1973] 2 All ER 621).

Where the court proposes to bind over a defendant who has been convicted (in other words, using the power to bind over as a form of sentence), the defendant must be given the opportunity to make representations and the amount of the recognizance must take account of the defendant's means (*R v Central Criminal Court ex p Boulding* [1984] QB 813; [1984] 1 All ER 766).

15.3.2   Refusal to enter into recognizance

If the person refuses to be bound over, the court can impose a custodial sentence.

Where the bind over is ordered under s 115 of the Magistrates' Courts Act 1980 the maximum period of the custodial sentence is six months. There is no statutory limit to the custodial sentence where the defendant refuses to be bound over under s 1 of the Justices of the Peace Act 1968, although it would seem to be wrong in principle for a magistrates' court to exceed the usual limit on its sentencing powers.

Although the penalty for failing to enter into the recognizance is expressed to be committal to prison, this is deemed to include detention in a young offender institution (and so the power to impose a custodial sentence applies to the offender who is aged 15 to 20) (*Howley v Oxford* (1985) 81 Cr App R 246).

Thus, a person under 15 could only be bound over if he agreed to be bound over (*Conlan v Oxford* (1983) 79 Cr App R 157).

15.3.3 Failure to comply with conditions of bind over

If the person who has been bound over fails to keep the peace and to be of good behaviour, the court may order the payment of some or all of the amount of the recognizance.

When the court orders forfeiture of the recognizance it must fix a term of imprisonment (or detention in a young offender institution) to be served in default of payment (s 31 of the Powers of Criminal Courts Act 1973).

Forfeiture proceedings in respect of a bind over ordered by a magistrates' court are commenced by means of a complaint to the court which made the original order (s 120 of the Magistrates' Courts Act 1980).

Forfeiture proceedings are regarded as civil, not criminal, and so the civil standard of proof (the balance of probabilities) applies (*R v Marlow Justices ex p O'Sullivan* [1984] QB 381; [1983] 3 All ER 578). Nevertheless, the person should be given an opportunity to present evidence (including calling witnesses) and to make representations as to why the recognizance should not be forfeited (*R v McGregor* [1945] 2 All ER 180).

15.3.4 Binding over parents and guardians: offenders under 16

See Chapter 17, 17.4 for details of the power to bind over the parent or guardian of an offender who has not attained the age of 16.

TABLE OF STATUTORY MATERIALS

STATUTORY MATERIALS

FINES

POWERS OF CRIMINAL COURTS (SENTENCING) ACT 2000

Section 126: Powers to order statement as to offender's financial circumstances.

(1) Where an individual has been convicted of an offence, the court may, before sentencing him, make a financial circumstances order with respect to him.

(2) Where a magistrates' court has been notified in accordance with section 12(4) of the Magistrates' Courts Act 1980 that an individual desires to plead guilty without appearing before the court, the court may make a financial circumstances order with respect to him.

(3) In this section 'a financial circumstances order' means, in relation to any individual, an order requiring him to give to the court, within such period as may be specified in the order, such a statement of his financial circumstances as the court may require.

(4) An individual who without reasonable excuse fails to comply with a financial circumstances order shall be liable on summary conviction to a fine not exceeding level 3 on the standard scale.

(5) If an individual, in furnishing any statement in pursuance of a financial circumstances order:

   (a) makes a statement which he knows to be false in a material particular;

   (b) recklessly furnishes a statement which is false in a material particular; or

   (c) knowingly fails to disclose any material fact, he shall be liable on summary conviction to imprisonment for a term not exceeding three months or a fine not exceeding level 4 on the standard scale or both.

(6) Proceedings in respect of an offence under sub-section (5) above may, notwithstanding anything in section 127(1) of the Magistrates' Courts Act 1980 (limitation of time), be commenced at any time within two years from the date of the commission of the offence or within six months from its first discovery by the prosecutor, whichever period expires the earlier.

Section 128: Fixing of fines

(1) Before fixing the amount of any fine to be imposed on an offender who is an individual, a court shall inquire into his financial circumstances.

(2) The amount of any fine fixed by a court shall be such as, in the opinion of the court, reflects the seriousness of the offence.

(3) In fixing the amount of any fine to be imposed on an offender (whether an individual or other person), a court shall take into account the circumstances of the case including, among other things, the financial circumstances of the offender so far as they are known, or appear, to the court.

(4) Sub-section (3) above applies whether taking into account the financial circumstances of the offender has the effect of increasing or reducing the amount of the fine.

(5) Where:

    (a) an offender has been convicted in his absence in pursuance of section 11 or 12 of the Magistrates' Courts Act 1980 (non-appearance of accused); or

    (b) an offender:

        (i) has failed to comply with an order under section 126(1) above, or

        (ii) has otherwise failed to co-operate with the court in its inquiry into his financial circumstances,

and the court considers that it has insufficient information to make a proper determination of the financial circumstances of the offender, it may make such determination as it thinks fit.

Section 129: Remission of fines

(1) This section applies where a court has, in fixing the amount of a fine, determined the offender's financial circumstances under section 128(5) above.

(2) If, on subsequently inquiring into the offender's financial circumstances, the court is satisfied that had it had the results of that inquiry when sentencing the offender it would:

    (a) have fixed a smaller amount; or

    (b) not have fined him,

it may remit the whole or any part of the fine.

(3) Where under this section the court remits the whole or part of a fine after a term of imprisonment has been fixed under section 139 below (powers of Crown Court in relation to fines) or section 82(5) of the Magistrates' Courts Act 1980 (magistrates' powers in relation to default), it shall reduce the term by the corresponding proportion.

(4) In calculating any reduction required by sub-section (3) above, any fraction of a day shall be ignored.

ENFORCEMENT OF FINES IMPOSED BY MAGISTRATES' COURT

MAGISTRATES' COURTS ACT 1980

Section 82: Restriction on power to impose imprisonment for default

(1) A magistrates' court shall not on the occasion of convicting an offender of an offence issue a warrant of commitment for a default in paying any sum adjudged to be paid by the conviction unless:

    (a) in the case of an offence punishable with imprisonment, he appears to the court to have sufficient means to pay the sum forthwith;

    (b) it appears to the court that he is unlikely to remain long enough at a place of abode in the United Kingdom to enable payment of the sum to be enforced by other methods; or

    (c) on the occasion of that conviction the court sentences him to immediate imprisonment, detention in a young offender institution for that or another offence, or he is already serving a sentence of custody for life, or a term of imprisonment, detention in a young offender institution, or detention under section 9 of the Criminal Justice Act 1982.

    ...

(3) Where on the occasion of the offender's conviction a magistrates' court does not issue a warrant of commitment for a default in paying any such sum as aforesaid or fix a term of imprisonment under ... section 77(2) which is to be served by him in the event of any such default, it shall not thereafter issue a warrant of commitment for any such default or for want of sufficient distress to satisfy such a sum unless:

    (a) he is already serving a sentence of custody for life, or a term of imprisonment, detention in a young offender institution, or detention under section 9 of the Criminal Justice Act 1982; or

    (b) the court has since the conviction inquired into his means in his presence on at least one occasion.

(4) Where a magistrates' court is required by sub-section (3) above to inquire into a person's means, the court may not on the occasion of the inquiry or at any time thereafter issue a warrant of commitment for a default in paying any such sum unless:

    (a) in the case of an offence punishable with imprisonment, the offender appears to the court to have sufficient means to pay the sum forthwith; or

    (b) the court:

        (i) is satisfied that the default is due to the offender's wilful refusal or culpable neglect; and

      (ii) has considered or tried all other methods of enforcing payment of the sum and it appears to the court that they are inappropriate or unsuccessful.

(4A) The methods of enforcing payment mentioned in sub-section (4)(b)(ii) above are:

    (a) a warrant of distress under section 76 above;

    (b) an application to the High Court or county court for enforcement under section 87 below [enforcement as if the fine were a judgment of the High Court/county court];

    (c) an order under section 88 below [supervision pending payment];

    (d) an attachment of earnings order; and

    (e) if the offender is under the age of 25, an order under section 17 of the Criminal Justice Act 1982 (attendance centre orders).

    ...

Section 84: Power to require statement of means

(1) A magistrates' court may, either before or on inquiring into a person's means under section 82 above ... order him to furnish to the court within a period specified in the order such a statement of means as the court may require.

(2) A person who fails to comply with an order under sub-section (1) above shall be liable on summary conviction to a fine not exceeding level 3 on the standard scale.

(3) If a person in furnishing any statement in pursuance of an order under sub-section (1) above makes a statement which he knows to be false in a material particular or recklessly furnishes a statement which is false in a material particular, or knowingly fails to disclose any material fact, he shall be liable on summary conviction to imprisonment for a term not exceeding 4 months or a fine not exceeding level 3 on the standard scale or both.

    ...

ENFORCEMENT OF CROWN COURT FINES

POWERS OF CRIMINAL COURTS (SENTENCING) ACT 2000

Section 139: Powers and duties of Crown Court in relation to fines and forfeited recognizances

(1) Subject to the provisions of this section, if the Crown Court imposes a fine on any person or forfeits his recognizance, the court may make an order:

    (a) allowing time for the payment of the amount of the fine or the amount due under the recognizance;

    (b) directing payment of that amount by instalments of such amounts and on such dates as may be specified in the order;

    (c) in the case of a recognizance, discharging the recognizance or reducing the amount due under it.

(2) Subject to the provisions of this section, if the Crown Court imposes a fine on any person or forfeits his recognizance, the court shall make an order fixing a term of imprisonment or of detention under section 108 above (detention of persons aged 18 to 20 for default) which he is to undergo if any sum which he is liable to pay is not duly paid or recovered.

(3) No person shall on the occasion when a fine is imposed on him or his recognizance is forfeited by the Crown Court be committed to prison or detained in pursuance of an order under sub-section (2) above unless:

    (a) in the case of an offence punishable with imprisonment, he appears to the court to have sufficient means to pay the sum forthwith;

    (b) it appears to the court that he is unlikely to remain long enough at a place of abode in the United Kingdom to enable payment of the sum to be enforced by other methods; or

    (c) on the occasion when the order is made the court sentences him to immediate imprisonment, custody for life or detention in a young offender institution for that or another offence, or so sentences him for an offence in addition to forfeiting his recognizance, or he is already serving a sentence of custody for life or a term:

        (i) of imprisonment;

        (ii) of detention in a young offender institution; or

        (iii) of detention under section 108 above.

(4) The periods set out in the second column of the following Table shall be the maximum periods of imprisonment or detention under sub-section (2) above applicable respectively to the amounts set out opposite them.

Table

An amount not exceeding £200	7 days
An amount exceeding £200 but not exceeding £500	14 days
An amount exceeding £500 but not exceeding £1,000	28 days
An amount exceeding £1,000 but not exceeding £2,500	45 days
An amount exceeding £2,500 but not exceeding £5,000	3 months

An amount exceeding £5,000 but not exceeding £10,000	6 months
An amount exceeding £10,000 but not exceeding £20,000	12 months
An amount exceeding £20,000 but not exceeding £50,000	18 months
An amount exceeding £50,000 but not exceeding £100,000	2 years
An amount exceeding £100,000 but not exceeding £250,000	3 years
An amount exceeding £250,000 but not exceeding £1 million	5 years
An amount exceeding £1 million	10 years

(5) Where any person liable for the payment of a fine or a sum due under a recognizance to which this section applies is sentenced by the court to, or is serving or otherwise liable to serve, a term of imprisonment or detention in a young offender institution or a term of detention under section 108 above, the court may order that any term of imprisonment or detention fixed under sub-section (2) above shall not begin to run until after the end of the first-mentioned term.

(6) The power conferred by this section to discharge a recognizance or reduce the amount due under it shall be in addition to the powers conferred by any other Act relating to the discharge, cancellation, mitigation or reduction of recognizances or sums forfeited under recognizances.

(7) Subject to sub-section (8) below, the powers conferred by this section shall not be taken as restricted by any enactment which authorises the Crown Court to deal with an offender in any way in which a magistrates' court might have dealt with him or could deal with him.

(8) Any term fixed under sub-section (2) above as respects a fine imposed in pursuance of such an enactment, that is to say a fine which the magistrates' court could have imposed, shall not exceed the period applicable to that fine (if imposed by the magistrates' court) under section 149(1) of the Customs and Excise Management Act 1979 (maximum periods of imprisonment in default of payment of certain fines).

(9) This section shall not apply to a fine imposed by the Crown Court on appeal against a decision of a magistrates' court, but sub-sections (2) to (4) above shall apply in relation to a fine imposed or recognizance forfeited by the criminal division of the Court of Appeal, or by the House of Lords on appeal from that division, as they apply in relation to a fine imposed or recognizance forfeited by the Crown Court, and the references to the Crown Court in sub-sections (2) and (3) above shall be construed accordingly.

(10) For the purposes of any reference in this section, however expressed, to the term of imprisonment or other detention to which a person has been

sentenced or which, or part of which, he has served, consecutive terms and terms which are wholly or partly concurrent shall, unless the context otherwise requires, be treated as a single term.

(11) Any reference in this section, however expressed, to a previous sentence shall be construed as a reference to a previous sentence passed by a court in Great Britain.

Section 140: Enforcement of fines imposed and recognizances forfeited by Crown Court

(1) Subject to sub-section (5) below, a fine imposed or a recognizance forfeited by the Crown Court shall be treated for the purposes of collection, enforcement and remission of the fine or other sum as having been imposed or forfeited:

(a) by a magistrates' court specified in an order made by the Crown Court; or

(b) if no such order is made, by the magistrates' court by which the offender was committed to the Crown Court to be tried or dealt with or by which he was sent to the Crown Court for trial under section 51 of the Crime and Disorder Act 1998,

and, in the case of a fine, as having been so imposed on conviction by the magistrates' court in question.

(2) Sub-section (3) below applies where a magistrates' court issues a warrant of commitment on a default in the payment of:

(a) a fine imposed by the Crown Court; or

(b) a sum due under a recognizance forfeited by the Crown Court.

(3) In such a case, the term of imprisonment or detention under section 108 above specified in the warrant of commitment as the term which the offender is liable to serve shall be:

(a) the term fixed by the Crown Court under section 139(2) above; or

(b) if that term has been reduced under section 79(2) of the Magistrates' Courts Act 1980 (part payment) or section 85(2) of that Act (remission), that term as so reduced,

notwithstanding that that term exceeds the period applicable to the case under section 149(1) of the Customs and Excise Management Act 1979 (maximum periods of imprisonment in default of payment of certain fines).

(4) Sub-sections (1) to (3) above shall apply in relation to a fine imposed or recognizance forfeited by the criminal division of the Court of Appeal, or by the House of Lords on appeal from that division, as they apply in relation to a fine imposed or recognizance forfeited by the Crown Court; and references in those sub-sections to the Crown Court (except the references in sub-section (1)(b)) shall be construed accordingly.

(5) A magistrates' court shall not, under section 85(1) or 120 of the Magistrates' Courts Act 1980 as applied by sub-section (1) above, remit the whole or any part of a fine imposed by, or sum due under a recognizance forfeited by:

(a) the Crown Court;

(b) the criminal division of the Court of Appeal; or

(c) the House of Lords on appeal from that division,

without the consent of the Crown Court.

(6) Any fine or other sum the payment of which is enforceable by a magistrates' court by virtue of this section shall be treated for the purposes of the Justices of the Peace Act 1997 and, in particular, section 60 of that Act (application of fines and fees) as having been imposed by a magistrates' court, or as being due under a recognizance forfeited by such a court.

CRIME (SENTENCES) ACT 1997

Section 35: Fine defaulters: general

(1) Sub-section (2) below applies in any case where a magistrates' court:

(a) has power under Part III of the 1980 Act to issue a warrant of commitment for default in paying a sum adjudged to be paid by a conviction of a magistrates' court (other than a sum ordered to be paid under section 71 of the Criminal Justice Act 1988 or section 2 of the Drug Trafficking Act 1994); or

(b) would, but for section 89 of the Powers of Criminal Courts (Sentencing) Act 2000 (restrictions on custodial sentences for persons under 21), have power to issue such a warrant for such default.

(2) The magistrates' court may:

(a) subject to sub-sections (4) to (6) and (11) below, make a community service order; or

(b) subject to sub-sections (7) to (11) below, make a curfew order,

in respect of the person in default instead of issuing a warrant of commitment or, as the case may be, proceeding under section 81 of the 1980 Act (enforcement of fines imposed on young offenders).

(3) Where a magistrates' court has power to make an order under sub-section (2)(a) or (b) above, it may, if it thinks it expedient to do so, postpone the making of the order until such time and on such conditions, if any, as it thinks just.

...

(6) In the case of an amount in default which is described in the first column of the following Table, the period of community service specified in an order under sub-section (2)(a) above shall not exceed the number of hours set out opposite that amount in the second column of that Table.

Table

Amount	Number of hours
An amount not exceeding £200	40 hours
An amount exceeding £200 but not exceeding £500	60 hours
An amount exceeding £500	100 hours

...

(9) In the case of an amount in default which is described in the first column of the following Table, the number of days to which an order under sub-section (2)(b) above relates shall not exceed the number of days set out opposite that amount in the second column of that Table.

Table

Amount	Number of days
An amount not exceeding £200	20 days
An amount exceeding £200 but not exceeding £500	0 days
An amount exceeding £500 but not exceeding £1,000	60 days
An amount exceeding £1,000 but not exceeding £2,500	90 days
An amount exceeding £2,500	180 days

(10) A magistrates' court shall not make an order under sub-section (2)(b) above in respect of a person who is under 16.

...

[Section 35(13) provides for the order under 35 to cease once full payment of the sum due has been made and for the pro rata reduction of the number of hours of community service or the number of days under a curfew order where part-payment is made.]

[Sub-section (14) empowers the Secretary of State to vary the figures given in s 35 for the number of hours of community service or the number of days for which a curfew order is to operate.]

...

Section 40: Fine defaulters

(1) This section applies in any case where a magistrates' court:

    (a) has power under Part III of the 1980 Act to issue a warrant of commitment for default in paying a sum adjudged to be paid by a conviction of a magistrates' court (other than a sum ordered to be paid under section 71 of the Criminal Justice Act 1988 or section 2 of the Drug Trafficking Act 1994); or

    (b) would, but for section 89 of the Powers of Criminal Courts (Sentencing) Act 2000 (restrictions on custodial sentences for persons under 21), have power to issue such a warrant for such default.

(2) Subject to sub-section (3) below, the magistrates' court may, instead of issuing a warrant of commitment or, as the case may be, proceeding under

section 81 of the 1980 Act (enforcement of fines imposed on young offenders), order the person in default to be disqualified, for such period not exceeding 12 months as it thinks fit, for holding or obtaining a driving licence.

...

ABSOLUTE AND CONDITIONAL DISCHARGES

POWERS OF CRIMINAL COURTS (SENTENCING) ACT 2000

Section 12: Absolute and conditional discharge

(1) Where a court by or before which a person is convicted of an offence (not being an offence the sentence for which is fixed by law or falls to be imposed under section 109(2), 110(2) or 111(2) below) is of the opinion, having regard to the circumstances including the nature of the offence and the character of the offender, that it is inexpedient to inflict punishment, the court may make an order either:

    (a) discharging him absolutely; or

    (b) if the court thinks fit, discharging him subject to the condition that he commits no offence during such period, not exceeding three years from the date of the order, as may be specified in the order.

(2) Sub-section (1)(b) above has effect subject to section 66(4) of the Crime and Disorder Act 1998 (effect of reprimands and warnings).

(3) An order discharging a person subject to such a condition as is mentioned in sub-section (1)(b) above is in this Act referred to as an 'order for conditional discharge'; and the period specified in any such order is in this Act referred to as 'the period of conditional discharge'.

(4) Before making an order for conditional discharge, the court shall explain to the offender in ordinary language that if he commits another offence during the period of conditional discharge he will be liable to be sentenced for the original offence.

(5) If (by virtue of section 13 below) a person conditionally discharged under this section is sentenced for the offence in respect of which the order for conditional discharge was made, that order shall cease to have effect.

(6) On making an order for conditional discharge, the court may, if it thinks it expedient for the purpose of the offender's reformation, allow any person who consents to do so to give security for the good behaviour of the offender.

(7) Nothing in this section shall be construed as preventing a court, on discharging an offender absolutely or conditionally in respect of any offence, from making an order for costs against the offender or imposing

any disqualification on him or from making in respect of the offence an order under section 130, 143 or 148 below (compensation orders, deprivation orders and restitution orders).

Section 13: Commission of further offence by person conditionally discharged

(1) If it appears to the Crown Court, where that court has jurisdiction in accordance with sub-section (2) below, or to a justice of the peace having jurisdiction in accordance with that sub-section, that a person in whose case an order for conditional discharge has been made:

    (a) has been convicted by a court in Great Britain of an offence committed during the period of conditional discharge; and

    (b) has been dealt with in respect of that offence,

that court or justice may, subject to sub-section (3) below, issue a summons requiring that person to appear at the place and time specified in it or a warrant for his arrest.

(2) Jurisdiction for the purposes of sub-section (1) above may be exercised:

    (a) if the order for conditional discharge was made by the Crown Court, by that court;

    (b) if the order was made by a magistrates' court, by a justice acting for the petty sessions area for which that court acts.

(3) A justice of the peace shall not issue a summons under this section except on information and shall not issue a warrant under this section except on information in writing and on oath.

(4) A summons or warrant issued under this section shall direct the person to whom it relates to appear or to be brought before the court by which the order for conditional discharge was made.

(5) If a person in whose case an order for conditional discharge has been made by the Crown Court is convicted by a magistrates' court of an offence committed during the period of conditional discharge, the magistrates' court:

    (a) may commit him to custody or release him on bail until he can be brought or appear before the Crown Court; and

    (b) if it does so, shall send to the Crown Court a copy of the minute or memorandum of the conviction entered in the register, signed by the justices' chief executive by whom the register is kept.

(6) Where it is proved to the satisfaction of the court by which an order for conditional discharge was made that the person in whose case the order was made has been convicted of an offence committed during the period of conditional discharge, the court may deal with him, for the offence for which the order was made, in any way in which it could deal with him if he had just been convicted by or before that court of that offence.

(7) If a person in whose case an order for conditional discharge has been made by a magistrates' court:

   (a) is convicted before the Crown Court of an offence committed during the period of conditional discharge; or

   (b) is dealt with by the Crown Court for any such offence in respect of which he was committed for sentence to the Crown Court,

   the Crown Court may deal with him, for the offence for which the order was made, in any way in which the magistrates' court could deal with him if it had just convicted him of that offence.

(8) If a person in whose case an order for conditional discharge has been made by a magistrates' court is convicted by another magistrates' court of any offence committed during the period of conditional discharge, that other court may, with the consent of the court which made the order, deal with him, for the offence for which the order was made, in any way in which the court could deal with him if it had just convicted him of that offence.

(9) Where an order for conditional discharge has been made by a magistrates' court in the case of an offender under 18 years of age in respect of an offence triable only on indictment in the case of an adult, any powers exercisable under sub-section (6), (7) or (8) above by that or any other court in respect of the offender after he attains the age of 18 shall be powers to do either or both of the following:

   (a) to impose a fine not exceeding £5,000 for the offence in respect of which the order was made;

   (b) to deal with the offender for that offence in any way in which a magistrates' court could deal with him if it had just convicted him of an offence punishable with imprisonment for a term not exceeding six months.

(10) The reference in sub-section (6) above to a person's having been convicted of an offence committed during the period of conditional discharge is a reference to his having been so convicted by a court in Great Britain.

Section 14: Effect of discharge

(1) Subject to sub-section (2) below, a conviction of an offence for which an order is made under section 12 above discharging the offender absolutely or conditionally shall be deemed not to be a conviction for any purpose other than the purposes of the proceedings in which the order is made and of any subsequent proceedings which may be taken against the offender under section 13 above.

(2) Where the offender was aged 18 or over at the time of his conviction of the offence in question and is subsequently sentenced (under section 13 above) for that offence, sub-section (1) above shall cease to apply to the conviction.

(3) Without prejudice to sub-sections (1) and (2) above, the conviction of an offender who is discharged absolutely or conditionally under section 12

above shall in any event be disregarded for the purposes of any enactment or instrument which:

(a) imposes any disqualification or disability upon convicted persons; or

(b) authorises or requires the imposition of any such disqualification or disability.

(4) Sub-sections (1) to (3) above shall not affect:

(a) any right of an offender discharged absolutely or conditionally under section 12 above to rely on his conviction in bar of any subsequent proceedings for the same offence;

(b) the restoration of any property in consequence of the conviction of any such offender; or

(c) the operation, in relation to any such offender, of any enactment or instrument in force on 1st July 1974 which is expressed to extend to persons dealt with under section 1(1) of the Probation of Offenders Act 1907 as well as to convicted persons.

CHAPTER 16

YOUNG OFFENDERS: CUSTODIAL SENTENCES

There are three types of custodial sentence which apply to offenders who have not attained the age of 21. The first is detention in a young offender institution under s 96 of the Powers of Criminal Courts (Sentencing) Act 2000 (18–20 year olds), detention and training orders under s 100 of the Act (offenders under 18), and long term detention under s 91 of the Act.

The two main differences between custodial sentences for those under 21 as against those over 21 are:

- young offenders and adults do not serve their sentences together: young offenders are detained separately from adult offenders;

- unlike a sentence of imprisonment, a sentence of detention in a young offender institution or a detention and training order cannot be suspended. A custodial sentence on an offender who has not attained the age of 21 must therefore be immediate.

16.1 DETENTION AND TRAINING ORDERS

Section 100 of the Powers of Criminal Courts (Sentencing) Act 2000 provides for the making of a detention and training order where an offender aged between 12 and 17 year old is convicted of an offence which (in the case of an adult offender) is punishable with imprisonment.

A detention and training order is a custodial sentence and so the requirements set out in ss 79 to 81 of the Powers of Criminal Courts (Sentencing) Act 2000 apply. In particular, the court must be satisfied that the seriousness of the offence requires such a sentence or, in the case of a violent or sexual offence, such a sentence is needed to protect the public from serious harm from the offender. Section 83 restricts the power of the court to impose a detention and training order on someone who is not legally represented.

Where the offender has not attained the age of 15 at the date of conviction, a detention and training order can only be imposed if he is a 'persistent offender' (s 100(2)(a)). The term 'persistent offender' is not defined, but would presumably require that the offender has been convicted on at least two previous occasions.

Where the offender is 10 or 11 at the date of conviction, a detention and training order cannot be imposed unless the Secretary of State extends such orders to offenders of this age group (and there are apparently no immediate plans to do so) and if such a sentence is the only way of protecting the public from further offending by that offender (s 100(2)(b)).

16.1.1   Duration of detention and training order

The total length of a detention and training order can be four, six, eight, 10, 12, 18 or 24 months (s 101(1)). However, the term of a detention and training order cannot exceed the maximum term of imprisonment that the Crown Court could impose on an adult offender for that offence (s 101(2)).

Where the offender is convicted of more than one offence for which a detention and training order could be imposed, the court can impose consecutive detention and training orders but the total term imposed must not exceed 24 months (s 101(3) and (4)).

Section 102(2) provides that the period of detention under a detention and training order is to be one half of the total term of the order.

Section 101 empowers both the Crown Court and a youth court to impose a detention and training order for up to 24 months. As half of the period of the detention and training order is spent in custody, this means that the youth court is empowered to impose 12 months custody (plus 12 months supervision) for a single offence. The youth court's powers in this regard are therefore greater than those of the adult magistrates' court, which can only impose 6 months' custody for a single offence on an offender who has attained the age of 18. In *R v Medway Youth Court ex p A* [2000] 1 Cr App R(S) 191, a youth court sentenced a young offender to a 12 month secure training order under s 1 of the Criminal Justice and Public Order Act 1994 (the secure training order was effectively the precursor to the detention and training order). It was argued that this sentence was unlawful, given the general restriction on the sentencing powers of magistrates to six months' custody for a single offence (or 12 months for two or more either way offences). The Divisional Court held that Parliament had clearly intended to permit magistrates to exceed the usual six months limit in the case of secure training centre orders. The court went on to refer to the new detention and training orders and noted that, so far as these orders are concerned, magistrates are to 'have the power to make the sentences of any length the Crown Court could impose' up to the limit of 24 months and that the old restrictions on the justices' powers were 'not to be presumed to apply to new sentencing powers'.

16.1.2   Supervision under a detention and training order

Section 103(1) provides that the period of supervision under a detention and training order begins with the offender's release from custody (whether that is at the half way point or not) and lasts until the expiry of the total term of the detention and training order. During the period of supervision, the offender is under the supervision of a probation officer, a social worker, or a member of a youth offending team (s 103(3)).

The offender receives a notice setting out any requirements with which he must comply during the period of supervision (s 103(6)(b)). Section 104 provides that failure to comply with such requirements will lead to the issue of a summons requiring the offender to appear before the youth court which made the order or the youth court for the area where the offender lives. If breach of the requirement(s) is proved, the court may order detention of the offender for a period of up to three months, or the remainder of the term of the detention and training order, whichever is shorter, or it may impose a fine of up to £1,000 (s 104(3)).

16.1.3 Commission of further offences during supervision period

Section 105 applies where a person is convicted of an imprisonable offence committed after release from detention but before the expiry of the term of a detention and training order (that is, during the period of supervision). The court which convicts him of the later offence may (as well as dealing with him for the later offence) order his detention for a period equal in the length to the period between the date of the commission of the later offence and the date when the original detention and training order would have expired.

16.1.4 Early release from a detention and training order

Section 102(4) provides for discretionary early release: in the case of an order for a term of 8 months or more but less than 18 months, one month before the half way point of the total term of the order; in the case of an order for a term of 18 months or more, one or two months before that half way point. If the youth court, on an application by the Secretary of State, so orders, release can be postponed until one month after the half way point (detention and training orders of eight months or more but less than 18 months) or one or two months after the half way point (detention and training orders of 18 months or more): s 102(5).

Time spent in custody on remand prior to the imposition of a detention and training order is not automatically deducted, so s 101(8) requires the court, when determining the duration of a detention and training order, to take account of any period for which the offender was remanded in custody in connection with that, or a closely related offence. In *R v Ganley* (2000) *The Times*, 7 June, the Court of Appeal highlighted the fact that time spent in custody on remand is not automatically deducted from the period to be served under a detention and training order but has to be taken into account by the court when passing sentence.

16.2 DETENTION IN A YOUNG OFFENDER INSTITUTION

Section 96 of the Powers of Criminal Courts (Sentencing) Act 2000 provides that, where an offender who has attained the age of 18 but is under 21 is convicted of an offence which is punishable with imprisonment in the case of an offender who has attained the age of 21, the court may impose a sentence of detention in a young offender institution.

The criteria for imposing a sentence of detention in a young offender institution (being a custodial sentence) are the same as for the imposition of a sentence of imprisonment on an adult offender.

These criteria are discussed in detail in Chapter 13; in summary, a sentence of detention in a young offender institution may be imposed if:

- the offence, or the combination of the offence and one or more offences associated with it, was so serious that only a custodial sentence can be justified for the offence; or

- the offence is a violent or sexual one and only a custodial sentence would be adequate to protect the public from serious harm from the offender; or

- the offender refuses to consent to the imposition of an additional requirement in a probation order where consent is necessary for that requirement.

It should be noted that the Criminal Justice and Court Services Bill 2000 proposes the abolition of the sentence of the detention in a young offender institution. Following the abolition of this sentence, a court imposing a custodial sentence on a defendant aged 18 or over at the time of sentence will impose a sentence of imprisonment.

16.2.1 Procedural requirements

Chapter 13 sets out the procedure which the court has to impose before imposing a sentence of imprisonment on an adult. The same provisions regarding the procedure are to be followed before imposing a sentence of detention in a young offender institution. In particular, the court must first obtain a pre-sentence report (and can only refrain from doing so if the offence in question in triable only on indictment) and must explain why it is imposing a custodial sentence (see ss 79–81 of the Powers of Criminal Courts (Sentencing) Act 2000).

Furthermore, s 83 of the 2000 Act prevents the court from imposing a sentence of detention in a young offender institution on an offender who is not legally represented unless either the offender has refused to apply for legal representation funded by the Criminal Defence Service.

16.2.2   Relevant date for determining the age of the offender

Section 96 of the 2000 Act refers to an offender aged 15 to 20 being convicted on an offence and s 1(1) of that Act says that an offender who has not attained the age of 21 at the date of conviction cannot be sentenced to a term of imprisonment.

In *R v Danga* [1992] QB 476; [1992] 1 All ER 624, it was confirmed that the sentence to be imposed is to be determined according to the offender's age at the date of conviction, not at date of sentence. Thus, an offender who is 20 when convicted, but 21 when the sentence is passed, is sentenced to detention in a young offender institution not to imprisonment (*R v Danga* (1992) was followed in *R v Starkey* (1994) 15 Cr App R(S) 576).

16.2.3   Length of detention

The minimum period of detention in a young offender institution is 21 days (s 97(2) of the 2000 Act).

The maximum period of detention is the same as the maximum sentence of imprisonment in the case of an offender who has attained the age of 21. It follows that, where a young offender aged between 18 and 21 is convicted of a single offence which is triable either way, the magistrates may impose up to six months' detention; where such an offender is convicted of two or more offences which are triable either way, the magistrates may impose up to 12 months' detention. The Crown Court may impose detention of any length up to the maximum sentence applicable to the offence in question (that is, the maximum prison sentence for an adult offender).

Section 97(4) of the 2000 Act allows the court to impose consecutive sentences of detention in a young offender institution in the same way that consecutive sentences of imprisonment can be imposed on an offender who has attained the age of 21.

16.3   CUSTODY FOR LIFE/DURING HER MAJESTY'S PLEASURE

Section 93 of the Powers of Criminal Courts (Sentencing) Act 2000 provides that, where an offender under 21 is convicted of murder, the Crown Court must sentence the offender to custody for life. An offender aged 10–17 who is convicted of murder is sentenced to be detained during Her Majesty's pleasure under s 90 of the 2000 Act.

Section 94 provides that where an offender aged 18–20 is convicted of an offence which carries discretionary life imprisonment in the case of an adult offender, the Crown Court may impose custody for life. Usually, custody for life is only appropriate in a case other than murder if the offender is dangerous and is suffering from mental instability (*R v Powell* (1989) 11 Cr App R(S) 113). The mental instability does not have to be sufficiently severe to amount to mental illness (*R v Silson* (1987) 9 Cr App R(S) 282).

Under the Criminal Justice and Court Services Bill 2000, offenders aged 18–20 who would have been sentenced to custody for life will be sentenced to life imprisonment instead.

The Criminal Justice and Court Services Bill 2000 also changes the way that tariffs are set in cases of detention during Her Majesty's pleasure. It provides that the tariff should be set by the sentencing judge, and not by the Home Secretary (the tariff continuing to represent the minimum period that the offender must serve before a case can be referred to the Parole Board to consider release). The period set by the court will be open to appeal by the offender (or referral to the Court of Appeal by the Attorney General if he or she considers it unduly lenient). This is to give effect to the decision of the European Court of Human Rights in *V v UK; T v UK* (1999) *The Times*, 17 December. The arrangements for setting tariffs in the case of detention during Her Majesty's pleasure will therefore be the same as those that currently apply to offenders serving discretionary life sentences.

16.4   DETENTION UNDER S 91 OF THE POWERS OF CRIMINAL COURTS (SENTENCING) ACT 2000

As we have seen, once an offender has attained the age of 18, the courts can impose the same length of custody (by way of detention in a young offender institution) that they could in the case of an adult (by way of imprisonment). However, in the case of an offender who is under 18 at the date of conviction, the usual custodial sentence (the detention and training order) is limited to a total of 24 months (of which only half is served in custody). Plainly, this would not be adequate punishment where an offender under the age of 18 committed a really serious offence. Section 91 of the Powers of Criminal Courts (Sentencing) Act 2000 provides for long term detention in the following cases:

- where a young offender who has attained the age of 10 but is under 18 is convicted of manslaughter;

- where a young offender who has attained the age of 10 but is under 18 is convicted of an offence which carries at least 14 years' imprisonment in the case of an adult offender;

- where a young offender who has attained the age of 10 but is under 18 is convicted of indecent assault on a woman contrary to s 14 of the Sexual Offences Act 1956 or indecent assault on a man contrary to s 15 of the Sexual Offences Act 1956;

- where a young offender who has attained the age of 14 but is under 18 is convicted of causing death by dangerous driving (contrary to s 1 of the Road Traffic Act 1988) or with causing death by careless driving while under the influence of drink or drugs (contrary to s 3A of that Act).

Section 91 only applies to an offender who has been convicted in the Crown Court. Thus, a youth court cannot impose a sentence under this section.

16.4.1 Length of detention

The maximum sentence which can be imposed under s 91 is the same as the maximum sentence of imprisonment which can be imposed on an adult offender (s 91(3)). If the offence carries life imprisonment in the case of an adult, detention for life can be ordered under s 91.

Usually, a sentence under s 91 of the Powers of Criminal Courts (Sentencing) Act 2000 will be for more than two years (cf the 24 month detention and training order). However, unless the Secretary of State exercises his power under s 100(2) of the Act to extend the scope of detention and training orders to 11–12 year olds, there is no custodial sentence for offenders in that age group apart from detention for life for murder (s 90) or detention under s 91. In the case of offenders in that age group, a relatively short sentence under s 91 may be appropriate. In *R v LH* [1997] 2 Cr App R(S) 319, for example, the Court of Appeal upheld a sentence of 12 months' detention under s 91 for indecent assault where the offender was too young for any other custodial sentence; also *R v Nicholls and Warden* [1998] 1 Cr App R(S) 66, where the Court of Appeal reduced a sentence on such a youngster of two years' detention to 12 months' detention.

16.4.2 Procedure to be followed before imposing a sentence under s 91

A sentence of detention under s 91 cannot be imposed on an offender who is not legally represented unless either the offender has refused to apply for legal representation funded by the Criminal Defence Service or representation has been withdrawn because of misconduct on the part of the offender (s 83 of the 2000 Act).

16.4.3 Effect of time spent on remand

Where a young offender has spent time in custody (or in local authority secure accommodation) because bail was withheld before conviction and/or sentence, the time spent in custody or in secure accommodation counts towards the service of any custodial sentence (whether detention in a young offender institution or long term detention under s 91 of the 2000 Act) subsequently imposed for the offence for which bail was withheld, and so that period will be deducted from the sentence which is imposed by the court in order to calculate how long the offender will actually have to serve in custody (s 67 of the Criminal Justice Act 1967, as amended by Sched 11, para 2, of the Criminal Justice Act 1991).

16.4.4   Early release

The provisions relating to early release from sentences of imprisonment (see Chapter 13) apply equally to sentences of detention in a young offender institution and to sentences of long term detention under s 91 of the 2000 Act.

TABLE OF STATUTORY MATERIALS

STATUTORY MATERIALS

POWERS OF CRIMINAL COURTS (SENTENCING) ACT 2000

Section 89: Restriction on imposing imprisonment on persons under 21

(1) Subject to sub-section (2) below, no court shall:

    (a) pass a sentence of imprisonment on a person for an offence if he is aged under 21 when convicted of the offence; or

    (b) commit a person aged under 21 to prison for any reason.

(2) Nothing in sub-section (1) above shall prevent the committal to prison of a person aged under 21 who is:

    (a) remanded in custody;

    (b) committed in custody for trial or sentence; or

    (c) sent in custody for trial under section 51 of the Crime and Disorder Act 1998.

Section 90: Offenders who commit murder when under 18; duty to detain at Her Majesty's pleasure

Where a person convicted of murder appears to the court to have been aged under 18 at the time the offence was committed, the court shall (notwithstanding anything in this or any other Act) sentence him to be detained during Her Majesty's pleasure.

Section 91: Offenders under 18 convicted of certain serious offences; power to detain for specified period

(1) Sub-section (3) below applies where a person aged under 18 is convicted on indictment of:

    (a) an offence punishable in the case of a person aged 21 or over with imprisonment for 14 years or more, not being an offence the sentence for which is fixed by law; or

    (b) an offence under section 14 of the Sexual Offences Act 1956 (indecent assault on a woman); or

    (c) an offence under section 15 of that Act (indecent assault on a man) committed after 30th September 1997.

(2) Sub-section (3) below also applies where a person aged at least 14 but under 18 is convicted of an offence under:

(a) section 1 of the Road Traffic Act 1988 (causing death by dangerous driving); or

(b) section 3A of that Act (causing death by careless driving while under influence of drink or drugs).

(3) If the court is of the opinion that none of the other methods in which the case may legally be dealt with is suitable, the court may sentence the offender to be detained for such period, not exceeding the maximum term of imprisonment with which the offence is punishable in the case of a person aged 21 or over, as may be specified in the sentence.

(4) Sub-section (3) above is subject to (in particular) sections 79 and 80 above.

Section 93: Duty to impose custody for life in certain cases where offender under 21

Where a person aged under 21 is convicted of murder or any other offence the sentence for which is fixed by law as imprisonment for life, the court shall sentence him to custody for life unless he is liable to be detained under section 90 above.

Section 94: Power to impose custody for life in certain other cases where offender at least 18 but under 21

(1) Where a person aged at least 18 but under 21 is convicted of an offence:

(a) for which the sentence is not fixed by law; but

(b) for which a person aged 21 or over would be liable to imprisonment for life,

the court shall, if it considers that a sentence for life would be appropriate, sentence him to custody for life.

(2) Sub-section (1) above is subject to (in particular) sections 79 and 80 above, but this sub-section does not apply in relation to a sentence which falls to be imposed under section 109(2) below.

Section 96: Detention in a young offender institution for other cases where offender at least 18 but under 21

Subject to sections 90, 93 and 94 above, where:

(a) a person aged at least 18 but under 21 is convicted of an offence which is punishable with imprisonment in the case of a person aged 21 or over; and

(b) the court is of the opinion that either or both of paragraphs (a) and (b) of section 79(2) above apply or the case falls within section 79(3),

the sentence that the court is to pass is a sentence of detention in a young offender institution.

Section 97: Term of detention in a young offender institution, and consecutive sentences

(1) The maximum term of detention in a young offender institution that a court may impose for an offence is the same as the maximum term of imprisonment that it may impose for that offence.

(2) Subject to sub-section (3) below, a court shall not pass a sentence for an offender's detention in a young offender institution for less than 21 days.

(3) A court may pass a sentence of detention in a young offender institution for less than 21 days for an offence under section 65(6) of the Criminal Justice Act 1991 (breach of requirement imposed on young offender on his release from detention).

(4) Where:

(a) an offender is convicted of more than one offence for which he is liable to a sentence of detention in a young offender institution; or

(b) an offender who is serving a sentence of detention in a young offender institution is convicted of one or more further offences for which he is liable to such a sentence,

the court shall have the same power to pass consecutive sentences of detention in a young offender institution as if they were sentences of imprisonment.

(5) Subject to section 84 above (restriction on consecutive sentences for released prisoners), where an offender who:

(a) is serving a sentence of detention in a young offender institution; and

(b) is aged 21 or over,

is convicted of one or more further offences for which he is liable to imprisonment, the court shall have the power to pass one or more sentences of imprisonment to run consecutively upon the sentence of detention in a young offender institution.

Section 99: Conversion of sentence of detention or custody to sentence of imprisonment

(1) Subject to the following provisions of this section, where an offender has been sentenced to a term of detention in a young offender institution and either:

(a) he has attained the age of 21; or

(b) he has attained the age of 18 and has been reported to the Secretary of State by the board of visitors of the institution in which he is detained as exercising a bad influence on the other inmates of the institution or as behaving in a disruptive manner to the detriment of those inmates,

the Secretary of State may direct that he shall be treated as if he had been sentenced to imprisonment for the same term.

(5) This section applies to a person:

    (a) who is detained under section 90 or 91 above; or

    (b) who is serving a sentence of custody for life,

as it applies to a person serving a sentence of detention in a young offender institution.

DETENTION AND TRAINING ORDERS

Section 100: Offenders under 18: detention and training orders

(1) Subject to sections 90, 91 and 93 above and sub-section (2) below, where:

    (a) a child or young person (that is to say, any person aged under 18) is convicted of an offence which is punishable with imprisonment in the case of a person aged 21 or over; and

    (b) the court is of the opinion that either or both of paragraphs (a) and (b) of section 79(2) above apply or the case falls within section 79(3),

the sentence that the court is to pass is a detention and training order.

(2) A court shall not make a detention and training order:

    (a) in the case of an offender under the age of 15 at the time of the conviction, unless it is of the opinion that he is a persistent offender;

    (b) in the case of an offender under the age of 12 at that time, unless:

        (i) it is of the opinion that only a custodial sentence would be adequate to protect the public from further offending by him; and

        (ii) the offence was committed on or after such date as the Secretary of State may by order appoint.

(3) A detention and training order is an order that the offender in respect of whom it is made shall be subject, for the term specified in the order, to a period of detention and training followed by a period of supervision.

(4) On making a detention and training order in a case where sub-section (2) above applies, it shall be the duty of the court (in addition to the duty imposed by section 79(4) above) to state in open court that it is of the opinion mentioned in paragraph (a) or, as the case may be, paragraphs (a) and (b)(i) of that sub-section.

Section 101: Term of order, consecutive terms and taking account of remands

(1) Subject to sub-section (2) below, the term of a detention and training order made in respect of an offence (whether by a magistrates' court or otherwise) shall be 4, 6, 8, 10, 12, 18 or 24 months.

(2) The term of a detention and training order may not exceed the maximum term of imprisonment that the Crown Court could (in the case of an offender aged 21 or over) impose for the offence.

(3) Subject to sub-sections (4) and (6) below, a court making a detention and training order may order that its term shall commence on the expiry of the term of any other detention and training order made by that or any other court.

(4) A court shall not make in respect of an offender a detention and training order the effect of which would be that he would be subject to detention and training orders for a term which exceeds 24 months.

(5) Where the term of the detention and training orders to which an offender would otherwise be subject exceeds 24 months, the excess shall be treated as remitted.

(6) A court making a detention and training order shall not order that its term shall commence on the expiry of the term of a detention and training order under which the period of supervision has already begun (under section 103(1) below).

(7) Where a detention and training order ('the new order') is made in respect of an offender who is subject to a detention and training order under which the period of supervision has begun ('the old order'), the old order shall be disregarded in determining:

    (a) for the purposes of sub-section (4) above whether the effect of the new order would be that the offender would be subject to detention and training orders for a term which exceeds 24 months; and

    (b) for the purposes of sub-section (5) above whether the term of the detention and training orders to which the offender would (apart from that sub-section) be subject exceeds 24 months.

(8) In determining the term of a detention and training order for an offence, the court shall take account of any period for which the offender has been remanded in custody in connection with the offence, or any other offence the charge for which was founded on the same facts or evidence.

(9) Where a court proposes to make detention and training orders in respect of an offender for two or more offences:

    (a) sub-section (8) above shall not apply; but

    (b) in determining the total term of the detention and training orders it proposes to make in respect of the offender, the court shall take account of the total period (if any) for which he has been remanded in custody in connection with any of those offences, or any other offence the charge for which was founded on the same facts or evidence.

(10) Once a period of remand has, under sub-section (8) or (9) above, been taken account of in relation to a detention and training order made in respect of an offender for any offence or offences, it shall not subsequently be taken account of (under either of those sub-sections) in relation to such an order made in respect of the offender for any other offence or offences.

(11) Any reference in sub-section (8) or (9) above to an offender's being remanded in custody is a reference to his being:

    (a) held in police detention;

    (b) remanded in or committed to custody by an order of a court;

(c) remanded or committed to local authority accommodation under section 23 of the Children and Young Persons Act 1969 and placed and kept in secure accommodation; or

(d) remanded, admitted or removed to hospital under section 35, 36, 38 or 48 of the Mental Health Act 1983.

(12) A person is in police detention for the purposes of sub-section (11) above:

(a) at any time when he is in police detention for the purposes of the Police and Criminal Evidence Act 1984; and

(b) at any time when he is detained under section 14 of the Prevention of Terrorism (Temporary Provisions) Act 1989;

and in that sub-section 'secure accommodation' has the same meaning as in section 23 of the Children and Young Persons Act 1969.

(13) For the purpose of any reference in sections 102 to 105 below to the term of a detention and training order, consecutive terms of such orders and terms of such orders which are wholly or partly concurrent shall be treated as a single term if:

(a) the orders were made on the same occasion; or

(b) where they were made on different occasions, the offender has not been released (by virtue of sub-section (2), (3), (4) or (5) of section 102 below) at any time during the period beginning with the first and ending with the last of those occasions.

Section 102: The period of detention and training

(1) An offender shall serve the period of detention and training under a detention and training order in such secure accommodation as may be determined by the Secretary of State or by such other person as may be authorised by him for that purpose.

(2) Subject to sub-sections (3) to (5) below, the period of detention and training under a detention and training order shall be one-half of the term of the order.

(3) The Secretary of State may at any time release the offender if he is satisfied that exceptional circumstances exist which justify the offender's release on compassionate grounds.

(4) The Secretary of State may release the offender:

(a) in the case of an order for a term of 8 months or more but less than 18 months, one month before the half way point of the term of the order; and

(b) in the case of an order for a term of 18 months or more, one month or two months before that point.

(5) If a youth court so orders on an application made by the Secretary of State for the purpose, the Secretary of State shall release the offender:

(a) in the case of an order for a term of 8 months or more but less than 18 months, one month after the half way point of the term of the order; and

(b) in the case of an order for a term of 18 months or more, one month or two months after that point.

(6) An offender detained in pursuance of a detention and training order shall be deemed to be in legal custody.

Section 103: The period of supervision

(1) The period of supervision of an offender who is subject to a detention and training order:

(a) shall begin with the offender's release, whether at the half way point of the term of the order or otherwise; and

(b) subject to sub-section (2) below, shall end when the term of the order ends.

(2) The Secretary of State may by order provide that the period of supervision shall end at such point during the term of a detention and training order as may be specified in the order under this sub-section.

(3) During the period of supervision, the offender shall be under the supervision of:

(a) a probation officer;

(b) a social worker of a local authority social services department; or

(c) a member of a youth offending team,

and the category of person to supervise the offender shall be determined from time to time by the Secretary of State.

(4) Where the supervision is to be provided by a probation officer, the probation officer shall be an officer appointed for or assigned to the petty sessions area within which the offender resides for the time being.

(5) Where the supervision is to be provided by:

(a) a social worker of a local authority social services department; or

(b) a member of a youth offending team,

the social worker or member shall be a social worker of, or a member of a youth offending team established by, the local authority within whose area the offender resides for the time being.

(6) The offender shall be given a notice from the Secretary of State specifying:

(a) the category of person for the time being responsible for his supervision; and

(b) any requirements with which he must for the time being comply.

(7) A notice under sub-section (6) above shall be given to the offender:

(a) before the commencement of the period of supervision; and

(b) before any alteration in the matters specified in sub-section (6)(a) or (b) above comes into effect.

Section 104: Breach of supervision requirements

(1) Where a detention and training order is in force in respect of an offender and it appears on information to a justice of the peace acting for a relevant petty sessions area that the offender has failed to comply with requirements under section 103(6)(b) above, the justice:

    (a) may issue a summons requiring the offender to appear at the place and time specified in the summons before a youth court acting for the area; or

    (b) if the information is in writing and on oath, may issue a warrant for the offender's arrest requiring him to be brought before such a court.

(2) For the purposes of this section a petty sessions area is a relevant petty sessions area in relation to a detention and training order if:

    (a) the order was made by a youth court acting for it; or

    (b) the offender resides in it for the time being.

(3) If it is proved to the satisfaction of the youth court before which an offender appears or is brought under this section that he has failed to comply with requirements under section 103(6)(b) above, that court may:

    (a) order the offender to be detained, in such secure accommodation as the Secretary of State may determine, for such period, not exceeding the shorter of three months or the remainder of the term of the detention and training order, as the court may specify; or

    (b) impose on the offender a fine not exceeding level 3 on the standard scale.

(4) An offender detained in pursuance of an order under sub-section (3)(a) above shall be deemed to be in legal custody.

(5) A fine imposed under sub-section (3)(b) above shall be deemed, for the purposes of any enactment, to be a sum adjudged to be paid by a conviction.

(6) An offender may appeal to the Crown Court against any order made under sub-section (3)(a) or (b) above.

Section 105: Offences during currency of order

(1) This section applies to a person subject to a detention and training order if:

    (a) after his release and before the date on which the term of the order ends, he commits an offence punishable with imprisonment in the case of a person aged 21 or over ('the new offence'); and

    (b) whether before or after that date, he is convicted of the new offence.

(2) Subject to section 8(6) above (duty of adult magistrates' court to remit young offenders to youth court for sentence), the court by or before which a person to whom this section applies is convicted of the new offence may, whether or not it passes any other sentence on him, order him to be

detained in such secure accommodation as the Secretary of State may determine for the whole or any part of the period which:

(a) begins with the date of the court's order; and

(b) is equal in length to the period between the date on which the new offence was committed and the date mentioned in sub-section (1) above.

(3)   The period for which a person to whom this section applies is ordered under sub-section (2) above to be detained in secure accommodation:

(a) shall, as the court may direct, either be served before and be followed by, or be served concurrently with, any sentence imposed for the new offence; and

(b) in either case, shall be disregarded in determining the appropriate length of that sentence.

(4) Where the new offence is found to have been committed over a period of two or more days, or at some time during a period of two or more days, it shall be taken for the purposes of this section to have been committed on the last of those days.

(5) A person detained in pursuance of an order under sub-section (2) above shall be deemed to be in legal custody.

Section 106: Interaction with sentences of detention in a young offender institution

(1) Where a court passes a sentence of detention in a young offender institution in the case of an offender who is subject to a detention and training order, the sentence shall take effect as follows:

(a) if the offender has been released by virtue of sub-section (2), (3), (4) or (5) of section 102 above, at the beginning of the day on which it is passed;

(b) if not, either as mentioned in paragraph (a) above or, if the court so orders, at the time when the offender would otherwise be released by virtue of sub-section (2), (3), (4) or (5) of section 102.

(2) Where a court makes a detention and training order in the case of an offender who is subject to a sentence of detention in a young offender institution, the order shall take effect as follows:

(a) if the offender has been released under Part II of the Criminal Justice Act 1991 (early release of prisoners), at the beginning of the day on which it is made;

(b) if not, either as mentioned in paragraph (a) above or, if the court so orders, at the time when the offender would otherwise be released under that Part.

(3) Sub-section (1)(a) above has effect subject to section 105(3)(a) above and sub-section (2)(a) above has effect subject to section 116(6)(b) below.

(4) Subject to sub-section (5) below, where at any time an offender is subject concurrently:

   (a) to a detention and training order; and

   (b) to a sentence of detention in a young offender institution, he shall be treated for the purposes of sections 102 to 105 above and of section 98 above (place of detention), Chapter IV of this Part (return to detention) and Part II of the Criminal Justice Act 1991 (early release) as if he were subject only to the one of them that was imposed on the later occasion.

(5) Nothing in sub-section (4) above shall require the offender to be released in respect of either the order or the sentence unless and until he is required to be released in respect of each of them.

(6) Where, by virtue of any enactment giving a court power to deal with a person in a way in which a court on a previous occasion could have dealt with him, a detention and training order for any term is made in the case of a person who has attained the age of 18, the person shall be treated as if he had been sentenced to detention in a young offender institution for the same term.

CHAPTER 17

YOUNG OFFENDERS: NON-CUSTODIAL SENTENCES

The main non-custodial sentences applicable to young offenders are supervision orders and attendance centre orders. A court dealing with a young offender also has the power to impose a fine or to order a conditional or absolute discharge.

17.1 POWERS OF ADULT MAGISTRATES' COURT

We saw in Chapter 5 that there are circumstances in which a juvenile may be sentenced by an adult magistrates' court. However, the range of sentences available to the adult court is very limited. An adult magistrates' court may:

- order an absolute or conditional discharge;
- impose a fine (see below);
- order the parents of the juvenile to enter into a recognisance to take proper care of, and to exercise proper control over, a juvenile who has not attained the age of 16 (see below);
- make ancillary orders such as compensation and disqualification from driving.

17.2 POWERS OF YOUTH COURT AND CROWN COURT

As regards non-custodial sentences, the powers of the youth court and the Crown Court are identical.

17.3 FINES

A fine may be imposed on a juvenile (that is, someone under 18) by a youth court, an adult magistrates' court and by the Crown Court.

17.3.1 Maximum fine

Under s 135 of the Powers of Criminal Courts (Sentencing) Act 2000, the maximum fine which may be imposed by a youth court or an adult magistrates' court on an offender who has not attained the age of 18 is £1,000.

Where the offender has not attained the age of 14, s 36 limits the fine to a maximum of £250. There is, however, no limit on the fine which may be imposed by the Crown Court.

17.3.2 Payment of fine

Under s 137(1) of the Powers of Criminal Courts (Sentencing) Act 2000, where the offender is under 16, the court must order that the fine be paid by the parent or guardian of the offender unless either:

- the parent or guardian cannot be found; or
- it would be unreasonable to order the parent or guardian to pay the fine.

Under s 137(3) of the 2000 Act, where the offender has attained the age of 16, the court has a discretion (not a duty) to order the parent or guardian to pay the fine.

Where a parent or guardian is ordered to pay the fine, s 136 of the 2000 Act provides that it is the means of the parent or guardian (not those of the young offender) which are taken into account in fixing the amount of the fine. Accordingly, s 136 empowers the court to make a 'financial circumstances order' requiring the parent or guardian to provide a statement of means.

17.4 PARENTAL RECOGNIZANCE

The power to bind over is dealt with in Chapter 15. As regards offenders under 16, however, there is a special form of bind over.

Section 150(1) of the Powers of Criminal Courts (Sentencing) Act 2000 empowers the Crown Court, a youth court or an magistrates' court to order the parent or guardian of an offender who has not attained the age of 18 to enter into a recognizance to take proper care of the offender and to exercise proper control over him. The effect of such an order is that the parent or guardian promises to pay a sum specified by the court, which must not exceed £1,000, if they fail to comply with the terms of the order.

Such an order can only be made if the court is satisfied that it is desirable to do so in the interests of preventing the offender from committing further offences.

Where the offender has not attained the age of 16 (that is, is under school-leaving age), the court must state in open court why it has not exercised the power under s 150 if it decides not to bind the parents over.

A parent or guardian can only be ordered to enter into a recognizance with their consent. However, a parent or guardian who unreasonably refuses to consent may be fined up to £1,000 (that is, a fine on level 3) (s 150(2)).

In fixing the amount of the recognizance, the court must take account of the means of the parent or guardian, whether this has the effect of increasing or reducing the amount of the recognizance (subject always to the maximum of £1,000): s 150(7).

Under s 150(2), when a court imposes a community sentence on a young offender, the order may include a requirement that the offender's parent or guardian enter into a recognizance to ensure that the young offender complies with the terms of the order.

17.5   SUPERVISION ORDERS

Section 63 of the Powers of Criminal Courts (Sentencing) Act 2000 enables a youth court or the Crown Court (but not an adult magistrates' court) to make a supervision order against an offender who has attained the age of 10 but who is under 18.

The effect of a supervision order is to place the juvenile under the supervision of a social worker, a member of a youth offending team, or a probation officer. The supervisor will usually be a social worker unless the probation service is already in contact with other members of the offender's family. The role of the supervisor, according to s 64(4) of the Act, is to 'advise, assist and befriend' the offender.

A supervision order is a community order and so has to be justified by the seriousness of the offence(s) being dealt with by the court (s 35(1) of the 2000 Act).

Before a supervision order can be made, the court must obtain a pre-sentence report if the supervision order is to contain any of the additional requirements set out below (s 36(3)(e) of the Act).

17.5.1   Duration of order

A supervision order may last for up to three years (s 63(7) of the 2000 Act).

17.5.2   Additional requirements

The following additional requirements (set out in Sched 6 of the 2000 Act) may be added to a supervision order under the Children and Young Persons Act.

17.5.3 Residence

Paragraph 1 of Sched 6 allows the court to require the offender to reside with an individual named in the order. Before such a requirement may be imposed, the person named in the order must agree to the offender residing with him.

17.5.4 Complying with directions of supervisor

Paragraph 2(1) of Sched 6 enables the court to require a person who is subject to a supervision order to comply with any directions given by the supervisor to:

- live at a specified place for a specified period;
- present himself to a specified person at a specified place on a specified day;
- participate in activities specified by the supervisor.

Paragraph 2(5) stipulates that the maximum number of days in respect of which the supervisor may give directions is 90. These days need not be consecutive.

The directions are at the discretion of the supervisor in that it is for the supervisor to decide whether to exercise any of the powers conferred by the order.

These directions are intended to help the offender to develop her abilities and to become involved in worthwhile activities. The object is to show the offender that spare time can be used constructively. Directions may involve, for example, learning a new skill or going on an outward-bound adventure holiday.

17.5.5 Court-nominated activities

Under para 3(2)(a)–(c) of Sched 6, the court may itself specify requirements that the offender live at a particular place or attend at a specified place or take part in specified activities. In other words, the court removes the discretionary element from the directions under para 2(1) of Sched 6 by deciding itself what the offender is to do.

The maximum number of days in respect of which the court may impose such requirements is 90 (para 3(3)).

17.5.6 Reparation

Paragraph 3(2)(d) of Sched 6 enables the court to add a requirement to a supervision order that the offender make the reparation (otherwise than by payment of compensation) to the victim(s) of the offence or to the community at large.

17.5.7   Night restrictions

Paragraph 3(2)(e) of Sched 6 enables the court to make an order that the offender remain in a specified place (or one of a number of places) for specified periods between 6.00 pm and 6.00 am.

The supervised person may not be required to remain at a place for longer than 10 hours on any one night (para 4(2)).

Night restrictions cannot be imposed in respect of more than a total of 30 days (para 4(4)) and cannot continue in operation for more than three months from the date of the making of the supervision order (para 4(3)).

17.5.8   Negative requirements

Under para 3(2)(f) of Sched 6, the court may order the supervised person to refrain from participating in specified activities on specified days or for a specified period. The restrictions may apply for the entire duration of the supervision order.

• Procedural requirements

Before making an order under any of the provisions of para 3(2), the court must be satisfied:

(a)   that compliance with the requirements is feasible (para 3(4)(a));

(b)   that the requirements are necessary for securing the good conduct of the supervised person or for preventing him from committing further offences (para 3(4)(b));

Where the offender is under 16, the court has to consider the likely effects of the requirements it wishes to impose upon the offender's family circumstances (para 3(4)(c)).

Where compliance with the requirement requires the co-operation of a third party, the requirement can only be imposed with that person's consent (para 5(6)).

17.5.9   Requirement of residence in local authority accommodation

Under para 5 of Sched 6, the court may add a requirement that the supervised person live in local authority accommodation for a specified period.

The maximum period which may be specified in a residence requirement is six months (para 5(6)).

The residence requirement may also stipulate that the supervised person must not live with a person named in the order (para 5(2)).

A residence requirement may only be added to a supervision order if each of the conditions laid down in para 5(2) are met. Those conditions are:

- a supervision order has previously been made in respect of the offender;
- that supervision order contained a requirement of residence, or compliance with supervisor's directions, or court-nominated directions or night restrictions, or negative requirements, or contained a local authority residence requirement;
- the offender has failed to comply with the requirement, or has been found guilty of an offence which was committed while the original supervision order was in force;
- the court is satisfied that the failure to comply with the requirement, or the behaviour which constituted the offence was due, to a significant extent, to the circumstances in which the offender was living.

A requirement may only be imposed under para 5 if the offender is legally represented or has refused to apply for representation funded by the Criminal Defence Service (para 5(9)).

The other requirements which may be added to a supervision order may be imposed in addition to a residence requirement (para 5(9)).

17.5.10 Treatment for a mental condition

Paragraph 7 of Sched 6 enables the court to insert a requirement that the offender receive treatment for a mental condition.

The court must have evidence from a duly qualified medical practitioner that the mental condition of the offender is such as requires, and may be susceptible to, treatment but is not sufficiently serious to require a hospital order under the Mental Health Act 1983.

Such a requirement may specify treatment by a qualified medical practitioner, treatment (as a resident or non-resident patient) at a place specified in the order or treatment in a mental hospital.

The consent of the offender is required if she has attained the age of 14.

A condition requiring mental treatment lapses when the offender attains the age of 18 (para 6(3)).

17.5.11 Educational requirements

Paragraph 7 of Sched 6 enables the court to add a requirement to a supervision order that the offender, so long as he is of compulsory school age (that is, under 16), must comply with arrangements made by his parents and approved by the local education authority for his education.

Under para 7(5), such a requirement may only be imposed if necessary to secure the good conduct of the offender or to prevent the commission of further offences by him.

17.5.12 Breach of supervision order

Schedule 7 of the Powers of Criminal Courts (Sentencing) Act 2000 deals with the enforcement of supervision orders. A person who fails to comply with a supervision order and who is under 18 will be summoned to appear before the youth court; if the offender has attained the age of 18, she will be summoned to attend before the adult magistrates' court. Paragraph 2 of Sched 7 enables the supervisor to take action in respect of a breach of a supervision order. Where it is proved to the satisfaction of the court that the offender has failed to comply with any of the requirements of the supervision order, the court may impose a fine of up to £1,000 or may make a curfew order or an attendance centre order (para 2(2)(a) of Sched 7).

The fine or curfew order or attendance centre order may be imposed in addition to, or instead of, the discharge of the order.

Under para 2(2)(b), where the supervision order was made by a magistrates' court, the court dealing with the breach can revoke the order and re-sentence the offender for the original offence. The court can impose any sentence which it could have imposed if it had had jurisdiction to try the offender for that original offence.

If the supervision order was made by the Crown Court the magistrates dealing with the breach may simply commit the offender (in custody or on bail) to the Crown Court (para 2(2)(c)). The Crown Court may revoke the supervision order and re-sentence the offender for the original offence (para 2(4)).

When an offender is re-sentenced following breach of a supervision order, the court must take into account the extent to which the offender has complied with the requirements of the order (and make any necessary reduction) (para 4(7)).

17.5.13 Revocation or amendment of order

We have already seen that a supervision order can be discharged under para 2 of Sched 7 if the offender fails to comply with any of its requirements.

Paragraph 5 of Sched 7 enables the supervisor or the supervised person to make an application for the order to be discharged or varied. The application is made to the youth court if the offender is under 18 and to the adult magistrates' court if he has attained the age of 18.

If the court decides to vary the order, it may do so by cancelling any of the additional requirements imposed in the original order or by adding new requirements; any of the requirements (except night restrictions) which could have been imposed originally may be added when the order is varied.

17.6   ATTENDANCE CENTRE ORDERS

An attendance centre is 'a place at which offenders aged under 21 may be required to attend and be given, under supervision, appropriate occupation or instruction' (s 62(2) of the Powers of Criminal Courts (Sentencing) Act 2000).

Attendance centres are generally run by off duty police officers or teachers on Saturday mornings or afternoons. Premises such as schools, youth clubs and church halls are often used.

The power to make an attendance centre order is conferred by s 60 of the 2000 Act:

- where the court is dealing with an offender who is under 21 for an imprisonable offence it may make an attendance centre order;
- an attendance centre order may be made as an alternative to the imposition of a custodial term for non-payment of a fine; and
- an attendance centre order may be used as a method of punishing a failure to comply with the requirements of a supervision order or a probation order.

An attendance centre order may only be made if an appropriate centre is reasonably accessible to the offender (s 60(6)).

17.6.1   Number of hours

The aggregate number of hours must be specified in the order.

- *Minimum*

  The total number of hours must not be less than 12, unless the offender is under 14 and the court takes the view that 12 hours would be excessive (s 60(3)).

- *Maximum*

  Section 60(4) provides that the aggregate number of hours should not exceed 12 unless the court takes the view that, in all the circumstances, 12 hours would be inadequate. In that case, the total number of hours must not exceed 24 in the case of an offender who is under 16 and must not exceed 36 hours if the offender is aged between 16 and 20.

  This maximum aggregate number of hours applies only to attendance centre orders made on the same occasion. If an attendance centre order is made against someone who has not yet completed the number of hours under an earlier attendance centre order, the earlier order is disregarded in fixing the number of hours under the later order (s 60(6)).

Under s 60(10), an offender may not be required to attend a centre on more than one occasion on any day and cannot be ordered to attend for more than three hours on any one occasion.

17.6.2 Use of attendance centre order

The object of an attendance centre order is partly punitive, in that the offender is deprived of free time on a Saturday morning or afternoon. The effect can also be preventive; Home Office Circular 69/1990 points out that such an order can be effective in keeping football hooligans away from matches.

There is also a substantial element of rehabilitation. The Home Office Circular says that such an order should benefit the offender by 'bringing him under the influence of representatives of the authority of the State' and by 'teaching him something of the constructive use of leisure'. Thus, there should be firm discipline at an attendance centre but the emphasis will be on physical exercise (for example, sports) and skills (for example, car maintenance).

17.6.3 Breach of attendance centre order

Paragraph 1 of Sched 5 of the Powers of Criminal Courts (Sentencing) Act 2000 empowers a magistrates' court to issue a summons where an information has been laid by the person in charge of the attendance centre alleging that the offender has failed to attend the attendance centre or has broken the rules of the centre.

Where the original order was made by a magistrates' court, the magistrates' court dealing with the breach may either impose a fine of up to £1,000 (para 2(1)(a)) or revoke the order and re-sentence the offender for the original offence. Any sentence which could have been imposed by the original court may be imposed by the court dealing with the breach (para 2(1)(b)).

If the original order was made by the Crown Court, the magistrates' court may impose a fine of up to £1,000 for the breach but it cannot re-sentence the offender for the original offence. It can, however, commit the offender (in custody or on bail) to the Crown Court to be dealt with for the breach. The Crown Court can re-sentence the offender for the original offence (para 3(1)).

Where the offender is re-sentenced for the original offence, account must be taken of the extent to which he has complied with the original order (para 2(5)(a) and para 3(3)(a)).

It should also be noted that if the offender has 'wilfully and persistently failed to comply' with an attendance centre order, the court may impose a custodial sentence notwithstanding anything in s 79(2) of the 2000 Act (para 2(5)(b) and para 3(3)(b)).

17.6.4 Discharge or variation of attendance centre order

As well as the power to deal with a breach of an attendance centre order under paras 2 and 3 of Sched 5, the court may discharge or vary an order, on the application of the person in charge of the attendance centre or of the offender, under para 4 of Sched 5. If the order is revoked, the court has power to re-sentence for the original offence under para 4(3) of Sched 5.

17.7 ACTION PLAN ORDERS

Section 69 of the Powers of Criminal Courts (Sentencing) Act 2000 provides for 'action plan orders'. Under s 69(1), where a person aged under 18 is convicted of an offence, the court may, if it considers it desirable in the interests of securing his rehabilitation or preventing him from re-offending (s 69(3)), make an action plan order.

This is an order which (under s 69(2)):

(a) requires the offender, for a period of three months from the date of the order, to comply with a series of requirements with respect to his actions and whereabouts during that period (the 'action plan');

(b) places the offender, for that three month period, under the supervision of a probation officer, a social worker, or a member of a youth offending team; and

(c) requires the offender to comply with any directions given by his supervisor with a view to the implementation of the action plan.

An action plan order cannot be made if the offender is already the subject of such an order (s 69(5)(a)). Furthermore, an action plan order cannot be combined with a custodial sentence, or with probation, community service, a combination order, a supervision order, or a referral order (s 69(5)(b)).

Under s 70 of the 2000 Act, the requirements under the action plan order itself and the directions given by the supervisor, can require the offender to participate in specified activities, to attend at a particular place at a particular time, to attend an attendance centre, to keep away from a particular place or places, to comply with arrangements for his education, and to make reparation (otherwise than by payment of compensation) to the victim of the offence (or to someone affected by it), provided that this person consents, or to the community at large.

The requirements specified in the order should avoid any conflict with the offender's religious beliefs, with the requirements of any community order to which he is subject as a result of a previous conviction, and with the times (if any) when he attends school or any other educational establishment (s 70(4)).

An action plan order is a community sentence and so can only be made if justified by the seriousness of the offence (s 35(1) of the 2000 Act). Before an action plan order is made, the court must have a written report from the proposed supervisor setting out the requirements he or she thinks ought to be included in the order, the benefits to the offender that these requirements are designed to achieve, the attitude of the parent or guardian of the offender to those proposed requirements, and (where the offender is under 16) information about the likely effect of the order on the offender's family circumstances (s 69(6)).

Before making the order, the court has to explain its effect, and the consequences which may follow from failure to comply with it, to the offender (s 69(11)).

17.8   REPARATION ORDERS

Section 73 of the Powers of Criminal Courts (Sentencing) Act 2000 provides for 'reparation orders'. These orders can only be made where a person aged under 18 has been convicted of an offence.

The order requires the offender to make the form of reparation specified in the order (but not payment of compensation) either to the victim of the offence or someone otherwise affected by it (in either case, the person must be named in the order) or to the community at large (s 73(1)).

A reparation order cannot require the offender to work for more than a total of 24 hours or to make reparation to any person without the consent of that person (s 74(1)(a)).

The form of reparation ordered must be commensurate with the seriousness of the offence(s) for which the offender is being dealt with (s 74(2)).

The reparation has to be made under the supervision of a probation officer, a social worker, or a member of a youth offending team specified in the order and has to be made within three months of the making of the order (s 74(8)).

The requirements specified in the order should avoid any conflict with the offender's religious beliefs, with the requirements of any community order to which he is subject as a result of a previous conviction, and with the times (if any) when he attends school or any other educational establishment (s 74(3)).

Before making a reparation order, the court must obtain and consider a report written by a probation officer, a social worker, or a member of a youth offending team, indicating the type of work that is suitable for the offender and the attitude of the victim(s) to the requirements proposed to be included in the order (s 73(5)).

Before making a reparation order, the court must explain to the offender the effect of the order and the consequences of failing to comply with it (s 73(7)).

Section 73(8)) requires the court to give reasons if it does not make a reparation order in any case where it has power to make such an order.

A reparation order cannot be made at the same time as a custodial sentence, a community service order, a combination order, a supervision order with additional requirements imposed under Sched 6 of the 2000 Act, an action plan order or a referral order (s 73(4)).

17.8.1 Breach of action plan order and reparation order

Schedule 8 of the Powers of Criminal Courts (Sentencing) Act 2000 deals with the enforcement of action plan orders and reparation orders.

If the magistrates' court, on the application of the supervisor, finds that the offender has failed to comply with the requirements of the order, it may impose a fine of up to £1,000, or make a curfew order, or make an attendance centre order (para 2(2)(a) of Sched 8).

Where the original order was made by a magistrates' court, the magistrates may revoke the order and re-sentence the offender (para 2(2)(b)). If the order was made by a Crown Court, the magistrates may commit the offender (in custody or on bail) to be dealt with by the Crown Court, which may re-sentence the offender for the original offence (para 2(2)(c); para 2(4)).

Where the offender is re-sentenced, account must be taken of the extent to which he complied with the requirements of the order (para 2(7)).

Paragraph 5 of Sched 8 contains a general power to revoke or amend the order on the application of the supervisor or of the offender.

17.9 REFERRAL ORDERS FOR YOUNG OFFENDERS: YOUTH OFFENDER PANELS

These orders were created by the Youth Justice and Criminal Evidence Act 1999 and are now contained in ss 16–28 of the Powers of Criminal Courts (Sentencing) Act 2000.

A referral order may be either compulsory or discretionary. The provisions apply where a youth court or adult magistrates' court is dealing with an offender aged under 18 and the court is not minded to impose a custodial sentence, or to make a hospital order under the Mental Health Act 1983, or to grant an absolute discharge (s 16(1)).

The court *must* make a referral order if the offender pleaded guilty to the offence and to any connected offence and has not previously been convicted of any offence (s 17(1)). The court *may* make a referral order if the offender is being dealt with for at least two connected offences, he pleaded guilty to at least one of them but also pleaded not guilty to at least one of them, and has not previously been convicted of any offence (s 17(2)).

A referral order requires the offender to attend meetings of a youth offender panel. The court may also specify the period for which any youth offender contract (see below) is to have effect; that period must be between three and 12 months. Where the court is dealing with the offender for more than one offence, separate periods may be specified; those periods may be concurrent or consecutive (but, if they are consecutive, the total period may not exceed 12 months): s 18(6).

Where the court makes a referral order in respect of an offence, the court is prohibited from imposing community service, a fine, a reparation order, or a conditional discharge in respect of that offence (s 19(4)). Where the court is dealing with the offender for two or more connected offences, and makes a referral order in respect of one of them, the court must either make a referral order or grant an absolute discharge in respect of the other offence(s): s 19(2).

Unless the child is in the care of the local authority, a parent or guardian is required to attend meetings of the youth offender panel established for their child, unless and to the extent it would be unreasonable so to require (s 20). Membership of the youth offender panel for an offender is governed by s 21 and will include a member of the youth offending team and two other appropriately qualified people. If the offender fails to attend a panel meeting, the matter may be referred back to the court (s 22(2)).

At the first meeting of the youth offender panel established for the offender, the panel seeks to reach agreement with the offender on 'a programme of behaviour the aim (or principal aim) of which is the prevention of re-offending by the offender' (s 23(1)).

Under s 23(2), the programme may include provision for:

- the offender to make financial or other reparation to the victim of the offence;

- the offender to attend mediation sessions with the victim;

- the offender to carry out unpaid work in the community;

- the offender to be at home at specified times;

- attendance by the offender at school, college or place of work;

- the offender to participate in specified activities (for example, activities designed to address offending behaviour or to assist with the rehabilitation of those who are dependant on or misuse alcohol or drugs;

- to stay away from specified people or places.

The programme cannot provide for electronic monitoring of the offender's whereabouts (s 23(3)). Where anyone else will be affected by a requirement in the programme, that persons consent must first be obtained (s 23(4)).

The programme is reduced into writing and is signed by the offender and a member of the panel.

If the first meeting with the panel does not produce a contract with the offender, there may be a further meeting (s25(1)). If it appears that there is no prospect of an agreement being reached within a reasonable period, the matter is referred back to the court (s25(2)).

Section 26 provides for progress meetings to review the offender's progress in implementing the programme. Progress meetings are also convened if the offender wishes the terms of the contract to be varied or if he wishes the order to be revoked because of a significant change in his circumstances (such that compliance with the contract is no longer practicable). A progress meeting is also appropriate if it appears to the panel that the offender is in breach of any of the terms of the contract.

Section 27 deals with the final meeting held when the compliance period of the contract is due to expire. At the final meeting the panel reviews the offender's compliance with the contract and decides whether he has satisfactorily completed the contract (s 27(2)). If the panel decides that the offender has complied with the contract, this has the effect of discharging the referral order (s 27(3)). Otherwise, the panel refers the offender back to the court (s 27(4)).

Schedule 1 makes detailed provision for what happens where a youth offender panel refers the offender back to the court or where the offender is convicted of further offences during the currency of the order.

Under para 5 of Sched 1, if the court is satisfied that the offender has failed to comply with the requirements of the referral order, the court may revoke the referral order and sentence the offender for the original offence as if the case were one where are referral was not appropriate.

Under para 12 of Sched 1, where the offender re-offends during the period of a referral order, the court may extend his compliance period, but only if there is evidence of exceptional circumstances indicating that an extension of the compliance period is likely to help prevent further re-offending by him. Otherwise, unless the court grants an absolute discharge for the subsequent offence, the court revokes the referral order and sentences the offender for the original offence as if the case were one where a referral order was not appropriate.

17.10   CRIME PREVENTION PROVISIONS

The Crime and Disorder Act 1998 introduced a number of crime prevention measures to reduce the amount of crime committed by young people.

17.10.1   Anti-social behaviour orders

Section 1 of the Crime and Disorder Act provides for 'anti-social behaviour orders'. The local authority or the police may apply to the local magistrates' court for such an order if:

(a) any person aged 10 or over has acted in an anti-social manner (defined as acting in a manner that caused or was likely to cause harassment, alarm or distress to one or more persons not in the same household as himself); and

(b) such an order is necessary to protect people in the area from further anti-social acts by that person.

The anti-social behaviour order is an order which prevents the defendant from doing anything described in the order; the prohibitions imposed under the order can be anything the magistrates consider necessary to protect people in the locality from further anti-social acts by the defendant.

The minimum period of such an order is two years (no maximum period is specified by the Act).

Section 1(10) provides that if, without reasonable excuse, a person does anything which he is prohibited from doing by an anti-social behaviour order, he commits an offence (carrying up to six months' imprisonment and/or a fine up to £5,000 following summary conviction or up to five years' imprisonment and an unlimited fine following conviction in the Crown Court).

Section 4 of the Act provides for an appeal to the Crown Court against the making of an anti-social behaviour order.

17.10.2   Parenting orders

Section 8 of the Crime and Disorder Act 1998 creates 'parenting orders'. Such an order can be made in respect of the parent or guardian of a child or young person if:

(a) a child safety order had been made in respect of the child;

(b) an anti-social behaviour order has been made in respect of the child or young person;

(c) the child or young person has been convicted of an offence; or

(d) there has been a conviction for an offence involving truancy.

A parenting order can only be made if the court considers that a parenting order would be desirable in the interests of preventing:

(a) the repetition of the behaviour which led to the making of the child safety order or the anti-social behaviour order; or

(b) to prevent the child or young person from re-offending; or

(c) to prevent the child or young person from truanting.

The order requires the parent to comply, for a period of up to 12 months, with such requirements as are specified in the order, and (during that period) to attend, for up to three months (but not more than once in any week), counselling or guidance sessions specified by the probation officer, the social worker or the member of the youth offending team specified in the order.

The requirements which may are imposed are anything that the court considers desirable in the interests of preventing repetition of the anti-social behaviour, preventing further truanting, or preventing the youngster from re-offending.

Section 9 of the Act provides that, where a person under the age of 16 is convicted of an offence, and the court is satisfied that any of the pre-conditions for the making of a parenting order are satisfied, a parenting order must be made.

Before making a parenting order, the court must explain to the parent the effect of the order and the consequences of non-compliance with it.

An application to vary or discharge the parenting order can be made by the probation officer or social worker specified in the order or by the parent. Where an application for discharge of the order is dismissed, a further application for its discharge can only be made with the consent of the court which made the order.

Failure by the parent without reasonable excuse to comply with the requirements of the order is a summary offence punishable with a fine up to level 3 (£1,000).

Section 10 provides that where a parenting order was made because a child safety order had been made, appeal lies to the High Court. Where the order was made because an anti-social behaviour order had been made, appeal lies to the Crown Court. Where the order is made following commission of an offence by the youngster and, in the case of truanting offences, there is the same right of appeal as if the order were a sentence passed by the court following commission of the offence.

17.10.3   Child safety orders

Section 11 of the Crime and Disorder Act 1998 creates 'child safety orders'. A magistrates' court, on the application of a local authority, is empowered to make a child safety order if the court is satisfied that one of more of the following conditions has been fulfilled with respect to a child under the age of 10:

(i) the child has committed an act which, if committed by someone over 10, would have constituted a criminal offence;

(ii) a child safety order is necessary for the purpose of preventing the child from doing so again;

(iii) the child has contravened a ban imposed by a curfew notice; or

(iv) the child has acted in a manner that caused, or was likely to cause, harassment, alarm or distress to one or more persons not in the same household as himself.

The effect of the order is:

(a) to place the child under the supervision of a social worker or a member of a youth offending team for up to three months (or 12 months if the court regards the circumstances of the case as exceptional); and

(b) to require the child to comply with requirements specified in the order. The court may impose any requirements which it considers desirable in the interests of:

(i) securing that the child receives appropriate care, protection and support and is subject to proper control; or

(ii) preventing any repetition of the kind of behaviour which led to the child safety order being made.

This order is made in the context of family proceedings (not the criminal jurisdiction of the magistrates); the standard of proof is therefore that applicable to civil proceedings (that is, the balance of probabilities): s 11(6).

Before making a child safety order, the court must explain to the parent the effect of the order and the consequences of non-compliance with it.

An application to vary or discharge the order can be made by the social worker or the member of the youth offending team specified in the order or by the parent/guardian. Where an application for discharge of the order is dismissed, a further application for its discharge can only be made with the consent of the court which made the order.

Where the child fails to comply with any requirement included in the order, the magistrates may, on the application of the social worker or the member of the youth offending team specified in the order, replace the order with a care order (under s 31(1)(a) of the Children Act 1989) or vary the child safety order.

Under s 13 of the 1998 Act, appeal against the making of a child safety order lies to the High Court.

17.10.4 Local child curfew schemes

Section 14 of the Crime and Disorder Act 1998 empowers a local authority to ban children of specified ages under 10 from being in a public place within a specified area, during specified hours (between 9 pm and 6 am), otherwise than under the effective control of a parent or responsible person aged 18 or over. The order can last for a maximum of 90 days and only comes into operation if confirmed by the Secretary of State. The scheme is publicised by means of curfew notices.

Where the police have reasonable cause to believe that a child is in contravention of a ban imposed by a curfew notice, they must inform the local authority and may remove the child to the child's place of residence (unless there is reasonable cause to believe that the child would suffer significant harm there).

TABLE OF STATUTORY MATERIALS

STATUTORY MATERIALS

FINES: 10–17 YEAR OLDS

POWERS OF CRIMINAL COURTS (SENTENCING) ACT 2000

Section 135: Limit on fines imposed by magistrates' courts in respect of young offenders

(1) Where a person aged under 18 is found guilty by a magistrates' court of an offence for which, apart from this section, the court would have power to impose a fine of an amount exceeding £1,000, the amount of any fine imposed by the court shall not exceed £1,000.

(2) In relation to a person aged under 14, sub-section (1) above shall have effect as if for '£1,000', in both places where it occurs, there were substituted '£250'.

Section 136: Power to order statement as to financial circumstances of parent or guardian

(1) Before exercising its powers under section 137 below (power to order parent or guardian to pay fine, costs or compensation) against the parent or guardian of an individual who has been convicted of an offence, the court may make a financial circumstances order with respect to the parent or (as the case may be) guardian.

(2) In this section 'financial circumstances order' has the meaning given by sub-section (3) of section 126 above, and sub-sections (4) to (6) of that section shall apply in relation to a financial circumstances order made under this section as they apply in relation to such an order made under that section.

Section 137: Power to order parent or guardian to pay fine, costs or compensation

(1) Where:

(a) a child or young person (that is to say, any person aged under 18) is convicted of any offence for the commission of which a fine or costs may be imposed or a compensation order may be made; and

(b) the court is of the opinion that the case would best be met by the imposition of a fine or costs or the making of such an order, whether with or without any other punishment, the court shall order that the fine, compensation or costs awarded be paid by the parent or guardian of the child or young person instead of by the child or young person himself, unless the court is satisfied:

 (i) that the parent or guardian cannot be found; or

 (ii) that it would be unreasonable to make an order for payment, having regard to the circumstances of the case.

(2) Where but for this sub-section a court would impose a fine on a child or young person under:

 (a) paragraph 4(1)(a) or 5(1)(a) of Schedule 3 to this Act (breach of curfew, probation, community service, combination or drug treatment and testing order);

 (b) paragraph 2(1)(a) of Schedule 5 to this Act (breach of attendance centre order or attendance centre rules);

 (c) paragraph 2(2)(a) of Schedule 7 to this Act (breach of supervision order);

 (d) paragraph 2(2)(a) of Schedule 8 to this Act (breach of action plan order or reparation order);

 (e) section 104(3)(b) above (breach of requirements of supervision under a detention and training order); or

 (f) section 4(3)(b) of the Criminal Justice and Public Order Act 1994 (breach of requirements of supervision under a secure training order),

the court shall order that the fine be paid by the parent or guardian of the child or young person instead of by the child or young person himself, unless the court is satisfied:

 (i) that the parent or guardian cannot be found; or

 (ii) that it would be unreasonable to make an order for payment, having regard to the circumstances of the case.

(3) In the case of a young person aged 16 or over, sub-sections (1) and (2) above shall have effect as if, instead of imposing a duty, they conferred a power to make such an order as is mentioned in those sub-sections.

(4) Subject to sub-section (5) below, no order shall be made under this section without giving the parent or guardian an opportunity of being heard.

(5) An order under this section may be made against a parent or guardian who, having been required to attend, has failed to do so.

(6) A parent or guardian may appeal to the Crown Court against an order under this section made by a magistrates' court.

(7) A parent or guardian may appeal to the Court of Appeal against an order under this section made by the Crown Court, as if he had been convicted on indictment and the order were a sentence passed on his conviction.

(8) In relation to a child or young person for whom a local authority have parental responsibility and who:

 (a) is in their care; or

 (b) is provided with accommodation by them in the exercise of any functions (in particular those under the Children Act 1989) which stand referred to their social services committee under the Local Authority Social Services Act 1970,

references in this section to his parent or guardian shall be construed as references to that authority.

(9) In sub-section (8) above 'local authority' and 'parental responsibility' have the same meanings as in the Children Act 1989.

Section 138: Fixing of fine or compensation to be paid by parent or guardian

(1) For the purposes of any order under section 137 above made against the parent or guardian of a child or young person:

  (a) section 128 above (fixing of fines) shall have effect as if any reference in sub-sections (1) to (4) to the financial circumstances of the offender were a reference to the financial circumstances of the parent or guardian, and as if sub-section (5) were omitted;

  (b) section 130(11) above (determination of compensation order) shall have effect as if any reference to the means of the person against whom the compensation order is made were a reference to the financial circumstances of the parent or guardian; and

  (c) section 130(12) above (preference to be given to compensation if insufficient means to pay both compensation and a fine) shall have effect as if the reference to the offender were a reference to the parent or guardian,

but in relation to an order under section 137 made against a local authority this sub-section has effect subject to sub-section (2) below.

(2) For the purposes of any order under section 137 above made against a local authority, sections 128(1) (duty to inquire into financial circumstances) and 130(11) above shall not apply.

(3) For the purposes of any order under section 137 above, where the parent or guardian of an offender who is a child or young person:

  (a) has failed to comply with an order under section 136 above; or

  (b) has otherwise failed to co-operate with the court in its inquiry into his financial circumstances,

and the court considers that it has insufficient information to make a proper determination of the parent's or guardian's financial circumstances, it may make such determination as it thinks fit.

(4) Where a court has, in fixing the amount of a fine, determined the financial circumstances of a parent or guardian under sub-section (3) above, sub-sections (2) to (4) of section 129 above (remission of fines) shall (so far as applicable) have effect as they have effect in the case mentioned in section 129(1), but as if the reference in section 129(2) to the offender's financial circumstances were a reference to the financial circumstances of the parent or guardian.

(5) In this section 'local authority' has the same meaning as in the Children Act 1989.

BINDING OVER PARENT OR GUARDIAN

POWERS OF CRIMINAL COURTS (SENTENCING) ACT 2000

Section 150: Binding over of parent or guardian

(1) Where a child or young person (that is to say, any person aged under 18) is convicted of an offence, the powers conferred by this section shall be exercisable by the court by which he is sentenced for that offence, and where the offender is aged under 16 when sentenced it shall be the duty of that court:

    (a) to exercise those powers if it is satisfied, having regard to the circumstances of the case, that their exercise would be desirable in the interests of preventing the commission by him of further offences; and

    (b) if it does not exercise them, to state in open court that it is not satisfied as mentioned in paragraph (a) above and why it is not so satisfied,

but this sub-section has effect subject to section 19(5) above and paragraph 13(5) of Schedule 1 to this Act (cases where referral orders made or extended).

(2) The powers conferred by this section are as follows:

    (a) with the consent of the offender's parent or guardian, to order the parent or guardian to enter into a recognizance to take proper care of him and exercise proper control over him; and

    (b) if the parent or guardian refuses consent and the court considers the refusal unreasonable, to order the parent or guardian to pay a fine not exceeding £1,000,

and where the court has passed a community sentence on the offender, it may include in the recognizance a provision that the offender's parent or guardian ensure that the offender complies with the requirements of that sentence.

(3) An order under this section shall not require the parent or guardian to enter into a recognizance for an amount exceeding £1,000.

(4) An order under this section shall not require the parent or guardian to enter into a recognizance:

    (a) for a period exceeding three years; or

    (b) where the offender will attain the age of 18 in a period shorter than three years, for a period exceeding that shorter period.

(5) Section 120 of the Magistrates' Courts Act 1980 (forfeiture of recognizances) shall apply in relation to a recognizance entered into in pursuance of an

order under this section as it applies in relation to a recognizance to keep the peace.

(6) A fine imposed under sub-section (2)(b) above shall be deemed, for the purposes of any enactment, to be a sum adjudged to be paid by a conviction.

(7) In fixing the amount of a recognizance under this section, the court shall take into account among other things the means of the parent or guardian so far as they appear or are known to the court; and this sub-section applies whether taking into account the means of the parent or guardian has the effect of increasing or reducing the amount of the recognizance.

(8) A parent or guardian may appeal to the Crown Court against an order under this section made by a magistrates' court.

(9) A parent or guardian may appeal to the Court of Appeal against an order under this section made by the Crown Court, as if he had been convicted on indictment and the order were a sentence passed on his conviction.

(10) A court may vary or revoke an order made by it under this section if, on the application of the parent or guardian, it appears to the court, having regard to any change in the circumstances since the order was made, to be in the interests of justice to do so.

(11) For the purposes of this section, taking 'care' of a person includes giving him protection and guidance and 'control' includes discipline.

MAGISTRATES' COURTS ACT 1980

Section 81: Enforcement of fines imposed on young offenders

(1) Where a magistrates' court would, but for section 89 of the Powers of Criminal Courts (Sentencing) Act 2000, have power to commit to prison a person under the age of 18 for a default consisting in failure to pay, or want of distress to satisfy, a sum adjudged to be paid by a conviction, the court may, subject to the following provisions of this section, make:

(a) an order requiring the defaulter's parent or guardian to enter into a recognizance to ensure that the defaulter pays so much of that sum as remains unpaid; or

(b) an order directing so much of that sum as remains unpaid to be paid by the defaulter's parent or guardian instead of by the defaulter.

(2) An order under sub-section (1) above shall not be made in respect of a defaulter:

(a) in pursuance of paragraph (a) of that sub-section, unless the parent or guardian in question consents;

(b) in pursuance of paragraph (b) of that sub-section, unless the court is satisfied in all the circumstances that it is reasonable to make the order.

(3) None of the following orders, namely:

(a) an order under section 60(1) of the said Act of 2000 for attendance at an attendance centre; or

(b) any order under sub-section (1) above,

shall be made by a magistrates' court in consequence of a default of a person under the age of 18 years consisting in failure to pay, or want of sufficient distress to satisfy, a sum adjudged to be paid by a conviction unless the court has since the conviction inquired into the defaulter's means in his presence on at least one occasion.

(4) An order under sub-section (1) above shall not be made by a magistrates' court unless the court is satisfied that the defaulter has, or has had since the date on which the sum in question was adjudged to be paid, the means to pay the sum or any instalment of it on which he has defaulted, and refuses or neglects or, as the case may be, has refused or neglected, to pay it.

(5) An order under sub-section (1) above may be made in pursuance of paragraph (b) of that sub-section against a parent or guardian who, having been required to attend, has failed to do so; but, save as aforesaid, an order under that sub-section shall not be made in pursuance of that paragraph without giving the parent or guardian an opportunity to be heard.

(6) A parent or guardian may appeal to the Crown Court against an order under sub-section (1) above made in pursuance of paragraph (b) of that sub-section.

(7) Any sum ordered under sub-section (1)(b) above to be paid by a parent or guardian may be recovered from him in like manner as if the order had been made on the conviction of the parent or guardian of an offence.

(8) In this section:

'guardian', in relation to a person under 18, means a person appointed, according to law, to be his guardian, or by order of a court of competent jurisdiction;

'sum adjudged to be paid by a conviction' means any fine, costs, compensation or other sum adjudged to be paid by an order made on a finding of guilt ...

SUPERVISION ORDERS

POWERS OF CRIMINAL COURTS (SENTENCING) ACT 2000

Section 63: Supervision orders

(1) Where a child or young person (that is to say, any person aged under 18) is convicted of an offence, the court by or before which he is convicted may (subject to sections 34 to 36 above) make an order placing him under the supervision of:

(a) a local authority designated by the order;

(b) a probation officer; or

(c) a member of a youth offending team.

(2) An order under sub-section (1) above is in this Act referred to as a 'supervision order'.

(3) In this Act 'supervisor', in relation to a supervision order, means the person under whose supervision the offender is placed or to be placed by the order.

(4) Schedule 6 to this Act (which specifies requirements that may be included in supervision orders) shall have effect.

(5) A court shall not make a supervision order unless it is satisfied that the offender resides or will reside in the area of a local authority; and a court shall be entitled to be satisfied that the offender will so reside if he is to be required so to reside by a provision to be included in the order in pursuance of paragraph 1 of Schedule 6 to this Act.

(6) A supervision order:

(a) shall name the area of the local authority and the petty sessions area in which it appears to the court making the order (or to the court amending under Schedule 7 to this Act any provision included in the order in pursuance of this paragraph) that the offender resides or will reside; and

(b) may contain such prescribed provisions as the court making the order (or amending it under that Schedule) considers appropriate for facilitating the performance by the supervisor of his functions under section 64(4) below, including any prescribed provisions for requiring visits to be made by the offender to the supervisor,

and in paragraph (b) above 'prescribed' means prescribed by rules under section 144 of the Magistrates' Courts Act 1980.

(7) A supervision order shall, unless it has previously been revoked, cease to have effect at the end of the period of three years, or such shorter period as may be specified in the order, beginning with the date on which the order was originally made.

(8) A court which makes a supervision order shall forthwith send a copy of its order:

(a) to the offender and, if the offender is aged under 14, to his parent or guardian;

(b) to the supervisor;

(c) to any local authority who are not entitled by virtue of paragraph (b) above to such a copy and whose area is named in the supervision order in pursuance of sub-section (6) above;

(d) where the offender is required by the order to reside with an individual or to undergo treatment by or under the direction of an individual or at any place, to the individual or the person in charge of that place; and

(e) where a petty sessions area named in the order in pursuance of sub-section (6) above is not that for which the court acts, to the justices' chief executive for the petty sessions area so named,

and, in a case falling within paragraph (e) above, shall also send to the justices' chief executive in question such documents and information relating to the case as the court considers likely to be of assistance to them.

(9) If a court makes a supervision order while another such order made by any court is in force in respect of the offender, the court making the new order may revoke the earlier order (and paragraph 10 of Schedule 7 to this Act (supplementary provision) shall apply to the revocation).

SCHEDULE 6

REQUIREMENTS WHICH MAY BE INCLUDED IN SUPERVISION ORDERS

Requirement to reside with named individual

1   A supervision order may require the offender to reside with an individual named in the order who agrees to the requirement, but a requirement imposed by a supervision order in pursuance of this paragraph shall be subject to any such requirement of the order as is authorised by paragraph 2, 3, 6 or 7 below.

Requirement to comply with directions of supervisor

2

(1) Subject to sub-paragraph (2) below, a supervision order may require the offender to comply with any directions given from time to time by the supervisor and requiring him to do all or any of the following things:

(a) to live at a place or places specified in the directions for a period or periods so specified;

(b) to present himself to a person or persons specified in the directions at a place or places and on a day or days so specified;

(c) to participate in activities specified in the directions on a day or days so specified.

(2) A supervision order shall not require compliance with directions given by virtue of sub-paragraph (1) above unless the court making it is satisfied that a scheme under section 66 of this Act (local authority schemes) is in force for the area where the offender resides or will reside; and no such directions may involve the use of facilities which are not for the time being specified in a scheme in force under that section for that area.

(3) A requirement imposed by a supervision order in pursuance of sub-paragraph (1) above shall be subject to any such requirement of the order as is authorised by paragraph 6 below (treatment for offender's mental condition).

(4) It shall be for the supervisor to decide:

   (a) whether and to what extent he exercises any power to give directions conferred on him by virtue of sub-paragraph (1) above; and

   (b) the form of any directions.

(5) The total number of days in respect of which an offender may be required to comply with directions given by virtue of paragraph (a), (b) or (c) of sub-paragraph (1) above shall not exceed 90 or such lesser number, if any, as the order may specify for the purposes of this sub-paragraph.

(6) For the purpose of calculating the total number of days in respect of which such directions may be given, the supervisor shall be entitled to disregard any day in respect of which directions were previously given in pursuance of the order and on which the directions were not complied with.

(7) Directions given by the supervisor by virtue of sub-paragraph (1)(b) or (c) above shall, as far as practicable, be such as to avoid:

   (a) any conflict with the offender's religious beliefs or with the requirements of any other community order to which he may be subject; and

   (b) any interference with the times, if any, at which he normally works or attends school or any other educational establishment.

Requirements as to activities, reparation, night restrictions, etc

3

(1) This paragraph applies to a supervision order unless the order requires the offender to comply with directions given by the supervisor under paragraph 2(1) above.

(2) Subject to the following provisions of this paragraph and paragraph 4 below, a supervision order to which this paragraph applies may require the offender:

   (a) to live at a place or places specified in the order for a period or periods so specified;

   (b) to present himself to a person or persons specified in the order at a place or places and on a day or days so specified;

   (c) to participate in activities specified in the order on a day or days so specified;

   (d) to make reparation specified in the order to a person or persons so specified or to the community at large;

   (e) to remain for specified periods between 6 pm and 6 am:

      (i) at a place specified in the order; or

      (ii) at one of several places so specified;

   (f) to refrain from participating in activities specified in the order:

      (i) on a specified day or days during the period for which the supervision order is in force; or

(ii) during the whole of that period or a specified portion of it,

and in this paragraph 'make reparation' means make reparation for the offence otherwise than by the payment of compensation.

(3) The total number of days in respect of which an offender may be subject to requirements imposed by virtue of paragraph (a), (b), (c), (d) or (e) of sub-paragraph (2) above shall not exceed 90.

(4) The court may not include requirements under sub-paragraph (2) above in a supervision order unless:

    (a) it has first consulted the supervisor as to:

        (i) the offender's circumstances; and

        (ii) the feasibility of securing compliance with the requirements,

        and is satisfied, having regard to the supervisor's report, that it is feasible to secure compliance with them;

    (b) having regard to the circumstances of the case, it considers the requirements necessary for securing the good conduct of the offender or for preventing a repetition by him of the same offence or the commission of other offences; and

    (c) if the offender is aged under 16, it has obtained and considered information about his family circumstances and the likely effect of the requirements on those circumstances.

(5) The court shall not by virtue of sub-paragraph (2) above include in a supervision order:

    (a) any requirement that would involve the co-operation of a person other than the supervisor and the offender, unless that other person consents to its inclusion;

    (b) any requirement to make reparation to any person unless that person:

        (i) is identified by the court as a victim of the offence or a person otherwise affected by it; and

        (ii) consents to the inclusion of the requirement;

    (c) any requirement requiring the offender to reside with a specified individual; or

    (d) any such requirement as is mentioned in paragraph 6(2) below (treatment for offender's mental condition).

(6) Requirements included in a supervision order by virtue of sub-paragraph (2)(b) or (c) above shall, as far as practicable, be such as to avoid:

    (a) any conflict with the offender's religious beliefs or with the requirements of any other community order to which he may be subject; and

    (a) any interference with the times, if any, at which he normally works or attends school or any other educational establishment,

and sub-paragraphs (7) and (8) below are without prejudice to this sub-paragraph.

(7) Subject to sub-paragraph (8) below, a supervision order may not by virtue of sub-paragraph (2) above include:

(a) any requirement that would involve the offender in absence from home:

(i) for more than two consecutive nights; or

(ii) for more than two nights in any one week; or

(b) if the offender is of compulsory school age, any requirement to participate in activities during normal school hours,

unless the court making the order is satisfied that the facilities whose use would be involved are for the time being specified in a scheme in force under section 66 of this Act for the area in which the offender resides or will reside.

(8) Sub-paragraph (7)(b) above does not apply to activities carried out in accordance with arrangements made or approved by the local education authority in whose area the offender resides or will reside.

(9) Expressions used in sub-paragraphs (7) and (8) above and in the Education Act 1996 have the same meaning in those sub-paragraphs as in that Act.

4

(1) The place, or one of the places, specified in a requirement under paragraph 3(2)(e) above ('a night restriction') shall be the place where the offender lives.

(2) A night restriction shall not require the offender to remain at a place for longer than ten hours on any one night.

(3) A night restriction shall not be imposed in respect of any day which falls outside the period of three months beginning with the date when the supervision order is made.

(4) A night restriction shall not be imposed in respect of more than 30 days in all.

(5) A night restriction imposed in respect of a period of time beginning in the evening and ending in the morning shall be treated as imposed only in respect of the day upon which the period begins.

(6) An offender who is required by a night restriction to remain at a place may leave it if he is accompanied:

(a) by his parent or guardian;

(b) by his supervisor; or

(c) by some other person specified in the supervision order.

Requirement to live for specified period in local authority accommodation

5

(1) Where the conditions mentioned in sub-paragraph (2) below are satisfied, a supervision order may impose a requirement ('a local authority residence requirement') that the offender shall live for a specified period in local authority accommodation (as defined by section 163 of this Act).

(2) The conditions are that:

(a) a supervision order has previously been made in respect of the offender;

(b) that order imposed:

(i) a requirement under paragraph 1, 2, 3 or 7 of this Schedule; or

(ii) a local authority residence requirement;

(c) the offender fails to comply with that requirement, or is convicted of an offence committed while that order was in force; and

(d) the court is satisfied that:

(i) the failure to comply with the requirement, or the behaviour which constituted the offence, was due to a significant extent to the circumstances in which the offender was living; and

(ii) the imposition of a local authority residence requirement will assist in his rehabilitation,

except that sub-paragraph (i) of paragraph (d) above does not apply where the condition in paragraph (b)(ii) above is satisfied.

(3) A local authority residence requirement shall designate the local authority who are to receive the offender, and that authority shall be the authority in whose area the offender resides.

(4) The court shall not impose a local authority residence requirement without first consulting the designated authority.

(5) A local authority residence requirement may stipulate that the offender shall not live with a named person.

(6) The maximum period which may be specified in a local authority residence requirement is six months.

(7) A court shall not impose a local authority residence requirement in respect of an offender who is not legally represented at the relevant time in that court unless:

(a) he was granted a right to representation funded by the Legal Services Commission as part of the Criminal Defence Service for the purposes of the proceedings but the right was withdrawn because of his conduct; or

(b) he has been informed of his right to apply for such representation for the purposes of the proceedings and has had the opportunity to do so, but nevertheless refused or failed to apply.

(8) In sub-paragraph (7) above:

(a) 'the relevant time' means the time when the court is considering whether or not to impose the requirement; and

(b) 'the proceedings' means:

(i) the whole proceedings; or

(ii) the part of the proceedings relating to the imposition of the requirement.

(9) A supervision order imposing a local authority residence requirement may also impose any of the requirements mentioned in paragraphs 2, 3, 6 and 7 of this Schedule.

Requirements as to treatment for mental condition

6

(1) This paragraph applies where a court which proposes to make a supervision order is satisfied, on the evidence of a registered medical practitioner approved for the purposes of section 12 of the Mental Health Act 1983, that the mental condition of the offender:

    (a) is such as requires and may be susceptible to treatment; but

    (b) is not such as to warrant the making of a hospital order or guardianship order within the meaning of that Act.

(2) Where this paragraph applies, the court may include in the supervision order a requirement that the offender shall, for a period specified in the order, submit to treatment of one of the following descriptions so specified, that is to say:

    (a) treatment as a resident patient in a hospital or mental nursing home within the meaning of the Mental Health Act 1983, but not a hospital at which high security psychiatric services within the meaning of that Act are provided;

    (b) treatment as a non-resident patient at an institution or place specified in the order;

    (c) treatment by or under the direction of a registered medical practitioner specified in the order; or

    (d) treatment by or under the direction of a chartered psychologist specified in the order.

(3) A requirement shall not be included in a supervision order by virtue of sub-paragraph (2) above:

    (a) in any case, unless the court is satisfied that arrangements have been or can be made for the treatment in question and, in the case of treatment as a resident patient, for the reception of the patient;

    (b) in the case of an order made or to be made in respect of a person aged 14 or over, unless he consents to its inclusion;

and a requirement so included shall not in any case continue in force after the offender attains the age of 18.

(4) Sub-sections (2) and (3) of section 54 of the Mental Health Act 1983 shall have effect with respect to proof for the purposes of sub-paragraph (1) above of an offender's mental condition as they have effect with respect to proof of an offender's mental condition for the purposes of section 37(2)(a) of that Act.

(5) In sub-paragraph (2) above 'chartered psychologist' means a person for the time being listed in the British Psychological Society's Register of Chartered Psychologists.

Requirements as to education

7

(1) This paragraph applies to a supervision order unless the order requires the offender to comply with directions given by the supervisor under paragraph 2(1) above.

(2) Subject to the following provisions of this paragraph, a supervision order to which this paragraph applies may require the offender, if he is of compulsory school age, to comply, for as long as he is of that age and the order remains in force, with such arrangements for his education as may from time to time be made by his parent, being arrangements for the time being approved by the local education authority.

(3) The court shall not include such a requirement in a supervision order unless:

(a) it has consulted the local education authority with regard to its proposal to include the requirement; and

(b) it is satisfied that in the view of the local education authority arrangements exist for the offender to receive efficient full-time education suitable to his age, ability and aptitude and to any special educational need he may have.

(4) Expressions used in sub-paragraphs (2) and (3) above and in the Education Act 1996 have the same meaning in those sub-paragraphs as in that Act.

(5) The court may not include a requirement under sub-paragraph (2) above unless it has first consulted the supervisor as to the offender's circumstances and, having regard to the circumstances of the case, it considers the requirement necessary for securing the good conduct of the offender or for preventing a repetition by him of the same offence or the commission of other offences.

Exercise of powers under paragraphs 3, 6 and 7

8

(1) Any power to include a requirement in a supervision order which is exercisable in relation to a person by virtue of paragraph 3, 6 or 7 above may be exercised in relation to him whether or not any other such power is exercised.

(2) Sub-paragraph (1) above is without prejudice to the power to include in a supervision order any other combination of requirements under different paragraphs of this Schedule that is authorised by this Schedule.

SCHEDULE 7

BREACH, REVOCATION AND AMENDMENT OF SUPERVISION ORDERS

Meaning of 'relevant court', etc

1

(1) In this Schedule, 'relevant court', in relation to a supervision order, means:

    (a) where the offender is under the age of 18, a youth court acting for the petty sessions area for the time being named in the order in pursuance of section 63(6) of this Act;

    (b) where the offender has attained that age, a magistrates' court other than a youth court, being a magistrates' court acting for the petty sessions area for the time being so named.

(2) If an application to a youth court is made in pursuance of this Schedule and while it is pending the offender to whom it relates attains the age of 18, the youth court shall deal with the application as if he had not attained that age.

Breach of requirement of supervision order

2

(1) This paragraph applies if while a supervision order is in force in respect of an offender it is proved to the satisfaction of a relevant court, on the application of the supervisor, that the offender has failed to comply with any requirement included in the supervision order in pursuance of paragraph 1, 2, 3, 5 or 7 of Schedule 6 to this Act or section 63(6)(b) of this Act.

(2) Where this paragraph applies, the court:

    (a) whether or not it also makes an order under paragraph 5(1) below (revocation or amendment of supervision order):

        (i) may order the offender to pay a fine of an amount not exceeding £1,000; or

        (ii) subject to paragraph 3 below, may make a curfew order in respect of him; or

        (iii) subject to paragraph 4 below, may make an attendance centre order in respect of him; or

    (b) if the supervision order was made by a magistrates' court, may revoke the supervision order and deal with the offender, for the offence in respect of which the order was made, in any way in which he could have been dealt with for that offence by the court which made the order if the order had not been made; or

    (c) if the supervision order was made by the Crown Court, may commit him in custody or release him on bail until he can be brought or appear before the Crown Court.

(3) Where a court deals with an offender under sub-paragraph (2)(c) above, it shall send to the Crown Court a certificate signed by a justice of the peace giving:

    (a) particulars of the offender's failure to comply with the requirement in question; and

    (b) such other particulars of the case as may be desirable; and a certificate purporting to be so signed shall be admissible as evidence of the failure before the Crown Court.

(4) Where:

    (a) by virtue of sub-paragraph (2)(c) above the offender is brought or appears before the Crown Court; and

    (b) it is proved to the satisfaction of the court that he has failed to comply with the requirement in question,

that court may deal with him, for the offence in respect of which the supervision order was made, in any way in which it could have dealt with him for that offence if it had not made the order.

(5) Where the Crown Court deals with an offender under sub-paragraph (4) above, it shall revoke the supervision order if it is still in force.

(6) A fine imposed under this paragraph shall be deemed, for the purposes of any enactment, to be a sum adjudged to be paid by a conviction.

(7) In dealing with an offender under this paragraph, a court shall take into account the extent to which he has complied with the requirements of the supervision order.

(8) Where a supervision order has been made on appeal, for the purposes of this paragraph it shall be deemed:

    (a) if it was made on an appeal brought from a magistrates' court, to have been made by that magistrates' court;

    (b) if it was made on an appeal brought from the Crown Court or from the criminal division of the Court of Appeal, to have been made by the Crown Court,

and, in relation to a supervision order made on appeal, sub-paragraph (2)(b) above shall have effect as if the words 'if the order had not been made' were omitted and sub-paragraph (4) above shall have effect as if the words 'if it had not made the order' were omitted.

(9) This paragraph has effect subject to paragraph 7 below.

...

Revocation and amendment of supervision order

5

(1) If while a supervision order is in force in respect of an offender it appears to a relevant court, on the application of the supervisor or the offender, that it is appropriate to make an order under this sub-paragraph, the court may:

    (a) make an order revoking the supervision order; or

    (b) make an order amending it:

(i) by cancelling any requirement included in it in pursuance of Schedule 6 to, or section 63(6)(b) of, this Act; or

(ii) by inserting in it (either in addition to or in substitution for any of its provisions) any provision which could have been included in the order if the court had then had power to make it and were exercising the power.

(2) Sub-paragraph (1) above has effect subject to paragraphs 7 to 9 below.

(3) The powers of amendment conferred by sub-paragraph (1) above do not include power:

(a) to insert in the supervision order, after the end of three months beginning with the date when the order was originally made, a requirement in pursuance of paragraph 6 of Schedule 6 to this Act (treatment for mental condition), unless it is in substitution for such a requirement already included in the order; or

(b) to insert in the supervision order a requirement in pursuance of paragraph 3(2)(e) of that Schedule (night restrictions) in respect of any day which falls outside the period of three months beginning with the date when the order was originally made.

(4) Where an application under sub-paragraph (1) above for the revocation of a supervision order is dismissed, no further application for its revocation shall be made under that sub-paragraph by any person during the period of three months beginning with the date of the dismissal except with the consent of a court having jurisdiction to entertain such an application.

Amendment of order on report of medical practitioner

6

(1) If a medical practitioner by whom or under whose direction an offender is being treated for his mental condition in pursuance of a requirement included in a supervision order by virtue of paragraph 6 of Schedule 6 to this Act:

(a) is unwilling to continue to treat or direct the treatment of the offender; or

(b) is of the opinion mentioned in sub-paragraph (2) below, the practitioner shall make a report in writing to that effect to the supervisor.

(2) The opinion referred to in sub-paragraph (1) above is:

(a) that the treatment of the offender should be continued beyond the period specified in that behalf in the order;

(b) that the offender needs different treatment;

(c) that the offender is not susceptible to treatment; or

(d) that the offender does not require further treatment.

(3) On receiving a report under sub-paragraph (1) above the supervisor shall refer it to a relevant court; and on such a reference the court may make an order cancelling or varying the requirement.

(4) Sub-paragraph (3) above has effect subject to paragraphs 7 to 9 below.

Presence of offender in court, remands, etc

7

(1) Where the supervisor makes an application or reference under paragraph 2(1), 5(1) or 6(3) above to a court he may bring the offender before the court; and, subject to sub-paragraph (9) below, a court shall not make an order under paragraph 2, 5(1) or 6(3) above unless the offender is present before the court.

(2) Without prejudice to any power to issue a summons or warrant apart from this sub-paragraph, a justice may issue a summons or warrant for the purpose of securing the attendance of an offender before the court to which any application or reference in respect of him is made under paragraph 2(1), 5(1) or 6(3) above.

(3) Sub-sections (3) and (4) of section 55 of the Magistrates' Courts Act 1980 (which among other things restrict the circumstances in which a warrant may be issued) shall apply with the necessary modifications to a warrant under sub-paragraph (2) above as they apply to a warrant under that section, but as if in sub-section (3) after the word 'summons' there were inserted the words 'cannot be served or'.

(4) Where the offender is arrested in pursuance of a warrant issued by virtue of sub-paragraph (2) above and cannot be brought immediately before the court referred to in that sub-paragraph, the person in whose custody he is:

(a) may make arrangements for his detention in a place of safety for a period of not more than 72 hours from the time of the arrest (and it shall be lawful for him to be detained in pursuance of the arrangements); and

(b) shall within that period, unless within it the offender is brought before the court referred to in sub-paragraph (2) above, bring him before a justice,

and in paragraph (a) above 'place of safety' has the same meaning as in the Children and Young Persons Act 1933.

(5) Where an offender is brought before a justice under sub-paragraph (4)(b) above, the justice may:

(a) direct that he be released forthwith; or

(b) subject to sub-paragraph (7) below, remand him to local authority accommodation.

(6) Subject to sub-paragraph (7) below, where an application is made to a youth court under paragraph 5(1) above, the court may remand (or further remand) the offender to local authority accommodation if:

(a) a warrant has been issued under sub-paragraph (2) above for the purpose of securing the attendance of the offender before the court; or

(b) the court considers that remanding (or further remanding) him will enable information to be obtained which is likely to assist the court in deciding whether and, if so, how to exercise its powers under paragraph 5(1) above.

(7) Where the offender is aged 18 or over at the time when he is brought before a justice under sub-paragraph (4)(b) above, or is aged 18 or over at a time when (apart from this sub-paragraph) a youth court could exercise its powers under sub-paragraph (6) above in respect of him, he shall not be remanded to local authority accommodation but may instead be remanded:

    (a) to a remand centre, if the justice or youth court has been notified that such a centre is available for the reception of persons under this sub-paragraph; or

    (b) to a prison, if the justice or youth court has not been so notified.

(8) A justice or court remanding a person to local authority accommodation under this paragraph shall designate, as the authority who are to receive him, the authority named in the supervision order.

(9) A court may make an order under paragraph 5(1) or 6(3) above in the absence of the offender if the effect of the order is confined to one or more of the following, that is to say:

    (a) revoking the supervision order;

    (b) cancelling a provision included in the supervision order in pursuance of Schedule 6 to, or section 63(6)(b) of, this Act;

    (c) reducing the duration of the supervision order or any provision included in it in pursuance of that Schedule;

    (d) altering in the supervision order the name of any area;

    (e) changing the supervisor.

Restrictions on court's powers to revoke or amend order

8

(1) A youth court shall not:

    (a) exercise its powers under paragraph 5(1) above to make an order:

        (i) revoking a supervision order; or

        (ii) inserting in it a requirement authorised by Schedule 6 to this Act; or

        (iii) varying or cancelling such a requirement,

except in a case where the court is satisfied that the offender either is unlikely to receive the care or control he needs unless the court makes the order or is likely to receive it notwithstanding the order;

    (b) exercise its powers to make an order under paragraph 6(3) above except in such a case as is mentioned in paragraph (a) above;

    (c) exercise its powers under paragraph 5(1) above to make an order inserting a requirement authorised by paragraph 6 of Schedule 6 to this Act in a supervision order which does not already contain such a requirement, unless the court is satisfied as mentioned in paragraph 6(1) of that Schedule on such evidence as is there mentioned.

(2) For the purposes of this paragraph 'care' includes protection and guidance and 'control' includes discipline.

9 Where the offender has attained the age of 14, then except with his consent a court shall not make an order under paragraph 5(1) or 6(3) above containing provisions:

(a) which insert in the supervision order a requirement authorised by paragraph 6 of Schedule 6 to this Act; or

(b) which alter such a requirement already included in the supervision order otherwise than by removing it or reducing its duration.

...

Appeals

11 The offender may appeal to the Crown Court against:

(a) any order made under paragraph 2(2), 5(1) or 6(3) above by a relevant court, except:

(i) an order made or which could have been made in the absence of the offender (by virtue of paragraph 7(9) above); and

(ii) an order containing only provisions to which the offender consented in pursuance of paragraph 9 above;

(b) the dismissal of an application under paragraph 5(1) above to revoke a supervision order.

Power of parent or guardian to make application on behalf of young person

12

(1) Without prejudice to any power apart from this sub-paragraph to bring proceedings on behalf of another person, any power to make an application which is exercisable by a child or young person by virtue of paragraph 5(1) above shall also be exercisable on his behalf by his parent or guardian.

(2) In this paragraph 'guardian' includes any person who was a guardian of the child or young person in question at the time when any supervision order to which the application relates was originally made.

ATTENDANCE CENTRE ORDERS

POWERS OF CRIMINAL COURTS (SENTENCING) ACT 2000

Section 60: Attendance centre orders

(1) Where:

(a) (subject to sections 34 to 36 above) a person aged under 21 is convicted by or before a court of an offence punishable with imprisonment; or

(b) a court would have power, but for section 89 below (restrictions on imprisonment of young offenders and defaulters), to commit a person aged under 21 to prison in default of payment of any sum of money or for failing to do or abstain from doing anything required to be done or left undone; or

(c) a court has power to commit a person aged at least 21 but under 25 to prison in default of payment of any sum of money,

the court may, if it has been notified by the Secretary of State that an attendance centre is available for the reception of persons of his description, order him to attend at such a centre, to be specified in the order, for such number of hours as may be so specified.

(2) An order under sub-section (1) above is in this Act referred to as an 'attendance centre order'.

(3) The aggregate number of hours for which an attendance centre order may require a person to attend at an attendance centre shall not be less than 12 except where:

(a) he is aged under 14; and

(b) the court is of the opinion that 12 hours would be excessive,

having regard to his age or any other circumstances.

(4) The aggregate number of hours shall not exceed 12 except where the court is of the opinion, having regard to all the circumstances, that 12 hours would be inadequate, and in that case:

(a) shall not exceed 24 where the person is aged under 16; and

(b) shall not exceed 36 where the person is aged 16 or over but under 21 or (where sub-section (1)(c) above applies) under 25.

(5) A court may make an attendance centre order in respect of a person before a previous attendance centre order made in respect of him has ceased to have effect, and may determine the number of hours to be specified in the order without regard:

(a) to the number specified in the previous order; or

(b) to the fact that that order is still in effect.

(6) An attendance centre order shall not be made unless the court is satisfied that the attendance centre to be specified in it is reasonably accessible to the person concerned, having regard to his age, the means of access available to him and any other circumstances.

(7) The times at which a person is required to attend at an attendance centre shall, as far as practicable, be such as to avoid:

(a) any conflict with his religious beliefs or with the requirements of any other community order to which he may be subject; and

(b) any interference with the times, if any, at which he normally works or attends school or any other educational establishment.

(8) The first time at which the person is required to attend at an attendance centre shall be a time at which the centre is available for his attendance in accordance with the notification of the Secretary of State, and shall be specified in the order.

(9) The subsequent times shall be fixed by the officer in charge of the centre, having regard to the person's circumstances.

(10) A person shall not be required under this section to attend at an attendance centre on more than one occasion on any day, or for more than three hours on any occasion.

(11) Where a court makes an attendance centre order, the clerk of the court shall:

(a) deliver or send a copy of the order to the officer in charge of the attendance centre specified in it; and

(b) deliver a copy of the order to the person in respect of whom it is made or send a copy by registered post or the recorded delivery service addressed to his last or usual place of abode.

(12) Where a person ('the defaulter') has been ordered to attend at an attendance centre in default of the payment of any sum of money:

(a) on payment of the whole sum to any person authorised to receive it, the attendance centre order shall cease to have effect;

(b) on payment of a part of the sum to any such person, the total number of hours for which the defaulter is required to attend at the centre shall be reduced proportionately, that is to say by such number of complete hours as bears to the total number the proportion most nearly approximating to, without exceeding, the proportion which the part bears to the whole sum.

SCHEDULE 5

BREACH, REVOCATION AND AMENDMENT OF ATTENDANCE CENTRE ORDERS

Breach of order or attendance centre rules

1

(1) Where an attendance centre order is in force and it appears on information to a justice acting for a relevant petty sessions area that the offender:

(a) has failed to attend in accordance with the order; or

(b) while attending has committed a breach of rules made under section 62(3) of this Act which cannot be adequately dealt with under those rules,

the justice may issue a summons requiring the offender to appear at the place and time specified in the summons before a magistrates' court acting for the area or, if the information is in writing and on oath, may issue a warrant for the offender's arrest requiring him to be brought before such a court.

(2) For the purposes of this paragraph a petty sessions area is a relevant petty sessions area in relation to an attendance centre order:

(a) if the attendance centre which the offender is required to attend by the order or by virtue of an order under paragraph 5(1)(b) below is situated in it; or

(b) if the order was made by a magistrates' court acting for it.

2

(1) If it is proved to the satisfaction of the magistrates' court before which an offender appears or is brought under paragraph 1 above that he has failed without reasonable excuse to attend as mentioned in sub-paragraph (1)(a) of that paragraph or has committed such a breach of rules as is mentioned in sub-paragraph (1)(b) of that paragraph, that court may deal with him in any one of the following ways:

(a) it may impose on him a fine not exceeding £1,000;

(b) where the attendance centre order was made by a magistrates' court, it may deal with him, for the offence in respect of which the order was made, in any way in which he could have been dealt with for that offence by the court which made the order if the order had not been made; or

(c) where the order was made by the Crown Court, it may commit him to custody or release him on bail until he can be brought or appear before the Crown Court.

(2) Any exercise by the court of its power under sub-paragraph (1)(a) above shall be without prejudice to the continuation of the order.

(3) A fine imposed under sub-paragraph (1)(a) above shall be deemed, for the purposes of any enactment, to be a sum adjudged to be paid by a conviction.

(4) Where a magistrates' court deals with an offender under sub-paragraph (1)(b) above, it shall revoke the attendance centre order if it is still in force.

(5) In dealing with an offender under sub-paragraph (1)(b) above, a magistrates' court:

(a) shall take into account the extent to which the offender has complied with the requirements of the attendance centre order; and

(b) in the case of an offender who has wilfully and persistently failed to comply with those requirements, may impose a custodial sentence notwithstanding anything in section 79(2) of this Act.

(6) A person sentenced under sub-paragraph (1)(b) above for an offence may appeal to the Crown Court against the sentence.

(7) A magistrates' court which deals with an offender's case under sub-paragraph (1)(c) above shall send to the Crown Court:

(a) a certificate signed by a justice of the peace giving particulars of the offender's failure to attend or, as the case may be, the breach of the rules which he has committed; and

(c) such other particulars of the case as may be desirable,

and a certificate purporting to be so signed shall be admissible as evidence of the failure or the breach before the Crown Court.

3

(1) Where by virtue of paragraph 2(1)(c) above the offender is brought or appears before the Crown Court and it is proved to the satisfaction of the court:

    (a) that he has failed without reasonable excuse to attend as mentioned in paragraph 1(1)(a) above; or

    (b) that he has committed such a breach of rules as is mentioned in paragraph 1(1)(b) above,

that court may deal with him, for the offence in respect of which the order was made, in any way in which it could have dealt with him for that offence if it had not made the order.

(2) Where the Crown Court deals with an offender under sub-paragraph (1) above, it shall revoke the attendance centre order if it is still in force.

(3) In dealing with an offender under sub-paragraph (1) above, the Crown Court:

    (a) shall take into account the extent to which the offender has complied with the requirements of the attendance centre order; and

    (b) in the case of an offender who has wilfully and persistently failed to comply with those requirements, may impose a custodial sentence notwithstanding anything in section 79(2) of this Act.

(4) In proceedings before the Crown Court under this paragraph any question whether there has been a failure to attend or a breach of the rules shall be determined by the court and not by the verdict of a jury.

Revocation of order with or without re-sentencing

4

(1) Where an attendance centre order is in force in respect of an offender, an appropriate court may, on an application made by the offender or by the officer in charge of the relevant attendance centre, revoke the order.

(2) In sub-paragraph (1) above 'an appropriate court' means:

    (a) where the court which made the order was the Crown Court and there is included in the order a direction that the power to revoke the order is reserved to that court, the Crown Court;

    (b) in any other case, either of the following:

        (i) a magistrates' court acting for the petty sessions area in which the relevant attendance centre is situated;

        (ii) the court which made the order.

(3) Any power conferred by this paragraph:

    (a) on a magistrates' court to revoke an attendance centre order made by such a court; or

    (b) on the Crown Court to revoke an attendance centre order made by the Crown Court,

includes power to deal with the offender, for the offence in respect of which the order was made, in any way in which he could have been dealt with for that offence by the court which made the order if the order had not been made.

(4) A person sentenced by a magistrates' court under sub-paragraph (3) above for an offence may appeal to the Crown Court against the sentence.

...

Amendment of order

5

(1) Where an attendance centre order is in force in respect of an offender, an appropriate magistrates' court may, on an application made by the offender or by the officer in charge of the relevant attendance centre, by order:

(a) vary the day or hour specified in the order for the offender's first attendance at the relevant attendance centre; or

(b) substitute for the relevant attendance centre an attendance centre which the court is satisfied is reasonably accessible to the offender, having regard to his age, the means of access available to him and any other circumstances.

(2) In sub-paragraph (1) above 'an appropriate magistrates' court' means:

(a) a magistrates' court acting for the petty sessions area in which the relevant attendance centre is situated; or

(b) (except where the attendance centre order was made by the Crown Court) the magistrates' court which made the order.

...

ACTION PLAN ORDERS

POWERS OF CRIMINAL COURTS (SENTENCING) ACT 2000

Section 69: Action plan orders

(1) Where a child or young person (that is to say, any person aged under 18) is convicted of an offence and the court by or before which he is convicted is of the opinion mentioned in sub-section (3) below, the court may (subject to sections 34 to 36 above) make an order which:

(a) requires the offender, for a period of three months beginning with the date of the order, to comply with an action plan, that is to say, a series of requirements with respect to his actions and whereabouts during that period;

(b) places the offender for that period under the supervision of the responsible officer; and

(c) requires the offender to comply with any directions given by the responsible officer with a view to the implementation of that plan;

and the requirements included in the order, and any directions given by the responsible officer, may include requirements authorised by section 70 below.

(2) An order under sub-section (1) above is in this Act referred to as an 'action plan order'.

(3) The opinion referred to in sub-section (1) above is that the making of an action plan order is desirable in the interests of:

(a) securing the rehabilitation of the offender; or

(b) preventing the commission by him of further offences.

(4) In this Act 'responsible officer', in relation to an offender subject to an action plan order, means one of the following who is specified in the order, namely:

(a) a probation officer;

(b) a social worker of a local authority social services department;

(c) a member of a youth offending team.

(5) The court shall not make an action plan order in respect of the offender if:

(a) he is already the subject of such an order; or

(b) the court proposes to pass on him a custodial sentence or to make in respect of him a probation order, a community service order, a combination order, an attendance centre order, a supervision order or a referral order.

(6) Before making an action plan order, the court shall obtain and consider:

(a) a written report by a probation officer, a social worker of a local authority social services department or a member of a youth offending team indicating:

(i) the requirements proposed by that person to be included in the order;

(ii) the benefits to the offender that the proposed requirements are designed to achieve; and

(iii) the attitude of a parent or guardian of the offender to the proposed requirements; and

(b) where the offender is aged under 16, information about the offender's family circumstances and the likely effect of the order on those circumstances.

(7) The court shall not make an action plan order unless it has been notified by the Secretary of State that arrangements for implementing such orders are available in the area proposed to be named in the order under sub-section (8) below and the notice has not been withdrawn.

(8) An action plan order shall name the petty sessions area in which it appears to the court making the order (or to the court amending under Schedule 8

to this Act any provision included in the order in pursuance of this sub-section) that the offender resides or will reside.

(9) Where an action plan order specifies a probation officer under sub-section (4) above, the officer specified must be an officer appointed for or assigned to the petty sessions area named in the order.

(10) Where an action plan order specifies under that sub-section:

    (a) a social worker of a local authority social services department; or

    (b) a member of a youth offending team,

the social worker or member specified must be a social worker of, or a member of a youth offending team established by, the local authority within whose area it appears to the court that the offender resides or will reside.

(11) Before making an action plan order, the court shall explain to the offender in ordinary language:

    (a) the effect of the order and of the requirements proposed to be included in it;

    (b) the consequences which may follow (under Schedule 8 to this Act) if he fails to comply with any of those requirements; and

    (c) that the court has power (under that Schedule) to review the order on the application either of the offender or of the responsible officer.

Section 70: Requirements which may be included in action plan orders and directions

(1) Requirements included in an action plan order, or directions given by a responsible officer, may require the offender to do all or any of the following things, namely:

    (a) to participate in activities specified in the requirements or directions at a time or times so specified;

    (b) to present himself to a person or persons specified in the requirements or directions at a place or places and at a time or times so specified;

    (c) subject to sub-section (2) below, to attend at an attendance centre specified in the requirements or directions for a number of hours so specified;

    (d) to stay away from a place or places specified in the requirements or directions;

    (e) to comply with any arrangements for his education specified in the requirements or directions;

    (f) to make reparation specified in the requirements or directions to a person or persons so specified or to the community at large; and

    (g) to attend any hearing fixed by the court under section 71 below.

(2) Sub-section (1)(c) above applies only where the offence committed by the offender is an offence punishable with imprisonment.

(3) In sub-section (1)(f) above 'make reparation', in relation to an offender, means make reparation for the offence otherwise than by the payment of compensation.

(4) A person shall not be specified in requirements or directions under sub-section (1)(f) above unless:

(a) he is identified by the court or (as the case may be) the responsible officer as a victim of the offence or a person otherwise affected by it; and

(b) he consents to the reparation being made.

(5) Requirements included in an action plan order and directions given by a responsible officer shall, as far as practicable, be such as to avoid:

(a) any conflict with the offender's religious beliefs or with the requirements of any other community order to which he may be subject; and

(b) any interference with the times, if any, at which he normally works or attends school or any other educational establishment.

Section 71: Action plan orders: power to fix further hearings

(1) Immediately after making an action plan order, a court may:

(a) fix a further hearing for a date not more than 21 days after the making of the order; and

(b) direct the responsible officer to make, at that hearing, a report as to the effectiveness of the order and the extent to which it has been implemented.

(2) At a hearing fixed under sub-section (1) above, the court:

(a) shall consider the responsible officer's report; and

(b) may, on the application of the responsible officer or the offender, amend the order:

(i) by cancelling any provision included in it; or

(ii) by inserting in it (either in addition to or in substitution for any of its provisions) any provision that the court could originally have included in it.

REPARATION ORDERS

POWERS OF CRIMINAL COURTS (SENTENCING) ACT 2000

Section 73: Reparation orders

(1) Where a child or young person (that is to say, any person aged under 18) is convicted of an offence other than one for which the sentence is fixed by

law, the court by or before which he is convicted may make an order requiring him to make reparation specified in the order:

(a) to a person or persons so specified; or

(b) to the community at large,

and any person so specified must be a person identified by the court as a victim of the offence or a person otherwise affected by it.

(2) An order under sub-section (1) above is in this Act referred to as a 'reparation order'.

(3) In this section and section 74 below 'make reparation', in relation to an offender, means make reparation for the offence otherwise than by the payment of compensation; and the requirements that may be specified in a reparation order are subject to section 74(1) to (3).

(4) The court shall not make a reparation order in respect of the offender if it proposes:

(a) to pass on him a custodial sentence; or

(b) to make in respect of him a community service order, a combination order, a supervision order which includes requirements authorised by Schedule 6 to this Act, an action plan order or a referral order.

(5) Before making a reparation order, a court shall obtain and consider a written report by a probation officer, a social worker of a local authority social services department or a member of a youth offending team indicating:

(a) the type of work that is suitable for the offender; and

(b) the attitude of the victim or victims to the requirements proposed to be included in the order.

(6) The court shall not make a reparation order unless it has been notified by the Secretary of State that arrangements for implementing such orders are available in the area proposed to be named in the order under section 74(4) below and the notice has not been withdrawn.

(7) Before making a reparation order, the court shall explain to the offender in ordinary language:

(a) the effect of the order and of the requirements proposed to be included in it;

(b) the consequences which may follow (under Schedule 8 to this Act) if he fails to comply with any of those requirements; and

(c) that the court has power (under that Schedule) to review the order on the application either of the offender or of the responsible officer,

and 'responsible officer' here has the meaning given by section 74(5) below.

(8) The court shall give reasons if it does not make a reparation order in a case where it has power to do so.

Section 74: Requirements and provisions of reparation order, and obligations of person subject to it

(1) A reparation order shall not require the offender:

    (a) to work for more than 24 hours in aggregate; or

    (b) to make reparation to any person without the consent of that person.

(2) Subject to sub-section (1) above, requirements specified in a reparation order shall be such as in the opinion of the court are commensurate with the seriousness of the offence, or the combination of the offence and one or more offences associated with it.

(3) Requirements so specified shall, as far as practicable, be such as to avoid:

    (a) any conflict with the offender's religious beliefs or with the requirements of any community order to which he may be subject; and

    (b) any interference with the times, if any, at which he normally works or attends school or any other educational establishment.

(4) A reparation order shall name the petty sessions area in which it appears to the court making the order (or to the court amending under Schedule 8 to this Act any provision included in the order in pursuance of this sub-section) that the offender resides or will reside.

(5) In this Act 'responsible officer', in relation to an offender subject to a reparation order, means one of the following who is specified in the order, namely:

    (a) a probation officer;

    (b) a social worker of a local authority social services department;

    (c) a member of a youth offending team.

(6) Where a reparation order specifies a probation officer under sub-section (5) above, the officer specified must be an officer appointed for or assigned to the petty sessions area named in the order.

(7) Where a reparation order specifies under that sub-section:

    (a) a social worker of a local authority social services department; or

    (b) a member of a youth offending team,

the social worker or member specified must be a social worker of, or a member of a youth offending team established by, the local authority within whose area it appears to the court that the offender resides or will reside.

(8) Any reparation required by a reparation order:

    (a) shall be made under the supervision of the responsible officer; and

    (b) shall be made within a period of three months from the date of the making of the order.

SCHEDULE 8

BREACH, REVOCATION AND AMENDMENT OF ACTION PLAN ORDERS AND REPARATION ORDERS

Meaning of 'the appropriate court'

1   In this Schedule, 'the appropriate court', in relation to an action plan order or reparation order, means a youth court acting for the petty sessions area for the time being named in the order in pursuance of section 69(8) or, as the case may be, 74(4) of this Act.

Breach of requirement of action plan order or reparation order

2

(1) This paragraph applies if while an action plan order or reparation order is in force in respect of an offender it is proved to the satisfaction of the appropriate court, on the application of the responsible officer, that the offender has failed to comply with any requirement included in the order.

(2) Where this paragraph applies, the court:

    (a) whether or not it also makes an order under paragraph 5(1) below (revocation or amendment of order):

       (i) may order the offender to pay a fine of an amount not exceeding £1,000; or

       (ii) subject to paragraph 3 below, may make a curfew order in respect of him; or

       (iii) subject to paragraph 4 below, may make an attendance centre order in respect of him; or

    (b) if the action plan order or reparation order was made by a magistrates' court, may revoke the order and deal with the offender, for the offence in respect of which the order was made, in any way in which he could have been dealt with for that offence by the court which made the order if the order had not been made; or

    (c) if the action plan order or reparation order was made by the Crown Court, may commit him in custody or release him on bail until he can be brought or appear before the Crown Court.

(3) Where a court deals with an offender under sub-paragraph (2)(c) above, it shall send to the Crown Court a certificate signed by a justice of the peace giving:

    (a) particulars of the offender's failure to comply with the requirement in question; and

    (b) such other particulars of the case as may be desirable,

and a certificate purporting to be so signed shall be admissible as evidence of the failure before the Crown Court.

(4) Where:

    (a) by virtue of sub-paragraph (2)(c) above the offender is brought or appears before the Crown Court; and

    (b) it is proved to the satisfaction of the court that he has failed to comply with the requirement in question,

that court may deal with him, for the offence in respect of which the order was made, in any way in which it could have dealt with him for that offence if it had not made the order.

(5) Where the Crown Court deals with an offender under sub-paragraph (4) above, it shall revoke the action plan order or reparation order if it is still in force.

(6) A fine imposed under this paragraph shall be deemed, for the purposes of any enactment, to be a sum adjudged to be paid by a conviction.

(7) In dealing with an offender under this paragraph, a court shall take into account the extent to which he has complied with the requirements of the action plan order or reparation order.

(8) Where a reparation order or action plan order has been made on appeal, for the purposes of this paragraph it shall be deemed:

    (a) if it was made on an appeal brought from a magistrates' court, to have been made by that magistrates' court;

    (b) if it was made on an appeal brought from the Crown Court or from the criminal division of the Court of Appeal, to have been made by the Crown Court,

and, in relation to a reparation order or action plan order made on appeal, sub-paragraph (2)(b) above shall have effect as if the words 'if the order had not been made' were omitted and sub-paragraph (4) above shall have effect as if the words 'if it had not made the order' were omitted.

(9) This paragraph has effect subject to paragraph 6 below.

...

Revocation and amendment of action plan order or reparation order

5

(1) If while an action plan order or reparation order is in force in respect of an offender it appears to the appropriate court, on the application of the responsible officer or the offender, that it is appropriate to make an order under this sub-paragraph, the court may:

    (a) make an order revoking the action plan order or reparation order; or

    (b) make an order amending it:

        (i) by cancelling any provision included in it; or

        (ii) by inserting in it (either in addition to or in substitution for any of its provisions) any provision which could have been included in the order if the court had then had power to make it and were exercising the power.

(2) Sub-paragraph (1) above has effect subject to paragraph 6 below.

(3) Where an application under sub-paragraph (1) above for the revocation of an action plan order or reparation order is dismissed, no further application for its revocation shall be made under that sub-paragraph by any person except with the consent of the appropriate court.

Presence of offender in court, remands, etc

6

(1) Where the responsible officer makes an application under paragraph 2(1) or 5(1) above to the appropriate court he may bring the offender before the court; and, subject to sub-paragraph (9) below, a court shall not make an order under paragraph 2 or 5(1) above unless the offender is present before the court.

(2) Without prejudice to any power to issue a summons or warrant apart from this sub-paragraph, the court to which an application under paragraph 2(1) or 5(1) above is made may issue a summons or warrant for the purpose of securing the attendance of the offender before it.

(3) Sub-sections (3) and (4) of section 55 of the Magistrates' Courts Act 1980 (which among other things restrict the circumstances in which a warrant may be issued) shall apply with the necessary modifications to a warrant under sub-paragraph (2) above as they apply to a warrant under that section, but as if in sub-section (3) after the word 'summons' there were inserted the words 'cannot be served or'.

(4) Where the offender is arrested in pursuance of a warrant issued by virtue of sub-paragraph (2) above and cannot be brought immediately before the appropriate court, the person in whose custody he is:

(a) may make arrangements for his detention in a place of safety for a period of not more than 72 hours from the time of the arrest (and it shall be lawful for him to be detained in pursuance of the arrangements); and

(b) shall within that period bring him before a youth court; and in paragraph (a) above 'place of safety' has the same meaning as in the Children and Young Persons Act 1933.

(5) Where an offender under sub-paragraph (4)(b) above is brought before a youth court other than the appropriate court, the youth court may:

(a) direct that he be released forthwith; or

(b) subject to sub-paragraph (7) below, remand him to local authority accommodation.

(6) Subject to sub-paragraph (7) below, where an application is made to a court under paragraph 5(1) above, the court may remand (or further remand) the offender to local authority accommodation if:

(a) a warrant has been issued under sub-paragraph (2) above for the purpose of securing the attendance of the offender before the court; or

(b) the court considers that remanding (or further remanding) him will enable information to be obtained which is likely to assist the court in deciding whether and, if so, how to exercise its powers under paragraph 5(1) above.

(7) Where the offender is aged 18 or over at the time when he is brought before a youth court other than the appropriate court under sub-paragraph (4)(b) above, or is aged 18 or over at a time when (apart from this sub-paragraph) the appropriate court could exercise its powers under sub-paragraph (6) above in respect of him, he shall not be remanded to local authority accommodation but may instead be remanded:

(a) to a remand centre, if the court has been notified that such a centre is available for the reception of persons under this sub-paragraph; or

(b) to a prison, if it has not been so notified.

(8) A court remanding an offender to local authority accommodation under this paragraph shall designate, as the authority who are to receive him, the local authority for the area in which the offender resides or, where it appears to the court that he does not reside in the area of a local authority, the local authority:

(a) specified by the court; and

(b) in whose area the offence or an offence associated with it was committed.

(9) A court may make an order under paragraph 5(1) above in the absence of the offender if the effect of the order is confined to one or more of the following, that is to say:

(a) revoking the action plan order or reparation order;

(b) cancelling a requirement included in the action plan order or reparation order;

(c) altering in the action plan order or reparation order the name of any area;

(d) changing the responsible officer.

Appeals

7   The offender may appeal to the Crown Court against:

(a) any order made under paragraph 2(2) or 5(1) above except an order made or which could have been made in his absence (by virtue of paragraph 6(9) above);

(b) the dismissal of an application under paragraph 5(1) above to revoke an action plan order or reparation order.

YOUTH OFFENDER PANELS (REFERRAL ORDERS)

POWERS OF CRIMINAL COURTS (SENTENCING) ACT 2000

Section 16: Duty and power to refer certain young offenders to youth offender panels

(1) This section applies where a youth court or other magistrates' court is dealing with a person aged under 18 for an offence and:

    (a) neither the offence nor any connected offence is one for which the sentence is fixed by law;

    (b) the court is not, in respect of the offence or any connected offence, proposing to impose a custodial sentence on the offender or make a hospital order (within the meaning of the Mental Health Act 1983) in his case; and

    (c) the court is not proposing to discharge him absolutely in respect of the offence.

(2) If:

    (a) the compulsory referral conditions are satisfied in accordance with section 17 below; and

    (b) referral is available to the court,

the court shall sentence the offender for the offence by ordering him to be referred to a youth offender panel.

(3) If:

    (a) the discretionary referral conditions are satisfied in accordance with section 17 below; and

    (b) referral is available to the court,

the court may sentence the offender for the offence by ordering him to be referred to a youth offender panel.

(4) For the purposes of this Part an offence is connected with another if the offender falls to be dealt with for it at the same time as he is dealt with for the other offence (whether or not he is convicted of the offences at the same time or by or before the same court).

(5) For the purposes of this section referral is available to a court if:

    (a) the court has been notified by the Secretary of State that arrangements for the implementation of referral orders are available in the area in which it appears to the court that the offender resides or will reside; and

    (b) the notice has not been withdrawn.

(6) An order under sub-section (2) or (3) above is in this Act referred to as a 'referral order'.

(7) No referral order may be made in respect of any offence committed before the commencement of section 1 of the Youth Justice and Criminal Evidence Act 1999.

Section 17: The referral conditions

(1) For the purposes of section 16(2) above the compulsory referral conditions are satisfied in relation to an offence if the offender:

    (a) pleaded guilty to the offence and to any connected offence;

    (b) has never been convicted by or before a court in the United Kingdom of any offence other than the offence and any connected offence; and

    (c) has never been bound over in criminal proceedings in England and Wales or Northern Ireland to keep the peace or to be of good behaviour.

(2) For the purposes of section 16(3) above the discretionary referral conditions are satisfied in relation to an offence if:

    (a) the offender is being dealt with by the court for the offence and one or more connected offences;

    (b) although he pleaded guilty to at least one of the offences mentioned in paragraph (a) above, he also pleaded not guilty to at least one of them;

    (c) he has never been convicted by or before a court in the United Kingdom of any offence other than the offences mentioned in paragraph (a) above; and

    (d) he has never been bound over in criminal proceedings in England and Wales or Northern Ireland to keep the peace or to be of good behaviour.

(3) The Secretary of State may by regulations make such amendments of this section as he considers appropriate for altering in any way the descriptions of offenders in the case of which the compulsory referral conditions or the discretionary referral conditions fall to be satisfied for the purposes of section 16(2) or (3) above (as the case may be).

(4) Any description of offender having effect for those purposes by virtue of such regulations may be framed by reference to such matters as the Secretary of State considers appropriate, including (in particular) one or more of the following:

    (a) the offender's age;

    (b) how the offender has pleaded;

    (c) the offence (or offences) of which the offender has been convicted;

    (d) the offender's previous convictions (if any);

    (e) how (if at all) the offender has been previously punished or otherwise dealt with by any court; and

    (f) any characteristics or behaviour of, or circumstances relating to, any person who has at any time been charged in the same proceedings as the offender (whether or not in respect of the same offence).

(5) For the purposes of this section an offender who has been convicted of an offence in respect of which he was conditionally discharged (whether by a court in England and Wales or in Northern Ireland) shall be treated, despite:

    (a) section 14(1) above (conviction of offence for which offender so discharged deemed not a conviction); or

    (b) Article 6(1) of the Criminal Justice (Northern Ireland) Order 1996 (corresponding provision for Northern Ireland),

as having been convicted of that offence.

Section 18: Making of referral orders: general

(1) A referral order shall:

    (a) specify the youth offending team responsible for implementing the order;

    (b) require the offender to attend each of the meetings of a youth offender panel to be established by the team for the offender; and

    (c) specify the period for which any youth offender contract taking effect between the offender and the panel under section 23 below is to have effect (which must not be less than three nor more than twelve months).

(2) The youth offending team specified under sub-section (1)(a) above shall be the team having the function of implementing referral orders in the area in which it appears to the court that the offender resides or will reside.

(3) On making a referral order the court shall explain to the offender in ordinary language:

    (a) the effect of the order; and

    (b) the consequences which may follow:

        (i) if no youth offender contract takes effect between the offender and the panel under section 23 below; or

        (ii) if the offender breaches any of the terms of any such contract.

(4) Sub-sections (5) to (7) below apply where, in dealing with an offender for two or more connected offences, a court makes a referral order in respect of each, or each of two or more, of the offences.

(5) The orders shall have the effect of referring the offender to a single youth offender panel; and the provision made by them under sub-section (1) above shall accordingly be the same in each case, except that the periods specified under sub-section (1)(c) may be different.

(6) The court may direct that the period so specified in either or any of the orders is to run concurrently with or be additional to that specified in the other or any of the others; but in exercising its power under this sub-section the court must ensure that the total period for which such a contract as is mentioned in sub-section (1)(c) above is to have effect does not exceed twelve months.

(7) Each of the orders mentioned in sub-section (4) above shall, for the purposes of this Part, be treated as associated with the other or each of the others.

Section 19: Making of referral orders: effect on court's other sentencing powers

(1) Sub-sections (2) to (5) below apply where a court makes a referral order in respect of an offence.

(2) The court may not deal with the offender for the offence in any of the prohibited ways.

(3) The court:

    (a) shall, in respect of any connected offence, either sentence the offender by making a referral order or make an order discharging him absolutely; and

    (b) may not deal with the offender for any such offence in any of the prohibited ways.

(4) For the purposes of sub-sections (2) and (3) above the prohibited ways are:

    (a) imposing a community sentence on the offender;

    (b) ordering him to pay a fine;

    (c) making a reparation order in respect of him; and

    (d) making an order discharging him conditionally.

(5) The court may not make, in connection with the conviction of the offender for the offence or any connected offence:

    (a) an order binding him over to keep the peace or to be of good behaviour;

    (b) an order under section 150 below (binding over of parent or guardian); or

    (c) a parenting order under section 8 of the Crime and Disorder Act 1998.

(6) Sub-sections (2), (3) and (5) above do not affect the exercise of any power to deal with the offender conferred by paragraph 5 (offender referred back to court by panel) or paragraph 14 (powers of a court where offender convicted while subject to referral) of Schedule 1 to this Act.

(7) Where section 16(2) above requires a court to make a referral order, the court may not under section 1 above defer passing sentence on him, but section 16(2) and sub-section (3)(a) above do not affect any power or duty of a magistrates' court under:

    (a) section 8 above (remission to youth court, or another such court, for sentence);

    (b) section 10(3) of the Magistrates' Courts Act 1980 (adjournment for inquiries); or

    (c) section 35, 38, 43 or 44 of the Mental Health Act 1983 (remand for reports, interim hospital orders and committal to Crown Court for restriction order).

Section 20: Making of referral orders: attendance of parents, etc

(1) A court making a referral order may make an order requiring:

    (a) the appropriate person; or

    (b) in a case where there are two or more appropriate persons, any one or more of them,

to attend the meetings of the youth offender panel.

(2) Where an offender is aged under 16 when a court makes a referral order in his case:

(a) the court shall exercise its power under sub-section (1) above so as to require at least one appropriate person to attend meetings of the youth offender panel; and

(b) if the offender falls within sub-section (6) below, the person or persons so required to attend those meetings shall be or include a representative of the local authority mentioned in that sub-section.

(3) The court shall not under this section make an order requiring a person to attend meetings of the youth offender panel:

(a) if the court is satisfied that it would be unreasonable to do so; or

(b) to an extent which the court is satisfied would be unreasonable.

(4) Except where the offender falls within sub-section (6) below, each person who is a parent or guardian of the offender is an 'appropriate person' for the purposes of this section.

(5) Where the offender falls within sub-section (6) below, each of the following is an 'appropriate person' for the purposes of this section:

(a) a representative of the local authority mentioned in that sub-section; and

(b) each person who is a parent or guardian of the offender with whom the offender is allowed to live.

(6) An offender falls within this sub-section if he is (within the meaning of the Children Act 1989) a child who is looked after by a local authority.

(7) If, at the time when a court makes an order under this section:

(a) a person who is required by the order to attend meetings of a youth offender panel is not present in court; or

(b) a local authority whose representative is so required to attend such meetings is not represented in court,

the court must send him or (as the case may be) the authority a copy of the order forthwith.

Section 21: Establishment of panels

(1) Where a referral order has been made in respect of an offender (or two or more associated referral orders have been so made), it is the duty of the youth offending team specified in the order (or orders):

(a) to establish a youth offender panel for the offender;

(b) to arrange for the first meeting of the panel to be held for the purposes of section 23 below; and

(c) subsequently to arrange for the holding of any further meetings of the panel required by virtue of section 25 below (in addition to those required by virtue of any other provision of this Part).

(2) A youth offender panel shall:

(a) be constituted;

(b) conduct its proceedings; and

    (c) discharge its functions under this Part (and in particular those arising under section 23 below),

in accordance with guidance given from time to time by the Secretary of State.

(3) At each of its meetings a panel shall, however, consist of at least:

    (a) one member appointed by the youth offending team from among its members; and

    (b) two members so appointed who are not members of the team.

(4) The Secretary of State may by regulations make provision requiring persons appointed as members of a youth offender panel to have such qualifications, or satisfy such other criteria, as are specified in the regulations.

(5) Where it appears to the court which made a referral order that, by reason of either a change or a prospective change in the offender's place or intended place of residence, the youth offending team for the time being specified in the order ('the current team') either does not or will not have the function of implementing referral orders in the area in which the offender resides or will reside, the court may amend the order so that it instead specifies the team which has the function of implementing such orders in that area ('the new team').

(6) Where a court so amends a referral order:

    (a) sub-section (1)(a) above shall apply to the new team in any event;

    (b) sub-section (1)(b) above shall apply to the new team if no youth offender contract has (or has under paragraph (c) below been treated as having) taken effect under section 23 below between the offender and a youth offender panel established by the current team;

    (c) if such a contract has (or has previously under this paragraph been treated as having) so taken effect, it shall (after the amendment) be treated as if it were a contract which had taken effect under section 23 below between the offender and the panel being established for the offender by the new team.

(7) References in this Part to the meetings of a youth offender panel (or any such meeting) are to the following meetings of the panel (or any of them):

    (a) the first meeting held in pursuance of sub-section (1)(b) above;

    (b) any further meetings held in pursuance of section 25 below;

    (c) any progress meeting held under section 26 below; and

    (d) the final meeting held under section 27 below.

Section 22: Attendance at panel meetings

(1) The specified team shall, in the case of each meeting of the panel established for the offender, notify:

    (a) the offender; and

(b) any person to whom an order under section 20 above applies, of the time and place at which he is required to attend that meeting.

(2) If the offender fails to attend any part of such a meeting the panel may:

(a) adjourn the meeting to such time and place as it may specify; or

(b) end the meeting and refer the offender back to the appropriate court,

and sub-section (1) above shall apply in relation to any such adjourned meeting.

(3) One person aged 18 or over chosen by the offender, with the agreement of the panel, shall be entitled to accompany the offender to any meeting of the panel (and it need not be the same person who accompanies him to every meeting).

(4) The panel may allow to attend any such meeting:

(a) any person who appears to the panel to be a victim of, or otherwise affected by, the offence, or any of the offences, in respect of which the offender was referred to the panel;

(b) any person who appears to the panel to be someone capable of having a good influence on the offender.

(5) Where the panel allows any such person as is mentioned in sub-section (4)(a) above ('the victim') to attend a meeting of the panel, the panel may allow the victim to be accompanied to the meeting by one person chosen by the victim with the agreement of the panel.

Section 23: First meeting: agreement of contract with offender

(1) At the first meeting of the youth offender panel established for an offender the panel shall seek to reach agreement with the offender on a programme of behaviour the aim (or principal aim) of which is the prevention of re-offending by the offender.

(2) The terms of the programme may, in particular, include provision for any of the following:

(a) the offender to make financial or other reparation to any person who appears to the panel to be a victim of, or otherwise affected by, the offence, or any of the offences, for which the offender was referred to the panel;

(b) the offender to attend mediation sessions with any such victim or other person;

(c) the offender to carry out unpaid work or service in or for the community;

(d) the offender to be at home at times specified in or determined under the programme;

(e) attendance by the offender at a school or other educational establishment or at a place of work;

(f) the offender to participate in specified activities (such as those designed to address offending behaviour, those offering education or training or those assisting with the rehabilitation of persons dependent on, or having a propensity to misuse, alcohol or drugs);

    (g) the offender to present himself to specified persons at times and places specified in or determined under the programme;

    (h) the offender to stay away from specified places or persons (or both);

    (i) enabling the offender's compliance with the programme to be supervised and recorded.

(3) The programme may not, however, provide:

    (a) for the electronic monitoring of the offender's whereabouts; or

    (b) for the offender to have imposed on him any physical restriction on his movements.

(4) No term which provides for anything to be done to or with any such victim or other affected person as is mentioned in sub-section (2)(a) above may be included in the programme without the consent of that person.

(5) Where a programme is agreed between the offender and the panel, the panel shall cause a written record of the programme to be produced forthwith:

    (a) in language capable of being readily understood by, or explained to, the offender; and

    (b) for signature by him.

(6) Once the record has been signed:

    (a) by the offender; and

    (b) by a member of the panel on behalf of the panel,

the terms of the programme, as set out in the record, take effect as the terms of a 'youth offender contract' between the offender and the panel; and the panel shall cause a copy of the record to be given or sent to the offender.

Section 24: First meeting: duration of contract

(1) his section applies where a youth offender contract has taken effect under section 23 above between an offender and a youth offender panel.

(2) The day on which the contract so takes effect shall be the first day of the period for which it has effect.

(3) Where the panel was established in pursuance of a single referral order, the length of the period for which the contract has effect shall be that of the period specified under section 18(1)(c) above in the referral order.

(4) Where the panel was established in pursuance of two or more associated referral orders, the length of the period for which the contract has effect shall be that resulting from the court's directions under section 18(6) above.

(5) Sub-sections (3) and (4) above have effect subject to:

    (a) any order under paragraph 11 or 12 of Schedule 1 to this Act extending the length of the period for which the contract has effect; and

    (b) sub-section (6) below.

(6) If the referral order, or each of the associated referral orders, is revoked (whether under paragraph 5(2) of Schedule 1 to this Act or by virtue of paragraph 14(2) of that Schedule), the period for which the contract has effect expires at the time when the order or orders is or are revoked unless it has already expired.

Section 25: First meeting: failure to agree contract

(1) Where it appears to a youth offender panel to be appropriate to do so, the panel may:

   (a) end the first meeting (or any further meeting held in pursuance of paragraph (b) below) without having reached agreement with the offender on a programme of behaviour of the kind mentioned in section 23(1) above; and

   (b) resume consideration of the offender's case at a further meeting of the panel.

(2) If, however, it appears to the panel at the first meeting or any such further meeting that there is no prospect of agreement being reached with the offender within a reasonable period after the making of the referral order (or orders):

   (a) sub-section (1)(b) above shall not apply; and

   (b) instead the panel shall refer the offender back to the appropriate court.

(3) If at a meeting of the panel:

   (a) agreement is reached with the offender but he does not sign the record produced in pursuance of section 23(5) above; and

   (b) his failure to do so appears to the panel to be unreasonable, the panel shall end the meeting and refer the offender back to the appropriate court.

Section 26: Progress meetings

(1) At any time:

   (a) after a youth offender contract has taken effect under section 23 above; but

   (b) before the end of the period for which the contract has effect, the specified team shall, if so requested by the panel, arrange for the holding of a meeting of the panel under this section ('a progress meeting').

(2) The panel may make a request under sub-section (1) above if it appears to the panel to be expedient to review:

   (a) the offender's progress in implementing the programme of behaviour contained in the contract; or

   (b) any other matter arising in connection with the contract.

(3) The panel shall make such a request if:

    (a) the offender has notified the panel that:

        (i) he wishes to seek the panel's agreement to a variation in the terms of the contract; or

        (ii) he wishes the panel to refer him back to the appropriate court with a view to the referral order (or orders) being revoked on account of a significant change in his circumstances (such as his being taken to live abroad) making compliance with any youth offender contract impractical; or

    (b) it appears to the panel that the offender is in breach of any of the terms of the contract.

(4) At a progress meeting the panel shall do such one or more of the following things as it considers appropriate in the circumstances, namely:

    (a) review the offender's progress or any such other matter as is mentioned in sub-section (2) above;

    (b) discuss with the offender any breach of the terms of the contract which it appears to the panel that he has committed;

    (c) consider any variation in the terms of the contract sought by the offender or which it appears to the panel to be expedient to make in the light of any such review or discussion;

    (d) consider whether to accede to any request by the offender that he be referred back to the appropriate court.

(5) Where the panel has discussed with the offender such a breach as is mentioned in sub-section (4)(b) above:

    (a) the panel and the offender may agree that the offender is to continue to be required to comply with the contract (either in its original form or with any agreed variation in its terms) without being referred back to the appropriate court; or

    (b) the panel may decide to end the meeting and refer the offender back to that court.

(6) Where a variation in the terms of the contract is agreed between the offender and the panel, the panel shall cause a written record of the variation to be produced forthwith:

    (a) in language capable of being readily understood by, or explained to, the offender; and

    (b) for signature by him.

(7) Any such variation shall take effect once the record has been signed:

    (a) by the offender; and

    (b) by a member of the panel on behalf of the panel; and the panel shall cause a copy of the record to be given or sent to the offender.

(8) If at a progress meeting:

    (a) any such variation is agreed but the offender does not sign the record produced in pursuance of sub-section (6) above; and

(b) his failure to do so appears to the panel to be unreasonable, the panel may end the meeting and refer the offender back to the appropriate court.

(9) Section 23(2) to (4) above shall apply in connection with what may be provided for by the terms of the contract as varied under this section as they apply in connection with what may be provided for by the terms of a programme of behaviour of the kind mentioned in section 23(1).

(10) Where the panel has discussed with the offender such a request as is mentioned in sub-section (4)(d) above, the panel may, if it is satisfied that there is (or is soon to be) such a change in circumstances as is mentioned in sub-section (3)(a)(ii) above, decide to end the meeting and refer the offender back to the appropriate court.

Section 27: Final meeting

(1) Where the compliance period in the case of a youth offender contract is due to expire, the specified team shall arrange for the holding, before the end of that period, of a meeting of the panel under this section ('the final meeting').

(2) At the final meeting the panel shall:

   (a) review the extent of the offender's compliance to date with the terms of the contract; and

   (b) decide, in the light of that review, whether his compliance with those terms has been such as to justify the conclusion that, by the time the compliance period expires, he will have satisfactorily completed the contract,

and the panel shall give the offender written confirmation of its decision.

(3) Where the panel decides that the offender's compliance with the terms of the contract has been such as to justify that conclusion, the panel's decision shall have the effect of discharging the referral order (or orders) as from the end of the compliance period.

(4) Otherwise the panel shall refer the offender back to the appropriate court.

(5) Nothing in section 22(2) above prevents the panel from making the decision mentioned in sub-section (3) above in the offender's absence if it appears to the panel to be appropriate to do that instead of exercising either of its powers under section 22(2).

(6) Section 22(2)(a) above does not permit the final meeting to be adjourned (or re-adjourned) to a time falling after the end of the compliance period.

(7) In this section 'the compliance period', in relation to a youth offender contract, means the period for which the contract has effect in accordance with section 24 above.

SCHEDULE 1

YOUTH OFFENDER PANELS: FURTHER COURT PROCEEDINGS

PART I

REFERRAL BACK TO APPROPRIATE COURT

Introductory

1

(1) This Part of this Schedule applies where a youth offender panel refers an offender back to the appropriate court under section 22(2), 25(2) or (3), 26(5), (8) or (10) or 27(4) of this Act.

(2) For the purposes of this Part of this Schedule and the provisions mentioned in sub-paragraph (1) above the appropriate court is:

   (a) in the case of an offender aged under 18 at the time when (in pursuance of the referral back) he first appears before the court, a youth court acting for the petty sessions area in which it appears to the youth offender panel that the offender resides or will reside; and

   (b) otherwise, a magistrates' court (other than a youth court) acting for that area.

Mode of referral back to court

2   The panel shall make the referral by sending a report to the appropriate court explaining why the offender is being referred back to it.

Bringing the offender before the court

3

(1) Where the appropriate court receives such a report, the court shall cause the offender to appear before it.

(2) For the purpose of securing the attendance of the offender before the court, a justice acting for the petty sessions area for which the court acts may:

   (a) issue a summons requiring the offender to appear at the place and time specified in it; or

   (b) if the report is substantiated on oath, issue a warrant for the offender's arrest.

(3) Any summons or warrant issued under sub-paragraph (2) above shall direct the offender to appear or be brought before the appropriate court.

Detention and remand of arrested offender

4

(1) Where the offender is arrested in pursuance of a warrant under paragraph 3(2) above and cannot be brought immediately before the appropriate court:

(a) the person in whose custody he is may make arrangements for his detention in a place of safety (within the meaning given by section 107(1) of the Children and Young Persons Act 1933) for a period of not more than 72 hours from the time of the arrest (and it shall be lawful for him to be detained in pursuance of the arrangements); and

(b) that person shall within that period bring him before a court which:

    (i) if he is under the age of 18 when he is brought before the court, shall be a youth court; and

    (ii) if he has then attained that age, shall be a magistrates' court other than a youth court.

(2) Sub-paragraphs (3) to (5) below apply where the court before which the offender is brought under sub-paragraph (1)(b) above ('the alternative court') is not the appropriate court.

(3) The alternative court may direct that he is to be released forthwith or remand him.

(4) Section 128 of the Magistrates' Courts Act 1980 (remand in custody or on bail) shall have effect where the alternative court has power under sub-paragraph (3) above to remand the offender as if the court referred to in sub-sections (1)(a), (3), (4)(a) and (5) were the appropriate court.

(5) That section shall have effect where the alternative court has power so to remand him, or the appropriate court has (by virtue of sub-paragraph (4) above) power to further remand him, as if in sub-section (1) there were inserted after paragraph (c); 'or

(d) if he is aged under 18, remand him to accommodation provided by or on behalf of a local authority (within the meaning of the Children Act 1989) and, if it does so, shall designate as the authority who are to receive him the local authority for the area in which it appears to the court that he resides or will reside;'.

Power of court where it upholds panel's decision

5

(1) If it is proved to the satisfaction of the appropriate court as regards any decision of the panel which resulted in the offender being referred back to the court:

(a) that, so far as the decision relied on any finding of fact by the panel, the panel was entitled to make that finding in the circumstances; and

(b) that, so far as the decision involved any exercise of discretion by the panel, the panel reasonably exercised that discretion in the circumstances,

the court may exercise the power conferred by sub-paragraph (2) below.

(2) That power is a power to revoke the referral order (or each of the referral orders).

(3) The revocation under sub-paragraph (2) above of a referral order has the effect of revoking any related order under paragraph 11 or 12 below.

(4) Where any order is revoked under sub-paragraph (2) above or by virtue of sub-paragraph (3) above, the appropriate court may deal with the offender in accordance with sub-paragraph (5) below for the offence in respect of which the revoked order was made.

(5) In so dealing with the offender for such an offence, the appropriate court:

    (a) may deal with him in any way in which (assuming section 16 of this Act had not applied) he could have been dealt with for that offence by the court which made the order; and

    (b) shall have regard to:

        (i) the circumstances of his referral back to the court; and

        (ii) where a contract has taken effect under section 23 of this Act between the offender and the panel, the extent of his compliance with the terms of the contract.

(6) The appropriate court may not exercise the powers conferred by sub-paragraph (2) or (4) above unless the offender is present before it; but those powers are exercisable even if, in a case where a contract has taken effect under section 23, the period for which the contract has effect has expired (whether before or after the referral of the offender back to the court).

Appeal

6 Where the court in exercise of the power conferred by paragraph 5(4) above deals with the offender for an offence, the offender may appeal to the Crown Court against the sentence.

Court not revoking referral order or orders

7

(1) This paragraph applies:

    (a) where the appropriate court decides that the matters mentioned in paragraphs (a) and (b) of paragraph 5(1) above have not been proved to its satisfaction; or

    (b) where, although by virtue of paragraph 5(1) above the appropriate court:

        (i) is able to exercise the power conferred by paragraph 5(2) above; or

        (ii) would be able to do so if the offender were present before it, the court (for any reason) decides not to exercise that power.

(2) If either:

    (a) no contract has taken effect under section 23 of this Act between the offender and the panel; or

    (b) a contract has taken effect under that section but the period for which it has effect has not expired,

the offender shall continue to remain subject to the referral order (or orders) in all respects as if he had not been referred back to the court.

(3) If:

    (a) a contract had taken effect under section 23 of this Act; but

    (b) the period for which it has effect has expired (otherwise than by virtue of section 24(6)),

the court shall make an order declaring that the referral order (or each of the referral orders) is discharged.

Exception where court satisfied as to completion of contract

8   If, in a case where the offender is referred back to the court under section 27(4) of this Act, the court decides (contrary to the decision of the panel) that the offender's compliance with the terms of the contract has, or will have, been such as to justify the conclusion that he has satisfactorily completed the contract, the court shall make an order declaring that the referral order (or each of the referral orders) is discharged.

Discharge of extension orders

9   The discharge under paragraph 7(3) or 8 above of a referral order has the effect of discharging any related order under paragraph 11 or 12 below.

PART II

FURTHER CONVICTIONS DURING REFERRAL

Extension of referral for further offences

10

(1) Paragraphs 11 and 12 below apply where, at a time when an offender aged under 18 is subject to referral, a youth court or other magistrates' court ('the relevant court') is dealing with him for an offence in relation to which paragraphs (a) to (c) of section 16(1) of this Act are applicable.

(2) But paragraphs 11 and 12 do not apply unless the offender's compliance period is less than twelve months.

Extension where further offences committed pre-referral

11. If:

    (a) the occasion on which the offender was referred to the panel is the only other occasion on which it has fallen to a court in the United Kingdom to deal with the offender for any offence or offences; and

    (b) the offender committed the offence mentioned in paragraph 10 above, and any connected offence, before he was referred to the panel, the relevant court may sentence the offender for the offence by making an order extending his compliance period.

Extension where further offence committed after referral

12

(1) If:

  (a) paragraph 11(a) above applies; but

  (b) the offender committed the offence mentioned in paragraph 10 above, or any connected offence, after he was referred to the panel,

  the relevant court may sentence the offender for the offence by making an order extending his compliance period, but only if the requirements of sub-paragraph (2) below are complied with.

(2) Those requirements are that the court must:

  (a) be satisfied, on the basis of a report made to it by the relevant body, that there are exceptional circumstances which indicate that, even though the offender has re-offended since being referred to the panel, extending his compliance period is likely to help prevent further re-offending by him; and

  (b) state in open court that it is so satisfied and why it is.

(3) In sub-paragraph (2) above 'the relevant body' means the panel to which the offender has been referred or, if no contract has yet taken effect between the offender and the panel under section 23 of this Act, the specified team.

Provisions supplementary to paragraphs 11 and 12

13

(1) An order under paragraph 11 or 12 above, or two or more orders under one or other of those paragraphs made in respect of connected offences, must not so extend the offender's compliance period as to cause it to exceed twelve months.

(2) Sub-paragraphs (3) to (5) below apply where the relevant court makes an order under paragraph 11 or 12 above in respect of the offence mentioned in paragraph 10 above; but sub-paragraphs (3) to (5) do not affect the exercise of any power to deal with the offender conferred by paragraph 5 or 14 of this Schedule.

(3) The relevant court may not deal with the offender for that offence in any of the prohibited ways specified in section 19(4) of this Act.

(4) The relevant court:

  (a) shall, in respect of any connected offence, either:

    (i) sentence the offender by making an order under the same paragraph; or

    (ii) make an order discharging him absolutely; and

  (b) may not deal with the offender for any connected offence in any of those prohibited ways.

(5) The relevant court may not, in connection with the conviction of the offender for the offence or any connected offence, make any such order as is mentioned in section 19(5) of this Act.

(6) For the purposes of paragraphs 11 and 12 above any occasion on which the offender was discharged absolutely in respect of the offence, or each of the offences, for which he was being dealt with shall be disregarded.

...

Further convictions which lead to revocation of referral

14

(1) This paragraph applies where, at a time when an offender is subject to referral, a court in England and Wales deals with him for an offence (whether committed before or after he was referred to the panel) by making an order other than:

(a) an order under paragraph 11 or 12 above; or

(b) an order discharging him absolutely.

(2) In such a case the order of the court shall have the effect of revoking:

(a) the referral order (or orders); and

(b) any related order or orders under paragraph 11 or 12 above.

(3) Where any order is revoked by virtue of sub-paragraph (2) above, the court may, if appears to the court that it would be in the interests of justice to do so, deal with the offender for the offence in respect of which the revoked order was made in any way in which (assuming section 16 of this Act had not applied) he could have been dealt with for that offence by the court which made the order.

(4) When dealing with the offender under sub-paragraph (3) above the court shall, where a contract has taken effect between the offender and the panel under section 23 of this Act, have regard to the extent of his compliance with the terms of the contract.

Interpretation

15

(1) For the purposes of this Part of this Schedule an offender is for the time being subject to referral if:

(a) a referral order has been made in respect of him and that order has not; or

(b) two or more referral orders have been made in respect of him and any of those orders has not,

been discharged (whether by virtue of section 27(3) of this Act or under paragraph 7(3) or 8 above) or revoked (whether under paragraph 5(2) above or by virtue of paragraph 14(2) above).

(2) In this Part of this Schedule 'compliance period', in relation to an offender who is for the time being subject to referral, means the period for which (in accordance with section 24 of this Act) any youth offender contract taking effect in his case under section 23 of this Act has (or would have) effect.

CHAPTER 18

ANCILLARY ORDERS

In this chapter, we consider the powers of the court to order an offender to pay compensation to the victim, to order forfeiture of articles used to commit crime and to confiscate the proceeds of drug trafficking. We also consider the special orders which can be made in respect of offenders who are mentally disordered. We also examine the power of the court to recommend that a person be deported. Finally, we look at various orders involving exclusion and disqualification.

18.1   COMPENSATION ORDERS

Section 130 of the Powers of Criminal Courts (Sentencing) Act 2000 empowers a court which has convicted someone of an offence to require that person to pay:

...

(a) compensation for any personal injury, loss or damage resulting from that offence or any other offence which is taken into consideration by the court in determining sentence; or

(b) to make payments for funeral expenses or bereavement in respect of a death resulting from any such offence, other than a death due to an accident arising out of the presence of a motor vehicle on a road.

The 'personal injury' does not have to be physical injury. It can include distress and anxiety (*Bond v Chief Constable of Kent* [1983] 1 WLR 40; [1983] 1 All ER 456). The Magistrates' Association Sentencing Guidelines point out that it can include terror or distress caused by the offence.

In *R v Donovan* (1981) 3 Cr App R(S) 192, Eveleigh LJ said that:

... a compensation order is designed for the simple, straightforward case where the amount of the compensation can be readily and easily ascertained.

The same approach was followed in *R v White* [1996] 2 Cr App R(S) 58, where the Court of Appeal said that where a case raises difficult or complex issues as to liability, a compensation order is not appropriate.

In *R v Watson* [1991] Crim LR 307, it was held that a compensation order should only be made if there is evidence of the amount of the victim's loss or else the prosecution and the defence agree on the amount of the order.

In *Holt v DPP* [1996] 2 Cr App R(S) 314, two youths stole £1,900 from an elderly lady. She died before sentence was passed on the youths. The Divisional Court held that the present case was a simple and straightforward one, and so a compensation order was appropriate. The amount of the loss was not in issue, nor was the defendants' responsibility for that loss. The youths had the means to pay and there were no factors which made it more appropriate to leave the matter of compensation to the civil courts. Furthermore, there was no reason why a compensation order could not be made in favour of the victim's estate if the victim had died by the time the compensation order was made.

Section 130(3) requires the court to give reasons if it does not make a compensation order where it has power to make one. A compensation order should be considered whether or not there is an application for compensation by or on behalf of the victim, although in practice the prosecution will normally indicate that there is a claim for compensation.

18.1.1 Causation

In *R v Horsham Justices ex p Richards* [1985] 1 WLR 986; [1985] 2 All ER 1114, it was held that the prosecution must show that the loss or damage suffered by the victim occurred as a result of the offence of which the offender has been convicted. However, in *R v Corbett* [1992] Crim LR 833, it was held that for a compensation order to be made, whilst there must be some cause or connection between the offence and the injury sustained by the victim, the offence need not be the sole cause of the injury. The question was whether the injury could fairly be said to have resulted from the offence.

For example, in *R v Derby* (1990) 12 Cr App R(S) 502, the defendant pleaded guilty to a charge of affray. It was accepted by the prosecution that the offender was not the person who used violence against the victim. Although the defendant was part of the disturbance he did not inflict any actual violence. It was therefore held that he could not be ordered to pay compensation to the victim of the violence, since the injury had been inflicted by someone else, albeit in the same incident.

See, also, *R v Deary* (1994) 14 Cr App R(S) 502, where the Court of Appeal quashed a compensation order because there was no proven causal link between the offender's part in an affray and the injury sustained by the victim.

However, other cases have placed less importance on the need to prove causation.

In *R v Taylor* (1993) 14 Cr App R(S) 276, the defendant was convicted of affray following an incident in which a person had been kicked while on the ground. Taylor was ordered to pay compensation to the person who was kicked. He appealed on the basis that it had not been proved that it was he who had kicked the victim. It was held that a compensation order may be made against someone who is involved in a fight in which someone is injured even if the injuries were not caused by that offender.

In *Taylor*, it was seen as important that the defendant's behaviour was a factor leading to the start of the fighting in which the injury to the victim was inflicted. A similar approach was taken in *R v Denness* [1996] 1 Cr App R(S) 159. In that case, there were three appellants. One of them was being arrested. There was a struggle as the other two appellants tried to pull the first away from the officer. Another police officer intervened and a struggle developed. One of the officers was injured. The appellants pleaded guilty to affray but were found not guilty of assault occasioning actual bodily harm. The Court of Appeal upheld the making of compensation orders against each of the appellants, on the basis that they were all involved in the incident in which the officer was injured.

Section 130(5) of the 2000 Act provides that, in the case of an offence under the Theft Act 1968, where the property is recovered but has been damaged while out of the owner's possession, the damage is deemed to result from the offence.

In *R v Ahmad* (1992) 13 Cr App R(S) 212, for example, the defendant pleaded guilty to taking a conveyance. Section 35(2) was held to apply to damage which had been caused to the car but not to the loss of property which had been in the vehicle (as the defendant had not been convicted of the theft of that property).

A compensation order for injury, loss or damage (apart from loss suffered by dependents where the victim dies) cannot be made where the loss is due to an accident arising out of the presence of a motor vehicle on a road unless either s 130(5) applies or else it is loss which is not covered by any insurance held by the offender or by the Motor Insurers' Bureau scheme (s 130(6)). Where an order is made in a road accident case, its amount can include compensation for loss of no claims bonus.

18.1.2 Amount of compensation

In calculating the amount of compensation, the court must have regard to any evidence as to the amount of the loss and to any representations made by the defendant or the prosecution (s 130(4)). In other words, the amount of the damage should be proved if it is not agreed between the parties.

Section 131(1) of the 2000 Act sets a limit of £5,000 compensation for an offence where the order is made by a magistrates' court. There is, however, no limit on the total amount of compensation ordered provided that not more than £5,000 is ordered in respect of any one offence. Thus, if there are five offences, the maximum is £25,000.

There is no limit on the amount of compensation which can be awarded in respect of an offence by the Crown Court.

However, it should be noted that where a compensation order includes an award in respect of bereavement, such an award can only be made in favour of the person entitled to damages for bereavement under s 1A of the Fatal Accidents Act 1976 (the spouse of the deceased or, if the deceased was a minor, her parents) and the amount of the award must not exceed the sum prescribed in the 1976 Act (currently £7,500) (ss 130(10) of the 2000 Act).

18.1.3   Home Office guidelines

The Magistrates' Association Sentencing Guidelines include guidelines (taken from a Home Office circular issued in August 1993) which should be used by courts as a starting point in deciding how much compensation to order. The guidelines include the following suggestions:

Graze (depending on size)	up to £50
Bruise (depending on size)	up to £75
Black eye	£100
Cut (no permanent scarring; depending on size and whether stitched)	£75–500
Loss of non-front tooth (depending on cosmetic effect and age of victim)	£250–500
Loss of front tooth	£1,000
Facial scar (however small – resulting in permanent disfigurement)	from £750
Fractured jaw	£2,750
Broken nose	£1,000–1,750
Broken arm or leg (simple fracture with full recovery within three weeks)	£2,500

18.1.4   Means of offender

Section 130(11) of the Powers of Criminal Courts (Sentencing) Act 2000 requires the court to take account of the offender's means in deciding whether to make a compensation order and, if so, the amount of the order.

So, in *R v Ellis* (1994) 158 JP 386, a compensation order was quashed because the judge made it without there being any evidence that the defendant, who was unemployed, would be able to pay it. Such an order could only be made against an unemployed defendant if there was evidence that he would be able to find employment. Similarly, in *R v Love and Tomkins* [1999] 1 Cr App R(S) 484, the Court of Appeal said that it is wrong to make a compensation order where the defendant has no assets and his means of earning income are being suspended or brought to an end by the imposition of a sentence of imprisonment. The court should also be very careful before making an order based on the defendant's capacity to earn money after release from prison. However, it is not necessarily wrong to combine a compensation order with a sentence of imprisonment. A compensation order may be appropriate in those cases where there is evidence that the defendant has assets or will have sufficient earning capacity after release from prison.

Co-defendants may (and indeed should) be required to pay different sums under compensation orders if their capacity to pay is different (*R v Beddow* (1987) 9 Cr App R(S) 235).

A compensation order should not generally be made if its effect would be to require the offender to sell his home (*R v Harrison* (1980) 2 Cr App R(S) 313). However, in *R v McGuire* (1992) 13 Cr App R(S) 454, it was held that a compensation order could properly be made, even though it would have the effect of forcing the offender to sell his home, at least if it appears that he will have sufficient money left over to buy a cheaper house.

Similarly, there is usually no objection to making an order which will require the offender to sell other assets (*R v Workman* (1979) 1 Cr App R(S) 335).

In *R v Barney* (1989) 11 Cr App R(S) 448, it was pointed out that the court should avoid giving the impression that the offender will receive a more lenient sentence if he has sufficient funds to pay compensation; in other words, the impression should not be given that a person can buy their way out of prison. However, the willingness of the offender to pay compensation is relevant in mitigation to the extent that it indicates remorse.

It should be noted that, if the offender misleads the court into thinking he can pay more compensation than he is in fact able to pay, the court will not subsequently vary the compensation order on the ground that he lacks the means to pay (*R v Hayes* (1992) 13 Cr App R(S) 454).

A compensation order should only be made if it is likely that the offender will be able to pay it (if necessary by instalments under s 75(1) of the Magistrates' Courts Act 1980) within a reasonable time. Ideally, compensation should be paid within a year; however, in *R v Olliver* (1989) 11 Cr App R(S) 10, it was said that a fine may be imposed if it can be paid within two or three years and presumably the same principle applies to a compensation order.

- Juveniles

  Where an offender who is under 18 is convicted of an offence, a compensation order may be made. However, where the offender is under 16, the court must order the parent or guardian to pay the compensation unless either the parent or guardian cannot be found or it would be unreasonable to require the parent or guardian to pay the compensation (s 137(1) of the Powers of Criminal Courts (Sentencing) Act 2000).

Where the offender is 16 or 17, the court has a discretion to order the parent or guardian to pay the compensation (s 137(3) of the 2000 Act).

Where the compensation is to be paid by a parent or guardian, it is their means (not the means of the offender) which are taken into account (s 136 of the 2000 Act).

18.1.5 Combining compensation orders and other orders

Section 130(1) of the Powers of Criminal Courts (Sentencing) Act 2000 allows the court to make a compensation order as well as, or instead of, imposing a punishment on the offender.

It should be noted that s 130(12) of the Act gives priority to compensation over fines. If the offender cannot afford to pay both compensation and a fine, the amount of the fine should be reduced or no fine should be imposed. The Magistrates' Association Guidelines remind the justices that 'compensation is an order in its own right and should be treated as such – particularly where the offender has insufficient means to pay a fine as well'.

It must be borne in mind that a sentence of immediate custody may well have the effect that the offender will not be able to pay compensation (as it will have the effect of preventing him from earning the money with which to comply with the order) and, in such a case, the custodial sentence would preclude a compensation order (*R v Webb* (1979) 1 Cr App R(S) 16; *R v Gill* (1992) 13 Cr App R(S) 36). This would not be the case if the offender had substantial savings or other realisable assets and so would be able to meet the order from his existing resources (*R v Panayioutou* (1989) 11 Cr App R(S) 535), or if he had good prospects of finding employment on release from custody (*R v Townsend* (1980) 2 Cr App R(S) 328), or if the custodial sentence is relatively short and there is evidence that the offender's previous job will be open to him when he is released from custody (*R v Clark* (1992) 13 Cr App R(S) 124).

18.1.6 Enforcement of compensation orders

Compensation orders are enforced in the same way as fines (see Chapter 15, 15.1.8). Enforcement is carried out by a magistrates' court, with a term of custody in default of payment. The maximum term of custody for non-payment of compensation is the same as the term for a fine of the same amount. Note, however, that the Crown Court does not have power to fix a term in default when making a compensation order (although it does when imposing a fine) (*R v Komsta* (1990) 12 Cr App R(S) 63).

As with a fine, if the offender has paid part of the compensation due under the order, the custodial term will be reduced proportionately.

Where the offender is in receipt of income support, the Fines (Deduction from Income Support) Regulations 1992 enable the court to order deduction of compensation from the offender's income support in the same way that fines may be deducted at source.

18.1.7   Other methods of obtaining compensation

Compensation orders should not be confused with the Criminal Injuries Compensation Board nor with the Motor Insurers' Bureau scheme (which provides compensation from a fund set up by insurance companies to compensate victims of road accidents where the driver at fault cannot be traced or is uninsured). The Criminal Injuries Compensation Act 1995 puts the criminal injuries compensation scheme on a statutory footing. Section 2 of the Act sets out the basis on which compensation is payable under the scheme. A standard amount of compensation is payable depending on the nature of the injury suffered by the victim, the amount being calculated according to a tariff published by the Home Secretary. Loss of earnings may also be recovered.

It is always open to a victim of crime to bring civil proceedings against the perpetrator. If the victim receives money under a compensation order from a magistrates' court or the Crown Court, that money will be deducted from any damages awarded by the county court or the High Court, and vice versa.

18.2   RESTITUTION ORDERS

Section 148 of the Powers of Criminal Courts (Sentencing) Act 2000 applies where goods have been stolen and a person is convicted of theft (or asks for theft to be taken into consideration) in respect of those goods.

Under s 24(4) of the Theft Act 1968, theft includes robbery, burglary, blackmail, obtaining property by deception and handling stolen goods.

Three orders are possible:

- The court may order anyone who has possession or control of the goods to restore them to the person who is entitled to have those goods (s 148(2)(a)).

    Where the person who has possession or control of the goods is not the offender but an innocent purchaser who bought them in good faith, the court may order the offender to pay compensation to the purchaser under s 148(2)(c) below (s 148(4)).

- Where the stolen goods have been sold and the proceeds used to purchase other goods which are in the possession of the offender, the court may order the offender to hand over those goods to the person who was entitled to the stolen goods (s 148(2)(b)).

- The court may order the offender to pay a sum not exceeding the value of the stolen goods to the person who was entitled to those goods provided that this sum can be paid out of money which was in the offender's possession when he was arrested (s 148(2)(c)). In *R v Ferguson* [1970] 1 WLR 1246; [1970] 2 All ER 820, it was held that this provision also applies to money seized from the offender after his arrest (in that case, £2,000 seized from a safe deposit box 11 days after the offender's arrest was held susceptible to an order under s 148).

An order should only be made under s 148 where it is clear that the person benefiting under the order owned the goods; if there is any doubt, the matter is best left to the civil courts (*R v Calcutt* (1985) 7 Cr App R(S) 385).

18.3   FORFEITURE ORDERS

Section 143 of the Powers of Criminal Courts (Sentencing) Act 2000 empowers a Crown Court or magistrates' court to make a forfeiture order in two situations.

- Under s 143(1), the court may make an order in respect of property which has lawfully been seized from the offender or which was in his possession or under his control at the time he was arrested for the offence (or when the summons was issued if proceedings were commenced by the laying of an information).

  This power only applies if the property was used for the purpose of committing, or facilitating the commission of, an offence committed by the offender or if it was intended by him to be used for that purpose.

  Section 143(6) of the 2000 Act provides that:

  (a) if the offence in question is either manslaughter or an offence under the Road Traffic Act 1988 which is punishable with imprisonment; and

  (b) the offence involved the use of a vehicle and the offender was driving or in charge of the vehicle,

  the vehicle is automatically regarded as having been used for the purpose of committing the offence.

- Under s 143(2) of the 2000 Act, the court may make a forfeiture order where the offence consists of unlawful possession of property which has lawfully been seized from the offender or which was in his possession or under his control at the time he was arrested for the offence (or when the summons was issued if proceedings were commenced by the laying of an information).

In deciding whether or not to make a forfeiture order, the court must have regard to the value of the property and to the likely effects of the order on the offender (s 143(5)). An order is inappropriate if it has a disproportionately severe impact on the offender (R *v Highbury Corner Magistrates ex p Di Matteo* [1991] 1 WLR 1374; [1992] 1 All ER 102).

18.3.1 Effect of forfeiture order

Property which is subject to a forfeiture order is taken into the possession of the police and is held by them under the Police (Property) Act 1897. If the property is owned by someone other than by the offender, that person has six months in which to claim the property (in which case the claimant must show that he did not consent to the offender having the property and did not know it was being used for the commission of an offence). Property which has not been claimed within six months is sold.

Section 145 of the 2000 Act provides that if the offender has been convicted of an offence resulting in loss in respect of which a compensation order could be made, or such an offence is taken into consideration by the court, but the offender does not have the means to pay compensation, the court may order that when property subject to a forfeiture order is sold, the proceeds should be paid to the victim.

18.3.2 Other powers of forfeiture

Other specific statutory powers to make forfeiture orders are contained in the following legislation:

- Section 27 of the Misuse of Drugs Act 1971 enables the court to order forfeiture (and destruction where appropriate) of property related to drugs offences or drug trafficking offences.

  For s 27 to apply, it must be shown that the property is related to the offence of which the offender has been convicted (*R v Morgan* [1977] Crim LR 488).

  In *R v Cuthbertson* [1981] AC 470; [1980] 2 All ER 401, it was held by the House of Lords that forfeiture orders apply to 'tangible' property such as the drugs, the equipment for making them, vehicles used for transporting them and cash handed over (or ready to be handed over) for them.

  The object of a forfeiture order is not to strip drug traffickers of the profits of their crime. This object is achieved by means of confiscation orders, which are dealt with in 18.4 below.

- Section 52 of the Firearms Act 1968 provides that, where a person is convicted of a firearms offence, or is convicted of a crime for which a custodial sentence is imposed, the court may order the forfeiture or disposal of any firearm or ammunition in his possession.

- Section 1 of the Prevention of Crime Act 1953 provides that where the offender is convicted of being in possession of an offensive weapon, the court may order the forfeiture or disposal of the weapon.

- Section 1 of the Obscene Publications Act 1964 states that where the offender is convicted of having obscene articles in his possession for gain (s 2 of that Act), the court may order the forfeiture of those articles.

- Section 24 of the Forgery and Counterfeiting Act 1981 empowers the court to order the forfeiture (including the destruction) of counterfeit currency.

18.4 CONFISCATION ORDERS UNDER THE DRUG TRAFFICKING ACT 1994

A confiscation order may be made by the Crown Court under Drug Trafficking Act 1994 provided that the defendant has been convicted of a drug trafficking offence. Drug trafficking offences are defined in s 1(3) of the Drug Trafficking Act 1994 and include production, supply, and possession for supply of controlled drugs (ss 4 and 5 of the Misuse of Drugs Act 1971) and illegal importation or exportation of controlled drugs (ss 50, 68 and 170 of the Customs and Excise Management Act 1979).

The objective is to enable the court to confiscate any profit made from drug trafficking.

The procedure is very complicated but basically requires the court to ask three questions when it has convicted someone of a drug trafficking offence:

- has the defendant benefited from drug trafficking?;
- if so, what is the value of that benefit?;
- does the value of the benefit exceed the realisable assets against which a confiscation order can be made?

18.4.1 Benefit from drug trafficking

The prosecution has to prove that the offender has benefited from drug trafficking. The standard of proof is the civil standard (that is, the balance of probabilities) (s 2(8) of the Drug Trafficking Act 1994).

Section 4(1) of the Drug Trafficking Act 1994 defines benefiting from drug trafficking as receiving any payment or reward in connection with drug trafficking carried on by the defendant or by someone else.

Section 4(2), (3) of the Drug Trafficking Act 1994 enables the court to assume that any property held by the defendant at any time since his conviction, or during a period of six years preceding the date when proceedings were instituted against him, is a payment or reward received in connection with drug trafficking. The court may also assume that any expenditure during this six year period was met out of the benefit of drug trafficking.

The court may not make such assumptions if the defendant is able to show (on the balance of probabilities) that the assumptions are not correct in his case (s 4(4A)).

18.4.2   The 'prosecutor's statement'

Section 11 of the Drug Trafficking Act 1994 requires the prosecution to produce a statement setting out the matters which the prosecution say are relevant in showing that the defendant has benefited from drug trafficking and in assessing the value of that benefit. A copy of this statement is served on the defendant, who can then be required to indicate the extent to which he accepts the contents of the statement and, in so far as he does not accept the statement, the matters he proposes to rely on in order to rebut the prosecution case. If the defendant fails to indicate the matters he proposes to rely upon, the court may treat the defendant as accepting the contents of the prosecutor's statement (s 11(8) of the Drug Trafficking Act 1994).

18.4.3   Amount of confiscation order

The amount confiscated should be the same as the value of the defendant's benefit from drug trafficking (s 5(1) of the Drug Trafficking Act 1994) unless the court is satisfied that the amount which may be realised from the defendant's assets is less than the value of the benefit, in which case the order is for the amount which may be realised (s 5(3) of the Drug Trafficking Act 1994).

The burden of proof is on the defendant to show (on the balance of probabilities) that his realisable assets are less than the value of his benefit from drug trafficking (*R v Islemann* (1990) 12 Cr App R(S) 398).

Realisable property (s 6(2) of the Drug Trafficking Act 1994) means property presently held by the defendant and property which the defendant has given away at any time during a period of six years before the institution of the present proceedings. The court must take account of the effect of any obligations which have priority (for example, a mortgage) (s 6(1)).

In *R v Chrastny (No 2)* [1991] 1 WLR 1385; [1992] 1 All ER 193, it was held that realisable property includes property which has been acquired legitimately: in other words, the actual property does not have to be the direct proceeds of drug trafficking. It was also held in that case that where the property is jointly owned by the defendant and someone else (for example, a spouse) who is not a defendant, the order may be made in respect of the whole of the property.

In *R v Porter* [1990] 1 WLR 1260; [1990] 3 All ER 784, it was held that where several defendants are convicted of drug trafficking offences, the court must consider each defendant separately when considering confiscation orders: the amount by which they have benefited from drug trafficking and their realisable assets may differ. Separate orders must therefore be made against each defendant who is found to have benefited from drug trafficking.

Where a confiscation order is made under the Drug Trafficking Act 1994 for an amount which is less than the amount by which the offender benefited from the drug trafficking (because his realisable assets are less than the amount of that benefit), the prosecution can apply to the court for an increase in the amount of the order if the offender acquires assets after the original order was made, even if there is no evidence that those assets were acquired by dishonest means (*R v Tivnan* [1999] 1 Cr App R(S) 92).

18.5 CONFISCATION ORDERS UNDER THE CRIMINAL JUSTICE ACT 1988

The Criminal Justice Act 1988 (as amended by the Proceeds of Crime Act 1995) essentially extends to all indictable offences the sort of confiscation powers which exist in relation to drug trafficking offences (by virtue of the Drug Trafficking Act 1994). It is therefore no surprise that the scheme created by the Proceeds of Crime Act 1995 is similar to the scheme created by the Drug Trafficking Act 1994.

The Criminal Justice Act 1988 contains two procedures. The first procedure applies where the court is minded to make a confiscation order only in respect of the offences which are presently being dealt with by the court (that is, offences of which the defendant has just been convicted or offences which the defendant has asked the court to take into consideration). The procedure can be brought about either by the prosecution serving a written notice on the court, or by the court deciding of its own motion that a confiscation order is appropriate (s 71(1) of the Criminal Justice Act 1988).

If the court decides that the offender has benefited from any of the offences being dealt with by the court, the court must make a confiscation order for the amount of that benefit or the amount of the defendant's realisable assets (whichever is the lesser amount). The court fixes a term of imprisonment to be served if the offender fails to satisfy the confiscation order.

This is subject to the proviso contained in s 71(1C) of the Criminal Justice Act 1988, that where a victim of any of the offences being dealt by the court has instituted, or intends to institute, civil proceedings against the offender, the court has a discretion whether to make a confiscation order or not (or to make an order for a smaller amount than would otherwise have been the case). Section 72(5)(b) enables a confiscation order to be combined with a compensation order; in that case, the proceeds of the confiscation order will be used to satisfy the compensation order (s 72(7)).

The second procedure applies where the court wishes to confiscate the proceeds of crimes other than those of which the offender has been convicted (or which are being taken into consideration). This procedure is set out in s 72AA of the Criminal Justice Act 1988 (inserted by the Proceeds of Crime Act 1995). Section 72AA applies where the offender has been convicted of a 'qualifying offence'. This means an indictable offence, other than one to which the Drug Trafficking Act 1994 applies, as a result of which the offender has obtained property or derived a pecuniary advantage. This procedure can only be started by the prosecution serving a written notice on the court (that is, the court cannot commence this procedure of its own motion). Once this written notice has been served, the court has to be satisfied either that the offender has been convicted in the present proceedings of at least two qualifying offences or that the offender (as well as being convicted of a qualifying offence in the present proceedings) has been convicted of a qualifying offence on at least one previous occasion in the six years prior to the institution of the present proceedings.

The court is then entitled to make similar assumptions (in the absence of evidence from the defence to rebut them) to those established under the Drug Trafficking Act 1994, namely, that the property currently held by the offender represents the proceeds of crime and that income and expenditure during the previous six years similarly represent the proceeds of crime.

Once again, the court will make a confiscation order in respect of the amount of the offender's benefit from the proceeds of crime, or the amount of the defendant's realisable assets, whichever is the lesser amount.

In *R v Delaney and Hanrahan* ((1999) 14 May, unreported, CA), the appellants were convicted of burglary. The police found substantial deposits in various building society accounts held by the appellants and could not establish any legitimate source of income. The prosecution invited the court to draw the inference that the money in these accounts represented the proceeds of burglaries. The court made a confiscation order, having applied the assumptions in s 72AA(4) of the Criminal Justice Act 1988. It was held that it is not necessary for the prosecution to establish a *prima facie* case that the unexplained money represents the proceeds of crime. Once it has been proved that the offender is guilty of at least two qualifying offences, the assumption can be made that the money in the defendant's possession is the proceeds from crime; it is then for the defendant to prove (on the balance of probabilities) that the assumption is incorrect and should not be applied. Significantly, the court went on to hold that there is no conflict with Art 6(2) of the European Convention on Human Rights, since the presumption of innocence is not violated where a defendant has the opportunity to rebut the assumptions. The same principles would apply to confiscation orders under the Drug Trafficking Act 1994 (see 18.4 above).

18.6   MENTALLY DISORDERED OFFENDERS

In an attempt to ensure that custodial sentences are not imposed unnecessarily on mentally disordered offenders, s 82 of the Powers of Criminal Courts (Sentencing) Act 2000 requires the court to obtain a medical report before imposing a custodial sentence on someone 'who is or appears to be mentally disordered'. Under s 82(3), the court must consider the likely effect of a custodial sentence on the person's mental condition and on any treatment which may be available for it.

There are a number of different orders which may be made in respect of a mentally disordered offender.

A probation order may contain a requirement that the offender undergo treatment for his mental condition (para 3 of Sched 2 of the 2000 Act); a supervision order may also contain such a requirement (para 6 of Sched 6 of the 2000 Act). See Chapter 14, 14.3.2 and Chapter 17, 17.5.9.

Where the offender's condition is more serious it may be necessary for the court to make an order under the Mental Health Act 1983. There are two main orders under this Act, the hospital order and the guardianship order.

18.7   HOSPITAL ORDERS

Section 37 of the Mental Health Act 1983 provides that where a person is convicted by the Crown Court or a magistrates' court of an offence which is punishable with imprisonment, the court may make an order for his admission to and detention in a mental hospital.

Under s 37(2) of the Mental Health Act 1983, a number of conditions have to be satisfied before a hospital order can be made. Those conditions are:

- The court must be satisfied on the evidence of two duly qualified medical practitioners that the offender is suffering from 'mental illness, psychopathic disorder, severe mental impairment or mental impairment' and either:
    - (a) the mental disorder is of a nature or degree which makes it appropriate for the offender to be detained in a hospital for medical treatment and, in the case of psychopathic disorder or mental impairment, such treatment is likely to alleviate or prevent a deterioration in his condition; or

(b) the offender has attained the age of 16 and his mental disorder is of a nature or degree which warrants a guardianship order (see below).

• The court must be of the opinion that such an order is the most suitable method of disposing of the case.

A hospital order may be made even if there is no causal link between the offender's mental disorder and the offence of which he has been convicted (*R v McBride* [1972] Crim LR 322).

As with compulsory civil committal under Pt II of the Mental Health Act 1983, the order lapses after six months, but may be renewed for a further six months and may thereafter be renewed for periods of one year at a time, where the doctors dealing with the offender consider further detention to be necessary for the protection of the public or in the interests of the health or safety of the patient (s 20 and Sched 1 of the Mental Health Act 1983). There is no limit to the total length of detention in the hospital, but an application for the patient's release may be made to the Mental Health Review Tribunal.

18.7.1   Interim hospital order

Section 38 of the Mental Health Act 1983 enables the court to make an interim hospital order before finally disposing of the case. The conditions which have to be met are the same as for a hospital order (so it is likely that a hospital order will be made when the case is finally disposed of). An interim order may last for up to 12 weeks; it may then be renewed for further periods of up to 28 days at a time; an interim order cannot last for a total of more than six months.

18.8   RESTRICTION ORDERS

Section 41 of the Mental Health Act 1983 empowers the Crown Court to make a 'restriction order' as well as a hospital order. The court may do so if it considers:

> ... having regard to the nature of the offence, the antecedents of the offender and the risk of his committing further offences if set at large, that it is necessary for the protection of the public from serious harm to do so.

The effect of the restriction order is that the offender cannot be discharged from the mental hospital without the permission of the Secretary of State or of the Mental Health Review Tribunal.

A restriction order may be for a fixed period (in which case it lasts for that period, with no need for it to be renewed when the hospital order is renewed) or it may be for an indefinite period.

Such an order can only be made where it is necessary to protect the public from serious harm: it cannot be made simply to reflect the gravity of the offence committed by the offender (see *R v Birch* (1990) 90 Cr App R 78).

18.9   HOSPITAL ORDERS AND LIMITATION DIRECTIONS

Section 46 of the Crime (Sentences) Act 1997 inserts two new sections – 45A and 45B into the Mental Health Act 1983. These sections provide for the making of a hospital order coupled with a limitation direction. Before making such an order, the court must be satisfied, on the basis of evidence from two medical practitioners (one of whom just give oral evidence) that the offender is suffering from a psychopathic disorder, that the disorder is of a nature or degree which makes it appropriate for him to be detained in a hospital for medical treatment, and that such treatment is likely to alleviate (or prevent a deterioration of) his condition. Such an order is made in addition to a sentence of imprisonment. When an order is made, the offender is conveyed to the hospital named in the direction. If the offender ceases to need treatment he is returned to prison; if he is still in hospital when the sentence expires, he will cease to be subject to restriction and will remain in hospital as if detained under an ordinary hospital order made under s 37 of the 1983 Act. The offender is eligible for release on the decision of the responsible medical officer.

18.10   GUARDIANSHIP ORDERS

Under s 40(2) of the Mental Health Act 1983, a guardianship order may be made to confer certain powers in respect of the offender on an authority or person. These powers are the same as those conferred by a guardianship order made in the civil context (see Pt II of the Mental Health Act 1983). The powers include determining where the offender will reside and the power to require him to attend for treatment, occupational therapy, education or training.

The pre-conditions for the making of a guardianship order are the same as those for making a hospital order, except that there is no requirement that the offender's mental disorder be treatable.

A guardianship order lasts for 12 months, but can be renewed.

18.11   JUVENILES

An adult magistrates' court may not make a hospital order or guardianship order on a juvenile (s 7(8) of the Children and Young Persons Act 1969). Otherwise, the same principles apply as to adult offenders.

18.12   OTHER ANCILLARY ORDERS

Finally, we consider various orders which can be made at the time the offender is being sentenced.

18.12.1 Recommendation for deportation

Under s 6(3) of the Immigration Act 1971, a court which is dealing with someone who is not a British citizen and who has been convicted of an imprisonable offence, may make a recommendation to the Home Secretary that the person be deported. In *R v Nazari* [1980] 1 WLR 1366; [1980] 3 All ER 880, Lawton LJ said that the seriousness of the offence and the extent of the offender's criminal record should be taken into account in deciding whether or not to make a recommendation for deportation. Such a recommendation may be combined with any sentence but is most common where the offender has received a custodial sentence; in such a case, the Home Secretary can order the offender's deportation once he is released from prison.

18.13   EXCLUSION ORDERS

The courts have various statutory powers to exclude offenders from particular places.

18.13.1 Licensed premises

Section 1 of the Licensed Premises (Exclusion of Certain Persons) Act 1980 empowers a court which is dealing with a person who has been convicted of an offence of violence to prohibit the offender from entering licensed premises without the express consent of the licensee for a specified period of between three months and two years.

18.13.2 Football matches

Section 30 of the Public Order Act 1986 empowers a court which is dealing with a person who has been convicted of an offence of violence connected with a football match to prohibit the offender from entering premises for the purpose of attending a football match for a specified period of not less than three months.

18.14   DISQUALIFICATIONS

The courts also have a number of disqualification orders at their disposal.

18.14.1 Company directors

Sections 1 and 2 of the Company Directors Disqualification Act 1986 apply where a court is dealing with a person who has been convicted of an indictable (including triable either way) offence which is connected with the formation, management, liquidation, receivership or management of a company. The effect of the order is to prevent the offender from being a company director or being involved in the setting up or running of a company. The usual maximum period of disqualification is five years (magistrates' court) and 15 years (Crown Court). Disqualification is usually appropriate where the offender has been guilty of dishonesty or gross incompetence, so that he would be a danger to the public if he were to be allowed to continue to be involved in the management of companies (*per* Hoffmann J in *Re Dawson Print Group Ltd* [1987] BCLC 601).

18.14.2 Animals

Section 1 of the Protection of Animals (Amendment) Act 1954 enables a court to disqualify the offender from keeping any animal where the offender has been convicted of causing unnecessary suffering to an animal.

18.14.3 Road traffic offenders

Under s 34 of the Road Traffic Offenders Act 1988, where a person has been convicted of a road traffic offence involving obligatory disqualification, the court must order that he be disqualified from driving for at least 12 months unless the court finds that there are special reasons for not disqualifying him or for disqualifying him for less than 12 months. A special reason must be connected with the commission of the offence itself; mitigation which is personal to the offender is not a special reason (*R v Wickins* (1958) 42 Cr App R 236).

Other road traffic offences carry discretionary disqualification (see Sched 1 of the Road Traffic Offenders Act 1988). In such cases, disqualification is only imposed in the more serious examples of those offences (*per* Morland J in *R v Callister* [1993] RTR 70).

Many road traffic offences carry a number of penalty points which have to be endorsed on the offender's driving licence in the event of conviction. The number of points to be endorsed is set out in Sched 1 of the Road Traffic

Offenders Act 1988; sometimes, the number is fixed, sometimes, there is a range, with a minimum and a maximum number specified. If the offender is convicted of more than one offence, the points to be endorsed are those which relate to the offence which carries the highest number of points (s 28); thus, if I am convicted on one occasion of careless driving (which carries three to nine points) and failing to comply with a traffic sign (three points), the maximum number of points which can be endorsed is nine.

Under s 35 of the Road Traffic Offenders Act 1988, where a person is convicted of an offence which carries discretionary disqualification and mandatory endorsement and the number of penalty points on the offender's driving licence (including those imposed for the present offence) number 12 or more, the court must disqualify the offender from driving for at least six months (if it is his first disqualification) or 12 months (if it is his second) or two years (if he has already been disqualified twice) unless the court takes the view that there are grounds for not doing so or for disqualifying for a shorter period. Penalty points are taken into account if they were imposed within the last three years (s 29(2)). This is known as a 'totting up' disqualification.

In deciding whether there is mitigation to justify not disqualifying the offender (or for shortening the disqualification), the court cannot take account of:

- circumstances alleged to make the present offence less serious;
- hardship (unless it is exceptional hardship); or
- circumstances which the offender has relied on to escape a 'totting up' disqualification within the last three years (s 35(4)).

In *R v Thames Magistrates' Court ex p Levy* (1997) *The Times*, 17 July, the defendant had been disqualified from driving after being convicted of various driving offences. He appealed against these convictions but did not apply to have the disqualification suspended pending the appeal. The convictions were subsequently quashed following a successful appeal. Prior to the quashing of the convictions, he drove a motor vehicle. He was charged with driving while disqualified. The Divisional Court held, unsurprisingly, that he was guilty of driving while disqualified because he drove a motor vehicle while an order for disqualification was lawfully in force.

18.14.4 Disqualification under the Crime (Sentences) Act 1997

Section 146 of the Powers of Criminal Courts (Sentencing) Act 2000 provides that, in addition to, or instead of, dealing with an offender in any other way, a court may disqualify him from driving for such period as it thinks fit. Thus, the penalty of disqualification from driving can be imposed for any offence, not just driving offences. When this Act was passing through Parliament, it was said that (HC Official Report, SCA, 10 December 1996):

... it is important that the courts regard disqualification from driving as a heavy penalty, especially if someone is employed. There will therefore be occasions when they will not apply this penalty if it might result in a person losing his job, because that may seem disproportionate ... The important point ... is the idea that the use of the sentence should be appropriate to the nature of the offence, and that in most if not all cases there should be some relevance to the use of a vehicle.

TABLE OF STATUTORY MATERIALS

STATUTORY MATERIALS

COMPENSATION ORDERS

POWERS OF CRIMINAL COURTS (SENTENCING) ACT 2000

Section 130: Compensation orders against convicted persons

(1) A court by or before which a person is convicted of an offence, instead of or in addition to dealing with him in any other way, may, on application or otherwise, make an order (in this Act referred to as a 'compensation order') requiring him:

    (a) to pay compensation for any personal injury, loss or damage resulting from that offence or any other offence which is taken into consideration by the court in determining sentence; or

    (b) to make payments for funeral expenses or bereavement in respect of a death resulting from any such offence, other than a death due to an accident arising out of the presence of a motor vehicle on a road,

but this is subject to the following provisions of this section and to section 131 below.

(2) Where the person is convicted of an offence the sentence for which is fixed by law or falls to be imposed under section 109(2), 110(2) or 111(2) above, sub-section (1) above shall have effect as if the words 'instead of or' were omitted.

(3) A court shall give reasons, on passing sentence, if it does not make a compensation order in a case where this section empowers it to do so.

(4) Compensation under sub-section (1) above shall be of such amount as the court considers appropriate, having regard to any evidence and to any representations that are made by or on behalf of the accused or the prosecutor.

(5) In the case of an offence under the Theft Act 1968, where the property in question s recovered, any damage to the property occurring while it was out of the owner's possession shall be treated for the purposes of sub-section (1) above as having resulted from the offence, however and by whomever the damage was caused.

(6) A compensation order may only be made in respect of injury, loss or damage (other than loss suffered by a person's dependants in consequence of his death) which was due to an accident arising out of the presence of a motor vehicle on a road, if:

    (a) it is in respect of damage which is treated by sub-section (5) above as resulting from an offence under the Theft Act 1968; or

(b) it is in respect of injury, loss or damage as respects which:

   (i) the offender is uninsured in relation to the use of the vehicle; and

   (ii) compensation is not payable under any arrangements to which the Secretary of State is a party.

(7) Where a compensation order is made in respect of injury, loss or damage due to an accident arising out of the presence of a motor vehicle on a road, the amount to be paid may include an amount representing the whole or part of any loss of or reduction in preferential rates of insurance attributable to the accident.

(8) A vehicle the use of which is exempted from insurance by section 144 of the Road Traffic Act 1988 is not uninsured for the purposes of sub-section (6) above.

(9) A compensation order in respect of funeral expenses may be made for the benefit of anyone who incurred the expenses.

(10) A compensation order in respect of bereavement may be made only for the benefit of a person for whose benefit a claim for damages for bereavement could be made under section 1A of the Fatal Accidents Act 1976; and the amount of compensation in respect of bereavement shall not exceed the amount for the time being specified in section 1A(3) of that Act.

(11) In determining whether to make a compensation order against any person, and in determining the amount to be paid by any person under such an order, the court shall have regard to his means so far as they appear or are known to the court.

(12) Where the court considers:

   (a) that it would be appropriate both to impose a fine and to make a compensation order; but

   (b) that the offender has insufficient means to pay both an appropriate fine and appropriate compensation,

the court shall give preference to compensation (though it may impose a fine as well).

Section 131: Limit on amount payable under compensation order of magistrates' court

(1) The compensation to be paid under a compensation order made by a magistrates' court in respect of any offence of which the court has convicted the offender shall not exceed £5,000.

(2) The compensation or total compensation to be paid under a compensation order or compensation orders made by a magistrates' court in respect of any offence or offences taken into consideration in determining sentence shall not exceed the difference (if any) between:

   (a) the amount or total amount which under sub-section (1) above is the maximum for the offence or offences of which the offender has been convicted; and

(b) the amount or total amounts (if any) which are in fact ordered to be paid in respect of that offence or those offences.

Section 132: Compensation orders: appeals, etc

(1) A person in whose favour a compensation order is made shall not be entitled to receive the amount due to him until (disregarding any power of a court to grant leave to appeal out of time) there is no further possibility of an appeal on which the order could be varied or set aside.

(2) Rules under section 144 of the Magistrates' Courts Act 1980 may make provision regarding the way in which the magistrates' court for the time being having functions (by virtue of section 41(1) of the Administration of Justice Act 1970) in relation to the enforcement of a compensation order is to deal with money paid in satisfaction of the order where the entitlement of the person in whose favour it was made is suspended.

(3) The Court of Appeal may by order annul or vary any compensation order made by the court of trial, although the conviction is not quashed; and the order, if annulled, shall not take effect and, if varied, shall take effect as varied.

(4) Where the House of Lords restores a conviction, it may make any compensation order which the court of trial could have made.

(5) Where a compensation order has been made against any person in respect of an offence taken into consideration in determining his sentence:

(a) the order shall cease to have effect if he successfully appeals against his conviction of the offence or, if more than one, all the offences, of which he was convicted in the proceedings in which the order was made;

(b) he may appeal against the order as if it were part of the sentence imposed in respect of the offence or, if more than one, any of the offences, of which he was so convicted.

Section 133: Review of compensation orders

(1) The magistrates' court for the time being having functions in relation to the enforcement of a compensation order (in this section referred to as 'the appropriate court') may, on the application of the person against whom the compensation order was made, discharge the order or reduce the amount which remains to be paid; but this is subject to sub-sections (2) to (4) below.

(2) The appropriate court may exercise a power conferred by sub-section (1) above only:

(a) at a time when (disregarding any power of a court to grant leave to appeal out of time) there is no further possibility of an appeal on which the compensation order could be varied or set aside; and

(b) at a time before the person against whom the compensation order was made has paid into court the whole of the compensation which the order requires him to pay.

(3) The appropriate court may exercise a power conferred by sub-section (1) above only if it appears to the court:

    (a) that the injury, loss or damage in respect of which the compensation order was made has been held in civil proceedings to be less than it was taken to be for the purposes of the order; or

    (b) in the case of a compensation order in respect of the loss of any property, that the property has been recovered by the person in whose favour the order was made; or

    (c) that the means of the person against whom the compensation order was made are insufficient to satisfy in full both the order and a confiscation order under Part VI of the Criminal Justice Act 1988 made against him in the same proceedings; or

    (d) that the person against whom the compensation order was made has suffered a substantial reduction in his means which was unexpected at the time when the order was made, and that his means seem unlikely to increase for a considerable period.

(4) Where the compensation order was made by the Crown Court, the appropriate court shall not exercise any power conferred by sub-section (1) above in a case where it is satisfied as mentioned in paragraph (c) or (d) of sub-section (3) above unless it has first obtained the consent of the Crown Court.

(5) Where a compensation order has been made on appeal, for the purposes of sub-section (4) above it shall be deemed:

    (a) if it was made on an appeal brought from a magistrates' court, to have been made by that magistrates' court;

    (b) if it was made on an appeal brought from the Crown Court or from the criminal division of the Court of Appeal, to have been made by the Crown Court.

Section 134: Effect of compensation order on subsequent award of damages in civil proceedings

(1) This section shall have effect where a compensation order, or a service compensation order or award, has been made in favour of any person in respect of any injury, loss or damage and a claim by him in civil proceedings for damages in respect of the injury, loss or damage subsequently falls to be determined.

(2) The damages in the civil proceedings shall be assessed without regard to the order or award, but the plaintiff may only recover an amount equal to the aggregate of the following:

    (a) any amount by which they exceed the compensation; and

    (b) a sum equal to any portion of the compensation which he fails to recover,

and may not enforce the judgment, so far as it relates to a sum such as is mentioned in paragraph (b) above, without the leave of the court.

DISQUALIFICATION FROM DRIVING AS A GENERAL PENALTY

POWERS OF CRIMINAL COURTS (SENTENCING) ACT 2000

Section 146: Driving disqualification for any offence

(1) The court by or before which a person is convicted of an offence committed after 31st December 1997 may, instead of or in addition to dealing with him in any other way, order him to be disqualified, for such period as it thinks fit, for holding or obtaining a driving licence.

(2) Where the person is convicted of an offence the sentence for which is fixed by law or falls to be imposed under section 109(2), 110(2) or 111(2) above, sub-section (1) above shall have effect as if the words 'instead of or' were omitted.

(3) A court shall not make an order under sub-section (1) above unless the court has been notified by the Secretary of State that the power to make such orders is exercisable by the court and the notice has not been withdrawn.

...

Section 147: Driving disqualification where vehicle used for purposes of crime

(1) This section applies where a person:

    (a) is convicted before the Crown Court of an offence punishable on indictment with imprisonment for a term of two years or more; or

    (b) having been convicted by a magistrates' court of such an offence, is committed under section 3 above to the Crown Court for sentence.

(2) This section also applies where a person is convicted by or before any court of common assault or of any other offence involving an assault (including an offence of aiding, abetting, counselling or procuring, or inciting to the commission of, an offence).

(3) If, in a case to which this section applies by virtue of sub-section (1) above, the Crown Court is satisfied that a motor vehicle was used (by the person convicted or by anyone else) for the purpose of committing, or facilitating the commission of, the offence in question, the court may order the person convicted to be disqualified, for such period as the court thinks fit, for holding or obtaining a driving licence.

(4) If, in a case to which this section applies by virtue of sub-section (2) above, the court is satisfied that the assault was committed by driving a motor vehicle, the court may order the person convicted to be disqualified, for such period as the court thinks fit, for holding or obtaining a driving licence.

...

(6) Facilitating the commission of an offence shall be taken for the purposes of this section to include the taking of any steps after it has been committed for the purpose of disposing of any property to which it relates or of avoiding apprehension or detection.

...

SENTENCING AT A GLANCE

NON-CUSTODIAL SENTENCES

Absolute discharge:	Any age
Conditional discharge:	Any age Maximum duration 3 years
Fine:	Any age (10–13 year olds: maximum £250 14–17 year olds: maximum: £1,000)
Compensation order:	Any age
Curfew order:	Any age Maximum duration: 10–15 year olds: 3 months 16+: 6 months
Community service order:	Age: 16+ Number of hours: 40–240 hours
Probation order:	Age: 16+ Duration: 6 months–3 years Additional requirements may be imposed
Combination order:	Age: 16+ Probation (12 months–3 years) + Community Service (40–100 hours)
Drug treatment and testing order:	Age: 16+ Duration: 6 months–3 years
Attendance centre order:	Age 10–20 year olds (up to 25 for non-payment of fines) Minimum number of hours 12 (but may be less if offender under 14)
Maximum number of hours:	24 hours (10–15 year olds) 36 hours (16–20 year olds)
Supervision order:	Age: 10–17 year olds Maximum duration: 3 years Additional requirements may be imposed

Action plan order:	Age: 10–17 year olds
Reparation order:	Age: 10–17 year olds
Referral order:	Age: 10–17 year olds
Binding parents over:	Age: 10–17 year olds (if offender aged 10–15 court must justify not binding parents over)

CUSTODIAL SENTENCES

Imprisonment	Age: 21+
Suspended sentence	Age 21+ Maximum term to be suspended: 2 years Operational period (period of suspension): 1–2 years
Detention and training order:	12–17 year olds (but for 12–14 year olds only if persistent offenders) Duration: 4, 6, 8, 10, 12, 18 or 24 months (of which $1/2$ custody and $1/2$ supervision)
Detention in a young offender institution:	Age: 18–20 year olds Maximum: as imprisonment for adult offender
Detention at HM pleasure:	Age: 10–17 year olds (murder)
Custody for life:	Age: 18–20 year olds (murder)
Detention (s 91 of the of the 2000)	Age: 10–17 year olds (14–17 year olds for road traffic fatalities) Scope: offences carrying 14 years or more imprisonment for adult offenders, plus indecent assault and road traffic fatalities Maximum: as imprisonment for adult offender

PLEA AND DIRECTIONS HEARING QUESTIONNAIRE

PLEA AND DIRECTIONS HEARING

The Crown Court at

Case No T
PTI URN
R v

Judge's Questionnaire

Date of PDH
Name of Prosecution
Advocate at PDH

(In accordance with the practice rules issued by the Lord Chief Justice)

Name of Defence Advocate at PDH

A copy of this questionnaire, completed as far as possible with the agreement of both advocates, is to be handed in to the court prior to the commencement of the Plea and Directions Hearing.

1(a) Are the actual/proposed not guilty pleas definitely to be maintained through to a jury trial?	Yes ❑ No ❑
(b) Has the defence advocate advised his client of section 48 of the CJPOA 1994?	Yes ❑ No ❑
(Reductions in sentence for guilty pleas)	
(c) Will the prosecution accept part guilty or alternative pleas?	Yes ❑ No ❑

2 How long is the trial likely to take?

3 What are the issues in the case?

4 Issues as to the mental or medical condition of any defendant or witness.

5 Prosecution witnesses whose evidence will be given.

Can any statement be read instead of calling the witnesses?

To be read (number):
To be called (number):
Names:

6 (a) Number of Defence witnesses whose evidence will be placed before the Court. Defendant +	Defendant +
(b) Any whose statements have been served which can be agreed and accepted in writing.	
7 Is the prosecution intending to serve any further evidence? If Yes, what area(s) will it cover? What are the witnesses' names?	Yes ❏ No ❏
8 Facts which are admitted and can be reduced into writing. (s 10(2)(b) of the CJA 1967)	
9 Exhibits and schedules which are to be admitted.	
10 Is the order and pagination of the prosecution papers agreed?	
11 Any alibi which should have been disclosed in accordance with CJA 1967?	Yes ❏ No ❏
12 (a) Any points of law likely to arise at trial? (b) Any questions of admissibility of evidence together with any authorities it is intended to rely upon.	
13 (a) Has the defence notified the prosecution of any issue arising out of the record of interview? (Practice Direction Crime: Tape Recording of Police Interview 26 May 1989) (b) What efforts have been made to agree verbatim records or summaries and have they been successful?	Yes ❏ No ❏

14 Any applications granted/pending for:

   (i) evidence to be given through live television links?   Yes ❏   No ❏

   (ii) evidence to be given by pre-recorded video interviews with children?   Yes ❏   No ❏

   (iii) screens?   Yes ❏   No ❏

   (iv) the use of video equipment during the trial?   Yes ❏   No ❏

   (v) use of tape playback equipment?   Yes ❏   No ❏

15 Any other significant matter which might affect the proper and convenient trial of the case?

(for example, expert witnesses or other cases outstanding against the defendant)

16 Any other work which needs to be done.   Prosecution

Orders of the court with time limits should be noted in 'other directions'.

Defence

17 (a) Witness availability and approximate length of witness evidence.   Prosecution

Defence

   (b) Can any witness attendance be staggered?   Yes ❏   No ❏

   (c) If Yes, have any arrangements been agreed?   Yes ❏   No ❏

18 Advocates' availability?   Prosecution

Defence

Case listing arrangements

Name of Trial Judge:

Custody Cases Fix or warned list within 16 weeks of committal

Fixed for trial on
Place in warned list for trial for week beginning
Further directions fixed for
Not fixed or put in warned list within 16 weeks because:

Bail Cases

Further directions fixed for
Fixed for trial on
Fixed as a floater/ backer on
Place in a reserve/warned list for trial for week beginning
List officer to allocate   ❏ within ❏ days/weeks
            ❏ before

Sentence

Adjourned for sentence on
(to follow trial of R v

Other directions, orders, comments

Signed: Judge   Date:

RECOMMENDED READING LIST

Stones Justices Manual (a three-volume annual publication) contains all the statutes and rules applicable to magistrates' courts and the law administered by the magistrates. It also contains helpful commentary on these materials. All justices' clerks have a copy of *Stones* nearby.

Practitioners in the Criminal Courts use either *Archbold: Criminal Pleading Evidence and Practice* (which concentrates mainly on the Crown Court) or *Blackstone's Criminal Practice* (which deals with magistrates' courts and the Crown Court).

Both are published annually and are available on CD-Rom.

INDEX

C

D

J

S

Index